REMINISCENCES OF RIMSKY-KORSAKOV

N. A. Rimsky-Korsakov

Painting by I. Repin. Original in the Tretyakov Gallery, Moscow. Photo courtesy of the Music Division, the New York Public Library at Lincoln Center, Astor, Lenox, and Tilden Foundations.

V. V. YASTREBTSEV

Reminiscences of

RIMSKY-KORSAKOV

Edited and translated by
FLORENCE JONAS

Foreword by
GERALD ABRAHAM

COLUMBIA UNIVERSITY PRESS
NEW YORK   1985

The Press gratefully acknowledges the
assistance of Thomas S. Brush in
the publishing of this volume.

Library of Congress Cataloging in Publication Data

IAstrebtsev, V. V. (Vasiliĭ Vasilévich), 1866–1934.
Reminiscences of Rimsky-Korsakov.

Translation and abridgment of: Nikolaĭ Andreevich
Rimskiĭ-Korsakov.
Includes index and bibliographical references.
1. Rimsky-Korsakov, Nikolay, 1844–1908.
2. Composers—Soviet Union—Biography.   I. Jonas,
Florence.   II. Title.
ML410.R52I233 1985   780'.92'4 [B]   84-16967
ISBN 0-231-05260-X (alk. paper)

Columbia University Press
New York   Guildford, Surrey
Copyright © 1985 Columbia University Press
All rights reserved

Printed in the United States of America

This book is Smyth-sewn and printed on
permanent and durable acid-free paper

Designed by Ken Venezio

To
Lillian and Jacob
for later

CONTENTS

FOREWORD BY GERALD ABRAHAM   ix

TRANSLATOR'S NOTE   xiii

CHAPTER 1.   1886–1891   1

CHAPTER 2.   1892   16

CHAPTER 3.   1893   26

CHAPTER 4.   1894   60

CHAPTER 5.   1895   103

CHAPTER 6.   1896   138

CHAPTER 7.   1897   172

CHAPTER 8.   1898   195

CHAPTER 9.   1899   219

CHAPTER 10.   1900   248

CHAPTER 11.   1901   277

CHAPTER 12.   1902   302

CHAPTER 13.   1903   324

CHAPTER 14.   1904   337

CHAPTER 15.   1905   350

CHAPTER 16.   1906   379

CONTENTS

CHAPTER 17. 1907 400

CHAPTER 18. 1908 430

NOTES 479

RIMSKY-KORSAKOV'S WORKS 539

INDEX 551

FOREWORD

It is regrettable that no one has managed to Boswellize any of the greatest composers. We used to think Anton Schindler had done something like that for a few years of Beethoven's life but Schindler has been exposed as a fraud. Cosima Wagner's diary comes much nearer but she was altogether too close to the subject. Probably the only day-by-day record of a notable composer's sayings and doings by an observer standing in much the same relationship as Boswell to Samuel Johnson are the reminiscences of Rimsky-Korsakov by Vasily Vasilyevich Yastrebtsev. Rimsky-Korsakov is not in the same class as Beethoven or Wagner and a less remarkable character than Johnson, though by no means a colorless one. (He is probably the only man to have composed a musical illustration of the *Mannequin pis* in Brussels.) Nor was Yastrebtsev a potential Boswell. But like Johnson and Boswell, composer and admirer were a strongly contrasted pair; a photograph of c.1908 suggests Don Quixote and Sancho Panza.

Yastrebtsev was born in Mogilev in 1866 and was thus Rimsky-Korsakov's junior by twenty-two years. He studied at the Novgorod Realnoe Uchilishche—what used to be called a "secondary modern school" in Britain—before entering the St. Petersburg Technological Institute. But engineering was not for him; he was crazy about music and wished to study at the St. Petersburg Conservatory. He surprised Rimsky-Korsakov, who was one of the entrance examiners, by his general knowledge of music and entered Julius Johansen's harmony class at the end of September 1890. But Johansen's "endless tables" bored him and by his own account he spent most of his time either drinking tea or coffee and discussing "new music" with fellow students or studying the scores of Berlioz, Wagner, and Rimsky-Korsakov. Feeling that the conservatory had really nothing to offer him, he left it—with Rimsky-Korsakov's approval—and entered the far from onerous service of the Dvoryansky Zemelny Bank which, since he had "influence" and cared nothing for a career as a banker, left him almost unlimited time to enjoy the society of musicians and attend rehearsals of orchestral concerts and operas. He kept his bank post until after the Revolution, when he became curator of the Glinka and Rubinstein museums of the conservatory, and lectured in the Vasileostrovsky Music School near his home. He died in 1934.

Since nineteenth-century Russia had a tradition of amateur composers, he had in his early days tried to write songs. But he had the sense to realize very soon that he had no creative gift and, despite his dislike of conventional harmony teaching, began to study Lisztian and post-Lisztian harmony—particularly Rimsky-Korsakov's—on his own. His closer personal connection with the master began in October 1891 as a result of a long letter inquiring about the precise program of the orchestral piece entitled *Skazka* (Fairy Tale), which bears a motto from the first canto of Pushkin's *Ruslan and Ludmila*. In his *Reminiscences of Rimsky-Korsakov* he describes how he was still asleep when they brought him Rimsky-Korsakov's reply:

I was so painfully agitated that I almost wept. . . . It seemed to me that if I opened the letter all my dreams would be shattered for ever.

And when he found inside an invitation to call on the following Sunday:

the previous night I hardly closed my eyes. I was too agitated. That which I had aimed at for several years was at last to be achieved.

He lived in that spirit of passionate hero worship until the fatal June day in 1908 when a telegram from Rimsky-Korsakov's son-in-law Maximilian Steinberg told him that "Nikolai Andreyevich died in the night." For more than sixteen years he had been in almost daily contact with his idol.

The idol himself was not unembarrassed by the worshipper. In the early days he wrote to his wife:

Yastrebtsev often comes to me in the evenings; he intends to write about my compositions. I'm afraid he may turn out to be only a talker and not produce any sense. But all the same he's devoted to music and in this respect passionate, and therefore sympathetic.

Yastrebtsev's first venture into print, a study of "The Second and Third versions of *The Maid of Pskov* and the folk themes borrowed by Rimsky-Korsakov in this opera"[1] is bare and factual, and that dry precision and narrow focus were to characterize all his writing. His interests were not, of course, limited to Rimsky-Korsakov. His first love had been Berlioz, later he became a Wagner enthusiast, and he widened and deepened his appreciation of Russian music in general not only in concert halls and theaters but in the private houses of singers and other performers to which his friendship with Rimsky-Korsakov and, later, Balakirev soon gave him easy access. But it was to Rimsky-Korsakov's own home that he returned more and more frequently and as a gradually more welcome guest. And when he came away he at once faithfully recorded, often verbatim, what had been said. He often sets down his own leading questions, much less often what others said. Both ears were pricked for Rimsky-Korsakov alone. Praising his hero, he sometimes artlessly praised himself. For instance (26 January 1897):

Speaking of Rimsky-Korsakov's admirers, I said that (sad as it was) it must be admitted that really only I and V. I. Belsky [later the librettist of *Tsar Saltan, Kitezh,* and *The Golden Cockerel*] were totally sincere and intelligent enthusiasts for his music; as for the rest, one could say in Ostrovsky's words in *Snegurochka:* "Joylessly and coldly Spring is greeted by her gloomy land." We laughed. "Worse than that," added Rimsky-Korsakov. "I'm absolutely convinced that, leaving aside the libretto, the music of my *Sadko* wholly pleases no one but you." Upon this I remarked that I'd finally come to the sad conclusion that anyone who wants to win lasting fame among his contemporaries must try to write music as commonplace as possible. "Just recollect," I said, "that in its day poor *Ruslan* didn't find in all Russia even a Yastrebtsev." We laughed again.

Only in politics did Yastrebtsev not see eye to eye with Rimsky-Korsakov. After the military massacre of the peaceful demonstrators before the Winter Palace in January 1905 the composer told Yastrebtsev he had become a "bright red" but refused to talk about such "awfully agitating" matters. Before long he was obliged to talk about them publicly, championed the striking conservatory students, and made an orchestral setting of the revolutionary song *Dubinushka*. Yastrebtsev, on the other hand, became a member of the local committee of the more moderate Party of National Freedom (later, the Constitutional Democrats, or "Kadets," as they were nicknamed). But he says little or nothing about all this, though for that matter he says little about anything but music. He will mention in passing that one evening the company talked about Tolstoy but he records nothing that was said. On another occasion he laments that "after tea there was no opportunity at all to talk about music." He sometimes seems even to have resented the presence of guests who distracted the host from himself. He probably distracted the host in another sense, too; for Rimsky-Korsakov—knowing that everything which passed his lips was liable to be recorded, and being by nature more reticent than Samuel Johnson—must have been on his guard. As it was, Yastrebtsev sometimes annoyed him—and faithfully recorded the annoyance.

Despite these reservations, Yastrebtsev's memoirs are a remarkable, even unique, achievement. What would we not give for such a day-by-day record of sixteen years of the life and thought of any other distinguished composer, particularly one—and there are not many—at the center of such a lively circle of friends and disciples?

Yastrebtsev began to publish his *Reminiscences* in 1917, also including a number of letters from and to Rimsky-Korsakov. But the Revolution put an end after the second installment, which goes only as far as 27 March 1895; deterioration in the quality of the paper tells its own tale. It was not until 1959–60 that the Gosudarstvennoe muzykal'noe izdatel'stvo (State Musical Publishing House) published the complete work, though minus the letters, in two volumes amounting to a thousand pages of main text— at a rough estimate a quarter of a million words—apart from notes and other editorial matter. A complete translation would be a formidable task, but Florence Jonas has put non-Russian readers heavily in her debt with this admirable selection.

GERALD ABRAHAM

Translator's Note

It is interesting, I think, that it took a Broadway show of the 1980s (*Amadeus*) to coax a Rimsky-Korsakov opera out of the closet—his one-act *Mozart and Salieri,* written in 1897 and the least representative of all his works in this genre. Even so, this little opera received only a few performances and these hardly of the caliber of the original production (how could it be otherwise with no Chaliapin to portray Salieri?).

Aside from *The Golden Cockerel* (which is in the New York City Opera repertory) and an occasional performance of *Christmas Eve* or *The Legend of the Invisible City of Kitezh,* the only music of Rimsky-Korsakov which most people ever hear are the three orchestral showpieces: *Sheherazade, Capriccio espagnol* and the *Russian Easter Overture.* From this one would never know that he was essentially an opera composer, author of fifteen works in this genre. In them is to be found everything that Rimsky-Korsakov was: sailor, nature lover, lyricist, orchestrator, teller of tales, singer of folk songs (traditional and his own), Russian to the core with a profound love of the fantastic.

Eleven of Rimsky-Korsakov's operas were written during the years 1894–1906, and all throughout this time, Yastrebtsev was on hand to record their conception, birth, and finally public appearance—from rehearsal to premiere, anxiety to review, all against the background of St. Peterburg's rich musical life. This is not to say that Rimsky-Korsakov was only creating operas. Not at all, for while busy with them, he found time to write fifty of his sixty songs (also unknown here), to teach, conduct, travel abroad, and engage in an active social life with colleagues and students. Through the "Wednesday evenings" at the Rimsky-Korsakovs' we catch intimate glimpses of a number of these students, among them Glazunov, Liadov, Steinberg (the composer's favorite, subsequently his son-in-law and the composition teacher of Dmitri Shostakovich at the Moscow Conservatory), and Stravinsky. Incidentally, nowhere in Yastrebt-sev's memoirs is there any mention of another of Rimsky-Korsakov's fa-mous students—Sergei Prokofiev. This is not so strange as it may seem, for Stravinsky was a young man in his twenties when he came to Rimsky-Korsakov, studied privately with him, and developed a close personal relationship with him. On the other hand, Prokofiev was a mere fifteen-year-old when he entered Rimsky-Korsakov's course in orchestration and not a particularly sympathetic one at that. He found the assignments tiresome, and his teacher found him, though talented, "immature."

Thus far the only access to Rimsky-Korsakov has been through his autobiography, *My Musical Life*. Written at various times in the composer's life, often years after the events recorded occurred, it is not always ac-curate. Besides, it closes almost two years before Rimsky-Korsakov's death. Faced with the task of doing justice to Rimsky-Korsakov and to Yastrebt-sev's voluminous two-volume work while also making it feasible for pub-lication, I have had to resort to a careful selection of the material. Often I have abridged and even excised entire entries which I considered of negligible interest. I hope that what is presented here will prove interest-ing to the general reader and of value to the scholar. In the translation I have sought to be faithful to the author while at the same time enriching his style.

On behalf of those who will read this book and for myself, as well, I wish to express my deepest gratitude to Dr. Gerald Abraham, my friend and mentor, for having introduced us to Yastrebtsev and through him to Rimsky-Korsakov. I shall always remember the encouragement and sup-port given me by another dear friend, the late Boris Schwarz.

For permitting me to consult him on some research questions, also my thanks to Professor S. F. Johnson. For her ever-willing aid in many ways, my deep thanks to Catharine Nepomnyashchy, and certainly not least of all, to Nina Bouis, a joy to work with on the often tedious chores necessary to preparing this manuscript for publication.

REMINISCENCES OF RIMSKY-KORSAKOV

CHAPTER I

1886–1891

As I now recall, the first time I saw Nikolai Andreyevich Rimsky-Korsakov was on February 15, 1886, the day of the seventh and last of Anton Rubinstein's historical concerts.[1] There was not a single ticket to be had, not even a five-ruble one, so, without a moment's thought, I set off for the Europa Hotel, where Anton Grigoryevich lived. Even though I was told there that on the day of a concert, Rubinstein receives no one, I waited for him to come out. In about ten minutes he appeared in the doorway. I advanced toward him and when we were face to face, I asked if he would be so kind as to afford me the opportunity of attending his concert that day. After gazing at me intently, as if deliberating (he probably recognized me as the young man who had stood in the curve of his piano at his previous concerts, listening in raptures to his encores), he finally said: "Very well, then, let us go together; I'll try to get you in somehow."

With this we started out for the Assembly Hall of the Nobility. While crossing the street, we were almost crushed by the throng of cabmen milling about there. Suddenly one of them, who had bumped right into Rubinstein, shouted angrily "Hey, you there, you devil, where do you think you're going? Can't you see—this is where the gentry ride!" Shortly afterward, however, we reached the steps to the hall, where we were greeted by a chorus of ardent admirers. Impervious to their tearful entreaties, without so much as a glance at any of them, Anton Grigoryevich kept replying curtly: "It's impossible, quite impossible. I can't do anything about it." But then, at the entrance to the hall, he turned to the guard and said, "Let them in." With these words and a perfunctory nod to me, he disappeared in the crowd.

Thus I found myself on the stage, surrounded by a select audience. The program, devoted entirely to Russian composers, opened with eleven études by Chopin (op. 10 and 25). Then followed Glinka's *Tarantella, Barcarolle,* and *Souvenir d'une mazurka;* Scherzo in B minor; a mazurka and *Islamey* by Balakirev; Cui's Scherzo in B flat and Polonaise in C; *Étude, Novellette,* and *Waltz* by Rimsky-Korsakov; Étude in A flat and an intermezzo by Liadov; *Song Without Words, Waltz, Romance,* and *Scherzo à la russe* by Tchaikovsky; Anton Rubinstein's own Sonata no. 3, Theme and Variations from his Sonata no. 2, and the Scherzo from his Sonata no. 4, and *Feuillet d'album* and Waltz in A flat by his brother, Nikolai Rubinstein. In addition, Anton Grigoryevich played four encores—his own Melody no. 1 and *Soirées de Saint-Petersbourg,* the March from Beethoven's *Ruins of Athens* and, finally, Schumann's "Vogel alls Prophet."

After Rimsky-Korsakov's *Waltz,* two of those seated on the stage—a middle-aged lady in a black dress, and a tall, very stately man with large, blue-tinted spectacles—rose quietly and slowly descended the steps. As they passed us, my friend Zapolsky whispered: "Do you know who they are? That's our famous composer, professor at the Petersburg Conservatory, Nikolai Andreyevich Rimsky-Korsakov, and his wife, the former Mlle Purgold, also a well-known musician." I must confess that I paid little attention to Zapolsky; at that time I did not yet know the music of Rimsky-Korsakov. And so, after watching the Rimsky-Korsakovs indifferently as far as the door to the artists' room, I continued to revel in the brilliance and beauty of Rubinstein's playing.

24 October 1887

As I was about to leave the Lishins' tonight, Grigory Andreyevich suggested that I accompany him to the first Russian Symphony Concert of the season,[2] which was to be conducted by Rimsky-Korsakov and devoted entirely to the works of the late Alexander Borodin.

Arriving late at the Maly Theater and finding our seats occupied, we sat down in the second row near Tchaikovsky, whom I was to meet for the first time that evening.

Borodin's Second Symphony received a thunderous ovation. After the Polovtsian March from *Prince Igor,* which had been orchestrated by Rimsky-Korsakov and was being performed for the first time, the conductor was presented with a large laurel wreath (probably from V̇. V. Stasov) bearing the inscription "In the Name of Borodin."

25 November 1889

At the third Russian Symphony Concert, conducted by Rimsky-Korsakov,[3] the program included Rimsky-Korsakov's *Antar*[4] and Piano Concerto in C-sharp minor, the Destruction of the Temple of Radegast from act 4 of the unfinished opera-ballet *Mlada* by Borodin,[5] Liadov's *Inn Mazurka,*[6] Balaikirev's *Islamey,*[7] and Glazunov's *Second Overture on Greek Themes.*

Even though the program was extremely interesting, the concert was very poorly attended. I sat in the gallery, over the stage, and thus I was able to watch Nikolai Andreyevich to my heart's content.

Today I also saw Anatoly Liadov for the first time, when he came out to take a bow.

10 December 1889

At this, the fourth Russian Symphony Concert of the season, Rimsky-Korsakov conducted his amazing *Sadko,*[8] and he conducted brilliantly! The effect was stupendous; I was overwhelmed by the genius, power, and beauty of this supremely original orchestral fantasy! And I was not alone; the entire audience shared my feeling.

Tchaikovsky also conducted today—his *Hamlet* and Concert Fantasy for Piano.[9]

During this period the Russian Musical Society's concerts[10] were also in full swing, under the direction of Leopold Auer.[11] At one of the open rehearsals, as the audience was dispersing, I noticed Rimsky-Korsakov leaving, too. Seizing a moment when he was alone, I went up to him and asked if I might have his autograph. Although he seemed little disposed to such a display of feeling from an utter stranger, he replied with great reserve, not to say coldly, that if it would give me pleasure, he would comply with my request. Somewhat embarrassed by this response, I hurried away to lose myself in the crowd.

In those days I did not yet know Rimsky-Korsakov's brilliant *Snegurochka*.[12] I first became acquainted with it on January 16, 1889. That day marked the beginning of a new period in my life. Instantly, almost instinctively, I sensed its superiority to Tchaikovsky's *Onegin* and suddenly this opera, which I had worshipped, fell in my esteem. The more I listened to Rimsky-Korsakov's poetic fairy tale, the more I realized its enormous significance in the annals of our national music. I was absolutely regenerated aesthetically.

11 September 1890

Thanks to an extraordinary, totally unexpected set of circumstances, without pulling any strings or satisfying a single formal requirement, I was accepted as a scholarship student in Professor Johansen's harmony class at the Petersburg Conservatory. (Rimsky-Korsakov was no longer teaching harmony, counterpoint, and fugue.)

This is how it came about. Permission to take the examination I owe, on the one hand to Anton Rubinstein and Rimsky-Korsakov and, on the other, to my broad musical knowledge. My examiners were Professor Johansen and Rimsky-Korsakov. The latter was regarded at the Conservatory as "a man of iron will and extraordinary strictness" who, if he wanted something, insisted upon it and got it.

They sat me down at the piano and had me play three of my own romances. Rimsky-Korsakov seemed to like them more or less. While I was playing (owing to nervousness, erratically), he kept humming and muttering compliments, and when, in the last little piece, I shifted suddenly from 6/8 to 3/4, he turned to Yuly Ivanovich and declared: "There can be no doubt about it; the musicality is too obvious." He asked me if I knew anything about elementary theory—I gave an ambiguous reply. Then: "Which scale has both F flat and F sharp?" Even though this was a most innocent question, I did not take any chances but answered meekly: "I don't know."

Nikolai Andreyevich burst out laughing. "Well, aren't you a curious fellow!" he exclaimed. "You can't answer such a nonsensical question, but when it comes to musical literature you seem to know more than our entire Conservatory.

"Only in Russia could you conceive of such people," he added, as if to himself.

When they left to inform Rubinstein of their opinion of me, I could see Rimsky-Korsakov in the distance, gesticulating excitedly. The final outcome was that I, who knew thoroughly almost everything of Wagner and Berlioz, Phrygian and Dorian cadences, augmented triads and whole-tone scales, but was unclear about the simple key of G minor, was accepted as a scholarship student.

At the Conservatory

30 September; 3, 7, 13, 14, 20 October; 19, 20, 22 December 1890
16 February, 16 March, 6 April 1891

My stay at the Conservatory was rather strange. I spent most of the time either at a café, heatedly discussing the new music with other students, or in the library, poring over the most interesting things I could find there: Berlioz' scores, Wagner's *Der Ring des Nibelungen, Tristan,* and *Lohengrin,* Rimsky-Korsakov's *Snegurochka,* etc. The last I even copied out, thus continuing the work I had begun at the public library in the fall with the help of Stasov. This routine was suddenly interrupted, however, by a series of events which revitalized my life and for a long time tore me away from Johansen's endless tables. These were: (1) a performance of Borodin's *Prince Igor;* (2) Rimsky-Korsakov's anniversary; (3) a performance of the third act of *Mlada;* (4) an evening of opera at the Conservatory, consisting of one act each from Cui's *Captive of the Caucasus* and Rimsky-Korsakov's *Snegurochka,* and two acts from Solovyov's *Vakula the Smith;*[13] (5) a performance of Beethoven's Ninth Symphony at the Assembly Hall of the Nobility conducted by Anton Rubinstein; and (6) a totally unexpected introduction to Balakirev (on January 16, 1891, through Nina Fried).

The performance of *Prince Igor* at the Marinsky Theater was truly an event for everyone who loves our national music and fully comprehends the importance of this remarkable work. To me, at least, it always seemed a second *Ruslan;* sometimes I felt that certain moments of it even surpassed Glinka's masterpiece. The orchestral rehearsals, which I got into thanks to Nina Fried (who sang Konchakovna) and the company's producer Gennady Kondratyev, began on September 30, 1890, and continued until October 20. The premiere took place on October 23. Nikolai Andreyevich conducted the rehearsals meticulously; at one of them he even showed the *corps de ballet* how it should dance and how to group itself on the stage.

During an intermission at one of the final rehearsals, seizing an opportunity to look through the score on the conductor's stand, I became so engrossed that I did not notice the tall figure of Rimsky-Korsakov standing behind me. When I did, I became terrified and was on the point of leaving, when suddenly I heard Nikolai Andreyevich's voice: "Where are you off to? Go right on looking through the score if it interests you. You're not disturbing me in the least."

Overjoyed, I did not budge from that sacred podium until the very end, even though, shortly afterward, Kazachenko, Glazunov, and even Napravnik came up to talk with Rimsky-Korsakov.

This period was followed by two anniversary celebrations—first in honor of Tchaikovsky, then Rimsky-Korsakov. Tchaikovsky had not intended to mark his anniversary,[14] but the Conservatory honored him on December 3, 1890, and we students were given permission to present an address. Later, on the twenty-second of the month, after much insistence, we were also permitted to join in paying tribute to Rimsky-Korsakov, again with an address, at a special concert organized by Belyaev in honor of the twenty-fifth anniversary of Nikolai Andreyevich's first public appearance as a composer.

For my part, I went to Stasov to enter my name on the "gilded scroll," which was to be presented to Rimsky-Korsakov on the day of his anniversary.[15] Although the plate had already been engraved, Vladimir Vasilyevich promised to make a special trip to the engraver that same day to see that my name was added. Besides this, I sent an anonymous congratulatory letter to Rimsky-Korsakov at his home (as a student I did not dare sign my name).

At last the long-awaited day arrived.[16] At about one o'clock we, friends and admirers of Rimsky-Korsakov, gathered at the Dominique Restaurant, from which we went, as an unofficial delegation, to the Rimsky-Korsakovs' apartment. Rimsky-Korsakov received us very warmly. First Cui spoke on our behalf. Then Stasov made a few remarks to the effect (certain to offend Cui) that "it was Nikolai Andreyevich alone, who all his life proudly carried the banner of Russian music and never once swerved from serving it honestly." We cheered. Rimsky-Korsakov thanked us.

The following day, at the end of the rehearsal for the anniversary concert, Rimsky-Korsakov gave me my first musical autograph—from *Sheherazade.*

The jubilee concert, consisting entirely of works by Rimsky-Korsakov, took place on December 22. The conducting was shared by Georgi Deutsch and Glazunov. Included in the program were the Symphony no. 1, *Sadko, Antar,* the *Easter Overture,* and the Piano Concerto in C-sharp minor (this last played by N. Lavrov).

At the end of the First Symphony, to the sounds of a fanfare composed especially for this day by Liadov and Glazunov, Rimsky-Korsakov was given a tremendous ovation. There was no end of wreaths, speeches, delegations, and gifts—from colleagues at the Conservatory, the orchestra of the Imperial Russian Opera, and former students. Rimsky-Korsakov appeared to be very happy.

16 February 1891

The third outstanding event of my Conservatory days was the sixth Russian Symphony Concert at which, among other things, the third act of *Mlada* was performed.[17]

I will not stop to describe the rehearsals, except to say that I gained from them a thorough knowledge of Glazunov's *Kremlin,*[18] the Introduction and Polonaise from Mussorgsky's *Boris Godunov* (in Rimsky-Korsakov's orchestration), and, especially, the third act of *Mlada.*

Throughout the rehearsals and on the day of the concert itself I was in a daze. It had been a long time since I had heard anything like that and, as a result, by the time I arrived home, I was so excited that I did not sleep a wink all night.

The last events which left an indelible impression on me were the opera evening at the Conservatory,[19] and the performance of Beethoven's Ninth Symphony, in which, by the way, I participated as a chorister. The former was given at the Conservatory on March 17, 1891; the latter at the Assembly Hall of the Nobility on April 6, 1891, under the direction of Anton Rubinstein.

As always in the case of Conservatory presentations, the hall was crowded and unbearably stuffy. Cui was seated next to Rubinstein; Rimsky-Korsakov and his wife in the back of the hall, among us students. Cui's *Captive of the Caucasus* went off fairly well, and the composer was applauded rather warmly. *Snegurochka* also went satisfactorily. At the end there was such a burst of applause that Rimsky-Korsakov had to take several bows. In contrast, Solovyov's *Vakula the Smith* did not elicit a single handclap. This I found astonishing.

I had attended all the rehearsals of *Snegurochka*. Rubinstein also attended several of them. At one I heard him remark, or rather, growl, shaking his lion's mane: "No matter what they say, there's certainly a great deal that's good in this opera." With that, he left, slamming the door behind him.

10 September 1891

Obviously evening is wiser than morning,[20] for while this morning I had finally decided to continue my studies at the Conservatory, now I am resolved to give them up and to study privately. This is how it came about. I hesitated to register at the Conservatory before consulting with Rimsky-Korsakov; he was the only one whose judgment I trusted completely. Accordingly, I went to see him at the Chapel. As luck would have it, he was there, in the precentor's class.[21] He was informed that I had come to see him, and I was taken directly to him on the second floor.

Rimsky-Korsakov was extremely kind. I poured out my heart to him. I spoke about what I planned to do with my training later on; I complained about the erroneous way in which harmony is taught here; I mentioned that Johansen had advised me to enroll in Liadov's class[22] as the best way to prepare for the special harmony class, etc. Rimsky-Korsakov made a helpless gesture with his hands, and, at the end, insisted that I quit the Conservatory and study privately, with his student N. A. Sokolov.

"Liadov is also an excellent teacher," he said, "but when it comes to basic principles, I'm sure that not only Sokolov but every other graduating theory student knows them better than even Beethoven and Glinka did." Then he added: "Last year I often spoke about you in my advanced classes. I realized that the Conservatory has nothing to offer you—the instruction here is more concerned with 'systems' than with knowledge. Besides, you'll never be a specialist in theory. Your artistic taste is too highly developed for you to apply yourself with enthusiasm to fifths and octaves. You have 'skimmed over' the basic principles and begun immediately with what is most important and most interesting. Finally, to be a thoroughly intelligent and knowledgeable musician, an informed critic or conductor, believe me, you don't really have to know that much. (I'm speaking to you honestly.) Much of what we teach is nonsense—trivia required by a 'school.' Much of it we ourselves, out of necessity, surround with a kind of forbidding aura. All this, I repeat, is actually much easier than it seems. By studying privately, you'll acquire a more thorough knowledge of harmony, counterpoint, and fugue—and more quickly. Then, if you feel you'd like to finish up with me, you're welcome to do so. However, I warn you in advance—contrary, perhaps, to what you may expect, you won't get a great deal from me, even about instrumentation, for at the Conservatory I teach it on a very limited scale. Otherwise, no one would learn anything. This I found out long ago.

"When it comes to talent," continued Rimsky-Korsakov, "as a rule, it's very difficult to judge *a priori*—it's so tricky. Sometimes you think someone has talent; suddenly you look and you can't find a trace of it—and vice versa. One thing I can say—a fertile imagination is a sure sign of talent. To all appearances, you have many of the essential gifts—such as an excellent ear, a remarkable memory. But again I repeat; you'll never become a real theorist. Therefore, while I believe that a general study of the basic principles and rules of music would be very, very useful to you, I see little need for you to delve deeply into the purely technical aspects of the art.

"As for orchestration, which seems to interest you so much, in this, too, I'd probably be of little help to you. What, specifically, could I possibly tell you about this branch of musical knowledge when you've already studied the scores of Berlioz, Liszt, Wagner, and us Russians and, I've heard, have even copied out my *Snegurochka?* Everything is there, and neither I nor anyone else is going to say anything more. Again I repeat: to become a musician in the full sense of the word, it's not absolutely necessary to be at a conservatory!"

When I remarked that I was used to being there and that if I were not, I would not be able to use the library, Rimsky-Korsakov replied that

that would be unfortunate, since "it has a few things," but then, by way of consoling me, he said that there will be no new additions as they have decided not to spend any money on the library for several years.

"And," he added, "you've probably long been well acquainted with what's there."

The conversation turned to the subject of absolute pitch. Nikolai Andreyevich observed that this is something which can always be cultivated and, conversely, can also be spoiled; that, on the whole, it is a very agreeable faculty to have, and one should always strive to develop it.

Discussing thus one thing and another, I spent about three quarters of an hour with Rimsky-Korsakov. When I rose to leave and began to apologize for having disturbed him with my unexpected visit, he assured me that he was very glad to have been of help to me, shook my hand warmly, and even accompanied me to the staircase—in short, he exceeded all the rules of kindness.

Understanding, gentle, simple and warm—this was Rimsky-Korsakov the very first time I saw him!

On the thirteenth, I withdrew from the Conservatory.

[On October 7, 1891, Yastrebtsev sent Rimsky-Korsakov a letter asking him to clarify the meaning of his *Skazka* and where to find a correct, detailed account of the program of *Sheherazade*.[23] He also asked the composer which melodies in *Snegurochka* are based on actual folk tunes. Here is Rimsky-Korsakov's reply]:

9 October 1891

Dear Sir and esteemed fanatic of Russian music,

Since I terribly dislike writing letters, if you wish to question me about various things, please come to see me. Weekdays you will not find me at home before eight-thirty in the evening, but on Sunday, barring some extraordinary occurrence, I will be here in the morning and afternoon. I shall be very glad to see you and have a talk with you.

Yours,   N. Rimsky-Korsakov. 8 October 1891.

P.S. You did not tell me your given name and patronymic.

13 October 1891

It was not yet ten-fifteen when I rang the bell at no. 66.[24] I will not attempt to describe the blissful feeling I experienced that memorable morning, except to say that seldom in my life have I been happier.

Nikolai Andreyevich kindly consented to point out to me the Russian folk themes he had used in *Snegurochka*. Leafing through the opera, he indicated the following as borrowings from folk sources:

In the Prologue. In the chorus of the birds:

Example 1

In the scene of the Farewell to Shrovetide, a motive in the chorus (example 2—see Rimsky-Korsakov's collection, *100 Russian Folk Songs,* pt. II, no. 46, "A my maslenitsu dozhidaem")[25] or a variant (example 3), and in the scene with the scarecrow, in the timpani (example 4):

Example 2

Example 3

Example 4

In act 1. Theme heard by Rimsky-Korsakov in his childhood in Tikhvin (example 5); theme of the wedding ceremony (example 6); see Rimsky-Korsakov's *100 Russian Folk Songs,* pt. II, no. 100, in praise of bachelorhood: "Kak za rechkoiu, da za bystroiu"; also Stakhovich's collection,[26] 3d ed., 1854. This is followed by another folk song (example 7), also from

Example 5

Example 6

Example 7

Rimsky-Korsakov's collection, no. 78, the wedding song: "Kak ne pava-svet po dvoru khodila" from Orlov Province, Maloarchangelsk District, village of Troitsk (1810–1820), reported by S. V. Rimskaya-Korsakova. This melody is found also in the third edition of Pratsch's collection.[27]

The tune "Ai, vo pole lipen'ka" (see Rimsky-Korsakovs' collection, pt. II, no. 54; also in Pratsch) [example 8].

Example 8

In act 3 there appears a variant of "Kamarinskaia" or, rather, "Kamar-itskaia" [example 9].

In scene 2 of the same act, Mizgir's phrase, "Da chto strashen' ia, to pravdu ty skazala" is also constructed on a Russian theme.

Example 9

Finally, the millet sowing chorus "Proso" in the last act (example no. 10) contains two melodies drawn from Balakirev's collection[28]: (1) minor, from Pskov Province and District (Balakirev's collection, no. 9—"A my proso seiali") and (2) major, from Nizhny-Novgorod Province, Semyonov District (Balakirev's collection, no. 8—"A my zemliu zaniali").[29]

Example 10

Thus, neither Lel's songs, the chorus of the blind gusli player, "Shrovetide," nor the final chorus "Svet i sila" was drawn from the folk, except the following phrase, which Nikolai Andreyevich borrowed from a folk song communicated to him by Liadov [example 11].

Example 11

It goes without saying that we did not get around to discussing all the questions I had brought with me. I did learn, however, that neither *Skazka* nor *Sheherazade* is to be taken as a literal depiction, musically, of the literary work on which it is based.[30]

Aside from this, I gathered some miscellaneous information, such as that Rimsky-Korsakov likes Grieg and Bach; that the Eastern themes in Borodin are not folk themes but his own, for he could not write on the themes of others (as is evident from his fantasy on the theme "Ei,

Ukhnem"); [31] that Rimsky-Korsakov has not written any of the *Treatise on Orchestration* [32] but should he ever decide to do so, he will consider me as a collaborator.

By now the time had come to leave, but I lingered on; I felt so comfortable. Finally, at quarter to twelve, I rose. Rimsky-Korsakov accompanied me to the door, helped me on with my coat and, as he bade good-bye, said, "Please feel free to drop in whenever you have something you'd like to chat about with me. I'll always be very glad to see you and talk with you."

26 November 1891

After the lecture at the Pypins', where N. A. Kotlyarevsky talked about the *raskol*, [33] I went to the Rimsky-Korsakovs'. It was not quite nine o'-clock when I reached the small square opposite no. 66. Nikolai Andreyevich received me in the anteroom and then we went into his study. This evening we seem to have discussed almost everyone—"Russian" and "Western"—Gluck, Weber, Mozart, Beethoven, Bach, Serov, Mussorgsky, Wagner. In the course of our conversation, I learned that Balakirev notwithstanding, Nikolai Andreyevich reveres Wagner and Bach. He does not consider Bach dry—he even discerns in him at times the most profound poetry—and he likes the Overture to *Die Meistersinger*.

Desirous of finding out what Rimsky-Korsakov thinks of Berlioz' *Harold*, I had brought the score with me. I had just recently collected as much information about it as I could and had even obtained the views of one of our greatest luminaries of music—Balakirev. How surprised I was when, after remarking that *Harold*, like all the other works of this genius, contains a great deal that is good, especially with respect to orchestration and rhythm (in which he is unequaled), Rimsky-Korsakov added that except for such things as the impeccable introduction to *The Flight into Egypt*, the Dance of the Nubians, the *Roman Carnival* Overture and the Waltz of the Sylphs, he does not care for Berlioz' music. He does not consider the Course à l'âbime from *Faust* "real music" but rather, extraordinarily brilliant musical decoration. Until now he has found it impossible to accustom himself to Berlioz, and he is certain that Berlioz himself could not remember his own compositions.

It was midnight when I passed the State Duma.

28 November 1891

I ran into Rimsky-Korsakov briefly at the next to last open rehearsal of the first Russian Symphony Concert.[34] I gave him my brochure on the leitmotives in *Parsifal,* as I had promised.

When they were going through "The Catacombs" from Mussorgsky's *Pictures from an Exhibition*[35] (as orchestrated by M. M. Tushmalov, a student of Rimsky-Korsakov) suddenly, at the moment when the skulls become illumined and the cellos move to the high register, Nikolai Andreyevich shouted: "Messrs. violoncellists, play a little more softly. Otherwise no one will enjoy it."

CHAPTER 2

1892

12 January

This morning at Rimsky-Korsakov's we talked and argued at length about the question of music drama[1] and the suitability of various subjects for musical treatment. In Rimsky-Korsakov's opinion, *Onegin* is still too near to us and therefore unsatisfactory as a subject; *Boris Godunov* and Ostrovsky's *Snegurochka* are another matter. I was about to suggest Gogol's story "The Terrible Vengeance" when Rimsky-Korsakov informed me that he had considered it but had decided that it is too gloomy for an opera.

"It might be used as the theme of a symphonic poem," he added. "At least the scene in the Carpathians."

"You've heard, haven't you?" he said suddenly. "I'm going to reorchestrate *The Stone Guest*. Does this surprise you? Well, I can tell you, there's nothing strange about it at all. When I made the first version, I didn't know how to orchestrate and therefore much of it came out very poorly. This is understandable; at that time I hadn't even written my *Sadko* yet!"[2]

"Tell me," I asked, "how do you account for the enormous difference in style, music, and orchestration between your First Symphony (except for the Andante) and *Sadko*? One might think these works were written by two different people."

"It's like this," replied Nikolai Andreyevich. "When I wrote the symphony we[3] knew only Beethoven, Schumann, and some of Glinka; by the time I began working on *Sadko* and *Antar,* I was deeply inspired by the beauty of Liszt's *Mephisto Waltz."*

Nikolai Andreyevich promised to read to me some time rough drafts on orchestration he had made long ago, adding that he may write a treatise on the subject some day. But I probably will not like it, he said, since it will deal primarily with instruction in technique.

"I shouldn't like to reveal the secrets of poetic combinations, poetic instrumentation," he went on. "As it is, these days everybody's beginning to orchestrate too poetically, and that's a great pity."

He suggested that I compile an instrumental anthology of the best examples of Russian music, with some, perhaps, from his own scores.

"Let them consider this superpatriotism, if they like," he said. "Let them even berate us for it. No matter. Such an anthology would be extremely desirable."

Just before I left, Nikolai Andreyevich asked if I would like to hear *The Stone Guest* and *Ratcliff*[4] at the home of one of their relatives. "If you wish, I'll introduce you to them," he said. "I'm sure they'll be glad to invite you. Meanwhile, it would be worth your while to make a closer study of these operas."

I thanked him and he promised to let me know when and where *The Stone Guest* will be given.[5]

4 February

I was at the rehearsal for the Tsar's concert in the Imperial Chapel,[6] where, among other things, they performed Chopin's Polonaise in A, arranged for wind instruments by Rimsky-Korsakov at the wish of His Majesty.[7] As I was leaving, I went over to Rimsky-Korsakov and asked if he would be good enough to name a day when I could see him. He set Sunday, February 9.

9 February

I was at Rimsky-Korsakov's from ten-fifteen to half past twelve. Among other things we talked about the new orchestration of *Boris Godunov,*[8] with the "orchestra + ½,"[9] which Rimsky-Korsakov is considering, and also the latest orchestration in general. This latter Nikolai Andreyevich finds excessively sumptuous, heavy, or rather, "fat" and, because of this, somewhat monotonous.

"After all," he said, "the orchestration in *Prince Igor* and *Snegurochka* is simple, almost Mozartean or Beethovenian, with the addition of two French horns, a harp, and an English horn. Yet, these operas sound fairly good and even more subtle somehow. Originally I had intended to orchestrate only certain pages of *Boris*—the more festive ones—brilliantly, leaving the intimate side of the opera alone. But later I feared that the splendor of the ball music might overshadow the rest. Often the best passages of a work will slip by unnoticed simply because the scoring is less colorful. This, of course, we wouldn't want.

"You know," he went on, "at the moment I'm reminded of the good landowner of the old days, accustomed to serfdom since his childhood, who, while aware of all the benefits and rightness of the new reform, nevertheless thinks now and then—to himself, of course—that things were also good, even better under the old system.

"Judge for yourself," he continued. "Let's suppose that I absolutely had to have four flutes—for the portrayal of your Kashchei,[10] let's say. But this episode lasts only seven measures and after that these four flutes are absolutely superfluous, only amounting to ballast. Now, if the composer doesn't suggest that two or three of them 'go home' and continue the rest of the piece in 'normal' colors, he'll have to give them more work to do, whether he wants to or not; he'll have to bring in these unfortunate three or four flutes which, far from improving the already reinforced orchestration, only serve to weaken it. For my part, I must say that I found it much more interesting to orchestrate before, with the more limited orchestral resources, than it is now, when there are more colors than we really need."

On leaving I took the orchestral score of *Snegurochka* with me. Nikolai Andreyevich asked me to do him the favor, when copying it, of indicating and correcting in the margins any misprints I notice.

4 March

This evening I went to the Assembly Concert[11] at the Marinsky Theater. The program consisted of Napravnik's *Don Juan*,[12] excerpts from

Mendelssohn's *Lorelei,* and the third act of Rimsky-Korsakov's *Mlada.* The last went poorly. The tenor (Yaromir) was bad; the performance, on the whole, cold, drawn out, and rather slovenly. The audience did not seem to like this work particularly. They did, however, recall Rimsky-Korsakov three times.

8 March

This morning Nikolai Andreyevich informed me that the quartet competition jury (Tchaikovsky, Laroche, Napravnik, and himself)[13] had awarded the first prize to some Miroslav Weber and the second to Nikolai Sokolov.

Speaking of an article on Verstovsky, which was published some years ago, he observed that in all likelihood *Askold's Tomb* had been composed not by Verstovsky but by Varlamov, since "Everything else of Verstovsky's is terribly bad!"[14]

Then, with regard to his own critical articles, he confessed that he has never been able to forgive himself. "At the time Cui simply put me on the spot, and I gave in," he said. "I denounced *Nizhegorodtsy* and didn't find a single flaw in *Ratcliff.* I've kept silent ever since."[15]

Nikolai Andreyevich asked me to return his score of *Snegurochka* before the summer as he may need it for the forthcoming Moscow production. At present, he said, he is revising *The Maid of Pskov* (he has discarded the entire prologue)[16] and has already finished the prologue to *Boris.*

"You know," he said, changing the subject, "I'm watching with horror the increasing degeneration of music. Having finally corrupted the public's taste with his 'Nutcrackers,' which are elegant on the surface but incredibly shallow musically, this gifted Tchaikovsky is going to ruin his own music and music in general. Had I been at the last concert, I'd have cheered Tchaikovsky for his *Romeo and Juliet* but hissed him for his *Suite."*[17]

In Rimsky-Korsakov's view the love theme of *Romeo and Juliet* does not lend itself to development, as is generally the case with long, self-contained melodies.

"On the other hand, how inspired it is!" he added. "What inexplicable beauty, what burning passion! It's one of the best themes in all Russian music."

We then considered the reasons for Cui's unpopularity and we agreed that to a large extent, he had brought this on himself with his caustic, imprudent, and combative critical articles and his arrogant statements about great musical figures, which antagonized many people.

"Truthfully speaking," said Rimsky-Korsakov, "it wasn't necessary to scoff at some of Beethoven's relatively weak pages, to insist, for example, that the finale of his Seventh Symphony is no better than the theme 'Ah, que j'aime les militaires' from Offenbach's *La Grande-Duchesse de Geroldstein*. After all, Beethoven was not a great melodist. His creative powers consisted in his striking and unique wholeness of conception. Meanwhile, statements like Cui's provoke irreconcilable and, if you like, justifiable animosity in loyal listeners. I'd compare this with what I would feel if someone were to speak disrespectfully, say, about my father."

As I was leaving, I mentioned that at the recent performance of the third act of *Mlada* I had heard someone comment that it contained neither melody nor harmony.

"You don't say," retorted Nikolai Andreyevich with mock sadness. "What was it then—a pause, perhaps?"

6 April

In the morning, before the rehearsal of *Boris* at the Molases', I dropped in on Rimsky-Korsakov. This time we talked about Mussorgsky and *Boris Godunov*.

"In the sixties," said Rimsky-Korsakov, "at the time of the renascence of Russian music, when the young Russian composers, conscious of their powers and aware of the many imperfections of the music of the classical period, wanted to shake off the yoke of routine and move forward along a new path, 'toward new shores,'[18] we were still very young and considerably illiterate musically. Besides, there prevailed in our close-knit circle, with whom Dargomyzhsky had strong ties and which was destined later on to develop into what is now known as the 'New Russian School,'[19] some curious preconceptions, which we then accepted blindly. We were certain, for example, that only the natural sounds of the French horn were good and suitable for orchestration; that compared with the woodwinds, the stringed instruments were too colorless and inexpressive; that the double basses were coarse and therefore should be avoided, etc. etc. Then, just at that time of struggle and doubt about the immutability of the old, along came Mussorgsky with his superbly brilliant and gifted *Boris Godunov*.

"You know," Nikolai Andreyevich continued, "I both adore and abhor this work. I adore it for its originality, power, boldness, distinctiveness, and beauty; I abhor it for its lack of polish, the roughness of its harmonies, and, in some places, the sheer awkwardness of the music. Of course, this is totally beyond the comprehension of our 'musical old believers'; they confuse style with the lack of it and often construe the illiteracy of the author of *Boris* as a sign of his extraordinary individuality."

After that we talked about critics and I told Rimsky-Korsakov that I was seriously thinking of becoming one. "Why do that!" he exclaimed. "Then I should have to dislike you, and I wouldn't want that!

"But joking aside," he added, "despite my general antipathy to critics, I heartily approve of your resolve and give it my blessing."

Speaking of *Sadko,* Rimsky-Korsakov mentioned that he has revised the orchestration and has already sent the manuscript to Jurgenson in Moscow.[20] At the end of our conversation, I told him I had recently heard a lady remark that she was literally worn out by the cacophony of the Prelude to Wagner's *Rheingold* (which, as we know, is constructed entirely on the E-flat major triad without the slighest hint of dissonance). "You have to admit one thing," remarked Rimsky-Korsakov. "The public hears absolutely nothing when it listens to music." We burst out laughing.

22 April

About thirty people (fourteen of them performers) attended the eighth rehearsal of *Boris* at the Molases' today.[21]

Rimsky-Korsakov worked with the chorus and soloists on intonation and tempi. At one point, just before the scene in which the vagabonds deride Khrushchev, he burst out: "This is sheer nonsense, some kind of *tiap-liap!*" And during the chorus "raskhodilas', razgulialas' udal' molodetskaia!" Stasov launched into a tirade, assuring us that this finale is really nothing but "rubbish," that in Mussorgsky, as in Schubert, the middle sections (that is, the development) are always unsuccessful, and, as a consequence, musically "rubbish."

21 May

This afternoon, regarding today's conductors, Rimsky-Korsakov offered the following observations:

"Nowadays everybody conducts—the Galkins, Krushevskys—anyone who wants to—and as a result, our symphonic concerts have deteriorated and become colorless! It didn't used to be like this. Formerly, when you went to a concert, you knew who would be leading the orchestra: Balakirev, Berlioz, von Bülow, Napravnik, Rubinstein—they all had names. And even if each of them had certain shortcomings, we knew them; they had shown what they could do; they had taken their place in the annals of music. These days, anyone who can lay his hands on a baton holds forth. That's why their performances lack color and individuality."

27 May

By ten o'clock I was at the Conservatory for the preliminary performance of the examination cantatas.[22] Soon afterward Rimsky-Korsakov arrived, and upon seeing me, he sat down beside me. Since the hall was still almost empty, we began talking, and I informed him that I had rejected Cui's suggestion that I write for the Moscow journal *Artist* in his stead,[23] feeling that I was not ready to assume such a task. Rimsky-Korsakov was delighted with my decision. "I can tell from this how seriously you regard criticism," he said. "There will be time for that. It's really not worthwhile writing feuilletons. When someone undertakes such extremely responsible work, he must offer something truly serious, meaningful, and interesting."

Then suddenly changing the subject, he declared: "You know, I'm absolutely incensed at the indifference of our administration—Johansen and Solovyov! After all, it's their students who are performing today. It wasn't like this in Rubinstein's day. Anton Grigoryevich was always the first to arrive and the last to leave."

Then he added that under the new regime at the Conservatory, Gabel will probably be put in charge of the opera class and Galkin the class in orchestration. "Surely the golden age is upon us!" and he laughed.

28 May

From the Conservatory I went to the Molases' to inquire about whether they had managed to set up some singing before the summer. How surprised and happy I was to find Nikolai Andreyevich there. He is leaving for Luga today and had come to say good-bye.[24] When he left, I accompanied him.

As we were driving along, I remarked on the fact that most of his operas revolve around the day of Ivan Kupala[25] and that, as a consequence, he has immortalized in music this summer folk holiday whose origin is lost in pagan antiquity.

"This is not by chance," he replied with a smile. "As for the reason— someday you yourself will supply the answer."

At the corner of Moshkov Lane we parted—until autumn!

14 October

Whether by chance or design (at the wish of Rimsky-Korsakov) my ticket for the dress rehearsal of *Mlada*[26] led me to a seat alongside Balakirev. Thus, through an exchange of remarks during the first three acts, I got to know his opinion of it.

Balakirev considers the music of the opera extraordinarily noble despite some shortcomings. "You won't find anything banal in it," he observed. "This is not Tchaikovsky." He was absolutely delighted with "Egypt."[27] "Now you're going to hear real music *à la Tamara*,"[28] he remarked. In general, he regards act 3 as the most important, even though he does not like the "fantastic *kolo*,"[29] (which, in his opinion, is devoid of music) or the chorus and "infernal *kolo*." He seemed completely indifferent to "Kashchei."[30] In act 1 his highest praise went to the "dreams"; he found the scene of Yaromir's appearance an imitation of Liszt's *Hungaria* and the *redowa*[31] of Chopin's *Rondo à la Mazur*. In act 2 he greatly admired the scene of divination by horses, praised the "Lithuanian dance," but did not care for the final *kolo*. However, so far as I could tell, in this case the fault lies not so much with the music as it does with the subject, for Balakirev intensely dislikes the cult of Kupala nights and the poetry of pagan worship associated with them. "Remember *May Night* and *Snegurochka!*" he exclaimed. "Now here's a third opera in this vein." However, the moment when Mlada plays the trick on Voyslava and Yaromir for the third time sent Mily Alexeyevich into ecstasies. "This is marvelous," he shouted unrestrainedly. "Postively ravishing! Though it, too, is Liszt."

Besides this, Mily Alexeyevich feels that just as act 2 ought to end not with the resumption of the *khorovod* but with these entrancing Lisztian false progressions, so act 3 ought to break off immediately after the cock's crowing; otherwise, according to him, what you get is a sort of dispirited scene of birds' singing à la Wagner's *Siegfried*.[32] "And why?" he asked. "It only spoils the amazing, brilliant music of 'Egypt.' "

During act 4 Balakirev was no longer sitting beside me, and, therefore, I was unable to learn what he thought of it.

20 October

Finally *Mlada* had its premiere. The theater was filled. The opera met with enormous success. In the course of the evening Rimsky-Korsakov was called out fifteen times, and, at the end, he was presented with five wreaths.

On the other hand, our press, with few exceptions, was extremely hostile toward this brilliant new work; with its characteristic brazenness it scoffed at *Mlada*'s best pages. Not so Tchaikovsky. He was so captivated by the opera that, when one of the "subscription ladies" asked him his opinion, he replied with an uncharacteristic sharpness: "Of course, the public is stupid and artistically undeveloped, and therefore a work like this means nothing to them. But for us musicians, it's something to listen to, something to study!"[33]

Meanwhile, everyone knows that the ignoramus's hatred for everything new and great is much stronger than the intelligent person's contempt for stupidity, so there's no use wasting time on the opinion of "the critics."

24 November

I dropped in at the Rimsky-Korsakovs' to acquaint Nikolai Andreyevich (at his request) with Słowacki's poem *Lilla Weneda*[34] and the opera-*bylina*[35] *Sadko* (after Findeisen's plan).[36] However, Glazunov was there, so I put this off until a more opportune occasion.

During tea the name of Pavel Petersen came up and this recalled an amusing incident which had occurred at the last Russian Musical Society concert.[37] It seems that after hearing Rimsky-Korsakov's song *Tikho vecher dogoraet* (which Nina Fried gave as an encore), the said Petersen, unaware

‚of who had composed it, began praising it to the skies. However, upon learning the composer's name and realizing his *faux pas,* he suddenly replaced the words "charmante" and "superbe" by the word "jolie" and, after glancing about timorously, bolted from the artists' room.

1 December

In the evening I went with Shtrup to the Rimsky-Korsakovs', again with the aim of setting forth subjects suitable for musical treatment. We managed to present Findeisen's plan of *Sadko,*[38] the Ryazan tale of Yevpaty Kolovrat[39] (after Semenov) and, finally, the biblical story of King Saul and David. Rimsky-Korsakov liked the last best of all; at one time he had even thought of working on it.[40] However, all three subjects suffer from the same shortcoming—a dearth of female characters—a circumstance which renders an opera dry and uninteresting.

By the time we finished with these subjects, it was late, and therefore the reading of the others—*Lilla Weneda, The Mines of Falun, Nal and Damayanti, The Beautiful Mélusine* (a legend of Provence), and *The Hussites*[41]—was put off until another time.

Meanwhile, what a mass of material we had collected: for symphonic poems: *The Flying Dutchman; Ahasfer, or the Wandering Jew;* Gogol's "Terrible Vengeance" (scene in the Carpathians);[42] *Tale of the City of Kitezh; Oleg the Prophet;* legend of *The Angel of Death;* and for operas: Zhukovsky's *Rustem and Zorab;* Ibsen's *Heroes of the North;* and Byron's *Heaven and Earth* and *Cain.*[43] The last named Rimsky-Korsakov adores. As for *Heaven and Earth,* he may tackle it some day; he finds it "terribly tempting."

As I was preparing to leave, Rimsky-Korsakov turned to me suddenly and said: "Well, what do you think? Tell me honestly—seeing me this past year, always sitting here in the same place, morning after morning, in dark spectacles, haven't you often thought to yourself: 'What a dried-up old man!' Well? Isn't that so?" and he burst out laughing.

It was one o'clock in the morning when I left.

CHAPTER 3

1893

28 January

Although I had expected to go to Moscow for the first performance of *Snegurochka*,[1] my plans fell through. I was in utter despair. All I could do was to send Nikolai Andreyevich a congratulatory telegram.

This morning I went to the Nikolayev station to welcome the Rimsky-Korsakovs home. After work I stopped by at their house to find out more about the performance of *Snegurochka*. Glazunov was also there. According to the Rimsky-Korsakovs, the opera met with great success; the Muscovites seemed to like it very much. Nikolai Andreyevich was called out many times and most of the arias had to be repeated. This, of course, lengthened the performance considerably; it did not end until twelve-thirty. The opera was given virtually uncut and, on the whole, the Moscow Directorate felt very favorably toward it.

"Just to give you an example," added Nikolai Andreyevich, "at the railroad station, as I was about to leave, Altani and I got into a discussion about the possibility of making some cuts in the opera, in view of the length of the performance. However, when I suggested omitting the trio between Kupava, Lel, and Snegurochka, he protested, saying that before omitting any of this marvelous music, he would try to 'cut' the intermissions. As you know, our Petersburg Directorate is absolutely incapable of such consideration, even verbally."

14 February

In a wide-ranging discussion about romanticism; the state of opera today; Wagner, Schumann, Berlioz, and the new Russian school, Rimsky-Korsakov stated that he regards Wagner as more of a romantic than Schumann and his music (the *Ring, Tristan, Lohengrin*), despite its long-windedness, striking and fascinating owing to its total originality and ex-traordinary pictorialness. These qualities, he feels, constitute its principal virtue.

We talked again about Dargomyzhsky's *Stone Guest* and concluded that, though a most remarkable and interesting work, it is by no means a work of genius. Mme Rimsky-Korsakov, Nadezhda Nikolayevna, I suspect, be-lieves that Dargomyzhsky was more gifted than Wagner. She especially dislikes *Rheingold;* Nikolai Andreyevich—*Tristan and Isolde.* What he finds particularly annoying about the latter opera is its static quality, which causes the music, from the very first measures, to weigh on the listener.

The conversation turned to the need to found a journal devoted spe-cifically to music criticism, with a section given over to a critique of criticism.

"In this way," said Rimsky-Korsakov, "thanks to you and others who are in sympathy with this idea, our criticism might at last pass into really good hands. Only then might there be some hope of vitalizing and regen-erating public taste. But, of course, this is a long way off; nothing hap-pens all of a sudden.

"Incidentally," he continued, "we now have it on good authority that our music is not liked at Court. The only works of Tchaikovsky that they approve of are *Eugene Onegin* and, perhaps *The Sleeping Beauty.* But then, Tchaikovsky himself is not considered a Russian there."

As I was bidding good-bye, I mentioned to Rimsky-Korsakov that I had only recently come to know his *Switezianka*[2] and liked it very much, especially as I detected in it a similarity to *Sadko.* It is, I said, a kind of second *Golden Fish.*[3]

"It's just because of this resemblance that I don't like this thing," he retorted.

It was past midnight when I finally left. I promised to bring Nikolai Andreyevich an amusing letter of Mr. S,[4] in which this intrepid Russian Scudo derides Rimsky-Korsakov and other representatives of his hated *kuchka.*[5]

18 February

This time Nikolai Andreyevich and I had a long talk about Hanslick's book[6] and the harmful effect it must surely have on music; also about Sacchetti's lecture[7] and its ridiculous examples of what was alleged to be program music but was nothing more than onomatopoeic music of the eighteenth century.

"It really would be much better if a person wouldn't take it upon himself to acquaint the public with something he doesn't understand," asserted Rimsky-Korsakov. "Otherwise what you have is a well-intentioned but senseless caricature, which only leaves the listener with the impression that the lecturer is making fun of the subject of his lecture.

"You know," he went on, "yesterday I ran into Sacchetti at the Conservatory, and when he asked me how I liked his talk, I confessed frankly that it had displeased me very much. 'Consider for a moment,' I said. 'How could I possibly like a lecture which stops at nothing in its efforts to ridicule the very artistic tenets I have served all my life. Why, you wrote off my entire artistic career, and not me alone but the entire nineteenth century.' As you can imagine, Sacchetti was dumbfounded!"

Over tea we talked about another S.[8] who, though adhering closely to Rimsky-Korsakov's lectures on harmony (evidently he considered them quite good), nevertheless spoke condescendingly, almost contemptuously, about Rimsky-Korsakov as a musician. Here, for example, is what he wrote to Lishin on May 28, 1887: "The psalms written by the graduating students of Korsakov's class were so *disgraceful* that Rubinstein did not want to give them diplomas (awards were out of the question), and only my marks and Johansen's saved these innocent victims of Korsakov's dilletantism."

After tea we discussed the form of *Sadko,* and I learned that it can easily be represented schematically as follows:

A . . . b—c—C—c (Variations) d A

Introduction   Allegro   Dance   Pre-Coda   Coda

Further, I learned that, besides its use in *Sadko,* the scale consisting of alternate tones and semitones, invented by Nikolai Andreyevich, is found also in *Skazka, Mlada* (act 3, "Egypt"), at the end of the third movement of *Antar,* and in the new coda of the finale of *The Maid of Pskov.*

Third, the theme given below is a folk theme, and it was borrowed by Nikolai Andreyevich from Balakirev's collection:[9]

Example 12

Finally, I learned that Rimsky-Korsakov employed analogous methods when depicting waves or choppy seas in *Sadko* and *Mlada,* which, he said, only evinces a kind of "poverty of invention."

I forgot to mention that Nikolai Andreyevich once told Shtrup that he would have liked to delete from the second edition of his symphonic poem *Sadko* the double repeat in the episode depicting Sadko being lured into the submarine kingdom, since it is a senseless redundancy, but he had left it in "to punish myself."

6 March

On the way to work this morning, I ran into Nikolai Andreyevich, who is celebrating his forty-ninth birthday today. When I congratulated him he invited me to drop by this evening, adding that some of his closest friends will be there.

Upon arriving at the Rimsky-Korsakovs', I found Liadov, Sokolov, Belyaev, and Glazunov. The evening began with a lively argument about duels, particularly Pushkin's. Nikolai Andreyevich is unalterably opposed to them. In his opinion "a duel proves nothing. All you do is wittingly put yourself on a level with the scoundrel." Then followed a discussion of the Antokolsky exhibition and the ridiculous polemic between Burenin and Stasov,[10] which has flared up again. In the midst of this, the doorbell rang and in walked Antokolsky himself. The conversation shifted to the problems and resources of art; the Middle Ages, critics, the public, etc. Antokolsky became positively animated. Evidently we had struck a sensitive chord, for he immediately launched into a fiery attack on the lack of objective criticism, not only here in Russia but in France as well—"which should be of no comfort to us," he observed, "since instead of one hump, mankind has two.

"I'm convinced," he went on, "that you very seldom find a truly objective critic. Actually, it's difficult to walk between two steep banks and therefore, in our country, as everywhere, the critic is always playing the role of either advocate or prosecutor."

Someone made reference to the Middle Ages and the limited technical means available to the artist in those days.

"And yet," retorted Antokolsky, "we painters and sculptors in particular (I don't speak about music. I'm an ignoramus when it comes to that!), abundantly equipped as we are with all the technical means of our day—we're children compared with Michelangelo, Leonardo da Vinci, Cellini, and Raphael. The loftiest ideas are simple—relatively, that is—but they're very difficult to achieve. No wonder Voltaire wrote Catherine II: "Forgive me, Your Majesty, for not writing briefly, but I have not the time."

Antokolsky is annoyed at the endlessly increasing number of bad painters being produced by the academies with their easy granting of titles and special privileges. In the West, height (loftiness) in art has been replaced by breadth. Even in this we are not original; we are only an echo.

The time had come to take our leave. It was three in the morning.

11 March

When I entered, Nikolai Andreyevich was going through proofs of *May Night*. After some discussion of the techniques and means of the various arts—their similarities and differences—he informed me that as soon as he has finished writing his book "on poetic images in music"[11] he is going to start a journal of music criticism.

17 March

Chatting about the comparative massiveness of the latest orchestration, Rimsky-Korsakov recalled that at one time it irritated him. "But in the end," he said, "I succumbed to the intoxicating effect of the amplified

Wagnerian orchestra with its three flutes, oboes, clarinets, and bassoons, three trumpets, four trombones, and horn. The result of this is to be found in my *Mlada* and the third version of *The Maid of Pskov.*"

Nikolai Andreyevich presented me with his portrait. For the musical autograph we chose an orchestral excerpt from the beginning of the March of the Berendeys (finale of the fourth act of *Snegurochka*).

18 March

Tonight Shtrup set forth his ideas about Rimsky-Korsakov's *Skazka,* ideas held as well by the Semenovs, Belsky brothers, Lapshin, and myself. When he concluded, Nikolai Andreyevich offered his view of the work. *Skazka,* he said, is first and foremost a symphonic piece. As such it requires a certain form—hence the repetition of movements, etc. However, he continued, if one looks closely, one can discern in it a number of different moods and poetic images from the Russian fairy tale epic. With this Nikolai Andreyevich pointed out themes and figures which may conjure up certain episodes from Pushkin's *Ruslan and Ludmila.* In the end, however, he maintained, as he had before, that *Skazka* does not represent an exact depiction of Pushkin's work; that the latter only served as a "starting point" for his poem. And the same, he said, applies to *Sheherazade* and the program which guided its composition—*Arabian Nights.*[12]

Apropos of the discussion of the latter, I learned something highly interesting—that the various keys suggest various colors, or rather, shades of color to Rimsky-Korsakov. For example, E major seems tinged with a dark blue, sapphirelike color (first movement of *Sheherazade*—"The Sea"; also the *rusalka* scene from act 2 of *May Night*). B major has a more somber character—it is dark blue with a touch of steel or even lead (the beginning of act 3 of *Mlada.* When the clouds scatter and disappear and night brightens, the key changes to E major). A major, on the other hand, has the bright, rosy hue of spring (Chorus of the Flowers and first cavatina of the King of the Berendeys from *Snegurochka,* Chorus of the Maidens from *The Maid of Pskov*—"Po malinu, po smorodinu"; "The Birds" from act 3 of *Mlada*). D major has the color of daylight (the sunrise from *Mlada;* morning from *Night on Bald Mountain,* Mussorgsky—Rimsky-Korsakov). F major (also B-flat minor and partly F-sharp minor) is green (first movement of Beethoven's *Pastoral* Symphony), while C-sharp minor has a purple, somewhat ominous, tragic cast (scene of the appearance of the apparition from *Mlada*). C-sharp minor, B-flat major, etc., suggest tints ranging from purple to bluish.

According to Nikolai Andreyevich, Balakirev really likes only two keys—D-flat major and B minor.

"He's quite indifferent to the others; in fact he doesn't like them very much," remarked Nikolai Andreyevich. "And so, when he heard that the introduction to *Snegurochka* begins in A minor, he urged me to transpose it from A minor to B minor."

Finally, considering the means and artistic purpose of music, Rimsky-Korsakov stated that what he values highly in this, as in the other arts, are conciseness and clarity of exposition. Thus, because of its utter formlessness, he finds the "Waldweben" from Wagner's *Siegfried,* while ravishing musically, unbearable.

23 March

Discussing Stasov and Cui as critics, Nikolai Andreyevich ventured the view that although, of course, they had accomplished some things, their jeering and scoffing have so alienated the public against Russian music that it (the public) has long ceased to admire what they were fighting for. On principle Rimsky-Korsakov is unalterably opposed to combative criticism (as he is to war). His motto is "fairness above everything."

After tea our attention turned to the subject of program music and Hanslick, who contends that music is a tonal form, a tonal arabesque devoid of spiritual and extramusical content. In support of his view, he cites Beethoven's famous sonata *Les adieux,* which was dedicated to a duke, not to the memory of meeting and parting of lovers.

"In my opinion," commented Nikolai Andreyevich, "this argument isn't even witty. But then, can you blame Hanslick if, in many instances, Serov's words: 'M—r, vous vous êtes trompé de porte' apply to him?"

Then Nikolai Andreyevich related to us something extremely interesting which Repin had told him recently, during one of the morning sittings.[13] It seems that the Venus de Milo had never been a Venus at all but, judging from an ancient medal they found, it had been a statue of the Goddess of Victory holding a shield in her arms. The discovery of the medal resolved the puzzling question of the unevenness of the statue's arms.

"Now," added Nikolai Andreyevich, "let someone dare to claim that music is powerless; that only painting and sculpture are pictorial. Nonsense! To a person who didn't know beforehand what the *Last Supper* is, who hadn't learned this as a child, Leonardo da Vinci's famous painting would be just as incomprehensible as any Beethoven symphony, if not more so. Just so, if someone hadn't found the long-forgotten medal, the statue of Victory with the broken arms would forever have been transformed into Venus, and people would have believed it. *Errare humanum est.*"

Next summer the entire Rimsky-Korsakov family is going to the Crimea.

29 March

Tonight I found Trifonov at Rimsky-Korsakov's. The main topics of conversation were: Stasov, Liadov, Cui, Glinka, Berlioz, Wagner, and Leoncavallo.

Regarding Stasov, Rimsky-Korsakov had this to say: "There's a man I deeply respect and dearly love. I love him for his courtesy and consideration for the people he cares for; he will never permit any harm to come to them. I respect him for his forbearance. He may literally detest someone, but if that person, even an enemy of his, should seek advice or information from him, he would always be ready to do whatever he could for him. And that's a rare quality!

"Yes," continued Nikolai Andreyevich, "Stasov is an exceptional person. Crusty, intemperate, and combative as he is as a publicist, he's always been gentle and extremely considerate in his home life. On the whole, I feel unusually sympathetic toward his views. In certain instances, however, Vladimir Vasilyevich has been absolutely impossible. For example, judging from some of his writings, the Overture to *Ruslan* is rubbish; Glinka's *Slavsia* chorus would be good if only it didn't have any minor thirds; works beginning with fifths or fourths are works of genius; Beethoven's major flaw was that he wrote in the symphonic form, and so on, and so forth."

Apropos of Liadov and his "hostility" toward Schumann and Berlioz, Nikolai Andreyevich said: "While at one time he worshipped Schumann, he never really liked Berlioz. Actually, Anatoly Konstantinovich has one strange quality: he cannot admire several people at the same time. For example, he could never fall in love with someone new until he had stopped loving his present ideal. The sole exceptions to this are Pushkin and Chopin. Time was when Liadov thought no one surpassed Lermontov, but then he became enamored of Tolstoy, and Lermontov was relegated to a secondary place. At present he's enamored of Turgenev and, in music, Wagner—and he doesn't care for the rest of them."

Rimsky-Korsakov took exception to Trifonov's view that Wagner is dry, saying that he has never considered him so.

"To be sure, his music is long," Nikolai Andreyevich asserted. "I don't know anything of his that's short. But, on the other hand, how magnificent and noble his music is, how infinitely rich the harmony, how pictorial his orchestration, and, though brief, how distinctive and original his leitmotives! Of course, *Ruslan* is more touching, but the *Ring of the Nibelungen* is more profound, more grandiose. Meanwhile, music is such a varied art that every genre, every new word is welcome and has a right to exist. Besides, although Wagner's style was already clearly defined in *Lohengrin,* Wagner never stood still; he was continually creating something new. One has only to recall the charming instrumental coloring (I'm not speaking of the form) of the 'Waldweben,' the marvelous storm at the beginning of *Die Walküre,* and many other things."

According to Nikolai Andreyevich, the weakest element in Wagner's music is the rhythm, which he finds somewhat artificial. Not so with Berlioz, whose rhythms are so rich that his music can hardly be played on the piano (though in all truthfulness, most of the transcriptions have been carelessly made and are incomplete). In sum, it might be said that Wagner is extraordinarily rich harmonically but poor rhythmically, while Berlioz is weak harmonically and strong rhythmically.

After tea, the conversation turned to Cui's Quartet, a work which Rimsky-Korsakov does not like, he said, because it contains more traces of Cui's "French style" than anything else of his, that is, "the most undesirable Cui!" This brought us to the subject of "the French," for whom Rimsky-Korsakov has so little love.

"Those endless 2/4, quadrille motives," he remarked "The customary little can-can hidden beneath a mask of exquisite harmony and excellent, though purely superficial orchestration. The exception, of course, is Berlioz, whose orchestration is woven out of poetic tonal ideas."

Asked by Trifonov what he thought of Leoncavallo's *Pagliacci,*[14] Rimsky-Korsakov gave us his first impression of it: "In terms of plot and stagecraft," he said, "it's highly successful. But when it comes to the music, it's sheer trickery—a mixture of bad Bizet and mediocre Boito with some 'clever' ninth or eleventh chords mixed in, used *à la* Wagner, against the background of which there'll be a suggestion now and then of a little can-can. There's one place I do like, though, despite the extremely cheap style of writing—the women's chorus against the continuous fourths in the men's voices, which sounds something like an imitation of pealing bells. I think, however, the theme of this chorus was probably drawn from a Calabrian folk song. It's very distinctive and stands out sharply from all the rest.

"As for the orchestration of *Pagliacci,* it's brilliant enough but it obviously aims at a coarse effect. For example, the orchestra literally thunders; the kettledrums and cymbals are set in motion and suddenly, for no reason whatsoever, the harmonics of the violins are heard and then the crash of the kettledrums again. What's more, in the Prologue, during the Overture, Pagliacci [sic] comes out and narrates the story in recitative and after this, the Overture continues. This is something like the famous 'frenzied cry' above the orchestra in *Cavalleria rusticana,*[15] which the audience took for high drama but in my opinion, only testifies to the composer's creative impotence."

On the way home Trifonov told me that Rimsky-Korsakov had strongly urged him not to write an anniversary article about him because, said he, "You like me too much to treat me and my works properly." However, when he learned that Stasov had also decided to write about him,[16] he went to Trifonov and asked him to write the article.[17]

1 April

While Shtrup was giving Rimsky-Korsakov's second son, Andrei, a cello lesson, Nikolai Andreyevich and I again discussed the necessity of publishing an independent music journal under his editorship to counter current views.

"Neither Stasov, Cui, nor even Balakirev is suited to head such a journal," I commented. "Stasov—because to begin with he's not a musician; Cui—because he can't stand anything that's superior to him; Balakirev—because he's extremely intolerant and inconsistent in his musical sympathies. For example, he absolutely refuses to recognize the music of Wagner, for some reason despises Grieg, hates Anton Rubinstein, and can't bear the Jews in general, though this doesn't prevent him from virtually worshipping Nikolai Rubinstein and even hanging his portrait above his piano between those of Berlioz and Glinka."

"I think," interjected Nikolai Andreyevich, "that Mily Alexeyevich's love for Liszt is based, secretly, on the fact that he was, after all, an abbé." We burst out laughing.

After this we talked about a diagram, worked out by Nikolai Andreyevich, which indicates clearly the relationship between the arts and sciences. We had a long and heated argument about the various elements of contemporary art—objectivity, subjectivity, the epic, the lyric, the dramatic, etc.

"Surely you've observed," remarked Nikolai Andreyevich, "that there are moments when music seems feeble in comparison with the word. But it only *seems* so, for, in all such instances, the word oversteps the bounds of its competency and lapses into caricature. Take the phrase, 'she entered . . . the whole world was reflected in her glance.' Very beautiful and poetic, to be sure, but it doesn't make too much sense."

We contemplated the state of contempoary art, agreeing that it has said everything and "we" (i.e., Russians) cannot devise anything essentially new.

In Rimsky-Korsakov's opinion, the Russian folk song has already been exhausted; as in painting, so in music, content has given way to technique and routine.

Nikolai Andreyevich is perplexed about what the future will bring. Perhaps the present forms of art will die, disappear, pass into the realm of legends and relics as did, in its time, the art of the Greeks, Egyptians, Chinese, and others. Following some speculation on this possibility, Nikolai Andreyevich turned to the state of art in our country.

"The trouble is," he said, "we Russians have assimilated Western culture too quickly; we've fermented too quickly—what if the excess of yeast should lead to a reverse course, to complete disintegration? In painting, for example, we may even have surpassed the West. Yet we've created nothing essentially new. Landscape and genre painting already existed in the West when we took it up. We've painted some parts of Russia. Suppose there aren't enough views of Siberia, the Urals, Viatsk

Province, or whatever. Given modern technique, this isn't difficult. But then what?"

This time Nikolai Andreyevich and I were alone. Before tea Nikolai Andreyevich talked at length about the round-the-world voyage he made during his years in the navy.[18]

Following this, we talked about Glazunov, and I remarked that while I like his music very much and I consider him an extremely talented composer, I have never been able to clarify for myself the nature of his individuality. His early works *(Stenka Razin* and *The Forest)* are surely more striking, fresher, and more interesting than his most recent ones (the Third Symphony, *The Kremlin*); in these one senses repetition and even a certain decline in his creative powers.[19]

"Glazunov has 'drunk' from all of us, if one might put it that way," remarked Rimsky-Korsakov, "especially from Borodin, from me, perhaps, and, of late, from Wagner. His fantasy *The Sea* bears a marked resemblance to the Wagner of the *Meistersinger* period; his *American March* smacks strongly of the *Huldingungsmarsch,* and the Andante from the Third Symphony clearly contains traces of *Tristan and Isolde."*

Tea was served and we went into Nikolai Andreyevich's study. I informed him of my intention of making an analysis of his works for a series of articles I wish to write, using for purposes of comparative study and elucidation of his individuality both the Western and the new Russian schools. I asked for his help with the Russian composers, especially his own works.

He received my proposal very warmly but added: "Don't you think, Vasily Vasilyevich, that you value me far too highly? Study Liszt and Balakirev more closely, and you'll see that a great deal in me is not mine. Still, if you have an irresistible desire to undertake such an extremely difficult and serious task, you have my full support, of course, for something really serious and intelligent needs to be done in this field. The mystery shrouding what is new in art must some day be dispelled; it is necessary to clarify for people the things they like but do not understand. There are many such wonders—by Berlioz and Wagner, for example— to which the public is blind. I'll be glad to help you in any way I can, but why have you chosen my music as a point of departure? I repeat (by no means from modesty), you overvalue me."

I showed Nikolai Andreyevich my table of distinguishing features of his orchestration. Some he accepted, others he rejected, maintaining that while such combinations are characteristic of his orchestration, they cannot be considered innovations.

"Take, for example, the effect of harmonics *tremolo*. That was invented by Borodin (see Yaroslavna's lament—her appeal to the sun). Generally speaking, I'm indebted to Borodin for the introduction of strings into my scores; before this, I had avoided them whenever possible, entrusting what was most important to the winds. This was wrong, since, when it comes to flexibility and expressiveness, the stringed instruments are beyond compare. On the other hand, the combination of the harmonics of the violins and piccolos *pianissimo* (in Spring's recitatives from *Snegurochka*); the use of the panpipe and the lowest tones of the contrabassoon with bassoons (see Morena's recitative from act 3 of *Mlada* at the words "Moi bessil'nye chary"); of the piccolo *pianissimo,* indeed the entire flute family (from the piccolo to the alto flute)—these are mine.

"By the way, since you're so interested in tracking down my supposed innovations, I'll point out one: I invented the orchestral reproduction of the sound of bells. The bells in the *Easter Overture, The Maid of Pskov, Prince Igor,* even in *Khovanshchina, Boris Godunov,* and *Night on Bald Mountain* were all orchestrated by me. Besides this, I may have been the first to use the tone-semitone scale, that is, if it's not in Liszt—I don't recall. As for my 'special orchestration,' sometimes I feel offended that it's called this, for to me it seems that in praising the scoring, they're deprecating my music. 'Of course, the picture is painted superbly but the drawing is poor!' What people refuse to understand is that the orchestration was created for the music, or, rather, *by* the music and not the other way around.

"Do you really think," he went on, "that I'm able to orchestrate everything in the same way? I tell you it's the reverse: give me a Schubert andante, and I won't be able to do anything with it; it will sound decent enough but no better than if it had been done by Laube or Napravnik.

"When it comes to orchestration," continued Nikolai Andreyevich, "I've observed three different procedures: first, when the music was composed with no thought of scoring it, this being done only later because the composer, for some reason, wanted to 'set it to instruments'; second, when a composer had an irrepressible urge to employ some sort of un-usual sound effect—flute *tremolo,* let's say—and sat down and fabricated music that would suit it; third, and most normal, when the orchestration was created at the same time as the piece itself.

"Of course," he concluded, "every orchestral composer—myself in-cluded—has worked in all three ways, but only the last one is truly artistic and desirable."

Speaking further about the wonders of Wagner's orchestration, Nikolai Andreyevich noted that besides his endless innovations (such as the piling up of sound, for example), one of his most remarkable inventions is the almost imperceptible transition from strings to winds, as in the Prelude to *Lohengrin,* where, just at the moment D major appears, the trombones enter, while the strings, which had been playing *fortissimo,* suddenly cease on a dissonant chord (A, C sharp, F sharp, G natural).

"The whole mass of sound is sustained by the winds," he went on. "And what is so extraordinary about this is the fact that the listener doesn't grasp immediately what's going on; he thinks he's still hearing the strings. I repeat, what wonders there are in Wagner's scores! His use of trombones *pianissimo* as a background for strings *forte!* I tried this for the first time in the opening movement of *Sheherazade* and the result was a superb sonority! By the way, Wagner was the first to introduce trom-bones *con sordini* into music (in *Götterdämmerung*). But then, what don't you find in his scores—and Berlioz'! Of course, their genius aside, they both came along at a time when there was nothing except the good Haydn-Beethoven orchestra, and they had a wide field for activity. Now, after Berlioz, Weber, Mendelssohn, Liszt, and Wagner, what can we say that's really new in orchestration? One might even possess some talent for discoveries in this sphere, but once everything has been discovered, you can't become a Columbus! It may be that in the future, new kinds of passing notes or even new melodic embellishments of some sort may be formed from the natural tones (after the sixteenth overtone), but it would be foolish to assume that harmony will be enriched by these third and quarter tones. Will the idea of several orchestras *à la* Berlioz' *Tuba mirum* or like the three-tiered choruses from Wagner's *Parsifal* be devel-oped further? I doubt it.

"You may have noticed," he continued, "that in *Mlada,* at Lada's ap-pearance, I tried placing a chorus of bright spirits in the gridiron above the stage, but owing to the abominable acoustics of the Marinsky Theater, it didn't work. I simply had to discard three of the four flutes which had been playing in unison with the French horn, for the combination of flutes and horn completely drowned out the voices, making them absolutely inaudible. Moreover, however good the idea of placing music in space may be, it's a purely superficial device and, consequently, of little value."

Later in the evening, we returned to the question of tonality, and Rimsky-Korsakov stated again that keys with sharps suggest colors to him, while those with flats convey moods. The alternation of C-sharp minor and D-flat major in the "Egypt" scene from *Mlada* was not fortuitous, he said, but, on the contrary, a deliberate attempt to convey a feeling of warmth, since bright colors always engender such sensations, while deep blues and violets suggest cold and gloom.

"This may explain why the brilliant Prelude to Wagner's *Rheingold* with its E-flat tonality (strange in this instance) produces a sort of gloomy impression on me," he added. "I myself would definitely have set it in E major." [20]

In conclusion Nikolai Andreyevich remarked that he has comparatively little aptitude for abstract symphonic music. He considers his First Symphony (except for the Andante) and his Third (except for the Scherzo) his weakest works. "To me even a folk theme has a program of sorts," he added.

15 April

I arrived at the Rimsky-Korsakovs' at nine in the evening to find that Nikolai Andreyevich was still at the Conservatory. When he returned, at ten, he told me that Galkin and Solovyov are being considered for the Directorship; also that Napravnik may agree to accept the post, but only on condition that the Conservatory passes from private to state ownership and becomes a kind of Musical Academy. Nikolai Andreyevich thinks this latter is likely, since the present financial situation is certain to force the Conservatory into bankruptcy.

This crisis, which had its beginnings as far back as Davydov's time, was brought to a head by the Tsar's gift, which necessitated the complete reconstruction of the Bolshoi Theater, the electrification of which alone will come to at least 12,000 rubles annually. There is no money; no one to borrow it from; no one who will donate it.[21]

Further, I learned that Rimsky-Korsakov is giving up his book *On Poetic Images in Music*, as this sort of work does not suit him.[22] He has also decided not to compile a textbook of orchestration, for he believes that such a study would require dozens of volumes. Besides, in his view, it is impossible to learn orchestration from a book—however thorough it may be; serious results can be obtained only from reading scores.

"For this," he said, "the scores of Glinka, Borodin, and my own, I think, are very useful. Wagner's scores are too complicated and massive for students. At present I'm waiting for the critical monograph you promised me.

"I repeat," he said, "I would have liked, like Arakcheyev, to put everything in order, but I didn't succeed in doing so. Obviously it's difficult for a man on the verge of fifty to undertake something he's never done before. I had enough time this year (since I somewhat neglected my work at the Chapel), and the best of intentions, but all I did was chatter about very lofty and interesting subjects and, thus, really did nothing worthwhile."

Nikolai Andreyevich is also giving up editing because he cannot manage it. He advised me to apply myself more energetically to writing, and, in order to facilitate the analysis of his works, to try to group them—that is, put *Sadko, Skazka,* and the *Easter Overture* under one heading, *Antar* and *Sheherazade* under another, since the latter are both Eastern suites.

"Before you write the analysis of *Sadko,*" he said, "take a look at Liszt's *Ce qu'on entend sur la montagne;* the use of B-flat major after D-flat major and C major after E major is obviously Lisztian. What's more, the typical harmonies on pages 14, 20, 27–28, and 41–42 of *Sadko* are likewise Lisztian, from his brilliant *Mephisto Waltz.*"

We discussed an argument I had recently with Alexandra Nikolayevna Molas about musical technique and its harmful effect on inspiration.

"It's positively outrageous," retorted Rimsky-Korsakov, "how freely everyone expresses himself on the subject of music. Just what do Stasov and Alexandra Nikolayevna know about theory, I'd like to know. Yet, how authoritatively they advance their absolutely groundless positions! Neither Mussorgsky nor Cui (both had relatively little training) would have made a judgment about this. As for me, I support the study of theory unequivocably—but selectively, not *en masse* as at our Conservatory, where some people think that talent can be drummed in through training. It cannot. In fact, Mussorgsky, though endowed with a truly outstanding creative gift, had a relatively poorly developed ear. Does this surprise you? Come to the piano and I'll prove it to you with any page from *Boris Godunov,* in which every measure is faulty—and there's no correlation between what's in the right and left hands."

With this, Rimsky-Korsakov played through about five pages, and, indeed, the harmonization in most cases proved not only illogical but downright illiterate.

"I'd like to know what would have happened to *Khovanshchina* if I hadn't cleaned it up. How would it have been orchestrated?" he speculated. "Just because something sounds fairly good on the piano doesn't mean it's going to sound good when set for voices and orchestra. Not at all! I once demonstrated this to Stasov with the Chorus of the Raskolniki from *Khovanshchina.* Now, although I know I'll be cursed for doing so, I'm going to revise *Boris,* for as it is, it's absolutely absurd harmonically and, at times, even melodically. Unfortunately this is something that Stasov and like-minded people will never understand."

At the end of the evening our conversation turned to the special qualities of various composers. Rimsky-Korsakov noted that while Beethoven and Glinka possessed inexhaustible technical resources, Borodin, for all the striking and brilliant qualities of his music, suffered from a certain monotony in this respect.

"Those everlasting sustained notes at the beginning, the organ points, the syncopations," he said. "We have only to recall the opening of every section of *Igor* and much of the rest of his music—all of them are in the same style: the Prologue, Yaroslavna's lament, and her arioso; the scene with the maidens; Konchak; Ovlur; Igor himself, etc. Besides, his figurations are formed predominantly of quarter and half-notes. As a consequence, in Borodin, in contrast to Beethoven and Glinka, one finds a kind of dullness, a lack of animation."

On leaving I asked Rimsky-Korsakov to inscribe the four-hand arrangement of *Sadko,* which I plan to give my mother on her name day.

20 April

Soon after I arrived at the Rimsky-Korsakovs', the doorbell rang and in walked Nikolai Andreyevich's nephew, Peter Voinovich Rimsky-Korsakov, a naval officer. Our conversation naturally turned to his forthcoming voyage, foreign lands, America, and the Americans. Rimsky-Korsakov again reminisced about his visit to the New World thirty years ago.

"I can just imagine what it's like there now," he said. "In that country technology has been raised to the level of inspiration. What energy, what amazing practical inventiveness! Say what you will, the Americans possess the secret of the future social system, the secret of the life of future generations. On the other hand, it's most unlikely they'll ever equal us in the field of the arts. As of now, having created nothing in the way of music, they've only a superficial knowledge of it and have somehow gone mad over Wagner, with no understanding of him at all, since, obviously, *Yankee Doodle* and the *Ring* and *Parsifal* are two different things, as Kuzma Prutkov would say.[23] But then, nothing ever fazes them!"

Before his nephew came, Nikolai Andreyevich had talked about Liszt. Generally speaking, he feels that Liszt's works are too drawn-out. He does not care for *Mazeppa, Tasso,* or the *Faust* Symphony. Of the remaining works, he values most the *Mephisto Waltz* and *Der nächtliche Zug* (except for one thoroughly weak passage in the middle of it). He also likes the second part of the *Offertorium* and the Magnificat from the *Dante* Symphony; *St. Elizabeth* (except for the Crusaders' march and one or two other passages); and of the symphonic poems—*Hunnenschlacht, Les préludes, Ce qu'on entend sur la montagne* (although this is too long), *Hungaria* (also very long), and *Orpheus.*

"In *Die Ideale,*" he concluded, "Liszt carried the programmatic element too far. Could he seriously have thought he was embodying in sound each line of the poem he inserted in the score?"

I mentioned two Serov letters recently published by Findeisen[24] and this elicited the following comment: "Curious, how late the need to compose manifested itself in this man." Then Nikolai Andreyevich added that although Serov did not possess an outstanding creative gift, his works always evidenced a "vital person," composing, not fabricating. He considers the music of the Shrovetide scene from *The Power of the Fiend* "definitely talented" despite its many flaws.

At the end we talked again about the contemplated revisions of *Boris Godunov,* and Nikolai Andreyevich declared that he is definitely thinking of giving up the job of cleaning up the harmonies of this work.

"Judge for yourself," he said, "why should I do this? After all, what right have I to change something that has already been submitted to the court of public opinion? It was another matter when something had to be finished; in that case I was to some degree the author of this thing. But in this case? The composer himself finished everything to the best of his ability. Bad or good—that's his affair. What sense does it make for me, an outsider, to poke my nose into something when I haven't been asked to? I did a couple of scenes for concert performance—that's enough, otherwise they'll curse me!"[25]

On leaving I took for informational and excerpting purposes the volume of Stasov's writings, including the article on Nikolai Andreyevich and one entitled "Twenty-five Years of Our Music."[26]

4 May

Someone was there on business when I dropped in on Rimsky-Korsakov, so his son Andrei and I went into the drawing room, where I accompanied him on something by Mendelssohn. When Nikolai Andreyevich appeared in the doorway and just as we started to converse, the doorbell rang and in walked Glazunov. Apparently, he, too, was there on business, for they went into the study. Accordingly, Andrei and I sat down at the piano and began going through *Khovanshchina* and *The Maid of Pskov.* I became so engrossed that I did not notice that Nikolai Andreyevich had entered the room just as I reached the final chorus of the latter opera.

"It's strictly forbidden to play the original version of this now," he said jokingly. "The new one has turned out much better. In the first place, this chorus has been lengthened; second, it's better worked out; and, most important, it ends with Olga's chords, which give both the chorus and the whole opera a greater sense of unity."

We spoke briefly about Rubinstein's recent interview in *Peterburgskaia gazeta,*[27] and then about the critical financial situation of the Conservatory which, as things now stand, will have to close down. If it comes to that, a group of the professors will open a private music school but on a much more modest scale. Glazunov told us that, according to N. Sokolov, Bessel is going to lease the Conservatory from the Imperial Russian Musical Society.

"Oh, if only he would publish *The Maid of Pskov!*" chuckled Nikolai Andreyevich. "Then he could do anything he wants to! Après moi le déluge!"

We also discussed next season's Russian Musical Society concerts. There are to be less than ten, but thus far, no one knows who will conduct them. Even Tchaikovsky, whom Rimsky-Korsakov proposed, has not yet been invited! Auer might have been willing but they say that Solovyov put him in an awkward position by telling him that all the Russians are declining "and therefore we don't dare ask you, Lev Semyonovich!"

"Do you know what Auer proposed for this season?" asked Rimsky-Korsakov. "First, Beethoven's Mass in D and an entire concert of Beethoven's works; second, Haydn's *Creation;* third, an evening devoted to Brahms and Schumann. When I suggested that they play something of Liszt, Auer replied that *Tasso* and *Mazeppa* had already been given and these are his best things. As for *Hunnenschlacht* and *Hungaria,* let him be spared that!"

Then we talked about Krushevsky, the "perfect assistant conductor," and also about last season. It seems that for a long time they refused to permit *Sheherazade* to be performed, claiming that it might corrupt the taste of our musical youth. Then, quite unexpectedly, Johansen came to Rimsky-Korsakov's defense. "Why not play it?" he asked. "Nikolai Andreyevich is strict in his teaching—he only takes liberties in his own works!" Thus the fate of *Sheherazade* was decided: it was included in the program. However, a new difficulty arose, for whereas the regulations of the Russian Musical Society stipulated that a composer's fee for the performance of a symphonic work should be one hundred rubles, the Conservatory Areopagus felt that Rimsky-Kosakov's symphonic suite was too light and playful to qualify for that fee. They resolved the dilemma by deciding to reduce the fee to fifty rubles. But then, in the world of such specialists as Tur, Petersen, and others, where Tchaikovsky's Fifth Symphony is thought to be "Eastern" you can hear even more atrocious things than that!

After tea, at Glazunov's request, we listened to him play through Alexander Taneyev's First Symphony. On the whole it is not bad, although it bears traces of Glinka, Borodin, and Tchaikovsky.

When it came time to go, Glazunov and I left together. As we walked along, we talked about Tchaikovsky. Alexander Konstantinovich is of the opinion that the introductory statement of his themes is brilliant, but that the same cannot always be said about the themes themselves.

"In my view, Peter Ilyich has a masterful technique," he said, "but he's not self-critical enough. *The Nutcracker, Sleeping Beauty,* and other works contain pages of pure genius alongside of a lot that's mediocre, insipid, even banal."

9 May

This evening, when I went to the Rimsky-Korsakovs', I found Tchaikovsky there.[28] The conversation, as usual, covered a variety of subjects: Serov's critical articles, *The Stone Guest* (which Tchaikovsky does not much care for), *A Life for the Tsar* (which, contrary to the general opinion, he likes no less than *Ruslan*), and *Judith* (with which he is enraptured, especially as it is intimately linked with memories of his youth).[29]

We talked about the Russian Musical Society and the need to resuscitate their concerts, which have deteriorated since the departure of Hans von Bülow (this "Messiah" of conductors, as Liadov calls him) and Anton Rubinstein. It was suggested that a prominent musician, someone like Tchaikovsky, Rimsky-Korsakov, or Balakirev, might be able to save them from utter ruin.

"You know," said Tchaikovsky, "I'm really not a conductor at all. Having performed only my own works—and Beethoven's Ninth Symphony, once—I'm by no means experienced in this field. Even supposing that by working exclusively at it, I didn't make a mess of it—what then? Could I really rouse the slumbering St. Petersburg subscription audience and raise the musical interest of our capital to its proper level? Not at all! I'd only have given up half a year of my life, offered myself as a sacrifice. And to whom? To some Petersen who, of course, would come to me every day insisting that I perform this or that work by Messrs. Ivanov and Solovyov, claiming that if I didn't, I would draw criticism from the Imperial Russian Musical Society which could damage its interests substantially.[30]

"Well, I don't consider Ivanov a composer," concluded Peter Ilyich, "and I can't stand Solovyov's music any more than that of such celebrated charlatans as Leoncavallo and Boito, with whom I had the mistfortune to be awarded a doctorate by Cambridge University."[31]

Interestingly, before Tchaikovsky's arrival, Rimsky-Korsakov, Liadov, Glazunov, and Belyaev had talked about the Italian composers. How surprised (perhaps even indignant!) the followers of the new Russian school would have been to hear their idols unanimously extol Verdi and Rimsky-Korsakov praise Donizetti, particularly *Lucia!* In the view of Nikolai Andreyevich, Donizetti was not only extremely gifted; his style of composing had a special elegance which set him apart from the others.

[The summer of 1893 was a tragic one for the Rimsky-Korsakovs. It was spent in Yalta, where they had gone in the hope of saving their ailing little daughter Masha. However, the child died on August 22. On Wednesday, September 8, Yastrebtsev received the following communication from Rimsky-Korsakov:]

I will be at home Thursday evening.

7 September. Yours, N. Rimsky-Korsakov.

9 September

On my arrival at the Rimsky-Korsakovs', I found that Nikolai Andreyevich had gone to Belyaev's to discuss the programs of the coming season of the Russian Symphony Concerts. Shortly afterward, however, he returned. After a discussion of the works being considered for the concerts, our conversation shifted to Liadov. I ventured the opinion that, generally speaking, his music is more beautiful than it is powerful. But Nikolai Andreyevich disagreed, saying that in his opinion Anatoly Konstantinovich "is capable of composing absolutely everything." After this he talked at length about Balakirev, his fortunes and eccentricities, tracing his career through the years 1868–74 to show how, when, and why certain character traits might have developed.[32]

"This was truly a terrible time for Balakirev," he said at the end.

"During these years he saw no one; he completely disappeared, vanished into thin air." [33]

I informed Nikolai Andreyevich that I had visited Balakirev at Peterhof during this past summer and had not only heard but seen a very neatly written score of part of the first movement (up to the development section) of his First Symphony. [34] Moreover, after playing it, Mily Alexeyevich had sat me down at the piano to play a pedal point on D flat, while he strummed a charming "Eastern" andante from his Second Symphony (which, alas, has never been written down).

When I hummed the first theme of the First Symphony for Nikolai Andreyevich he exclaimed: "Just as I thought! That's the very same symphony whose sketches Balakirev played for us thirty years ago. By the way, Ludmila Ivanovna Shestakova recently received a letter from Mily Alexeyevich informing her that the first movement of his symphony was now finished and orchestrated.

"You won't believe," continued Nikolai Andreyevich, "what an enormous and important role he played in the education of all of us—this energetic young Balakirev, who had just returned from the Caucasus and played for us the little Eastern songs he had heard there! If they still appeal to you even now, you can just imagine what they meant in those days to us, who had never before heard anything like that. Those new sounds were a revelation to us; we were all literally reborn. As for me, I certainly owe a great deal to Balakirev. Of all of us I'm the one he influenced most, I think; his personality left an indelible imprint on my music.

"You know what," said Nikolai Andreyevich suddenly, "I'm going to write my autobiography, or rather, reminiscences of the early sixties, of the young Balakirev, and those days in general. There's a great deal of interest to tell." [35]

As I was taking my leave, Nikolai Andreyevich told me that the Theater Directorate refuses to put on his *May Night* until he changes the third act, as in their view, this act is "unsuccessful" and can ruin the whole opera.

15 September

This morning I ran into Nikolai Andreyevich just as he was leaving the Conservatory and I decided to accompany him to his new apartment. [36]

"Have you read Napravnik's interview?"[37] he asked as we walked along Chernyshev Pereulok. "No? It's really interesting how far a person will go sometimes. Just listen. I'll read it to you."

And then and there he read the following: "The lack of musical education reveals itself not only in our performers but in most of our composers, as well. Take the most talented—the late Mussorgsky. In this regard, he was an utter ignoramus. True, Rimsky-Korsakov, a former naval officer, studied music, but not until later on. Cui is certainly gifted; so is Glazunov, but he, too, is untrained and consequently all of his compositions are pretty weak. The most awful thing about these composers, however, is their new direction; soon they will arrive at a point where they will deny the need for melody in music. What pleasure is there in listening to something forced, fabricated? I do not understand."

"And I, in turn, don't understand," declared Rimsky-Korsakov, "how Napravnik can shamelessly emulate Messrs. Baskin and Solovyov. You know, last year I refused to be interviewed but now, who knows, if somebody came to me for my views on music, in general, and particularly that of Napravnik, whom many regard as an authority, I might very well give up my antipathy to official statements and speak out in defense of Russian music. I can hardly refrain from giving, at long last, a proper assessment of Napravnik, whose music is often really labored and artificial—his *Don Juan,* for instance—the texture often elementary and crude, and even the orchestration only that of a military bandmaster. And he dares to judge and condemn this school, which he has striven so hard to emulate all his life, without success, of course."

I have never seen Rimsky-Korsakov more agitated. Wishing to change the subject, I asked him why Tchaikovsky, who flatly refused to conduct last May, has given in now and is going to direct three or four concerts.

"Oh, that's nothing," he replied. "In the spring, when Peter Ilyich refused, he simply thought that he didn't want to conduct. That's all."

We parted.

1 October

During tea Rimsky-Korsakov talked a great deal about Wagner and his *Lohengrin.* This time it did not strike him as drawn-out and tedious. However, in his view, despite the fact that the Prelude, the scene with the Swan, the procession to the Cathedral, and the amazing trumpet fanfares before act 3 are creations of genius, this opera does not contain quite enough pure music. There are a great many inspired touches here and there but that is all. Besides, the leitmotives are not developed fully, as they are in the *Ring*.

"And how can we reconcile this," continued Nikolai Andreyevich, "that the music of Wagner, where he is not Wagner, is positively weak, nothing more than a kind of Kücken.[38] There's no in-between with him! Remember the ensemble from the first act of *Lohengrin*, the music preceding the mighty fanfares of the Prelude to act 3, and, finally, the song contest (rather, torture) from *Tannhäuser?* Yet, when you consider his music as a whole, you realize how overwhelmingly ingenious, how original Wagner was! Just recall his 'Venus grotto' with the echoes of the pilgrims' chorus, his dazzling Overture to *Tannhäuser,* his *Ring of the Nibelungen,* etc. Involuntarily you will ask yourself which is better—to be forever beautiful and unoriginal or to compose an impossibly awkward theme like the *double idée fixe* of the *Symphonie fantastique* and be a Berlioz or a Wagner? I dare say the latter is the more enviable."

13 October

When Shtrup, Nikolai Andreyevich, and I entered the drawing room, Nadezhda Nikolayevna was playing Nikolai Andreyevich's charming *Paraphrases* on a theme composed in his childhood by his eldest son, Mikhail Nikolayevich.[39] Shortly afterward tea was served and we got into a conversation about new books. Nikolai Andreyevich said he has read absolutely nothing but proofs for a month. "Much better and more useful," he added.

After some talk about Findeisen's projected music journal and my collaboration on it,[40] we got onto the subject of my forthcoming wedding and Nikolai Andreyevich's "ritual responsibilities."[41] He assured me that he will be at my house between four-thirty and five o'clock and will be wearing his frock coat but not his decorations. He asked me not to be angry about this, explaining that for some reason he always feels very awkward, not himself, when he wears them.

In conclusion I wish to cite several additional examples of Rimsky-Korsakov's sense of key-color relationships. To him C major seems white:

E-flat major—rather dark, gloomy; G major—bright, joyous. A-flat major has a violet, or rather, grayish violet tinge; A minor is somewhat rosy (through association with A major)—like the glow of sunset on a cold, snow-covered winter landscape. With A major, on the other hand, it is already daybreak, a spring or summer morning—brilliant, fiery, full of life, youth, and beauty. B minor has a rather greenish tint—it is somewhat stern and cruel; F major is bright green, the color of birch trees in spring. As for dominant seventh chords—that of D major has a bright, springlike character and rosy cast turning into the yellowish gold of sunlight, for with D major it is already day (Procession of the Berendeys from act 4 of *Snegurochka*); the dominant seventh chord of A major, on the other hand, which borders on the dark blue of E major and at the same time strives toward the rosy A major (though here the blue E major predominates) has a violet cast.

Just before I left, Rimsky-Korsakov inscribed the proofs of the score of *May Night,* which he had given me last spring. I was so moved by his kind inscription[42] that I rushed up to him and embraced him firmly.

22 October

By about one o'clock my wife and I were at the Rimsky-Korsakovs', where, as expected, we were received very warmly. They talked about *Tannhäuser,* which they heard yesterday. As before, Rimsky-Korsakov maintains that the scene of the song contest is very unsuccessful, for although each one claims he is going to sing something new, in fact they all keep singing the same thing.

"Say what you will," he said, "the Overture, being extremely brilliant and containing the best music, completely destroys the opera, rendering what follows uninteresting and long-winded. Even the Venusberg is spoiled, somewhat, by the rather formal love duet (between Venus and Tannhäuser). Besides this, the boring shepherd's song is weak and colorless, unlike the famous English horn solo from the third act of *Tristan and Isolde,* which in the old days the critics called the 'solo of the mad oboist.' "

Before we left, Andrei showed us a photograph of Nikolai Andreyevich, taken when he was still a cadet at the Naval Academy, which according to Nikolai Andreyevich, makes him look like a sleepyhead.

23 October

This evening, quite by chance, I found myself at the first quartet evening of the Russian Musical Society, which, incidentally, was honoring Leopold Auer on his twenty-fifth anniversary.[43] During the intermission I ran into Rimsky-Korsakov, who confirmed the rumor that Tchaikovsky is critically ill; he had called at Peter Ilyich's house today and learned this.

It seems that last Wednesday (October 20) Tchaikovsky went to the Chamber Society. Afterward he dropped in at Leiner's restaurant, where he ate some macaroni and then drank a glass of unboiled water. That night he was taken ill with all the symptoms of Asiatic cholera—writhing and convulsing. This is the crisis period, but the doctors (Bertenson and others) fear that the cholera may affect his kidneys. If so, that would be the end. Still (according to the doctors), there is a slight hope that the illness may turn out to be typhus. In that case, God willing, Tchaikovsky would pull through. But who knows? Such an exhausting illness could have a pernicious effect upon his psychological makeup.

"You know," said Rimsky-Korsakov, "about two years before he died, Borodin came down with this abominable illness, cholera.[44] And what do you think? After he recovered, he was scarcely recognizable. He had lost his creative gift almost completely. What's going to happen now?"

24 October

Today there arrived, by messenger, from the Rimsky-Korsakovs a cake and two scores—*Antar* bearing the inscription: "24 October 1893—To Dear Vasily Vasilyevich Yastrebtsev from N. Rimsky-Korsakov—*sol'* (see Symphony no. 1 of Borodin)" and Borodin's First Symphony inscribed: "24 October 1893—To Dear Vasily Vasilyevich Yastrebtsev from N. Rimsky-Korsakov—*khleb*[45] (see *Antar*. Rimsky-Korsakov)."

Attached to the cake was a card reading "Nikolai Andreyevich Rimsky-Korsakov and Nadezhda Nikolayevna Rimskaya-Korsakova planned to visit the young couple today but were prevented from doing so by certain circumstances. In view of this, we send material and spiritual greetings, 24 October 1893."

I was extremely flattered and overjoyed by this attention from the Rimsky-Korsakovs.[46]

25 October
(Day of Tchaikovsky's death)

On my way home, I dropped in for a minute at the Rimsky-Korsakovs' to inquire about the sudden death of Tchaikovsky. But neither Nikolai Andreyevich nor Nadezhda Nikolayevna was at home—they had gone to the memorial service. And so, after asking Andrei to convey to his father my heartfelt gratitude for his kindness and the scores, I left.

Obviously we were not fated to see Tchaikovsky after the first Russian Musical Society concert on the sixteenth, where he had conducted his Sixth Symphony, which ends so unexpectedly, so enigmatically with the tragic harmonies of the final Adagio. Of course, no one listening to these sepulchral, concluding chords could possibly have imagined that these were to be Tchaikovsky's last moments of public service to his art; that we were bidding him farewell forever.

What a strange coincidence: I first met Tchaikovsky six years ago last night at the Russian Symphony Concert in honor of Borodin. Early the next morning I went to his house and he gave me an inscribed portrait and also an autograph from *The Enchantress,* which was about to be staged at the Marinsky Theater. Exactly six years later, on the night of October 24, he was no more.

27 October

On entering Kononov's Hall for the first performance of *Khovan-shchina,*[47] I ran into the Rimsky-Korsakov family. We talked, of course, about Tchaikovsky's funeral and I was given a ticket to the funeral services at the Kazan Cathedral and also to the interment in the Alexander Nevsky Cemetery.

The performance of *Khovanshchina* was exceedingly uneven, particularly on the part of the orchestra, which made a great many mistakes.[48] Among those attending, besides the Rimsky-Korsakovs, were the Molases, the Stasovs, Shtrup, and even Baskin.[49]

31 October

Today, just one week after sending the *khleb-sol',* Nikolai Andreyevich and Nadezhda Nikolayevna paid us a visit. As soon as Nikolai Andreyevich had made himself comfortable, I took him into my study to show him my scores and various mementoes I had collected, among them a wreath from his anniversary celebration, earth from Wagner's grave, the baton which Tchaikovsky had used to conduct the premiere of his *Francesca* at the Philharmonic Society's concert on March 5, 1887.

"You probably think," remarked Nikolai Andreyevich, turning to me, "that there will be a large audience at the memorial concert for Tchaikovsky.[50] Well, I can assure you, on the basis of past experience, you're mistaken. Despite the public's seeming burning interest in Tchaikovsky's music nowadays, the hall will be almost empty, as usual. You know, several years ago when he conducted his *Tempest* at one of the Russian Symphony Concerts,[51] the audience was smaller than ever. Now, how would you explain that?"

Then we spoke about the second performance of *Khovanshchina*. It had gone much better than the first, but had drawn a very small audience; of the "kuchkists," only Dianin and Belsky were there.

Mention of Mussorgsky's opera recalled to Nadezhda Nikolayevna a very amusing incident which had occurred in connection with a performance of excerpts from it at a Free Music School concert.[52]

"The Dance of the Persian Girls was listed on the program," she said, "but there was no sign of a score. What was to be done? Mussorgsky didn't feel like doing it. So, Nikolai Andreyevich, without a second thought, sat down and orchestrated it. The piece had an enormous success. Mussorgsky was called out many times. He was exceedingly happy and, when he finally returned from the stage, he kept repeating with childlike naïveté that he was very glad that everything had gone off so well; that he himself would have orchestrated the dances 'exactly' as Rimsky-Korsakov had; and that he was simply amazed at how astutely Nikolai Andreyevich had guessed all his intentions. Meanwhile, Mussorgsky took absolutely no notice of the harmonic changes Nikolai Andreyevich had made when scoring the piece."

One more thing—Nikolai Andreyevich would like to subscribe to the entire Wagner cycle.[53] The only trouble is—it is terribly expensive!

8 November

Nikolai Andreyevich told me that he recently heard Gounod's *Romeo and Juliet* for the first time[54] and in terms of the orchestration, which he characterized as delicate and refined, he liked it very much.

Then he turned to me and asked, "Have you heard the news? I'm resigning from the Chapel, where I spent more than ten and a half years, and Liapunov is being appointed to replace me.[55] The latter is supposed to be a secret, but the whole Chapel knows about it. For some reason, Balakirev did everything he could for a long time to conceal it, even though he did take Liapunov to see his future apartment."

Rimsky-Korsakov seems very pleased with his new situation; at least he will have more free time to work on the counterpoint textbook.

"You know," he added, "being a true Russian, I tried to do everything at once. I even wanted to include in this manual theoretical ideas about the harmonization of church modes. But I restrained myself and put this aside for a subsequent independent work which might serve as a complement to my two previous textbooks of harmony and counterpoint."[56]

20 November

On the day of the concert,[57] I did not see Nikolai Andreyevich at all; he was not even in the artists' room in the intermission.

The first movement of Tchaikovsky's Fourth Symphony was performed rather lifelessly. On the other hand, the Scherzo (pizzicato), second movement, and finale sounded excellent. As for Tchaikovsky's brilliant Francesca, it, too, was played superbly, with enthusiasm. It is only a pity that the orchestra's harp was rather small and therefore, the ravishing L'istesso tempo (solo English horn) did not sound sufficiently bewitching, in my opinion. Of course, this was not Rimsky-Korsakov's fault.

21 November

At seven o'clock, when I arrived at the Rimsky-Korsakovs', Nikolai Andreyevich was still resting, so Nadezhda Nikolayevna and I went into the dining room. Our conversation centered on Khovanshchina, which, I learned, had been completed and orchestrated by Nikolai Andreyevich in 1882 during their second summer in Stelyovo. According to Nadezhda Nikolayevna, while working on it, Nikolai Andreyevich became so carried away that he said again and again: "At times I really feel I'm not Korsakov but Mussorgsky."

"By the way," Nadezhda Nikolayevna added, "when Nikolai Andreyevich decided to study theory, after becoming a professor at the Conservatory, Cui, Stasov and even Balakirev expressed great hostility toward the idea. Cui told Nikolai Andreyevich right out: 'Here's where we part company.' And Stasov, after hearing *May Night,* declared that, while he didn't like it, 'it had turned out better than he had expected from Rimsky-Korsakov.' Nikolai Andreyevich had to write *Snegurochka* in order to recover his good name."

When Nikolai Andreyevich joined us we got onto the subject of Laroche (or "Larokhia," as Mussorgsky used to call him) and his outrageous article about *Khovanshchina.* [58]

"At times Laroche's hatred of Mussorgsky's music drives him to the point of absurdity," I remarked, "as when he maintains that Mussorgsky was totally lacking in musicality, incapable of composing anything decent. On the other hand, there's one statement of his with which I thoroughly agree—that despite majority opinion, everything Rimsky-Korsakov has touched has not only been improved but has turned out to be exemplary, as, for example, Marfa's song ('Iskhodila mladeshen'ka')."

"But I'm really afraid this article will set the rabid Mussorgists loose on me," countered Nikolai Andreyevich. "And then what will I do? How will I reply if they start prying, asking me whether I changed anything in the opera or, even worse, added something of my own? I'll simply have to confess that I did both; that I not only added but rewrote here and there. Just imagine what they'll do to me then! Beat me probably!" And he burst out laughing.

"This morning," he continued, "I saw Laroche at the Galkin concert,[59] and I told him he'd better be prepared to write a new article because, despite his denunciation of Mussorgsky, I've started revising *Boris Godunov* again."

"Is it true that you changed the bell notes in the final chorus of the first act of *Khovanshchina?*" I asked.

"Yes, it's true," replied Nikolai Andreyevich. "As far as I can recall, instead of C—F sharp, Mussorgsky had B—F natural, which was not good. Besides this, I transposed the chorus 'Batia, batia' from E-flat minor to D minor, for in Mussorgsky the key of E-flat minor predominated throughout almost four numbers, and this was exceedingly boring. Also, I eliminated the scene of the destruction of the Scrivener's booth, in which the music was extremely poor. As for folk themes, the only ones are Marfa's song, which you mentioned; 'Ladu, ladu,' Andrei Khovansky's song from act 5; and, perhaps, the theme of the final chorus—that is, if you don't count the tune 'Stoi, moi milyi khorovod' (no. 26 from Balakirev's collection), which appears in extremely awkward and melodically corrupted form in the chorus of the Raskolniki, 'Posramikhom, prerekokhom i preprekhom,' from act 3, or the first little song of the Strelets Kuzka 'Podoidu, podoidu . . . pod Ivan-gorod,' which is somewhat reminiscent of the folk song 'Vdol' da po rechke.'"

Apropos of the music he had deleted, feeling it was superfluous and extremely weak, Nikolai Andreyevich made the following rather significant observations regarding Mussorgsky and his style.

"The more I think about it," he began, "the clearer it becomes to me that Mussorgsky was hardly cut out for the extreme naturalism on which he so prided himself. If you look at his early works, you'll see in them a striving for beauty, an unmistakable penchant for form (Scene at the Fountain, *Alla Marcia,* etc.) and a tendency towards correct part-writing ('S gornei nepristupnoi vysoty' from *Boris Godunov*). But then he wrote *Savishna, The Nursery,* and other things, in which music is called upon to depict 'a wicked nurse,' 'stitches,' 'thread' and 'riding on a stick,' and he began searching for sounds that could embody all this. From that moment, I believe, a crisis occurred in Mussorgsky's musical style. Encouraged by his friends (Stasov, Molas, et al.), he ended up persuading himself that he had been summoned to completely reform the art of music. He became a fanatic about his artistic direction, and everywhere, even where it was not called for, he wrote lavishly, in exaggerated, concentrated tones and colors, fully convinced that every musical utterance of his was sacred, every combination of sounds, however fortuitous, artistic and in keeping with the canons of art. He went even further—he lapsed into a kind of self-delusion and insisted that the first theme of his B minor Intermezzo *in modo classico*[60] had been inspired by a Bach fugue—'secretly Russian'— and that it depicted a crowd of peasants stumbling in snowdrifts as they struggled to cross the fields. This unmitigated conceit drove him to compose the initial, utterly senseless D minor Chorus of the Raskolniki, with its continuous parallel fourths. Fortunately, later on he himself destroyed it and replaced it with a new one. This deeply grieved Stasov; he even upbraided me several times for having distorted it. All I did, really was to make it a little easier for the singers to perform.

"This notion of infallibility," continued Nikolai Andreyevich, "gave

Mussorgsky free rein to use the very same music, often indiscriminately, in different works. Thus, he transferred an entire melodic phrase from a song about a woman rebuking her husband for drunkenness[61] to the scene of Boris' death ('Ne vveriaisia navetu boiar kramol'nykh'). And the music of *Salammbô?* Practically all of it was incorporated in *Boris Godunov.* Let me observe here, by the way, that the only parts of *Khovanshchina* which were orchestrated by Mussorgsky were the Chorus of the Streltsy, Shaklovity's aria, and Marfa's song 'Iskhodila mladeshen'ka' (the latter with somewhat different harmonization and instrumentation with *tremolo*). However, the score of Shaklovity's aria got lost and it had to be orchestrated again, along with other numbers of this opera. Thus, neither the scene of the divination, nor the introduction, nor the Dance of the Persian Girls was ever scored by Mussorgsky himself."

1 December

Shtrup and I, who had been at the Molases' on Sunday for the performance of *Boris,* were curious as to why Nikolai Andreyevich had not come but had preferred instead to go to the Russian Musical Society's quartet evening in memory of Tchaikovsky.[62]

"And permit *me,* in turn, to ask *you* why you were there, when you know every note of this opera by heart and the performances keep getting worse and worse each year," retorted Nikolai Andreyevich. "No, to tell the truth, I've no desire these days to listen to this earlier version of *Boris.* I've set about 'cleaning it up,' and I already have such a clear picture of its new form that the old one no longer interests me. When, God willing, I finish with *Boris,* I'll take up *The Nursery* and then everything of Mussorgsky's will have been completed, orchestrated, and edited by me. That will irritate the musical Khovanshchina!"[63]

I informed Nikolai Andreyevich that the next opera to be given at the Molases' would be his *May Night.*

"Well," he remarked, "while I'm not particularly elated about that, since the performance will be far from subtle, I must say it's better and more useful for them to get to know something new than to spend their whole lives listening to *Boris Godunov* and *The Stone Guest.*"

We talked at length about Taneyev's *Oresteia.*[64] Nikolai Andreyevich finds much that is good in it, called it "very intelligent, artistic, noble." "In short, everything is as it should be," he continued, "but it lacks something—exactly what that is it's difficult to define. Something elusive. Could it be life, inspiration?"

During tea, mention of Konius' suite *From Childhood* sparked a heated discussion about whether an artist can portray well and truthfully something he himself has not experienced. Opinions were divided. Without going into detail, I will summarize the points made. Shtrup (who, in typical Stasov fashion, did not listen to anyone else's arguments) maintained that a composer can express truthfully and realistically only that which he himself has actually experienced, that man's sensibilities are limited. Nikolai Andreyevich contended, on the contrary, that an artist will never communicate what he has felt truly deeply and spontaneously; that the creative person differs from ordinary mortals only in an enormous susceptibility to weak emotions. As proof of this he cited himself.

"For example," he began, "I doubt if you would find anyone in the entire world more skeptical of everything supernatural, fantastic, phantasmal, or otherworldly than I. And yet, as an artist, it is just these things that I love most. And ritual? What could be more intolerable than a ritual? I feel positively embarrassed, as though I were acting out a *commedia* when I attend them, and this goes even for funerals. Yet with what delight I've depicted rituals in my music! No—I firmly believe that art is essentially the most fascinating and intoxicating of lies!"

In passing someone referred to Nikolai Andreyevich's new pieces for violin and cello.[65] After that, Trifonov told us that these days Stasov cannot bring himself to go to see Tolstoy.[66] While he adores him for *War and Peace* and *Anna Karenina,* he does not much like Tolstoy's recent writings, and therefore he is afraid to go.

They say that on Stasov's last visit to Yasnaya Polyana a curious thing happened. As Vladimir Vasilyevich and Lev Nikolayevich were on their way to bed and about to say good night, suddenly, on the threshold to their rooms, they became so engrossed in conversation that, without noticing, they stood there talking, with the candles in their hands until morning.

As I took my leave I apologized for not having read Nikolai Andreyevich's notes on aesthetics.

"Don't feel badly," he replied. "There's nothing of interest in them. Besides, there are so few of them that they're really not worth talking about."

CHAPTER 4

1894

2 January

At ten-thirty, when I arrived at the Public Library for the celebration in honor of Stasov, I found that I had missed the opening addresses.[1] Therefore, after listening to the remaining speeches and embracing the guest of honor, I went home, where Findeisen and I drank tea while awaiting Anton Rubinstein's concert, scheduled for one-thirty.[2]

Stasov replied to all the speeches with a ready wit, felicity, warmth, and intelligence. The sight of this seventy-year-old man, crowned with gray hair, with an eternally youthful fighting spirit, imprinted in my memory the words from Antokolsky's congratulatory letter, comparing Vladimir Vasilyevich to "an oak which would sooner break than bend."

Among those present, besides the Rimsky-Korsakov family, were T. I. Filippov, Ludmila Shestakova, Liadov, Glazunov, Belyaev, and the venerable and recently honored D. V. Grigorovich,[3] one of the last of the Russian literary Mohicans.

21 January

Being, as usual, the first to arrive at the rehearsal of the third Russian Symphony Concert,[4] I utilized the opportunity to leaf through the scores on the conductor's stand. To my surprise, inserted in the introduction to

Ratcliff was a sheet of staff paper, containing five newly scored measures, which had obviously been sketched in hastily, in Rimsky-Korsakov's hand. Here and there the bass had been reinforced, French horns doubled with strings *pizzicati,* etc.

On entering the hall, Nikolai Andreyevich's first words to me were: "Where have you been hiding? We thought you were coming yesterday—we waited and waited, but there wasn't a trace of you! You know, on the twenty-seventh my wife and I are going to Odessa for two concerts. We'll be back on the sixteenth of February."[5]

During the intermission Nadezhda Nikolayevna told me that Nikolai Andreyevich is finally leaving the Chapel today and is to go there at two o'clock for the official farewell. I promised to drop in on the Rimsky-Korsakovs tonight.

The first thing we talked about when I arrived was Glazunov's Fourth Symphony, which was on today's program.[6] Nikolai Andreyevich finds the orchestration a bit cumbersome, especially in the third movement. Actually, it would benefit from being made brighter, more transparent, closer to Glinka's.

Later Nikolai Andreyevich showed me the original score of *Ratcliff,* on which Balakirev had scribbled caustic comments such as: "What are these magpie hops?" and "What kind of Asiatic part writing have we here?"

"By the way," said Nikolai Andreyevich, "before orchestrating something, I always scrutinize the harmonization and part writing thoroughly, for correct and clear part writing is just about one of the most important requisites for sonorous orchestration. I wanted terribly to reorchestrate the excerpts from *Ratcliff* before performing them, but I was afraid of offending our César. Really, the wisest thing he could do right now would be to entrust me with the rescoring of the whole opera. I can assure you it would turn out well! In its present form, with its incredible orchestration, it's absolutely impossible to perform. Working on it would give me a rest from *Boris Godunov.* It can become tedious working continually on the same thing."[7]

20 February

Today Nikolai Andreyevich gave me a detailed account of the concerts in Odessa. The audiences, he said, were not especially large, but they were enthusiastic. For example, at the second concert, *Sadko,* Lel's song, and all of the *Capriccio espagnol* had to be repeated, and at the end, Rimsky-Korsakov was presented with a silver baton. *Antar* was not played, as planned, because no decent harpist could be obtained; it was replaced by Nikolai Andreyevich's First Symphony.

As for the orchestra, it was so used to playing everything in a slipshod fashion that, despite excellent sight-reading (in Odessa, operas are given with one rehearsal), it was necessary to hold five rehearsals—and even so it did not really come out right.

During the Rimsky-Korsakovs' visit, the Odessa branch of the Russian Musical Society gave a concert in Nikolai Andreyevich's honor at which, among other things, they performed two of his women's choruses.

I forgot to mention that besides the scheduled concerts, Nikolai Andreyevich conducted a third one for the benefit of the orchestra, at which his *Capriccio* was given again together with several numbers from Tchaikovsky's *Nutcracker Suite.* On this occasion, the orchestra presented Nikolai Andreyevich with a silver wreath.

On their return journey, the Rimsky-Korsakovs stopped for a day in Moscow to discuss with Pchelnikov—the "Moscow Pogozhev"—the possibility of a production there of *The Maid of Pskov.*[8] Pchelnikov fully approved the idea, especially since the Grand Duke[9] will probably not succeed in presenting *Die Walküre* next year, as he intended (the libretto has not yet been translated and, besides, the opera is very complicated), and therefore there will be an opening. Of course, everything depends upon I. A. Vsevolozhsky, Director of the Imperial Theaters, Pchelnikov added. Thus, the matter was only half settled.

"And so," continued Rimsky-Korsakov, "after having returned to St. Petersburg, I went again to Moscow on the nineteenth for a 'diplomatic' visit with Ivan Alexandrovich Vsevolozhsky. I wanted, once in my life, to clear up the question of why not a single one of my operas is given on the imperial stage. Vsevolozhsky explained very politely that in view of the extraordinary expenses expected to be incurred by the production, next winter, of Taneyev's *Oresteia,* Napravnik's *Dubrovsky,*[10] and Blaramberg's *Tushintsy*[11] it will be absolutely impossible to revive my *Snegurochka;* that he deeply regrets not having managed to give my *Mlada* once this entire season."

In reply Rimsky-Korsakov pointed out that he has two more operas—

May Night and *The Maid of Pskov;* that he finds most strange the contention of Kondratyev and Napravnik that *May Night* cannot possibly be staged, that it would surely fail, because of the "memorial service" in the third act which, they maintain, spoils the entire work.

"Mark you," said Rimsky-Korsakov, turning to me, "this imaginary ceremony lasts only sixteen measures and conceptually it's very poetic."

"As for Kondratyev and his advice regarding what changes or improvements must be made in my operas," Nikolai Andreyevich told Vsevolozhsky, "I beg to differ with him and to state, once and for all, that I do not consider him a judge of such matters. It is not he but I who know best what revisions should be made in my works, especially since, as far as I can judge, the most felicitous act in *May Night* is act 3, the very one he rejects. What's more, it has always met with success on the stage. Therefore, the Directorate's apprehensions are groundless."

Vsevolozhsky thanked Rimsky-Korsakov for bringing all this to his attention and for reminding him of his (Rimsky-Korsakov's) operas. In conclusion he promised to keep them in mind when drawing up the repertoire.

Yesterday Cui gave Nikolai Andreyevich permission, if he wishes, to again do some work on the rescoring of *Ratcliff,* the Entr'acte and Introduction to which are already finished. He even expressed a desire to hear these sections of the opera at one of next year's Russian Symphony Concerts.

Besides this, Nadezhda Nikolayevna told me that in Odessa they made the acquaintance of the painter Kuznetsov, an extremely interesting man, strikingly handsome and virile—a veritable Levko.

22 February

At eight-thirty my wife and I were at the Rimsky-Korsakovs'. Nikolai Andreyevich seemed somewhat preoccupied. First we played through Deutsch's collection of folk songs from Archangel and Olonets provinces. Except for a few fairly good ceremonial songs, the collection does not offer anything particularly noteworthy.

After that we talked about the latest journalistic squabble between Stasov and Burenin[12] (according to Repin, "a malicious and despicable liar") and about the outrageously stupid little article entitled "A False

Alarm" and signed "Anonymous," describing the celebration of Cui's twenty-fifth anniversary of the Molases'. Here is what we read in *Peterburgskaia gazeta* of February 21, 1894:

On the night of February 13, the good burghers of the Third District of the Spassky Precinct were frightened out of their wits by an unusual racket issuing from house no. 666. They came running into the street in their underwear. Once there, however, their minds were set at rest; the two fire engines of the city's Second Department, which had come in response to the alarm, had left. The alarm had turned out to be false. It seems that admirers of the noted composer Artakserks Tpryu had simply gathered at no. 666 to celebrate the twenty-fifth anniversary of his opera *Ukhvatom po kocherge* (About an Oven Fork and a Poker), which, by the way, was performed only once at the Bolshoi Theater, because on that occasion the roof caved in and therefore no further performances could be given.

The festivities were marked by great warmth of feeling. The honoree was greeted by the beating of an oven fork against copper pots and pans and ecstatic cries of "clever fellow" and "well done." Following that, the devotees performed the composer's famous opera on saucepans, copper pots, oven doors, pails, tubs, and other domestic musical instruments. The one who played the role of the Oven Fork sang continuously, as called for in the score, with his head stuffed in an empty barrel, which produced such a powerful effect that many of the ladies could not stand it and fainted dead away. The woman who performed the part of the Poker sang holding a two-year-old cat in her arms. At the high notes she gently twisted the cat's tail. This too produced no small effect. In fact it threw the esteemed critic Volodimir Skif into such ecstasy that he forgot himself and began shouting: "Don't say honored guest—that's a disgusting word—cry 'My Little One.' " And with this he grabbed the honoree in his arms and rushed off to toss him into the Marinsky Theater, while intoning in a wild voice:

> Toward evening of a foul autumn
> The maiden walked through the wasteland,
> Holding the secret fruit of an ill-starred love
> In her trembling arms.

The performance of the opera continued from eight in the evening until eight the next morning. Although the walls of house no. 666 cracked, no one was injured.

I cite this for the edification of future generations, that they may know our press's attitude toward the fate of the finest creations of our time.

After tea tonight Rimsky-Korsakov and I had a discussion about the harmonic dissonances in Mussorgsky's Dance of the Persian Girls, which I discovered when comparing the rough sketches [see example 13] with the published score (in Rimsky-Korsakov's orchestration) [example 14].[13] Such a comparison clearly reveals the difference between the artistry of these two composers.

Example 13

Example 14

Many such fine, such subtle touches are to be found throughout *Khovanshchina,* for it was completed and revised by Nikolai Andreyevich. Let us take, for example, the Introduction; the scene of the prediction and Marfa's song; the love episode in the scene with Susanna (with its chromatic harmonization); the chorus "Ladu, ladu"; the amazingly beautiful accompaniment (chromatically descending violins *tremolo con sordini*) to Marfa's words: "Zharko bylo, kak noch'iu sheptal ty mne pro liubov' svoiu" with the funereal tolling of the monastery bells at the words "Hallelujah" (added by Rimsky-Korsakov); and, finally, the inspired closing chorus (based on a Molokane[14] theme left by Mussorgsky[15]) sung during the Old Believers' self-immolation.[16]

6 March

This afternoon, apropos of Laroche's recent article on Suvorin,[17] we (Belyaev, Trifonov, Rimsky-Korsakov, and I) got into a heated argument about the unscrupulousness of all militant criticism and the virtual impossibility of its being impartial and fair. We had in mind Serov and Cui as well as Laroche. Then someone mentioned Kopylov and Balakirev and their continuing antagonism toward each other. There upon Rimsky-Korsakov rose to the defense of Kopylov, declaring that he is a splendid teacher of choral singing, that it would be a great misfortune for the Chapel if they should lose him and it can end in this.

After this Nikolai Andreyevich showed us a Chopin autograph, which Count Sheremetyev had found in an old album of his mother's.[18] It appeared to be the first figure of a kind of nocturne in E major and, apart from the name of Chopin, represents a certain musical interest.

After Belyaev and Trifonov left, Nikolai Andreyevich took me into his study and showed me part of the scene at the fountain from *Boris Godunov,* which he had just finished and orchestrated (forty-eight pages in all).[19] He had cut it considerably.

"They needn't think," he remarked, "that, in orchestrating *Boris,* I'm only going to score it. Nothing of the kind. I intend to change and clean up many things. Let them curse me for this, but I'm certain that, when it's all finished, no one will think of performing it as it was before."

Finally, Nikolai Andreyevich praised Findeisen's magazine to the skies, especially Petrovsky's lively and provocative article titled "On Compulsory Enjoyment at the Marinsky Theater."[20]

Evening of the Same Day

I returned to the Rimsky-Korsakovs' for Nikolai Andreyevich's fiftieth birthday party. Ludmila Shestakova was already there when I entered, as were Belyaev, Sokolov, Liadov—about twenty-five guests in all. Thus any kind of serious conversation was out of the question. Besides, "music" took over as a matter of course.

First, Anna Grigoreyvna Zherebtsova sang a number of songs by Rimsky-Korsakov, Tchaikovsky, Glinka, Rubinstein, and Cui. Nadezhda Nikolayevna accompanied her—and elegantly, even though, because of lack of time, she has barely played for many years. When I mentioned this to Nikolai Andreyevich, he replied with mock seriousness that I was telling him nothing new, that he knew this better than I and had known it the very first time he met her.

"You won't believe it," he added, "but at one time Nadezhda Nikolayevna alone bore the entire burden of *Boris, Ratcliff,* and *The Maid of Pskov*—and how marvelously she played!"[21]

After the singing, Liadov and Glazunov played "for their own pleasure" the first movement of Nikolai Andreyevich's First Symphony. Then Nadezhda Nikolayevna and Liadov played the Andante from this symphony and Rimsky-Korsakov's *Fantasia on Serbian Themes.*[22] After this, Liadov sat at the piano and began banging out the theme of *Paraphrases,*[23] all the while assuring us that he can play this theme from memory even in passages where he is required to play two notes against three—yet no one praises him for it. Finally, Nadezhda Nikolayevna joined him to play several of the little pieces from this work, ending with Liadov's own *Procession.* (Incidentally, I learned that Liadov composed his *Paraphrases* at the same time as his cantata *The Bride of Messina.*)

In the course of the evening, while looking through some manuscripts on Nikolai Andreyevich's writing table, I came upon three of his scores, which I had long known about but had never seen: unpublished manuscripts of three orchestrated songs entitled *V temnoi roshche zamolk solovei, Noch',* and *Tikho vecher dogoraet,* dated Lucerne.

25 March

The rehearsal of *May Night* at the Molases' went more smoothly then before. Koryakin sang untiringly, in full voice and from memory.[24] During one of the breaks, I mentioned to Nikolai Andreyevich that I am going to hear *The Damnation of Faust*[25] for the thirty-first time. "And I—I'm not going for the fourth time!" he exclaimed.

We spoke about Kruglikov's recent article in *Artist*[26] on Cui's *Ratcliff,* in which the critic compared Cui with Schumann, finding a certain similarity in their music and mistakenly attributing to Schumann a gift for brilliant rhythmic inventiveness.

"That's absolutely untrue," declared Nikolai Andreyevich. "Schumann wasn't at all rich rhythmically; on the contrary, he was excessively symmetrical. When it comes to rhythm, the only indisputable genius in all music is Berlioz. Take, for example, the opening theme of his *Roman Carnival* Overture. Why, there's more rhythm here in the space of a few measures than in any other entire work."

Regarding the three principal elements of music and their interrelationship—melody, harmony, and rhythm—Nikolai Andreyevich expressed the view that it is rhythm—the most universal and freest of all musical means—which exerts the greatest influence on the character of melody—not harmony, which has its limits.

After that, the conversation turned to Nikolai Andreyevich's *Aesthetics,* and he remarked that it is not worth reading, for it is really "terrible" nonsense, a lot of "serious talk" about trifles and "trivial talk" about things of paramount importance. If he could have brought himself to do it, he said, he would have burned it long ago. "However," he added, "if this manuscript interests you so much, take it from Shtrup. I've lent it to him again."[27]

4 April

I went to Nikolai Andreyevich's to show him my draft of the tables of "false progressions."[28] So far as I could tell, he seemed pleased with them; he added only that it might not be a bad idea later on for me to investigate the question of church modes.

"Bear in mind," he said, "how much we modern Russians have already done in this field, how far we have outstripped the Netherlands school and the old Italian school headed by Palestrina, in whose works you'll sometimes run across a C sharp in the Dorian mode. You won't find that in our music, and you don't have to go far for an example. Take Lel's first song with its purely Dorian cadence, something they never dreamed of in the West; or the Mixolydian chorus "Proso" from act 1 and the double chorus from act 3 of *May Night;* or, finally, Lumir's strictly Phrygian song from act 2 of *Mlada.* There are many such examples in Russian music."

Our conversation shifted from Greek modes to the subject of parallel V^2 chords [dominant seventh chord in the third inversion] in second, fifth, and third relationships, and I learned that Rimsky-Korsakov had used parallel V^2 chords in the scene with Pannochka intentionally, to heighten the fantastic quality of Levko's dream.

Here are examples of parallel V^2 chords in second relationship: (1) Levko's recitative: "Kak sladok zapakh topolei," (2) the scene between Levko and Pannochka, (3) the scene in which the *rusalki* lure the step-mother into the water, (4) the finale of *May Night,* at the words: "Krasnoi devitse slava, slava." Still another typical example is the end of the love duet between Mizgir and Snegurochka, at the words: "Smotri, vse iarche i strashnee gorit vostok! Sozhmi menia, sozhmi v svoikh obiatiakh, drug!" Here there is a succession of five parallel V^2 chords—G flat, A flat, B flat, C, and D. Let me draw your attention to this special feature of these remarkably sonorous V^2 chords, that when they appear in an identical sequence in the final chorus of *Snegurochka* (in the hymn to Yarilo-Sun), they are used in such a way that there's hardly a single minor triad in this episode, a fact that lends even greater force and brilliance to the B-flat chorus in 11/4 time. In this respect (that is, the lack of minor chords) this Hymn to the Sun surpassed even Glinka's brilliant *Slavsia* from *A Life for the Tsar.* Incidentally, it saddened Stasov considerably that the latter contained minor chords—on the second, third, and sixth degrees of the normal major scale.

As examples of parallel V^2 in a fifth relationship I cited the Headman's stupidly perplexed phrases from *May Night:* "Da, ia vizhu, chto eto ty." Finally, as an example of parallel V^2 chords in a third relationship I pointed to the scene of the eclipse from *Prince Igor.*

We noted that in Russian music the Wagnerian leitmotiv has been somewhat transformed; in its new homeland it acquired a new coloring, becoming simply *Leitharmonie,* which was undoubtedly more correct and expedient.

In conclusion, apropos of the women's choruses from *May Night* and the so-called theory of *podgoloski,* which at one time caused quite a sensation,[29] Nikolai Andreyevich had this to say: "You know what hurts me most about this whole affair? It's that not one of those who cried out against or in support of Melgunov ever took the trouble to look at the score of *May Night,* where, even before the publication of his collection, I used—quite artistically—in the *troitskaia* song (act 1) the notorious *podgoloski* allegedly discovered by him. I repeat, no one took notice of this; no one has ever said a word about their existence. It's as though they really didn't exist at all."

This chorus, by the way, was written in the strict Phrygian mode.

I will not stop to report our entire conversation of this evening, which flitted from one question to another, but will mention one very interesting fact, that is, that the French horn phrase in the *troitskaia* song from act 1 of *May Night,* which occurs again in the introduction to act 3 and in the music of the *rusalki,* depicts the rising of the moon.

"You know," said Rimsky-Korsakov, "at the time I was composing *May Night* and right up to the completion of *Snegurochka,* I was positively in love with the cult of sun worship and its ritual songs, and not only with that but with the whole period preceding it, with all sorts of *troitskie* and *rusal'nye* songs and *vesnianki.*[30] Therefore, it should come as no surprise to you that—contrary to the opinion of the Ukrainian gentlemen, accustomed only to such romantic songs of theirs as "Viyut vitry" and, unacquainted unfortunately with their own ritual *bytovye*[31] songs—my opera is filled with pure folk elements. You have only to recall Levko's first song; the *troitskaia* song; the beginning of the trio from act 2 ("Skoro l' dumayete vy"); the little themes in Svoyachenitsa's part; the melodic contour of the comical march in the scene between the Scribe and the Golova; the *rusalki* choruses ("Barvinochek" and "Sviataia nedelia") from act 3. All these, I repeat, are authentic Ukrainian folk tunes and songs. You will find them in the collection of A. I. Rubets,[32] who did much more for the music of the Ukrainians than is commonly thought and, in any case, more than the 'renowned'[33] Lysenko."

At the end, Nikolai Andreyevich thanked me for having come and asked me, if possible, to look in on him again this week, except for Wednesday, when he will be at Dmitri Stasov's for the performance of *Angelo,*[34] in which the composer himself will sing all the parts.

Tonight Nikolai Andreyevich announced suddenly and quite unexpectedly that now that he has given up "all his aesthetics," he has decided to write a new opera.[35]

"Don't think, though, that it's going to be *King Saul,*"[36] he declared. "I'm telling you right now, it's not. I'm not going to tell anyone what the subject is until I've finished the whole thing; even if you should guess, I won't confirm it. It will contain chords and orchestration which will probably be in your notebook. I've already worked out some of it in my mind but a few changes have to be made.

"When I was writing *The Maid of Pskov*," he went on, "everybody knew about it. I even played excerpts from it bit by bit as soon as they were composed. Everybody also knew *May Night*, especially Liadov; I played the third act to him several times. Some others also knew this act. On the other hand, it was different with *Snegurochka*, my longest opera; that was written in less than no time, in a single summer, and came as a complete surprise to everyone, even my closest friends. *Mlada*, again, was composed in full view of everyone, as it were, but no one heard a note of it until it was finished and, in this sense, it, too, was a secret. At the present time I want terribly to write a new work; that much I'm telling you and a few others, like Stasov, Liadov, Glazunov, Shtrup, and Sokolov. But neither they, you, nor anyone else is going to find out what its subject is and, believe me, I find this rather amusing. You mustn't think, however, that *Saul* is going to escape his fate. Not at all. But first I'll compose this opera. Then I'll start working on *Zoryusha,*[37] which, alas, Liadov has not written,[38] and after that, *King Saul.*

"Oh, yes," added Nikolai Andreyevich teasing me good-naturedly, "I'm not even going to tell you what 'it' will be called. You may as well not ask. And don't rack your brains to find out; you won't. Meanwhile, I'm going to write the text myself, as I did for *May Night* and *Mlada.*"

And he chuckled.

Later a conversation arose regarding the plot of *Snegurochka,* which Rimsky-Korsakov so adored that he spent days on end working on it to the point where even his wife almost became jealous of it. He started out making a fair copy in full score straightaway, but this method proved too slow and he had to abandon it.

As Nikolai Andreyevich explained, ever since his childhood he had always been inclined toward pantheism and so, when he became involved with the marvelous subject of *Snegurochka,* which gave full range to every sort of ritual, he began to pray to nature: to an old, twisted, weathered stump, a shrub, an ancient oak, a forest brook, a lake, even to a large head of cabbage, a black ram, or a cock crow, seemingly shattering the magic of the night.

"In all this I perceived something special, supernatural," he said. "At times I felt that, when it comes to the magical, the fantastic, animals, birds, and even trees and flowers are more knowing than human beings; that they have a much deeper understanding of the language of nature.

"You must admit," he concluded, "that all this was terribly exaggerated, illogical, but to me it seemed real. I believed in it passionately, like a child, a dreamer who has surrendered himself totally to his daydreams. The strange thing is that at those moments the world seemed closer to me, more comprehensible; I felt merged with it. Even now, when the epic of sun-worship has lost some of its earlier fascination for me, I still can't rid myself completely of pantheistic ideas, and, while I'm by no means a clericalist—especially since my religious convictions are rather tentative—yet, as an artist I'm carried away by the whole ritualistic, so to say, pagan side of religion. I love it profoundly in others, and I see the beauty in Lent, in religious processions, in funeral feasts with blini, even though I myself will not participate in the processions nor eat the funeral blini."

21 April

Nikolai Andreyevich told me some additional facts about his new opera. It will consist of four acts and nine scenes; the libretto was written during Holy Week, and some of the music has already been sketched. So saying, he drew from his pocket a small notebook and leafed quickly through it. It was, indeed, filled.

"You know," he said, "Liadov thinks that if this is not *King Saul* and if the subject is not foreign, it must be *The Fair at Sorochintsy*. As you know, I'm not going to discuss this matter with anyone. Everyone is free to think whatever he likes."

Turning then to the subject of key colors, Nikolai Andreyevich pointed out yet another peculiarity of his perception of them—that is, not only do the various tonalities suggest colors and moods, but even seventh chords seem "decked out in bright colors," their hue depending upon the tones of which they are formed. For example, to him there are three independent diminished seventh chords: (1) C sharp, E, G, B flat—purplish bluish golden (somewhat dark); (2) D, F, A flat, B—yellowish greenish violet with a grayish tinge (very motley); and (3) E flat, F sharp, A, C—bluish greenish rose-colored (rather bright because of the C and A, though darkened somewhat by the E flat).

Besides this, there are four types of augmented triads: (1) C, E, G sharp (A-flat)—bluish-violet (tender); (2) D flat, F, A—purplish greenish rose-colored; (3) D, F sharp, A sharp (B flat)—yellowish greenish (rather dark); and (4) E flat, G, B—gray bluish greenish. Wherever C occurs, it always brightens the harmony, B darkens it, and A endows it with a clear, springlike, rosy tinge.

The episode in act 3 of *Mlada,* in which the full orchestra ascends in a chromatic sequence constructed on intervals of diminished fifths in the basses, the point where "shadows fall on the cliffs and trees and the rising moon fills the heavens with a golden glow," produced on Rimsky-Korsakov the impression of the "play and interplay of the color spectrum in the nocturnal clouds." [39]

I forgot to mention that earlier, when speaking about the key of E-flat major—"dark, gloomy, gray-bluish" (the tonality of cities and fortresses), Nikolai Andreyevich commented: "Remember the chorus of the boyars from *Prince Igor:* ('Nam, kniaginia, ne vpervye pod stenami gorodskimi'), which is written in E-flat major? Well, in the scene of the geography lesson from *Boris Godunov* ('Kak s oblakov, edinym vzorom ty mozhesh obozret vse tsarstvo—granitsy, reki, grady'), at first Mussorgsky had the word *grady* (with the same music and the same harmonization) before the word *reki.* This irritated me, for the E-flat major chord was not where I thought it ought to be. So, I prevailed upon Mussorgsky to rearrange the words and it came out just as it is now—this E-flat major gives me great satisfaction."

When I remarked that the fountain scene from *Boris* is also in E-flat major and that Nikolai Andreyevich is probably not particularly pleased about this, he replied that, while, of course, E major would have been preferable, in this case E-flat major is not at variance with the coloring.

"If this scene had been written in F," he added, "that wouldn't have done at all, so far as the color is concerned. But don't forget—Mussorgsky was by nature also a colorist and he certainly would never have made such a blunder."

Further, apropos of the harmonic curiosities which will appear in Rimsky-Korsakov's forthcoming opera and the new use of the interval of the diminished fifth—of the "Stasovian" elements of the New Russian School, we talked about (1) tritones; (2) the juxtaposition of tonalities adjacent to each other in the space of the augmented fourth (or diminished fifth); (3)

parallel fifths strewn about lavishly even where they are inappropriate and where, consequently, they serve no artistic purpose whatsoever (as, for example, in Cui's *Ratcliff* in the scene when Margareta rises slowly and walks through the crowd, or at MacGregor's words "Vrag moego spokoistviia," where these fifths might have been eliminated without the slightest harm to the music); (4) Borodin's epic parallel seconds; and (5) Balakirev's keys of B minor and D-flat major, which were so brilliantly and, obviously, deliberately introduced into the early works of the Russian school and without doubt left a deep imprint on all the latest Russian music, partly from force of habit, partly also because D flat sounds especially grateful, beautiful, and mellow in orchestration. We have only to recall the "kiss scene" from *Snegurochka;* "Egypt" from *Mlada;* the last kiss of the peri Gul Nazar ("Joy of Love") from the fourth movement of Rimsky-Korsakov's *Antar;* Maria's first song, the "blessing" scene, love duet, and final chorus from *Ratcliff;* the love theme from Tchaikovsky's *Romeo and Juliet;* the end of Balakirev's *Tamara;* the third movement (bayan) from Borodin's B minor Symphony, etc.

To conclude the discussion of Rimsky-Korsakov's sense of key-color, I should mention that to him C minor, like C major, seems white but somewhat darker than C major, with a slight yellowish tinge; D-flat major—rather dark, warm. D major suggests daylight—sunny, yellowish golden, regal, powerful.[40] A-flat major, as the dominant of D-flat minor, has a somewhat austere, though pensive, character; its color is grayish violet, since A-flat already has a tinge of violet with a slight grayish cast. A-flat (G-sharp) minor bears a vague resemblance to A-flat major, except that it is paler and hazier as, on the whole, every minor is compared to its relative major. The same may be said of D minor and E-flat minor. E minor is bluish, like a reflection of A major; F minor—greenish, like a reflection of the brilliantly green "pastoral" F major; F-sharp (G-flat) major—grayish green; F-sharp minor—a pale grayish green.

G major, according to Rimsky-Korsakov, has a brownish golden tinge; G minor, on the other hand, lacks a clearly defined coloring. It has the character of an elegy, an idyll.[41] In Rimsky-Korsakov's view, B-flat major is somewhat dark, strong; B-flat minor is one of the gloomiest keys; B major is somber, dark blue, with a steel-like, perhaps even grayish, lead-colored tint. B minor is steel gray with a greenish tinge (somewhat stern and harsh). Finally, E major is sapphire blue, glittering, nocturnal, dark azure. In cases where this color cannot play any role, as, for example, in the music of the Polonaise, all of the inherent brilliance of the tonality is transferred, as it were, to the character of the music itself, from which, according to Rimsky-Korsakov, it acquires a particularly vivid and festive coloration.

2 May

When I walked in, Nikolai Andreyevich looked absolutely shattered, as though he had been stricken by some enormous grief. Never before have I seen him so depressed and irritable. As it turned out, the reason for this change in him is that two days ago he gave up smoking. This seemingly insignificant act has made him very nervous.

Yesterday, Nikolai Andreyevich told me, he went alone and rented a dacha (for three hundred rubles) called Vechasha, with a marvelous park, lake, and orchard. It is located on the estate of Ogaryova some eleven or twelve versts from the Plyuss station.[42] Nikolai Andreyevich invited me to visit them this summer. He also told me that he is thinking of giving up his new opera, after having shown several of us the completed first scene.

"You know, only lyrical music is good," he said suddenly, as if continuing aloud a private thought. "The rest is nothing but trickery. I've reached an impasse. It's pointless for me to write the new opera, for lyricism is just what I lack. Generally, speaking, I'm no longer good for anything. If I ever did have any creative power, it's left me and, of course, forever. And this is such a glorious plot that I wanted so terribly to set to music just a short while ago! I suppose I ought to take comfort in the fact that there was a time when things were different. But that thought only makes the present creative void weigh even more heavily."

When I rose to leave, Nikolai Andreyevich proposed that he accompany me to Troitsky.[43] However, it turned out differently; we became so involved in conversation that we walked to the Nevsky, turned around, passed my house at no. 24, and found ourselves again on Zagorodny, opposite his house. By then Nikolai Andreyevich seemed slightly tired, but he was more composed. He even said that he still has not decided whether he would only orchestrate *Boris Godunov* this summer or would also take up his new opera again.

"What of it if I repeat myself here and there?" he mused. "Some new fine points will come to the rescue. After all, every person is extremely original. Besides, who knows, perhaps the music of the future will be defined only by fine points."

4 May

Despite a heavy rain, I was at the Rimsky-Korsakovs' exactly at eight-fifteen. Nikolai Andreyevich was absolutely unrecognizable; he was so gay and talkative, without a trace of his former melancholy. Soon afterward Shtrup and Trifonov arrived.

After tea, Nikolai Andreyevich announced that he had brought us together to acquaint us with the Introduction to his new opera[44] and he would like us to tell him what we think it portrays.

"I warn you," he declared, "this music does not characterize the whole opera as, for example, the Overture to *The Maid of Pskov* does. On the contrary, like the Introduction to *Mlada,* it depicts only an isolated moment."

At our request, Nikolai Andreyevich and Nadezhda Nikolayevna then played this Introduction three times. After that we discussed and argued about it. On one point, however, we all agreed—the music depicts a clear, cold, starlit night of undisturbed tranquillity.

At the end, Nikolai Andreyevich divulged the subject of the opera and read his libretto. He is depressed that so little has been done thus far: only the text, the Introduction, and the first few scenes.

"Now you can understand, I hope," said Nikolai Andreyevich, "the nature of the responsibilities facing me, to which I alluded once when discussing the question of subject matter. For a long time I've had a desire to poeticize in sound the last remnants of the sun cult, namely *Kolyada* and *Ovsen.*[45] Now, as you see, I'm doing this. Moreover, I've always wanted to write an opera on this marvelous subject, but somehow I procrastinated. The public will undoubtedly think that I composed my opera only with the aim of competing. But, in all honesty, despite some excellent pages, Tchaikovsky's opera on this subject[46] contains a great deal of bad music (to say nothing of the wretched libretto). I wanted to present the material in a completely new light—as I understand it. I don't think there's anything reprehensible in what I'm doing. After all, a number of plays and operas were written on the legend of the famous Dr. Faustus, before and after Goethe, and no one seems to have denounced either the dramatists or composers for choosing that subject again."

We left at about quarter past one.

14 May

"Do you know whom I've acquired as an enemy?" asked Rimsky-Korsakov tonight. "Who would you think? Colonne. And do you know why? Because I didn't go to see him immediately upon his arrival. He was offended at my 'extreme' ingratitude; after all, he performed *Antar* in Paris. On the whole, he's had a bad time of it ever since he came here. Napravnik didn't return his visit but simply replied to his visiting card with one of his own. How stupid and arrogant these Europeans are sometimes—putting on airs for no reason whatsoever!"

After this Nikolai Andreyevich told me that as usual during examination period, he and Solovyov are on friendly terms, that whenever they meet, Solovyov tries to say something nice to him. For example, he told Nikolai Andreyevich that he had recently had an argument about the *Easter Overture* with one of his friends when he (Solovyov) tried to persuade him that this was not a fantasy but an overture. Again, on learning that Nikolai Andreyevich is at work on a new opera, Solovyov marveled at his stamina, saying: "Oh, I wouldn't be able to compose anything in the face of such unfriendliness on the part of the Theater Directorate. After all, *Cordelia* was dropped for no apparent reason—it was even playing to full houses—and when I mentioned in passing the possibility of their presenting *Vakula the Smith*[47] at the Marinsky, Vsevolozhsky flatly refused and, by way of consoling me, said that not only my opera but even Tchaikovsky's *Cherevichki* will never be given."

"How do you think I felt listening to this," commented Nikolai Andreyevich, "when I myself have started on a third 'Vakula'?"

Finally, Solovyov had added: "You know, Vsevolozhsky is taking his revenge on me because once, when he suggested that I write an opera on a scenario of *The Queen of Spades* which he had drawn up, I told him that I didn't think this a suitable subject for an opera. I can assure you he has never forgiven me."

At this point the doorbell rang and in walked Nikolai Andreyevich's former teacher and friend, F. A. Kanille, to whom, by the way, Nikolai Andreyevich dedicated his First Symphony. The conversation covered a wide range of subjects and people, from Glinka to the latest music— Wagner, Liszt, Liapunov, Glazunov, etc. There was much talk, also, about Balakirev. Regarding him, Nikolai Andreyevich observed that while he is an enormous natural talent, owing to the unfortunate circumstances of his life and also—this is the main thing—a morbid indolence and dilatory method of composing, he has gone to seed.

From Mily Alexeyevich we turned to Anton Rubinstein, a first-rate artist (in Nikolai Andreyevich's view), to whom music is everything. Indeed, while working out a fugue at the piano, he would lose himself so completely that if someone were to tell him that the world is about to come to an end, he would probably not budge an inch, but would simply reply absentmindedly: "I know, fine, in a minute, only let me finish!"

Someone noted that nowadays there are no longer any singers, pianists, conductors, or composers, even though everybody plays, sings, composes, and even conducts choruses and orchestras.

"This is understandable," declared Nikolai Andreyevich. "In Glinka's day and before that, art was a kind of 'cottage industry.' A person had to have real talent to break through to fame. Today it's become a factory enterprise."

We returned to the subject of Liapunov and Glazunov. Asked by Kanille which of them is the more talented, Nikolai Andreyevich replied that while he considers Liapunov highly gifted, Glazunov is far superior to him.

"Since you wish to know what I think," said Nikolai Andreyevich, "I must say that, perhaps contrary to many others, I regard Glazunov as the foremost composer of our day, not only here in Russia but in all Europe. I'm speaking of the younger generation of artists, of course.

"All I know," he continued, turning toward me, "is that when I'm dead, you'll still have Glazunov. And when you're old—remember my words—not only won't you not have Glazunov, but there won't be any composer with even the slightest talent. Art, then, won't amount to anything, I believe."

I forgot to mention that while talking with Rimsky-Korsakov about his new opera (before Kanille's arrival), Nikolai Andreyevich played for me his three-tiered imitation of the main theme, which depicts the bright, cold, glittering night at the end of the first act. We also talked about subjects like that of *The Maid of Pskov* and he told me that despite their merits, they would hardly inspire him today.

"I even think," remarked Rimsky-Korsakov, "that if someone were to suggest that I write *The Maid of Pskov* at the present time I would refuse."

Besides this, I learned that Nikolai Andreyevich plans to introduce a completely new orchestral effect into the magic scene of the new opera, that is, harmonics glissando on the open strings of the cello, to produce a kind of fantastic sonority, backed up by a more or less constant, sustained ninth chord.

19 May

Today, in addition to me, Trifonov and Shtrup were also at the Rimsky-Korsakovs'. Before they came, we talked a great deal about my mother and her imagined heart trouble. Nikolai Andreyevich told me that despite a severe heart condition, his mother had lived to the ripe old age of eighty-four, and therefore I had no need to be particularly apprehensive.

When Trifonov arrived, a conversation arose about Liadov and his plan to compose an orchestral fantasy called *Baba Yaga.*[48]

"But I'm telling you from experience," contended Nikolai Andreyevich, "Liadov won't do anything this year. Someone or something will surely prevent him and, in the fall, when you ask him about his *Baba Yaga,* he'll tell you that he hasn't even started it, that it's not worth doing and, furthermore, he's been reading a great deal. It's a pity; the fragments of it that I heard once I liked very much. But you'll see, he'll succumb to his laziness. Just recently, after listening to his plans, I said to him: 'How glad I am to see you an active *kuchkist,* if only for a few minutes. I'm grateful even for that.'"

We talked briefly about Glazunov and his reconciliation with Laroche.

After tea Nikolai Andreyevich played through twice the entire first scene of the first act of his new opera (dated May 16). When he finished, we had a long discussion about it. Nikolai Andreyevich pointed out here and there how he plans to score it. He will employ neither the bass clarinet nor the English horn; of late he has become tired of these timbres.

Nikolai Andreyevich's parting words, spoken apropos of his new opera, were: "I repeat, the main thing in music is not melody nor even harmony, but rhythm and only rhythm."[49]

22 May

I dropped in on Rimsky-Korsakov for a minute, but instead I stayed for more than an hour and a half. I showed him what I had written from memory about our last visit (on the nineteenth). It proved to be a "photographic likeness." Then we talked about the performance of the new version of his symphonic poem *Sadko,* Borodin's *Petite Suite,* and Mendelssohn's Fourth Symphony[50] at Pavlovsk on the twentieth.

Regarding Mendelssohn, Nikolai Andreyevich declared: "No matter what anyone says, Mendelssohn was a first-rate composer and a superlative orchestrator as well. His music to *A Midsummer's Night Dream* is brilliant; his symphonies, octet, and overtures are wonderful, especially *Fingal's Cave,* with its ravishing middle section. And even the *Lieder ohne Worte* are charming. If some people call them 'bittersweet,' it's only the epithet that's bad."

This led us to consider the general state of talent among the young musicians of today.

"Surely, Nekrasov and Lev Steinberg are gifted, and I'm convinced that even Sheffer, who's never been able to pass a single examination at the Conservatory, has a talent," said Nikolai Andreyevich. "But they lack one thing—individuality. And that's the main thing."

While we were on this subject, Nikolai Andreyevich showed me two new scores which he had received yesterday as a present from Glazunov —*Chopiniana* and *Valse de concert.*[51]

"Imagine this—what a strange coincidence," remarked Rimsky-Korsakov. "I was walking about the room, pondering over the music of Oxana which I had just played, when suddenly I heard someone in the apartment above playing it in the very same key and almost exactly. There's writing in privacy in Petersburg for you!" And he laughed.

After making arrangements about my visit to the Rimsky-Korsakovs at Vechasha[52] (according to Nikolai Andreyevich, a marvelous place, which even has a wonderful lake, as in *Snegurochka,* where we shall, without fail, go on St. John's night to look for the flower of the fern),[53] we somehow got onto the subject of the old gentry, whereupon I learned something very interesting—that Rimsky-Korsakov's paternal grandmother was a priest's daughter, whom his grandfather abducted, and his maternal grandmother a simple peasant woman, a serf who belonged to Skaryatin, a landowner of the Maloarkhangelsk District, Orlov Province.

"Without these 'regenerative influences,'" declared Rimsky-Korsakov, "we probably would have degenerated, but now, at least, there's a legitimate justification for my passion for everything pertaining to religious rites and ceremonies, for 'cassocks' and the priesthood, for these Christian holy men of today; and finally, for *khorovody* and *troitskie* and *rusal'nye* songs. So, you see, that's where I inherited my ideas (atavism) and my wholehearted love for everything relating to real, everyday life, to the folk. Therein, most likely, lies the secret and the reason for the appearance of my *Easter Overture* and my *Kupala khorovody*."

My First Visit to Vechasha

4 June

Leaving St. Petersburg on the morning train, I arrived at the Plyuss station by two-thirty. There I hired a tarantass to drive to Vechasha. The road was so bad that I did not reach my destination until about quarter to five.

Before I had time to pay the driver, great shrieks of excitement issued from the house, and Volodya, Nadya, and Andryusha came rushing toward me and threw their arms around my neck. Even Nadezhda Nikolayevna began making such a fuss that one would have imagined something of extraordinary interest had occurred.

At the time of my arrival, Nikolai Andreyevich was still napping, but the racket awakened him and, beaming with delight and waving his arms joyfully, he, too, came running toward me and embraced me. Scarcely had I managed to change my clothes and make myself presentable than I was dragged from Nikolai Andreyevich's study (where I was to stay)— first to the lake, then to the siskins and bullfinches, and, finally, to little Nadyusha's newly acquired hare. Following this, they literally stuffed me with all kinds of food and cocoa made especially for me.

After dinner we all went for a stroll to the Lyubensk forest, which borders on the neighboring estate. Here Nadezhda Nikolayevna gathered wildflowers and the children picked forget-me-nots and caught tadpoles, while Nikolai Andreyevich searched out a four-leaf clover, which he handed to me with mock solemnity, saying: "This is from Snegurochka!"

Upon returning home, we proceeded to eat again and, finally, tea was served. Everyone was in a very good humor. Both before and after tea we took long walks through the garden with its magnificent allées bordered by linden trees, and we also went several times to the lake to feast our eyes on the wondrous reflection of the moonlight on the reeds and on the smooth, mirrorlike surface of the lake itself. A breathtaking sight!

As we strolled along, Nikolai Andreyevich told me that just today, shortly before my arrival, he completed the last measures of scene 2 of *Christmas Eve* and, thus, now all of act 1 is finished. Among the other things we discussed were the *Revue Wagnérienne* and the articles by Chamberlain carried there;[54] the unsuccessful French translations of *Die Walküre* and *Tristan,* made by one Wilder; the monotony of Serov's Simferopol letters to his sister S. N. Dyutur, currently appearing in *Russkaia muzykal'naia gazeta;*[55] Schumann's ideas on music, which have already lost much of their original interest;[56] and Findeisen's scenario of *Sadko* (which I had brought with me).[57]

Finally, after more chatting about this and that, the time came for us to retire. It was midnight when I blew out my candle. Nikolai Andreyevich was quietly strumming something on the piano, apparently improvising. Suddenly he stopped, and I fell asleep.

5 June

This morning I rose at about seven-thirty. After morning tea, Nikolai Andreyevich worked on the final draft of the libretto of scene 2, and I read some of my "reminiscences" to Andrei. Then we all went swimming. (Nikolai Andreyevich, by the way, is an excellent swimmer.)

Before dinner Nikolai Andreyevich played his new scene for Nadezhda Nikolayevna and me. Nadezhda Nikolayevna did not seem completely satisfied with it, but, on the basis of this first hearing, I found much superb music in it. Rimsky-Korsakov was visibly depressed. After dinner he lay down for an hour's rest. When he arose, we took long walks, before and after tea and supper, despite a light rain. Nadezhda Nikolayevna joined us. And what didn't we discuss—everything from Nikolai Andreyevich's

Christmas Eve and Wagner's *Waldweben* to Mussorgsky's realism, which at times verges on caricature;[58] Liadov's laziness (what one French novelist characterized as "l'improductivité slave"); and Findeisen's article on the thematic scheme of *Snegurochka*.[59] Regarding the latter, I learned that Nikolai Andreyevich considers Findeisen's division of all the themes into three independent groups correct. I learned, too, that he regards *Snegurochka* as definitely superior to *Mlada,* indeed to everything he has ever written.

"You know," he said, "I could really be called 'the leading progressive of the conservative trend,' 'the one who now and then picks up what was left lying around by the "Mighty Handful" *(moguchaia kuchka).'* Judge for yourself. Opera—this artistic genre which is essentially false yet so alluring in the range and variety of its form—has now reached the very limits of its possibilities. And what excesses has it not endured on its way—from the concert with senseless roulades—this "École de petits chiens" as Berlioz called it—to virtual drama with orchestra and polyphony, as in Wagner. Meanwhile music is above all an abstract language with endless and in most cases colorless recitatives, the ones in my operas, at least. I'm no Mussorgsky; he could do something with them. But then what an amazing wealth of timbres lies hidden in any good human voice!

"You know," he went on, "according to our code, the primary requisite of genuinely good music was an absence of fioritura; only in works of an Eastern character, such as Konchakovna's cavatina, *Georgian Song* and *Hebrew Song,* etc., was this kind of 'virtuosity' permitted. However, here it was given an odd, fantastic cast. As for me, I love this virtuosity when it is not an insipid collection of sounds but a fast melody of beautiful, original design as, for example, in Chopin. Sometimes I even admire the technique itself of a soloist, provided it is extraordinary (as in the case of Joachim, Auer, Thomson, Rubinstein, etc.). In my new opera, I'm giving the coloratura an important place, in Oxana's part. Let anyone who likes denounce me—I'll still do it."

We talked about Balakirev and his enthusiastic, though typically harsh criticism of *Mlada*.[60] Earlier, in 1891, he had not even wanted to acquaint himself with it, considering it a product of Wagnerism, which he detests.

"Evidently, Glazunov was correct in his explanation of Mily Alexeyevich's utterly senseless hostility toward the brilliant creator of the *Nibe-*

lungen," I commented, "for when I asked him what accounts for it, he replied 'I suspect it's this: Balakirev has always approved and loved in music only what he himself has discovered.'"

"That's possible," said Nikolai Andreyevich, "especially since from his early youth, Balakirev was always morbidly vain, at times even strange. Besides this, his character and views were wont to change so much that often I could have sworn there was not one Balakirev but several, none of whom had anything in common with the rest.

"Actually," he went on, "I'm convinced that Balakirev's deep hatred for Anton Rubinstein stems partly from stubbornness and partly from the fact that Anton Grigoryevich, being himself an individual of stature and very proud, would never kowtow or give in to him, and Balakirev could not bear anyone to disagree with him. In short, he met his match."

Further, we talked about Rubets' marvelous collection *216 Little Russian Folk Songs,* from which Nikolai Andreyevich is going to borrow something for his new opera; at least the *kolyada* "Holy Night" (no. 34) with a revised Belorussian text (from Shein's collection);[61] and, finally, about Sinkiewicz and Byron's *Cain,* specifically the scene in The Realm of Death which, for some reason, was deleted from the Russian translation by the censors.

Before going to bed, Nikolai Andreyevich, Nadezhda Nikolayevna, and I stood for a long time on the brick walkway leading to the bathhouse, feasting our eyes on the heat lightning and the magnificent crimson-orange reflection of the moon in the lake. The air was warm and still; nature seemed to have stopped breathing.

By eleven-thirty I was in bed.

I forgot to mention that after evening tea, everyone, including Nikolai Andreyevich, climbed trees and played hoopla.

6 June

When I arose (at about quarter to eight), I was told that Nikolai Andreyevich had gone swimming, so I set off toward the lake. On the way I met him, returning to the house. I observed that, like yesterday, he was somewhat out-of-sorts. He started to talk about his new opera, saying that perhaps he will not finish it—"it's not worth the trouble."

"You know," he said, "I see clearly that this music is not at all on a par with that of *Snegurochka,* that my talent is on the wane. Yet it's difficult not to write. Idleness crushes the artist, whose very nature is divided between the creative life, the life of the creative imagination, and real life—between art and the family. And the one can never, under any circumstances, take the place of, much less become one with the other.

"By the way," he continued, "you think that friendship and friends just come your way without any effort. Well, I think just the contrary. I believe that friendship is based either on personal interest or on the expectation of something. Suddenly the years pass and there's absolutely nothing. Do you think that friends won't give you up? You can be sure they'll lose interest in you and just take off! I've observed this more than once in former friends of mine, people who knew me in the days when I was composing *May Night, Snegurochka,* even before then. I've often heard them say things like 'Of course, Nikolai Andreyevich, we have a very high regard for you,' and somehow the rest remained unsaid. In my opinion personal acquaintance with any artist, while undoubtedly good in some respects, is, in most cases, detrimental to a correct appraisal of his work, for friends look upon his compositions with different and usually prejudiced eyes. You've only to recall Beethoven's caustic pun about Goethe, after he'd come to know him better and was somewhat disillusioned with him as a person. 'I used to think,' said Beethoven, 'that he was a king of poets; now I see that he is a poet of kings.'

"You know," went on Nikolai Andreyevich, "Tchaikovsky hated to play his music for anyone before it was finished, and he justified this very wittily: 'If I were certain in advance that my listeners would go into ecstasies over my new thing, I'd play it. But if I have any doubts, if I think that their rapture will be less than complete, I won't play a single note, for such a response would paralyze my creative impulse and my desire to continue composing.'

"Believe me," concluded Nikolai Andreyevich, "I completely agree with him. He was absolutely right in acting like that. Analysis destroys creativity. If people were to give themselves up to endless metaphysical probing, they'd go out of their minds. Nothing would ever be written, as we see, for example, in the case of Balakirev, whose extremely morbid self-criticism literally ruined him, compelling him to write and rewrite his *Tamara* over a period of twelve years."

Strolling back and forth along the linden-lined allée, we talked about many things—Cui, his songs, his lack of foresight and the liberalism he affected while working on *Peterburgskie vedomosti*—in short, during the glorious period of the crusade of the "Mighty Handful"; also about the prodigious productivity of Beethoven and Wagner; the antipathetic characters of Chopin and Berlioz, etc., etc.

At mid-morning Nikolai Andreyevich excused himself and went to his study to do some work on his opera. Later, in the afternoon, he offered to play his new variant of the end of scene 2 for Nadezhda Nikolayevna and me. He had scarcely begun when he stopped.

"No," he exclaimed in a voice choked with sadness, even despair. "I can't play anymore—it won't do. I'm really able to play all this but I have to work it up."

So saying, he began to pace back and forth nervously, looking at neither of us. Obviously, yesterday's depression and doubts about his powers had taken hold of him. He was terribly agitated.

After dinner Nikolai Andreyevich lay down to rest, while Nadezhda Nikolayevna and I went to the fields to gather cornflowers for Nadyusha. By the time we returned, Nikolai Andreyevich had gotten control of himself and he played his new version to the end. Nadezhda Nikolayevna remained silent as before. Then Rimsky-Korsakov stood up, closed the music and declared, not without humor: "Well, if someday my future biographer should wish to describe this evening, he'll have to exclaim solemnly: 'Our famous composer's second scene was played by the author himself amid the deadly silence of the listeners!' "

This little joke evidently pleased him, for he became cheerful.

"Do you know what our dear departed Borodin used to do when he didn't like something he was playing? 'Oh,' he'd exclaim, looking intently, for no reason, at some pause or glancing absentmindedly at some opening triad, 'how successfully it (i.e., the pause) has managed to insert itself between the lines; really, what a splendid D major.' "

And Rimsky-Korsakov began to laugh good-naturedly. Obviously, his depression had passed. "And now, let's go into the garden," he said.

During supper, when they brought the farmer's cheese, which Rimsky-Korsakov did not eat but his wife ate with relish, Nikolai Andreyevich smiling good-naturedly, turned to me and said: "You know, Vasily Vasilyevich, my taste and Nadezhda Nikolayevna's often differ, and not only in the case of cheese, buttermilk, and sour cream but even sometimes in music: there have been times—often—when I liked something which Nadezhda Nikolayevna did not care for at all."

After evening tea, at our request, he played all of act 1. The evening was quite cool but even so, when the music ended, we went out for a breath of fresh air before retiring.

I forgot to mention that before playing his opera, Nikolai Andreyevich, in jest, improvised for a while in the style of Wagner. He claims that, given a certain facility for harmonization, there is nothing easier than to write recitatives in this style, preserving throughout the noble character inherent in the music of this giant.

7 June

After our customary morning milk and coffee, Nikolai Andreyevich and I went for our last stroll on the lower linden allée. Nikolai Andreyevich told me that he is somewhat apprehensive about the last scene of *Christmas Eve*, which, like the final one of *May Night*, is, strictly speaking, not stageworthy, since everything that was expected to happen has happened and consequently the rest is, in a sense, no longer interesting. In such a case, he said, music, however successful (as in the finale of *May Night*), cannot save the situation.

Our conversation turned to *Sadko*, which Nikolai Andreyevich is thinking of taking up in the very near future. He would like to sketch out the libretto as soon as possible but is being held up because he does not have at hand the folklore collections of Rybnikov, Kirsha Danilov, and Kireyevsky.[62]

"When I complete this opera (the Introduction is already finished)," he said, "it will become clear to you at once how far and in what way I've advanced beyond the music of my earlier period, for then, although many things were already foreshadowed, not everything was, as certain people think."

He urged me to make every effort to secure Laroche's article on Glinka[63] from Findeisen and to send it to Trifonov, who needs it for an article he wants to write on Russian opera over the past twenty-five to thirty years.

Just before I left, Rimsky-Korsakov began to talk about the Crimea and a journey he and Nadezhda Nikolayevna had planned to take there this summer, if their family could have been left in Pargolovo with their relatives, the Sokolovs.

"Then we could have gone to Yalta and visited the grave of our daughter,"[64] said Nikolai Andreyevich. "But this is out of the question now. You know, I should like terribly to visit at least one more time in my life the town of Tikhvin, where I was born, and also the village of Troitskoe, where my grandmother and, together with her, my *khorovody* were born."

At last the time came for me to leave. We said good-bye. The horses started off, the bells jingled, and soon the estate and, with it, its residents disappeared behind the hills.

2 September

Having an idea that Rimsky-Korsakov had returned from the country by now and, desirous of seeing him as soon as possible, I went to the Conservatory. Once there, however, I had to wait a good three-quarters of an hour to see him, as he was busy with Johansen. When he finally emerged from the Director's office, we were so happy to meet again after our relatively long separation that we embraced heartily, much to the consternation of the custodians and students who happened to witness this scene.

After that we went together to Bessel's, where I learned that the vocal score of *The Maid of Pskov* will probably be completed by the end of September and the final installment of the whole opera will be published in October. While strolling about, we chatted about the forthcoming musical and opera season, the proposed concerts in honor of Tchaikovsky, Wagner, and Beethoven, respectively, the production of *May Night* which is to take place later this month, etc. Finally we arrived at Zagorodny.

Before I had a chance to say hello to everyone, Nikolai Andreyevich took me into his study to show me the manuscript of *Christmas Eve,* which had been finished, as it turned out, on August 15. On the writing table lay the full score of the first scene, which had been orchestrated obviously in Vechasha, as the last page bore the date August 29.

"You will not believe this," remarked Rimsky-Korsakov, "but what I like most of all is orchestrating my things, more even than composing them. This is because I realize that only when orchestrating am I writing exactly what is destined to be inviolable, that each note I write is just the right one and that thus, there's no guesswork, nothing tentative about any of it."

We got onto the subject of the double bass, which unquestionably produces the tenderest tone of all the bass instruments, a quality at first spurned vigorously by the leading lights of the Russian school. Then Nikolai Andreyevich set forth his views about the orchestration of the classicists.

"You know," he said, "the relatively thin and at times even poor, dull sonority of their orchestration does not result from economy of means. (Saint-Saëns has an entire symphony—the one in A minor—scored only for small orchestra, with one flute, one oboe, a clarinet, and two French horns. Nevertheless, it sounds marvelous.) Instead it results primarily from an inability to orchestrate chords, to assign and distribute the instrumental voices among them, and also from an inadequate acquaintance with the orchestral resources at their disposal."

8 September

When I arrived at the Rimsky-Korsakovs', at seven-thirty, Nikolai Andreyevich was still resting and Nadezhda Nikolayevna was playing Chopin for Andrei. Soon, however, Nikolai Andreyevich appeared. At our insistence, Nadezhda Nikolayevna ("pianist to the court of Andrei Rimsky-Korsakov," as she called herself) played several Chopin pieces, concluding with the ravishing E major Étude, whose melody Rimsky-Korsakov considers the finest, the most perfect that ever existed—"truly celestial sounds," as he put it.

"It's absolutely incomprehensible," he remarked, "this combination in one person—Chopin—of two brilliant gifts—the gift of a supreme melodist and a harmonist of genius and originality. You won't believe it, but in his A-flat Étude, where the very harmony seems to sing, there are chord sequences which even today's composers, headed by Wagner, have not yet attained to. It will probably be many, many years before people finally learn to appreciate them as they should. Indeed, after the infinitely poetic sounds of Chopin, all other music seems crude and ponderous, including the works of such giants as Beethoven and Schumann. Leave Liszt aside, but Wagner—you could even come to loathe him and his strange and complicated music. As far as I'm concerned, it's this Chopin kind of pianoforte improvisation that's the real music. To me it's far superior to all those long drawn-out orchestral proceedings, if only because they require a whole army of trombones, violins, and kettledrums."

During tea, apropos of the unfortunate *cornet à pistons*, which Berlioz, for some reason, considered faulty but used continuously in his scores, Nikolai Andreyevich described to us the usual course of development of the aesthetic tastes of all dedicated creative artists. During the first phase, he said, the enthusiast has an irrational passion for percussion instruments, especially the triangle. This is followed by a period during which he values only the harp and the harmonics of the violin or violins *con sordini*—and only *con sordini*. During the third period he prefers the English horn to all other instruments. In conclusion, Rimsky-Korsakov stated that only the musician who values the strings above all—what's more strings *senza sordini*—is finally and truly mature.

22 September

Alexandra Nikolayevna and Nikolai Pavlovich Molas were at the Rimsky-Korsakovs' when I arrived tonight, but they soon left. Almost at once, Nikolai Andreyevich began to reproach me for playing his opera to "everyone" without his permission, adding that, in view of this, he will never again play a new work for me. It was extremely unpleasant to be reproached in this way, especially since I knew very well who had put the idea into his head.[65] However, the conversation quickly took another direction, to the forthcoming production of *May Night* at the Mikhailovsky Theater, for which Rimsky-Korsakov has reserved tickets for me.

After this, Nikolai Andreyevich gave an account of a curious visit he had had from some young man named Diaghilev, who fancies himself a great composer but, nevertheless, would like to study theory with Nikolai Andreyevich. His compositions proved to be absurd, and Nikolai Andreyevich told him so bluntly, whereupon he became offended and, on leaving, declared arrogantly that nevertheless he believes in himself and his gifts; that he will never forget this day and that some day Rimsky-Korsakov's opinion will occupy a shameful place in his (Rimsky-Korsakov's) biography and make him regret his rash words, but then it will be too late. . . . .

Apropos of this, I recalled Lombroso's[66] theory about the existence of a certain type of deranged person who, though undoubtedly gifted, never creates anything that is not bizarre, inane, and even downright stupid. To illustrate this point, Nikolai Andreyevich suggested that I listen to a number of strange works by the composer d'Indy (author of the symphonic trilogy *Wallenstein*), who is well known in the West and has the approval of such people as the young Belgian composer Gilson, and who claims to be a passionate follower of Wagner and the Russian (!) school.

"I'm inclined to think," added Nikolai Andreyevich, "that either he has no ear whatsoever or he's decided to make fun of us. We've only to recall his *Petite sonate,* thirty-five pages with a senseless elementary melody. He's published a number of examples of Kuzma-Prutkov music, in the style of the famous advertisement 'about sperm for the breeding of fish on dry land,' and we've permitted ourselves to be taken in."

Before tea, Nadezhda Nikolayevna gave an imitation of d'Indy.

By eleven o'clock, we managed to persuade Nikolai Andreyevich to play the first scene of the second act of *Christmas Eve.* Even though he was obviously out of sorts, I took the chance of asking him to play the *kolyadka* (from scene 2, act 1), which he did.

28 September

Tonight, after a lapse of twelve years, *May Night* was finally revived at the Mikhailovsky Theater.[67] This time, despite many shortcomings in the performance (Chuprynnikov, as Levko, could scarcely be heard; Slavina's voice seemed coarse for the tender role of Hanna; the theater's abominable acoustics rendered the French horns dull and colorless; and even the solo trumpet at the end of act 2 was scarcely audible), Rimsky-Korsakov was received enthusiastically by the audience. He was called out several times after each act and, at the end of the second scene of act 2, he was presented with an enormous and very effective laurel wreath designed by Stasov and Mme Shestakova.

The theater was filled. The performance lasted from eight o'clock until eleven. There were only a few cuts—two short ones in the *rusalki khorovod,* one in the scene of the Headman's explanation, and one in the last scene—all made with Nikolai Andreyevich's consent.

As for the rest of the cast, Runge was excellent as Pannochka; the same may be said of the chorus. Ugrinovich (Vinokur), Koryakin (the Headman), and Dolina (Svoyachenitsa) handled their roles splendidly, with much life and humor. Goncharov (Kalenik), Klimov (the Scribe), and even Slavina, though the timbre of her voice is not suited to the young beauty Hanna, were all fairly good.

Following the opera, I went with a few others to the Rimsky-Korsakovs' where we stayed until midnight.

8 October

Tonight I took to Nikolai Andreyevich some little souvenirs my mother had brought him from Italy—a desk set, an album with scenes of Rome, a small ashtray from Florence, etc. He was clearly touched by my mother's thoughtfulness; he said at once that tomorrow, without fail, he will drop in at Chernyshev Lane to thank her in person for "the whole museum of gifts."

We spoke about the forthcoming tribute to be paid to Bessel[68] on the twenty-fifth anniversary of his publishing firm. Then Rimsky-Korsakov played for me scene 4 from *Christmas Eve*.

During tea we talked about Laroche and his growing influence on the musical youth who, thanks to him, have already begun to reject their former artistic views, in short, everything on which they were nurtured and to which they owe everything. Our conversation turned to Brahms (this ponderous but honest composer of the West) and proceeded to Hanslick. With this, Rimsky-Korsakov recounted a scandalous incident which had occurred between the latter and Schütt, a one-time pupil of Rimsky-Korsakov. According to Esipova, Hanslick wrote scathingly about this young composer's compositions until someone advised him to grease Hanslick's palm. And then what? The great Hanslick accepted the offering and thenceforth changed his tactics completely toward the young maestro.

"What a character!" exclaimed Rimsky-Korsakov as he ended his tale. "No wonder I've always detested him and his harmful book *The Beautiful in Music,* which many people, including Laroche, have praised so highly."

After tea Nikolai Andreyevich played the new *terzetto* he has written to replace the original little duet in act 4 ("Cherevichki ia dostal"), which he feels was not altogether successful.

When he finished, he closed the music and said, "Well, now no one is ever going to hear another note of this opera until it is performed—not Stasov, Liadov—no one except old Mme Shestakova. So as not to offend her, I'll play bits of it for her; it would be a sin to refuse. I'll even pay her a special visit for this. However, I'm not going to perform any numbers from *Christmas Eve* at the Russian Symphony Concerts, as I intended. There's really no point in making myself a target once again."

Shortly before I left we got onto the subject of Mozart who, though certainly a genius of the first magnitude, did not say the last word, with his *Don Giovanni,* in the history of the development of operatic style.

"I'm not arguing," asserted Rimsky-Korsakov, "Mozart is not Gluck[69] and his *Don Giovanni* is not a minuet, but it by no means has the extraordinary significance that some people once ascribed to it and very likely still do. I don't deny that in *Don Giovanni* a new trend manifested itself (musical characterization and even a certain formlessness in recitative). But this opera was only a first step toward the latest music drama which, despite the fact that it had much in common with its prototype, far outstripped it and, in the persons of Wagner and Glinka, achieved heights unattainable by Mozart."

15 October

The Russian Musical Society began its winter season with a program consisting of Rimsky-Korsakov's *Skazka* and Schumann's *Das Paradies und die Peri.* Despite Krushevsky's questionable conducting and Valter's inability to sustain high notes, Rimsky-Korsakov was called out twice.

18 October

Today Nikolai Andreyevich was in a fine mood and visibly delighted with my visit. We had a discussion about Tchaikovsky's orchestration, which, though excellent on the whole, suffers from insufficient variety, insufficient instrumental contrast. Almost continuous *tutti* and frequent doubling of voices results in a certain degree of monotony. Besides this, the winds almost always "sing through the nose," something which Rimsky-Korsakov repeatedly brought to Peter Ilyich's attention and the latter completely agreed with. In this connection, I recalled to Rimsky-Korsakov what Tchaikovsky had said about Berlioz' music, when I visited him back in 1887 on October 25:

"In Berlioz' music and mine, the texture is highly complicated but with this difference, that his works, though generally presenting enormous difficulties, are rather easy for the individual players, while my music is complex and not too easy to perform. This is so not only for the orchestra as a whole but for the individual players as well, since it demands thorough virtuosity of them. I don't mean that my music is impossible to play—not at all. I wish to state only that writing in a technically difficult manner is my principal shortcoming, one which, despite all effort, I cannot free myself from. Thus, it is the major and essential defect of my style."

"I hope the orchestra won't dare to say this about me," commented Rimsky-Korsakov, "for my scores are considerably easier and more elementary technically than Tchaikovsky's, except for 'Egypt,' perhaps, and some other really complicated things."

Apparently poor Nikolai Andreyevich did not suspect that the "highly cultivated" hacks, not knowing what to carp at, what to vent their spleen and secret envy on, had begun to persuade the public that his scoring is incredibly difficult for every instrument and, apropos of *Snegurochka* had even made up a derisive little ditty on the motive of the Hymn to the Sun, beginning with the words: "Rimsky-Korsakov has played dirty tricks on us."

Our conversation turned somehow to the lack of beauty in the "false progressions" and harmonic fabrications of the modern Italian school from Verdi *(Otello)* to Mascagni *(Cavalleria rusticana)* and such others as Boito, Sgambati, etc.

"Evidently, harmonic refinement is not in their nature," remarked Rimsky-Korsakov. "They are not Wagners."

Finally, we addressed ourselves to the subject of Glinka's enormous gift for virtuoso orchestral writing, recalling such pages from *Ruslan* as the Bard's two songs (with piano and harp); the "mystic canon" following Ludmila's abduction in act 1 (with the ethereal flute fioritura); the orchestration of the Persian Chorus "Lozhitsia v pole mrak nochnoi;" Chernomor's March (with the fantastic glockenspiel solo in the trio); the Chorus of the Flowers, etc.; in all of which the very latest instrumental combinations are employed.

"Only someone who, for some reason, finds this to his disadvantage, could fail to see it," concluded Rimsky-Korsakov.

23 October

I spent this entire evening at the Rimsky-Korsakovs'. We had a long discussion about the curious articles by Sementkovsky, which appeared in *Istoricheskii vestnik*[70] under the high-flown title "The Ideals of Art." While nothing whatever was said about "ideals," there was a statement to the effect that neither Antokolsky nor Repin is a genius and that everything about their work is haphazard and fortuitous.

"Obviously," commented Rimsky-Korsakov, "these gentlemen haven't arrived at the simple truth that no one in the world has yet been able to define the real tasks, purposes, and means of art, and that, even after creating great works, artists themselves have never fully understood what they did or why art exists."

As for Repin's painting of Ivan the Terrible, mentioned in these articles, despite the striking color and amazing realism (or rather, naturalism), Nikolai Andreyevich does not like it. He finds it repugnant, because of the excessive amount of blood and "for overstepping the bounds of pure art."[71]

After a brief silence during which he seemed to be pondering, Nikolai Andreyevich added, "You know, at the present moment I feel in particularly good spirits. I've long since forgotten the aesthetic abracadabra on which I wasted almost three years. I've given up spouting lofty truths about art, which are of no use to anyone. I am composing. I finished my choruses today, the twenty-third of October, instead of the middle of November, as I had expected to. And I repeat, I'm profoundly happy. The day I finally finish scoring the opera, which will probably be sometime next February, I'm going to start working on *Sadko*. It will open with a brilliant feast *à la Ruslan,* something new for me. And it will come out marvelously.

"Really," he said in conclusion, "it's not for us to write articles or delve into analysis. If we do, in our declining years we'll find ourselves blushing over our ignorance, our rash and intemperate judgments. You don't have to go far to find examples of this—you've only to remember Cui's feuilletons on Wagner, particularly the one titled '*Lohengrin,* or Curiosity Punished,'[72] and Serov's and Rubinstein's no less regrettable writings about Glinka's *Ruslan*.[73] And all this because, sometimes for want of judgment of our own, we've repeated the words of others."

28 October

This time, besides me, Shtrup was also at the Rimsky-Korsakovs', but Nikolai Andreyevich and I saw little of him as he spent almost the entire evening at the piano in the drawing room, preparing for the choral rehearsals of *The Maid of Pskov*.[74]

Rimsky-Korsakov was in an excellent mood. He spoke about Mussorgsky's *Fair at Sorochintsy*,[75] the introduction to which he had at one time planned to perform at the Russian Symphony Concerts. The orchestration, he said, was particularly outrageous. For example, it contained a number of chords (with identical disposition of the voices) scored for trumpets with trombones and violins *divisi*. In some places you would find open fifths of double basses, violas, and violins without any doubling of the cellos. There were many such blunders.

At about ten-thirty Nikolai Andreyevich and I left the house and I accompanied him as far as Belyaev's. On the way we talked about my "many-volumed" (as Nikolai Andreyevich put it) reminiscences, which obviously take up a great deal of my time.

"But is it really going to be interesting for future generations to read so much about me alone?" he asked. And then he again asked me to let him see at least a bit of it.

3 November

Rimsky-Korsakov told me something very interesting about the Chorus and Dances of the Birds from *Snegurochka*, that is, that the opening oboe figure is nothing but the screech of a startled young hawk or merlin and that, in addition to the voice of a cuckoo, this number contains another tiny rhythmic phrase on the English horn, likewise drawn directly from nature. That is the way some unknown bird sang in Stelyovo, according to Nikolai Andreyevich. The little oboe phrases (likewise those of the English horn) in the introduction to this opera, beneath which, in one of the rough drafts (June 10, 1880), the composer, for fun, wrote "cock-a-doodle-doo," imitate exactly the crowing of a cock. This is not something contrived but, as in *Mlada,* it is authentic. According to Nadezhda Nikolayevna, this is really the way one Stelyvo cock crew.

Into those enchanting moments in the prologue and act 4, during which the most delicate lacelike sounds are heard in the violins with sparkling flashes of light from the violin harmonics and piccolos *pp,* Rimsky-Korsakov introduced the whistle of their beloved bullfinch (likewise drawn from nature). This bird, by the way, always sang this melodic figure in the same key but a tone higher.

7 November

The brilliant pianist and gifted composer Anton Grigoryevich Rubinstein passed away at 2:00 A.M. in Petersburg. May he rest in eternal peace!

The Rimsky-Korsakovs were at dinner when I arrived, so I, took my customary place between Nadezhda Nikolayevna and Nikolai Andreyevich and, as usual, drank a glass of wine with water and ate *pirozhki.*

We embarked on a discussion about Cui's recent article in *Artist,*[76] agreeing that it is high time Cui gave up his worthless role as critic and took a clear, hard look at things, since these preconceived, superficial judgments and half-baked ideas only do harm and lead to all sorts of misunderstandings. For example, according to Cui, Rimsky-Korsakov is "a landscape painter." So be it. But what is better in *May Night* than the first scene of act 2, which is a genre scene without a trace of landscape, and genre in the style of Mussorgsky to boot. Also, in Cui's opinion, Rimsky-Korsakov writes only brief "little phrases and themes." Thus, it must be that during his entire thirty years of composing, he cannot have written a single real phrase or theme. On the other hand, this same Cui states that, despite all expectations, the best number of the entire opera *(May Night)* is the love duet from act 1, that is, precisely what, Cui contends, Rimsky-Korsakov is least capable of.[77]

"Really, it's a pity," said Rimsky-Korsakov, "when you come to think of it, if you believe the critics, you'll arrive at the unexpected conclusion that after Glinka there was only one operatic composer—Dargomyzhsky—and not because of *Rusalka* (what's *Rusalka!*), but because of *The Stone Guest.* Tchaikovsky, who wrote some ten operas and I, who've composed five, we don't count, because Peter Ilyich was a 'lyricist and symphonist' and I 'only a symphonist,' even though, strictly speaking, I haven't written a single successful nonprogrammatic symphony!"

This reminded Nikolai Andreyevich of the following incident, which he related to me. There was a run-through of *Snegurochka*. Evidently Napravnik didn't care for it very much, for, while listening to it, he seemed occupied only with trying to find every possible cut that could be made. It was terribly long, he claimed.

"When I protested," concluded Rimsky-Korsakov, "that they really do put on long operas and cited as an example *The Huguenots,* he couldn't bear it and declared sharply, categorically that my argument didn't prove anything since *The Huguenots* is a live work and my *Snegurochka*—dead."

14 November

During a brief visit to Rimsky-Korsakov, I learned that Balakirev has resigned from the Court Chapel.[78]

In passing I mentioned Ivanov's laudatory article about Rubinstein,[79] who, in the critic's opinion, lacked only one quality to make him a complete genius—Rimsky-Korsakov's gift for orchestration. This caused Nikolai Andreyevich to remark with comic sadness: "Well then, I guess the only thing I lack is Rubinstein's creative power."

The only one of all the critics who assessed correctly Anton Grigoryevich's significance as a musician was Solovyov, who called him a pianist of genius and an important composer.

21 November

When I dropped in on the Rimsky-Korsakovs, I found them exultant. It seems that on Saturday (the nineteenth), Nikolai Andreyevich played through his entire new opera for Liadov and Blumenfeld and they had both been delighted with it.

After reporting this, they told me that on the twenty-sixth Nikolai Andreyevich is going to play the whole opera for other friends and acquaintances who have not heard it.

26 November

Christmas Eve was given tonight at the Rimsky-Korsakovs. Felix Blumenfeld, Nadezhda Nikolayevna, and Nikolai Andreyevich took turns accompanying. The latter also filled in the voice parts wherever possible, that is, except for Oxana's technically difficult song from scene 2 (the first one), which he played on the piano, and the church clerk's chant, which Nikolai Alexandrovich Sokolov sang from sight.

Among those present were Stasov, Liadov, Glazunov, Belyaev, Shtrup, and Trifonov. The music began at about nine o'clock and ended at midnight, with only one break of an hour or so, during which tea was served. So far as I could tell, the opera made a favorable impression. The *kolyadki,* folk scenes, and clerk's chant met with loud approval, to say nothing of act 3, especially the "matins" and "the procession of Kolyada and Ovsenya," which impressed all the listeners not only by its bewitching, inspired music but also by the unusual beauty and originality of its conception. Besides this, Stasov and Liadov praised the libretto. The only one who said nothing was Glazunov, who sat silently on the divan beside Trifonov the whole time, following the score of the new, "not too successful" opera (in his opinion).

28 November

When I arrived, Nikolai Andreyevich was at the piano in the drawing room, reading through Anton Rubinstein's Third Symphony in preparation for the rehearsal.[80] He did not like this job and he was visibly exhausted from it. Scarcely had I entered the room, when he stood up, availing himself of the opportunity to interrupt his work, at least temporarily.

Stretching and yawning, Nikolai Andreyevich closed the score with a bang and said: "I simply cannot understand why I'm conducting the Russian Symphony Concerts when there's Glazunov, who could replace me— and successfully. I've really been sick of this sort of work for a long time now. Who really needs *me* to conduct them? Who benefits from saddling *me* with this business year in and year out? The traditional style of performing the works of us oldsters[81] I established long ago. Therefore, it's unnecessary for me to meddle further in this field, especially since nowadays our new Russian school, as such, has completely disintegrated and the word "kuchkist," once a swearword on the lips of our enemies, has become just about the same to those, like Liadov and Glazunov, whom our school nurtured and reared, as the saying goes.

"To be perfectly honest," continued Nikolai Andreyevich, "such an attitude on the part of our *own* (I'm not speaking about enemies) secretly outrages me. It puts me in mind of Krylov's fable.[82] Who doesn't know it? But, remember, what I just said must remain between us for now. I certainly wouldn't want to solicit farewell ovations. I really don't care for them, I find them too painful and sad. I'd like to retire from this business quietly, peacefully, without any fanfare and, as far as possible, on good terms with everyone—and most important—without revealing and emphasizing the reason. And now I have to conduct Rubinstein's works, most of which I actually don't like, for I find them colorless, unoriginal, and totally unsatisfying.

"You know," Nikolai Andreyevich went on, "I'm coming to the sad conclusion that Anton Grigoryevich's symphonic music can be characterized as follows: if, while listening to something you don't know, you have the feeling that it's either bad Beethoven or poorly orchestrated Mendelssohn, and if, at the same time, it never strikes you as downright tasteless or ugly but, on the other hand, there's nothing daring about it—on the contrary everything about it seems proper and decent, even if hopelessly monotonous—then you can be sure you're listening to one of Rubinstein's many works of this kind. I would exclude from this category, of course, a few excerpts from his vocal and Eastern music (the choruses from *The Tower of Babel,* the dances from *The Demon* and *Feramors,* some of *The Maccabees, Azra,* the *Persian Songs,* etc.). The only more or less pleasing exception from among his symphonic pieces is, I, think, *Don Quixote,* which Rubinstein once said he composed as a parody of Liszt. God must have punished him, for, as luck would have it, this 'parody' turned out to be his greatest success."

Besides this, we spoke at length about Balakirev's resignation from the Court Chapel.

"To us," said Nikolai Andreyevich, "Balakirev is a man of genius—author of *Tamara, Islamey,* the *Song of the Golden Fish*—and we esteem him and admire his works. But, in the Chapel, he's only the Director and at times he's extremely erratic and even carping. No wonder the majority there dislike him."

In further conversation, apropos of the present-day, so-called Laroche, or rather, Laroche-Taneyev trend of thinking among the Petersburg musicians,[83] Nikolai Andreyevich observed, not without bitterness: "Whenever I criticized shortcomings in the new Russian school, I always tried, insofar as possible, to correct them. The best proof of this is what I've done with Mussorgsky, almost all of whose works I've harmonized and scored anew. Now all they can do is reproach me, but when it comes right down to it, they won't have a leg to stand on. I don't include Glazunov among them; he's really done a great deal for Borodin."

3 December

Today the first Russian Symphonic Evening, dedicated to the memory of Anton Rubinstein, took place under the direction of Rimsky-Korsakov. And what happened? Neither the name of the revered artist nor the comparatively interesting program[84]—nothing saved the concert, and the hall was almost completely empty. There's the public's famed love for Rubinstein!

5 December

Nikolai Andreyevich gave me an account of the official tryout of *Christmas Eve,* which took place on the evening of December 1 in the foyer of the Marinsky Theater before Napravnik, Laroche, Modest Tchaikovsky, Pogozhev, and most of the artists of the Marinsky company. It scored a complete success, although, of course, the most subtle points, such as "the aerial procession of Kolyada" and the Dawn, were not understood. Blumenfeld played magnificently and even Rimsky-Korsakov himself was in good form. Napravnik praised the libretto.(!)

At the rehearsal at the Molases' the following day, Koryakin declared that *Christmas Eve* had "certainly exceeded all expectations." Mravina was so taken with Oxana's first aria that she wrote Nikolai Andreyevich for permission to sing it at a concert even before the opera itself was given. And Dolina, who had been unable to attend the tryout, sent Nikolai Andreyevich a congratulatory telegram the very next day.

The program of the second Russian Symphony Concert included, besides the premiere of Glazunov's new suite *Scènes de ballet,* the suite from Rimsky-Korsakov's *Snegurochka.*

I saw Rimsky-Korsakov briefly and he broke the news that he has declined the post of Director of the Court Chapel, offered to him by Count Vorontsov-Dashko, Minister of the Court.

"My visit to the Count did prove of some benefit to me, however," he added, "for I brought up the question of staging my new opera, which had been forbidden by the censor. The Count promised that if I present a written petition to him, appending to it the libretto and the judgment of the censor, he would bring this to the attention of the Emperor."[85]

CHAPTER 5

1895

1 January

Nikolai Andreyevich told me that last night, exactly at midnight, he received an official communication from Polovtsev, Director of the Administrative Department of His Majesty's Cabinet, to the effect that the censorship of *Christmas Eve* has been rescinded and the Emperor has granted permission for the opera to be performed in full on the imperial stage.

Further, speaking of Mendelssohn, Rimsky-Korsakov observed that today's composers, having made wide use of devices strewn lavishly throughout the *Midsummer Night's Dream* Overture (with its superbly original introductory bars for woodwinds) ought to bow down before him, since what is beautiful in their works originated with him. As examples of his own debt to Mendelssohn, Rimsky-Korsakov cited the Introduction to *Christmas Eve* and the opening of *Sheherazade*.

In conclusion, we talked about our young musicians' exaggerated adoration of Dargomyzhsky and his *Stone Guest* and their equally exaggerated love for Mussorgsky, which has been magnified considerably by the articles of Stasov and others.

2 January

When I arrived at the Rimsky-Korsakovs', I found Arensky[1] at the entrance, about to ring the bell. After we were admitted, he and Rimsky-Korsakov went into the study, where they conversed until he left.

Rimsky-Korsakov was in very good spirits; he talked animatedly about Vsevolozhsky and his extraordinary kindness. Besides, he told me that *May Night* was given today at the Marinsky Theater instead of *The Barber of Seville* and that Shtrup had obtained a box for them.

During dinner they read a lot of poetry which Rimsky-Korsakov had jotted down "under the inspiration of his first trip to Stelyovo" (in 1880), as well as some written in Taitsa, including a description of a parrot. After that followed an account, also in verse, of a trip to Nizhny and other things. There was much laughter.

After everyone had left the room, Nikolai Andreyevich drew from his pocket a notebook, on which appeared the words *"Sadko* (libretto), December 31, 1894. January 1, 1895." Obviously Rimsky-Korsakov is not wasting any time.

4 January

Tonight my wife and I heard *May Night* in a very uneven (more bad than good) performance. The subscription audience was cold, as usual. The singers lapsed into caricature continually and, at times, strove for a coarse effect. The second scene of act 2 was greeted with silence. It was not until the end of the performance that some people began to applaud. But this was short lived, for beginning with the *rusalki,* people started to leave and during the finale, there was a virtual stampede toward the exit. Thus, not only Levko's story (act 1) but Pannochka's brilliant "farewell" passed completely unnoticed.

On Monday (January 2) at the end of the performance, with practically no one in the hall, some unknown person presented Rimsky-Korsakov with a laurel wreath. There's an empty gesture for you!

5 January

When I arrived at the Rimsky-Korsakovs', at eight-thirty, Nikolai Andreyevich was orchestrating *Christmas Eve* and Nadezhda Nikolayevna was working on its vocal score. Nikolai Andreyevich was visibly distressed over last night's poor reception of *May Night* (due, in no small measure, to the singers' weak voices). This led to a discussion about Cui and the harm he had caused Rimsky-Korsakov as the first one to express the opinion that Rimsky-Korsakov is above all a symphonist and, consequently, not an opera composer; that he lacks sweep and a gift for melodic inventiveness, that most of his music is superficial; finally, that, as a composer he is entirely without humor and passion (Stasov agreed). All this notwithstanding, Nikolai Andreyevich cannot wait to begin his next opera, *Sadko*.

From further conversation, I learned that *Snegurochka* is going to be given in Kiev.[2]

"I really don't know whether it's worth going there," said Nikolai Andreyevich. "Altani maintains there's no use expecting anything of the Kievans. According to him not long ago they ruined an opera called *Aleko* by some budding young composer by putting it on after only one rehearsal.[3] Meanwhile, Bessel is pressing me to go, arguing that the presence of the composer at a premiere always heightens the festive atmosphere."

During tea we got onto the subject of composers' fees and Nikolai Andreyevich told me that he had sold Bessel all the rights to *Snegurochka* for fifteen hundred rubles, which, in those days and for Bessel, was a very respectable sum. Nowadays, Belyaev pays as much as three thousand rubles for an opera, even though he does not care much for program music in general and opera in particular. He likes only quartets.

Our conversation ended with a discussion of the ever-increasing superficiality of the standards by which contemporary composers choose their subjects (music boxes, marionettes, puppets, and other such rubbish). Rimsky-Korsakov attributed this, on the one hand, to a natural reaction against the strict artistic demands of Balakirev and Stasov, who felt that art should concern itself only with what is great (a reaction initiated, obviously, by Tchaikovsky in his last works), and on the other hand, to the high fees paid by Belyaev.

"Strange," said Nikolai Andreyevich suddenly, "one curious thing has escaped your attention—the rather sad fate that has befallen our 'cheap Hanslickians' (Ivanov and Solovyov). So long as they were on good terms with us, they occasionally composed something. Now, however, their creativity has evaporated completely and the more they envy us, the worse their compositions are."

11 January

When I arrived at the Rimsky-Korsakovs', I found Nikolai Andreyevich feverishly orchestrating the Polonaise with chorus from *Christmas Eve*. On learning that he was including *piccolo clarinets* in the score, I began to poke fun at him. Such refined orchestration, I said, could only indicate a decline of truly artistic ideals; the Polonaise would sound rich and splendid only if it were entrusted to the strings alone, and what's more, strings *senza sordini*.

"Don't sneer at me," retorted Rimsky-Korsakov with a laugh. "Exclude the string instruments from the most magnificent orchestration and you'll end up with the flat, vulgar sonority of a regimental band."

Over dinner we talked about Grechaninov's B minor Symphony, which is to be given its premiere on the fourteenth of this month at the third Russian Symphony Concert under Rimsky-Korsakov.

"It's really not good," noted Nikolai Andreyevich, "if someone, who has a natural inclination to compose in the style of Rubinstein and writes fairly well in this style, suddenly takes a fancy to Borodin and begins to compose in his style. It won't work."[4]

13 January

Rubinstein's sonata was played well by Hildebrand and Borovka at the Music Society tonight. Besides this, the three choruses from *The Maid of Pskov*[5] were conducted with such fervor that they had to be repeated and after the last one, Rimsky-Korsakov was called out.

During intermission Cui showered Nikolai Andreyevich with compliments, assuring him that it was a long time since he had heard anything like this, that he was struck by the magnificence, sweep, and power of the music, etc. Meanwhile, I was engaged in a heated discussion with Nadezhda Nikolayevna about Laroche's outrageous article in *Ezhegodnik*.[6] But then out came Arina Andreyevna Fedosova,[7] the famous narrator of folk tales, who proceeded to relate numerous laments, *byliny*, etc. My mother and I moved to the first row. I regretted terribly that I had no pencil and paper with which to fix the singing in my memory. Nikolai Andreyevich and Blumenfeld took down as many of the tunes as they could, and thus, Nikolai Andreyevich added new ones to the five he had recorded before.

23 January

At dinnertime I dropped in at the Rimsky-Korsakovs' only to learn that Nikolai Andreyevich had left for Kiev on the eighteenth and Nadezhda Nikolayevna is to go on the twentieth.

Andrei was so carried away by Safonov's conducting at the Russian Musical Society[8] that he pounced on me for singling out for praise only the tonal beauty of the performance.

After noting the rather good reception given *May Night* at the Mikhailovsky Theater on the twenty-second, I left.

29 January

Nadezhda Nikolayevna did not care much for the Kiev performance of *Snegurochka* because they introduced a great deal of "clowning" into it. For example, the choristers danced unnecessarily in the scene of the Farewell to Shrovetide, during Lel's third song, and in the scene of the Chorus of the Flowers, and, besides this, Bobyl hopped about excessively. Nikolai Andreyevich, on the other hand, was quite pleased with his visit. The people of Kiev responded warmly to the opera—a new one for them—and the artists put a great deal of effort into the performance. At the premiere, Rimsky-Korsakov was presented with a silver wreath and, in addition, a musical evening was given in his honor.[9]

After Kiev, we talked about the *Coronation Cantata*,[10] which was commissioned from Glazunov after Rimsky-Korsakov declined. "Wouldn't it be fine," exclaimed Rimsky-Korsakov, "if the Directorate would suddenly decide to commission me to compose a new opera—of my choice—*Sadko,* say. I certainly wouldn't refuse that!"

1 February

Tonight Nikolai Andreyevich and I got onto the subject of Napravnik's *Dubrovsky,* which, while not marked by any great originality so far as its musical ideas are concerned, is, nevertheless, Napravnik's best opera. In this case, Nikolai Andreyevich and I agreed completely about the music. We considered the best passages to be: Vladimir's quasi lullaby; the end of the love duet and the piano prelude in the scene between Vladimir and Masha; some of the interlude depicting the stuffy air and the impending storm. The worst, we thought, were the portrayal of the Frenchman, the endless repetition of "Good day, Master," the music of the contradance and the lesson.

"This makes you feel as though music had retrogressed seventy-five years!" exclaimed Nikolai Andreyevich.

6 February

Nikolai Andreyevich informed me this afternoon that of all the excerpts from *Christmas Eve* performed at the Russian Symphony concert,[11] Cui liked only the Introduction and the little chorus "Sviatoi vecher"; he objected to the Polonaise and Oxana's aria, the latter because of its resemblance, stylistically, to *Snegurochka.*

Being in an excellent mood, Nikolai Andreyevich related the following amusing conversation overheard at the concert by one of his acquaintances. It seems that after the playing of Liadov's *Scherzo,* the audience began to call for the composer. The latter, however, did not come out. Meanwhile, Stasov, as head of the delegation carrying the wreath, walked over to Belyaev, said something to him and then proceeded to deliver an address. At his, a lady in the parterre turned to the one next to her and said: "Tell me, why did they call for Liadov but give the wreath to Belyaev?"

"Why is this so hard to understand?" replied the other. "Liadov is dead and now only his editor Belyaev is left."

"Isn't she an idiot?" asked Nikolai Andreyevich in conclusion. "And this is the 'cream of society' that goes to concerts and passes judgment on music! No wonder even a Baskin has a wide circle of enthusiastic admirers!"

I forgot to mention that during dinner I read to Nikolai Andreyevich Ossovsky's article about Baskin from *Russkaia muzykal'naia gazeta,*[12] which begins caustically with the words of Shakespeare's Portia: "God made him, and therefore let him pass for a man."

13 February

Nikolai Andreyevich and I had a rather extended discussion about Laroche's exceedingly strange article about Tchaikovsky.[13] I say "strange" because, despite its one hundred and one pages, it adds up to absolutely nothing. It is so full of contradictory statements that reading it, you begin to doubt that the author really understood it himself.

Let me cite a few of Laroche's opinions about Rimsky-Korsakov's music and his artistic makeup in general. First (on page 101), we find the rather surprising notion that, as of now, *May Night* is the chef d'oeuvre of Rimsky-Korsakov's entire thirty-year career; then that Rimsky-Korsakov's preoccupation with Russian subjects is limiting him. Why, asks Laroche, shouldn't the creator of *Sheherazade, Antar,* and *Capriccio espagnol* give us one Spanish, one Arabian, one fantastic opera? To this senseless question he offers the following answer of sorts: one cannot say with certainty now that some time in the future he (Rimsky-Korsakov) will not be able to wear foreign dress; one can say only that he will wear Russian dress wonderfully.

Later, speaking of the young girls' chorus from *Onegin* ("Devitsy, krasavitsy"), Laroche remarks (on p. 139), not without malice:

Faced with this problem (that is, the necessity to write this chorus), a composer of the young Russian school would go about solving it in a far more thorough fashion (than Tchaikovsky). He would dig up a folk song in some collection or record one himself somewhere in the region of the Sheksna. Then he would compose a number in couplet form with variations *soprano ostinato,* following all the rules of the Glinka school. It would come out both Russian and piquant. . . . I find that it would come out too well.

Laroche's article contains one very interesting observation, but it was made not by the author but by Tchaikovsky in conversation with him:

"How amazingly good Nikolai Andreyevich's orchestration sounds," Tchaikovsky said to Laroche in 1889–90. "The horns, trumpets, stringed instruments—all are kept within bounds, all are where they are needed, everything is as it should be. In mine, on the other hand, the brasses keep blowing as hard as they can, page after page, needlessly and to no purpose."

No wonder that, when comparing the orchestration of the classicists with that of Tchaikovsky, Laroche said: "His orchestration is not the limpid stream of the Golden Age, but a turbid and angry torrent." Fine praise indeed!

20 February

This afternoon, when I arrived at the Rimsky-Korsakovs', I found Nikolai Andreyevich working on the orchestration of the second act of *Christmas Eve,* the completion of which had been greatly delayed by the Russian Symphony Concerts and the trip to Kiev.

First we discussed Laroche's recent article in *Novosti* [14] in which, among other things, this paradoxical critic complains about the excessive and undeserved luck of the Russian composers, whom he views as the true darlings of fortune.

"I'm absolutely certain," declared Nikolai Andreyevich, "that now, thanks to this strange article, they'll make things even harder for us Russians and, as a result, we'll appear even more seldom on the posters of the Russian Musical Society, which isn't treating us all that favorably as it is."

During dinner, Nikolai Andreyevich told me that the judges at the last Quartet Competition (Napravnik, Arensky, and himself) had awarded the third prize to Glazunov [15] (first and second prizes were out of the question).

"I think this will teach Alexander Konstantinovich a good lesson. He's become somewhat conceited, if you'll forgive my saying so," remarked Rimsky-Korsakov.

Then he spoke highly of one of the contributors to Findeisen's *Russkaia muzykal'naia gazeta*—Ossovsky—and he wanted to know whether this was a pseudonym, for Petrovsky, perhaps.

"He seems to be a sensible fellow with a clear understanding of music," he added. [16]

27 February

Last night, Rimsky-Korsakov told me, he went to Balakirev's with a view to hearing the first movement of his new symphony. [17]

"I must tell you," said Nikolai Andreyevich, "only a fourth of this symphony is new; all the rest is old. I've known it for a long time. Besides this, the form is rather strange. On the whole I rather liked the first Allegro."

In addition to Rimsky-Korsakov, there were also some "Chapel geniuses"[18] at Balakirev's, and the latter made Nikolai Andreyevich listen to a mazurka by one of them. After it had been played, Mily Alexeyevich asked Rimsky-Korsakov what he thought of it. Rimsky-Korsakov replied in a guarded affirmative, adding only that he found the harmonization of the piece overly sumptuous and refined.

"It seemed as though I were listening to some kind of *Mephisto Waltz* of Liszt," remarked Rimsky-Korsakov, to which Balakirev retorted: "Well, now it's clear that the Conservatory has devoured you."

After some further talk about this and that, I started to leave. With that Nikolai Andreyevich presented me with the manuscript of the second half of scene 2 from *Christmas Eve* (the scene at Oxana's). On the Young Girls' *Kolyadka* he wrote the following comical inscription in honor of the Mondays: "To Dear Vas. Vas. Yastrebtsev—I give this manuscript as a keepsake and to ponder. N. R-Korsakov, February 27, '95. 7 P.M. (There was no *kisel'* but there was chocolate)."[19] Then on the Introduction to *Snegurochka,* to commemorate the fifteenth anniversary of the first sketch of this work, Rimsky-Korsakov scribbled (the pen would not write) the following inscription, a paraphrase of Spring's recitative from the Prologue:

> 'Tis fifteen years since I, for fun
> And to amuse my inconstant nature,
> Fickle and capricious,
> Began the opera *Snegurochka*—February 27, 1895.
>
> N. R-Korsakov
> To V. V. Yastrebtsev as a keepsake.

Tomorrow Scriabin is supposed to be at the Rimsky-Korsakovs', so Nikolai Andreyevich invited me to come at eight-thirty.

28 February

There were already a few people at Rimsky-Korsakov's when I arrived, among them Stasov, with whom Rimsky-Korsakov was carrying on an animated conversation about his recent visit to Balakirev.

"And what about the symphony?" Stasov interrupted.

Nikolai Andreyevich told him what he thought of it.

"Just as I surmised," retorted Stasov. "I had good reason to keep insisting to Balakirev that not writing can destroy talent completely, that an artist can become rusty from such inactivity. You see, what I said is coming true; as you say yourself, this Allegro is really rather dry!

"You've not forgotten, I'm sure," growled Stasov, good-naturedly, "Balakirev's famous—his astonishing statement of the sixties: 'When I compose, each tack must be hammered in its proper place.' And remember how he recommened that everyone compose collectively, since only such 'filtered' music can be truly good? What an idea, eh?"

And Stasov burst out laughing.

But just then Scriabin entered with Liadov and shortly afterward, the music began. Scriabin played, among other things, his own D-sharp minor and G-sharp major études. Both were very vigorous and beautiful. The distinguishing feature of the first one is its impetuosity (Stasov was in raptures), and of the second—thunderous basses.

After tea, at Nikolai Andreyevich's request, Arensky performed several numbers from his opera *Nal and Damayanti,* his "Greek Rhythms," and the well-known *Basso ostinato.*[20] The music ended and the conversation began.

"I may be mistaken," said Rimsky-Korsakov turning to Stasov, Sokolov, Liadov, and me, "but in my opinion, although Scriabin is the more gifted of the two, Arensky's music is more appealing and more varied. I would even go so far as to say that, despite Scriabin's unquestionable talent, his devotion to the piano exclusively and his complete indifference toward the works of others will keep him from going further and, thus, he won't leave the vicious circle of piano études."

By the way, tonight I informed Stasov and Liadov that I am writing my reminiscences of Rimsky-Korsakov. Liadov was utterly delighted and Stasov obviously interested, for with his typical spontaneity, he asked me to read them to him.

6 March

I dropped in on the Rimsky-Korsakovs to congratulate Nikolai Andreyevich on his birthday. We turned again to the subject of Laroche, whereupon Nikolai Andreyevich told me that Tchaikovsky did not like him all that much, never deferred to him but, on the contrary, often ridiculed him, for some reason calling him "Manya."[21] When he became irritated with Laroche, he would ask: "Tell me, Manya, how much money did you manage to squeeze out of the merchant who commissioned your *Carmosine?*"[22] To which Herman Augustovich would only reply with a sigh.

During dinner we discussed Napravnik's senseless "prolonging" cuts in Schubert's C major Symphony.[23]

"I call them 'prolonging,'" explained Nikolai Andreyevich, "because by cutting out the modulation or development section, they compel the listener to remain longer in the same key. This is extremely damaging to a work, for when the harmony is not 'freshened up,' little by little the music begins to be wearisome. And all this because of a cut!"

27 March

Before dinner, I showed Nikolai Andreyevich Baskin's wretched brochure on Mussorgsky[24] and after that we talked about the latest squabble between Laroche and Ivanov, in which this time Ivanov rebuked him soundly.[25]

In further conversation, Nikolai Andreyevich informed me that at present he is striving in orchestration "for the brightest combinations of orchestral timbres," for the kind of "overall clarity of tone" (especially in the middle register, which usually sounds nasal) "that makes everything seem suffused with brilliant sunlight."

"From this point of view," he added, "the orchestration of *Christmas Eve* will be the most perfect and *The Maid of Pskov* the most colorless."

After dinner, Nikolai Andreyevich set forth his view of music, a view he had alluded to recently, at the last musical evening with Scriabin.

"Music, like every other art," he said, "means something different to each person and the aesthetic views and standards of one are not binding on another, though, of course, there are many fewer views and standards than there are individuals. Any definition of the aims and purposes of art is, at the very least, meaningless gibberish, like any effort to find out the 'beginning of all beginnings.' And this applies particularly to music, for music is a dream (at least, that's how I understand it). And even though now and then little sparks of this nonexistent dream flash by, they are embodied only in sounds."

31 March

I went to Rimsky-Korsakov's tonight with the aim of acquainting him, for the first time, with my "reminiscences." At my request, we went alone into his study, where I proceeded to read to him from eight-thirty until twelve-twenty-five. Apparently, Nikolai Andreyevich found my writings very satisfactory, for at the end he thanked me for the pleasure I had afforded him, assured me that I have a certain literary gift (as shown by my descriptions of nature, etc.), and, when we bade good-bye, he kissed me three times (Russian fashion) and asked me to read more to him later on. I was, of course, terribly happy.

6 April

The Maid of Pskov was given at the Panayevsky Theater under the auspices of the Music Society before a full house.[26] Despite many shortcomings in the performance, Nikolai Andreyevich was called out many times. Among the critics attending were Ivanov (with the score), Laroche, Veimarn, and Trifonov; among the musicians—Arensky and Cui.

Cui did not care much for the opera and complained to Mme Shestakova that he was bored after the first act. In turn, she admonished him not to be a hypocrite. She understood full well that Cui was not saying what he thought, only that "Miltiades' laurels were giving him no rest."

9 April

The third performance of *The Maid of Pskov,* scheduled for tonight, did not take place, for the simple reason that Olga (Sokolovskaya) did not put in an appearance. The audience waited patiently for more than half an hour. Finally, when Mr. Solovyov announced that the performance was canceled, angry whistling broke out in the gallery and suddenly it seemed as if the topmost reaches of the Panayevsky Theater were filled with a detachment of nightingales. Someone, it is said, announced to the whole theater that he would never come there again. In short, it turned into a scandal! I had just about decided to go home when, suddenly, I thought better of it and set off for the Rimsky-Korsakovs'.

Nadezhda Nikolayevna was deeply distressed over what had happened but, thanks to his "morbidly" (as he puts it) optimistic nature, Rimsky-

Korsakov was not much put out. He even tried to calm Shtrup by engaging him in conversation about the libretto of *Sadko*. The first two acts have already been written, he said, and he expects to finish the third and fourth in the next few days. Work has already begun on the music.

Turning, then, to his *Maid of Pskov*, Nikolai Andreyevich told us that the opera contains only three folk motives: (1) the melody which accompanies the dialogue of the nurses in the opening scene, (2) the theme of the love duet from act 1, and (3) Tucha's song of farewell to Pskov. All the remaining themes are Nikolai Andreyevich's own. As for the melody of the girls' chorus in the scene between Ivan and Olga in Tokmakov's house, it cannot be counted as a folk song, even though it was used (in somewhat simplified form in his *Kallistrat*) by Mussorgsky, who heard it in Pskov Province, since, here, it has been altered considerably by the composer. The same may be said about the profoundly folklike phrase (example 15), repeated at the end of each stanza of Tucha's song "Raskukuisia, kukushechka," for although it is reminiscent of the melody from Ryazan Province "Podui, podui, nepogodushka"[27] (example 16), the resemblance is purely superficial.

Example 15

Vo tem- nom le- su dub-   vush-, ke

Example 16

Ekh,   ne ma- len'- ka- ia

In this connection, Nikolai Andreyevich cited Vaksel's article[28] denouncing *The Maid of Pskov* for its mediocrity and misuse of folk themes. (In the critic's opinion, this opera is even dryer and more artificial than *Prince Igor* and *Khovanshchina*.)

"I've gotten it all my life for these folk themes!" remarked Rimsky-Korsakov, chuckling. "They railed at me not only when I borrowed them from collections, but even when my own melodies had the misfortune to strike the critics as folk themes.[29] They were all following Cui's example. Meanwhile, there are quite a few folk themes not only in the cantatas and inventions of Bach and the Netherlanders, but even in Glinka's *Ruslan*. Yet, it's never occurred to anyone to denounce Glinka for this. But those were different times."

14 April

Not finding Nikolai Andreyevich at home, I left a comical note, beseeching him to accede to Findeisen's request and send me a short autograph, suggesting as best, the opening three or four measures of the overture to *The Maid of Pskov*.[30]

From conversation with Nadezhda Nikolayevna I learned that the late Tsar[31] did not like Rimsky-Korsakov's music, did not know it, (save, perhaps, his *Kheruvimskaia*),[32] was not interested in the "new Russian music" at all and, once, after the *Easter Overture* was played for him, forbade it ever to be played again in his presence. Nadezhda Nikolayevna also told me about another curious thing—the effect that Laroche's *Novosti* article on Russian composers[33] had had on a commission for *Sadko*.

"Just imagine," she said, "prior to this letter, Vsevolozhsky was extremely kind and courteous; he even proposed that Nikolai Andreyevich set to work on an opera—*Sadko,* for example—with the thought that he (Vsevolozhsky) would stage it immediately. But then Laroche's article was published and prospects changed. The Directorate seemed to be equivocating, and when Nikolai Andreyevich, finally realizing what was going on, went to Vsevolozhsky and officially declined the commission, Ivan Alexandrovich was overjoyed and said immediately that now that his hands were not tied, it would be better not to wait for *Sadko* but to revive . . . Rubinstéin's *Feramors.*"[34]

17 April

During dinner, mention of Ekaterina Lebedeva's examination in orchestration, at which she was required to orchestrate an excerpt from Berlioz' *Damnation of Faust,* reminded Nikolai Andreyevich of Bernhard's[35] dread of hearing the names of Borodin, Rimsky-Korsakov, Berlioz, etc. In such cases, they say, he would usually interrupt the student with: "Yes,

yes, you can find everything in them, of course. But it would be better for you to tell me how Weber, for example, employed the clarinet."

3 May

When I entered the Rimsky-Korsakovs', I found Nikolai Andreyevich going through the orchestral proofs of the first scene of *Christmas Eve,* which had arrived the day before yesterday. While he was very glad to see me, I sensed that he was feeling ill and troubled. My suspicions were soon confirmed, for he began to talk about the illness—arteriosclerosis— which has been plaguing him for more than six years now.

"Last summer," he said, "this unpleasant illness, from which Borodin also suffered and, in fact, died, filled me with a fear of death which is totally alien to me. You wouldn't believe it, but at times I became so terrified about dying before completing my new opera that I was absolutely at my wit's end."

During dinner, however, the atmosphere changed somewhat when he talked about yesterday's visit of Glazunov and Kanille. He praised Glazunov's new symphony[36] and also the variations he wrote for a quartet honoring Belyaev on the tenth anniversary of his publishing activity.[37]

We also conversed about an article by Ivanov, in which he took Trifonov to task for his insipidity[38] and, among other things, expressed regret over the withdrawal from the repertory of the Marinsky Theater of two such worthy operas as Rimsky-Korsakov's *Snegurochka* and Solovyov's *Cordelia.*

5 May

Tonight I found Shtrup at the Rimsky-Korsakovs'. Our conversation at first concerned *The Queen of Spades,* a piano score of which lay open on the piano. Nikolai Andreyevich thinks very highly of the musical portrayal of the old Countess and had words of high praise, also, for the scene in Liza's boudoir, with the elegant duet between Liza and Polina.

After this the conversation drifted imperceptibly to the subject of Cui's *Ratcliff* and its amazingly unintelligible declamation, whereupon Nikolai Andreyevich told us that Borodin always called the festive chorus from act 1 "the chorus of the famished guests," since in this scene the guests just keep dashing to and fro and singing, without ever getting a chance to eat anything.

We then went into the study where, as promised, Nikolai Andreyevich read us the libretto of *Sadko*. It appears that he has already sketched out quite a bit of the music for this opera and has also decided upon the orchestration.

We got onto the subject of *May Night* and it turned out that, for the most part, Nikolai Andreyevich himself likes only act 1 and the first (the magic) half of act 3. These he always listens to. He either spends the remainder of the time in the smoking room or else he goes home right after the duet and "sunrise."

"It's wearisome somehow," he added, "to listen to these fools—the Headman, the Scribe, and the rest—after the *rusalki* and Pannochka, whom I love and will always love as much as I do Snegurochka, Mlada, and the Sea Queen."

14 May

Just as I had finished reading Tolstoy's *Confession,* the doorbell rang and in walked Nikolai Andreyevich.

"You're probably surprised that I've come to you in such nasty weather," he said, "but I figured—and rightly, as you see—that you wouldn't go anywhere on such a cold, rainy day and therefore I'd find you at home without any advance warning."

As a housewarming gift, Rimsky-Korsakov had brought us a torte and three books of his songs, comprising opus nos. 3, 4, and 7, recently published by Belyaev. Each book bore an inscription. On the first was written: "To dear V. V. Yastrebtsev from the composer and reviser— May 14, 1895"; on the second: "From the composer and reviser of (his own) compositions N. R-Korsakov—May 14, 1895"; on the third: "From the composer and reviser of (his own and others') compositions—May 14, 1895."

We talked about Findeisen's article on *The Maid of Pskov*.[39] Rimsky-Korsakov does not much care for it. For one thing, it contains many confused and inaccurate statements despite its clearly favorable tone. For another thing, Nikolai Andreyevich cannot understand why Findeisen considers the end of scene 1, act 2 "too trite and readily found in many mediocre works of the operatic repertoire."

"This is absolute nonsense," he declared, "for it's here, in the finale, that the music is as fanciful as can be—that's its chief defect. It's a kind of continuous augmented triad.

"Besides this," he continued, "for some reason, Findeisen regards the phrase of the flute and harp [example 17] as a theme of lightning, which is again completely erroneous, since it depicts rather the sound of rain and has nothing whatever of the character of fire (or the Wagnerian Loge), as he maintains.

Example 17

"Further, it's not true that the Putivl fanfares were inspired by my *Maid of Pskov,* since they were composed first by Borodin for Gedeonov's *Mlada* and, therefore, in all likelihood, preceded my own. However, I cannot say exactly. I don't remember.

"By the way," added Rimsky-Korsakov, suddenly changing the subject, "do you know what Mussorgsky sometimes called me when he wanted to express to me special warmth and delight? What do you think? This: 'my abomination, my vile thing' (*moia merzost, moia gadost'*). This was his highest praise."

Chatting thus, we did not notice how the time had passed. By now it was five o'clock—we had been talking for three hours. On the whole Nikolai Andreyevich was extremely cheerful and pleasant during this visit. He held our dear Ksenechka in his arms, kissed her hands, and was obviously very pleased with her.

On leaving, Rimsky-Korsakov promised to visit us again before leaving for Vechasha.

15 May

During dinner at the Rimsky-Korsakovs' we fell to talking about the "Russian style" and "church modes." Mindful of Laroche's earlier attacks on what he considered pseudo-Russian music, Nikolai Andreyevich declared, not without irritation: "How angry it makes me when some half-German, half-Frenchman, who has never spent any time in the country-side, dares to ridicule what, to him, is 'ridiculous folk music' and has the impertinence, out of ignorance, to maintain that there can be no such style in music, that it's only the Utopia of frivolous minds, etc. The fact is, there are many such gentlemen in our Russia, aren't there . . . ?"

20 May

This afternoon I was at the Conservatory and just as Nikolai Andreyevich and I were beginning to talk, Lavrov came up to us, then Blumenfeld, Liadov, and some others. They became involved in a discussion of a recent article about the Court Chapel,[40] which asserted that if one sensed a slight neglect of choral singing in the Chapel, this was surely the fault of its leaders (Balakirev and Nikolai Andreyevich), who, though first-rate musicians, were not composers of church music and, therefore, were not completely conversant with it.

"You can be sure," retorted Nikolai Andreyevich, "that if I wanted to become a composer of sacred music, I could do so at once, and I could compose the most excellent music in this style. Nothing is easier than that. Indeed, everybody would begin crossing themselves in time with it."

From sacred music we turned to Nikolai Andreyevich's Piano Concerto, which the composer himself cannot stand.

"There's not a single note of my own in it," he declared. "All of it is either folk music, Liszt, or 'routine piano writing'—that's all it is.

"By the way," he added, turning to me, "you won't believe this, but there are times when I not only dislike the piano—I begin to hate it. This happens when suddenly there's a rumbling in the bass which I actually don't hear, don't understand, and therefore cannot endure.

"In my opinion," he concluded, "Chopin's *Berceuse* will forever remain the ideal expression of the piano style."

24 May

By nine o'clock in the evening, when I entered the Rimsky-Korsakovs', Shtrup was already there, arguing vehemently with Nikolai Andreyevich about the libretto of *Sadko*.

My appearance in no way interrupted the conversation. Indeed, more heated debates (entirely peaceful, however) arose over whether, in the finale of act 2, choruses should be introduced after the "transformation of the fish into gold" or simply rejoinders by the "elders" of Novgorod, displeased with Sadko's extravagance; whether, in the second scene of act 1, the twelve-year period, for which no explanation is given, should be eliminated and replaced by a simple foreboding of the inevitable destruction of the power of the Sea King, about which the Sea Queen had learned from the clear streams; whether the youngest and fairest daughter of the Sea King should fall in love with the blue seas like her sisters—the rivers—or with the comely youth and marry him. On this they seemed decided. Nikolai Andreyevich, however, remained slightly depressed.

"I fear," he said, "that the same thing will happen to me as happened once to Borodin, when he was writing *Igor*. You won't believe it, but he came to Nadezhda Nikolayevna several times to ask where, in which act, Konchakovna should sing her cavatina—the second or the third. Borodin felt that without it, the second act was more like a concert, a series of separate arias, than like an opera."

We all burst out laughing, including Nikolai Andreyevich.

After tea, Nikolai Andreyevich and I went into his study, where he talked about the music of *Sadko*. He is thinking of composing it, as he did in the old days, episode by episode, which he will then orchestrate immediately.

"The music gains a great deal from this method of composition, from having been rendered more finished artistically," he said. "Otherwise what has happened (in the case of *Mlada* and *Christmas Eve*) is that in a fit of haste, when I was eager to finish one scene or another as quickly as possible, I jotted down some fairly conventional music here and there, intending to replace it with something novel, real, later on, when orchestrating. And what happened? When the time came, I was tired and, instead of working over these passages, I scored them, consoling myself with the thought that I have good music also—so 'the devil with these unfinished bits.' "

The proofs for scene 3 of *Christmas Eve* have already been sent to Leipzig, Nikolai Andreyevich told me. Partly from this he has so tired his eyes that he has decided to do nothing for three days after his arrival in Vechasha. He does not want to damage them still further.

At the end, Nikolai Andreyevich advised me to spend the summer happily and busily and not to forget to write him. Again he repeated his invitation to visit them in Vechasha in August. When we bade good-bye, we kissed each other three times after the Russian fashion. I started to thank Nikolai Andreyevich for the interest and cordiality he has shown me, but he interrupted me, saying that he has shown me no special cordiality—it is simply that he likes me sincerely.

And so we have said good-bye until autumn! On the twenty-fifth of May, at nine o'clock, the train left for Vechasha and with it disappeared, for the summer, my "winter sunshine."

12 August

Desirous of seeing Nikolai Andreyevich and, besides, eager to hear his new opera as soon as possible, I undertook my second journey to Vechasha. On my arrival, I was greeted by almost the entire family, who had come to meet me at the forest a verst and a half from the estate. Nadezhda Nikolayevna and Nadyusha set out for the house in the carriage, while Nikolai Andreyevich, Volodya, Andryusha, and I proceeded on foot. On the way, I learned that Rimsky-Korsakov finished composing the music for *Sadko* on August 10 and is about to work on the orchestration.

Everyone was in an excellent mood, which was aided not a little by the delightful weather. Once at the house, I gave Nikolai Andreyevich a somewhat revised reprint of my little article on the second and third versions of *The Maid of Pskov*.

After tea we walked to the lake to look at the stars. In the course of our walk, Nikolai Andreyevich told me that he is not going to write any more operas on Russian subjects, as this would inevitably lead to a repetition of what is already known. Further, he feels that in reality there is as little pure music in the dramatic music so hailed and made famous by our critics as there is genuine, sincere feeling and warmth in people.

"As you know," he said, "I'm no admirer of heart-rending sounds; one can write as much music of that kind as he'd like to and whenever he wants to. It requires neither profound inspiration nor profound talent.

"Isn't this the reason why, in the dramatic music hailed by our critics," added Nikolai Andreyevich smiling, "art, however strange it may seem at first glance, has almost always defended and still defends 'free,' illicit love, since most often it is this love which is honest and enduring and consequently beautiful."

We returned to the house at about midnight. I was promised a performance of *Sadko* tomorrow.

13 August

Today Nikolai Andreyevich played through his entire opera from the draft manuscript. This obviously tired him, but he held out till the very end. I had difficulty sorting out my impressions. A great deal of it I liked very much, but many things did not seem sufficiently clear.

Besides this, I read to Nikolai Andreyevich my notes on last year's visit to Vechasha. He seemed very pleased with them.

Later, during a stroll in the garden, Nikolai Andreyevich asked me not to tell anyone that he had played the opera for me, so as to spare him having to do the same for others. He pointed out that here and there he had used "last year's" material (as, for example, the theme of Nezhata's first *bylina;* the closing scene between the *skomorokhi* and Nezhata with the glorification of the Sea and the Volkhova River). This had not been the case with *Christmas Eve,* he said, which had been written "at one stroke" and entirely of new material.

"Now, I'm free of all sorts of musical leftovers," he added. "By the way, if you happen to notice folk themes in *Sadko*—I'm warning you, there are very few—don't mention it to anyone. I'd like to test our public and critics once more and hear them reproach me again for those 'folk tunes,' which were never sung by the folk but are entirely my own."

15 August

During our morning stroll in the garden, Nikolai Andreyevich told me that he is considering writing a serious critical essay sometime in the future on the music of *Boris Godunov*—pro and con.

"As it is now," he said, "you keep praising this opera, you go into ecstasies over it, but when it comes to giving an example, you don't know what to point to, what to cite—it's all illiterate."

Shortly before my departure, we took one more walk through the garden. The weather was glorious.

"You know something?" asked Rimsky-Korsakov, as we were descend-

123

ing the lower linden allée. "Say what you will, the music aside, my operas are in essence very religious, for in them I'm either worshipping nature or extolling the worship of it."

At five o'clock the horses were brought. Practically the whole Rimsky-Korsakov family came out on the porch to see me off. This time I was particularly sad to leave, because I felt that I was leaving forever this place where I had, on both visits, spent such happy moments.

4 September

At about five o'clock, following my customary Monday visit to my mother, I dropped by at Zagorodny to find out whether the Rimsky-Korsakovs had returned. It turned out that they had come from Vechasha on the first of the month but have still not gotten their apartment in order as they have no servant.

Nikolai Andreyevich seemed somewhat out of sorts and tired. He had just seen Stasov, who had "showered" him with all kinds of news. He and Balakirev, Stasov said, are once again on friendly terms, and he is apparently in the latter's good graces. Balakirev has given up his symphony for the time being and has taken to writing songs (he needs money). He has already written four or five, but he plans to increase that number to ten or twelve. Finally, Stasov reported that on a recent visit to the home of his brother, Dmitri Vasilyevich, he met Balakirev, who played the first two songs for him and he liked them very much.

During dinner, Nikolai Andreyevich recounted to me the following interesting anecdote relating to the critic Lenz, author of the book on Beethoven and his three styles. Once, at one of the musical evenings at the home of Grand Duke Konstantin Nikolayevich, wishing to please the Grand Duke, Lenz confirmed a statement he had made to the effect that Beethoven had written three overtures to *Fidelio*. Rimsky-Korsakov, who was also there, begged to disagree, pointing out that Beethoven had written not three but four overtures: three in the key of C and one in E. I can just imagine how the obsequious Lenz must have felt at that moment.

7 September

Today, apropos of Serov's enthusiastic review of Rimsky-Korsakov's *Fantasia on Serbian Themes*,[41] we discussed Serov—the critic.[42]

"Nevertheless," remarked Nikolai Andreyevich, "I still dislike him even more as a critic than as a composer. But then, perhaps I'm being unfair to him."

We also talked about the reminiscences which Rimsky-Korsakov is writing.

"It will be long and interesting, not, of course, for the style of writing, but for the content," said Nikolai Andreyevich. "Moreover, these reminiscences will be of the sort that can hardly be published in their entirety even after my death, for they deal with too many different people. Therefore, I shall bequeath this work to my wife and children and will request that, insofar as it is possible, only some passages be published. The right to edit the writing will be granted, but it will be strictly forbidden to change anything. As of now these reminiscences cover two periods of my life: (1) from my childhood and acquaintance with Balakirev to my return from the voyage around the world and the death of my father (1862), when I paid my last visit to Tikhvin, where, by the way, I lived continuously until I was twelve years old, and (2) from my marriage in 1872 to the year 1878, when I composed *May Night*.

"At the present time," he added, "I spend my mornings scoring *Sadko* (act 3) and my evenings writing my 'Reminiscences.' "

18 September

Before Nikolai Andreyevich arrived, Nadezhda Nikolayevna gave me a lengthy account of their recent visit to Ludmila Shestakova, where among other things, they ran into Balakirev. Nadezhda Nikolayevna had not seen him since the funeral of young Deutsch in 1891.[43]

On this occasion Balakirev was extraordinarily pleasant. He talked at length with Rimsky-Korsakov about his intention of giving two concerts so as to make some money to pay for two Chapel boys at the Conservatory. Finally, at everyone's request, he played his fourth song, *Ne penitsia more*, which is written in the best Glinka style and dedicated to Ludmila Ivanovna. Everyone liked it very, very much.

Yesterday afternoon Stasov visited the Rimsky-Korsakovs. Nadezhda Nikolayevna played (and their daughter Sofia Nikolayevna sang) *Bylina o Volkhe Vseslav'eviche* from *Sadko* for him. Whether he liked it or not it is difficult to say, but I think that he did not, since he likes to give his opinion of a work immediately, and this time he only remarked, "You can't tell anything from a first impression." He was certain in advance, however, that he would like all the rest of the opera very much, since he is so fond of Nikolai Andreyevich and his *Sadko* fantasy.

22 September

After tea tonight we discussed the possibility of Erdmannsdörffer's[44] appointment as conductor of the Russian Musical Society, which, if it goes through, will surely signalize the exclusion of all Russian music, since he neither likes, knows, nor understands it. Then we got onto the subject of the various publishing houses, noting that the only operatic scores of Tchaikovsky that Jurgenson has published are *Eugene Onegin* and *The Nutcracker* (we were speaking of orchestral, not vocal scores, those have been printed).

"Yet everybody praises him," remarked Rimsky-Korsakov, "and they berate Belyaev, who publishes everything that falls into his hands. There's justice for you."

As I was about to leave, we somehow began talking about the performance of Bach fugues on the harpsichord.

"I've never been able to understand," declared Rimsky-Korsakov, "what satisfaction, much less enjoyment, can possibly be derived from listening to this powerful music on a flaccid, worthless fortepiano from the end of the last and beginning of this century. Yet the public goes into raptures over these sounds. I'm sure you've observed in Bach's orchestral scores a striving for virtuoso instrumentation—a solo English horn or viola, flute *ostinato*, even a whole quartet of English horns or oboes. Strange as it may be, this propensity for special coloring in Bach's works was purely fortuitous, without rhyme or reason, for the music he assigned one day to the woodwinds, he gave the next day to the strings or even converted into a flute solo without the slightest suggestion of the earlier instrumentation."

8 October

Despite the foul weather, Nikolai Andreyevich came to visit us this afternoon at one-thirty. We drank tea and chatted about this and that until five o'clock. As we were saying good-bye, he informed me that he intends to write a two-act opera called *The Barber of Baghdad,* based on a story from *Thousand and One Nights.*[45] I will not like it, he said, because it will not contain any unusual chords or woodwinds tremolo.

10 November

This evening Nikolai Andreyevich told me that the first scene of act 3 of *Sadko* (numbering fifty pages) was orchestrated between the first and seventh of this month. Mindful of the difficulties encountered with the censor during the production of *Christmas Eve,* he believes that he faces a great deal of difficulty with the libretto of *Sadko.*

"What if the censor won't permit my Father Nikola?" he conjectured. "It would be unthinkable to replace him by a 'Most Serene Highness.' "[46]

In further conversation, it came out that Balakirev thoroughly dislikes Liadov's new variations on what he considers the "extremely poor theme" of Glinka's *Venetian Night.*[47]

"This is especially surprising," remarked Nikolai Andreyevich, "since Mily Alexeyevich himself made a choral arrangement of this very Glinka melody during his days at the Chapel Choir, and the students there used to sing it."

In this connection Nikolai Andreyevich expressed deep regret over his own orchestration of the famous folk song *Slava,*[48] adding that it was virtually thrust on him by Rubets and he "had not had the heart to refuse." Meanwhile, this work is not only exceedingly weak, long, and musically untalented, but the part writing is abominable. Talk of this brought Rimsky-Korsakov to note that "in terms of ease of performance, of all us Russians, the one who wrote the worst was Mussorgsky, when more than one voice was involved and if three, four, or more voices were required—Cui, the reason being that in such cases, a knowledge of theory is absolutely indispensable, and that is something neither of them could boast of."

13 November

When I entered today, Rimsky-Korsakov greeted me with the words: "How happy I am! I've been informed by the censor's office that I may keep my Nikola if he's listed as 'an unknown old man.' "

This morning at the rehearsal of *Christmas Eve*,[49] Nikolai Andreyevich chose the crown for Catherine II (Piltz). He had rejected all of them so a new one had to be ordered. Of the two Tsaritsas (Piltz and Nosilova), he prefers Nosilova, but for some reason she will not be singing at the first performance. The Grank Dukes Vladimir Alexandrovich and Mikhail Nikolayevich are going to attend the dress rehearsal. Of the general public only Balakirev will be permitted in. As for me, Rimsky-Korsakov will try to get me a seat in his loge (as his "son") for the preliminary rehearsal.

We talked again about Erdmannsdörffer. On the whole, Rimsky-Korsakov does not much care for him, especially when he conducts Beethoven. Apparently, he does not understand this composer at all, for he introduces an absurd *ritardando* or begins to sentimentalize for no reason whatsoever. The best example of this was his performance of the *Eroica* Symphony the day before yesterday.

18 November

I was at the Marinsky Theater by eleven-forty-five, but the rehearsal did not begin until after twelve-thirty. Owing to repetitions, it lasted until four-thirty-five. Besides the Rimsky-Korsakovs, those present included Shtrup, Trifonov, Kanille, Napravnik, Belyaev, and Laroche, as well as Vsevolozhsky, Kondratyev, and other officials of the Theater Directorate.

On the whole, the rehearsal went tolerably well. The curtain did not rise or fall on time; the "procession of Kolyada and Ovsenya" was all but invisible; the scene of Vakula's leavetaking of Oxana and that with Catherine failed completely—the first because of the unrhythmical singing of the chorus, the second because of the abominable singing of Mme Piltz. On the other hand, the sets are superb and Mravina (Oxana) sang beautifully and acted very well.

During the interval, I told Nadezhda Nikolayevna that I had played excerpts from the opera at the Pypins' recently and seemed to have achieved the desired result, since I had literally "compelled" them to take an interest in it. I also reported an exchange which took place between Timofeyev and Slavina. When the latter asked her what she thought of the opera, she replied that she had been "terribly bored" and was amazed that anyone could like such a work. When Timofeyev took issue with her, she, with complete equanimity, called him a "Chinaman"; in other words an Asiatic, that is, a person devoid of taste and a musical sense.

And these are the judges and high priestesses of art! Poor art!

20 November

When Nikolai Andreyevich returned from the dress rehearsal of *Christmas Eve,* he informed us that there is a possibility that the opera will not be given tomorrow, because the Grand Dukes Vladimir Alexandrovich and Mikhail Nikolayevich dislike it intensely. What is more, they are highly indignant at the appearance of the Tsaritsa[50] and the Devil on the same stage, etc. Grand Duke Mikhail did not even stay until the end. They intend to report on this to His Majesty tomorrow.[51] We were thunderstruck by this news. Rimsky-Korsakov is going to visit Vsevolozhsky after dinner today to ask that the scene with Catherine be deleted, if this is absolutely necessary to save the opera.

In the evening, when I was again at the Rimsky-Korsakovs', Nikolai Andreyevich told me that he had not found Vsevolozhsky at home and, therefore, he had left a letter for him. We reflected on our "high society's" ignorance about the arts. Small wonder that in his day Turgenev suffered only because he dared to openly defend Gogol.[52]

"Actually," commented Rimsky-Korsakov, "it would be better if all of Gogol's works were banned along with my opera. Then, at least, no one would be tempted to write on his subjects."

Finally, we speculated on the devastating effect the Grand Duke's decision would have upon the performers and noted that if, for some reason, *Christmas Eve* is not given, not only will the 18,000 rubles spent on the production be lost but also Paleček's benefit and the entire subscription of 6,000 rubles.[53] What a dismal prospect!

Poor Rimsky-Korsakov!

21 November

At about three o'clock I was again at the Rimsky-Korsakovs'. *Christmas Eve* has been postponed until next Tuesday. What is going to happen? Rimsky-Korsakov saw Kruglikov and Kashkin, who have come here from Moscow just for this premiere.

This morning Rimsky-Korsakov went to the theater and also to Vorontsov-Dashkov's. The latter was at home but did not receive him.

Really, here in Russia they don't especially encourage our gifted people. No wonder in the West they consider us barbarians; it must be said that when it comes to self-awareness, we have not progressed much beyond our ancestors the Scyths.

24 November

Consumed with impatience to learn the fate of *Christmas Eve*, I once again dropped by at the Rimsky-Korsakovs'. This time I found Nikolai Andreyevich in an extremely melancholy mood. It seems that yesterday the report on the opera was finally submitted to the Emperor. His Majesty "deeply regretted" that lack of time prevents his attendance at the rehearsals, and, consequently, the scene at the Tsaritsa's will have to be changed.[54] Rimsky-Korsakov does not appear to be upset so much about the fate of *Christmas Eve* as he is about the possibility that *Sadko* may not be staged, even after the censor's having permitted his "unknown old man" (Nikola).

"The censor will give permission," he said, "Pobedonostsev will take it away. And in this case, a 'Most Serene Highness' will not come to the rescue.

"In any case, now there's no need to rush with this opera," he added, "and, therefore, I'm going to begin work on revising and completing Mussorgsky's *Fair at Sorochintsy*. Perhaps they'll stage that; the subject is pleasant and they even have many of the sets already."

I was about to take my leave, but Nikolai Andreyevich detained me. We went into the dining room. His face continued to bear the mark of profound sadness, even when he smiled.

"Do you know what the situation is with my works?" he asked, as if continuing our conversation of the other day. "Nowadays, they don't understand them (let's console ourselves with this flattering assumption). Later on no one will take any interest in them, for art will become a relic of the past, and future generations will study with curiosity only the most important works, those which were characteristic of a certain period in the historical development of the music of one or another country. They'll listen (with commentaries, of course) to the operas of Gluck, to Mozart's *Don Giovanni*, Weber's *Freischütz*, Rossini's *Barber of Seville*,

Meyerbeer's *Huguenots;* and of the later ones—Gounod's *Faust,* perhaps; Wagner's *Lohengrin* and *Ring of the Nibelungen,* Glinka's *Ruslan* and *A Life for the Tsar*—in Russia. But the other things, the small things, they won't pay any attention to at all. Really, who will want to spend 18,000 out of curiosity about the past to listen to some *Christmas Eve* or other, some *Sadko?*"

But now it was time for me to leave. My parting words to Nikolai Andreyevich were: "Everything you've been saying today is untrue. *The Maid of Pskov, Snegurochka,* and *Sadko* are infinitely superior to everything you've mentioned (excepting the *Ring,* of course), and sooner or later, I'll be proven right."

"You may think so," replied Rimsky-Korsakov, smiling bitterly, "but I have no such hopes. After a while they'll forget my music just as completely as they've disliked and rejected it during my lifetime. Save for some fragments, it will sink into oblivion."

Upon returning home I found the following note from Nikolai Andreyevich:

Dear Vasily Vasilyevich: Today I've searched my house in vain for Mussorgsky's *Fair at Sorochintsy.* I recall that you took it away. If you have it, bring it to me. I need it very badly.

Christmas Eve will be given on Tuesday with the Tsaritsa changed to a "Most Serene Highness." They forget the saying: "Don't give your word unless you intend to keep it." A great pity.

24 November 1895   Your N. Rimsky-Korsakov

25 November

At about nine o'clock this evening I ran into Nikolai Andreyevich as he was on the way to the Russian Musical Society to hear Liszt's *Festklänge.*[55] "You know," he remarked, "I've glanced hurriedly through *The Fair* and, I must say, there's little that's good in it. Besides this, the text is crude—very crude."

28 November

Christmas Eve met with great success. Despite the exceedingly high prices, the theater was filled to overflowing. At the end of act 1, the audience called loudly for the composer, but he was not in the theater. Evidently, he was offended at the Directorship's last minute servile tricks, such as listing the Church Clerk on the posters as "Student," etc.

Following act 3, Paleček was given a tremendous ovation and tendered many testimonials and gifts.

Mravina (Oxana) sang and acted delightfully; Yershov (Vakula) was also good, especially in the upper registers; Chuprynnikov (the Devil) and Ugrinovich (Church Clerk) acted excellently, as did Koryakin (Chub). Stravinsky, in the small role of Panas, overacted, as usual. Kamenskaya handled the part of Solokha magnificently, particularly in hut scene.

After the performance, I took our group's wreath to the Rimsky-Korsakovs'. Nikolai Andreyevich was very moved; he embraced me and asked me to convey his gratitude to the others. He inquired about the performance and was very pleased to learn that the Grand Duke Konstantin Konstantinovich, Prince Paul Mavrikiyevich, and Grand Duchess Elizaveta Mavrikiyevna had attended the performance.[56] He was also happy that the boys' and girls' *kolyadka,* on which Paleček had worked for almost a year, had been encored.

During the performance, I learned, the Rimsky-Korsakovs went for a drive along the embankment and to the islands.[57]

1 December

Not having received the box tickets promised me for the third performance of *Christmas Eve,* I dropped in on the Rimsky-Korsakovs to inquire whether, by chance, there was an empty seat in their box. As it turned out, they have no box—only two seats in the front of the parterre.

From our conversation, I learned that today Nikolai Andreyevich had been at the censorship office. The chief censor, Adikayevsky, showered him with compliments on the opera and apologized for having been obliged, against his will, to change the "clerk" to "student" (though without altering the text).

"What would you have me do?" he asked. "The libretto was sent to me twice for review."

The censor said that what he liked most in the whole opera was the chorus in memory of Gogol.

"Unfortunately," said Rimsky-Korsakov, "this memorial turned out to be 'corrupting.'"

4 December

Having, by chance, received a ticket for *Christmas Eve,* after dinner at my mother's, I dropped in on the Rimsky-Korsakovs. Nikolai Andreyevich was also going to tonight's performance, so we went together.

On the way, Nikolai Andreyevich brought up the subject of Solovyov's "covert" articles (or rather, denunciations) in *Birzhevye vedomosti* and *Svet,* and his desire to put as bad a light as possible on *Christmas Eve.* Indeed, in an effort to make his criticism more convincing he even dragged in the question of religion.[58] All this only because he himself has written a poor opera on the same subject which the Theater Directorate refuses to put on.

"Yes," said Rimsky-Korsakov in conclusion, "they've launched an all-out campaign against me. One thing does surprise me: why are these people so hostile to every new work? It's inconceivable to me that, however weak my opera may be, there's not a single passage or scene in it which might appeal to the listener. Why is it that whenever a new musical work makes its appearance it's greeted with such abuse and ridicule?"

I must say that tonight's performance came off rather badly; it was very sloppy.[59] Nevertheless, at the end of the first act, the audience called out the artists and, after their third bow, the composer. At the conclusion of the opera, there was also scattered applause but no outburst of enthusiasm. It seems that the articles of our "Midas-critics," the opinion of the grand dukes, the lack of coordination in the performance, and the audience's disinterest in Gogol's story all had their effect. Nothing was encored; the wonderful scene of the great *Kolyadki* passed without a single clap; this, like the music of "Kolyada's procession" went totally unnoticed.

My neighbor assured her companion with great earnestness that this was the worst opera she had ever heard; that it is a preposterous piece of buffoonery, it has not a single Little Russian tune—indeed, no music whatsoever; and the artists sing some kind of Italian arias.

But as I was leaving, I heard a little old man, on the verge of tears, mumble ecstatically: "What music and what breadth!"

This afternoon Nikolai Andreyevich and I had a discussion about Laroche's article of yesterday in *Novosti*,[60] in which this cultured Hanslick, after speculating on how the twentieth and twenty-first centuries will regard Rimsky-Korsakov's music (without offering a single thought of his own about *Christmas Eve,* as usual), with his characteristic gallantry, again expressed envy over the "Russian Liszt's" success with contemporary society, despite the fact that he (Rimsky-Korsakov) possesses so little "inventiveness" when it comes to melody.

We talked, too, about the continuing silence of friends, from which one could only conclude that they did not like the opera; about a marvelous pianist, Josef Hofmann, who has turned up in Petersburg; and about a curious incident which had occurred in a tramway between some man, who denounced *Christmas Eve* vociferously, and a lady, who came to its defense. The unknown man, incidentally, turned out to be the critic Ivanov.

18 December

When I entered, Rimsky-Korsakov was orchestrating *Boris Godunov* (act 4, scene 1)—Prince Shuisky's account to the boyars, to be precise. This naturally led us to talk about Mussorgsky, particularly his outrageous harmonization of the scene between Boris and Shuisky.

"You're wondering, I'm sure, how I could have liked this music," remarked Nikolai Andreyevich, "but there really was a time when I did."

Then we spoke of Arensky's suite,[61] which, in Nikolai Andreyevich's view, "is boring not because it's long but, on the contrary, is long because it's boring."

19 December

I was at the Rimsky-Korsakovs' for dinner. I had invited myself there yesterday, not only because I wanted to be with Nikolai Andreyevich on this day but, more particularly, because I was certain that no one from among our "Humperdincks"[62] would take any notice of the thirtieth anniversary[63] of his career as a composer. And I was not mistaken. Indeed, why should we honor the greatest of our own artists when the West has given us *Hänsel and Gretel?*

To commemorate the occasion, I presented Nikolai Andreyevich with a small bronze paperweight. So far as I could tell, he was very pleased with it.

During dinner we discussed the staging of *Boris* at the Marinsky Theater.

"Do you know the person from the theatrical world who wouldn't oppose this?" asked Rimsky-Korsakov. "Napravnik. In the main he even likes this opera, but, of course, he feels that it must first be reorchestrated and cleaned up harmonically."

Nikolai Andreyevich complained that he will probably never live long enough to be able to arrange his day according to his own wishes and tastes, that is, to enjoy "peace of mind."

"I spend my whole life either composing or revising my own or someone else's scores," he said. "Because of all this, I'm always working against time, for I'm burdened by all sorts of work that was begun and not finished. That's the case now with *Boris.* If they succeed in staging it, I'll be obliged again to work without a break, even though I've already finished the Prologue to scene 1, act 1; scene 2 (only the vocal score); all of the Polish Act (in two scenes), the scene in Pimen's cell, and part of the boyars' duma.

"You know," he went on, "I firmly believe that this opera ought to end with the scene of Boris' death, not with the Pretender and the Simpleton, as Mussorgsky has it. Such an ending is inartistic and if it is good at all, it's good only in theory and then even that is questionable."

25 December

As always on Mondays, at dinner time, I was at the Rimsky-Korsakovs'. In a discussion of Kashkin's article about *Christmas Eve,* Nikolai Andreyevich said that, despite the author's erroneous idea that the legendary and fantastic elements were introduced into the opera for purely superficial effect, he is, for the most part, pleased with it, since he considers it to a certain degree fair.[64] Further, apropos of the liturgical melodies in the opera, Nikolai Andreyevich pointed out that the bright, com-

Example 18

Po- ko- ri- sia kres- tu, cha-do t'my

Example 19

Deacon

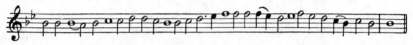

pelling phrase of Vakula's incantation, which forms the basis of the music of "Vakula's ride on the Devil" is his own (example 18); that the theme of the final chorus of scene 8, act 3 "Na vostoke svet zasiial Bozhei pravdoi" is that of a troparion and, finally, for Solokha's song of praise, he introduced a melody composed in the style of *znammeny* chant (example 19).

One thing more: Grand Duke Konstantin Nikolayevich, despite his seeming great musicality, like Laroche, cannot stand the music of Mussorgsky, Borodin, and Cui, is indifferent toward Balakirev (he only tolerates him), and likes only Tchaikovsky and then only some things.

31 December

On my visit this evening, Nikolai Andreyevich and I had a long talk about yesterday's Bleichmann concert,[65] particularly Liszt's *Faust* Symphony. This is a work which Nikolai Andreyevich has never liked particularly. He sharply criticized the purely harmonic opening melodies, constructed on parallel descending augmented triads, finding them ugly and unmusical. He considers the orchestration of the beginning of the second movement—depicting Marguerite and so loved by Glazunov—unsuccessful, as flutes in the low register are totally undesirable here. In his opinion, the third movement (Mephistopheles) of this excessively long and prolix symphony, with its "extremely magnificent and piercingly brilliant orchestration," is the best part of the work. However, the final *Chorus mysticus,* which is based on Goethe's marvelous text (in an inconceivably poor, though accurate translation by the poet Fet) has little appeal to him.

Turning to other subjects, we agreed that Paganini was a most ghastly (antimusical) composer, and we noted that Cui has once again taken up his pen, replacing "Père Laroche" on *Novosti.*

CHAPTER 6

1896

5 January

The Rimsky-Korsakovs have just left. They dropped by briefly to extend to my wife and me an open invitation to Sunday musicales to be held at their home beginning on the seventh.

6 January

When my wife and I arrived at the Rimsky-Korsakovs' this afternoon, we found them in excellent spirits. Nikolai Andreyevich played the new version of the Inn Scene from *Boris* (as far as Varlaam's song) and the beginning of the love duet between Marina and the Pretender (in E major instead of E-flat major), also in corrected and reworked form.

During tea, Nikolai Andreyevich told us that Belyaev and Scriabin have gone to Paris to give concerts [1] but that, as of now, nothing has been heard from them. Then we spoke about Glazunov (now completely Larochified) who, in a recent conversation with Stasov, solemnly expressed the *pleasant* thought that what he values most in music is technique! Not unexpectedly, this threw poor Vladimir Vasilyevich into despair.

In the evening, at Bleichmann's concert, I saw Rimsky-Korsakov in the distance, when he came out to take a bow after the performance of his

Sinfonietta. At this concert, too, I heard, for the first time, the new, young musical luminary Josef Hofmann.[2]

7 January

Besides the Rimsky-Korsakov family, there were not a great many people at the first "musical evening"—only the Frieds, Blumenfelds, Belskys, Glazunov, Timofeyev, and a few others—and therefore it was very lively. Before tea Nina Fried sang: Lenepveu's *Deuil d'avril,* Saint-Saëns' *Peut-être,* and five of Rimsky-Korsakov's songs: *Noch', Pesnia Zuleiki, Taina, Tikho vecher dogoraet,* and *Chto v imeni tebe moem.*

Among other things, our conversation touched on poetry, with general agreement that for style and beauty of exposition Lermontov and Count Alexei Tolstoi are the most perfect of all Russian poets.

We moved into the study, where a discussion arose about the two published excerpts from Cui's *Ratcliff*—the Introduction to the opera and the Entr'acte to act 3, which Rimsky-Korsakov orchestrated back in 1894—and about the ridiculous corrections the proud and touchy Cui made in the Korsakov score.[3]

After tea Sofia Nikolayevna, the Rimsky-Korsakovs' elder daughter, sang Ratmir's aria from *Ruslan* ("I zhar i znoi") and one of Rubinstein's *Persian Songs* and Glazunov played four excerpts from his *Coronation Cantata.* Rimsky-Korsakov flatly refused to play anything from *Sadko.*

The evening ended at about twelve-thirty. All in all it had been very enjoyable.

9 January

Today the eighth performance of *Christmas Eve* finally took place. It was directed by Napravnik in a slipshod fashion, worse than that of Krushevsky. The theater was almost full, but the audience arrived rather late, and this made it very difficult to hear the music.

The greatest success was scored this time by Yershov, Mikhailova, and Ugrinovich. Indeed, the latter, as the Church Clerk, was obliged to repeat the whole scene of "Solokha's song of praise" (a boring scene, in the opinion of the critics!).

Rimsky-Korsakov was not called out.

Evidently, S. Bulich was correct in maintaining that this is a *chamber* opera; in other words, it is so fine and elegant that it must be listened to in complete silence and in a small theater, although, of course, with a full orchestra. Otherwise, not only "the procession of Kolyada," the Introduction, the scene of the "Stars," and "Vakula's ride through the air," but even the highly effective finales of scenes 1 and 4 and the brilliant Polonaise will pass unnoticed.

15 January

Nikolai Andreyevich and I had a talk today about Petrovsky's article on *Christmas Eve*.[4] Despite a certain unnecessary long-windedness, Nikolai Andreyevich is pleased with this article. In the case of the "Dance of the Stars," the critic correctly divined Rimsky-Korsakov's purpose in presenting a series of dances most easily understandable to Vakula, dances which he could have heard about somewhere, since he was a Slav and had Polish pans and Hungarians of Galicia close by. This explains why the stars dance a *khorovod,* mazurka, and czardas but do not dance a waltz. On the whole, Petrovsky's basic view of the heroes of Rimsky-Korsakov's opera, in which nature and the *kolyadki* were assigned a major role, does credit to the young critic.

Later our conversation touched on Mussorgsky's *Seminarist,* which, despite Nikolai Andreyevich's liking for it and his contention that it is lifelike, moves me little.

With this Nikolai Andreyevich remembered Mussorgsky's letters, and then and there he got them out and began reading from them. He happened upon one in which Mussorgsky spoke about the orchestral fantasy *Sadko* (then in the process of composition), whose initial idea he had given to Nikolai Andreyevich. In this same letter he also gave his opinion of the German approach to music (he considered it ruinous for art), of the fourth movement of *Antar,* and called Rimsky-Korsakov "a Glinka of aesthetics."[5]

20 January

My wife and I attended the first Russian Symphony Concert of the season. The program consisted of Rimsky-Korsakov's Third Symphony, songs by Cui and Anton Rubinstein (sung by Zherebtsova, accompanied by Lavrov), Rachmaninov's fantasy *The Rock,* Ippolitov-Ivanov's *Caucasian Sketches,* and the Overture to Borodin's *Prince Igor.*

As usual, the audience was not especially large. Others, besides those of us who ordinarily attend these concerts, included Ludmila Shestakova, Cui, Bloch, the "musical pen-pusher" Laroche, the two quasi-heroes of the contemporary musical "Nibelheim"—Solovyov (Mime) and Stanislavsky (Fafner),[6] Baskin, Liadov, and Stasov.

Following his symphony, Rimsky-Korsakov was called out twice. Cui also came out to acknowledge the thunderous applause and shouts of "author," which greeted his songs.

Rachmaninov's *Rock* (dedicated last year to Nikolai Andreyevich), is positively charming for the beauty and richness of its orchestration. It is sort of "half-Liszt, half-Glazunov," with a dash of instrumental touches from the third act of Rimsky-Korsakov's *Mlada,* which is a kind of holy of holies of modern orchestration. I do not mean to imply that this fantasy is devoid of the composer's own musical personality. Not at all.

As for Rimsky-Korsakov's Third Symphony, which was composed back in 1872–73 and somewhat reorchestrated and revised in 1886, I agree thoroughly with the opinion expressed by Cui in *Novosti.*[7]

21 January

The Rimsky-Korsakovs' second musical evening was not particularly exciting. Of the twenty-two guests, the only one who performed was Anna Zherebtsova-Yevreinova. She sang Nikolai Andreyevich's *Vostochnyi romans* and *Na kholmakh Gruzii* and two of Rubinstein's *Persian Songs.* She was not in good voice, however, and seemed tired. Lavrov provided the accompaniment.

Glazunov presented Nikolai Andreyevich with the score of his ballet suite (*Scènes de ballet,* op. 52) which, like Rimsky-Korsakov's *Capriccio espagnol* was dedicated to the orchestra of the Imperial Russian Opera.

Before tea, Nadezhda Nikolayevna, Liadov, and I had a long discussion about Humperdinck's *Hänsel and Gretel,*[8] which Glazunov likes very much but Rimsky-Korsakov cannot stand.

Tonight I noticed on Nikolai Andreyevich's table the proofs of the opening scenes of *Boris Godunov* in Rimsky-Korsakov's new, "cleaned up" version.

29 January

This time Nikolai Andreyevich gave me an account of his recent visit to Vsevolozhsky and their conversation about the operas being considered for the coming season (1896–97). These include a production of *Boris Godunov* at the Marinsky Theater, provided, of course, that Tsar Nicholas does not strike it from the repertoire submitted for his approval as the late Alexander III did.

"You know," said Nikolai Andreyevich, "Vsevolozhsky, indeed our entire Theater Directorate, is completely dependent on the Court. That's how things stand. Vsevolozhsky told me right out: 'First of all, we have to please the imperial family, then the public's taste, and only after that, the demands of art. Here it is Shrovetide, and among the operas submitted for the Tsar's consideration was *Christmas Eve*. But not a word has been said about it, which is tantamount to "don't give it." And so it's not in the repertoire. Nevertheless, this opera will be given without fail both after Easter and in the fall.'

"As for next season," continued Nikolai Andreyevich, "in accordance with His Majesty's wishes, they'll give Tchaikovsky's *Oprichnik* and Massenet's *Esclarmonde,* for which they'll invite Sanderson,[9] and mine will wait.

"It's clear to me," concluded Nikolai Andreyevich, "that the tsars don't think highly of my operas, that *Christmas Eve* is in disfavor, especially since, according to Vsevolozhsky, His Majesty not only did not attend it but, in all likelihood, never will. It would be a good thing, Ivan Alexandrovich told me, if somehow the Tsar could be lured to *Mlada,* if only to see the stage sets."

4 February

The Rimsky-Korsakovs' third musical evening was highly successful, even though the guests did not begin to arrive until late and thus, tea was not served until about eleven o'clock.

Before then, the time passed imperceptibly, however, due to the constant stream of conversation. They talked about Cui's recently published article on the Russian song[10] (which, despite many interesting and witty observations, has serious flaws and omissions); Meyerbeer (whom Glazunov considers the most intelligent and gifted operatic composer of the West); Aivazovsky's charming exhibition;[11] the tendentiousness of Vereshchagin's paintings; and the coming opera season. Regarding the latter, it appears that, in accordance with the Tsar's wishes, the Marinsky will present Boito's *Mefistofele,* Massenet's *Esclarmonde* and *La navarraise, Don Giovanni,* Tchaikovsky's *Oprichnik,* Saint-Saëns' *Samson et Dalila, Pagliacci,* and Minkus' ballet *Mlada.*[12] Obviously, *Boris Godunov* is not to be given.

From what Koryakin said, Vsevolozhsky has not yet lost hope of finding some way by which Rimsky-Korsakov's opera-ballet *Mlada* may be revived simultaneously with Minkus' ballet. Cherepnin was right in maintaining that at present it is useless to expect the Imperial Theaters to do anything for Russian music and, therefore, we must set up our own theater through private means, with Belyaev at the head and Rimsky-Korsakov as musical director and conductor.

Thus went the discourse until after tea, when Koryakin sang Konchak's aria from *Prince Igor,* the Headman's aria from the first act of *May Night,* and Grandfather Frost's song from *Snegurochka.* Then Glazunov and Cherepnin played, four hands, some of the Prologue of the last opera.

Earlier in the evening, I had an interesting conversation with Nikolai Andreyevich about the scene from act 2 of *Boris Godunov* with Xenia's lament in B minor instead of B-flat minor. It has now been scored by Nikolai Andreyevich, and, according to him, it contains much that is interesting and curious in the way of orchestration. I also learned when Mussorgksy composed and revised the opera and when it was first performed in Petersburg and Moscow.

5 February

This being Monday, I went, as always, to the Rimsky-Korsakovs', only to find that Nikolai Andreyevich was not at home. When he returned, shortly before seven o'clock, he told me that he had not seen Vsevolozhsky (the Committee was with him) but his assistant, Hershelman, who is temporarily replacing Pogozhev, as the latter has been appointed to the Corononation Commission. Hershelman corroborated what Koryakin had said, namely, that when Ivan Alexandrovich presented to His Majesty the question of staging *Boris Godunov* in Nikolai Andreyevich's newly revised and rescored version, the Tsar had only grimaced and remarked: "No, we don't need this opera for now. After all, it's still the music of the Balakirev school."

Nikolai Andreyevich has decided to try to get up a subscription and present *Boris* himself at the beginning of next season.

"This will be my final appearance as a conductor," he added. "It's a role I've never liked, but this time I must make an exception, and I'll do it. And now, just to spite everybody, I'm going to orchestrate this opera and orchestrate it particularly well. This will be my revenge." [13]

After completing *Boris*, Nikolai Andreyevich plans to finish *Sadko* and present it to the Directorate.

"It will be interesting, won't it, to see Minkus' *Mlada* next year? To hear how a real ballet composer has depicted the scene of the 'divination by the horses' and Mount Triglav with the *khorovod* of the spirits. All this ought to be there, you know."

In conclusion, Nikolai Andreyevich gave me Cui's version of a scurvy trick Solovyov played on Koptyaev. It seems that as critic of *S.-Peterburgskie vedomosti*, Koptyaev wrote a favorable article about *Christmas Eve*. When the article did not appear, he went to the editor for an explanation. There he ran into Solovyov, who told him right out that articles of this kind cannot be published, since they praise something which, in point of fact, must be condemned.

Here is another example of the outrageous behavior of this son of Feopemt,[14] this time having to do not with music but with a music publisher.

"You know," Solovyov once remarked to Bessel, "I used to write for *Novosti*. Be grateful that I didn't play a mean trick on you." (The very words of this Professor of the Petersburg Conservatory.)

"What a scoundrel!" said Rimsky-Korsakov. "Really, you ought to begin keeping a diary. All this is terribly interesting. Otherwise I'm afraid you'll forget or not tell it as it was."

11 February

Hurrah! *Boris* is going to be given in September under the direction of Rimsky-Korsakov. Twenty-one hundred rubles have already been collected.

Tomorrow morning (February 12), Rimsky-Korsakov will finish orchestrating the entire act which takes place in Boris' private apartments;[15] all that remains to be done is one page with the line "Chur, chur, ne ia. . . ."

"Remember last year when you came to us in Vechasha," said Nikolai Andreyevich, "I told you that I intended sometime to write a severely critical article about *Boris* and its merits and defects. Well, now I don't think there's any need for such an article. The new, corrected vocal score and new orchestral score will convey to future generations more eloquently than words my views not only of this work as a whole but of every measure of it, particularly since the 'transcription of the opera for orchestra' made by me is not *mine* personally but only what Mussorgsky himself ought to have done but could not solely for lack of compositional technique.

"As you see," continued Nikolai Andreyevich, "in my intention to reorchestrate and reharmonize Mussorgsky's great opera, there was absolutely nothing reprehensible, much less criminal. In any case, I don't feel I've sinned.

"And now," he concluded, "as soon as *Boris* and *Sadko* are finished, I must go through the score of Dargomyzhsky's *Stone Guest* again, and if there's anything in the orchestration that strikes me as bad (and there will probably be many such things), I'll correct it, so that later on, no one will be able to accuse me of a careless attitude toward the works of others. After that, I'll be able to retire, since I've gone through everything of Mussorgsky's. Therefore, my conscience is clear, for with respect to his works and his memory, I've done everything that I could and should have done."

18 February

The Rimsky-Korsakovs' fourth musical evening did not come off too well. The reason was that Nikolai Andreyevich had suddenly fallen ill—he had spit blood—and the news of this upset all of us terribly. As a result, there was relatively little music. Chuprynnikov sang a song by Liszt (badly), Levko's Serenade from *May Night*, Balakirev's *Vzoshel na nebo mesiats iasnyi* and, at Dianin's request, Konchak's aria from *Prince Igor*.

On the whole the evening passed quietly. After tea Blumenfeld played Solovyov's mock quadrille *Klin Klinom*[16] and Nikolai Andreyevich performed, as a jest, an old-fashioned lancers' quadrille, arranged by Borodin on the melody of a church chant.[17]

19 February

Nikolai Andreyevich is considerably better, but, of course, he is by no means in a sparkling frame of mind. We talked about the programs of the next two Russian Symphony Concerts and also about *Boris*. Even though twenty-six hundred rubles have been collected, Nikolai Andreyevich seems to feel weighted down by his intention to perform the opera—he is too old, he says.

26 February

This afternoon we got into a heated argument about Berlioz' *Faust*. Nadezhda Nikolayevna contended that the music of "The Death of Faust" is banal and loathsome from beginning to end. She is amazed that I can like such "rubbish," she said, adding that the sole reason for Balakirev's love of Berlioz is obstinacy, and such taste compels her to doubt his musicality.[18] I, of course, felt no need to refute this nonsense until Nadezhda Nikolayevna asserted that any page of *Khovanshchina* would wipe out all of Berlioz' *Faust,* at which point, I, smiling, called her a *kuchkistka*.

Rimsky-Korsakov also dislikes *Faust,* his reason being, he explained, that he has "outgrown it." He, too, expressed surprise at my enthusiasm for it.

"Here you are," he said, "such a confirmed lover of harmony, precisely the element in Berlioz that lacks variety and beauty—it's nothing but a continuous amazingly clumsy juxtaposition of the major, minor, and diminished seventh chord—that's all."

I, in turn, maintained that Rimsky-Korsakov's antipathy toward Berlioz' music lies in his own nature and flows from an incompatibility in their makeups and temperaments. However, our argument was interrupted by dinner, and the question of the artistic ideas of the brilliant creator of *Les Troyens,* which we had begun to discuss, was postponed to a future time.

Later, I mentioned to Nikolai Andreyevich that tomorrow our "Pypin group" is going to honor Balakirev on the fortieth anniversary of his debut as a pianist. I added that there will be no Balakirev concert as the doctor has dissuaded him from giving one because of his extreme nervousness.

To this, Nikolai Andreyevich retorted, with a smile, "Oh, if only some doctor would forbid me to give *Boris!* How wonderful that would be!"

3 March

The Korsakov musical evenings seem to have deteriorated into "at homes." A lot of fuss and not much point.

Today Nina Fried was indisposed, so she did not come. For some reason neither did the Chuprynnikovs. There were many of the Rimsky-Korsakovs' relatives, but of the musicians, only Liadov, Blumenfeld, Lavrov, and Glazunov.

After tea Alexandra Molas sang a number of songs of Cui, Rimsky-Korsakov, and Mussorgsky, and Blumenfeld and Lavrov played (very badly) the introduction to *Christmas Eve.*

Nikolai Andreyevich told me that in a day or two he will finish the piano arrangement of *Boris,* which at present is consuming all his spare time.

4 March

When I saw Nikolai Andreyevich today, we returned to the subject of Berlioz, "this genius of rhythm and color" (as Nikolai Andreyevich put it), a fascinating personality though, perhaps, acerbic and not very likeable in everyday life; a man thoroughly convinced of and devoted to his own musical tendency; finally, a composer, a romantic, romantic to the point of ecstasy.

"Surely Berlioz must have had something," said Nikolai Andreyevich, "for him to have been able to subjugate Glinka, Schumann, and even Liszt, that at times recherché but always flawless harmonist. Lack of doubt about the rightness of his ideal—this alone is a mark of genius. Finally, the love you and people like you have for Berlioz makes me wonder, against my will, if his music really is depraved."

6 March

After work I went directly to the Rimsky-Korsakovs', where I had dinner. Nikolai Andreyevich informed me that he has finished the vocal score of *Boris* and is terribly exhausted from working on it. Then he turned the conversation to the symphonic works of Richard Strauss, his absurd *Till Eulenspiegel,* and his incredibly massive and complicated orchestration of rather poor musical material.

"It strikes me," he said, "that one might well apply to the works of young Richard Strauss the old proverb: 'The mountain has labored and brought fourth a mouse.' It's quite different with Glazunov—his music is rich in content. You'll never find anything ornate or artificial in it."

18 March

This time at the Rimsky-Korsakovs', I looked through the manuscript score of part of act 2 of *Boris Godunov,* which was begun on March 10. It turned out that the orchestration of Varlaam's Song was completed on March 15 and the rest, as far as the classical trio ("Vot edet on")—on March 17.

Apropos of Mussorgsky, we talked again about Cui's article "The Russian Song,"[19] in which the author calls Mussorgsky, to some extent, an "antimusical composer," a statement which caused quite a stir among his ardent admirers.

"Actually," said Rimsky-Korsakov, "for all the striking originality of Mussorgsky's works, at times you come upon something so strange that you have to agree with Cui in spite of yourself. The irregularities and illiteracy which you encounter are of two kinds: first, mistakes and orthographic absurdities, which are easily corrected, and second, usages of harmony, which almost defy correction. The latter have to be rewritten. There's quite a bit of such music in Mussorgsky—for example, the entire scene between Prince Shuisky and Boris from act 2, the chiming clock, etc."

I suggested that Nikolai Andreyevich publish the principal cuts he had made in the opera, such as the story of the Tsars, etc., as an appendix to the piano reduction. At least then he will protect himself against excessive criticism by his ill-wishers and sham experts on Mussorgsky.

As I was leaving, I remarked that this year, with its wondrous clear, cold, and glittering winter nights and bright stars—the first such as this in St. Petersburg in a long time—nature seems to be paying tribute to his *Christmas Eve.*

"It's only a pity," replied Nikolai Andreyevich with a smile, "that you alone have noticed this protest of nature."

24 March

This afternoon I learned that on March 21, Nikolai Andreyevich completed the orchestration of the Inn Scene, beginning with the trio. Thus, in a single day he wrote twenty-three pages of full score.

"One other time in my life," he said, "when we were living in Nikolsky, I wrote twenty-four pages in one day. That was when I was orchestrating the first Polovtsian dances from Borodin's *Igor.* I've never written more than that."

At present he was taken up *Sadko* again with the idea of rescoring the beginning of the second scene so as to make this entire scene—up to the arrival of the King of the Sea—still more transparent and give the music sharper definition.

25 March

In the evening at about ten o'clock, I went to the Rimsky-Korsakovs' knowing that I would find Belsky there.[20] They read some corrections which Vladimir Ivanovich had made in the libretto.

After tea, at our request, Nikolai Andreyevich played all of act 1 of the opera, excepting the song of the Venetian guest, which he is planning to discard.[21] After that, he played this song and all of the first scene of Act 3.

In a discussion about *Sadko,* I learned that Nikolai Andreyevich would like to develop it into two separate short operas with three scenes each. However, he probably will not do this, and why should he?

2 April

On this visit Rimsky-Korsakov and I had a long discussion about Schumann's *Genoveva* and its notable passages:

(1) the Overture, which begins very originally with a diminished chord of the ninth. This is heard later in the Tchaikovsky of the period of *Eugene Onegin,* Cui of the time of *Ratcliff,* and even in the Tchaikovsky of the last period, that of *The Queen of Spades;*

(2) the magnificent chords, suggestive of something mysterious which serve as a kind of transition from the first chorale to Golo's recitative "Konnt'lich mit Ihnen."

The amazingly original combination of chords of the major and minor triads (at a relationship of a major third) owed its appearance in the musical literature of the second half of the nineteenth century entirely to Schumann, not to Liszt and Wagner, as might have been expected. Taken in reverse order (B-flat minor and D), these triads form that harmonic combination which gave us the "chords of death" and "fate" (in *Mlada*). It must be pointed out, however, that Rimsky-Korsakov has come to know *Genoveva* only now; at the time he was composing his *Skazka, Sadko* fantasy, and *Mlada,* he had no idea of this Schumann opera at all.[22]

Further, we discussed:

(3) the march-like chorus (no. 5 in E), in which lay hidden, in embryo, Mussorgsky's *Destruction of Sennacherib* and even his *Oedipus;*

(4) the inspired, purely "Lohengrinian" music which accompanies the scene in which Golo kisses Genoveva and she, half-asleep, utters the name of Siegfried;

(5) the ravishingly sad and tender music of the beginning of act 2;

(6) the very charming and elegant duet (no. 9 in E minor) between Genoveva and Golo, which exudes something archaic, medieval;

(7) the brilliant scene of Golo's oath to Genoveva, with its unusually daring and novel ending;

(8) the marvelous conclusion of Genoveva's Prayer (no. 11 in B-flat) in which is heard the most subtle, purely Schumannesque interweaving of harmonies, something our most elegant Schumannist César Cui never hit upon;

(9) the daring, mocking, and totally unexpected (from a harmonic standpoint) F-sharp minor after the dominant of E-flat major and before a new E-flat major in the rejoinder of the sorceress Margareta (see the concluding scene of act 2);

(10) and the brilliant music at the beginning of scene 2, act 3 (in the sorceress' cave).

One must, however, listen all the way through this strikingly gloomy scene in order to judge the amazing power and expressiveness, which only the deeply inspired music of the creator of *Manfred* was sometimes capable of attaining.

We went on to consider:

(11) the rather interesting (from a musical point of view) Incantation of Margareta and the first magic chorus (the second and third choruses are less so), which calls to mind the future love scene from Wagner's *Walküre;*

(12) the gloomily majestic scene between Margareta and the ghost of the dead Golo, constructed on a menacing and mysterious theme, very close to the principal melody of Chopin's posthumous F-minor étude as well as to the theme of Chernobog and the Black Service from Rimsky-Korsakov's *Mlada;*

(13) the unusually noble and meditative Introduction to act 4, stylistically calling to mind Wagner's *Tristan,* except that this *Tristan* style was created by Schumann before Wagner;

(14) the music preceding the funereally cynical song of Caspar and Balthasar, which sort of foreshadows the stars in Rimsky-Korsakov's *May Night;*

(15) the wonderful moment when, having despaired of salvation, Genoveva suddenly sees a cross and hears voices from heaven;

(16) the brilliant music accompanying the scene of Golo's departure.

At the end, Rimsky-Korsakov summed it up thus: "Most surprising of all, is the fact that despite its many superb passages and considerable scenic interest, these musical beauties pass unnoticed by many, owing to the awfully dull orchestration, in which the individual instruments are completely inaudible and you hear only the general *tutti.* Meanwhile, what a wealth of music there is here—real, not leitmotivic music."

9 April

According to Nikolai Andreyevich the three performances of Schumann's *Genoveva* took in only thirty-two hundred rubles.[23] As a consequence, even though the theater, orchestra, and chorus were free, the concert barely paid for itself. We talked again about this opera, noting that Schumann was undoubtedly a "highly intelligent person" and, so far as operatic style is concerned, he far surpassed Meyerbeer.

From this we turned to the subject of Cui's article,[24] which, though intelligent, unfortunately underestimated completely the music of the beginning of act 4 and the absolute genius of the scene of Golo's departure after he finds that he cannot bring himself to kill Genoveva. Then we considered the stupid twaddle of our 'congenitally blind" connoisseurs of art—Ivanov and Solovyov,[25] these everlastingly dissatisfied, ill-starred musician-clowns. Ivanov, for example, even solemnly put forth the curious notion that *Genoveva* is a "stillborn" creation and that the Society's choice of last year *(The Maid of Pskov)* was much more successful. Solovyov, on the contrary, wrote that we ought to rejoice that this season the Society gave *Genoveva,* since last year it condemned the public to listen to the "stillborn" *Maid of Pskov.*

Apropos of Ivanov, bear in mind that Auer went to hear the opera mainly because he had read Ivanov's review in the morning and took it to mean the opposite of what it said. Auer did not make a mistake, for he liked both the opera and the performance.

As I was leaving the Rimsky-Korsakovs', I learned that Belsky would be there this evening, so I returned again at about eleven o'clock. We got onto the subject of the enmity between Cui and Tchaikovsky, an enmity so deep-seated that the latter even took the congratulatory telegram Cui sent him on the hundredth performance of *Eugene Onegin* at the Marinsky Theater as "a malevolent joke played on him by someone unknown to him." This implacable enmity stemmed from a very malicious article which Cui wrote on the occasion of Tchaikovsky's debut as a composer, something which Peter Ilyich could never forgive.[26]

Mention of this called to mind that pretentious scoundrel Hanslick and his stupid derision of Tchaikovsky's brilliant *Romeo and Juliet* Overture. Taking the introduction for a depiction of Juliet's funeral (!?), Hanslick quipped that the Allegro in B minor, which follows, must represent the funeral banquet with a drinking-bout and fistfight. At this point the critic heard the cracks of a whip. The incomparably beautiful second theme in D-flat left him only with the impression of the alternation of two dissonant chords, reminding him of the scraping of a knife against a plate.[27]

"You know," interjected Nikolai Andreyevich, "in its day my symphonic poem *Sadko* also received cruel treatment from the notorious Dr.

Hanslick. In his opinion, the music could be likened to the sounds "d'une seringue mal graissée." That's witty, isn't it? Why, it's even worthy of our Baskin. After that, I lost all my respect for Hanslick and stopped believing in his erudition."

After this we discussed the question of what our critics mean when they call a composer "nonoperatic."

"As far as I'm concerned," said Nikolai Andreyevich, "anyone who is capable of composing songs well, can write recitatives, and has some talent for symphonic and descriptive music is a true composer of operatic music—one much to be desired—that's obvious—since these are the elements which go to make up opera. The false notion that such composers are "nonoperatic" has arisen only from the fact that in their works they deviate from the operatic style of Meyerbeer and Verdi, a style which has been artificially elevated to the ideal by the public (and after them the critics)."

15 April

According to Nikolai Andreyevich, the chorus is rehearsing diligently for the production of *Boris,* but these rehearsals are becoming burdensome to him.[28]

"Besides this," he added, "I have to write a foreword to the reorchestrated score, and this is not easy to do, for, in explaining what prompted me to undertake this task, I must at the same time not offend Mussorgsky's memory nor show insufficient respect for his truly outstanding talent and the enormous contribution he made to the history of the development of Russian national music drama."

25 April

Today my wife and I attended the twenty-fourth performance of *Prince Igor.* Despite the spring weather, the theater was filled, so much so that we had difficulty obtaining tickets in the third row. Because of its outstanding success and many encores, the performance lasted until twelve-thirty.

Here I consider it appropriate to remind the reader precisely which parts of *Igor* were orchestrated by Rimsky-Korsakov.

As is known, Glazunov orchestrated the overture (44 pages) and part of act 3, after the March of the Polovtsi (113 pages), that is, a total of 157 pages (out of 710).

Borodin himself orchestrated the Choruses of Praise (beginning and end of the Prologue); Galitsky's recitative and song (act 1); recitative and girls' chorus (with fast five-beat ending); Konchakovna's cavatina (act 2) without choral accompaniment; Vladimir Igoryevich's cavatina; Konchak's aria; the Polovtsian Dances (no. 17) with chorus (a great part of these dances, however, was orchestrated by Rimsky-Korsakov and even Liadov with the agreement of the composer); Yaroslavna's lament; the peasants' chorus and part of the finale of act 4—185 pages in all.

All of the rest was orchestrated by Rimsky-Korsakov in 1887, that is: from the Prologue—the eclipse scene (pp. 25–34) and, further, up to the final chorus (pp. 35–55).

From act 1: the scene at Prince Galitsky's (pp. 68–78), as far as the song; the recitative ("Sestra-to"); the girls' chorus and the following scene with Galitsky; Skula's scene ("Stoi, rebiyata, slukhai") with chorus; the prince song ("Skula, Eroshka, i narod"); the chorus—"Da, vot komu by kniazhit na Putivle" (93–138); Yaroslavna's arioso (139–151); scene between Yaroslavna and Vladimir; Finale (chorus of the Boyars and the tocsin with the "wailing" of the women).[29]

From act 2: the Polovtsian girls' song (the beginning of which was composed by Glazunov); Polovtsian girls' dances (no. 8) with a quintuple phrase added by Rimsky-Korsakov (214–38); recitative "Podrugi-devitsy," etc. (beginning and end of which were composed by Rimsky-Korsakov and Glazunov):

Example 20

by Rimsky-Korsakov   by Glazunov

The chorus written down "from memory" by Glazunov (to words by Rimsky-Korsakov: "Dai gospod' zdorov'ia, krasnye devitsy"); the Polovtsian Patrol—"Solntse za goroi ukhodit na pokoi" (pp. 248–260); the recitative ("Ty li, Vladimir moi") and duet between Vladimir and Konchak-ovna; recitative which follows it ("Nu chto zh otets tvoi"); Prince Igor's aria ("Ni sna, ni otdykha izmuchennoi dushe") with the famous B-flat clarinet and gloomy pizzicato of the cellos and double basses at the end; the scene between Igor and Ovlur (268–323); and Konchak's recitative "Gei, plennits privesti siuda" (344–350).

From act 3: the March of the Polovtsi with chorus (421–454), the scenario of which was written by Rimsky-Korsakov.

Finally, from act 4: the recitative ("Kak unylo vse krugom") and duet between Yaroslavna and Igor; song of the gudok players; the scene and chorus (584–648); final chorus: "Guliai vo zdravye kniaz'ia" . . . "Zdrav-stvui, batiushka, nash kniaz zhelannyi" (649–667).[30]

Besides this, all of the Borodin manuscripts and the above were tran-scribed by Nikolai Andreyevich and given in this form to the printer.

Thus, Glazunov scored 157 pages, Borodin—185 pages, and Rimsky-Korsakov—368 pages (out of a total of 710 pages).

Small wonder, then, that Belyaev, when presenting Rimsky-Korsakov with a copy of the score of Prince Igor, inscribed it as follows: "To dear Nikolai Andreyevich Rimsky-Korsakov, thanks to whose talent, love for the late composer, and selflessly energetic labor the world is indebted for the publication of this opera. From the publisher."

Indeed, I do not imagine that there have been many such artists as Rimsky-Korsakov, not only here in Russia but even in the West.

Visit to Smerdovitsy[31]

22 August

Nikolai Andreyevich was very glad to see me when I arrived from Petersburg this evening. Almost immediately after tea, we went into the garden, even though it was quite cool and completely dark.

We began to talk, naturally, about Sadko. The opera, Nikolai Andrey-evich said, will probably be divided into three acts, with the scenes grouped as follows: act 1—two scenes (Feast and Scene at Lake Ilmen); act 2—two scenes (In Sadko's Rooms and Scene of the Wager); act 3—three scenes (On the Ship, In the Underwater Realm, and again On the Shore of Lake Ilmen). At present all that remains to be done is for Rimsky-

Korsakov to complete the orchestration of some twenty pages of the "dance."

Later Rimsky-Korsakov informed me, sadly, of the death of Porfiry Alexeyevich Trifonov on July 22.

It was nearly midnight when we entered the house and settled down to read my analysis of the fantasy *Sadko*. However, because of the lateness of the hour, we did not finish it.

23 August

This morning, after tea, we went out into the garden and, despite a light drizzle, we strolled along the wonderful oak-lined allée.

We discussed at length the new version of *Boris Godunov* and the necessity of expanding the piano score—restoring the most important cuts. Somehow we became caught up in a discussion of what constitutes genius. In the view of Rimsky-Korsakov, the measure of this quality in a composer is the degree to which his creativity predominates over that of others. Thus, among the Russian composers we find the following: Mussorgsky equals Glinka + Dargomyzhsky + Schumann and Liszt +, finally, his own; Borodin—again Glinka + Beethoven + Schumann + his own; Cui—Chopin + Schumann + something of his own. Thus, not one of them is a genius but, as Belinsky put it, they are "brilliant talents." This is not so with Beethoven, Chopin, Wagner, Glinka, or even Berlioz, whose works, though lacking in pure music, contain a multitude of brilliant innovations. When it comes to our latest composers, only Balakirev can rightly be considered a man of genius, for in his youth he expressed his musical talent especially brightly. Then, however, he suddenly fell silent and remained so for almost thirty years. And now, for all their elegance, his latest songs are a far cry from his earlier ones (*Pridi ko mne, Pesnia Selima, Pesnia zolotoi rybki,* etc.).

Our conversation turned to Nikolai Andreyevich's *Sadko,* and I learned that it contains relatively few folk themes. There is one borrowed from T. I. Filippov's collection (no. 4) and incorporated into the wandering pilgrims' chorus (song about Falsehood and Truth); another borrowed from the *Obikhod*[32] and reworked in the scene of Nikola's appearance in the underwater kingdom as well as in the final chorus in his honor, from the last act. There is no question, however, that in its melodic pattern the theme of the sailors' chorus "Vysota l', vysota podnebesnaia" resembles Kirsha Danilov's folk tune "O solov'e Budimiroviche" (see no. 3 from Rimsky-Korsakov's collection), and the melody of the wedding rite ("Rybka shla, plyla iz Novgoroda") is similar to the tune of the *khorovod* from Nizhegorod Province, Arzamassky District: "Stoi, moi milyi khorovod, stoi, ne raskhodis' " (see Balakirev's collection, no. 26).

Later in the morning, at my request, Nikolai Andreyevich played all of the new scene 3, some of scene 4 (with the big crowd, wandering pilgrims, people of Novgorod, soothsayers, *skomorokhi*, Nezhata, etc.), and all four songs of the foreign guests—that of the Viking, that of the Indian, and the two of the Venetian in praise of Venice. The first of the latter (newly written) was in strict Catholic, I would even say "pre-Raphaelite" style, with a continual, highly original, canonic accompaniment.

After dinner Rimsky-Korsakov played all of act 4 (scene 3, act 3, according to the new enumeration), which begins, after an effective introduction, with the Sea Princess' lullabye and ends with Sadko's tale. Since act 3 is not quite finished, he put off playing it for me until St. Petersburg.

"I hope," Rimsky-Korsakov remarked as we went out into the garden, "that this time Glazunov won't say that my opera hasn't much counterpoint. By the way, as I already told you once, I intend to spend some time working on this method of composition once more in my life."

In the evening we went through parts of the second scene of act 1, that is, the somewhat revised beginning, Sadko's song (in which the two last verses are worked out contrapuntally), and the new C major ending (the point at which the swans swim away through the peaceful waters to the azure tower).

At midnight we went to our rooms, but just as I was about to blow out the candle, in walked Nikolai Andreyevich. He sat down on the divan and began telling me that he never again wanted to write another opera, that he is going to devote himself either to chamber music or to a textbook of orchestration, and if not he will make a draft of "his thoughts on music and on musical aesthetics in general," not following any particular system. I urged him first to finish the ill-fated *Anchar,* then try to write a few short cantatas or a one- or two-act opera on the subject of "The Feast at the Palace of King Alcinous" (from *The Odyssey*) or Byron's *Heaven and Earth.*

On leaving, Rimsky-Korsakov said that he will rise without fail tomorrow morning to see me off. It was about one o'clock when I blew out my candle.

24 August

Indeed, despite the fact that I had to leave for the station at quarter to six, Nikolai Andreyevich kept his word and came out to bid me goodbye.

While I was having coffee, he remarked, quite unexpectedly: "What is good is that which has survived from a long-forgotten past. You know, when I composed the theme for the final chorus of *Sadko* [33] I decided that I'd never again write an opera on a Russian subject, especially since the subjects of my operas are both incomprehensible and ridiculous to most of our public. This is very regrettable, since it testifies to their ignorance and total lack of interest in their past."

When he bade good-bye, Rimsky-Korsakov thanked me for having come to visit them. The horses started off. Soon I passed the small thicket beside the road, and we proceeded at a slow trot toward the village of Vreda and then to the railroad station.

10 September

The Belskys were at the Rimsky-Korsakovs' when I arrived. Soon afterward Shtrup also appeared. They talked about the recent production of *May Night* in Prague,[34] and the strong impression it had produced on both the public and the critics.[35] The public liked best acts 1 and 3, the critics, act 2. The latter were especially enthusiastic over the strikingly lifelike (in their opinion) and colorful comic scenes and the surprisingly beautiful music in the opera's lyrical moments, and only the *rusalki* were almost unnoticed or not understood. Some of the Czech critics found influences of Smetana here and there, which pleased them greatly. This they ascribed to Rimsky-Korsakov's acquaintance with the works of their compatriot.[36] At the same time, they felt it their duty to point out that conversely the music of Rimsky-Korsakov had influenced the style of Dvořák.

We also talked about the seven performances of *Snegurochka* at the Nizhegorod Exhibition where, despite the small orchestra (twenty players), thanks to the wonderful sets by Mamontov and the splendid Snegurochka (Tsvetkova), it had a great success and played to full houses, according to the reports of people present.

After tea, Nikolai Andreyevich played all of acts 2 and 4 of *Sadko,* but, despite our requests, he flatly refused to play act 3, claiming that he has completely forgotten it. As it was, both acts were played rather indifferently, with many mistakes. Rimsky-Korsakov seemed to be either fatigued or absentminded; he played as though he were forcing himself. After act 2 he said: "From now on I shall play my *Sadko* worse and worse, for I've 'over-learned' it, as they say."

Regarding the magnificent (in every respect, not excluding the contrapuntal) final scene of the opera, he remarked half seriously, half in jest: "I'm certain that almost everyone is going to criticize me severely, since there's not a particle of so-called 'scenic interest' in it. It's a sort of hymn to old times and Novgorod with the Volkhova river. Oh well, let them abuse me—I'm used to that."

30 September

At the choral rehearsal of *Boris* tonight, I learned from Nikolai Andreyevich that a certain Pierre d'Alheim[37] (author of a book on Mussorgsky) has come to Petersburg and will be at the Molases' tomorrow. Nikolai Andreyevich has also been invited to be there, as d'Alheim wants very much to meet him. He is thinking of presenting Nikolai Andreyevich's songs (and those of Borodin and Balakirev) in Paris this winter.

On the twenty-fifth, Cui visited Rimsky-Korsakov to discuss the program for the concert planned for the opening of the new Conservatory.[38] It is to consist entirely of works by Russian composers and will be conducted by Rimsky-Korsakov.

"Just imagine," said Nikolai Andreyevich, "our esteemed critic (Cui) didn't even know Balakirev's new songs. At least, that's what he told me."

According to Nikolai Andreyevich, upon being tested, the new large hall of the Conservatory has turned out to be absolutely impossible accoustically.

14 October

Rimsky-Korsakov and I chatted about d'Alheim and his intention of taking Rimsky-Korsakov to task for his revision of *Boris Godunov* [39] on his return to Paris; also about Delines' absurd article in *Figaro,* in which, although he had been sent the official biography of Nikolai Andreyevich, this scatterbrained Frenchman offered the totally false information that Nikolai Andreyevich had begun to occupy himself with music under the influence of Turgenev's advice.

I learned that *Snegurochka* had been given in Kharkov [40] and saw two telegrams: one from the conductor Esposito, informing Nikolai Andreyevich of the performance and asking him to *favor* them with a visit, and the other from the entire company congratulating him on the opera's success.

Speaking of *Sheherazade* and its success abroad, Rimsky-Korsakov said, laughingly: "Mark my words. This work of mine will be played all over Germany for a long time to come, and, in spite of its success, no one will even think of playing anything else."

19 October

Today the first staged rehearsal of *Boris* took place under the direction of Osip (Josef) Paleček. They went through the entire Prologue. Simultaneously, in adjoining rooms, several of the soloists prepared their parts, accompanied in turn by a student, Goldenblum, Alexei Davidov, and Nikolai Andreyevich. In the course of the evening they managed to go through all of the Inn Scene as well as the Polish Act, the latter twice, with Nosilova and Sukhomlina playing the role of Marina by turns.

During the interval, I learned from Nikolai Andreyevich that Count Sheremetyev has consented to let them use his sets of *Boris.* Thank heavens! At least that will make it easier for our musical brotherhood.

28 October

This morning Nikolai Andreyevich and I talked about the two private concerts being planned in memory of Tchaikovsky, one to be conducted by Nikisch and the other by Napravnik. [41] They are thinking of performing, among other things, the Fifth and Sixth symphonies, the *Romeo and Juliet* Overture, and the symphonic poem *Francesca da Rimini.*

By coincidence, last Thursday on the eve of the third anniversary of Peter Ilyich's death (October 25, 1893), they celebrated Nikolai Andreyevich's twenty-fifth anniversary as a professor at the Conservatory.[42]

In the evening I ran into Nikolai Andreyevich at the rehearsal of Boris, or more correctly, the "dance class," for today the chorus and Marina (Ilina) were learning the polonaise under the supervision of Paleček.

4 November

Nikolai Andreyeivch and I had a long talk about d'Alheim's book, which is not bad, for a foreigner, even though the sections dealing with the everyday life of the Russian peasant are absolutely ridiculous.

As for the French translations of Mussorgsky's text, with a few exceptions, they have been done conscientiously, aside from this comical word-for-word rendering of the text of the song Savishna: "Ma lumière Sawichna, mon clair faucon, aime-moi, l'insensé."[43]

"Just imagine," said Rimsky-Korsakov, "while we Russians find much of what d'Alheim has written ridiculous, in Paris his lectures on Mussorgsky have created a sensation. He has received scores of letters on the subject, which he has published."

Here is a sample of some of some of the views expressed:

Bourgault-Ducoudray: "Had Mussorgsky written nothing but the score of Boris Godunov, he would still be worthy of being counted among the most daring and original creative musicians of our epoch."

Raymond Bouyer: "The composer of Boris Godunov is a strong and vital personality who carried to the extreme the voluptuousness of grief. Borodin and Balakirev, more sumptuous, are less subjective. It was said of Berlioz: 'He did not have enough talent for his genius.' The same may be said of Mussorgsky."

Jules de Brayer: "How perfect his (Mussorgsky's) musical technique is! In this respect how much he could teach even César Franck himself, and many others reputed to be faultless."

André Fontainas wrote that "I imagine Mussorgsky's orchestration to be dense, new, somewhat shrill (like Balakirev's)."

Alexandre Georges said: "I would be even more capivated by the 'Persian Dance' and its Eastern wildness, languor, and brutality if I had not recognized in it the influence of that sensualist—Balakirev."

What an opinion!

However, among the masses of flattering statements received by d'Al-heim about Mussorgsky[44] there were some which were very derogatory and rather cruel. Thus, Clément Lippacher wrote:

"Mussorgsky's work seems to me difficult to judge. Musically, it is incoherent, distorted, debauched, artistically insane. Nevertheless, I really believe that it can have a great success in the sphere of the sublime, since whatever else, it is free from banality and staleness."

Alfred Bruneau asserted that "all the ridiculous critics who have been converts to the music of Wagner have attached themselves to Mussorg-sky." And Saint-Saëns stated unashamedly that "Mussorgsky is nothing but a crazy, fatuous, ugly declaimer."

When I ran into Nikolai Andreyevich again, tonight, at the rehearsal of *Boris,* I passed on to him a stupid remark (made by a German) which Lapshin had once told me: "In Russland sind nur zwei berühmte Com-ponisten: Rimsky-Korsakow und . . . Nischny Novgorod." I also told him of the following ludicrous explanation of Dargomyzhsky's *Kazachok,* which was published in *Figaro,* October 17, 1896: " 'La Cosatchoque' de Dar-gomijsky est célèbre à Saint-Petersbourg. C'est une danse militaire que ce compositeur a développée et dont il a fait une rapsodie difficile à jouer, mais excellente pour les doigts."

11 November

Nikolai Andreyevich was in a wonderful mood today. Only one prob-lem: the Conservatory's new building is to be opened officially tomorrow, and Nikolai Andreyevich has misplaced his decorations. What is more, he has no idea of how many to wear and in what order.

The subject of Tchaikovsky's memorial concert came up, and Nikolai Andreyevich said again, referring specifically to Nikisch's inspired perfor-mance of the Fifth Symphony, that he does not know a better conductor.

For *Boris* they plan to invite the most "heterogeneous orchestra possi-ble." "There will be Barbarians, Scythians, Ostrogoths, Visigoths, Cher-emissians, and Mordvinians, all in pairs," said Nikolai Andreyevich. The first orchestral rehearsal has been set for the thirteenth; the second, with soloists and chorus, for the fourteenth.

Tonight, at the piano rehearsal of *Boris,* they went through the whole opera. The new Varlaam (Stravinsky)[45] proved to be very good and in character.

After the Coronation Scene, Nadezhda Nikolayevna remarked to me, not without irritation, that this chorus now sounds much worse than Mussorgsky's. "I don't excuse any alterations or revisions whatsoever," she said.

Shortly afterward, Rimsky-Korsakov commented to me: "You cannot imagine how much I regret now that I made so few changes, relatively, in the Prologue, for on trying it out, it turns out that what was left untouched is clumsy."

On November 28 *Boris Godunov* finally received its first performance, under the direction of Rimsky-Korsakov.[46] It was attended by a very large audience. The opera went rather smoothly, except for the first scene of the Prologue, in which the chorus of wandering mendicants lagged behind a bit.

Boris was sung by Lunacharsky; Xenia by Larina; Xenia's nurse—Sukhomlina; the Tsarevich—Mme Vardot; Varlaam—Stravinsky; Missail—Varzar; Marina—Ilina; the Pretender—Morskoi; Prince Shuisky—Safonov; Pimen—Zhdanov; the Jesuit Rangoni—Kedrov; the Hostess of the Inn—Mme Varlikh; and the Simpleton—Karklin.

Among those attending, besides the Rimsky-Korsakovs, were: Stoyanovsky, Cesar Cui, the Stasovs, the Molases, the Dianins, Glazunov, Liadov, Johansen, Auer, Samus, Solovyov, Baskin, and Ivanov, who followed the opera from the old orchestral score. Laroche was not there.

The staging of *Boris* was very good—even the scene at the fountain was lifelike—and the costumes were magnificent, especially Marina's.

The second performance of *Boris* went still better than the first, but the audience was small. The box office return was only 500 rubles.

Nosilova performed the role of Marina superlatively. Ilina was an exceedingly charming Tsarevich. Varlikh sang the Nurse's part well. Timofeyev was good as Missail and Varzar good, too, as Shuisky. Incidentally, the gong was much improved—it came in on time—the reason being that it was played by Rimsky-Korskov himself. The conductor today was Goldenblum.

The audience gave *Boris* a very warm reception and called out Rimsky-Korsakov both after the scene at the fountain and at the end of the performance. Kamenskaya went into raptures over the opera, and when Rimsky-Korsakov suggested that they stage it at the Marinsky Theater, she replied: "This is just what I've been berating our fools about all day today."

2 December

Rimsky-Korsakov told me that there may not be a fourth performance of *Boris* because Morskoi (the Pretender) is singing at the Marinsky all week. The only hope is that tomorrow they will present him and Stravinsky with wreaths and the day after, they will give Nosilova a basket of flowers. Meanwhile, the tickets are selling very well.

We spoke of Ivanov's strange article in *Novoe vremia*[47] and Stasov's ecstatic one in *Novosti.*[48] As for the orchestration of *Boris,* Nikolai Andreyevich told me that he did not finish scoring the Introduction and the Polish Act during Mussorgsky's lifetime, as Stasov asserts in his article, but did so after looking through the score of Wagner's *Walküre,* that is, in 1889, when the *Ring* was given in St. Petersburg.

Nikolai Andreyevich is going to *Samson et Dalila*[49] so that he may have another talk with Morskoi and try to persuade him to sing on Wednesday.

3 December

Like the premiere, the third performance of *Boris* drew a large audience. This time the role of Xenia's Nurse was sung by Rimsky-Korsakov's daughter, Sofia Nikolayevna. The opera went smoothly. Goldenblum conducted and Rimsky-Korsakov, as before, was at the gong. Of all the costumes, Marina's wonderful silver gown with its charming diamond belt was probably the most striking. Incidentally, both Stravinsky and Morskoi received wreaths.

During part of the opera, I sat in a box with Rimsky-Korsakov and learned that he had scored many passages, as for example, the scene in the cell, the love duet, and others just as Mussorgsky himself wished.

Tomorrow the fourth performance will take place. Already tickets in the amount of five hundred rubles have been sold.

Thank God!

4 December

The fourth performance of *Boris* went particularly well, thanks to the performances of Nosilova (Marina), Stravinsky (Varlaam), Lunacharsky (Boris), and Morskoi (the Pretender). The hall was very well filled. Goldenblum conducted again as Rimsky-Korsakov has a sore arm.

In the course of the evening, wreaths were presented to Stravinsky, Lunacharsky, and Nikolai Andreyevich and flowers to Nosilova. During the presentation of the wreath to Nikolai Andreyevich, the orchestra played a flourish and the soloists and chorus, who preceeded Nikolai Andreyevich onto the stage, greeted him with applause and bravos. With this the whole audience joined in, from the balcony down to the very last rows of the parterre.

Just one more thing: again neither Malozemova, Laroche, Shestakova, Balakirev, nor Findeisen was present today.

6 December

This afternoon Rimsky-Korsakov dropped in on us to congratulate Nadya in person, he said, on the birth of Sonya.

He is planning to finish all of *Boris* and publish the cuts as a separate supplement. Meanwhile, along with the new piano scores, Bessel has sold several old copies of the opera.

Today Nikolai Andreyevich was in a splendid mood. He took special delight in recalling how he had insisted on having his own way and, under the pretext of a sore arm, had not conducted the final performance of *Boris,* firstly to give Goldenblum this enormous pleasure and secondly, so that he could listen to the opera from beginning to end, calmly, free of worry.

After tea, I showed Rimsky-Korsakov a marvelous portrait of Liszt I had obtained from Weimar.

8 December

Rimsky-Korsakov and I had a rather long talk about Tchaikovsky's Fifth and Sixth symphonies. He praised the Andante from the Fifth Symphony highly, even though the very beginning of it is reminiscent of the well-known aria from Massenet's Le roi de Lahore. In the Sixth Symphony we both like mainly only the first and fourth movements; the second (in 5/4 time) sounds rather like a ballet number.

We talked about Tchaikovsky's Manfred, with its semi-Russian melody characterizing the hero, and Rimsky-Korsakov remarked that he does not care very much for it except for certain marvelous passages in the first and third movements and the coda of the second movement. To him the Scherzo seems insufficiently ethereal and poetic, particularly the trio, despite the violin solo and even the harp.

9 December

Following a discussion of Boito's Mefistofele, Rimsky-Korsakov remarked that he had come to the conclusion recently, that if it is impossible to put together a potpourri from a work, "this clearly indicates that the music is of a poor quality."

Later, on the subject of conductors, after noting that the Italians are, in a way, caricatures of Nikisch, Rimsky-Korsakov observed: "This, you see, appeals to our public, whose artistic development is too backward even for Verdi without embellishments."

Talking of Boris, I learned that Rimsky-Korsakov is bent on revising the Coronation Scene once more, since he finds that it contains little development and splendor—which is bad.

After tea we talked at length about Félicien David's Le Désert and how the charming song "O nuit, O belle nuit" had undoubtedly had an influence on the poetic music of the King Berendey's second cavatina ("Ukhodit den' veselyi") from the first scene of act 3 of Snegurochka:

Example 21

O nuit, o bel- le nuit, ta fraî-cheur nous ré-jou-it com-me une a-man-te com-ble l'at-ten-te d'a-mour

Rimsky-Korsakov rejects completely the idea that a profoundly artistic work can leave a depressing impression on the listener, however gloomy the subject may be (the Finale of act 2 of *Boris,* for example). He disagrees as well with the idea that it is necessary to depict a nasty person by means of "nasty" music or a timid person by "timid," clumsy vocal writing.

19 December

By dinnertime I was at the Rimsky-Korsakovs' with a bouquet of hyacinths for Nadezhda Nikolayevna. Since Nikolai Andreyevich was somewhat late, we had quite a long chat, in the course of which I learned that Nikolai Andreyevich recently received a very cordial letter from Balakirev, asking him to take part in the harmonization of a new collection of Russian folk songs. This work, he said, he would not like to entrust to anyone but himself, Rimsky-Korsakov, Liapunov, or Liadov. Nadezhda Nikolayevna does not think that "Nika" will do it, however—he has not the time. "In all likelihood Liadov will," she added.

When "Korsinka" returned, we discussed at length his new orchestration of *Boris,* especially the second half of act 2 with its strikingly unprecedented instrumentation (we have only to recall the scene of Prince Shuisky's report and that of Boris' hallucinations). Clearly, Rimsky-Korsakov meant it when he said, last winter, apropos of the Directorate's refusal to stage this opera at the Marinsky Theater, that "just to spite everybody" he was going to score it as well as could be.[50]

At about half past seven we rose from the table, Nikolai Andreyevich to go to the Marinsky Theater to hear *Christmas Eve* (on the second subscription) and I to Khessin.

In conclusion I will set down, in chronological order, the following facts pertaining to Rimsky-Korsakov's revision of the score of *Boris Godunov:*

From January 30 to February 4, 1892, Rimsky-Korsakov orchestrated the second scene of the prologue; between February 5 and 13, 1892—the first scene of the prologue; from April 3 to 14 and from November 20 to December 15, 1893—the first scene of act 3; from February 25 to March 21, 1894—the second scene of act 3; from March 27 to April 5, 1894—the first scene of act 1.

From December 15 to 27, 1895, Rimsky-Korsakov orchestrated the second scene of act 4. As we shall see below, this was revised again during the period between May 6 and May 9, 1896. Besides, at the end of the scene there is the notation: 23 December 1895.

Act 2 was orchestrated from January 21 to February 11, 1896; the second scene of act 1—from March 10 to 26, 1896; the first scene of act 4—from April 19 to May 5, 1896 and, finally, the second scene of act 4—from May 6 to 9, 1896.

Here is a detailed record of Rimsky-Korsakov's work on *Boris Godunov*, scene by scene, together with rather interesting notations found here and there on his manuscript:

Prologue: Scene 1 was begun on February 5 and finished on February 13, 1892. Scene 2 was begun on January 30 and finished on February 4, 1892.

Act 1: Scene 1—(in Pimen's cell) from the beginning up to Grigory's words: "I, padaia stremglav, ia probuzhdalsia" is dated March 27–29, 1894; further, to his words: "zachem i mne ne teshitsia v boiakh" —April 3, 1894; still further, to Grigory's words: "Davno, chestnoi otets"—April 4, 1894; and, finally, the conclusion of this scene—"Boris, Boris, vse pred toboi trepeshchet"—April 5, 1894.

Scene 2—(In the Inn) was started on March 10, 1896. Varlaam's song "Kak vo gorode bylo vo Kazani" is dated March 15, 1896; after that, up to "Kak edet on"—March 17; the rest, up to "Startsy smirennye, inoki chestnye"—March 20, 1896.

The end of the scene bears the date March 21, 1896, but there is a special note that the entire scene was completed not on the twenty-first but on the twenty-sixth of March 1896. There is also a remark by Rimsky-Korsakov: "Thanks to *Glazun* for looking through it."

Act 2 (in Godunov's private apartments) was begun on January 21, 1896 (Xenia's lament, etc.). "Pesnia pro komara" "Skazochka," etc., up to Boris' words "A ty, moi syn, chem zaniat?" bears the date January 31, 1896; the rest, continuing to the words "Tiazhka desnitsa groznogo sud'i"— February 1, 1896; Boris' aria itself—February 3, 1896 (the orchestral score has four flats, the vocal score seven, but the tonality remains the same, since the "occasional" flats were put into the orchestral score wherever necessary); the rest to Prince Shuisky's words "V Litve iavilsia samozvanets" is dated February 4, 1896.

On the margins of the manuscript score we find the following curious notes:

(1) On page 87, near the clef, at the beginning of the "informer's" reply, Rimsky-Korsakov wrote the three letters: "N.F.S.," which stand for "Nikolai Feopemptovich Solovyov."

(2) On page 92, in the scene between Godunov and Shuisky there is the comment: "Tonight at 8 P.M. the Mar. Theater rejected *Boris*. N. R-Kor."

But let us return to the time schedule:

The remainder of the scene between Godunov and Shuisky (as far as Shuisky's account) is dated February 8, 1896; Shuisky's account itself—"V Ugliche, v sobore" ending with Boris' retort—"Dovol'no" —February 9; then, as far as Boris' words "Von, von tam . . . chto eto?"—February 10, 1896. The rest, that is, the brilliantly orchestrated scene of Boris' "hallucinations" to the end of act 2 (pp. 126–132 of the manuscript) is dated February 11, 1896.

Act 3 (the Polish Act): scene 1—(in Marina's apartments). Female chorus "Na Visle lazurnoi" is dated April 3 to 8, 1893. Marina's recitative "Dovol'no, krasotka-panna blagodarna" to the words "U nog ee lezhali, v blazhenstve utopaia"—April 14, 1893.

The rest of the scene (scene of Marina's sadness), starting with the words "Net, ne etikh pesen' nuzhno panne Mnishek" and ending with Rangoni's entrance—November 20–23, 1893. Here, too, we find a curious note made by Rimsky-Korsakov: "Begun anew on November 20, 1893 (after Laroche's article)." (As we see, even Laroche, through his articles, can sometimes be of service to Russian music.)

As for Marina's scene with the Jesuit, ending with her words: "Proch' s glaz moikh" it is dated December 14, 1893, and the very end of the scene (adagio)—"Plamenem adskim glaza tvoi zablesteli"—December 15, 1893.

Scene 2—(at the fountain) was begun on February 26, 1894. The polonaise is dated March 6, 1894; the love scene between Marina and the Pretender, up to the words "Sviatuiu zhazhdu liubvi" —March 9, 1894; the rest, ending with the brilliantly reworked love duet—March 21, 1894.

Act 4: Scene 1—(In the forest near Kromy) from the beginning up to and including the chorus "honoring the boyar Krushchov" is dated April

19, 1896. Here is also a note by Nikolai Andreyevich: "After the rehearsal of this chorus."

The scene of the Simpleton and the wandering mendicants "Solntse, luna pomerknuli" bears the date April 20; the chorus "Raskhodilas', razgulialas' udal' molodetskaia" to the entrance of the Jesuits—April 30, 1896; the Jesuits ("Domine, domine salvum fac") to the march—May 1, 1896; the rest, that is, the march, the scene with the Pretender, the chorus glorifying him, and the Simpleton's lament: "Leites', leites', slezy gorkie"—May 5, 1896 (S.-Petersburg).

Scene 2—(Boyar's Duma and death of Boris). As we mentioned earlier, Rimsky-Korsakov was already pondering over this scene in December 1895[51] (the manuscript bears the date December 15 and 27, 1895). Nevertheless, in its final version, it was orchestrated between May 6 and May 9, 1896. The Boyar's Duma, Shuisky's tale about Boris, Boris' appearance and Pimen's tale, the scene of Godunov's farewell to the Tsarevich Feodor, to the end of the opera—all this is dated May 9, 1896.

CHAPTER 7

1897

This afternoon Rimsky-Korsakov came to see me to find out more about Słowacki's *Lilla Weneda,* of which I had once spoken to him.[1] I read an abridged version of it to him, and after serious consideration, we both arrived at the conclusion that, though suitable for musical treatment, this story is too gloomy and symbolic.

On the way to visit me, Rimsky-Korsakov had dropped in on Napravnik to leave the vocal score of *Sadko,* with which Napravnik had recently expressed a desire to become better acquainted. Apropos of the Theater Committee's meeting on the fourteenth of this month,[2] he told Rimsky-Korsakov that it is only a formality since his works are beyond discussion and all of them, without exception, ought to be staged.

"On the whole, Napravnik and I have been on very friendly terms all this time," added Rimsky-Korsakov. "There are several reasons for this. First, we're both older now and we realize that we've never really engaged in intrigues against each other; then, the views of the so-called Kuchka have changed considerably; you know, I myself made many revisions in *The Maid of Pskov,* which Napravnik did not like in its earlier version. Finally, perhaps, because after Blaramberg's irritable letter blaming Napravnik alone (despite the fact that there is a Committee) for the failure of his opera *The Wave,* I suggested that an official reply to his tactless letter be sent to Blaramberg in the name of the full Committee. As it turned out, this touched Napravnik very much."

Finally, we spoke about Laroche, who, they say, never leaves his house, reads, or sees anyone. From time to time he weeps bitterly; he is awaiting his death and is in a very depressed and humble moral state.

6 January

During dinner today, a terribly heated argument arose about Wagner (in general) and Dargomyzhsky's *Stone Guest* (in particular). Nadezhda Nikolayevna stood up for the latter, with her characteristic vehemence, declaring that she cannot stand Wagner's "false" tendencies and his "infernally long and boring music." I, for my part, had little good to say for the music of *The Stone Guest* except, of course, for the part of Don Carlos and some of Don Juan.

"Now, I'll tell you what I dislike mainly about Wagner," said Rimsky-Korsakov. "That's 'Wagnerism,' for it's a kind of a cult, a sort of religion in art. Now, by its very nature, no religion tolerates criticism, and this is bad.

"But then," he went on, "I've always criticized most harshly everyone I had a special love for, such as Beethoven, Wagner, etc. To me it's always been especially painful when I found something mediocre or bad in such geniuses."

Our conversation concluded with a lengthy discussion of Hugo Riemann's article on *Sheherazade*.[3] I shall not go into it at this point, except to say that thus far Rimsky-Korsakov has not had such a sound and intelligent article about this work in the Russian language nor is he likely to in the near future.

19 January

Just as I was in the midst of copying the score of *Boris,* the bell rang and Rimsky-Korsakov appeared, quite unexpectedly. He was obviously depressed. He has finally become convinced that no one likes either *Christmas Eve* or *Sadko,* and this he ascribes to the music.

"Probably these works are not very inspired," he said. "You can't imagine how I envy Beethoven that he could say to his friend Stephan

Breuning, a few hours before he died, 'I did have talent, didn't I.' These days I'm coming more and more to love the classics: Bach, Beethoven, Haydn, and the others, whose music is still so fresh and full of life.

"You may not believe this," he went on, "but Beethoven had such inexhaustible resources when it came to form and modulation that, in this regard, alongside of him all other composers are pygmies. And what about Haydn's Twelfth (B-flat) Symphony[4]—isn't it really new even now? Isn't it marvelously orchestrated?

"At this moment," he continued, "when I'm becoming increasingly disillusioned about myself and my latest operas, I find comfort in talking with you, even though I can't trust your taste completely, for you're necessarily biased in my favor. After all, both *Christmas Eve* and *Sadko* were written before your eyes. But I feel that here I myself and my music are genuinely loved."

I suggested that it might be a good idea for him to finish *Antar,*[5] but he replied that it was not worth doing, since the music is not very good.

As I began to inquire further about this, Nikolai Andreyevich suddenly interrupted me, saying: "I've definitely come to the conclusion that if I should die today, music would suffer no loss whatsoever. My family would be in a less favorable financial situation, that's all. You cannot imagine how painful the awareness of this is for me. Therefore, I think I'm going to stop writing altogether. In that way I can leave this profession honorably.

"I completely forgot to tell you last time," continued Rimsky-Korsakov, "that there was a runthrough of *Sadko* on the fourteenth, but apparently no one understood it at all. As you know, Napravnik is not the sort of person given to handing out compliments, even to the author himself.

"You understand, of course," concluded Rimsky-Korsakov, as he rose to leave, "I worry very little about death. I don't expect hell in that world; I don't believe in such things. That would be outrageous."

It grieved me terribly to see Rimsky-Korsakov in such a melancholy mood and to realize that his morale has been shattered for no other reason than that his music is too good, too fine for his time; that it is not fully understood and valued as it deserves by the best representatives of our musical world. And so, in a desire to offer him some comfort, I wrote him a letter which I posted at 2 A.M. However, for some incomprehensible reason, it did not reach its destination until almost a month later.

20 January

Mindful of Nikolai Andreyevich's love for flowers, to cheer him up I brought him a small basket of hyacinths. He was clearly touched but felt he had to scold me for my extravagance.

This time we had a rather long discussion about Mussorgsky's music to Gogol's *Marriage*, which was written in four weeks. The first page of the manuscript bears the words:

Began to write on Tuesday 11 June/68 in Petrograd. Finished the act on Tuesday 8 July/68, in the Tula village of Shilovo.
M. Mussorgsky.[6]

As was to be expected, all eighty-nine pages of the music proved to be so bad, so illiterate and naive that one could readily understand why Stasov, when donating this manuscript to the Public Library, forbade its performance anywhere during his lifetime.

"Just imagine," said Rimsky-Korsakov, "in this work there are musical illustrations of such things as gray hair, which, for some reason, is depicted by a minor second."

Nadezhda Nikolayevna read to us Mussorgsky's curious dedication, which she had copied from the title page of (the one and only) act 1. Here it is:

I hand over my student work
to the eternal possession
of dear Vladimir Vasilyevich
Stasov on his birthday
2 January 1873.
Modest Musoryanin,
That is to say, Mussorgsky.
Written with a quill pen
in the Stasovs' apartment:
Mokhovaya, house of Melikhov,
in the presence of a sizable crush of people.
Mussorgsky.

After hearing Mussorgsky's song cycle *The Nursery* at the Molases' recently, Nikolai Andreyevich said, he suddenly got the idea to write a "simplified" *Niania* ("Nanny").[7]

"Because, you know," he added, "Mussorgsky's harmony in this cycle is unusually absurd. It's a kind of continuous 'musical E-flat major.' Remember the prelude to *Rheingold,* in which, by using the E-flat major chord throughout, Wagner obviously aimed at conveying the idea that up to the time when the guards stole the gold, the world had been a complete void? Well, from a purely musical point of view, *The Nursery,* too, is a kind of 'E-flat major.' "

27 January

Rimsky-Korsakov greeted me with the news that he is going to write an overture on the theme of "God Save the Tsar." Noting my surprise, he added: "They're not going to give *Sadko*—that's definite. I went to the theater today to see Kondratyev about this, and afterward I dropped in on Vsevolozhsky. He received me very cordially, as usual, but just as cordially informed me that on the twenty-fourth, when confirming the repertoire for the coming year, the Tsar declared, despite all his (Vsevolozhsky's) representations, 'We can do without that opera.' "

"This is what happened," Vsevolozhsky reported to Rimsky-Korsakov. "Since the Tsar doesn't remember the Sadko legend in detail, I had to give him a brief summary of the content of the opera. I even had to explain that the folk tradition about Sadko calls for the appearance of St. Nikola, but that Rimsky-Korsakov had taken him out and replaced him by a character called simply 'unknown old man,' which is totally acceptable to the censor. Finally, I pointed out that this is the only new opera by a well-known Russian composer, and, for this reason alone, it ought to be given at the Marinsky Theater. When His Majesty asked what the music is like, I told him it's somewhat reminiscent of *Mlada* and *Christmas Eve.* At that he crossed it off the list, saying, 'In that case, there's no point in putting on *Sadko.* Let the Directorate try to find something more cheerful.' "

(Here Nikolai Andreyevich interrupted his account: "Evidently they've even begun to censor music.")

"But you know what's good about all this?" added Vsevolozhsky, as if in jest. "We've been spared the terrible bother of preparing the production." (A fine joke!)

"Another curious thing about this whole episode," continued Nikolai Andreyevich, "is that today, when greeting me, Kondratyev didn't grasp my hand, as he used to, and inquire about my wife's health. And while the rest of the artists were polite, they seemed to be avoiding me. Even Pchelnikov, on meeting me at Vsevolozhsky's, disappeared immediately. The only conclusion to be drawn from all this is that the proposed production of *The Maid of Pskov* is a long, long way off. There's no use in my troubling the Directorate ever again with any of my operas, new or old, for my access to the stage has been cut off forever."[8]

Obviously Rimsky-Korsakov was deeply distressed, even though he was trying hard not to show it.

By the way, this coming season, the Marinsky Theater plans to give Félicien David's *Lalla Rookh, Don Giovanni,* Tchaikovsky's *Oprichnik, Andrea Chénier,* some stupid opera by Puccini, *Hänsel and Gretel,* and something else more amusing than the boring and untalented *Sadko.*[9]

10 February

On the whole, this time I found Nikolai Andreyevich in a rather good mood. He showed me the score of Borodin's *Sleeping Princess,*[10] which he completed on January 25 of this year. In it he very cleverly avoided the alternating seconds of the original. [Example 22] shows these "seconds without seconds."

Later, in a discussion of Findeisen's magazine *(Russkaia muzykal'naia gazeta),* Nikolai Andreyevich said, "You know, I'm absolutely certain that the only reason Findeisen didn't write anything about the revision of *Boris* is that, on principle, he didn't want to praise it but didn't know how to demonstrate what's wrong with it."

Turning again to the subject of *Sadko,* I remarked that there is some speculation about whether Vsevolozhsky had even thought of bringing up the question of it to the Tsar, to which Nikolai Andreyevich replied, "Now, I'll tell you another funny thing. When it became known that my opera wasn't going to be given, not one of my friends, except Stasov, uttered a word in protest against this strange decision. It never entered anyone's head to devote one of the concerts to the music of *Sadko.* And this is typical. In general, Glazunov terribly dislikes to protest about anything (it's not in his nature). Besides, under the influence of Laroche, they've all become convinced that no one has ever really persecuted Russian music, on the contrary, it's always been extraordinarily lucky and

Example 22

that if it occasionally 'caught it' from the critics, this was only because it was deserved."

We chatted about the first Russian Symphony Concert, at which the audience numbered about a hundred fewer people than usual, despite the visitors from Moscow (Count Leo Tolstoy's wife and Kashkin). Obviously, Taneyev's Overture to *Oresteia* and Glazunov's Sixth Symphony[11] so frightened our timid music lovers that, alas, even Tchaikovsky's new poetic Andante[12] could not attract a decent-sized audience.

As I was leaving, Nikolai Andreyevich informed me that Belyaev is planning to give a "test" concert in Moscow. There, they say, there is some hope for good box office returns, since the Muscovites on the whole are more enthusiastic about Russian music.

Example 22 *(cont.)*

spit kniazh-na vol shebnym snom;

spit pod kro-vom son sko val ei

fem-noi no chi krep-ko o chi

17 February

Today Nikolai Andreyevich brought up the subject of Glazunov and his opinions about music, which are becoming increasingly strange.

"Just imagine," he said, "Alexander Konstantinovich now flatly opposes color in music and values only beauty of sound—this, of course, in the broadest sense of the word. What's more, not long ago, he solemnly expressed a very odd opinion—that anyone who doesn't like the Finale of Tchaikovsky's unfinished Piano Concerto (op. 79)[13] is a fool.(!)

"You will agree," concluded Nikolai Andreyevich, "that if this continues, we're going to have to go our separate ways, without falling out, of course."

24 February

Apropos of a remark by Goldstein, we began talking about Borodin and his legendary absentmindedness, thanks to which he once addressed a letter to himself in Perm. Another time, at a frontier, when their passports were being visaed, he completely forgot his wife's name (which, naturally, aroused the suspicion of the customs official). Fortunately, Ekaterina Sergeyevna arrived soon afterward. On seeing her, Borodin exclaimed joyfully, "Katya, for Heaven's sake, tell them your name."

They also recalled the time when Borodin, told of his promotion to Councillor of State, suddenly, to everyone's embarrassment, began sobbing and replying to all questions, "Old age." They recollected another episode, one which caused a sensation and a lot of excitement at the time—the occasion of the Grand Duke's telegram to Borodin, reading:

Jena. Excellenz A. Borodin. Erwarte sie Morgen Abend. Alexander.

The telegram was for Borodin, but no one in Jena knew of any such "Excellency." How surprised and embarrassed the haughty Germans were when this important "general," to whom the Grand Duke of Weimar himself had sent a telegram, turned out to be the genial "fat man" ("der Dicke") Borodin, whom they had all known for a long time and who lived very simply with two young students (Dianin and Goldstein) in a virtual garret and often went to the market and even to the baker's. All this taken together really shook up the famous city.

"Do you know," said Rimsky-Korsakov "what Glazunov once said in all seriousness to Tchaikovsky at an occasion in his (Tchaikovsky's) honor? 'Peter Ilyich, you are God, since you make everything from nothing.'

"I don't think, however," added Rimsky-Korsakov, "That Tchaikovsky felt particularly flattered by such praise."

6 March

This evening I was at the Rimsky-Korsakovs' from eight-fifteen until twelve-thirty. Nikolai Andreyevich was sleeping when I rang, but he appeared in the drawing room soon afterward. So far as I could tell, he was in a very good mood. He drank his coffee with mock enthusiasm, while I swallowed some chocolate.

We had a long talk about Berlioz, in the course of which Nikolai Andreyevich observed, "His music is a sort of revolution, for while it has freed our hands considerably and breathed new life into music, in and of itself (like every revolution), it's not very good. I exclude from this his real masterpieces, such as the scene of the Sylphs, the *Rákóczy March,* the very fine Dance of the Nubians, and a few other things."

We touched on the subject of ballet, a genre which is so fashionable these days, thanks to the success of Tchaikovsky's *Sleeping Beauty* and *Nutcracker.*

"As I see it," said Rimsky-Korsakov, "setting oneself the goal of writing good music, where there's really little need of it, already invites a sort of criticism and in any case points to an incorrect statement of the problem as well as to the thanklessness of the task itself."

10 March

In the course of discussing this season's symphonic concerts, I remarked to Nikolai Andreyevich, "Thank heavens, the winter is coming to an end, and soon we won't have to go to all those evenings at the Conservatory and the Hall of the Nobility."

In saying this I had in mind the low level of interest generated by the Erdmannsdörffer and Belyaev concerts (save for the second one, in memory of Borodin).

"If music is becoming a burden to you," retorted Rimsky-Korsakov, "what can we expect from others? Believe me, this testifies more eloquently than words to the fact that music has already experienced the period of its highest development and is now finally on the decline. The fact is that by now even I am tired of many things. During the entire winter, I honestly profoundly enjoyed only three performances: first, that of Glinka's inspired *Ruslan;* second, Haydn's Twelfth Symphony (102) (which remains charming and fresh to this day); third, Beethoven's *Leonore* Overture no. 3, conducted in a mediocre way by Galkin."

23 March

I quite unexpectedly found myself at the Rimsky-Korsakovs' for the performance of *Sadko.* Blumenfeld seemed very pleased with the opera, for after playing it through from beginning to end, he declared that the musical interest grows continuously with each act. For his part, Liadov praised the work for its very interesting, stageworthy libretto. And Stasov (for whom this performance was given), while disapproving the Venetian guest and most of the recitatives, nevertheless congratulated Rimsky-Korsakov heartily on the birth of this new, great opera, which, he said, occupies about the same place among Rimsky-Korsakov's works as the *Ring* does among the operas of Wagner.

The conversation turned to Laroche, and Glazunov told us something curious, that is, that Herman Augustovich really dislikes Tchaikovsky's operas, especially *The Enchantress*. This partly explains why his article on Tchaikovsky as a dramatic composer[14] turned out to be so ridiculous. They say that he was pressured to write this article by friends of Tchaikovsky and he did so against his will.

"By the way," said Liadov, "I have a very interesting letter which Laroche sent me early in our acquaintanceship, in which he says, among other things, that with Gluck, Mozart, Meyerbeer, Wagner, Glinka, and Rimsky-Korsakov the music illustrates the text, while in Tchaikovsky there is seldom any relationship between the music and what they're singing about."

24 March

Commenting on yesterday's performance of *Sadko* and Stasov's "congratulations," Nikolai Andreyevich said that he would be willing to bet anything that Vladimir Vasilyevich did not understand the opera at all, even though he compared it with the *Ring.*

10 April

This evening I discussed with Nikolai Andreyevich the influence of Balakirev's music on his own. Indeed, upon careful analysis of the works of these two composers, we find some resemblances. Thus in Balakirev's *Lear* Overture there are certain elements which were incorporated later into the melodic characterization of Ivan the Terrible (in *The Maid of Pskov*). His *Tamara* and *Georgian Song*[15] introduced into contemporary music the new, so-called Balakirevian East,[16] reflections of which are to be found in Egypt and the Indian dance (with chorus) in *Mlada*, in the third movement of *Sheherazade* (at the point where the Queen is carried in on the palanquin), etc. Besides this, *Tamara* also left its mark on the clarinet cadenzas from *Sheherazade* as well as on the theme of *Mlada*, although, of course, the true source of the latter was not *Tamara* but Liszt's *St. Elizabeth* or Wagner's *Parsifal*. Melodic elements of the poetic duettino between Pannochka and Levko (in *May Night*) and the harmonic episode (example 23) incorporated in the poetic portrait of the gazelle (the Peri Gul Nazar) in Rimsky-Korsakov's *Antar* were foreshadowed—in part at least—in Balakirev's *Song of the Golden Fish*. Again, in his *Barcarolle*, at the words "Pogovori so mnoiu," one detects a suggestion of the charming melodic phrase (example 24) later encountered in Rimsky-Korsakov's song "Ia veru, ia lubim" at the words "ne mozhet litsemerit"—though here this phrase is much more beautiful and moving.

Example 23

Example 24

I have not even mentioned the last song (no. 20, *Dream*) of Balakirev's first song cycle, in which—at the words "Slovo liubvi preryvala poroiu" or "Tusklye zvezdnye ochi" (examples 25 and 26)—there occur melodic phrases absolutely identical with excerpts from Korsakov's *Iuzhnaia noch'* (examples 27 and 28) which, by the way, Rimsky-Korsakov dedicated to Balakirev.

These examples by no means exhaust the question of Balakirev's influence on Rimksy-Korsakov.

Example 25

(slightly faster)

Slo- vo lub- vi pre- ry- va- la po- ro- u

(slightly faster)

Example 26

Tusk- ly- e zvezd-ny- e o- chi

(softer)

(softer and slower)

ppp

Example 27

Di- koi vo- li pol- na, za- kho- di- la vol- na,

mf

Example 28

Po- spe- shai na svi- da- n'e lub- vi!

(a tempo)

Later we talked about the second movement of *Antar*,[17] which contains intimations of the future "harmonies of Morena" (in *Mlada*), and also about the fourth movement of this suite. The latter is Rimsky-Korsakov's favorite movement, especially the very end, which seems to melt away in the mysteriously tender chords of the ninth.

"All the same," remarked Rimsky-Korsakov, "some of *Antar* will have to be rescored somewhat, mainly to heighten the importance of the strings."[18]

On my remarking that much of the new Russian music has already entered a period of intelligent and sober criticism, Rimsky-Korsakov said; "That's because the cycle has been completed; everything has been said. With Glazunov's latest symphonies—the Fifth and Sixth—and the works of Scriabin something new is already emerging. What the outcome will be is still open to question."

9 May

This being Nikolai Andreyevich's name day, I visited him in the evening. Glazunov was also there. Chatting with me about this and that, Nikolai Andreyevich mentioned that during this period he has composed sixteen songs, to words by Maikov, Fet, Pushkin, Mey (after Mickiewicz), Alexei Tolstoi, Lermontov, and so on.[19] He is thinking of writing more things in this genre, also of completing *Anchar*.

"However, you won't care for any of the songs I've written," he added, "for they are not marked either by particularly profound harmony or by supernatural beauty."

Besides this, Nikolai Andreyevich informed me that he has agreed to take the chairmanship of our Music Society temporarily and is considering beginning his activity with a revival of *Boris Godunov,* but only God knows. . . .

The Korsakovs have rented a dacha on Lake Cheremenetskoye, twenty versts from Luga and five from Stelyovo. The estate, which belongs to Glinka-Mavrin, is called Smychkovo.

19 May

Realizing that Rimsky-Korsakov is very busy at this time, I decided not to disturb him with a separate farewell visit but simply to drop by today, as I always do on Monday, to return the rough draft of *Sadko* and four-hand music *(Sheherazade,* quartet, etc.) which I had borrowed.

Rimsky-Korsakov seemed to be in excellent spirits. He told me that he has dedicated one of his new songs, *Redeet oblakov letuchaia griada* (words by Pushkin), to me.

"I haven't played these songs for you," he added, smiling, "because you once forbade me to write anything after *Sadko.*"

When I asked what kind of song it is, he replied that it contains none of the sequences I love so much but has an unusually difficult accompaniment.

Since Nadezhda Nikolayevna had to go for the final shopping and Nikolai Andreyevich had to be at the Conservatory by eight o'clock, I left with him at about seven-thirty. At the gate I embraced him heartily, thanked him again for his dedication, and we took leave of each other for the summer.

And so we have come to the end of the season, a season not without interest.

Visit to Smychkovo

30 June and 1 July

I arrived at Smychkovo just after noon on the day of the Rimsky-Korsakovs' silver wedding anniversary [June 30]. Nikolai Andreyevich, indeed everyone, was very glad to see me, especially since I had brought mail, newspapers, and telegrams from Luga.

At about two o'clock, lunch was served, and then we all went for a stroll, first along the picturesque banks of the Luga River, and after that to a high hill before which lay a wonderful panorama of fields, meadows and, in the distance, a mill.

Nikolai Andreyevich mentioned that during the month of June, he had composed seventeen new songs, including duets, and that he is thinking of continuing to write in this genre. Besides this, he has carefully gone through the piano score of Dargomyzhsky's *Stone Guest* and has come to the sad conclusion that it contains a good deal of harmonic nonsense, which would have to be corrected before it could be rescored. In Nikolai Andreyevich's opinion, it is in this opera that the "harmonic evil" of Mussorgsky's works is rooted.

"I definitely want to write an article on the question of the deafness of composers," said Nikolai Andreyevich, "a deafness which afflicted not only Mussorgsky and Dargomyzhsky of the *Stone Guest* period but also Beethoven, Wagner, Liszt, and even Tchaikovsky, to say nothing of Messrs. d'Indy and co. Just recall the beginning of the second presto from the Finale of the Ninth Symphony, before the recitative 'O Freunde, nicht diese Töne,' where the orchestra plays C sharp, D E F G A B flat [example 29]. Remember the musically absurd characterization of Hagen in Wagner's *Götterdämmerung* [example 30], the strange F sharp against F natural in the double basses (on pages 46–47 of the score) of Liszt's *Mephisto Waltz;* or the equally incomprehensible D-flat triad on a pedal point in D natural found in Tchaikovsky.

Example 29

Example 30

"One is forced to conclude," he continued, "that in music, as in the other arts, there are 'divine laws,' which had their origin in spontaneous creativity, and 'human laws,' which were introduced into the art by the whim of some artist or other, as, for example, the use of the 6/4 chord, not in a final cadence or as a 'passing triad' but in the form of an independent chord in the middle of a musical statement; the former—'the divine laws'—are infinitely superior to the second. That's why, strictly speaking, it's hardly possible now to blaze really new trails in music, only to continue in the direction provided long ago if only in embryo by classical music. For if an artist has deviated sharply like, for example, Berlioz, Mussorgsky, Richard Strauss, d'Indy, the result has turned out to be absolute nonsense."

As we approached the house, Rimsky-Korsakov resumed our conversation.

"You cannot imagine," he said, "how moved I am by the fact that, at the very beginning of his career, Tchaikovsky was able to renounce everything for music. This resolution attested more eloquently than words to his deeply artistic nature. Here I am, for example, I couldn't bring myself to take such a step and I continued to serve [in the Navy]. And this is regrettable for, if I hadn't, then I wouldn't have later had to revise *The Maid of Pskov, Sadko,* and *Antar.*"

Thanks to the magnificent weather, dinner waas served in the garden. What with the ices, *zakuski,* and champagne, it lasted from six until seven-thirty and was very merry and lively. After dinner everyone went into the sitting room, where, at our request, Nikolai Andreyevich played all of his "June" songs and duets except the ballad *Switezianka,*[20] which has not yet been completely finished.

The following is a list of these songs, including dates of composition:

June 5:(1) *On spit, velikii Pan* (Maikov).[21] Duet in strict Lydian A major. (N.B. this duet was begun in St. Petersburg on May 9).

June 5 also saw the composition of two more songs: (2) *Ne veter, veia s vysoty* (A. K. Tolstoi) and (3) *Srezal sebe ia trostnik* (Maikov).

June 6:(4) *Zvonche zhavoronka pen'e* (A. K. Tolstoi).

June 7:(5) *Probuzhdenie* ("Mechty, mechty, gde vasha sladost'?") (Pushkin) and (6) *Oktava* (Maikov).

June 8:(7) *Svezhi dushist tvoi roskoshnyi venok* (Fet).

June 9:(8) *Ne penitsia more* (A. K. Tolstoi).

June 10:(9) *Drobitsia, i pleshchet, i bryzzhet volna* (A. K. Tolstoi).

June 19:(10) *Ekho* (Pushkin).

June 22:(11) *Prorok* (Pushkin).

June 23:(12) Duet set to words from *The Song of Songs* ("Ia tsvetok polevoi") translated by Mey; (13) completion of *Anchar* (Pushkin), which had been started on September 3, 1882.

June 25:(14) *Tikho, tikho more goluboe* (Maikov) and (15) *Mezh tremia moriami bashnia* (Maikov, after modern Greek poets).

June 29:(16) *Nenastnyi den' potukh* (a very gloomy song to words by Pushkin).[22]

Between the performance of the songs, we talked about the writer Vladimir Korolenko and at about midnight, we all went to our rooms.

I rose fairly early. However coffee soon appeared, after which Nikolai Andreyevich and I went for a stroll in the garden. We talked first about his new duet—*Pan* (to words by Maikov), written in a severe Greek style and which, owing to its antique vein, will never please the public; then about the strikingly inspired and airy beginning and end of the Chorus of Flowers in Glinka's *Ruslan*.

Later we had a detailed discussion of Haydn's wonderful symphonies (the first twelve)[23]—full of life and musical content—in which you sometimes come upon the most novel harmonies.

"And of these works, full of life and sound," said Rimsky-Korsakov, "Cui used to write that, like other classical music, they are dry and devoid of musical content."

Returning to the house, with Rimsky-Korsakov's permission, I looked through his new songs at the piano and, as always in such cases, learned some things by heart. When the time came to say good-bye, Rimsky-Korsakov embraced me warmly, thanked me again and again for my interest in his work and for having taken the trouble to visit him in the country. At about six o'clock in the evening, Andrei, the Akhsharumovs, and I set out on our journey, and soon the homestead disappeared behind the trees.

6 October

When I arrived at the Rimsky-Korsakovs', at about six o'clock, I found the whole family in great agitation. It seems that there had recently appeared in the Czech newspaper *Národní Listy* an outrageous article denouncing Napravnik not only for failing to make Czech music known in Russia but even for deliberately suppressing "Russian art," not giving new Russian works a chance to be heard, all because of an agreement with Anton Rubinstein (!) so that, for instance, if *Sadko* is not given on the Imperial stage, the fault is solely and exclusively Napravnik's. In conclusion, to substantiate his claim, the author gave as the source of his information Rimsky-Korsakov's well-known friend Shtrup.

"What the devil is the meaning of this!" shouted Nikolai Andreyevich. "This misunderstanding must be cleared up as soon as possible. Where could it have come from? Just what did Nikolai Martynovich say? Napravnik will be terribly offended with me; he'll think that I'm the chief source of this undeserved charge."

My appearance somewhat quieted Rimsky-Korsakov and we began to talk about my meeting with Balakirev at Pypin's yesterday, where he interestingly played a program devoted entirely to Chopin's works: *Polonaise-Fantaisie;* two preludes (C minor and E-flat major); *Étude* (E-flat minor); Ballade no. 4 (F minor); Sonata in B-flat minor and the wonderful, infinitely sad Mazurka in F minor.[24] Mily Alexeyevich had recently received a letter from Warsaw and four little piano pieces ("Lullaby," "Autumn Night," "At the Source," and "En valsant") from a Polish woman named Wanda Landowska, completely unknown to him. The young composer, to whom music means everything (as she puts it), asked Balakirev to give her his opinion of her compositions.

"And you know," said Mily Alexeyevich, "contrary to expectations, I was absolutely delighted with them, for despite some insignificant, purely technical faults, they showed a striking talent."

During dinner, Rimsky-Korsakov related a very curious discussion he had with Stasov today, while chatting with him about a proposed new edition of Mussorgsky's *Banquet*[25] (with French text). He (Stasov) told Nikolai Andreyevich that recently, while writing in the words of the song, he had noticed quite by chance that despite the changes in the rhythm, the declamation was faulty. In view of this, he strongly urged Rimsky-Korsakov to make some corrections for the new edition. "Willingly," Rimsky-Korsakov said, "but I'm sure that while correcting the declamation, I shall also have to correct chords here and there; and not only in this song, but in the flawless *Nursery* as well."

"But why, Nikolai Andreyevich, didn't you tell Mussorgsky this in his lifetime?" asked Stasov.

"For two reasons," replied Rimsky-Korsakov. "First of all, I almost never told Modest Petrovich what I thought of him and his music; I didn't want to offend him to no purpose. Second—and this is the main reason—because at that time there was a very great deal that I myself didn't know and understand."

14 October

The Rimsky-Kosakovs' first musical evening of the season took place tonight. Among the many guests were Stasov, Belyaev, Glazunov, Liadov, the Blumenfelds, Shtrup, Dianin, and Belsky and his wife.

The evening began with a performance of Rimsky-Korsakov's poetic ballad for chorus, tenor, and soprano *Switezianka* (from the manuscript). After that, Anna Zherebtsova sang nine of Nikolai Andreyevich's new songs. After tea, the Blumenfeld brothers performed two marvelous songs, *Anchar* and *Prorok,* repeated at the request of Stasov who was completely enraptured by them; and also Mussorgsky's *Raek.*

The evening was very lively and we did not leave until two o'clock in the morning.

5 November

At the Rimsky-Korsakovs' second musical evening, the Blumenfeld brothers performed *Mozart and Salieri.* Looking through the orchestral manuscript of this work, I noted that it was not only composed but also orchestrated at Smychkovo by August 5; also that Nikolai Andreyevich intends to dedicate it to the memory of Dargomyzhsky.

After tea, Glazunov played his new song *Muza* (to words by Pushkin), which is dedicated to Nina Fried, and four numbers from his ballet *Raymonda.* Besides this, Felix Blumenfeld played Korsakov's *Pan.* At the end, at our request, *Mozart and Salieri* was repeated. Stasov is very enthusiastic about it.

"I always said, Nikolai Andreyevich," he said, "that you cannot write recitatives. Today I take this back, for I'm absolutely captivated by your

Mozart. What's more, I'm amazed at your courage—writing an opera in the style of *The Stone Guest.* All honor to you!"

To this Rimsky-Korsakov replied, half in jest, half seriously, that he had written the opera mainly "from self-esteem," and that if, sometime in the future, he feels old age coming on, he will certainly compose *The Covetous Knight* and *The Feast in Time of Plague,* since it is much easier to write in this style (that of *The Stone Guest*).

"Otherwise I shall return to my own former style," he said.

Liadov and Stasov, I learned, adore *Die Walküre,* but Glazunov is completely indifferent to it and, conversely, worships *Siegfried.*

15 November

The program of the first Russian Symphony Concert consisted of the following works: Rimsky-Korsakov's *Antar* (in the new version);[26] Lyubava's aria from *Sadko; Intermezzo*—Mussorgsky–Rimsky-Korsakov; Liadov's *Musical Snuffbox;* Borodin's *Central Asia;* songs by Balakirev, Cui, and Rimsky-Korsakov; and Balakirev's *Rus'.*

Regarding *Antar,* the most interesting number on the program, let me draw attention to the following two details: firstly, this Eastern suite lasts 30–31 minutes (first movement—13 minutes; second—6 minutes; third—4.5 minutes; fourth—7 minutes); second, in its original version (that is, the manuscript of 1868), the program of the fourth movement differed slightly from the present published version. Here is the original text in full with italics to designate those episodes of the program omitted from the published edition.

Fourth movement: Antar returned to the ruins of Palmyra, *never to leave there again.* The third and last delight was the joy of love. Antar implored the Peri to take away his life as soon as she perceives in him the slightest sign of estrangement, and she vowed to do this. When, after a long period of mutual happiness, the Peri noticed one day that he was lost in thought and gazing pensively into the distance, *two large tears flowed from her eyes,* she embraced Antar passionately, the force of her love inflamed his heart, and the Peri, with a last kiss, united Antar's soul with hers, and he went to his eternal rest on her breast.

Antar died but his soul will live forever lovingly in the soul of his beloved, never tasting the bitterness which follows this pleasure.

Meanwhile how can one explain the final 12 measures of the coda of *Antar,* the music of which suggests his languishing in the endless bliss of love, without the program cited above and, mainly, its concluding lines.

Stasov was very dissatisfied with the revised version of *Antar.* This in no way prevented him, however, from being the first to shout *bis* following The Joy of Revenge.

6 December

The program of the third concert of the Russian Musical Society consisted of Beethoven's *Eroica* Symphony, Tchaikovsky's B-flat minor Piano Concerto, and the so-called Suite for Orchestra and Chorus from Rimsky-Korsakov's opera-ballet *Mlada.*

The soloist in the Tchaikovsky Concerto, Osip Gabrilovich, scored a tremendous success; he was recalled many times and had to play an encore. As for Safonov, tonight he impressed me as a very mediocre conductor. His conducting of Beethoven's symphony and the *Mlada* suite was extremely coarse and banal. On the whole I am becoming increasingly disenchanted with our native conductors.

8 December

This evening I met Rimsky-Korsakov at my mother's. He had come to invite her, in person, to their musical evening.[27] We talked about Berlioz' *Harold,* which I find little to my liking, infinitely less so than the *Damnation of Faust.*

"It may strike you as strange," commented Rimsky-Korsakov, "but Berlioz' orchestration, despite its undeniable merits, is now somewhat out of date—through no fault of its own."

Further, regarding *Mozart and Salieri,* which is scored for small orchestra, Rimsky-Korsakov expressed the view that "when writing operas in the style of *The Stone Guest,* you have to strive consciously to be more spare."

I learned that Cui has recently completed his *Saracen,* an opera on the subject of Dumas père's drama *Charles VII chez ses grands vassaux;*[28] that this fall Rimsky-Korsakov's *Snegurochka* was given three times at the Bolshoi Theater in Moscow; and that later on this month, *Sadko* is going to be given at the Solodovnikov Theater,[29] under the direction of Esposito. "I think, though, this performance," he said "will be extremely weak, as both the chorus and orchestra are small. However, what God gives . . ."

Rimsky-Korsakov has asked Belyaev to publish the orchestral score of act 3 of *Mlada* separately so that it may be given in concert performance.

29 December

At about six o'clock, I went to the Rimsky-Korsakovs' only to find that they were just about to leave for Moscow for the third and fourth performances of *Sadko*. Therefore, after congratulating Nikolai Andreyevich on the striking success of this marvelous opera (as reported by eyewitnesses), I took my leave.

At this point it is of interest to report what Moscow's leading newspapers had to say about *Sadko*. *Russkie vedomosti* carried a lengthy article by the well-known Moscow critic Kashkin, in which he said: "The Russian Private Opera of the Solodovnikov Theater has been granted the honor and even the historic mission of presenting the first performance of this most remarkable work, with which we became acquainted on December 26."

On the day after the premiere, *Moskovskie vedomosti* carried a very favorable article, signed "V" (actually written by Yevgeny Petrovich Veinberg, son of Peter Isayevich Veinberg).

Sadko without doubt enjoyed tremendous success in Moscow. The entire press received it with extreme warmth and, in this regard, has far outstripped our arrogant and envious Petersburg critics.

CHAPTER 8

1898

9 January

At the dress rehearsal of the third Russian Symphony Concert I saw Nikolai Andreyevich only in passing.[1] However I did have a talk with his son Mikhail Nikolayevich, from whom I learned that at the third and fourth performances of *Sadko*[2] Rimsky-Korsakov had received four laurel wreaths[3] and a magnificent, large silver one from Mamontov; also that at the fourth performance the theater was filled to overflowing.

On that occasion the Sea Princess was sung by Zabela (whom Rimsky-Korsakov regards as truly ideal for this important and vocally difficult role) and the Viking Guest, impromptu, by Chaliapin, who had already caused a sensation in Moscow with his wonderfully original portrayal of Ivan the Terrible (in *The Maid of Pskov*).

Besides this, Mikhail Nikolayevich told me that Nikolai Andreyevich recently wrote a duet, *Gornyi kliuch,* to words by Maikov,[4] and that he plans to go to Moscow again to conduct (gratis, of course) a concert of Russian music,[5] which Mamontov is thinking of giving at his own expense.

At the concert today[6] I did not get to see Rimsky-Korsakov, since I did not go down during the interval. I only followed from the distance his calm, assured, and, at the same time, artistic and intelligent conducting, which, for these very qualities, is considered by many cold and even lifeless. No wonder, for here, as everywhere else, everything is judged by outward appearances, without a thought being given to the inner meaning of anything.

Late in the afternoon I went to the Rimsky-Korsakovs' to see Nikolai Andreyevich after his return from Moscow and to congratulate him once more on the increasing success of *Sadko* and, above all, to learn some details about the meeting of Rimsky-Korsakov and Count Leo Tolstoy[7]—these two antipodes on questions of aesthetics.[8]

Regarding *Sadko,* Rimsky-Korsakov told me that both the third and the fourth performances had gone quite well, and that most of the soloists—Sekar-Rozhansky (Sadko), Chaliapin (Viking Guest), Negrin-Shmidt, and Zabela (the Sea Princess)—were positively charming.

I remarked that I myself never expected that an opera, and what is more, an opera-*bylina* like *Sadko,* could have found such immediate favor with the Muscovites.

"Who would have thought it possible?" said Rimsky-Korsakov with a smile. "I wasn't counting on a success. Now, however, I'm convinced that the public can respond to absolutely any kind of music, from the very worst to the very best, provided the performance is interesting to watch and, at the same time, intelligible. That's the whole secret."

We went on to discuss the two highly sympathetic articles by Veinberg and Kashkin[9] (in *Moskovskie vedomosti* and *Russkie vedomosti,* respectively),[10] citing Veinberg's true and wise observation that the Viking Guest's brilliant barcarolle (which Kashkin hates), with its echoes of Schubert's "Auf dem Wasser zu singen," contains a great deal of subtle irony and intentionally simple effects, such as the hold on the high G sharp at the end.

"You must have noticed in reading Kashkin's article that he didn't understand my St. Nicholas at all," said Rimsky-Korsakov, "since, regarding Lyubava's prayer (in scene 3) and the scene in which the Apparition appears (scene 4), he wrote: 'At the very end (of scene 3), the music goes off-key. In the eight measures of Lyubava Buslayevna's prayer, the accompaniment of the orchestra sounds as though it is imitating the highest registers of an organ with a sustained low pedal point. Such a Catholic mode of expression[11] is not in keeping with the sentiments of the wife of a merchant of Novgorod.'

"And further: 'When the Apparition appears—the Starchishche Moguch-Bogatyr in the dress of a wandering pilgrim—and strikes Sadko's *gusli* with a stick, this causes the dancing to stop immediately.'

" 'Here,' writes Kashkin, 'the characterization of this Apparition is not entirely comprehensible to us. It seems as though there is an organ in the orchestra and, at the end of the old man's speech, we hear Lyubava Buslayevna's prayer from the end of scene 3[12] again. This does not seem quite Russian in form.'

"Meanwhile, all this is actually simple," continued Rimsky-Korsakov. "The fact is that Veinberg understood this scene when he wrote: 'The old man's splendid arioso "Ai, ne v poru raspliasalsia grozen Tsar' morskoi" with organ-like accompaniment has a liturgical character and, unquestionably, indicates the supreme power, which all the monsters of the sea and their king—all the dark forces of nature—obey.' "

On the whole, Rimsky-Korsakov seemed very pleased with the Moscow reviews of *Sadko,* especially Kashkin's.

At the end, Nikolai Andreyevich gave me an account of their totally unexpected introduction to the wife of Count Leo Tolstoy (through Vladimir Vasilyevich Stasov), their evening visit to the Tolstoys, and the nonsensical views on aesthetics which the writer obviously regards as the truth.

"When we arrived at the Tolstoys'," began Rimsky-Korsakov, "we found the author of *War and Peace* and *Anna Karenina* sitting as usual in his workman's blouse, worn over a nightshirt. His hands had been scrubbed with a sweet-smelling toilet soap, but his boots (which, by the way, were exceedingly filthy) stank of tar! During the conversation, Lev Nikolayevich often became terribly excited, grabbed my hands, and interrupted repeatedly.

"Besides us," continued Rimsky-Korsakov, "there were Vladimir Stasov (who didn't stay to the end; at the height of our argument he became terrified and ran off home in my fur coat), the sculptor Ginsburg, and someone else, whom I didn't know and was never introduced to.

"Before tea the conversation was rather general, but after tea, as Nadezhda Nikolayevna and I were about to leave, Lev Nikolayevich insisted that we stay, saying he would like very much to question me personally about something. We remained, and immediately we fell to talking about problems of art, about beauty—this 'putrifying,' 'stinking' (in Tolstoy's view) 'ulcer' on art; about Balakirev, of whom Lev Nikolayevich knew nothing, or rather, whose song *Slyshu li golos tvoi* he likes very much (he even remembered that it is in the key of C, though he didn't know the author of it and whether he is alive)."

As the conversation continued, it became clear that Tolstoy hates Beethoven because of his outbursts of passion, but, until now, he has not been able to give up Chopin's music altogether, something which depresses him beyond words.[13]

"I told him," said Rimsky-Korsakov, "that I, on the contrary, am very happy that I idolize not only Chopin but also Beethoven, and I don't regret it for a minute."

"Every genuine, really good work of art," continued Count Lev Nikolayevich, "must above all be simple and clear, so that it can be understood equally by a 'coachman' and a 'nobleman,' as, for example, Handel's *Aria*[14] or Chopin's Nocturne in E flat. Otherwise, it's worthless," etc., etc.

"When I began to tell him," said Rimsky-Korsakov, "that if, as even he himself acknowledges, art ennobles and elevates man's soul, then it can only uplift, it cannot debase; that his *Childhood* and *Boyhood, War and Peace,* and *Anna Karenina* are strikingly artistic creations, and yet they're not simple and are filled with beauty, Lev Nikolayevich did not stop to hear me out, saying that he despises himself for these novels, and what's more they're absolutely worthless."

Tolstoy has never seen the opera *Sadko*—he doesn't keep up with contemporary music. He hates Wagner, obviously without knowing him at all, since, on his own admission, he was so irritated by *Siegfried*—this "revolting" opera—that he could barely sit through the first act of it.[15]

At about twelve-thirty, when the Rimsky-Korsakovs began to take their leave, Lev Nikolayevich came out to see them off. And as they stood in the entrance hall, in reply to Nadezhda Nikolayevna's apologies for having, perhaps, disturbed him, he muttered: "Not at all. To me it's been very interesting today to come face to face with gloom."[16]

"These words," said Nikolai Andreyevich, "I'm going to have engraved on a little gold plate as a memento and set it before me on my writing table for my greater edification. However, I'm certainly not going to read his book on art. I can just imagine how much nonsense it contains and how much harm it will do to our young people, who are confused enough without this and, generally speaking, not much interested in art."

8 February

Rimsky-Korsakov visited us from four o'clock until five-thirty. We had a rather long discussion about Glazunov's ballet *Raymonda*—its wonderful music, superb orchestration, and utterly mediocre plot.

Then we exchanged ideas about Mozart's *Don Giovanni*—the delightful duet "Là ci darem la mano," Don Giovanni's poetic serenade with its charming mandolin accompaniment, the interesting music expressing Leporello's fright, and the majestic, even grandiose scene with the Commendatore.

"All this is still new," remarked Rimsky-Korsakov, "almost contemporary."

Besides this, we discussed the contemplated visit to Petersburg of the Moscow Company of the Solodovnikov Theater (Mamontov's) and their intention to give *Sadko, The Maid of Pskov, May Night, Khovanshchina,* and *Orpheus* during Lent.

At present Rimsky-Korsakov is writing a prologue to *The Maid of Pskov.* Following this he will start working on another Russian opera.

"Russian without fail," he said with a laugh, then added: "I'll never be unfaithful to our fatherland, save in little things."

11 February

When I arrived at the Rimsky-Korsakovs' at about half past eight, I found Nikolai Andreyevich alone. We looked through the orchestral score of *Mozart and Salieri.* Then we chatted about the newly published collection of the critical articles of the late Peter Ilyich Tchaikovsky from the years 1868–1876 (with a foreword by Laroche),[17] which was presented to

Rimsky-Korsakov by Modest Ilyich Tchaikovsky with the following inscription: "To the great composer and friend of Peter Ilyich—Nikolai Andreyevich Rimsky-Korsakov—from a devoted M. Tchaikovsky. 16/1/1898." Interestingly, Peter Ilyich's critical activity had begun with an article in defense of Rimsky-Korsakov's *Fantasia on Serbian Themes*.[18] Years later, upon hearing *Sadko*, Modest Tchaikovsky was so taken with it that in a letter to Stasov he called it the foremost opera after Glinka's *Ruslan*.

After tea, at my request, Nikolai Andreyevich and Nadezhda Nikolayevna played (four-hands) Strauss, *Also sprach Zarathustra*, which was written, according to the title, "frei nach Nietzsche." You have only to recall the middle of this musically incomprehensible symphonic poem with its utterly banal and insipid waltz, constructed on the C-major triad, or its absolutely senseless ending (in B and C major simultaneously) and you will agree with Rimsky-Korsakov that d'Indy, Fauré, and the rest are "innocent babes" when it comes to "cacophony" and that Strauss is surely a madman, musically.

"But then, who knows," said Nikolai Andreyevich, "perhaps this poem and his other orchestral works are nothing more than a hoax, a mockery of contemporary music and the people (like Nikisch and others) who might be able to understand such utter nonsense.

"I can just imagine," he continued, "how ecstatic the composer of *Zarathustra* must be when conducting Mozart's *Don Giovanni!*"

22 February

This morning I went to the rehearsal of *The Maid of Pskov*.[19] As of now it is not going too well.

When the rehearsal ended, I accompanied Rimsky-Korsakov to Zagorodny[20] to pick up a copy of the score of *Sadko*. On the way, we talked about the orchestration of *The Maid of Pskov*, and Nikolai Andreyevich said that he finds it heavy, but that now, in *Sadko* (and to some extent earlier, in *Christmas Eve*), he has completely "recovered" from this aberration to which the *Ring* had led him at one time. For despite Wagner's undeniable genius (he concluded), he erred a great deal not only with respect to questions of music drama but even in the sphere of orchestration. One has only to recall his *Tristan*.

This evening the opera-*bylina Sadko* was given its first performance in the Hall of the Conservatory. The theater was filled to overflowing. In-

cluded in the cast were Sekar-Rozhansky (Sadko), Zabela (Princess Vol-
kova), Selyuk-Raznatovskaya (Lyubava Buslayevna), Strakhova (the *gusli*
player Nezhata), Sokolov (St. Nicholas), Bedlevich (Sea King), Chernenko
(Sea Queen), Mutin (Viking Guest), Karklin (Indian Guest); Petrov (Venetian Guest), et al. Esposito conducted. The sets and costumes were by
Korovin and Malyutin.

The performance ended around twelve-thirty. There was no end of
curtain calls. Rimsky-Korsakov was presented with a wreath. At the conclusion of the opera, a large group of students went to the artists' room
to thank him for the enormous pleasure he had given them.

"I'm glad, very glad, gentlemen, that you're pleased with my *Sadko,*"
said Rimsky-Korsakov smiling, as he shook hands with each one of them.

23 February

I attended the performance of *The Maid of Pskov* tonight. Chaliapin was
brilliant in the role of Ivan the Terrible, Zabela very charming as Olga.
At the end of act 2, she was presented with a basket of flowers. Even
though the theater was not filled, the opera enjoyed an overwhelming
success.

3 March

Tonight I heard *Die Meistersinger* for the first time in my life. I was
absolutely transported, although the long-windedness here and there (usual
with Wagner) did mar the overall effect.

As my wife and I were leaving the theater, we ran into the Rimsky-
Korsakovs, and then and there, on the staircase, we got into an argument
about Wagner.

"Awfully long. I'm completely exhausted," declared Nikolai Andreyevich.

I, on the contrary, was terribly taken with this marvelous opera.

6 March

At five o'clock, after dinner at my mother's, I dropped in on Nikolai
Andreyevich to congratulate him on his fifty-fourth birthday. Glazunov
and Stasov were also there. We read Cui's article on *Sadko,*[21] which, like

all his articles on Rimsky-Korsakov, abounds in half-derogatory, half-laudatory statements and, incidentally, refers to Lyubava as Sadko's "home-port wife." In general, there was a great deal of arguing and laughter.

Rimsky-Korsakov mentioned that someone from *Peterburgskaia gazeta* had tried unsuccessfully to interview him.

"You know, I didn't receive him," he said, "saying that I don't grant interviews, but if I did, I certainly wouldn't be inclined to say anything to this newspaper, for the work of whose principal critic (Baskin) I've always had nothing but contempt.

"So, he left empty-handed," he added with a chuckle.

At tonight's performance of *The Maid of Pskov,* they are going to play the entire introduction to act 3 (the storm, royal hunt, and the chorus "Dubravushka"), and Chaliapin will sing his arioso (in *modo phrygico*) in this act, which, by the way, was dedicated to him.[22]

In the evening, at the end of the performance, I saw Nikolai Andreyevich again, in the artist's room. He had been presented with a wreath of artificial laurels, and on Wednesday (the fourth) at the only performance of *May Night* (which I had not attended) he was also given two wreaths.

14 March

I went to the so-called dress rehearsal of *Snegurochka.* Zabela is not singing the title role; she has been replaced by a new protégée of Mamontov, one Mlle Paskhalova, a graduating student at the Moscow Conservatory, a not bad-looking young lady with a thoroughly mediocre voice. Clearly, all the trouble with Russian music stems from the fact that it is propagated not by artists, but by rich men and merchants, Mitrofans and Savvas.[23] This is why Zabela does not sing, the Felix Blumenfelds play, and even Sigismund Blumenfeld accompanies in the Assembly Hall of the Nobility.

Rimsky-Korsakov was obviously tired—"worn out," as he put it. They somehow managed to go through the prologue and first two acts four times without Lel and the fourth French horn and second clarinet. When the rehearsal ended, there suddenly occurred a small but nevertheless very unpleasant incident. As they were about to repeat the final chorus of the Berendeys (at the end of act 2), Nikolai Andreyevich, in an effort to make clear to them where to start, began to sing the theme of the chorus. At that moment, one of the choristers mimicked him in a squeaky voice. Rimsky-Korsakov flew into a rage.

"It's not my fault that I have no voice," he shouted, turning to the chorus. "I can't help that. But then perhaps I have something else, which not one of you has."

He was terribly agitated; he struck the conductor's stand so hard with his baton that he almost broke it. When they had gone through the entire chorus, he stood up and without a good-bye to anyone, exclaimed for all the hall to hear, " 'Till tomorrow . . . with Esposito!"

16 March

Thanks to the absence of Zabela and the presence of Paskhalova, Lyubatovich, and Bedlevich, *Snegurochka* went very badly; it was only in the third and fourth acts that it created a relatively better impression. Nikolai Andreyevich himself directed, but this was of little help. When he entered, the orchestra greeted him with three flourishes, and at the beginning of each act, they applauded him loudly.

Although the theater was not filled, the performance was fairly well attended. It dragged on until twelve-thirty.

29 March

About thirty people attended the musical evening at the Rimsky-Korsakovs' tonight, among them Liadov, Glazunov, Stasov, Lapshin, Morskoi, Chaliapin, Larina, Zabela and her husband, the two Blumenfelds, and the Belskys.

In the course of the evening, Zabela, Morskoi, Larina, Chaliapin, Sigismund Blumenfeld, and Sofia Nikolayevna sang songs and operatic arias (more than twenty-five in all), mostly by Rimsky-Korskaov. In addition to the Song of the Viking Guest (from *Sadko*) and Ivan the Terrible's arioso (from the second version of *The Maid of Pskov*), Chaliapin sang Mussorgsky's *Trepak* and Varlaam's "Kak vo gorode bylo vo Kazani" (from *Boris Godunov*) and Dargomyzhsky's *Staryi Kapral*. Larina sang three songs by Strauss and one by d'Indy. They were all accompanied by Felix Blumenfeld.

I forgot to mention that when I arrived, Nikolai Andreyevich presented me with the copybook containing his song cycle *U more,*[24] appropriately inscribed.

All in all, it was a wonderful evening.

11 April

The concert given by the Free Music School could not have gone better.[25] It was even well attended. The works presented before intermission were Liapunov's *Solemn Overture on Russian Themes* (premiere) and *Ballade* for orchestra, two choruses from Liszt's *Prometheus,* and three songs by Balakirev. The second half of the program was devoted to the premiere of Balakirev's Symphony no. 1 in C, with the composer conducting.[26]

During intermission, before the Symphony began, Balakirev was presented with a host of wreaths, to three flourishes by the orchestra and great bursts of applause. Istomin then came out onto the stage and read a mediocre address (written, they say, by Terty Ivanovich Filippov), and Liapunov presented the guest of honor with a cast of Liszt's hand. More wreaths were brought out. In short, the tribute to Mily Alexeyevich was a great success.

At the end of the symphony, Balakirev was recalled many times. Finally, when the audience crowded around the stage and insisted that he come out again, he descended the steps and embraced many of the men and kissed the ladies' hands.

12 April

I spent the entire afternoon (from noon until six o'clock) at the Rimsky-Korsakovs'. Besides me there were Krugilov and Valentin Alexandrovich Serov (son of the composer), who was painting a portrait of Nikolai Andreyevich. With mock seriousness, Rimsky-Korsakov tried to convince Serov that he wanted terribly to look younger in the portrait and most important of all, he would like his frock coat and cravat to be slightly darker blue. This occasioned much laughter.

We read a pompous and stupid little article on *Sadko* by Yevgeny Petrovsky.[27] Clearly, there will always be Bulgarins and Baskins in Russia!

Commenting later on Russian composers, Nikolai Andreyevich said that official duties had always severely hampered their creative activity, and that he does not consider himself as having become a real musician and composer until 1873, when he finally shed his hated naval uniform and was appointed inspector of the naval bands.

From further conversation, I learned that *Mozart and Salieri* is not going to be given,[28] because after six weeks Chaliapin has not managed to learn his role and cannot sing it without the music.

Besides this, Feodor Ivanovich has lost the proofs of *Anchar* and *Prorok.*[29]

I leafed through the orchestral manuscript of the prologue to *The Maid of Pskov,* which had been partly composed anew and partly revised. It was titled "In the Chambers of Boyarina Vera Sheloga" and dated 1877–81 and 1898.[30]

On the whole, Rimsky-Korsakov was exceedingly warm and affable today.

19 April

The final performance of *Sadko* attracted a relatively large audience. After the fourth scene, Rimsky-Korsakov was called out twice, after the sixth—three times. The opera enjoyed a considerable success.

Thus, the Petersburg season of the Moscow Private Opera has ended. From February 22 to April 19, *Sadko* was given nine times: on February 22, 24, and 27; March 5, 17, and 25; April 10, 15, and 19. If we add to this the fact that this opera was given fifteen times in Moscow, then we can see that between December 26, 1897, and April 19, 1898, *Sadko* was presented twenty-four times.

21 April

Besides me, the other guests at the Rimsky-Korsakovs' tonight were Nikolai Mikhailovich Nolle, Sigismund Blumenfeld, Belsky, Shtrup, and Zabela and her husband, M. A. Vrubel.

Before tea they engaged in a long and lively argument about Count

Leo Tolstoy's brochure *What Is Art?*, a work devoted to a total rejection of everything usually considered art, and above all, beauty.

After that, the conversation centered on Mamontov's theater, which is planning to give Cui's *Angelo* and Mussorgsky's *Boris Godunov* (as completed by Rimsky-Korsakov) next season. Savva Ivanovich Mamontov, it seems, has his own very special opinion about the voice. For example, he divides mezzo-sopranos into "pure ones" (Mme Rostovtseva) and "roof-shakers" (Balbanova, Chernenko).

After tea Nolle sang three fairly good songs: *Slykhali l' vy,* by Anton Rubinstein, and two by Felix Blumenfeld. Then, although she did not feel entirely well, Zabela sang Rimsky-Korsakov's *Nespiashchikh solntse* (twice), *O chem v tishi nochei,* and *Ne penitsia more* (also twice).

In conclusion, at Nikolai Andreyevich's request, Zabela also sang the Sea Princess' wonderful, poetic lullaby from *Sadko,* and with this the evening came to a close.

By now it was late, so we all stood up and began to say good-bye. Thus, the season of Korsakov musical evenings has ended.

9 May

I went to Pargolovo to congratulate Nikolai Andreyevich on his name day and to bring him a basket of artificial flowers from my mother.

Before lunch, just as I was about to read to him my analysis of the *Sadko* fantasy, in walked, one after the other, Belsky, Belyaev, Shtrup, A. N. Purgold, Dr. Spengler, Timofeyev, and some others, who had also come to pay their respects. Rimsky-Korsakov was in an excellent mood. They admired Serov's marvelous portrait of him, which was finished on May 5 and far surpasses Repin's.

Nikolai Andreyevich is eager to complete his new opera as soon as possible. He hopes to finish the first act by May 15, that is, within a month's time, so that he can begin work on another one.[31]

"You won't believe it," he said, "but even in the face of all the difficulties of getting them produced, it's extraordinarily tempting to write an opera. Such scope for the artist, such contrasts and variety!"

As we were going into the dining room, I mentioned to Rimsky-Korsakov that Balakirev was highly pleased with *Sadko,* though he maintained that the most wonderful moments in it, musically, were those in which one hears echoes of the earlier fantasy,[32] as, for example, "In the underwater realm."

"Well, I can't agree with this at all," countered Rimsky-Korsakov, "since neither the love duet in scene 2 nor the Sea Princess' lullaby in scene 7, both of which I myself like very much, was in the fantasy."

We touched briefly on the subject of singers, and Rimsky-Korsakov stated frankly that of all the voices, his favorite is the true soprano. To him this is the ideal, purely feminine voice.

We crossed the room and as we approached the window and caught sight of the buds just beginning to sprout on the shrubs and trees, Rimsky-Korsakov turned to me and said suddenly: "You know, in the spring, living in the city, as I must, I absolutely cannot look at foliage with indifference. Even when I pass by a public garden, I literally turn away from it—that's how strongly I'm affected by the very sight of green, reminder of the country, which I love so passionately and to which I'm drawn so irresistibly at this time of year."

Later, I brought up the subject of Rimsky-Korsakov's "sacred" music, whereupon he remarked, with a smile, that the "sacred" music in his secular works is much better than that which he had composed specifically for the church.[33] And indeed, we have only to recall his amazingly original introduction to St. Nicholas' speech (in *Sadko*) to agree with him:

Example 31

22 May

When I dropped in on Rimsky-Korsakov before work, I found him looking through the vocal score of *Snegurochka,* making changes here and there in preparation for a new edition with Russian and German texts (the latter translated by Bernhard).[34] He told me that he had promised

Shtrup and Belsky that he will play the first half of the prologue to *The Maid of Pskov* tonight, so I returned at around seven-thirty.

Speaking of his new opera, which begins immediately with a fast overture, Nikolai Andreyevich said that after he completes it, he thinks he will write another one, this time a "thoroughly decadent opera"[35] which will require the entire arsenal of Mamontov's lighting effects. After that he will compose nothing more for the stage.

For my part, I expressed the thought that an "introduction" following directly after a long overture, as, for example, in *Prince Igor* and *The Maid of Pskov,* mars somewhat the overall artistic effect; that however good the music may be, the sense of wholeness is destroyed. It is as though first you were to find yourself in a sumptuous hall, then in a small anteroom, and after that you again came into a series of magnificent salons.

"I agree with you," said Nikolai Andreyevich. "Actually, double introductions of this kind, double beginnings, as in my *Maid of Pskov,* are clearly an artistic blunder."

After tea he played the first half of his prologue twice. I was thoroughly enchanted by the power and, at the same time, extraordinary elegance of the Korsakov writing. What opera he is working on now, I do not know, but there is reason to believe it is *The Tsar's Bride.* In any case, the first act of this "secret" opera was completed May 17.

29 May

Today, two days before Rimsky-Korsakov's departure for Vechasha,[36] I dropped in on him to say good-bye. Belsky and Lapshin were also there. We got into a conversation about the musical decadents (Strauss, Schillings, d'Indy), Fauré, and César Franck. Reference was made to Mussorgsky's fairly good but very strange song *Noch'* (to a mutilated Pushkin text),[37] and to the fact that despite his amazingly original talent, of all the Russian composers, Mussorgsky was the most inclined to decadence and artistic chaos.

After tea, at our request, Rimsky-Korsakov played part of his prologue to *The Maid of Pskov* and four of his most recent songs: *Ia umer ot schast'ia* (to words by Uland, composed March 28, 1898), *Grechanka* (to words by Pushkin, composed March 31), *Snovedenie* (from Voltaire, Pushkin, composed April 12), and *Nimfa* (to words by Maikov, composed May 25). He played the songs several times, with Lapshin supplying the "voice" as best he could.

When Belsky and Lapshin left and Rimsky-Korsakov and I were alone, we talked about his latest works, noting that in them one senses a kind of "new style," a style which could be characterized by the word "flexible." This type of music is clearly evident especially in the songs of 1897–98 (except, of course, *Anchar* and *Prorok*) and in the arioso style of the recitatives of *Sadko* and *Mozart and Salieri*.

At about twelve-thirty I rose and began to take my leave. We embraced and bade good-bye until autumn.

19 September

At dinnertime, when I arrived at the Rimsky-Korsakovs', Nikolai Andreyevich was in his study going over the proofs of the overture and prologue to *The Maid of Pskov,* which he had just received from Bessel. We greeted each other warmly.

After inquiring about my summer at Parlovo, our little son, my mother and my wife, Nikolai Andreyevich told me that he will soon finish the orchestration of the second act of *The Tsar's Bride,* the opera he wrote in July, in Vechasha, on the subject of Mey's play of the same name (in a version by Tyumenev).[38] As of now it is in four acts.

"But the third act came out too short," he said, "so I'm going to combine it with the fourth into one act. That will be better."

Then he told me that they are preparing *Snegurochka* at the Marinsky Theater without him and even assigning roles without consulting him.

"One thing they needn't worry about," he added. "I won't go to the dress rehearsal even if they invite me, since by then my presence won't be of any use whatsoever. After all, Napravnik isn't going to 'rip apart' the score once it's been 'sewn up.' "[39]

In conclusion, we talked about Wagner. While Rimsky-Korsakov still retains his earlier respect for this composer's genius, he is coming more and more to dislike his style of writing, which has produced in the West, among his present-day (and incidentally untalented) followers, such ugly and outrageous creations as Strauss' *Guntram* and *Zarathustra* and Bruneau's *Messidor*.

10 October

I brought Rimsky-Korsakov Max Schillings' *Ingwelde,* Eugène d'Albert's *Gernot,* and Anton Bruckner's Mass in D minor to look through.

Chatting with him about this and that, I learned that *Snegurochka* has been postponed until November 6;[40] that on the thirteenth he is going to Moscow to conduct a concert on the seventeenth[41] in a program consisting of his own Third Symphony, the introductions to the first and third acts of Cui's *William Ratcliff,* Tchaikovsky's *Andante and Finale* (op. 79), the introduction to the Scene in the Temple from Taneyev's *Oresteia,* and the suite from Glazunov's *Raymonda.*

Finally, we discussed the songs of Schubert and Schumann—how enormously important they are in a historical sense, even though most of them have lost their former freshness and originality and, as a consequence, very few can stand up to strict criticism nowadays.

"Of course, such gentlemen as the German Bernhard will never understand this," remarked Rimsky-Korsakov.

22 October

I spent the entire evening with Rimsky-Korsakov. He told me he had received three laurel wreaths at the concert in Moscow on the seventeenth; also that he attended three rehearsals (two with piano and one with orchestra) of the second half of *Christmas Eve,* which is to be given soon at the Bolshoi Theater. On the eighteenth, the day of his departure, he attended the dress rehearsal of *Sadko,* which went very well. After that he dined at Mamontov's (they are on the best of terms again),[42] where he listened to his *Mozart and Salieri* (with Chaliapin and Inozemtsev) and *Boyarina Vera Sheloga* (with Mmes Gladkaya and Zabela), then went directly to the railroad station. Evidently he was very pleased with his Moscow visit.

We spoke about the new newspaper *Vestnik teatra i muzyki,*[43] published under the editorship of A. P. Koptyaev, to which I plan to contribute articles on the new Russian music and its representatives.

During tea G. N. Timofeyev appeared. The conversation concerned Napravnik's ill health and the fact that Felix Blumenfeld will conduct *Snegurochka,* the problems of Koptyaev's publication, and the need for clearly defined views and a certain measure of civic courage and even bravery on the part of both the editor and the contributors. Despite the many shortcomings of Findeisen's journal and even Petrovsky's stupid articles, Rimsky-Korsakov will not be unfaithful to Findeisen.

Apropos of music journals, we were reminded of an interesting interview with Tchaikovsky, which appeared in issue no. 2, 1892, of *Peterburgskaia zhizn'*.[44] It is also interesting to note, I said, that throughout his life Tchaikovsky held to the opinion of Rimsky-Korsakov expressed in his very first critical article.[45]

10 November

Tonight Rimsky-Korsakov and I talked about the Moscow production of *Christmas Eve*.[46] Judging from a letter from Kruglikov, the first four performances played to full houses.

We also took note that *Sheherazade* was played recently in London and that a heated controversy had broken out among the English over whether the clarinet runs in the third movement depict kisses!

Example 32

We discussed Schillings' *Ingwelde* and the unbearable boredom such music induces in the sober-minded listener; how poor it is in every respect, including the harmonic (despite its seeming seriousness and complexity). Then we turned our attention to the "neo-German" school, which recently has fallen deeply in love with sequences and stupid resolutions [see example 33].

Just before I left, we spoke briefly about A. P. Koptyaev's curious article "New Russian Music from a Cultural Point of View" (see *Severnyi vestnik* for 1897).[47]

Example 33

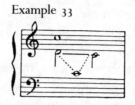

14 November

At the second concert of the Russian Musical Society, where, by the way, the incomparable French pianist Raoul Pugno[48] made his first appearance before the Petersburg public, they performed Rimsky-Korsakov's *Switezianka*. Safonov conducted; the soloists were Mme Butkevich and Morskoi (the latter was almost totally inaudible). The Cantata met with considerable success, despite the very mediocre performance. The composer was recalled at the end.

29 November

Rimsky-Korsakov reported to me that *Mozart and Salieri* had a favorable reception in Moscow, where it was given on November 25 together with Gluck's *Orpheus*.[49] It is being performed again today, this time not with *Orpheus* but with *May Night*. *Boris Godunov*[50] is to receive its first Moscow performance tomorrow (November 30).

After tea, Rimsky-Korsakov played through Scriabin's Prelude in E Minor (from the score), which is going to be performed at the Belyaev concert.[51] It proved to be a very charming little thing with piquant harmonization and fairly good orchestration.

I forgot to mention that speaking about Koptyaev and his strange views on art, Rimsky-Korsakov declared that in his opinion, there cannot nor should not be any such thing as a national form, whatever Mr. Koptyaev may claim; on the contrary, the form should be universal and the content—national, folk.

5 December

The first Russian Symphony Concert of the second season took place today, and it was very successful, even though, as usual, it was not well attended. The beginning, dance, and finale of Balakirev's *Tamara* are brilliant. The same can almost be said about Glazunov's incomparable Fifth Symphony.

Nikolai Andreyevich, Glazunov, his Symphony, and *Tamara* were received with great warmth, even though the Balakirev group did not applaud Rimsky-Korsakov at the end of *Tamara,* feeling that he had "made a mess of it" and had even done so "intentionally." I myself can testify that I have never heard this work played better; if the orchestra sounded thin, here and there, it was due not to some imagined ill will on Nikolai Andreyevich's part, but to Balakirev's orchestration, which is not flawless throughout.

12 December

When Rimsky-Korsakov arrived home for tea, he was obviously terribly upset. It seems that with the next Russian Symphony Concert scheduled for Friday, December 18[52] (only a week away), he has learned that the Assembly Hall of the Nobility will be occupied that entire day, and therefore the rehearsals will have to be held on Tuesday, Wednesday, and Thursday, with the last being the dress rehearsal. Zabela must be notified of this immediately.

Besides this, of late, certain critics, taking their cue from Bloch (Cui), have finally launched a campaign against the conductor Korsakov and the Russian Symphony Concerts in general.[53] In view of this, it would be most desirable to arrange to have a laurel wreath presented from the audience to Zabela at the coming concert.

During tea I related to Nikolai Andreyevich the following remark made by some general after he had heard *Mozart and Salieri* in Moscow. "I was so exasperated by this work," he said, "that I wanted to get my hands on Mozart and box his ears. And then I'd have liked to get hold of Salieri and box his ears, too."

"As you can see," I concluded, "neither *Christmas Eve, Switezianka,* nor *Mozart and Salieri* has had any luck."

"And what's more," said Rimsky-Korsakov, "it probably won't be long before they drop my *Snegurochka* from the repertoire."

15 December

Tonight, December 15, 1898, the long-promised performance of *Snegurochka* took place at the Marinsky Theater.[54] The theater was filled; all the critics were on hand. The cast included, among others: Snegurochka—Mravina (who, alas, has retained only the high notes), Mizgir—Yakovlev (only so-so), Spring—Fried (very good), Lel—Dolina (good), Kupava—Kozakovskaya (excellent), King of the Berendeys—Morskoi (generally poor, though he handled certain scenes, mainly the recitatives, well), Grandfather Frost—Serebryakov (fair), Bermyata—Maiboroda (?!), Bobyl—Urgrinovich (good); Bobylikha—Yunosova (fair). The orchestra was conducted by Felix Blumenfeld (poorly, lacking in nuance). The sets were good, even sumptuous (for example, the Palace of the King of the Berendeys), but lacking in style. The same may be said about the costumes, including the senseless attire of Lel (who looked more like a circus rider than a curly-headed shepherd boy) and the pseudo-Olympian tunic of Grandfather Frost, doomed to freeze for lack of sandals.

Despite all this, the opera had an enormous success. The cast and composer were called out many times after each act. In fact, Nikolai Andreyevich had to take twenty-one bows. Besides this, Mravina was presented with two baskets of flowers.

The opera ended at twelve-thirty. As we left, we were witnesses to a full lunar eclipse.

In conclusion permit me to quote the following excerpt from V. V. Stasov's reminiscences and notes about Viktor Mikhailovich Vasnetsov and his works (see the December volume, no. 3, of *Iskusstvo i khudozhestvennaia promyshlennost'* for 1898) regarding the question of the Berendeys: "Baron M. P. Klodt," writes Stasov, "conceived the idea of dressing the Berendeys in the costume of the Scyths,[55] so many wonderful examples of which are to be found in the Hermitage, made of gold, stone, terracotta, and other materials. However, this undertaking did not correspond fully to history, since the Berendeys were neither Scythian horsemen nor Slavonic farmers (Ostrovsky favored the latter), but some kind of unique, wild Turkic tribe. But, never mind, Baron Klodt's idea was original and well executed on the stage.

"Thus," adds Vladimir Vasilyevich, "everyone was satisfied."

19 December

The second Russian Symphony Concert of the season took place on the thirty-third anniversary of Rimsky-Korsakov's musical career.[56] The program consisted of Arensky's Second Symphony; Overture, Lullaby, Scene, and Narrative from Rimsky-Korsakov's musico-dramatic prologue *Boyarina Vera Sheloga* (with Zabela as Vera and Maximovskaya, a student of Iretskaya, as Nadezhda); *Elegy for Orchestra* (in Memory of Tchaikovsky) by Grechaninov; Aria from the opera *The Tsar's Bride* (also sung by Zabela); and *Dramatic Overture* by Wihtol.[57]

Maximovskaya's voice proved to be beautiful and powerful but still insufficiently developed. Zabela had an enormous, outstanding success. She repeated the aria with the orchestra (kneeling) and sang superlatively two new works by Rimsky-Korsakov: the song *Nimfa* (which was dedicated to her) and Marfa's second aria from *The Tsar's Bride* (scene 2, act 3). She was accompanied by Felix Blumenfeld. Following Vera Sheloga's Narrative, Nadezhda Ivanovna was presented with a large basket of flowers "From Petersburg admirers," and after Marfa's aria—with our laurel wreath.

After the overture to the Prologue, Rimsky-Korsakov was presented with a large laurel wreath from the students.

On the whole, the concert assumed a festive air.

20 December

I spent almost the entire day (from two o'clock until midnight) at the Rimsky-Korsakovs'. We talked at length about the orchestration and the music of *Vera Sheloga*. Somehow the Lullaby did not come out well, despite a relatively simple problem: the counterpoint in the violas was scarcely audible (should they not be doubled with a clarinet?). Meanwhile, the ending sounded coarse, since the flutes and clarinets stood out, not blending with the strings. In the overture the melodic passage in the strings was taken at too fast a tempo. When Ivan the Terrible's theme is stated, before Vera's words *"On . . . on,"* the scene drags and this is particularly noticeable during concert performance. At the end of Vera's Narrative, when the fanfare is repeated, the trumpets play too symmetrically, which perhaps is somewhat unnatural. However, all the rest is wonderful.

From further conversation I learned that Nikolai Andreyevich wrote not only *Nimfa* but *Son v letniuiu noch'* and the entire role of Marfa (in *The Tsar's Bride*) especially for Nadezhda Ivanovna's voice; that on December 18, as a memento of the hundredth anniversary of the Academy of Medicine, Nikolai Andreyevich received a special engraved medal (for Borodin's *Prince Igor*); that on the same day, *Sadko* had its first performance in Kharkov, under the direction of the well-known Kapellmeister Suk, and Prince Tsereteli (Impresario of the Kharkov Theater) sent him a telegram reporting its "brilliant success."

We talked about the fact that Chaliapin has already signed a contract with the Moscow Imperial Theater and that Mamontov learned of this only indirectly, since Feodor Ivanovich could not bring himself to tell him. What with Sekar-Rozhansky and Zabela also planning to leave, this probably means the end of the Solodovnikov Theater.

Mention of Chaliapin recalled the mishap which had occurred at the first performance of *The Maid of Pskov*. It seems that at the beginning of the second scene of act 3, Chaliapin, as he had forewarned, started to sing his recitative. Meanwhile the conductor, Truffi, through carelessness, began the accompaniment of the cavatina. As a result, the curtain had to be lowered and the act begun all over again.

We turned our attention again to the production of *Snegurochka,* which, as already mentioned,[58] was sumptuous but without style. And really, why did they release such ludicrous birds in the Prologue? Why did they make the King of the Berendeys wear such comical earmuffs? Why, indeed, could they not have thought of something more clever for Snegurochka than a satin ball gown, satin slippers, a diadem on her head, and *sortie de bal* over her shoulders, etc., etc.?

There were also many curious things about the sets and lighting. For example, in the last act the sky was bright rose, while the water in the lake remained bright green as before; the sun's ray fell on Snegurochka from the left, while Yarilo (the Sun) appeared above a startlingly high cliff (supposedly representing Yarilo's mountain) on the right.

In conclusion, Nikolai Andreyevich related a strange encounter he had with Figner at the second performance of *Snegurochka.* Upon catching sight of Nikolai Andreyevich from afar, Figner (with whom in all truthfulness he has never been on particularly friendly terms) rushed up to him, embraced him, and began congratulating him on the success of *Mozart and Salieri* in Moscow. Then he suggested that the opera be staged at the Marinsky Theater (as though this depended on Rimsky-Korsakov!)

and declared that in such a case, he would certainly want to play the part of Mozart.

26 December

The fourth symphonic concert of the Russian Musical Society took place today at the Conservatory, under the direction of Felix Weingartner. The program consisted of Weber's overture to Der Freischütz, Borodin's Symphony no. 2, Weingartner's symphonic poem Die Gefilde der Seligen (premiere), and Beethoven's Symphony no. 7.

Without going into great detail about Weingartner's conducting, let me say only that Beethoven's symphony went so-so; Borodin's symphony and Weingartner's own work sounded quite acceptable; Weber's Freischütz—superb, the effect here helped, in no small measure, of course, by its somewhat augmented orchestration.

During the intermission, I went below to see Nikolai Andreyevich to obtain from him Zabela's Moscow address and also to tell him about a letter I had received from her, complaining about an extremely hostile article about her singing at the recent Russian Symphony Concert.[59]

After that, we got into a discussion about Weingartner's Die Gefilde der Seligen, which was new to Petersburg. As it turned out, Nikolai Andreyevich had already heard it three times and had even gone through the score. These "Elysian Fields" actually have little appeal for him, despite the superb, brilliant (though pretentious) orchestration. In his view, this symphonic poem is almost totally lacking in melody. What is more, in the middle movement, the upper voices do not correspond to the bass, even though they are both in E flat. As Rimsky-Korsakov sees it, there is nothing special about the fact that this work sounds very noble, not banal. To write a quadrille that is not banal is unusually difficult, but to compose music in a purely Wagerian style that lacks clearly defined, finished melody but at the same time is not trite—nothing is easier, because the harmony can never be banal. At worst, it can only be bad, uninteresting.

27 December

Rimsky-Korsakov visited us between four and six o'clock this afternoon. He urged me to write an article in defense of the Belyaev Concerts and Zabela, since, of late, thanks to the reviews of Ivanov and Bloch, a campaign has literally been unleashed against both the concerts and everyone connected with them.[60]

Then we talked briefly about Borodin's music, specifically that in it there are no transitions from *piano* to *forte*. This is a flaw from which both *Central Asia* and the Second Symphony (particularly the Andante and Finale) suffer.

Before leaving, Nikolai Andreyevich played through the second scene of at 3 of *The Tsar's Bride* twice. Much of it (such as Marfa's aria) is wonderful. Nikolai Andreyevich promised to acquaint me with the entire opera as soon as the proofs arrive.

"What do you think?" he asked after the music had been removed and the piano closed. "I haven't degenerated completely yet, have I?"

On December 30, Nikolai Andreyevich is going to Moscow where he will stay until the sixth or eighth of January.

CHAPTER 9

1899

11 January

Before dinnertime, I dropped in on the Rimsky-Korsakovs. Nikolai Andreyevich had an excellent stay in Moscow. He attended *Christmas Eve,* where he was given a tremendous ovation[1] by the audience, which filled the theater to overflowing, even though this was the opera's seventh performance. The prologue to *The Maid of Pskov* is not enjoying any particular success; apparently it is being taken for the first act of the opera. Rimsky-Korsakov did not see *Mozart and Salieri.* As for *Sadko,* at this time it is going worse in Moscow than it did in Petersburg.

Our conversation turned to *Snegurochka,* which nowadays has little appeal to our society. Time and again I heard people in the audience say that although the music is very boring, it is better than the libretto, which is based on the extraordinarily senseless, muddled subject of Ostrovsky's spring tale, or that the entire opera is very boring, ponderous, untalented, and only fools could possibly like it. On the other hand, the first issues of Findeisen's magazine carried very favorable articles on both *Mozart and Salieri* and *Vera Sheloga.*[2]

Before dinner we chatted briefly about Stasov's article on Vasnetsov,[3] and his (Vladimir Vasilyevich's) nonsense about Vrubel's ornaments, which he at first took for Vasnetsov's and praised, and later, when he recognized them, tore to pieces mercilessly. Then we got onto the subject of the

219

Russian Symphony Concerts, noting that in Petersburg there are people who do not go to them only because they cannot listen to the new Russian music performed so outrageously as it is at these concerts under the totally ungifted, clumsy direction of Rimsky-Korsakov.

25 January

Tonight Rimsky-Korsakov and I got into a discussion about the "Italians' " outrageous performance of *Ruslan* (with its distorted tempi and melodies)[4] and the arrogant view of Mr. Podesti[5] that any measures of Puccini's *Bohème* are superior to all Russian music.

After that, we turned our attention to the conducting of Weingartner, Schuch, and Richter, agreeing that of the three the best is Richter. A man totally devoted to his art, he worships the music of Wagner (though he has little interest in his theories), knows all the classics (headed by Wagner) from memory, and yet is extremely modest, courteous, considerate, and obliging.[6] For example, upon learning, when going through the score of *Tristan* with Felix Blumenfeld, that he receives only eighteen hundred rubles at the Marinsky Theater, Richter immediately suggested that Blumenfeld join him in Vienna. With this purpose in mind, he put on his frock coat and went to see Vsevolozhsky the very next day, and the result was an increase in Blumenfeld's salary.

Richter went to see *Snegurochka* twice (seated in the orchestra pit or "factory," as he called it), and afterward quoted von Bülow: "At present the best German music is being written only in Russia." While in Moscow he dropped in on *Dubrovsky*,[7] but he left before the end of the first act, declaring that he "can't stand Kapellmeister music." He greatly admires Rimsky-Korsakov's *Sheherazade* and has performed it some twenty times all throughout England. Not long ago Nikolai Andreyevich presented him with the score of the suite from *Snegurochka* and the overture-fantasy *Skazka* (a pity it was not *Sadko* or *Antar*).

We talked about the music of the first act of *The Tsar's Bride*—the piquant fifth in the overture [example 34]; the striking harmonies associated with Ivan the Terrible, also in the overture [example 35]; Grigory Gryaznoy's restrained aria (B-minor *larghetto*) with its very interesting middle section of a somewhat "Bach-Handelian" character; the elegant characterization of Ivan Lykov (his entrance); the magnificent *fughetto* at the words "Slashche medu laskovoe slovo"; the wonderful dance with chorus *"Iar-khmel'"*); the typical harmonies of the "magic potion" [examples 36 and 37]; "Lyubasha's song (extremely difficult vocally); Malyuta's highly successful phrase *"Groza—to milost' bozh'ia, groza gniluiu sosnu izlomaet, da tselyi bor dremuchii ozhivit"*; and, finally, the profoundly sad, gripping duet between Lyubasha and the boyar Gryaznoy.

Example 34

Example 35

Example 36

Example 37

3 February

After work, I dropped in on Nikolai Andreyevich to pick up the proofs of *The Tsar's Bride*. We chatted about Glazunov's new suite, *The Seasons*, over which, they say, Stasov went into ecstasies after hearing it on the piano. Liadov is now going around making quips about Vladimir Vasilyevich, asserting that of late he is absolutely beside himself, not knowing what to say about the new things, and therefore he has decided to praise every sixteenth one to the skies.

"You know," added Rimsky-Korsakov, "when Glazunov's First Symphony was played for the first time, Stasov declared immediately that, even though, of course, Alexander Konstantinovich has enormous talent, he will never be able to orchestrate well because it's not in his nature. Well, he was wrong."

17 February

Nikolai Andreyevich returned home fairly late this afternoon, the reason being that after the Conservatory, he had gone with Liadov to the Vasnetsov exhibition.[8] He was in raptures over it, especially the marvelous painting *The Departure of the Bogatyrs*.

I finally brought him the proofs of the first scene of act 3 of *The Tsar's Bride*. I would have liked to ask if I might look through the rough draft of the opera, but since I saw him only briefly, I hesitated to do so. In noticed only a rather caustic inscription of Rimsky-Korsakov's hand on the cover of the second scene of act 3: "Expiation for Koptyaev."

While I was there, Nikolai Andreyevich received a letter from Edouard Colonne, inviting him to come to Paris to conduct a concert of his works.

Before Rimsky-Korsakov had come home, I had a long talk with Nadezhda Nikolayevna about Glazunov, whom the Rimsky-Korsakovs had met originally through Balakirev. He studied with Nikolai Andreyevich two winters[9] (at the time of *Mlada*). At first he was an enthusiastic admirer of the music of Rimsky-Korsakov and even presented him with a photograph inscribed: "To the musical sorcerer." Later, however, under the influence of Taneyev (and perhaps Laroche, too), he grew somewhat cool toward both Rimsky-Korsakov and Borodin and became attracted to Tchaikovsky and Brahms.

"These days," continued Nadezhda Nikolayevna, "he seems less interested in the composer of the *German Requiem*. At any rate, he seldom mentions him."

We chatted about Cui's equivocal behavior toward Ivanov (with whom he is on friendly terms) and Napravnik (whom he is always flattering).

Purely by chance it came out that since their marriage, the Rimsky-Korsakovs have never been to the Cuis'.

19 February

This morning I went to the dress rehearsal of the final concert of the Russian Musical Society under the direction of Hans Richter. The hall was swarming with people.

After listening to Beethoven's Ninth Symphony and Tchaikovsky's *Romeo and Juliet* Overture, I left and went to Mme Fried's for the Balakirev musical morning.

Mily Alexeyevich was at his best today. Besides his new nocturne, dedicated to Bessel, he played Liszt's *Concerto pathétique,* Schumann's *Carnaval,* and the first two movements of Chopin's brilliant Sonata in B-flat minor. There was much talk about Richter, whom Balakirev greatly admires, and also about the pianist Paderewski, who, in Mily Alexeyevich's view, plays like a charlatan, despite his marvelous velvety touch and amazing, faultless technique.

It should be noted, however, that at first Balakirev was in raptures over Paderewski's playing. It was only later that he suddenly changed his opinion.

24 February

My mother's "at home" today attracted a rather large group of people, among them the Rimsky-Korsakovs. In a discussion about opera, Nikolai Andreyevich stated that to him Saint-Saëns' *Samson et Dalila* represents the "ideal operatic form"; further, that Wagner's *Tristan and Isolde* is a kind of long drawn-out "chromatic" affair, while *Die Meistersinger* is a drawn-out "diatonic" affair.

"There was a great deal of the dilletante in Wagner, even in *Tannhäuser,*" he said. "He had to 'strain himself,' as they say, to achieve the style of *Der Ring des Nibelungen* (*Die Meistersinger* and *Parsifal*). In the love duet from *Tristan and Isolde* the hero sings repeatedly in parallel sevenths.

"You know," he added, "Richter told me recently that except for his opera *Rienzi,* Wagner didn't remember his own music. Once, for example, he didn't even recognize his *Meistersinger.* He had no gift whatsoever for the piano, couldn't play anything or accompany even something of his own."

As for Richter himself, he really does not particularly like to conduct concerts; he enjoys only preparing musical works for performance. On the whole, he has little interest in public approval, but he values highly the opinion of experts. Even now, despite his enormous success, he returned from the last concert dissatisfied, as he himself said, with his performance of Beethoven's Ninth Symphony.

According to Felix Blumenfeld, Richter's eyes almost filled with tears when he spoke of the warmth expressed to him by Nikolai Andreyevich and Glazunov.

"We mustn't forget," remarked Rimsky-Korsakov, "that, not being a composer himself, Richter regards composers with a special esteem. He considers them people of a 'higher order.' This is extremely touching."

He then told me that he has already replied to Colonne's letter, agreeing to conduct the concert but on condition that his trip to Paris and return is fully guaranteed.

By the way, Richter's name for Felix Blumenfeld is "that walking sack of notes."

25 February

My wife and I attended the thirty-sixth performance of *Snegurochka.*[10] The Marinsky Theater was filled to overflowing. Kozakovskaya sang the role of Kupava; Chuprynnikov—King of the Berendeys; Slavina—Lel; Nosilova—Spring; and Smirnov—Mizgir. The only numbers encored were the duet between the King and Kupava, the King's Cavatina, the Dance of the Skomorokhi, and Lel's third song (his first song passed without a single clap thanks to the abominable performance of Slavina). At the end, the artists and composer were recalled many times.

Listening to this opera today, I was made aware of Nikolai Andreyevich's great fondness for oboe solos and the fact that he writes many of them.

6 March

I went directly from work to the Rimsky-Korsakovs'. Nikolai Andrey-evich was very glad to see me. He was certain, he said, that I would be there on this day.[11] He told me that he has read my little article on Tchaikovsky, which has finally been published in Findeisen's newspaper (no. 10), but, alas, without the names of Ivanov and Solovyov.

We chatted about many things: Mamontov and the chill which seems to have developed in his relations with Rimsky-Korsakov; Hans Richter, who recently sent Nikolai Andreyevich his portrait, inscribed "Dem lie-ben Meister Rimsky-Korsakow der dankbare Kapellmeister Seiner herr-lichen 'Scheherazada.' Hans Richter"; *Die Meistersinger,* remarking on how cleverly Wagner had introduced music from *Tristan and Isolde* into the first scene of act 3 at Hans Sachs' words: "Mein Kind, von Tristan und Isolde kann' ich ein Traurig-Stück," a device found also in Rimsky-Korsakov, in three of whose works (*The Maid of Pskov,* the prologue to *The Maid of Pskov,* and *The Tsar's Bride*) Ivan the Terrible is delineated by one and the same theme.

Shortly before the guests arrived, we also talked about Liszt's brilliant *Mephisto Waltz* and its influence on the music of the fantastic scene in the forest in *Snegurochka,* that is, on the part of Mizgir.

In the evening the other guests at the Rimsky-Korsakovs', besides my mother and me, were Liadov, Glazunov, Zabela, Felix Blumenfeld, Be-lyaev, Chuprynnikov and his wife, V. V. Stasov, G. N. Timofeyev, Belsky, Lavrov, Dr. Spengler, and the four students—Mitusov, Richter, Fedorov-sky, and Mironov.

Upon meeting me, Stasov began to berate me severely for my article on Tchaikovsky.

"Of course," he said, "I have no right to impose my views on you, but, nevertheless, I can't help pointing out that I disagreee completely with your definition of the character of Tchaikovsky's music.[12] In what way is he the spokesman of his epoch? And indeed who has been such a spokesman? Schumann was not the spokesman of his time. Beethoven— he was superior to all the people around him, including Goethe, and, consequently, he stood outside his time. Even though Peter Ilyich suc-ceeded so well with his Sixth Symphony, which you praise and I, too, adore, this proves nothing, since it's a kind of autobiography. *The Nut-cracker*—that, too, is excellent. I repeat, although your article didn't send me to my grave (it was good to hear that, I must say!), nevertheless, I was shocked. I never expected that you had such a high opinion of Tchai-kovsky."

I confess this unexpected monologue had quite an unpleasant effect on me; it made me feel uncomfortable, but there was nothing I could do about it. The article has been published, and therefore it is now my turn to listen to all kinds of remarks. Soon afterward, however, the music began and I calmed down completely.

First Zabela and Chuprynnikov sang duets by Rimsky-Korsakov; then Nadezhda Ivanovna and Sofia Nikolayevna sang the duet *Gornyi Kliuch*. After that Chuprynnikov sang Rimsky-Korsakov's *Tikho, tikho more goluboe* (dedicated to him), the King of the Berendey's first cavatina, and Glazun-ov's charming *Nereida* (also dedicated to him). Zabela concluded the vocal part of the program with Marfa's last aria from scene 2, act 3 of *The Tsar's Bride* and two more songs by Nikolai Andreyevich, *Eshche ia poln, drug moi milyi* and *Nimfa* (both dedicated to her).

The evening ended with piano music. At the insistence of Timofeyev, Blumenfeld and Glazunov played (very badly, to tell the truth) the *King Lear* Overture and part of a serenade by Weingartner. After this Alexan-der Konstantinovich performed Spring and the beginning of Summer from his new ballet *The Seasons*.

On the whole, it was a lively evening. It broke up after three o'clock.

8 March

I went to hear *Sadko*.[13] The cast included Sekar-Rozhansky (Sadko); Zabela (Princess Volkhova), Rostovtseva (Lyubava), and Strakhova (Ne-zhata). Following scene 3, Rostovtseva (who sang her F minor aria very charmingly) and Rimsky-Korsakov were recalled many times. At the end of the opera, Nikolai Andreyevich took four bows.

The audience was relatively small. This can be explained in part by the ridiculous prices of parterre tickets (the gallery was filled to overflowing). As for the performance, with few exceptions, it was far from perfect. Oh, well, this is the usual misfortune of all private undertakings.

10 March

On Wednesday March 10 *Mozart and Salieri* was given its first perfor-mance.[14] Neither Shkafer (as Mozart) nor Chaliapin (as Salieri) sang particularly well. The overall effect was not bad, but, I repeat, the performance was less than satisfactory. At times, even the orchestra left much to be desired. On the other hand, the singing of the chorus (off-stage) in Mozart's *Requiem* and all of scene 2 of Nikolai Andreyevich's one-act opera, ending with Salieri's powerful recitative *"Ty zasnesh' nadolgo, Motsart,"* and the strong, mysteriously macabre characterization of the "man in black" produced a profound impression on me.

At the end of the opera, Rimsky-Korsakov was recalled four times.

I liked very much some parts of Gluck's *Orpheus,* which was also performed tonight.

17 March

I attended the first performance of *Boyarina Vera Sheloga* (with Tsvetkova as Vera) and *The Maid of Pskov* (with Chaliapin as Ivan the Terrible and Tsvetkova as Olga). Scene 1 of act 3 (In the Forest) and even the symphonic picture preceding it were omitted from the latter opera.

This year *The Maid of Pskov* is going somewhat better, more smoothly. Even Bedlevich (Prince Tomakov) strove to do the best he could, given the limitations of his voice. After Olga's arioso (in scene 1, act 2), Tsvetkova was presented with a charming basket of white flowers. Throughout the evening Rimsky-Korsakov was applauded frequently; in all he was recalled sixteen times.

After the performance, I rushed to the artists' room, where I managed to see Nikolai Andreyevich just long enough to tell him how deeply impressed I was by the second scene of *Mozart and Salieri* and to exchange a few words with him about Cui's vile articles in *Novosti* (March 9 and 12, 1899) directed against the Korsakov revision of *Boris Godunov* and Korsakov's *Mozart and Salieri.*[15]

19 March

I went to the dress rehearsal of the last Russian Symphony Concert of the season. This time, except for "A Child's Dreams" I did not care much for Tchaikovsky's Second Suite. As for Glazunov's fantasy *The Sea,* despite the splendid and powerful orchestration, I found it rather poor in melodic content and, besides this, very unoriginal. The novelty on the program was the overture of Rimsky-Korsakov's *Tsar's Bride,*[16] which was played twice (it lasts five minutes).

At the end of the rehearsal I spoke with Rimsky-Korsakov about Cui's articles and his letter of reply.[17] We also chatted about revisions he had made in the orchestration of The Maid of Pskov because Mamontov's orchestra lacked a tuba.

"You know," said Rimsky-Korsakov, "in Boris I also had to change something in the Scene at the Fountain where, because the orchestra did not have a sufficient number of strings, the trombones completely drowned out the upper voices."

It was time to go and we parted. I went to work and Rimsky-Korsakov to the Conservatory for a rehearsal of the change he had made in Boris at the end of the love duet between Marina and the Pretender.

20 March

During the intermission at the Russian Symphony Concert, I ran into Nikolai Andreyevich, who then and there made me read Petrovsky's outrageous article about Mozart and Salieri.[18]

Besides that, we talked about yesterday's performance of Boris (with Chaliapin in the title role), and Rimsky-Korsakov told me that he regards the scene of the Tsar's death as the finest moment in the opera.

As he was leaving, he invited me to them on Wednesday at eight-thirty "for a rehearsal."

24 March

By eight-forty-five I was at the Rimsky-Korsakovs' for the preliminary rehearsal.[19] When I entered the drawing room with Lunacharsky, whom I met on the staircase, the guests were already assembled.

Before tea they sang the quartet from act 2 of The Tsar's Bride four times. After tea they went through various duets and arias. Nikolai Andreyevich and Nadezhda Nikolayevna took turns accompanying. The music ended at about twelve-thirty, but Karklin and Lunacharsky stayed behind to go over certain parts once again in preparation for the Rimsky-Korsakovs' musical evening on Wednesday (March 31) or Monday (April 5).

They talked about the fact that Mozart and Salieri "had fallen flat," as the saying goes; also about Stasov's scathing letter to Findeisen, protesting the outrageous article on *Mozart and Salieri* which he published in his journal.[20]

8 April

The music began relatively late at the Rimsky-Korsakovs's (at about eleven o'clock) and continued almost without interruption until two in the morning, at which time supper was served. As a result the evening did not break up until after three o'clock.

Zabela and Lunacharsky began with Rimsky-Korsakov's duet *Angel i Demon.* This was followed by Marfa's first aria (Zabela) and the quartet from act 2 of *The Tsar's Bride* (Zabela, Karklin, Sofia Nikolayevna, and Lunacharsky). Then came more songs and arias by Rimsky-Korsakov, with Chaliapin singing *Anchar, Prorok, Gonets,* Varlaam's song from *Boris Godunov,* and the Song of the Viking Guest from *Sadko.*

In the course of the evening Rimsky-Korsakov and I had a long discussion about Puccini's *Bohème,* at the end of which he remarked that "for all his shortcomings, Puccini far surpasses both Leoncavallo and Mascagni." Then we turned to the subject of Cui's mediocre review of *Prince Igor* in *Novosti,*[21] which begins with the words "The shortcomings of *Igor*" and includes the following "pearls" (I cite here several exact quotations from this extremely ambiguous article):

(1) In Yaroslavna's melancholy aria, which opens the second scene, the melodic outlines are rather pallid. Nevertheless it (i.e., the aria) is not devoid of tonal beauty and even a rather poetic mood.

(2) The song of the Polovtsian maiden is undeniably beautiful, but not outstanding; Konchakovna's cavatina is far better and more poetic.

(3) "Yaroslavna's Lament" is a rather commonplace and boring plaint in the Russian spirit. . . . It does not brighten the colorless characterization of Yaroslavna.

(4) This "Lament" is followed by a more successful chorus of the townspeople. . .

(5) "Borodin's Eastern music" calls to mind, at times, Rimsky-Korsakov, at other times, Beethoven, in his chorus of dervishes.

And, finally, as if in reproach:

(6) In their librettos both Glinka in *Ruslan* and Borodin in *Prince Igor* were concerned only about scenes suitable for music and to write music of the highest quality for these scenes.

I have an irresistible urge to sing, about César Antonovich, a line from his *William Ratcliff,* "Oh, old fox!"

Before tea we talked about Glazunov's new ballets—*The Seasons* and *Ruses d'amour* (both of which are distinguished, aside from their music, by unusual mastery of writing and extremely pictorial tonal beauty) and also about the complimentary articles on Rimsky-Korsakov and his *Snegurochka,* republished in *Muzykal'naia gazeta.* Here is what appeared in no. 14 of that newspaper regarding the second concert for the benefit of the Tchaikovsky Fund, held on March 28 under the direction of A. I. Siloti, at which they played, among other things, two excerpts from Tchaikovsky's *Snegurochka:* [22] "Spring's Monologue" and "Kupava's Complaint to the King of the Berendeys."

The marvelous subject of the tale (Ostrovsky's *Snegurochka*) has become so intimately linked with the brilliant music of Rimsky-Korsakov that all throughout you are disappointed that you are hearing not the music of Korsakov but the rather prosaic, though elegant, melodramatic murmuring of the orchestra.

And further:

There are plays and subjects which become so intimately associated with, even embodied in certain music that you do not seek nor wish to listen to other, new sounds. Of such a nature are parts of Beethoven's *Egmont,* Glinka's *Life for the Tsar,* Mendelssohn's *Midsummer Night's Dream,* and Rimsky-Korsakov's *Snegurochka.*

14 April

I dropped in on Rimsky-Korsakov at about five o'clock to pick up the manuscript of *Sadko.* I found there Konstantin Alexandrovich Iretsky (brother of Natalya Alexandrovna Iretskaya, Professor of Singing at the Petersburg Conservatory), a former schoolmate of Nikolai Andreyevich's at the Naval Academy, with whom Rimsky-Korsakov is on intimate terms. [23] We spoke about Chaliapin and the letter he sent Nikolai Andreyevich entreating him to orchestrate his song *Prorok* for the Pushkin evening; [24] about I. F. Tyumenev, a wealthy landlord, antiquarian, writer, and translator of Wagner's

Ring and *Meistersinger,* as well as singer, painter, even composer (a former pupil of Rimsky-Korsakov) and, besides all this, an extremely intelligent, well-educated, and modest man.

I learned that the vocal score of *Sadko* is already finished; also that in Moscow it has been announced that, during Easter Week, the Mamontov company is going to give *Sadko, Boris* (several times), and *The Maid of Pskov* (for the last time).

At the end of my visit we talked about M. Davydova's[25] reminiscences of Anton Grigoryevich Rubinstein, published in the April 1899 issue of *Istoricheskii vestnik.* There the author stated that Rubinstein was extremely superstitious. He feared that he would be forgotten after his death. He said repeatedly that he was going to Russia to die, and, as he approached the border, after having conversed very calmly with his traveling companions, he suddenly became highly agitated. He rushed to the window, peered out intently and, finally, when he caught sight of the little river which separates us from Germany, his face lit up. He removed his cap and cried: "There she is, Russia!" and bowed down to the ground.

After this, let Balakirev and Pypin try to tell me that Rubinstein loved only himself and hated Russia!

24 April

When I arrived at the Rimsky-Korsakovs' this afternoon, Nikolai Andreyevich, who was writing something, suddenly began fussing, then quickly hid some note paper and books in his desk, adding jokingly that "for the time being this is a secret," since he may never write "it."

This time, our conversation centered mainly on Artur Nikisch,[26] over whom both Nadezhda and Sofia Nikolayevna have literally gone mad. As before, I remained faithful to Hans Richter, placing him above Nikisch— this "virtuoso" of the orchestra with his successful but rather limited repertoire (as it always is with virtuosos). Actually, his posturing and exaggerated gestures are quite unnecessary except to naive listeners, especially the ladies who take them as a sign of his genius and strong, imperious temperament.

"I can see," said Nadezhda Nikolayevna, "that for some reason you're prejudiced against him or, perhaps, you're only mature enough for Hans Richter."

I laughed and replied, "In that case, Nadezhda Nikolayevna, I'm going to begin telling everyone that you're only mature enough to appreciate Nikisch."

Of late, these endless and pointless disputes about conductors have obviously begun to bore Rimsky-Korsakov (secretly he agrees with me on many things). Not wishing to irritate Nadezhda Nikolayevna further—she was already terribly agitated[27]—he kept silent and joined in the conversation only to offer the thought that he would like very much to test how enthusiastic the public would be if they did not know the name of the conductor, and particularly if they did not see him, if, for example, he were standing behind the screen. When, at last, we stopped arguing Nikolai Andreyevich, who was pacing the room, solemnly delivered himself of the following aphorism: "Ladies, and gentlemen, however gifted Nikisch may be, the public is a great and complex fool."

Earlier, before Nadezhda Nikolayevna had come in, we had talked about conducting, the fact that the principal gift for a conductor (in a musical sense) consists in his ability to gauge the true (most desired) speed at which an orchestra can play and still maintain its full sonority. In this connection, I contended that, perhaps, there is no such thing as a special genius for conducting but simply an overall gift for music, but that, besides this gift, a first-rate conductor must at the same time possess several other qualities, such as a critical gift, a thorough acquaintance with all the tonal peculiarities of the orchestra, etc.

"What's this? What are you suggesting?" asked Rimsky-Korsakov. "That a conductor—even Nikisch himself—has a right to arbitrarily change a composer's tempi, whether the result proves to be beautiful or not? (I'm thinking of his totally unwarranted slowing down of the tempo, almost by half, in the first movement of Tchaikovsky's Fifth Symphony.) In my view—no. I believe the composer knows his own intentions best, and he shouldn't be treated so cavalierly."

2 May

Nikolai Andreyevich visited us between three and five o'clock. We talked about the two interesting and extremely favorable articles by Emil Bormann which appeared in St.-Petersburger Zeitung, one on Boyarina Vera Sheloga,[28] the other on Mozart and Salieri. For example, regarding the Lullaby from *Vera Sheloga,* the author writes: "Der souveräne Techniker und der geniale Melodist reichen sich hier ebenbürtig die Hände. And in the article on *Mozart and Salieri* we find the following:

Wie grossartig einfach hat Rimski-Korssakow hier Seine wunderbare Melodik Seine grossartige Technik und seine sourveräne Beherschung der Ausdruckswahreit angewandt; letzteres bewog den genialen Komponisten auf die Mozart-Beethovensche Harmonisations-und Modulationseveise zurückzugreifen. Doch war sie ihm bloss zur Charakteristik des Zeitgeistes und der Persönlichkeiten nötig; niht dass er uns einfach eine geschikte Übung im alten Stil vorführte wie wir solches bei Tschaikowski antreffen. Er benutzte blossdas alte Material, welches er durchaus modern behandelte . . .

And further: " 'Russlan,' 'Pique Dame,' die Briefzene aus dem "Onegin" und "Mozart und Salieri"—sind die genialsten—vielleicht die einzig genialen—musikalischen Schöpfungen, die zu Puschkinschen Texten geschaffen wurden."

Rimsky-Korsakov and I talked about Mamontov's tactlessness, such as his suddenly returning the score of *Prorok* without any explanation (subsequently it came out that Chaliapin had had a falling out with Savva Ivanovich, had left him before he was supposed to and, as a consequence, the plan for the Pushkin evening had had to be abandoned) and his cancellation, also without any notice, of the benefit performance promised Ludmila Ivanovna Shestakova for the sixth week of Lent, at which scenes 2 and 4 of *Sadko* and two scenes from *The Maid of Pskov* were to have been given.

Rimsky-Korsakov then told me about his recent visit to Nikisch and their conversation about Richard Strauss. In Nikisch's view, Strauss is a major talent but one with a strong leaning toward decadence. His latest tone poems, said Nikisch, are the acme of the unbelievable in music.

"To this," continued Rimsky-Korsakov, "I replied that I not only fail to see a brilliant compositional gift in Strauss' works, but I consider even his orchestration abominable in a certain sense.

"And we were right," added Nikolai Andreyevich, turning toward me, "like Glazunov, Nadezhda Nikolayevna, and some others to 'hiss' Strauss' *Don Juan* at Nikisch's last concert."

Again we talked about Nikisch, this time about his colossal success in Moscow, where he was not only kissed as he is here in Petersburg but was literally smothered with flowers. We also discussed M. Ivanov's laudatory article about Rimsky-Korsakov's *Mozart and Salieri* in the section *Muzykal'nye nabroski* of *Novoe vremia* (May 3, 1899), no. 8325.[29]

"All the same," remarked Rimsky-Korsakov, "God only knows what this thing is—my *Mozart and Salieri*. Of course, the second scene is better than the first."

Then Rimsky-Korsakov showed me some (insignificant, of course) corrections in harmony, which Glazunov had made in *Snegurochka*.

"Thank heavens there are people like Alexander Konstantinovich," he said. "Otherwise there might be an 'unnecessary octave' or even an 'unnecessary harsh harmony' here or there, for all my 'regal' technique (as Emil Bormann puts it)."

With this, he began leafing through the proofs of *Snegurochka,* singing with comic seriousness, as if to himself, "Star ia stal i shalovliv, za mnoi prismatrivat' ne khudo."[30]

As she said good-bye, Nadezhda Nikolayevna invited me to visit them in Vechasha. I will probably go there when I return from my vacation.

I forgot to mention that when composing the music for the scene from *May Night* in which the Golova importunes Hanna ("Polubi, polubi menia, devitsa dusha"), Rimsky-Korsakov was inspired by the singing of three itinerant monks, which he heard once in Petersburg during Easter Week in the Eliseyevs' shop on the corner of Furshtadskaya and Liteinaya, where he had gone for wine. The motive with which they were "extolling God" had approximately the same character:

Example 38

Furiously

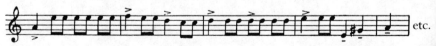

etc.

With tickets which I received from Nikolai Andreyevich, my mother and I attended the graduation exercises at the Conservatory. Two students completed the course in composition: Kalafati (student of Rimsky-Korsakov) and Alexander Borisovich Khessin (student of Solovyov).

Third Visit to Vechasha

August 5, 6, 7, and 8

At three-sixteen on the afternoon of August 5, I set out by train for Vechasha, as planned, arriving there at ten in the evening.

Scarcely had we exchanged greetings, when a conversation arose regarding Tchaikovsky's symphonies and the outstanding talent they evince. (At the time Nadezhda Nikolayevna and N. I. Richter[31] were playing his Fourth Symphony.) Rimsky-Korsakov is coming to love Tchaikovsky's music more and more, he said—not only the music but also the melodies, even though sometimes they are not sufficiently well-defined. As before, Nadezhda Nikolayevna went into ecstasies over Nikisch's conducting, insisting with the greatest earnestness that, being a creative genius, he often surpassed Tchaikovsky himself in the performance of his symphonies.

After drinking some milk and tea, Nikolai Andreyevich and I went into the garden. It was all as before, except that the allées seemed even more lush. Rimsky-Korsakov imparted the following bits of information to me: Oleg the Wise[32] is still not finished—he is having difficulty handling the form; on July 28 he composed a new song to the words of Pushkin's Poet; at present he is writing something for orchestra,[33] but just what is his secret for the time being; later on he would like to undertake an opera on an ancient Polish or Lithuanian subject—he asked me to give some thought to this theme.

Returning once more to the subject of Wagner, Rimsky-Korsakov and I agreed that his music seems to have generated some kind of "microbe" (true, one which science has not yet discovered). How else could one explain the sheer ecstasy which not only his music but each separate note of it evokes in so many people?

We talked about Belyaev's proposed publication of The Tsar's Bride and the fact that this score is going to disconcert many people, mainly the Wagnerites, who will dislike it terribly.

6 August

This morning Nikolai Andreyevich literally "sang a hymn" to the "olden days" and its geniuses—Beethoven, Haydn, Mozart, et al. He even expressed something of an antipathy to program music, saying that he would like to write a "pure" symphony.[34] This is a sure sign that he is engaged in a large-scale work—an opera or cantata.[35] So far as I can make out, Belsky is involved in it.

Then, suddenly changing the subject, Nikolai Andreyevich asked, "Do you know what I was called upon to do recently? What do you think? To give my opinion about Dreyfus! The French journal *La Vogue* wrote me, inquiring what I think about this case. I replied, somewhat evasively, with the words of Catherine II that 'it is better to acquit ten guilty men than to condemn a single innocent one.'"

We also discussed the natural desire of a composer to be understood, and the anxiety he suffers the first time he shows a new work to someone. We touched upon a very interesting question: inspiration and the signs of it.

"How all this comes about, I myself don't know," said Rimsky-Korsakov. "I know only that sometimes when working on a scene of an opera, you suddenly become aware that at the very moment you're composing a certain number, other themes and harmonies, not needed at all on the face of it, come into your head, and you jot them down. What's most surprising of all is that later on these very themes and chords turn out to be the ones best suited to some later scenes, which you seemingly had not been thinking about—not consciously at least—at the moment you were jotting them down."

In the evening Belsky came and they talked about a melody in 6/8; 5/8; 4/8; 3/8; 2/8; 1/8 time. As a result of this conversation, in finishing his *Oleg*, Rimsky-Korsakov, as a joke, used this melodic phrase not only in the final measures but also in the scene of the dialogue between Oleg and the Soothsayer, just before the latter's words: "Volkhvy ne boiatsia moguchikh vladyk."

Then there was a discussion about the Germans' lack of understanding of Glinka, and Rimsky-Korsakov mentioned that he intended to reorchestrate Glinka's *Prince Kholmsky* someday[36] and also to write a sort of critique of himself. Besides this, someone expressed the view that Pushkin's text should not have been changed in the songs *Doride* and *Na kholmakh Gruzii.* Rimsky-Korsakov concurred fully, saying that if he were to write these songs now, he would not think of violating Pushkin's text.

After tea Nikolai Andreyevich told me several things: that he considers the Dance of the Skomorokhi in *Snegurochka* superior to the one in *Sadko,* though he is fully satisfied with the song of Duda and Sopiel; that he is terribly fond of the key of B-flat minor but for some reason never writes in it; that this summer he conceived another new type of harmonization of the tone–half-tone scale, but that for the time being this is his secret. Finally, Nikolai Andreyevich gave a very witty explanation of the unusual chord in the part of the Wood Sprite (in the Scene in the Forest).

"It's nothing but the ninth chord of F major," he said, "in which the fifth note (G) is simultaneously raised and lowered chromatically."

7 August

We rose relatively late. No sooner had we said good morning than Nikolai Andreyevich went to the piano and played the following chord:

Example 39

"What do you think, Vasily Vasilyevich?" he asked. "Do you think it's possible to combine sounds in this way? And is it beautiful or sort of like Richard Strauss?"

I thought it sounded like Strauss.

"Nevertheless," he replied, "you're going to hear this harmony today, only it will be prepared slyly and you'll probably like it." And he burst out laughing.

Indeed, Nikolai Andreyevich was right, for after seeing Richter off, he played his new song three times for me,[37] and I liked it very much, especially its marvelous, harmonically very original and daring ending [example 40].

Example 40

However, Nikolai Andreyevich did not seem particularly pleased with this song. Both he and Belsky felt that the music did not quite suit the words.

"Of course, this is understandable," he observed. "Pushkin's words are too great to be set to music. Besides, this song is strongly reminiscent of those of my last period, and I'd rather it resembled *Chto v imene tebe moem?* That was somewhat more original."

We continued our talk in the garden and it turned automatically to Wagner, the strikingly underscored sensuality of his subjects *(Die Walküre, Tristan,* etc.). Laroche certainly hit the mark when he quipped, apropos of *Die Walküre:* "The curtain falls and Sieglinde falls."

"And yet," said Nikolai Andreyevich, "when speaking of Wagner, we must first acknowledge that he was unquestionably a genius; then we can go about enumerating his shortcomings, which, I repeat, are numerous. Would one of you venture (for fun) to write a philosophical treatise on Wagner's use of four horns to express 'Weltschmerz'? I can just imagine how Messrs. Koptayev and other Wagnerites of that ilk would rejoice!"

We discussed Petrovsky's extremely strange article of last year on *Sadko,*[38] in which the author asserted that one can readily acknowledge that Rimsky-Korsakov is the most national composer after Glinka, "even though the themes in *Sadko* are in themselves trivial and quite insignificant. For just as tiny seeds of opium secrete within themselves the beauty and satiny lustre of great visions, so these trivial themes evolve into a captivating symphony, an enchanting nocturne in which the rays of the moon and warm, languorous moisture of watery mists become sounds." And further, because of its musical content, *Sadko* is "too thick a book to encompass at one stroke."

Nevertheless, this did not prevent Petrovsky from saying that Sadko's wife "turns one's stomach" or that in the finale, Rimsky-Korsakov drives away all his stage marionettes. Then, at the very end of the article Petrovsky states once again that even though the subject of *Sadko* is boring and empty, "anyone who believes in Russian national music" and "wishes to acquaint himself with the beauty and originality of the forms of our art at this stage of its development, will find the best and most complete guide in *Sadko*."

"You have to admit," remarked Rimsky-Korsakov, "that although *Russkaia muzykal'naia gazeta* is an honest journal, it won't be of much use to Russian music, because it hasn't a firmly defined direction. Even the Wagerian cult among them (Findeisen, Petrovsky) are rather dispassionate, apparently without being aware of it. For example, they carried a long article on *Parsifal* by Vsevolod Cheshikhin,[39] stating flatly that the music of this opera becomes particularly inspired at the end—almost at the very moment when Wagner seems to be renouncing his theory of 'leitmotivs.' This is what they've come to!"

Nikolai Andreyevich is also displeased with Petrovsky's incomprehensible carping at Felix Blumenfeld's conducting.[40]

In the evening, we all strolled in the garden and admired the lake. Someone brought up the subject of Petrovsky's article on Rimsky-Korsakov's "flawless" (his word) song *Nimfa*.[41]

"Rimsky-Korsakov becomes a true Greek," wrote Yevgeny Maximovich,

when he turns to the no less Greek verses of Maikov. From such a felicitous union of poet and musician issue such masterpieces as *Nimfa*. Persons susceptible to perceiving *colors in sound* would undoubtedly find this thoroughly charming, plaintive, beautiful song shot through with an alluring shade of blue, limpid and captivatingly cool. . . . In the solitary corners of a park, nature joins its tender voice, its slight movement to the white creation of a human dream. . . . In the air of such corners, one senses something sacred: "Here God dwells." He dwells also in Korsakov's song.

"Well, I guess there couldn't be higher praise than that," remarked Rimsky-Korsakov.

However, Petrovsky wrote quite differently about Nikolai Andreyevich's song *Son v letniuiu noch'* (also to words by Maikov). Here he found the music "somewhat monotonous" owing to a "lack of passion" in the depiction of the ardent flame of youth, the sensual fantasies which seize the body and soul of "a shy and innocent young maiden."

The music is really as light and airy as an apparition, an enchanting haze; its pearly tints (the exquisitely beautiful scales at the words *"Ia blazhenstvo nebes"*) transport us at once into a fantastic, phantasmal state, but the coursing of the blood, the quivering of the heart and body, expressed by such breathless melody in the lines of the poem ("Nad dykhan'em ego obessilela ia, na grudi rasomknulisia ruki"), remain outside the domain of the music.

"Evidently Petrovsky wanted me to portray the sensual passion of an experienced woman of his day, rather than the poetic fantasy of an innocent young girl," commented Nikolai Andreyevich. "In this case, I thoroughly disagree with him."

11 September

Tonight Rimsky-Korsakov informed me that he has almost completed his new opera and has scored half of it. He has only to finish composing the final (seventh) scene. This opera, he said, will be his "farewell to the fairy tale." Its libretto, after Pushkin, was drawn up by Belsky. It turned out that Nikolai Andreyevich has written an opera on the subject of Pushkin's famous *Tale of Tsar Saltan, of His Son, the Famed and Mighty Hero, Prince Guidon Saltanovich, and of the Beautiful Swan Princess.* It consists of four acts and a prologue. Rimsky-Korsakov related the story of the opera to me act by act.

The cantata *Song of Oleg the Wise* has not only been completed but also orchestrated. Rimsky-Korsakov would like to ask Safonov to perform it at one of the symphonic concerts in Moscow, since this year there will be no soloists at the Belyaev concerts.

Besides this we chatted about the speech given by Prince Volkonsky,[42] in which the new director stated categorically that the "task of the Imperial Theater is to be the leader of the artistic tastes of the people, not the slave of their humdrum caprices, especially since, besides Glinka, we Russians have such composers of genius as Borodin, Tchaikovsky, and Rimsky-Korsakov, of whom we can, we should be proud."

In the future Nikolai Andreyevich plans to publish a separate suite from *Tsar Saltan,* consisting of the preludes to acts 1 and 2 and the third scene of act 4, accompanied by their corresponding epigraphs from Pushkin.

I completely forgot to mention that as a consequence of the repairs being made on the Assembly Hall of the Nobility, the Russian Symphony Concerts are going to be given in the Large Hall of the Conservatory; also, that all seven scenes of *Tsar Saltan* will open with the same fanfare [example 41], which I advised Nikolai Andreyevich to have printed on the title page of the opera. It should be noted that in this opera the arias, duets, and trios will not stand out from each other as separate numbers, as in *The Tsar's Bride,* but each of them will blend harmonically with all the rest.

Example 41

3 October

Nikolai Andreyevich has given Prince Tsereteli permission to present *The Tsar's Bride* in Odessa and after that, in Kharkov.[43] It will also be performed in Moscow this month immediately following Serov's *Power of the Fiend.*

On another subject—folk songs—Nikolai Andreyevich said that if he were to publish his collection of them now, he would harmonize them much more simply. He believes that both his collections, Balakirev's, and Liadov's transgressed greatly in this regard, since they are not simple recordings of folk music but rather a series of short arrangements of tunes which, though artistic, perhaps even good, are not entirely faithful to the original.

By the way, I learned that Belyaev pays composers from twenty-five to seventy-five rubles per song, but Rimsky-Korsakov received nothing— not a single kopeck—for the first four of his songs which Belyaev published (among them *Vostochnyi romans* and the Lullaby from *Vera Sheloga*), and later, for *El' i pal'ma, Iuzhnaia noch',* and *Na kholmakh Gruzii*—ten rubles each.

15 October

I attended the thirty-eighth performance of *Snegurochka* with Dulova as Snegurochka, Fried—Spring, Serebryakov—Grandfather Frost, Chuprynnikov—King of the Berendeys, Dolina—Lel, etc.

The theater was almost completely filled. (The only empty places, as in most cases, were the loges.) The artists and the composer were called out many times. After act 3 Rimsky-Korsakov took three curtain calls and at the end of the opera—two. Dulova was only so-so as Snegurochka.

27 October

I dropped in on the Rimsky-Korsakovs for half an hour. As it turned out, Nikolai Andreyevich had stayed in Moscow for the second performance of *The Tsar's Bride* and had not returned until yesterday.[44] Judging from the response to the first two performances (October 22 and 24), the opera scored a complete success among the Muscovites. Moscow critical opinion, as expressed by Messrs. Rozenov and Kashkin,[45] was, on the whole, extremely favorable. Rimsky-Korsakov maintains that *The Tsar's Bride* enjoyed a greater success than *Sadko*.

4 November

I found Nikolai Andreyevich somewhat upset tonight. He has not been able to finish *Saltan* because Belsky has not yet finished writing the libretto. The score of the opera will most likely be published by Bessel,[46] since Belyaev seems to find the publication of it burdensome.

We discussed Nikolai Andreyevich's adherence to form in *May Night, Snegurochka,* and *Sadko,* and he pointed out that his use of this procedure in *The Tsar's Bride* is not entirely fortuitous. It only seemed so to the critics, who find it difficult to grasp anything they cannot read in books.

"However, time is the best judge," added Rimsky-Korsakov. "Nowadays, for example, it wouldn't occur to anyone to say that I should have done some studying, but in the days of *The Maid of Pskov* they often wrote about this and, in part, it was even true."

7 November

The young people were visiting us and we were playing Balakirev's First Symphony, when suddenly the bell rang and in walked Nikolai Andreyevich. The room became alive with talk of the news of the day: the story of Safonov and Konius;[47] Stasov's article in defense of Timofeyev;[48] the Moscow performance of *The Tsar's Bride*;[49] and, finally, A. Suvorin's highly sympathetic piece about *Snegurochka* and its author in today's *Novoe vremia*,[50] which was occasioned by the publication of a fine article on this opera by Camille Bellaigue in the latest issue of *Revue des Deux-Mondes*.

"Of course it's a nice little piece, but it's a good eighteen years late," commented Rimsky-Korsakov.

On leaving, he took with him his manuscript of act 3 of *Tsar Saltan*—this "Russian Siegfried."

3 December

I attended the dress rehearsal of the second Russian Symphony Concert. Following the performance of excerpts from *Tsar Saltan*, Nikolai Andreyevich was given something of an ovation. Upon learning from Nadezhda Nikolayevna that he has already finished his new opera (of the same name), Stasov congratulated him warmly, saying that in all likelihood he had composed it at night, since he (Stasov) did not even suspect that it existed. He praised the excerpts played today and then added: "Remember, Nikolai Andreyevich, my advice to you—no, not advice but a request or the last will and testament of an old man—and sometime, when you're in the mood, write three or four musical settings of the Apocalypse."

"Well, then," replied Rimsky-Korsakov with a chuckle, "the title page will have to read: 'Music by Rimsky-Korsakov, Libretto . . . St. John!' How amusing!"

"I'm really not joking," interrupted Stasov. "I'm sure you'd write wonderful music on this subject. However, you'd have to have a rain of red frogs, and so on and so forth."

Thus, the "secret" about the new opera is out, and I am very, very glad.

8 December

When I arrived at the Rimsky-Korsakovs' today, Nikolai Andreyevich was giving Spendiarov a lesson, and therefore I was obliged to wait a short while to see him. When he came out of his study, we talked about the critics' response to the excerpts from *Tsar Saltan*[51] (performed at the second Russian Symphony Concert), and Nikolai Andreyevich observed that, while he had progressed heaven knows how much during the twenty years or so since his *Snegurochka,* the critics had also managed to grow a bit during these years, and this accounts for their more sympathetic tone toward him.

Somehow our conversation turned to the subject of the eleventh chord, which some theoreticians do not recognize as an independent chord, and with this Rimsky-Korsakov told me about an extremely amusing thought expressed by one of his friends to the effect that absolutely no one lives in London. And when they began to protest to this friend that London is a city of some three million inhabitants, he stubbornly repeated: "Nevertheless, there's not a living soul in London!" The same can be said about the eleventh chord.

18 December

The program of the fifth symphonic evening of the Russian Music Society included Glazunov's Sixth Symphony; Beethoven's Fourth Piano Concerto with Edouard Risler as soloist; Rimsky-Korsakov's *Song of Oleg the Wise* (premiere);[52] Liszt's *Tasso,* and César Franck's *Symphonic Variations* (also for the first time). The latter I did not hear, since I left before the concert ended.

Glazunov was called out at the end of the first movement and also at the end of his symphony. The *Song of Oleg the Wise* opened the second half of the evening. When the composer came out on the stage, he was greeted with long, thunderous applause. However, the performance of the work was far from satisfactory and, although the audience liked it, they were not overly enthusiastic. For one thing, the chorus was poorly prepared; for another, Morskoi's singing was almost inaudible. Besides this, Nikolai Andreyevich's unsteady tempo was too fast, and this served to mar the entire work. Sharonov was not bad as Oleg, but he bungled the exquisite *Cantabile* "Proshchai, moi tovarishch, moi vernyi sluga" (from

Oleg's farewell to his horse), and as a consequence it passed almost unnoticed.

22 December

When I visited Rimsky-Korsakov this evening, the talk concerned the
unsuccessful performance of *Oleg* and its reception by the critics.[53] In
Rimsky-Korsakov's view, the orchestration is too thick, since here and
there it drowned out the voices. He is resolved not to show the manuscript to anyone for a long time, to "hold it back."

Rimsky-Korsakov has orchestrated Mussorgsky's *Field Marshal*[54] for
Sekar-Rozhansky and has also composed a big aria in C major for Lykov,[55] to be inserted in the first scene of act 3 of *The Tsar's Bride* after
Lykov's words: "Neuzheli, Dunyasha? Byt' ne mozhet!" He has decided
to go to Moscow on January 1 for a few days, first, for a brief rest and
secondly, (this is the main reason) to hear his new aria. He has already
sent the manuscript there.

I reported to Nikolai Andreyevich Stasov's opinion of his *Oleg the Wise*.
While he likes it, "he is in two minds about it," as he put it. He finds
the recitatives poor but the "grobovaia zmeia"—matchless. Taken as a
whole, though it is not bad, it seems to have been written "backwards"
somehow, and the funeral feast in Balakirev's *Tamara* is far superior.

I forgot to mention that Nikolai Andreyevich feels that something has
surely happened to Solovyov of late, as he has suddenly begun to treat
him (Nikolai Andreyevich) and his works "differently."

25 December

My mother and I went to the Rimsky-Korsakovs' for their amateur
theatricals. They gave Chekhov's *Bear* and Shcheglov's *Nonsense*.[56] Among
those participating were Nadezhda and Sofia Nikolayevna, Andrei and
Volodya Nikolayevich Rimsky-Korsakov, N. I. Richter and his brother
Mikhail Ivanovich, and the student Troitsky. The makeup was done by
Stepan Stepanovich Mitusov; costumes and coiffures by startlingly pretty
Alexandra Kapitonovna Rogova (the Rimsky-Korsakovs' dressmaker), who
made herself look like a real china doll.

During the second play, the curtain was drawn and closed by Nikolai

Andreyevich himself. At the end of the performance, Volodya read "on behalf of Leonid Durnoshapov" (a character in Shcheglov's play), the following humorous poem "on critics" which Nikolai Andreyevich had written, on his own admission, "without any pangs of creation":

> The critic's task is not easy:
> A play has just been given,
> You have to report on it to the newspaper at once.
> I'll try to solve this problem.
> And so, to work!
> But I'll be bold.
> Only one decision I have to make:
> To begin with praise or censure?
> If you praise, you won't please
> The liberal section of the press;
> If you criticize, watch out—
> You'll get it from the actors.
> I decide to praise: Listen! "Oh!"
> (Five kopecks a line).
>> Being devoted to art with all their heart,
>> The actors outdid themselves.
>> A new era is upon us.
>> From Aristophanes to Molière
>> Right up to our own day
>> Who could have acted so effortlessly
>> And so expertly?
>> Who could have better interpreted the roles?
> Shakespeare's ghost brings them laurels
> For setting an example to the whole world.
>> But now I must end my article.
>> Glorious actors, hurrah!

(Detailed account in the next issue of the newspaper *Myl'nyi puzyr'*.)[57]

Later, in a discussion about the arts and creativity in general, Rimsky-Korsakov said that of all creative workers, he values writers least since, in his opinion, only true geniuses such as Pushkin, Lermontov, Turgenev, Gogol, and Leo Tolstoy are really good. He esteems compositional talent most and, after that, painters and sculptors. Generally speaking, he does not believe much in the so-called "pangs of creation," which he thinks can be explained in most cases either by a lack of talent or by insufficient compositional technique.

On leaving I took one of the three copies of the "playbill"—the one written in Nikolai Andreyevich's hand. Nadezhda Nikolayevna promised to give me a photograph of Serov's portrait of Rimsky-Korsakov, which hangs in the Tretyakov Gallery in Moscow.

On the whole, the evening went wonderfully.

31 December

On New Year's Eve I dropped in on Nikolai Andreyevich to return the score of the suite from Glazunov's *Raymonda* and the playbill, which Sofia Nikolayevna needs for some reason. When I entered Rimsky-Korsakov quickly hid something in his writing table. Can it be that he is already composing something else besides the opera, something smaller—a song perhaps?

We talked about the performance of *The Tsar's Bride* in Kharkov (on December 22, with Insarova and Kampionsky). Nikolai Andreyevich has received two reviews of it, one of which appeared in the *Kharkovskii vestnik* and the other in *Iuzhnyi krai*.[58]

Tomorrow Rimsky-Korsakov is going to Moscow.

CHAPTER 10

1900

2 January

This afternoon, between one and two o'clock, I visited Nadezhda Nikolayevna and received the promised portrait of Rimsky-Korsakov but, alas, without an inscription. Last night, as planned, Nikolai Andreyevich went to Moscow.

In the evening, upon returning home, I found on my table a greeting card from Nikolai Andreyevich with the message, "V.V.! Congratulations on your Name Day! N.R.K. January 1, 1900":

Example 42

Po-zdra vlia-u Vas s dnem Va-she-go an- ge-la

9 January

At about quarter to five I dropped in on the Rimsky-Korsakovs only to learn that just today Nikolai Andreyevich had decided to visit me.

Thus we missed each other. Speaking with Nadezhda Nikolayevna, I learned that during this visit to Moscow, Nikolai Andreyevich was presented with a large laurel wreath by the Russian Private Opera Company and a testimonial signed by all the soloists, the chorus, and the orchestra of the Solodovnikov Theater.

At around six o'clock, Rimsky-Korsakov returned home. He told me that he had been at my house and had left a letter for me; also that he had inscribed his portrait and had used as an autograph, as I had asked, the opening bars of the overture to *The Maid of Pskov*:

For his name day
as a keepsake.
N. R.-Korsakov

1 January
1900

(*Maid of Pskov*)

He was very pleased with his Moscow trip, even though the evening of his songs, planned by Mme Kerzin, had not materialized.[1]

We talked about the forthcoming concert in Brussels,[2] where Rimsky-Korsakov will certainly go and where he is considering performing the overture to Glinka's *Ruslan,* his own *Sheherazade* (at the request of the concert's organizers), the suite from Glazunov's *Raymonda,* the introduction to act 3 of Taneyev's *Oresteia,* and Dargomyzhsky's *Kazachok.*

Then we spoke about my proposed collaboration with *Russkii vestnik* (thanks to F. Romer) and about the new attitude at *Novoe vremia,* where young Suvorin and many other contributors to this paper clearly support the new Russian school with Rimsky-Korsakov at the head.

I brought to Nikolai Andreyevich's attention the new collection of thirty Russian folk songs arranged by Balakirev for four hands[3] and dedicated to "Posterity." He had not been acquainted with it.

Referring to the testimonial given him by the Solodovnikov Company, Nikolai Andreyevich remarked with a smile that it was a kind of "promissory note," since in signing it, the Directorate seemed to be soliciting permission to stage *Tsar Saltan* in Moscow next year.[4]

Besides this, Nikolai Andreyevich told me something curious: Cui believes that in his opera *The Saracen,* he finally achieved the "ideal fusion of word and music" and thus, he was the first Russian composer to have written a real opera, since, as he sees it, neither *Ruslan* nor *Prince Igor* can be counted! This astonishing idea César Antonovich expressed without a trace of shame on the day of his new opera's premiere.[5] No, clearly, Cui has gone absolutely mad.

26 January

As always, on Wednesday I dropped in on the Rimsky-Korsakovs. Nikolai Andreyevich was in an excellent mood. It seems that the other day, Prince Volkonsky informed him that next season, by order of the Tsar,[6] the Marinsky Theater is going to present his *Sadko*[7] and Wagner's *Walküre.*[8] Moreover, not only the sets but the costumes for *Sadko* are to be executed from sketches by the artist Apollinary Mikhailovich Vasnetsov and the entire production, including the selection of the cast, is to be under the supervision of Rimsky-Korsakov.

Further, I learned that no. 4 of *Le courrier musical* of January 27, 1900 (N. S.) carried an enthusiastic article by Jean d'Udine on Rimsky-Korsakov's *Antar,* which was performed in Paris at the Concerts Lamoureux under the baton of Camille Chevillard; also that the title page of the journal carried a picture of Nikolai Andreyevich (from Mrozovskaya's photograph of 1895).

9 February

I went to Rimsky-Korsakov's to pick up scene 1 of act 4 of *Tsar Saltan.* He reported on the reception at Prince Volkonsky's (on February 4), which was attended by all the "cream" of the music and theatrical world and, because of the throng of guests, was "so boring" that he and Glazunov left early.

Our conversation then touched on Rimsky-Korsakov's *Collection of Sacred Music,*[9] which was published by the Court Chapel in 1884. We considered the simple but original alternation of triads in *The Creed* and *Mercy of Peace;* the ending of *We Praise Thee* with its beautiful setting of the words "I molimtesia, Bozhe Nash"; the musically charming episode from *It Is Truly Meet* at the words "Chestneishuiu kheruvim," which was later incorporated in the accompaniment of the Kupalskoye *kolo*[10] (see act 2 of the opera-ballet *Mlada*).

"Since you're interested in my church music," said Rimsky-Korsakov, "I suggest that you take a look at my 'arrangements'—they are much better."

Speaking about Wagner's opera *Tristan,* which, during these days, Nikolai Andreyevich has attended repeatedly, going to all the rehearsals and studying the score, Nikolai Andreyevich expressed his thoughts about it as follows:

"Since *Tristan,* for all its shortcomings, is really an extraordinarily great work, we should not speak about it 'off-handedly,' as is often done here.

"I, for example," he continued, "go to *Tristan* with a purpose, for while listening to this extremely complex and tangled, though at times superb music, I continually learn how one should write and how one must not write under any circumstances."

16 February

Tonight, in a talk with Nikolai Andreyevich about the trip he is to make to Brussels for the concert there (on March 5/18), I learned that he will leave on Tuesday, the first week of Easter (February 22) and return at the beginning of the third week.

Once again we fell to talking about *Tristan and Isolde,* which Rimsky-Korsakov has been studying with exceptional zeal. He holds the view that it is unquestionably a major work, despite its often very considerable flaws; that in it Wagner expressed himself in an unusual way; that the music is real music, without trickery or empty, extramusical (decorative) effects; that for all its cumbersomeness, even the orchestration is exemplary, at times profoundly inspired and amazing. Most important of all, in this opera both the harmony and orchestration are *his own,* "Wagnerian,*" and in this sense, it is an extraordinary work.

I mentioned to Rimsky-Korsakov that I'm almost "beside myself" with excitement over *Saltan.* He raised no objection; indeed, he even showed me what he considers an interesting harmony in the scene between Guidon and the Swan Princess [example 44].

The other day, *Novoe vremia* carried a curious report to the effect that recently, while Safonov was conducting Rimsky-Korsakov's *Sheherazade* at

Example 44

one of the regular concerts of the Academy of St. Cecilia in Rome, the electricity suddenly failed and with that the concert ended, leaving Rimsky-Korsakov's work unfinished.[11] What a fine state of affairs!

24 February

Last night Nikolai Andreyevich left for Brussels with Liadov and Glazunov, and, therefore, I did not see him when I dropped in at his house today. Nadezhda Nikolayevna told me that the other day he received the following telegram from Safonov:

Mineralniye Vody. 19 February.
I read *Saltan* all night, while waiting for the train. I was moved, filled with admiration for the genius of the author. Regards. Safonov. I am going to Moscow.

Safonov has been courting Rimsky-Korsakov with particular zeal of late.

7 March

This morning I received a postcard from Nikolai Andreyevich in Brussels with a picture of the famous Mannequin Pis and a musical phrase [example 45], evidently by way of illustrating the famous Brussels fountain, although this "clarinet phrase" was drawn from the moment in act 1 of *Tsar Saltan* when the playful young Tsarevich Guidon runs out of the Court and all seven nurses chase after him in a desperate effort to catch him.

Example 45

In conclusion, let me say that the first performance of *The Tsar's Bride,* which took place on March 2, 1900, was reviewed by P. Veimarn, Solovyov, Koptyaev, Bormann, and Cui in seven of the most important Petersburg newspapers: *Novoe vremia, Syn otechestva, Birzhevye vedomosti, Rossiia, S.-Peterburgskie vedomosti, Severnyi kur'er,* and *Novosti.*[12]

8 March

Mindful that Rimsky-Korsakov was to have returned from Brussels last night, I went to his house directly after work. However, he had not yet come home when I arrived. Noting a new book on his desk entitled *Account of les concerts populaires de Bruxelles,*[13] which had been compiled for the twenty-fifth anniversary of their principal director Joseph Dupont (who died on December 21, 1899), I leafed through it quickly and learned which of Rimsky-Korsakov's works had been performed at these concerts. They were: the *Sadko* fantasy (in the original version)[14] on January 14, 1877; the *Fantasia on Serbian Themes*—January 10, 1886; *Antar*—January 23, 1877, and May 10, 1888; the Easter Overture and *Capriccio espagnol*—April 13, 1890; *Skazka*—December 9, 1894; the *Sadko* fantasy (new version) and *Sheherazade*—March 18, 1900. Listed among the foreign conductors invited were such notables as Hans Richter, Hermann Levi, Camille Saint-Saëns, Richard Strauss, and Felix Mottl.

At around six o'clock Rimsky returned. We talked about his trip.

"Generally speaking," he said, "the cult of Strauss, d'Indy, and others like them seems to hold sway in Brussels and therefore, when Hans Richter performed Tchaikovsky's wonderful Sixth Symphony there last year, it passed unnoticed.

"You know," he continued, "I've finally come to the conclusion that, thanks to our enormous ability to assimilate, we Russians have considerably outstripped the West of today. What still excites them keenly—for example, the Wagnerian tendencies and, especially, the absurd and utterly senseless creations of all sorts of Richard Strausses, we've already experienced to a considerable degree. After all, in terms of his artistic tendency, wasn't Dargomyzhsky, in the period of *The Stone Guest,* a kind of a Russian Wagner? And Mussorgsky, with his opera *The Marriage* and 'gray hair,' depicted in the accompaniment by a 'minor second'—wasn't he an absurd, grotesquely blatant innovator of the Richard Strauss type? And what happened? It's all past, finished! Meanwhile, even today, the Brussels public can get excited, even ecstatic over such rubbish. The best example of this is their response to Strauss' *Also sprach Zarathustra.*

"We didn't have their Bachs and Palestrinas—that's true," concluded Rimsky-Korsakov, "but then the West didn't have our Glinka, who at one stroke absorbed all of Western culture of the preceding centuries. He made his appearance in the history of Russian music totally unexpectedly, like the Greek Minerva, fully equipped with all the artistic ideas and compositional techniques of his time. In this sense Glinka was unique!"

In the evening I attended the second Concert Colonne,[15] at which Berlioz' grandiose romantic *Requiem* was performed, but I did not see Rimsky-Korsakov there.

11 March

This morning, during the intermission at the dress rehearsal of the third Russian Symphony Concert, Rimsky-Korsakov and I talked about his String Quartet in F and its wonderful first movement, the middle of which turns into a beautiful fugato, constructed on the melody [given in example 46]; which is reminiscent, partly, of the basic theme of Wagner's *Meistersinger* and is brought to a close with a charming coda with trills and figuration in the cello. The Andante, constructed on a theme of a

Example 46

somewhat liturgical character, used by Rimsky-Korsakov subsequently in Yaromir's second Dream in *Mlada* is, in mood, a worthy pendant to the prelude to The Flight into Egypt from Berlioz' oratorio *L'enfance du Christ*. Less successful is the third movement, a scherzo, of a Schubert-Mendelssohnian character. The charming singing second theme of the Finale is harmonized elegantly and, at the same time, naturally by Rimsky-Korsakov.

I informed Nikolai Andreyevich about the following amusing report which was carried in the March 2 issue of *Peterburgskaia gazeta* (no. 60) in the section *Teatral'noe ekho* (Theatrical echo). According to the Odessa interviewers, N. Figner expressed the thought that while he admires Rimsky-Korsakov's outstanding talent, from an artistic point of view all his operas share one flaw—the lack of a grateful role for tenor. At least, he has not been able to find one. He praised the part of Ivan (in *The Tsar's Bride*), but this is for baritone not for tenor.

The program this evening, under the direction of Rimsky-Korsakov, included Tchaikovsky's relatively little-known Third Symphony, a brilliant overture (in F) by V. Zolotarev (premiere), a beautiful but very drawn-out legend by F. Akimenko (premiere), and excerpts from Rimsky-Korsakov's *Tsar Saltan*. Rimsky-Korsakov, Zolotarev, and Akimenko were greeted with prolonged applause.

As I was leaving the concert, I met V. V. Stasov, who seemed extremely pleased with the performance of *Tsar Saltan*.

14 March

I dropped in on the orchestral rehearsal of act 3 of *The Tsar's Bride*. Thanks to A. Zverzhansky, I was introduced to V. I. Suk, Conductor of the Kharkov Opera, who proved to be an extremely amiable and likeable man.

Rimsky-Korsakov also attended the rehearsal. We talked about the absolute necessity of restoring one of the cuts since, in a purely musical sense, the sextet is the most important moment in the first scene of act 3 (it will be restored). Rimsky-Korsakov pointed out, too, that owing to the paucity of strings (there are only four first violins), one can really get to know the whole "anatomy" of the orchestration.

"You know," he said, "I can once again relax and enjoy myself thoroughly, listening to the sound of the Russian oboes; in Brussels, their timbre is particularly brazen, impudent. This is a characteristic shared by all French oboes, unlike here, where the timbre of the oboe has an unusually sad, pure, chaste quality."[16]

In the evening I attended the Kharkov Private Opera Company's second performance of *The Tsar's Bride*.[17]

The theater was almost completely filled. Both the artists and the composer were recalled many times. At the end of the second act, Rimsky-Korsakov received a tremendous ovation: six flourishes were played, one after the other; everyone applauded—the audience, orchestra, soloists, and chorus—and Nikolai Andreyevich was presented with a beautiful silver wreath from Prince Tsereteli.

As for the performance, the first act was the worst; the second and third went fairly well. Kampionsky sang the role of Gryaznoy wonderfully; Feodorov was good as Marfa's father; and Insarova was matchless as Marfa, handling this vocally difficult role exquisitely throughout. What is more, she literally stunned the audience with her profoundly poetic, sensitive acting and charming appearance. The scene of Marfa's delirium could not possibly be performed better. All in all, today's performance had a festive air about it, obviously because of the presence of the composer.

18 March

The program of the fourth and final Russian Symphony Concert of the season consisted of Taneyev's overture to *Oresteia,* Cherepnin's choruses *Night* and *Old Song,* Glazunov's *Intermezzo Lirico,*[18] Borodin's Third Symphony (unfinished), Wihtol's *Bard of Beverin,* Mussorgsky's chorus *The Destruction of Sennacherib,* and Rimsky-Korsakov's *Overture on Three Russian Themes.*[19]

On the whole, the concert went fairly well. Mussorgsky's chorus had to be repeated, and at the end of the concert, Nikolai Andreyevich was recalled many times.

11 April

The evening at the Rimsky-Korsakovs' with Insarova was quite lively, even though Maria Nikolayevna did not arrive until almost ten-thirty and did not sing a note. Besides her, there were the singer Kampionsky, V.

Stasov, Liadov, Lavrov, Spendiarov, V. I. Belsky and his wife, Yanova and her husband, et al.

There was not much music. Kampionsky sang arias from *Prince Igor* and *Sadko*, songs by Cui, Liszt, and Spendiarov; Yanova sang a number of songs by Rimsky-Korsakov and, at the request of Stasov, Sofia Nikolay-evna Rimskaya-Korsakova sang an aria from *The Maid of Pskov*. Rimsky-Korsakov played his comic duet between the Old Man and the Buffoon from the first act of *Tsar Saltan,* which not only sent Stasov into raptures but even reduced him to tears.

Before tea I had a rather detailed discussion with Rimsky-Korsakov about his collection of settings of sacred music, which are used at the "highest Court." It consists of the following: no. 1—*Cherubic Song;* no. 2—*Let All Mortal Flesh Keep Silent,* extraordinarily calm in character; no. 3—a Sunday Communion hymn, a variant of the *Cherubic Song* no. 1, of little importance from a musical point of view; no. 4—*See the Bridegroom Cometh*—very good musically, with a severe "Alleluia," a beautiful begin-ning and interesting episode at the words "Ne snom otiagotisia," some-what reminiscent in its harmonic structure to *Alexei, Man of God;* no. 5— *I Enter Thy Mansion, My Savior,* with unusually expressive music of a purely liturgical character; no. 6—the Psalm *By the Waters of Babylon,* a znamenny chant with a superb opening phrase and extremely successful harmoni-zation in the middle and end, which hypnotizes the listener with its original repetitiousness. As an example I cite the following three passages from the Psalm: the opening introduction of the chorus at the words "Vsegda pomianuti nam Siona," the original Alleluia, and the music which precedes this chorus.

I should like to point out here, by the way, that this collection of Rimsky-Korsakov's sacred music arrangements was published by the Court Chapel in 1886.

We also talked about Rimsky-Korsakov's double chorus "Tebe, Boga, khvalim," arranged from a Greek chant in three voices.

The manuscript of this worthy pendant to Berlioz' "Tibi amni Angeli" ("Te Deum," no. 2) was dated by Rimsky-Korsakov 18 July 1883 (Taitsa).

24 April

I attended the fortieth performance of *Snegurochka* with Mikhailova in the leading role, Kozakovskaya (Kupava), Slavina (Lel), Fried (Spring),

Chuprynnikov (King of the Berendeys), Smirnov (Mizgir), Bukhtoyarov (Grandfather Frost), Maiboroda (Bermyata), et al.

Even though the King's duet and cavatina, the Dance of the Skomorokhi, and Lel's third song were repeated, the performance as a whole was poor. After act 2, Rimsky-Korsakov was recalled three times, after act 3—twice.

It is regrettable that works like *Snegurochka, Ruslan,* and *Prince Igor* are given such bad and careless performances at our Imperial Theater.

9 May

I spent the evening at the Rimsky-Korsakovs'. Also there were Felix Blumenfeld, Liadov, Belyaev, Glazunov, and Belsky.

I mentioned that this morning at the graduation exercises I had run into my old friend Alexander Borisovich Khessin, who recently returned from abroad. He worked with Arthur Nikisch all winter, attending all the rehearsals of the twenty-two concerts he gave at the Gwendhaus in Leipzig and nine or ten concerts in Berlin, and he also went with him to Hamburg and Hanover. Thanks to help from Nikisch (and Siloti), Khessin conducted Yarov's military band for three months (from January to March), during which time he played a great deal of German and Russian music. On March 8–21 of this year he also conducted a concert at the Albert-Holle (Crystal Palace) in Leipzig, consisting entirely of works by Tchaikovsky.[20] It was attended by all the representatives of the Gwendhaus, headed by Nikisch. After that, on the advice of the latter, Khessin went to Karlsruhe to Felix Mottl (at the Court Theater), with the aim of becoming acquainted in more detail with the techniques of operatic conducting. He spent about five weeks there and intends to return in the fall.

We talked about *The Tsar's Bride,* and Rimsky-Korsakov said that in time to come this opera will have much greater importance in the history of Russian music than it is thought to have today by musicians, who are bewildered by its old-fashioned form.

After tea Felix Mikhailovich played (from the score) the first scene of act 3 and all of act 2 of *Tsar Saltan.* He seemed very pleased with it. He and Rimsky-Korsakov had a very long private conversation, most likely about Prince Volkonsky and *The Tsar's Bride.*[21]

On the way home, with Glazunov (at two o'clock in the morning), I learned, among other things, what he thinks of Rimsky-Korsakov's most recent works. In his opinion, in his last operas *(Christmas Eve, Sadko, The Tsar's Bride,* and *Tsar Saltan),* Nikolai Andreyevich has reached the point of cliché.

"Take the finale of the second act of *Saltan,*" he said. "The music may not be bad, but there isn't any real symphonic development."

15 May

I went to the Rimsky-Korsakovs' to bid them good-bye for the summer. We talked at length about *The Tsar's Bride.* Belyaev seems in no hurry to publish Lykov's new aria, which is quite understandable since the Belyaev circle (with Mitrofan Petrovich in the lead) does not care too much for this opera.

I reported to Nikolai Andreyevich what Balakirev thinks of *The Tsar's Bride,* namely, that it is a thoroughly unsuccessful opera; that the overture is poor; that whereas hitherto Rimsky-Korsakov was able to compose elegantly and interestingly, of late he seems to have written himself out; that the "Iar-khmel'" chorus was taken *in toto* from Liszt's Second Rhapsody; and that only the scene of Marfa's delirium is really good. (This latter seemed to irritate Rimsky-Korsakov somewhat.)

"I, on the other hand, am convinced they're all deeply mistaken about this work," said Rimsky-Korsakov. "It didn't just happen fortuitously. Not at all. It wasn't for nothing that before writing it, I composed fifty-five songs and *Mozart and Salieri;* thus they served as preparatory studies, as it were, for *The Tsar's Bride.*"

We discussed Prince Volkonsky's extremely strange proposal that Rimsky-Korsakov write a new opera, which he has promised in advance to stage at the Marinsky Theater (thereby passing over *Tsar Saltan* and *The Tsar's Bride).* As for producing *The Maid of Pskov* in Moscow, even though Chaliapin (the ideal artist for the role of Ivan the Terrible) is a member of the company, Telyakovsky, Assistant Director of Theaters there, has still to take a definite position on that matter since, on his own admission, he does not know the opera at all! How's that for a director!

On leaving, I promised Rimsky-Korsakov that I would drop in on him once more before he went abroad.

26 May

Late in the afternoon I went to the Rimsky-Korsakovs' as planned. We spoke about Suk's recent visit to Nikolai Andreyevich.

"You know," he remarked, "Vyacheslav Ivanovich is unquestionably an excellent musician with a superb ear, but as a man, he can't always be relied on—he plays both ends against the middle."

Then, speaking about his future plans vis-à-vis the Conservatory, Rimsky-Korsakov told me that beginning with next year, he is no longer going to teach harmony—it bores him. He is going to hand over this course to Liadov.

"In the first place," he said, "this will give me two days a week free of work at the Conservatory—Wednesday and Saturday (the days of the orchestral rehearsals at the Marinsky Theater). Second, I won't have to lecture on this subject, which really bores me so terribly that I couldn't give it the kind of conscientious attention my students have a right to expect of me."

We spoke briefly about Laroche and his extremely pitiful situation. He was literally turned out of his house and is having a difficult time making ends meet, living in a furnished room, which he rented from relatives of the Tchaikovskys.

In conclusion, Rimsky-Korsakov and I discussed the question of whether we exaggerate the importance of all the composers of the new Russian school or whether, compared with the really great composers, they are not something on the order of the Marschners and Spohrs.

"You won't believe it," said Rimsky-Korsakov, "but I myself have often wondered about this, and I must say frankly, the idea has greatly distressed me."

After dinner and coffee, we said good-bye for the summer, as usual, with a hearty embrace. The Rimsky-Korsakovs are leaving by steamer on June 3 or 4 for Lübeck, from where they plan to drive along the Rhine and then settle near Andrei or somewhere in the Schwarzwald,[22] or even in the Vosges.

I forgot to mention that before dinner Rimsky-Korsakov told me that Stasov had tried recently in all seriousness to persuade him to write an opera dealing with the time of Ghengis Khan and Prince Mikhail of Tver and to be sure to introduce into it the wild, religious dancing of the Siberian aborigines.

2 June

This morning, before work, I took a chance and dropped in again on the Rimsky-Korsakovs. When I entered the study, I found Nikolai Andreyevich looking over the last scene of *Tsar Saltan*. We got onto the subject of S. Bulich's article on Russian music,[23] which appears in *Brockhaus' Encyclopedic Dictionary*.

"You know," said Rimsky-Korsakov, "of late I've begun to resent the view expressed repeatedly in journals and newspapers—and it must be taken into consideration whether we like it or not—that only my *Maid of Pskov* and, perhaps, *Snegurochka* are good, while all the rest is ignored as though it didn't exist. Meanwhile, I believe that many of my latest things are on a par with these earlier ones. I venture to say the same about my songs. Moreover, what irritates me most about all this is the incredible stupidity and inability of the public (and artists as well) to form their own opinions."

"Even if they erred," I said, "at least their errors would be their own, while as it is, their opinions are both stupid and not their own.

"And indeed, in this respect," I continued, "it's not only the dilettantes who sin but also such major artists as Glazunov, Cui, and Liadov. Who else should understand music if not they? They have the knowledge, enormous musicality and taste—they even belong to the same school.

"However," I concluded, "we must admit that very few composers have a real critical sense. Unfortunately, this has always had and continues to have a very deleterious effect on music. Glazunov, for example, is thoroughly indifferent to operatic music—he prefers ballet. Liadov once tried seriously to convince you that you don't always have to begin an opera with a chorus."

"And when I pointed out to him," said Nikolai Andreyevich, "that not only does *The Tsar's Bride* begin with a solo (Gryaznoy's aria) but that *Snegurochka, Christmas Eve,* and even *Saltan* begin almost at once with recitatives, Anton Konstantinovich disagreed with me and continued to stand his ground."

Speaking then about the flexibility of operatic forms, Rimsky-Korsakov observed that Dargomyzhsky's *Stone Guest,* with its recitative style, differs from other operas mainly quantitatively, and not qualitatively, since the most superb examples of melodic recitative were already to be found in both Glinka and Mozart. One need only recall the part of Donna Anna in *Don Giovanni* or the brilliant scene from Glinka's *Ruslan*—"O pole, pole, kto tebia useial mertvymi kostiami."

"I'm of the opinion," he continued, "that one of the most important tasks facing an opera composer is to have a good idea of the right form, that is, the one fully suited to the given subject, before he begins to compose the music, especially since, strictly speaking, operatic form is far from rigid as the Wagnerites think."

Further, we talked about Nikolai Andreyevich's preface to *Tsar Saltan*, in which he states, among other things, that an opera is not written to be cut, and if someone undertakes to violate the artistic and scenic demands of a work of his or begins to alter his score arbitrarily, without his knowledge and consent, then he, Rimsky-Korsakov, will forbid its performance.

"I can imagine," he added, smiling, "that some people will be angry at me for saying this. Well, so be it."

Regarding the Kharkov Company's appearances in Moscow,[24] Rimsky-Korsakov remarked that, judging from the newspaper reports, the Muscovites were not particularly impressed by Insarova, though they did praise her portrayal of the "delirium scene" (in *The Tsar's Bride*). Also, the audiences were not especially large, but this can be explained partly by the fact that this opera had already been given at the Solodovnikov Theater about thirty times this winter (a fact pointed out by the Moscow critics).

Finally, we spoke of this, that in most of Rimsky-Korsakov's major works we find the same distinctive device, a kind of musical "kriuk"[25] [see example 47], which, for all its singularity, in each case takes on a somewhat different coloring.[26]

Example 47

We then considered the fact that the fantastic portrayal of the Swan Princess has something of the overall quality of Schumann's famous "Vogel als Prophet," a quality which had appeared before *Saltan* in Rimsky-Korsakov's *Skazka, Snegurochka* (scene between the Snegurochka and Spring), and even in *Sadko* (in the musical characterization of the Sea Princess Volkhova).

By now it was time for me to go to work. Once again, we said our good-byes, and this time Nikolai Andreyevich embraced me and kissed me heartily.

7 September

Having learned that the Rimsky-Korsakovs had returned from abroad on September 1, I dropped in on them after dinner to find out all about their impressions of their travels.

When I entered Nikolai Andreyevich was still resting. Not wishing to disturb him, I went directly into the drawing room. While waiting for him to appear, Nadezhda Nikolayevna, at my request, began to tell me about their trip. As it turned out, they had traveled throughout most of Germany and Switzerland, staying in Berlin, Strasbourg, Mainz, spending a whole month in the Schwarzwald and had visited Cologne, Lucerne, Interlaken, Geneva, Lausanne—in short, everywhere. Next summer, if all is well, they will go abroad again.

But now Nikolai Andreyevich appeared and we went into his study. He told me that in December, *Sadko* will most likely be given at the Marinsky Theater here, and in October—*Saltan,* at the Solodovnikov Theater in Moscow, and that he plans to go there for the performance of this opera.

Once again we returned to the subject of Wagner's music, noting that although it seldom remains for long in the same tonality, Wagner does use key signatures. He thereby seems to be indicating the "principal key," that is, the tonality around which, despite the most bizarre digressions and modulations, everything else seemingly groups itself as though about a fixed center.

"Isn't it possible," said Rimsky-Korsakov, "that the persistent return to B major in the scene of Walther's meeting with Eva (in act 2 of *Die Meistersinger*) reveals a kind of instinctive urge on Wagner's part 'not to break completely with form?' And what a fascinating result he achieves by constantly returning to the same tonality! Thus it seems that in these moments, the life of mankind, with its daily concerns, unpleasantnesses, and joys recedes into the background and in its place, before the very eyes of the listener, rises nature itself in all its charming beauty. The listener automatically imagines a quiet, enchanting summer night, suffused with the delicate, scarcely perceptible fragrance of lilac."

14 September

This afternoon Rimsky-Korsakov visited me between four and five-thirty. I mentioned to him the new and extremely cheap Payne edition of the works of Berlioz.[27] He thinks that such low prices (the full score of the *Symphonie fantastique* costs only three marks; *Romeo and Juliet*—four marks) ought to be kept for something better. There really is no crying need for Berlioz' works, he said; they probably ought to be held in li-braries and other places of that sort. To this I replied that not only shall I acquire this entire edition but that I could not possibly consider "spit-ting" on this composer, who, through his brilliant innovations, has so greatly advanced the art of music.

The conversation naturally became more heated and, as luck would have it, there on my table lay Timofeyev's article on *The Tsar's Bride,* which ended with the words: "While sharing the opinion that the music of *The Tsar's Bride,* with some exceptions (such as, Marfa's aria, the sextet, the last scene) does not attain the heights of inspiration and power of creation which Rimsky-Korsakov attained in his other four operas—*The Maid of Pskov, Snegurochka, Mlada,* and *Sadko*—nevertheless we think that *The Tsar's Bride* ought to be ranked with the remarkable Russian operas, which have enriched the Russian operatic repertoire."[28]

"I don't like this conclusion at all," declared Rimsky-Korsakov. "What it adds up to is this: the man heaped praise upon praise and, in the end, all this praise amounted to nothing but empty words, since in his opinion, *The Tsar's Bride* doesn't measure up to my other operas, and this just isn't true."

I'm convinced that Nikolai Andreyevich exaggerates the musical im-portance of this opera without realizing it. He thinks that everyone else is wrong. When I asked him point blank which is better—*The Tsar's Bride* or *Snegurochka*—he declared, not without irritation, that he is not going to give his opinion on this subject, that this is his secret (?!) but that I should not think that his opinion is simple.

"You, like everyone else," he said, "out of a certain perverseness, don't understand a great deal about me. You may even overestimate me, giving me ten or even eleven points for my works (according to the twelve point system), whereas I myself give them no more than six or seven. Nevertheless, I'm absolutely certain that in some cases I err less than you do.

"Here you are, even now," he concluded, "hoping very much that I'm wrong, and this I don't like."

"And I, in turn," I retorted, "would find it extremely painful to be mistaken, or still worse, disillusioned about my ideals."

On the whole, today's visit was not one of the most pleasant. We both felt hostile somehow toward each other. And all this because of Berlioz and *The Tsar's Bride*.

3 October

I spent the entire evening—from eight until midnight—at the Rimsky-Korsakovs'. No one else was there and therefore I felt wonderful, especially as both the host and hostess gave me an especially cordial welcome. We talked about various things: since Ippolitov-Ivanov's *Asya* [29] has already been given, *Saltan* will be performed in Moscow around the twentieth of this month. Nikolai Andreyevich plans to go there in about ten days. *Sadko* will not be performed before January.

This season there will be only three (instead of four) Russian Symphony Concerts. The programs are to include, among other things, the Fourth Symphony and a new overture by Glazunov; Borodin's First Symphony; Rimsky-Korsakov's *Sinfonietta,* and the first five of the six movements of Scriabin's First Symphony. Beginning this year, the Belyaev concerts will be conducted by Glazunov and Liadov.

"You won't believe this," remarked Rimsky-Korsakov, "but during the entire fourteen years that I've conducted the Russian Symphony Concerts, I've never been able to accustom myself to the audience's inattentiveness, even their dislike of them. Each time I've come out on the stage, I've experienced an unpleasant feeling, seeing the almost empty hall."

Following this we discussed the great importance of Glazunov's Fourth, Fifth, and Sixth symphonies. At the present time, Rimsky-Korsakov has grown quite cold toward his *Sea, Forest,* and even *Stenka Razin.*

After tea, Nikolai Andreyevich and I looked through new sacred works by Verdi. [30] Neither of us liked them, especially as the scale taken as the basis [example 48]; in itself it does not amount to anything.

Example 48

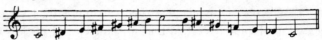

"His 'La donna è mobile' really shows much more talent," commented Rimsky-Korsakov jokingly. "If only Verdi had tried to harmonize this thing a little better, it would have come out quite nicely."

21 October

The first performance of *Tsar Saltan* was greeted by a thunderous ovation.[31] Following the prologue, Rimsky-Korsakov was called out three times to the blare of a fanfare and deafening applause from the audience, who jumped up from their seats at the sight of him; then he was presented with an immense laurel wreath from the Kerzin Society of Lovers of Russian Music. After the first act he was recalled again—four times—and after the second act—six times, at which point he was presented with a large silver lyre from the "grateful artists of the Private Opera."

Besides this, Nikolai Andreyevich was literally showered with small wreaths and bouquets. Never has any artist been accorded such an ardent and festive reception, not in Petersburg, at least. I repeat—it was overwhelming, spontaneous. By the end of the opera, Rimsky-Korsakov had taken twenty-five curtain calls!

Thus, the opera enjoyed an immense success. The cast for this premiere included Mutin as Saltan; Strakhova—Barbarikha; Tsvetkova—the Youngest Sister Militrissa; Rostovtseva—the Middle Sister; Veretennikova—the Eldest Sister; Sekar-Rozhansky—the Tsarevich Guidon; Zabela—the Swan Princess; Shkafer—Old Man; Shevelev—the Courier. The staging was by M. V. Lentovsky; the opera was directed by V. P. Shkafer and Ya. L. Kravetsky and conducted by M. M. Ippolitov-Ivanov.

The performance began at eight-twelve and ended at one in the morning.

14 November

Rimsky-Korsakov visited us this afternoon from two-thirty until quarter past three. When he rang, I had just finished reading *Servilia*. I do not know why, but I suddenly had a feeling that he is writing an opera on this subject, and I decided to reread Mey's play.

Today Rimsky-Korsakov was in a wonderful mood. We talked about the laudatory reviews of *Saltan*. For example, regarding the Moscow premiere of this opera, I. Lipayev declared (in *Russkaia muzykal'naia gazeta*, November 5, 1900, no. 45) that "N. A. Rimsky-Korsakov's creative powers are limitless and indefatigable. Not long ago we were all captivated by his *Mozart and Salieri, Sadko*, and *Tsar's Bride*. Now, in his new opera, *The Tale of Tsar Saltan*, we again have mysterious worlds, nature, people. Here is a phantasmagoria of color and sound."

Further, this reviewer wrote that "the march of Saltan's warriors is the embodiment of playful humor; the raging sea—an overpowering elemental force; the three wonders have no equal in operatic literature"; that in "act 2 the composer lifts the veil from truly fantastic lands"; that here "his inspiration shows itself in all its power; the instrumental color (in the scene of Guidon's meeting with the people) displays the same audacity and abandon."

In his musical sketches of November 6/19, 1900 (*Novoe vremia*, no. 8871),[32] Ivanov wrote that *Tsar Saltan* has already had seven performances before full houses; the eighth has been announced for this week, and the ninth is not far off, since the opera is enjoying an outstanding success.

19 November

I had arranged with Ossovsky to be at the Rimsky-Korsakovs' tonight, but he did not come—Belsky came instead. The evening passed imperceptibly, with much argument and laughter. We chatted about Glinka's music to *Prince Kholmsky*, noting that its quality is rather poor, but that this can be explained by the fact that it was written and orchestrated in barely a week.[33]

I suggested that Nikolai Andreyevich write an opera based on Count Alexei Tolstoi's *Tsar Feodor Ionnovich*, Ostrovsky's *Vasilisa Melentyeva*, or Mey's *Servilia*.

"You know," he replied, "in Moscow they tried to persuade me to write *Feodor*. When I tell you what I am writing, all of you are going to be terribly surprised."[34]

We spoke about Balakirev's symphony.[35] Rimsky-Korsakov severely criticized its form.

"For example, the first movement consists entirely of closing statements," he said, "but in the end they never arrive at a real conclusion. The scherzo is something else again—it's charming. As for the finale, it's a combination of the most heterogeneous themes, which in artistic terms can't possibly be combined."

In a discussion of Saint-Saëns' *Danse macabre* I learned that despite what Mussorgsky thought of it,[36] Nikolai Andreyevich truly admires it; in fact, he has an extremely high regard for Saint-Saëns' music in general.

"It may strike you as strange," he said, "but very few contemporary composers fully satisfy me as orchestrators—only Wagner (aside from his music), Glazunov, and Saint-Saëns. The rest—only with certain reservations—including even such an outstanding orchestrator as Tchaikovsky."

At the present moment, not only Ivanov, who went to Moscow purposely to hear *Saltan,* but even Solovyov have become better friends of Rimsky-Korsakov. For example, the latter recently asked him to select numbers from the opera which might be most suitable to play at a reading for children of Pushkin's *Tale of Tsar Saltan.* That this was no empty gesture is evident from the following newspaper report, which appeared soon after this conversation:

The Society for Children's Entertainment is arranging a literary and musical program for Wednesday afternoon in the Hall of the Pedagogical Museum at which, among other things, *The Tale of Tsar Saltan* will be presented, illustrated by lantern slides and music from Rimsky-Korsakov's opera. Participating soloists will be the mezzo-soprano Mme Shaskolskaya and tenor Klemantovich. . . . Two entr'actes from this opera will be performed on the piano by Mme Vengerova.

21 November

Talking with Rimsky-Korsakov about his use of folk tunes in *Saltan,* I learned that he had used several others besides the one in the "Lullaby of the Seven Nurses" and the theme "Vo sadu li, v ogorode." First of all, Prince Guidon's basic phrase is a variant of the well-known children's song [example 49], and second, the Sailors' theme [example 50].

This song Stepan Stepanovich Mitusov heard in Tver Province (not far from the Bologoye Station), sung by mendicants to the words: "Ia strem-

Example 49

Za- in- ka po-plia· shi.

Example 50

lius k tomu chertogu" and "Ia postavliu Bogu svechku." When visiting
the Rimsky-Korsakovs in Vechasha, he often sang it as a joke. Nikolai
Andreyevich liked it and used it in the opera to characterize the merchants.

Third, the theme of the Old Man's song (with chorus) at the end of
scene 2, act 4 [example 51]. This theme Rimsky-Korsakov took from his
own collection of Russian folk songs (see vol. 2, no. 98, "Velichal'naia
zhenikhu," which he had in turn borrowed from M. Stakhovich's *Collection of Russian Folk Songs,* 1854).

Example 51

Vot- do- moi ver- nus, na- shim po- khva- lus.

Fourth, the theme of the chorus greeting the Prince Guidon in the
finale of act 2 [example 52]. Actually this is nothing but a somewhat
modified version of the well-known znamenny chant for three voices,
"Tebe, Boga, khvalim."

Example 52

Voz- ne- si- te khva-lu,vsia zem-lia, mi-lost' bo- zhi- ia nam vos-si- ia

"Don't spread this last around too widely," remarked Rimsky-Korsakov with a smile, "or I fear Pobedonostsev may forbid my entire opera, and then what?"

The First Tribute to Rimsky-Korsakov.[37]

25 November

The first half of the program of the third Russian Symphony Concert was under the direction of Rimsky-Korsakov and consisted of Tchaikovsky's symphonic ballad *The Voyevoda,* Rimsky-Korsakov's symphonic picture *Sadko,* and the Procession of the Princes from his opera *Mlada.*[38] The second half, conducted by Liadov, presented *Elegy* by Zolotarev, *Intermezzo* by Liadov (both premieres), and Glazunov's Symphony no. 4 (in E flat).[39]

Following the performance of *Sadko,* Nikolai Andreyevich was given a long ovation. Belyaev and Stasov delivered speeches, and Rimsky-Korsakov was presented with five wreaths to the accompaniment of fanfares.

First came Belyaev, the energetic organizer of these concerts, who explained in his welcoming address that although the celebration of the anniversary should have been held at a later date (the real one),[40] it was being given on this evening because it had been impossible to arrange another Russian concert this season.

After Belyaev, Stasov delivered a highly emotional, profoundly sincere speech, which evoked a rapturous response from the audience. He compared the guest of honor with Sadko, pointing out that Nikolai Andreyevich, too, had been a sailor who journeyed around the world. Also, like Sadko, through his talent, he, too, had captivated a Princess—that is, Russia—and many other Princesses and Queens in Europe as well. And again, like Sadko, he, too, had his "cohorts"—his famous students. In line with this comparison, the inscription on one of the wreaths read: "To the great Sadko-musician of our time."

11 December

When I arrived at the Rimsky-Korsakovs' at dinner time, I found Nikolai Andreyevich very upset and extremely irritated by the "chronic" celebration of his thirty-fifth anniversary.[41]

"Any minute now," he said, "you're going to run across me in *Obozrenie Peterburga* in a feuilleton by Doroshevich."[42]

Besides this, because of Napravnik's sudden illness, he has to conduct his suite from *Saltan* at the Fourth Symphonic Concert of the Russian Musical Society on December 16, and after that he must make a special trip to Moscow to conduct an entire symphonic concert[43] in place of Safonov, who is also ill and begged Rimsky-Korsakov to help him out. In its turn, the Moscow Opera Company has informed him that, to mark his anniversary, it is going to present *Saltan* on December 19 and *Sadko* on December 20; that the whole company would like to honor him and thus he must be present. Finally, Bartsal wrote him that in honor of his anniversary, *Snegurochka* will be given at the Bolshoi Theater also on December 19.

"And now, suddenly, the Society of Musics Teachers has decided that they have to celebrate my thirty-fifth anniversary,"[44] said Nikolai Andreyevich. "They sent notices throughout all Russia and chose me to be their first honorary member. It's too much; I simply can't stand all this; I'll get sick. I haven't the strength.

"This time," he added, smiling, "shouldn't I just follow Laroche's advice and not go to the operetta on the nineteenth? That would even be amusing in a certain sense, wouldn't it?"

As we walked to the study, our conversation turned to Saturday's concert for the benefit of deaf-mute children,[45] arranged by Dolina in the Assembly Hall of the Nobility, at which, the program included, besides Tchaikovsky's Fourth Symphony, the overture to Gluck's *Iphigénie en Tauride* (with Wagner's finale) and the overture to the second act of Max Schillings' *Ingwelde,* two songs by Rimsky-Korsakov: *Vostochnaia pesnia* (Tartakov) and Lyubasha's song from *The Tsar's Bride* (Dolina).

"You know," said Nikolai Andreyevich, "after the concert I received a large laurel wreath from Maria Ivanovna with the most charming inscription: 'To the pride of Russian music, our glorous nightingale—Sadko N. A. Rimsky-Korsakov, a modest gift from the performer of Nezhata—M. I. Dolina. 19/XII 1900.'

"As you see," he added, "my anniversary has begun."

Turning from this to Wagner, Nikolai Andreyevich told me that Nadezhda Nikolayevna has fallen head over heels in love with *Die Walküre;* she even considers the boring scene between Wotan and Fricka good, though somewhat less successful than the rest.

"I truly believe," remarked Rimsky-Korsakov jestingly, "that if such music turned up in a different opera by a different composer (not Wagner), she would have thought it bad. But in Wagner, this scene is 'only weaker' than the others."

As we were saying good-bye, I told Rimsky-Korsakov that on December 17, the day he is to be honored by the Music Teachers, my article about him will appear in Findeisen's newspaper;[46] that thus, not only Dolina and Nikolai Feodorovich[47] but I, too, have resolved to persecute him on the day of his thirty-fifth anniversary and that, obviously, such is his bitter fate.

16 December

Tonight, at the fourth Symphonic Evening of the Russian Musical Society, Rimsky-Korsakov led the orchestra in his musical pictures from *Saltan* and the Choirmaster of the Imperial Russian Opera, G. A. Kazachenko, conducted Brahms' *Requiem* and de Swert's Cello Concerto no. 1.

Following the performance of the *Saltan* suite (the last number of which—the "Three Wonders"—had to be repeated), Rimsky-Korsakov was given a thunderous ovation and congratulatory telegrams were read from the Grand Duchess Alexandra Iosifovna, Grand Duke Konstantin Konstantinovich, the Moscow Branch of the Russian Musical Society (signed by Safonov), etc. In addition, Nikolai Andreyevich was presented with a testimonial from the St. Petersburg Branch of the Russian Musical Society, signed by fifty-eight members of the society and professors of the Conservatory, and a large laurel wreath from A. V. Ossovsky. Then P. N. Cheremisinov read a congratulatory message from the Central Board of the St. Petersburg Branch of the Russian Musical Society. Besides all this, Rimsky-Korsakov received many other greetings and telegrams from all over Russia.

17 December

This morning *Muzykal'nyi-teatral'nyi sovremennik* (no. 2) carried a warm, though brief article by Emil Bormann, pointing out Rimsky-Korsakov's enormous importance to Russian music.[48] In the same issue there also appeared a very charming poem by A. A. Kalinovsky, entitled *In Commemoration of Rimsky-Korsakov's Thirty-Fifth Anniversary*.

At two o'clock in the afternoon, the forty-second Public Symphonic Concert was given in Kononov's Hall, with the first half of the program devoted entirely to works by Rimsky-Korsakov. Despite the freezing weather, the Hall was filled to overflowing. Nikolai Andreyevich was called out many times and was presented with a large laurel wreath bearing the number XXXV. The second half of the program consisted of Saint-Saëns' *Oratorio de Noël*.

In the evening, the Society of Music Teachers and Other Workers in the Field of Music held its sixth meeting in the hall of the Petropavlovsky Academy. The entire evening was given over to paying tribute to the society's honorary member, Rimsky-Korsakov.

So many admirers of Nikolai Andreyevich came that the hall could not seat all of them, and many people had to stand. Shortly after eight o'-clock, the guest of honor entered to the festive sounds of his *Slava*. With this the entire audience, including Grand Duke Sergei Mikhailovich (the Society's patron) rose to its feet. Rimsky-Korsakov was pale and seemed very agitated. Beside him, on the arm of Findeisen, walked Nadezhda Nikolayevna, carrying a beautiful bouquet of white roses. Some twenty delegations, representing the widest possible range of civic and professional institutions, from the St. Petersburg Municipal Council to the Court Chapel, the St. Petersburg Philharmonic Society, the Society of Music Publishers, the Russian Musical Society, music critics, and the Writers' Union. Even architects participated in the festivities.

After the presentation of each wreath and the accompanying congratulatory address, Count Sheremetyev's "brass orchestra" played a fanfare from the pen of Rimsky-Korsakov.[49]

At the conclusion of this part of the celebration, the guest of honor and his wife took reserved seats in the front row, and the concert began. When it ended Rimsky-Korsakov was recalled again to enthusiastic applause.

At the entrance to the Hall, handbills bearing a portrait of Rimsky-Korsakov and also a special issue of *Russkaia muzykal'naia gazeta* (no. 51) were given out. The latter included a biography of Rimsky-Korsakov, a review of his career, a complete list of his works,[50] articles by Petrovsky, Findeisen, and others, Kalinovsky's poem, several pictures of Rimsky-

Korsakov, two facsimiles from his operas *(Maid of Pskov* and *Tsar Saltan),* a picture of the house in Tikhvin where he was born, etc.

The evening ended with a supper (by subscription) in Nikolai Andreyevich's honor at the Hôtel de France. It was attended by some eighty persons, among them F. and S. Blumenfeld, Lavrov, Liadov, Belyaev, Glazunov, Arensky, Cherepnin, Bessel, professors, and artists. During the supper numerous toasts were offered. Finally, at about two in the morning, the evening was brought to a close with these words from the guest of honor himself: "Even the best work has a Finale."

19 December

Today (December 19, 1900), the actual day of Rimsky-Korsakov's anniversary, there appeared in *Novoe vremia* the following letter to the editor:

Dear Sir:

Because of my departure for Moscow and because I cannot possibly thank personally all the institutions, societies, and individuals of Petersburg and elsewhere who paid tribute to me on the thirty-fifth anniversary of my musical career, I wish to express to them, through the press, my profound and heartfelt gratitude for the honor which they have paid me.

N. Rimsky-Korsakov.

Other newspapers please copy. 18 December.

25 December

At the invitation of Andrei Nikolayevich, I went to the Rimsky-Korsakovs' on the first day of Christmas for the amateur theatricals, which continued from one-thirty until five-thirty. They gave Gnedich's *Burned Letters,* Bilibin's *The Proprieties,* and Kuzma Prutkov's *The Hasty Turk, or Do You Like Being a Grandson?* [51]

Even though Nikolai Andreyevich had only returned from Moscow at ten o'clock this morning, he felt perfectly strong and cheerful. As usual there were many guests—various members of the family as well as the Belskys, Lapshin, Liadov, et al.

We talked about Rimsky-Korsakov's trip to Moscow, with which he was highly pleased. He showed us an elegant silver blotting pad, which he had received from the Directorate of the Moscow Private Opera on the day of his anniversary (December 19, 1900), during the performance of *Sadko;* also two tributes which had been presented to him on December 23, when he directed the Fourth Symphonic Evening of the Russian Musical Society—one from the teachers of the Conservatory and the other from people who attended the Society's symphonic concerts, this latter with one thousand signatures.

The program of the concert which Rimsky-Korsakov conducted on December 23 consisted of Glazunov's Symphony no. 1,[52] his own *Skazka* for orchestra; Haydn's Cello Concerto in D (with Edouard Jacobs as soloist); aria from *Prince Igor* ("Ni sna, ni otdykha izmuchennoi dushe"), sung by V. S. Sharonov; and Liszt's *Mephisto Waltz.*

How deeply affected Nikolai Andreyevich was by the ovations and the reception, in general, given him by the Muscovites is evident from this, that on the day of his departure, he sent the editor of a Moscow newspaper a letter similar to that of December 19th.[53]

31 December

This afternoon Rimsky-Korsakov visited me from two o'clock until quarter to five. He had come, he said, to thank me for participating in his anniversary and for my article about him. Besides this, he brought me a copy of the score of Liszt's *Mephisto Waltz,* on which he had written: "Directed by me at the Symphonic Evening of the Russian Musical Society in Moscow on December 23, 1900. N. Rimsky-Korsakov."

"I took the liberty of writing this on your music," he said, "only because I thought it might give you some pleasure."

Then I asked Rimsky-Korsakov for a musical autograph of his own to commemorate today and also the last day of the nineteenth century, whereupon he selected a few bars of Spring's opening recitative[54] from the Prologue to *Snegurochka* [example 53]. But he did not write in the

Example 53

words, leaving me to guess the meanings: "Razgadai zagadku, milostivyi gosudar'."[55] [He wrote only]: "This is my music. N. R-Korsakov, December 31, 1900."

Again at my request, he inscribed the vocal score of *Tsar Saltan,* as a memento of my October trip to Moscow: "To dear Vasily Vasilyevich Yastrebtsev—the Swan Princess. N. Rimsky-Korsakov. October 21, 1900—Moscow":

Example 54

Dlia zhi- vykh chu-des ia so- shla s ne-bes.

Rimsky-Korsakov also signed an excerpt from the score of scene 8 of *Christmas Eve,* adding alongside the date "17 December 1900" (the day on which he was honored by the Society of Music Teachers): "27 degrees below zero. N. R-Korsakov."

"You know," he said, "that freezing weather on the day of my anniversary had no effect whatsoever on me and my music." We laughed.

Then Nikolai Andreyevich talked about the influence of Liszt's *Mephisto Waltz* on his *Sadko* fantasy.

"Generally speaking," he said, "on the programmatic side, this marvelous work of Liszt's exerted an influence on the poetic legend about Sadko. Mephistopheles snatches a violin, plays, and everyone around becomes caught up in the whirlwind of a waltz. Sakdo seizes a *gusli,* plays, and the whole underwater kingdom, including the Sea King, breaks into a dance. Surely there's a similarity of motives here!"

I forgot to mention that Nikolai Andreyevich tried to convince me that he dreads my "reminiscences" and therefore, from now on, he is going to write me two different kinds of letters: some which may be published and others—forbidden ones, which must not be made public but must be burned as soon as they have been read.

Upon leaving, he wished me and my wife, Nadya, happiness in the coming twentieth century and also congratulated me on my name day. I have not seen him warmer and more affectionate in a long time.

CHAPTER 11

1901

5 January

The post brought me, from Nikolai Andreyevich, the program of a musical evening and lecture by V. V. Annenkov, which had been given in his honor in Kishinev on December 19. It had been arranged by V. P. Gutor for the students in his school. Also included was an article by Gutor devoted to Rimsky-Korsakov's thirty-fifth anniversary, which had been published in the January issue of *Bessarabets*.[1]

Among the works presented on the program were a four-hand arrangement of the *Sadko* fantasy, the First Symphony, *Capriccio espagnol*, arias from *Snegurochka, Maid of Pskov, May Night, Mlada, Christmas Eve, Sadko*, and numerous songs and piano pieces.

Accompanying all this was a laconic note: "Why do they keep writing about me? They only irritate me! N. R-K. January 4, to V. V. Yastrebtsev."[2]

24 January

Due to the very long intermissions, the rehearsal of *Sadko* which began at eleven-forty did not end until four-twenty. The production is good. Davydov (Sadko) is much better than Morskoi, and Bolska (the Sea Princess) took the high D in the Lullaby (which Rimsky-Korsakov added especially for her) with unusual ease and grace.

During the intervals I saw Insarova, Glazunov, Liadov, and Stasov. I also chatted in snatches with Nikolai Andreyevich, from whom I learned that he was highly amused by the closing words of Laroche's recent article in *Rossiia* (January 22, 1901), no. 626.[3]

"Go to the benefit performance for the orchestra (that is, *Sadko*)," wrote Laroche, "and applaud. Reconcile yourselves to the fact that the music (of Rimsky-Korsakov) does not smack of Leoncavallo; that the performance does not remind you of one by the Gramen family.[4] Applaud on faith, applaud for no reason whatever. After all, you don't know anything about how real musicians play and compose."

Thus Laroche spoke out in favor of Rimsky-Korsakov for the first time in his life.

In conversation with Stasov, Nikolai Andreyevich maintained that by now he (Nikolai Andreyevich) is so accustomed to being a guest of honor that he can easily "hire himself out" anywhere, not only as a composer fêted on a chance occasion, but as an honored guest of any sort whatsoever—without speeches, with speeches, even with speeches, a tear, and gestures.

26 January

The first performance of *Sadko* went off successfully. The theater was filled to overflowing, despite the extremely high prices of the "benefit" tickets.

After the first scene, Rimsky-Korsakov was presented with several wreaths—from the artists of the Russian opera, the orchestra, the audience, Mme Fried, etc. The singers and Rimsky-Korsakov were recalled after each act and, at the end, Nikolai Andreyevich was called out eight times.

The cast included Davydov as Sadko; Fried—his wife, Lyubava Buslayevna; Dolina—Nezhata; Stravinsky and Kravchenko—the *skomorokhi;* Serebryakov—the Sea King and Belskaya—his daughter, Volkhova. Napravnik conducted.

All the Imperial family, save for the Empress, was present, as well as all the music critics, save for Cui. As of now, it is difficult to say what the Petersburg public thinks of this brilliant opera, especially since the audience seemed to approve least the inspired scene of the underwater dance.[5]

I forgot to mention that although the Tsar arrived promptly at eight o'clock, at his request, the opera did not begin until ten after (as they were waiting for Maria Feodorovna) and, owing to the endless intermissions, it dragged on until one in the morning.

16 February

Upon returning from work I received the following note from Nikolai Andreyevich:

Vasily Vasilyevich:
Maria Nikolayevna[6] has promised to be with us on Saturday evening. Will you come? In general, I have heard nothing of you for a very long time:[7]

Example 55

Ni- ko- lai   An- dre- ev   Rim- skii   Kor- sa- kov

Nikolai Andreyev Rimsky-Korsakov. 1901.

17 February

I spent the entire evening at the Rimsky-Korsakovs'. Insarova was not there; she had sent a note of apology this morning. Besides me, the guests included Stasov, the young Rimsky-Korsakovs, Belsky and his wife, and the students Troitsky and Richter. During tea they argued about whether manuscripts hold any interest. Rimsky-Korsakov thinks not; he maintained that once a composition or any other work has been printed during the author's lifetime, his manuscript loses its importance. Stasov and I disagreed.

"But, after all, you, Vasily Vasilyevich, are the most famous 'general of manuscripts,' " retorted Rimsky-Korsakov.

Then Nikolai Andreyevich told us about a letter he had received from Prince Volkonsky, inviting him to become a member of the Opera Committee, since, as the Prince put it, "you stand at the summit of our musical world and we cannot do anything without you." At Popov's request, he became a member of the Society of the Folk Theater, but both he and Glazunov have refused to join Suvorin's new Russian Society.[8]

"You can just imagine what kind of founding member I'd be," Nikolai Andreyevich commented, "when I could never attend a meeting of the Society.

"To begin with," he continued, "I'm an 'armchair' person. But most important—I'm solely a musician—and nothing more. Besides, I don't know anyone there except Mr. Suvorin and Mr. Romer, and I know them only by hearsay."

After tea, Richter played several Chopin pieces, Liszt's Eighth Rhapsody, a few excerpts and the Wedding Song from *Sadko,* etc., and Sofia Nikolayevna sang two duets (*Pan* and *The Song of Songs*) with Volodya and Mitusov and something from *The Tsar's Bride.*

Nikolai Andreyevich told me that in response to a request from England for biographical material, he is sending them my article.

"Can you imagine what they'll make out of the sun cult!" he said. "Oh, well, let them do what they like."

24 February

At the end of the tenth and final Symphonic Evening of the Russian Musical Society I ran into Nikolai Andreyevich. We talked about Mendelssohn's incidental music to *Athalie,*[9] which we had just heard, agreeing that it is third-rate and, what is more, extraordinarily stale, quite unlike the eternally youthful Overture to the *Magic Flute* or the works of Beethoven. Even the overture sounded dull, colorless—something quite uncommon for Mendelssohn.

"I really believe," declared Rimsky-Korsakov, "that nowadays, of all Mendelssohn's music, only his *Midsummer Night's Dream* has remained really fresh and unfaded. All the rest, even the wonderful *Hebrides* overture, sounds quite old-fashioned."

27 February

I dropped in on Nikolai Andreyevich mainly to find out something about Liadov for Ossovsky, but I had little success. All I learned was that in his childhood, Liadov and his sister were abandoned to the mercy of fate by their father, a handsome libertine and, consequently, they were often obliged to live on charity—not infrequently (though only temporarily) on the money of their servants.

After this I read to Nikolai Andreyevich Kashkin's extremely laudatory review of his *Mozart and Salieri* in the journal *Zhizn'*.[10]

At around nine-thirty Glazunov appeared and they began to talk about a musical evening to take place next Tuesday at the Rimsky-Korsakovs'. Nikolai Andreyevich asked Glazunov to bring with him some two-piano music: Saint-Saëns' *Phaëton* or *Le rouet d'Omphale;* something by Richard Strauss, Schumann's *Andante,* and the "Procession of the Sea Monsters" from *Sadko.* When the Molases went abroad, they left their piano at the Rimsky-Korsakovs', and this was a good opportunity to play two-piano music.

After tea Alexander Konstantinovich played his wonderful new Sonata in B-flat minor (dedicated to Nadezhda Nikolayevna).[11] It is extremely difficult technically and highly interesting musically.

So then, until Tuesday.

6 March

Among the guests at the Rimsky-Korsakovs' tonight were V. V. Stasov, the Chuprynnikovs, Insarova, Markovich, Glazunov, Liadov, Felix Blumenfeld, Belsky and his wife, et al.

The conversation touched on Count Leo Tolstoy's excommunication from the church (preposterous for the twentieth century). Further, they talked about the relations between Liapunov and Arensky,[12] which have become so strained that they do not speak to each other at all and, when they have to discuss something regarding the Chapel, they do so by letter, as Rimsky-Korsakov and Balakirev did.

But now the music began. Before tea Felix Mikhailovich and Glazunov played (on the two pianos): Liszt's *Orpheus,* Saint-Saëns' *Caprice arabe,* the Introduction to *Die Meistersinger,* and the Wedding Rite from *Sadko.*

After tea Chuprynnikov sang arias and songs by Rimsky-Korsakov, F. Blumenfeld, and Cui, and Insarova songs by Rimsky-Korsakov, Tchaikovsky, Cui, and Yaroslavna's arioso from *Prince Igor* and Militrissa's tale from *Tsar Saltan.*

Finally, at our request, Glazunov played the first two movements of his new piano sonata.

18 March

This afternoon Rimsky-Korsakov visited my mother from one-thirty until three o'clock. (It was his last visit to her.) Among other things, we talked about his recent article on the need to reorganize the teaching of music theory in our conservatories;[13] also about the success of M. Ivanov's *Zabava Putyatishna,* ridiculously and impudently exaggerated by the *Novoe vremia* claque and artists; also about Findeisen's "at homes," and whether or not Rimsky-Korsakov is composing a new opera, etc. After that, Nikolai Andreyevich told me that recently Valter had confirmed his long-held suspicion that Laroche regards himself as a composer.

"Very well, then," Nikolai Andreyevich had replied, "from now on I can consider myself a 'music critic.' After all, I did write a couple of critical articles (on Cui's *Ratcliff* and Napravnik's *Nizhegorodtsy*)[14] and made several statements which are published in the newspapers."

23 March

I spent the whole evening at the Rimsky-Korsakovs'. Before tea, there was no music, but afterward they played two works by Rimsky-Korsakov—a string sextet in A,[15] written in Kabalovka in 1876 and marked op. 19,[16] and a relatively recent string quartet in G, composed in Smychkovo in 1897, of which I knew absolutely nothing.

The evening ended with supper. During the conversation, mention was made of Chaliapin's overwhelming success at the Teatro alla Scala, Milan, where he appeared as Mefistofele in Boito's opera of the same name.[17]

25 March

This morning I received the following letter from Rimsky-Korsakov:[18]

[Example 56.] I am writing you, dear Vasily Vasilyevich, about something mysterious and even mystical. It is this: if you give me your word to keep silent, that is, to speak to no one about a secret which will interest you (I guarantee),

Example 56

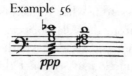

ppp

then come to us tomorrow, Sunday, at eight-thirty in the evening. If you cannot keep silent—do not come, and, if you do not, that will prove you are not interested and, in that case, you will know sometime but much later on. [Example 57.]

Example 57

March 24, 1901. Your N. R-K.[19]

At exactly eight-thirty this evening I was at the Rimsky-Korsakovs'. Belsky was also there, as were the Vrubels, Mikhail Rimsky-Korsakov, and the students Troitsky and Mironov. Although Zabela (Mme Vrubel) did not feel quite well, she sang an aria, "Tsvety moi," from Nikolai Andreyevich's new opera, and thus the secret was out. Besides us, the only ones who know about *Servilia* are Glazunov, Liadov, Bessel (who is going to publish it), and Bernhard (who is going to translate it into German).

After tea Zabela also sang Rimsky-Korsakov's songs: *O chem v tishi nochei, Eshche ia poln, drug moi milyi,* and *Nimfa.*

From conversation with Nikolai Andreyevich, I learned that he would like his new opera to be given its premiere at the Marinsky Theater; that he intends to omit both Silia, who is in love with Valerius (a sketchy character and, on the whole, of little interest) and the cynic Demetrius; the first act opens with the appearance of the conspirators. Rimsky-Korsakov himself drew up the libretto after Mey's drama. Although the fifth act is not quite finished, the first three and a half acts have already been scored.

Speaking about his new Quartet in G (which, by the way, Nadezhda Nikolayevna does not particularly like), Rimsky-Korsakov said he is not going to publish it.[20] This is a pity, for some of it is very charming and appealing, for example, the first Allegro non troppo, Variation no. 5 from the Largo (which resembles somewhat Rimsky-Korsakov's song *Nenastnyi den' potukh*), and the trio from the Alla polacca.

Rimsky-Korsakov has not yet decided whether he will write an overture to precede the introduction to *Servilia*. I think not, however, for he shares my opinion that, from an artistic point of view, an overture is not desirable if it does not lead immediately into the opera.[21]

Thus, Rimsky-Korsakov now has nine operas.

5 April

This evening, during tea, we talked about Glazunov (who, in Nikolai Andreyevich's view, is "completely exhausted" as a composer) and his passionate dislike of operatic music. Then we discussed Liadov, who, after Johansen, entered Rimsky-Korsakov's class but studied with him less than a year. At the end of the first term, he stopped going to lectures and continued to stay away throughout the following year, despite reprimands and threats. Finally, the authorities had no choice but to expel him from the Conservatory. When the time came for the examinations, Anatoly Konstantinovich presented his cantata *The Bride of Messina*,[22] so, in order to make it possible for him to take the examinations, they registered him again as a student of Rimsky-Korsakov.

At the end, Rimsky-Korsakov gave me a copy of his two women's choruses, *Tuchki nebesnye* and *Nochevala tuchka zolotaia* (op. 13), with the following inscription:

To dear Vasily Vasilyevich. My worst composition—for censure and remembrance. N. R-Korsakov. April 3, 1901.

22 April

Nikolai Andreyevich visited us between four and five o'clock. After greeting me, his first words were: "You, Vasily Vasilyevich, live far away and seldom drop in on me, while Vladimir Ivanovich Belsky lives nearby and drops in often, and so I've played my *Servilia* for him, but you still don't know it. That's not right.

"However," he added, "at the beginning of May, as soon as I've finished and orchestrated the second half of the last act (beginning with the appearance of the tribune Valerius), I'll gather some people together at my house and play the opera for them—without the beginning of act 5, of course, which I'll finish writing at the dacha. The rest I'll make known in the fall."

For the tenth anniversary of Galkin's conducting career, Rimsky-Korsakov, Liadov, Glazunov, and some others have decided to write an orchestral piece in variation form, which they will dedicate to him.[23] Nikolai Andreyevich has chosen for the theme a Russian folk song from Balakirev's collection (no. 28, Tula Province, Chernsky District):

Example 58

Slowly

Uzh ty po- le mo- e, po-le chi- sto- e, svet raz-dol'- e mo-e ty shi-ro- ko- e.

During the summer, Rimsky-Korsakov would like to finish his trio of 1897 and start work on *Nausicaä*,[24] for which Belsky is drawing up the libretto.

When Rimsky-Korsakov rose to leave, I offered to accompany him as far as Mikhail Nikolayevich's, and we left together. On the way, we had a discussion about the summer of 1897.

"You know," said Nikolai Andreyevich, "the year '97 when I wrote some fifty songs, duets, a trio, quartet, *Mozart and Salieri,* and other things, played a significant role in my life, for from that year on, I began to give much more attention to singers. In this sense, *Saltan* is closer in style to *The Tsar's Bride* than to *Sadko*. With *Sadko* the period of *Mlada* ended."

9 May

Knowing that Rimsky-Korsakov would be at the Conservatory for the graduation exercises in the afternoon, I went to see him in the evening. The only others there were Bessel and Glazunov.

Nikolai Andreyevich has already finished not only writing but also scoring the second half of the fifth act of *Servilia*. He plans to play through the entire opera for us soon. He is very tired from working on it and reading the proofs of *Saltan* and *Song of Oleg the Wise*.

We got onto the subject of the extremely confused situation at the Conservatory, Mme Benois' resignation (because Malozemova's student was awarded the piano prize instead of her student), and so on.

"All of this results from the fact that we haven't a real director," observed Rimsky-Korsakov. "I wonder whether these people would attempt to stir up trouble if Anton Rubinstein or Safonov were in charge instead of the kind but totally weak Bernhard."

We also talked about Arensky's resignation from the Chapel and the fact that for six years of service, he is to receive a pension of 6,000 rubles, while Balakirev was given only 3,000 (plus 1,500 rubles for his work with the Free Music School), despite his ten years there and the late Emperor Alexander III's high regard for him.

Thus far no one knows anything about the appointment of Professor Smolensky to replace Arensky, nor has the matter of Prince Volkonsky's resignation been clarified.

Recently Rimsky-Korsakov was at Andreyev's,[25] where he heard a fantasia on themes from his opera *Sadko* performed on balalaikas.

"As you might suspect," he said, "I went there resolved in advance to dislike both the piece and its performance. How surprised I was then, when I heard the 'first chorus of the Novgorodians,' 'Sadko's farewell aria to the ship,' the 'submarine dance,' the music accompanying Nikola's appearance and the chorus 'Vysota l', vysota podnebesnaia' in a very skillful transcription for balalaikas (obviously from the score), almost free of distortions of the original harmonies and modulations (which I had expected, and, in truth, feared most of all), and played excellently, with all the contrapuntal embellishments faithfully retained. Obviously, all I could do was to thank Mr. Andreyev and the Great Russian Orchestra and grant them permission to perform this fantasia, if they wish.

"You won't believe it," concluded Rimsky-Korsakov, "but despite my dislike for the balalaika, in this case I was delighted to hear my music in new 'tonal attire.' "

17 May

I was at the Rimsky-Korsakovs' at exactly eight o'clock.[26] Nadezhda Nikolayevna was not there; she had gone to Arcadia[27] for the third performance of *The Tsar's Bride*. According to Nikolai Andreyevich and Belsky, the opera is going relatively well under Maksakov's management. What is most important, it is being given without cuts. Rimsky-Korsakov attended the first performance, on May 11, and was presented with a laurel wreath. He did not go to the second one two days later, but Belsky was there, and he witnessed the following amusing incident. Unaware that the composer was not present, the audience called insistently for him. When he did not appear, someone shouted loudly: "Why are you applauding? Korsakov will be coming to Arcadia every day. He's writing a new opera now and he's collecting material for it everywhere."

Nikolai Andreyevich liked this capricious idea very much.

When Liadov arrived (at around nine o'clock), he immediately began to play *Servilia*. Since he already knew act 1 and the first half of act 3, he started with act 2, that is, with the "Banquet of the Stoics." (Pakopius' tale about Messalina is superb; the fast dance of the Maenads, in Mixolydian modes, is very piquant and original.)

At the end of act 2, we had tea, and then Liadov played the second half of act 3 (with the wonderful, deeply inspired love scene between Valerius and Servilia and the effective entrance of the Centurion), all of act 4 (at Locusta's), and, finally, the second half of act 5 (the very moving scene of Servilia's death), which was finished on April 17 and orchestrated on May 1. At times the opera made a very strong impression on me, but, as always, on a first hearing, it was extremely difficult to take it all in. I was struck by the wide use of modes and so-called double and even triple auxiliary notes (this is typical of *Servilia*). Stylistically the music proximates, partly, that of Rimsky-Korsakov's latest songs, partly *Mozart and Salieri* and, partly *The Tsar's Bride*. When I remarked about this, Rimsky-Korsakov agreed fully. Thus, the secret is out, though Stasov still knows nothing about it.

During tea, Liadov told us that, unlike Tchaikovsky, Anton Rubinstein was completely indifferent to the beauties of nature and that, in general, he was a "typical bachelor."

"Now, there's someone of whom I have the fondest memories," remarked Rimsky-Korsakov, "despite the considerable difference in our musical views."

Finally, we talked about the sixth part of *The Life of Peter Ilyich Tchaikovsky* and an extremely interesting letter Tchaikovsky once sent Rimsky-Korsakov. I will quote the first half of it (the second half is less interesting).

Moscow, 10 September 1875

My dear Nikolai Andreyevich,

Thank you very much for your kind letter.[28] You must know how I admire and revere your noble artistic modesty and amazing strength of character. These innumerable exercises in counterpoint, these sixty fugues and countless other musical intricacies which you accomplished—all this is such a great feat for a man who eight years before had already written *Sadko,* that I want to proclaim it to the whole world. I am astounded and do not know how to express my boundless respect for your artistic nature. How small, pitiful, self-satisfied, and naive I feel in comparison with you! I am only an artisan in composition. You will be an artist, in the full sense of the word. I hope you will not take these words as flattery. I am really convinced that with your immense gifts and the conscientiousness with which you approach your work, you will produce music which will far surpass everything that has thus far been written in Russia.

Here is an excerpt from a letter P. I. Tchaikovsky wrote to N. F. von Meck (see her correspondence with Tchaikovsky): [29]

. . . Korsakov was the only one of them [the *kuchka*—V. V. Ya.] who realized, five years ago, that the ideas preached by this circle had no sound basis, that their contempt for schooling, for classical music, their hatred of the authorities and the masterpieces was nothing but ignorance. I possess a letter of his dating from that time which moved me very deeply. He was overcome by despair when he realized how many years he had wasted and that he was following a path which was leading nowhere. He considered what he should do, and it became clear that he must study. And he began to study but with such zeal that before long the mastery of technique became indispensable to him. During one summer he wrote countless exercises in counterpoint and sixty-four fugues, ten of which he immediately sent me to look over. The fugues proved to be perfect, in their way, but I noted that his reaction had been too sudden. From contempt for study, he turned suddenly to the cult of musical technique. At present he is passing through a crisis, and it is difficult to predict how this crisis will end. Either he will emerge from this a great master or he will become mired in the intricacies of counterpoint.

On the whole, the evening passed very quickly. Belsky left somewhat earlier than Liadov and I. We remained until about one-thirty.

When Nikolai Andreyevich and I took leave of each other, we kissed three times, Russian fashion. His last words were: "I didn't ask whether your mother, Alina Andreyevna, received my note. Give my very warm regards to her and also to your wife and enjoy the summer."

When I arrived home (at two o'clock), it was as light as day, but the city was asleep.

First Visit to Krapachukha (5–6 August 1901)

Having left [Petersburg] on Saturday night, August 4, I arrived at the Krapachukha estate around ten o'clock in the morning. The dacha is charming, the situation magnificent, and the flower garden beautiful.

5 August

We talked about my mother's final days [30] and her threefold love for Nikolai Andreyevich—as a musician, a composer, and a man, who treated her only son with tenderness and affection.

Then, speaking about Modest Tchaikovsky's Reminiscences [31] of his brother, Peter Ilyich, Rimsky-Korsakov remarked that before the publication of this work, he had had no idea that Tchaikovsky had dedicated his song Pogodi (op. 16, no. 2) to him.

Further we chatted about the People's House, the Rome orchestra, and the flute of Pan, whose timbre has a tinge of eroticism. Rimsky-Korsakov praised highly the music of Gounod's Faust (the overture and the song about the King of Thule, from act 3) and the "chords of fate" from Bizet's Carmen.

6 August

Rimsky-Korsakov told me that Oleg has already been published, with a dedication to the memory of Pushkin; also that he has finished writing and orchestrating a prelude-cantata (From Homer) [32] with an orchestral section depicting a storm, followed by a women's chorus to the words "Vstala iz mraka mladaia s perstami purpurnymi Eos." It was begun on July 28 and is to serve as an introduction to the opera Nausicaä.

Speaking of Mlada, Christmas Eve, and Sadko—his three works most notable in terms of orchestration—Rimsky-Korsakov pointed out that his latest operas (for example, The Tsar's Bride) are much simpler in this respect. He also mentioned that with the exception of the "underwater kingdom" and some other places, he is not particularly fond of *Sadko*. He complained about the fate of his operas, including *Snegurochka*. He attributed the public's coolness toward them to something lacking in his talent.

"I can always picture how each of my heroes will feel," he said, "but when it comes to investing them with flesh and blood, I myself feel nothing.

"My works are skillful," he continued, "but they have little spontaneous warmth, little feeling. They're all rather like Snegurochki. This may even be very good, but not as far as the public is concerned. That's why they're indifferent to all my music. Lyricism and love—there's the supreme power, beauty, and poetry."

(Rimsky-Korsakov drinks milk with iodine; it lifts his spirits.)

I mentioned to Nikolai Andreyevich my critical article on his revisions of Mussorgsky (without text). He fully approves of its publication.[33] Then he began to complain that he has done little this summer. (He is undoubtedly composing something, but for the time being he is not talking about it.) He is deeply disappointed in his powers—a sure sign that he is working on some large-scale composition.

Our conversation turned to Nikolai Rubinstein and his strange opinion of Tchaikovsky's B-flat minor Piano Concerto.[34] An astonishingly flippant attitude for such an artist as Rubinstein.

Before dinner we played (four hands) Scriabin's E major Symphony and the first two movements of Taneyev's symphony. We argued about whether the latter work is or is not "Glazunov," whether, despite its many good qualities, it is really original. With this, Rimsky-Korsakov declared that at present Glazunov is the foremost composer in the whole world.

Nikolai Andreyevich is not writing the article about himself. This is a great pity.

"You know," he said, "I'd probably surprise many people if I wrote a critique of myself (my works). Apropos of *Snegurochka,* for example, I'd mention the influence that Bellini and Donizetti had on its style (the high notes at the end!). Before this I'd never have risked taking such a step."

Then I asked him point-blank whom he values more—Chopin or Glinka—and despite his veneration for Glinka, he replied, after some thought, Chopin, for in him were combined two geniuses—a genius for melody and a genius for harmony. He is puzzled by Tchaikovsky's dislike of Chopin's music (completely incomprehensible to musicians) and Chopin's dislike of the music of Schumann.

At the conclusion of our conversation, Rimsky-Korsakov related a preposterous incident which had occurred when he met Balakirev at Paderewski's concert: Mily Alexeyevich refused to shake hands with him.

"I hope I never run into him again," he said.

After evening tea, I left Krapachukha. The train pulled out at eleven-fifteen.

23 September

After dinner at Fried's, I went to the Rimsky-Korsakovs'. Nikolai Andreyevich was not at all surprised by my unexpected visit. He was in an excellent mood. He gave me the score of Lykov's inserted aria (in *The Tsar's Bride*) and a piano arrangement of his *Easter Overture* by Paul Gilson.

After tea we thought we might look through the works of Richard Strauss, but the conversation turned unexpectedly to Tolstoy's absurd book on art, and Nikolai Andreyevich became so agitated that for one hour he paced back and forth across the room. I simply cannot understand why Nadezhda Nikolayevna, who knows perfectly well how irritating the very mention of this book is to Rimsky-Korsakov—why she is the first one to bring it up in conversation.

The Maid of Pskov is going to be given in Moscow with Chaliapin at the beginning of October. Bartsal has managed to persuade Nikolai Andreyevich to take charge of the rehearsals.

I asked Rimsky-Korsakov what he is working on now, but he evaded my question, saying that some time he will tell me, but he would rather not talk about it today.

"Only you shouldn't think it's *Nausicaä*," he said. "I've definitely decided to give up the thought of writing this opera, since Nausicaä's love for Odysseus has little appeal for me; I simply don't understand it at all."

16 October

I was at the Rimsky-Korsakovs' from eight-thirty until eleven-thirty. We talked about Moscow,[35] where Nikolai Andreyevich was presented with three wreaths: from the artists of the Russian Opera, the Moscow Private Russian Opera, and the Kerzin Society.

Further, we discussed the unfair review given Glazunov's Piano Sonata in *Russkaia muzykal'naia gazeta;* [36] also the wonderful introduction to Liszt's oratorio *St. Elizabeth* and its influence on the characterization of Olga in Rimsky-Korsakov's *Maid of Pskov* and on Pimen's tale about the Tsarevich Dmitri in Mussorgsky's *Boris Godunov.*

When I left, I took with me two articles about Nikolai Andreyevich, which appeared in *Russkoe obozrenie* for the year 1901 (pp. 291–304), entitled: "Baian nashikh dnei" (Manykin-Nevstruyev) and "Skazka o Tsare Saltane" (P. A. Karsaev).

26 October

After work, I dropped in on the Rimsky-Korsakovs to find out the day and hour of the dress rehearsal of *The Tsar's Bride.* After informing me that it will be tomorrow at noon and giving me his visiting card as a pass to the Marinsky Theater, Nikolai Andreyevich related an "ultracomical" incident from the life of Tchaikovsky. It seems that once, to spare himself an irksome visit from Korsov,[37] Peter Ilyich lay absolutely still for three hours beneath the divan in his study, on which Korsov had settled himself in the hope of getting to see the composer and persuading him to write a special aria for him in *The Oprichnik.* [38]

"Finally, when Korsov left," said Peter Ilyich, "I rushed to my writing table like a madman and, choking with rage, I wrote what he had asked for. You can just imagine what kind of aria *that* was!"

30 October

I attended the first performance of *The Tsar's Bride.* [39] It scored a tremendous success. The composer and the artists were called out many times after each act; Rimsky-Korsakov had to take three curtain calls alone. Marfa's first aria and Lykov's inserted aria had to be repeated. Owing to some mistake made during the introduction, the singers were not together in the quartet.

The cast was as follows: Sobakin—Serebryakov (sang tenderly and expressively), Marfa—Bolska (sang very well but did not act well nor have a firm command of her role), Gryaznoy—Yakovlev (looked and acted marvelously but sang poorly), Malyuta Skuratov—Antonovsky (excellent in every respect), Lykov—Morskoi (so-so; he sang his interpolated aria very warmly, simply, and beautifully), Lyubasha—Slavina (good on the whole but died abominably), Bomelius—Kravchenko (overacted terribly), Domna Saburova—Gladkaya (excellent throughout), Dunyasha Saburova—Nosilova (her dancing during the wedding ceremony could not have been better).

The opera was conducted by Napravnik.

18 November

Rimsky-Korsakov called on us this afternoon from four until five-thirty. "The devil only knows how long it is since we saw each other," he said, as he entered the anteroom and was removing his coat. Actually, it had been about a month since my last visit to him, and then it was only for half an hour.

We talked about Count Sheremetyev's public concert on November 4,[40] where, among other things, they played the Suite from the opera *Tsar Saltan,* and the poster repeated for the hundredth time the hackneyed and groundless statement: "As an orchestrator, Rimsky-Korsakov could be called the Russian Berlioz."

We got into a discussion about *The Tsar's Bride*—certain drawn-out passages in the first act and the marvelous sextet with the strikingly bright, sparkling "chorus of praise."

"You know," I said, "my wife is so enamored of this opera that when she met you, she wanted to tell you that if she were rich, she'd arrange that when you left the theater after a performance of it, your way would be strewn with flowers."

We had to confess, however, that even though the public likes *The Tsar's Bride,* the third performance did not evoke the expected demand for encores; also that from a dramatic point of view, Bolska is not a convincing Marfa. Antonovsky, on the other hand, is surprisingly good as Malyuta Skuratov, acting like a kind of "host," "the life of the party," in the first act.

We turned our attention to Stasov's article,[41] which claims that, in terms of style and importance in the history of human culture, *Mozart and Salieri* is the zenith and *The Tsar's Bride* the nadir.

"Isn't it a fact, though," asked Rimsky-Korsakov, "that Mozart puts constraints on the artist, which hamper and limit his creativity?"

19 November

This evening at the Rimsky-Korsakovs', in a discussion of the orchestration of certain passages in *The Tsar's Bride,* Nikolai Andreyevich drew particular attention to the tremolo in the scene of the "Tsar's word" and the use of chords of brasses (in compressed spacing) in the scene between Marfa and Gryaznoy. On the whole, he considers this opera the most mature and best thought-through of all his works, since he wrote it after having had a great deal of experience in the writing of opera.

"This view I'll always defend, whatever others may think or say about *The Tsar's Bride,*" he declared.

"Just imagine." he continued, "while preparing their roles, neither Papayan nor even Bolska noticed that during Marfa's recitative (in the 'delirium' scene), at her words, 'Akh, posmotri,' the theme of her first aria is stated by the orchestra, and therefore this recitative cannot be sung *tempo rubato.* The question arises then—if the artists don't give any thought to their roles but simply learn them by rote, how much can they possibly communicate to the public? Nothing, of course. Meanwhile, I've come to the conclusion that nowadays absolutely no one truly cares for real, good music."

Then Nikolai Andreyevich told me that recently, when he dropped in at the theater on some business, by chance he heard the second act of Wagner's *Lohengrin* [42] and this time, for some reason, he did not like it very much. The music with which the act opens struck him as nothing more than a strange, unnatural collection of sounds.

He also told me that he is going to compile a textbook of orchestration with examples drawn from his own works and arrangements. [43]

"You'll agree," he said, "that only I know for certain what I wanted and to what degree I succeeded."

After this, we read a review by Charles Joly from *Le Figaro* (no. 322) of November 18, 1901 (N. S.), which recounts the story of *The Tsar's Bride* rather intelligently, though for some reason Bomelius is taken for a sorcerer ("sorte de sorcier").

Finally, we turned to Kruglikov's recent article about the Moscow production of *The Maid of Pskov*.[44] Nikolai Andreyevich was very pleased with the introduction to it, which did not surprise me since it expounds a number of ideas he himself has often expressed.

Upon leaving I received as a gift the two just published overtures—to *The Maid of Pskov* and to *Vera Sheloga*—as well as the orchestral manuscript of the latter. The first bore the inscription: "To dear Vasily Vasilyevich Yastrebtsev (too great an admirer of my works). N. R.-K.—19 November 1901"; the second, "To Vasily Vasilyevich who knows every note of mine, from a devoted N. R.-K.—19 November 1901"; he also gave me the orchestral manuscript of *Vera Sheloga,* with the inscription: "To dear Vasily Vasilyevich Yastrebtsev as a memento of our ten-year acquaintance and friendship. Affectionately, N. R-Korsakov. October 13, 1901."

30 November

After the bank, I dropped in on the Rimsky-Korsakovs. Nikolai Andreyevich did not return home until six o'clock and, even though I was in a hurry to get to Khessin's, he kept me for dinner. (Incidentally, he is very favorably impressed by Khessin.)

We got onto the subject of Tchaikovsky, specifically, his attitude toward *Paraphrases*,[45] whereupon Nikolai Andreyevich expressed the view that it was very wrong and, what is more, unworthy of him to criticize the work so harshly.[46]

"Take, for example, his *Snegurochka*,"[47] said Nikolai Andreyevich. "On the whole, it's a rather unsuccessful work, poorly suited to the subject, yet Peter Ilyich had it published anyhow, and he didn't consider himself a dilettante for this.

"By the way," he continued, changing the subject quite unexpectedly, "I've recently come to the conclusion that the French of today have completely forgotten how to write beautifully. Both Charpentier's *Louise* and Saint-Saëns' *Les Barbares* are very bad."

In conclusion, speaking of Glinka's song *The Gulf of Finland*, Nikolai Andreyevich remarked that at one time it had exerted an influence on both Balakirev and himself. Here is the passage which left a deep mark on the new Russian music [example 59].

Example 59

(7)   (6)   (5)   (4)

Trip to Moscow (14–17 December 1901)

14 December

Nadezhda Nikolayevna, Andrei, and I left Petersburg on the thirteenth and arrived in Moscow on the morning of the fourteenth.[48] At about noon Rimsky-Korsakov returned to the hotel from the rehearsal. He reported to Andrei and me that this time—alas!—the orchestra is made up of a heterogeneous group of players, including members of the Kerzin Society, and, consequently, he cannot achieve very good results. Besides this, he related an incident which had occurred yesterday with Chaliapin. It seems that Feodor Ivanovich was supposed to sing two new ballades, which had been composed especially for him (by Keneman and Sakhnovsky),[49] but no one knew where he was. Finally, at about nine o'clock, they tracked him down, but he did not know the songs, so the rehearsal (with piano) dragged on until three in the morning. Again today, despite all efforts, Feodor Ivanovich did not arrive at the dress rehearsal until the very end (that is, eleven-thirty) and, as before, he hardly knew what he was singing.

Yesterday the Kerzin Society presented a musical evening, the first half of which was devoted entirely to works by Rimsky-Korsakov. According to Nikolai Nikolayevich, the best of the participating artists were Sobinov, Sinitsyna, and Donskoy.

At dinner tonight they talked about Olenine-d'Alheim, who, according to Kruglikov, sings better than Chaliapin. However, she does not sing Rimsky-Korsakov's songs, probably because she resents his revisions of Mussorgsky's *Boris*. She forgets that he revised and finished *Khovanshchina*.

In the evening we attended *The Maid of Pskov*. The first overture (to

Vera Sheloga) went very badly. Evidently, the artists were not yet ready for this opera. The second overture went better. However, on the whole, the opera sounded rather dull. The audience did not call for the composer (perhaps they did not realize that he was there).

Vera Sheloga is marvelous, but it is an intimate work and therefore both it and *Mozart and Salieri* should be performed at the Maly Theater, not at the Bolshoi—in any case it ought not be given with such a large-scale, sweeping folk drama as *The Maid of Pskov.*

This time Chaliapin was not in good form. In the scene of Olga's death, his sobbing was so loud that it sounded like a dirge.

Incidentally, I learned that in the summer of 1877, when the Rimsky-Korsakovs were living in the Red Dacha,[50] the following incident occurred. Evidently, Nadezhda Nikolayevna did not care much for Vera Sheloga's theme:

Example 60

This so annoyed Nikolai Andreyevich that, with the words: "If that's how it is, we don't need it," he threw his manuscript over the fence, and Nadezhda Nikolayevna had to run out into the street and gather up the sheets to keep them from getting lost.

15 December

This morning we discussed yesterday's rehearsal and the incident with Chaliapin. There had even been catcalls, and 154 people (out of the 270 there) demanded their money back.

At twelve-thirty I went to the Tretyakov Gallery with Nadezhda Nikolayevna and Andrei, and Nikolai Andreyevich went to Bartsal's.

On our return, as I was changing my clothes, Rimsky-Korsakov suddenly burst into my room to ask if I knew whether he could wear a soft white shirt with a starched collar with his frockcoat.

"I'm afraid I may cause a scandal with such attire," he said.

How much time we wasted over this stupid matter of dress! In the end, he left, obviously annoyed that I had not been able to offer him practical advice. However, when I dropped into his room on the way to the concert, I found he had changed the soft shirt for a starched one and was in an excellent mood.

Acoustically the new hall of the Conservatory is truly ideal.

The first half of the program consisted of the third act of *Mlada* in a concert version for orchestra alone. It went brilliantly. When Rimsky-Korsakov came out, he was greeted by a fanfare played by the whole orchestra, then presented with a testimonial with seventy-seven signatures and, at the end, he was called out four times. The second half of the program was less interesting.

After the concert we set out for supper at Safonov's. As we crossed the courtyard of the Conservatory, a large group of young people earnestly ogled Chaliapin and Rimsky-Korsakov.

Among those invited for supper were Keneman, Rimsky-Korsakov, Andrei, Nadezhda Nikolayevna, Vera Ivanovna Scriabina, Chaliapin and his wife,[51] and Sakhnovsky. Thanks to Chaliapin's great talent as a raconteur, the evening passed imperceptibly. He told many stories about himself. His life has been one long Odyssey. What has he not been! He was twice apprenticed to a shoemaker (once to his uncle); he served as a clerk in a district military court; he was a chorister in a bishop's choir, a member of a Zemstvo Council. He worked as a bookbinder, served in a Ukrainian troupe, was a storyteller at a Nizhegorod inn, served in a consistory, sang in French operetta and, following that, he studied with Usatov for two months. He has sung at the Panayevsky Theater, the Marinsky Theater, with the Mamontov Company and is currently with the Moscow Opera.

17 December

On the train [to St. Petersburg], Nikolai Andreyevich complained that he feels he is growing old. It was different in the days of *Snegurochka,* he said, when thanks to his studies, many things had become accessible to him and he was faced with writing "Spring" for the first time.

"Recently, while composing Marfa's role (for *The Tsar's Bride*), I once again felt a considerable satisfaction, and that's why I have a special affection for this heroine.

"You know," he continued, "I'm coming to the conclusion that I've composed many things almost solely out of vanity. Chechott, the Kiev critic, writes that I'm first and foremost a symphonist. This hurts me somewhat, so I do my best to write operas. S. K. Bulich says that my folk scenes are particularly successful—so I begin to devote special attention to singers, and I write *The Tsar's Bride, Tsar Saltan,* and *Servilia,* in which attention is centered on the solo parts. Laroche rejects Mussorgsky—so I take it upon myself to revise *Boris Godunov.* Stasov claims that I don't know how to write recitatives—so I compose an opera in recitative style—*Mozart and Salieri,* etc.

"You won't believe it," added Rimsky-Korsakov, "but the awareness of this greatly diminishes the value and significance of my talent in my own eyes.

"Finally," he concluded, "I've discovered in myself incontrovertible signs of a kind of 'Salierism.' For example, I'm rather irked by the success of Chaliapin, Scriabin, Nikisch, d'Alheim, and others, and I feel more favorably disposed toward talented mediocrity, though I don't envy such artists as Anton Rubinstein, Glinka, Glazunov, and Hans Richter."

"But isn't this simply an outraged sense of unfairness?" I asked.

"Maybe so," replied Nikolai Andreyevich.

Then he added that despite his inclination to compose out of contrariness, he will never write a "pure" symphony, since this is not for him— his musical ideas immediately become unoriginal and shallow.

19 December

Following the precedent of previous years, I dined at the Rimsky-Korsakovs' today. We talked about the fact that *Servilia* will be given at the Marinsky Theater next year (talks are already underway with the stage designer and Blumenfeld) and *Mozart and Salieri* will probably be given at the Hermitage Theater[52] (with Sobinov and Chaliapin).

After dinner we looked through the orchestral score of act 2 of *Servilia,* and I promised to return the proofs of act 4 and 5 on Friday.

This being the thirty-sixth anniversary of Nikolai Andreyevich's career and mindful that my late mother always sent him flowers on this day, I brought him a pretty little basket of lilies of the valley, and, besides this, three roses for Nadezhda Nikolayevna.

22 December

I attended the sixth Symphonic Evening of the Russian Musical Society, at which Khessin conducted for the first time. The program consisted of Berlioz' *Symphonie fantastique,* two choruses by Taneyev—*Russian Song* and *Nocturne* (conducted by Konstantin von Bach), the Prelude to Wagner's *Parsifal,* Saint-Saëns' Third Violin Concerto (played by B. O. Livshits), and the March of the Magi from Liszt's *Christus.*

Khessin achieved a brilliant success, for which I am sincerely glad. Cui and Napravnik sent Nikisch a congratulatory telegram. During the intermission I ran into Rimsky-Korsakov, who said that in his opinion, Khessin conducted the Berlioz symphony excellently.

26 December

Khessin and I were at the Rimsky-Korsakovs'. We got onto the subject of foreign conductors: Nikisch, with his innumerable concert tours and somewhat monotonous programs; Mottl, a superb opera conductor but rather indifferent symphonic conductor (according to Khessin); Weingartner, unpleasant and overbearing; Hans Richter, currently conducting in Manchester; and Muck, who is in the service of Cosima Wagner. We also noted that these days Bayreuth is beginning to deteriorate mainly because of ever-deepening intrigues, plots, and servility.

Following this there was a lengthy discussion about Strauss and Wagner. I will not stop here to go into the conversation in detail as I have already presented Nikolai Andreyevich's views on these composers many times. Nothing essentially new was added, except for what Rimsky-Korsakov had to say about Wagner.

"It's a strange thing," he said, "I always like Beethoven, even though he could, I think, become boring. But Wagner—you've only to get out of the habit of [listening to] him, and when you hear him again, you don't like him (I don't, at least). Obviously, there's something wrong with his music. What's more, there's hardly another composer whose works can be cut so easily and, I may say, almost without even noticing it. And all because Wagner's works lack real form, the necessary proportion.

"You can't do this with Glinka," concluded Rimsky-Korsakov. "In *Ruslan,* you've only to omit Bayan's second song, and the finale of the Prologue will seem long!"

During tea we had a discussion about the absurd staging of *May Night* in Frankfurt am Main. Suffice it to say that the serious-minded Germans took the *fugato* in the second scene of act 2—"Satan, Satan!"—for a prayer to Satan, and the artists sang it kneeling! (What could be more stupid?)

Further, Nikolai Andreyevich related to us two amusing incidents about Anton Rubinstein.

"Once," he said, "when he was conducting one of his operas in Moscow, suddenly in the middle of the act, he put down his baton and in a loud voice shouted to the regisseur backstage: 'What about the moon?' Can you imagine what an impression this aside made on the audience?"

Another time, at a rehearsal of *The Demon* in Petersburg, Rubinstein began to berate the singers so rudely that Napravnik had to intervene and ask him to leave the podium.

At the end, Rimsky-Korsakov asked Khessin to show him his article on Strauss (this great "poet-musician," as Khessin calls him), adding jestingly: "I warn you, if you succeed in proving to me that Strauss' music 'is ushering in something new, unknown in art' (as Serova says), I'll do, in a certain sense, what the famous Petronius did and, that very same day, I'll shoot myself!"

I have no doubt whatsoever that Khessin will not succeed one iota in shaking Rimsky-Korsakov's faith in his artistic beliefs, especially since, even without Khessin, Nikolai Andreyevich was excellently informed about Strauss' music.

CHAPTER 12

1902

On my name day I received the following note from Nikolai Andrey-evich:

13/8 has been chosen as the meter, since it proved to be the most satisfactory during the trip to Moscow: N. R-K. [Example 61.] January 1, 1902. (Day of St. Vasily the Great).

Example 61

4 January

Nikolai Andreyevich was in a fine mood today when I dropped by with the scores of *Mlada* and *The Tsar's Bride*. He would like very much to make Khessin into a thoroughly intelligent musician, one with a sober view of things.

"What I value so highly," he said, "is that a musician's artistic taste and ear not be spoiled. I'm certain that someone who can like Strauss' *Heldenleben* doesn't really perceive the true beauty of sound, for one thing precludes the other.

"And these paradoxical statements of an avant-garde feuilletonist," continued Nikolai Andreyevich, "to the effect that 'the ugliest person can be expressive and produce an impression' and consequently 'the crux of the matter is not the beauty, smoothness, and symmetry of forms but expressiveness'—this I find totally unconvincing."

Further, we spoke about Liapunov, whose music, though very noble, is almost entirely lacking in originality—sometimes it's Balakirev, sometimes Glazunov (of the *Poème lyrique* period).[1]

Finally, we talked about the performance of *The Tsar's Bride* on December 29, 1901, which went very badly, unrhythmically. How curious that Balakirev deigned, at last, to attend it.

12 January

I went to the second Russian Symphony Concert, conducted by Liadov. The program consisted of Scriabin's Second Symphony (premiere), Kalafati's *Adagio* and *Scherzo* (also a premiere), Rimsky-Korsakov's *Skazka,* and the Entr'acte from Taneyev's *Oresteia*.

Even though *Skazka* went badly (especially the end), Rimsky-Korsakov was recalled three times. As for the works of Kalafati and Taneyev, the former's *Scherzo* proved to be reasonably good. Of Taneyev's Entr'acte, I can only say that the first half sounded really marvelous but the second was weak musically and orchestrated in a banal manner.

I sat next to the Rimsky-Korsakovs, and during the performance of Scriabin's Symphony (especially during the unusually wild harmonies), Nikolai Andreyevich and I exchanged glances. After hearing this work for the second time, Rimsky-Korsakov has become totally disenchanted with it. The harmonies of the Andante recalled to him a comical little poem and he wrote it on his visiting card:

> Dogs bark, cats moan,
> But the young girl's heart remains untouched.
> Sad and solitary
> She moves through the grove like the moon.

He was on the point of giving me the card, but then reconsidered and put it in his pocket.

During the intermission, we agreed that it would not be difficult to produce pounds of music like Scriabin's Symphony. It is so boring and lifeless that it fits Schopenhauer's well-known aphorism (if I am not mistaken) regarding the voluminous but talentless creations of most learned craftsmen, that is, that it was probably easier to write such works than it is to read them.

17 January

I went to a concert (or rather Liederabend) at Mme Olenine-d'Alheim's, which, by the way, was attended by all the "musical aristocracy" of the capital, including even Balakirev. They sang songs by Grieg, Chopin, Brahms, the entire *Dichterliebe* of Schumann, many songs by Schubert, many by Mussorgsky, including all of his *Nursery,* etc., etc.—thirty-nine songs in all and all from memory!

In the interval Rimsky-Korsakov told me that at supper at Belyaev's on Saturday after the concert, he had created something of a "scandal" by offering a toast which apparently angered Scriabin and his musical "co-religionists." "Permit me, gentlemen," he said, "to propose a somewhat capricious toast to the health of a musical figure I esteem highly— namely 'consonance'—for when 'consonance' will be healthy, then, too, will 'dissonance' be healthy, expressive, and beautiful."

Nikolai Andreyevich also reported to me that the eleventh performance of *The Tsar's Bride* (on January 15) had gone quite well. Yakovlev was extraordinarily good as Gryaznoy; he sang magnificently and overacted very little.

On taking leave, Nikolai Andreyevich asked me to bring him Strauss' *Heldenleben.* He needs it for the Conservatory, where he has already given a lecture on that composer's *Don Quixote* with the desired "negative success."

No, clearly you're not going to fool us Russians with such musical rubbish! Neither Koptyaev nor even the great Nikisch himself is going to get anywhere in our country!

20 January

Rimsky-Korsakov visited us this afternoon from four until quarter past five. Among other things, he speculated about the fate of his music after his death.

"At first, there will be a certain surge of interest," he declared. "They will probably even write a few brochures about me. But then eternal and irrevocable oblivion will set in, and I will play the same role in the history of music with my operas as Bellini and Donizetti, without, of course, ever attaining their fame.

"By the way," he continued, "here's what Telyakovsky told me recently. 'Next year we're going to give your *Servilia,* but after that we'll probably have to wait awhile, otherwise they'll begin reproaching me, saying that I put on only your operas.'

"As you can see," concluded Nikolai Andreyevich, "the immediate prospects for my operas are not too good."

5 February

In Rimsky-Korsakov's opinion, however beautiful, however grandiose the "magic scene" of Wotan's farewell to Brunnhilde, despite even the magic fire, something is lacking. It is as though Wagner had not yet hit upon the supreme moment in the characterization of Loge. It was not until the "fire scene" in *Siegfried* that he produced the most perfect, most profoundly inspired music of this type.

"Just think how advanced Liszt and Wagner were for their time," said Nikolai Andreyevich. "Why, all these 'Dichtungen'[2] and 'Nibelungen' were written in the fifties and the brilliant, dazzlingly orchestrated overture to *Tannhäuser* even earlier—at the beginning of the forties—in other words, at a time when we were still 'sucking on pacifiers.' Yet how new, how fresh and original all this still is!"

Nikolai Andreyevich suggested that sometime I should acquire the scores of *Die Walküre, Siegfried,* and *Tristan.*

Later on, we talked about our circle and the critics.

"Actually," said Nikolai Andreyevich, "a critic should not become involved in any way with the interests of the composers he criticizes but should pronounce his judgments from afar. But how to achieve this?"

When I left, I took with me Liadov's new collection: *35 Russian Folk Songs.*

"They're done wonderfully but they're too refined," remarked Rimsky-Korsakov. "They're all variations on folk themes—not ethnographic recordings. But then, Balakirev's collection and both of mine are guilty of the same shortcomings. If I were to record folk songs now, I'd harmonize them altogether differently."

6 March

After work I went to Rimsky-Korsakov's to congratulate him on his fifty-eighth birthday and to bring him a basket of pale pink hyacinths (as my late mother always did). We drank chocolate and talked about Mahler's conducting[3] (motionless but strikingly good, though somewhat mannered in Beethoven) and also about Wagner's music, which is captivating almost the entire Rimsky-Korsakov family.

Glazunov came and we discussed the problem of becoming flustered on stage. As an example of this, Alexander Konstantinovich told us about a curious experience he had had at a recital by Verzhbilovich, whom he had offered to accompany.

"I came out on the stage (the usual business, it would seem)," he said, "and suddenly I felt I couldn't make head or tail of anything. I began at once with preliminaries—a 6/4 chord; then I looked at the music and became so nervous that I could hardly make it out. It was terrible! For a moment I thought of getting up and leaving, but fortunately I didn't."

They spoke about Felix Blumenfeld, and Nikolai Andreyevich expressed the thought that as soon as he entered the Marinsky Theater,[4] Blumenfeld ceased being one of the Belyaev circle and by now has become a "theater drudge" in the full sense of the word.

Neither Glazunov nor I stayed for dinner. We walked together as far as Kazan Street, and on the way, we had a long talk about Khessin. In

Glazunov's opinion, Khessin is given to lying and boasting and, like all of Solovyov's students, he is not knowledgeable about music. Alexander Konstantinovich believes that of all the Russians, the only real symphonic conductor is Safonov, and neither Blumenfeld, Khessin, Klenovsky, nor Krushevsky can be compared with him.

8 March

Nikolai Andreyevich was at the People's House for a rehearsal of *May Night,* and from what he reported to me about it, he was rather favorably impressed. Even though nearly all of the soloists were poor, the orchestra played quite cleanly and, what is more, the opera was given without cuts. Rimsky-Korsakov also attended a rehearsal of the Mahler concert, and he found that, like most contemporary conductors, Mahler mutilated Beethoven's *Egmont.*

16 March

Tonight I went to the Rimsky-Korsakovs' for a belated party in honor of Nikolai Andreyevich's birthday. Among the guests there were M. N. Rimsky-Korsakov, Stasov, Glazunov, Liadov, N. Sokolov, Belyaev, Artsybushev, the Blumenfeld brothers, Belsky, and some of Rimsky-Korsakov's students.

The conversation turned to the subject of conductors and conducting. As Rimsky-Korsakov sees it, what is most important is that the orchestra should be favorably disposed. As an example, he pointed to his experience conducting the premiere of his *Capriccio espagnol,* which, he said, went "superlatively" because the musicians liked it; he himself had nothing to do with it.

Between tea and supper there was a great deal of playing and singing. Felix Blumenfeld played Glazunov's Second Sonata; then the Blumenfeld brothers played Liszt's *Hunnenschlacht;* Sigismund Blumenfeld, with his brother Felix accompanying, sang Mussorgsky's *Seminarist* and all of Liadov's *Children's Songs;* etc.

During supper Sokolov regaled us with comical stories. After supper, with Felix Blumenfeld as the orchestra, Sigismund Blumenfeld and Nikolai Sokolov improvised a one-act Italian opera of the good old days with a great deal of "tragedy" and one death. Stasov was in raptures. After the "opera," Mitusov did a "frenzied dance of a savage" to an accompaniment improvised by Glazunov. At the end Felix Blumenfeld played the "Butterweek" scene, Dance of the Skomorokhi, Hymn of the Berendeys, and the final song to the Sun-God Yarilo from *Snegurochka.* We all joined in singing the chorus of the last two numbers.

Stasov and I were almost the first to leave. By then it was already going on five in the morning.

"It's been a long time since there was such merriment at the Rimsky-Korsakovs'," I remarked to Vladimir Vasilyevich, as we reached the staircase.

"And all because there were so many talented people there," he replied.

"We used to have something like this at Dargomyzhsky's and Borodin's," he added.

I forgot to mention that after hearing Liadov's *Songs,* Nikolai Andreyevich declared, with comic seriousness, that tomorrow at the Conservatory he is going to scold Anatoly Konstantinovich for contenting himself with writing nothing but graceful parodies of Chopin when, with so much talent, he could become a fine, serious Russian composer.

Besides this, I learned that Malozemova has finally gotten her way: Schumann's *Carnaval* is going to be orchestrated; Rimsky-Korsakov himself has already scored *Florestan.* [5]

24 March

Rimsky-Korsakov visited us this afternoon from four o'clock until quarter to five. We drank champagne. With the first glass I toasted him and his *Servilia;* the second he drank to my health and the third—to the memory of my late mother.

We talked about the absolute necessity of protesting in the press against the slipshod, harmonically distorted piano arrangements of Tchaikovsky's *Romeo and Julet* and *The Tempest.* Otherwise, some naïve amateur musician might be led to believe that the only way to "harmonize" Tchaikovsky is to "overharmonize" him, as in this unfortunate Jurgenson edition.

How is it that such a reputable firm as Jurgenson is not ashamed to publish such rubbish!

Rimsky-Korsakov informed me that his purpose in coming today had been to reveal his long-kept secret, namely, that he has not only written but has already orchestrated a new, extremely fantastic opera in three scenes on the subject of a little "autumn" folk tale, and that it is to be called *Kashchei the Immortal.*

Initially the libretto of this opera was offered to Rimsky-Korsakov by Yevgeny Petrovsky, but on the first reading, he did not like it and he laid it aside. He liked the idea and the folk-tale subject, outside of time and place, but he objected to the vague and confused way in which it was set forth and also to the poetry, which was not particularly good. Petrovsky reworked it three times, but each time the scenario became more and more muddled and obscure. Thus the text of this tale remained until the summer, when Nikolai Andreyevich and his family went to the dacha in Krapachukha. There, in the country, on seeing the poppies in full bloom, he suddenly was seized with an overwhelming desire to write an opera on the subject of *Kashchei,* and, without hestiating, he composed the first scene (on a somewhat altered text), which he orchestrated at once. He also made a rough draft of the second scene. Then he stopped working on it until he returned to the city.

Upon returning from Krapachukha, Rimsky-Korsakov met with Petrovsky, informed him of what he had composed and of his revisions in the text and asked him to make some further alterations along these lines and also to write a third scene.

"Evidently Yevgeny Maximovich was annoyed at my changes in his libretto," said Rimsky-Korsakov, "for he flatly refused to rework the text any further, claiming that he perceived this subject differently than I did. Thus my half-composed opera 'fizzled out' until January 1902, when I felt drawn to this tale once again and quickly finished the missing third scene."

The subject on which Korsakov's *Kashchei* was based differed considerably from that originally proposed to him by Petrovsky and therefore, he decided to revise the lines of the first scene again.[6]

"This morning, before coming to you," said Rimsky-Korsakov, "I went to Petrovsky's and told him that *Kashchei the Immortal* is finished. Thank heavens, everything turned out perfectly. To all appearances Yevgeny Maximovich is no longer angry at me. Moreover, he would not hear of any compensation for his libretto, which I had utilized to some extent, and so this time we parted amicably, for which I'm exceedingly glad."

Rimsky-Korsakov then gave me a rather detailed account of the opera's plot, which I liked very much. According to him the work will contain very tricky harmonies, suitable for every possible "table of harmonies."

"By the way," said Rimsky-Korsakov, "you might take note of the fact that this is the first opera of mine which ends in the sunny D major."

"It would be interesting to know," I remarked, "what our 'advanced' musicians will think of *Kashchei.*"

"I can satisfy your curiosity in part," he replied jokingly, "for I've already shown some of the first scene to Glazunov, and, despite his dislike for opera in general and program music in particular, this time he declared that he didn't expect anything like this 'from me.' "

At the end Nikolai Andreyevich invited me to visit him on Tuesday (March 26), when he will play his *Kashchei* for Glazunov, Liadov, and Belsky. (Stasov will not be there. He will be introduced to the opera separately, because he makes a lot of noise and prevents others from listening attentively.)

When we parted, we kissed heartily and drank a liqueur from a silver cup in honor of Nikolai Andreyevich's new opera. Then I gave him one of the cups as a memento of October 13, 1901. Thus, my long overdue celebration of the tenth anniversary of my acquaintance with Nikolai Andreyevich proved to be the best possible.

It is a long time since Rimsky-Korsakov was so cheerful and animated.

25 March

Today I went again to the Rimsky-Korsakovs'; I was eager to look through Nikolai Andreyevich's new manuscript. From the rough draft and the score, it became clear that *Kashchei the Immortal* was composed between June 26 and September 1, 1901, and February 14 and March 11, 1902, and it was scored between July 24, 1901, and March 19, 1902.

We talked about Glazunov's Second Sonata. This time Nikolai Andreyevich praised it very highly. When I remarked that he is a much better composer than Glazunov, he only shrugged his shoulders and said: "What kind of talent do I have? I used to have it, but now? You know, I write everything out of contrariness."

Now, he said, he wants very much to write an opera on a subject completely different from that of *Kashchei*.

Finally, he complained that in recent years he has begun to lose his memory, and this distresses and alarms him very much.

I forgot to mention that during our conversation, Nikolai Andreyevich suddenly had difficulty breathing; he even turned pale. However, this lasted no more than a quarter or half a minute.

26 March

This evening Rimsky-Korsakov was in an excellent mood. At nine o'-clock Belsky came, then Liadov, and after tea, Felix Blumenfeld and Glazunov. The talk was about Liszt's *Christus*. Rimsky-Korsakov praised, in particular, the Introduction, "March," "Adoration of the Magi," "Entry into Jerusalem" and "Stabat mater speciosa."

Rimsky-Korsakov gave me the new edition of his *Textbook of Harmony*,[7] a ticket for Nikisch's rehearsal, and also one for the balalaika concert directed by Andreyev (an ardent admirer of Nikolai Andreyevich), at which they will perform a fantasia based on *The Tsar's Bride*.[8]

The music began at eleven o'clock and continued until one-thirty, after which supper was served. We did not leave until about three o'clock.

Kashchei was played twice. Overall it left a powerful impression. When it ended, a dispute arose about certain chords. It was evident that Nikolai Andreyevich is highly pleased with what he calls his "layered harmonies" (the shining skulls, snowstorm, Kashcheyevna's enchanted garden, scene of Kashchei's death, etc.). Thus, when Felix Blumenfeld expressed doubt that there's such a harmony as that used at the moment of Kashchei's death (when one hears chromatic progressions in the orchestra dissolve against the background of a diminished seventh chord—C, E flat, F sharp, A—played loudly by trumpets, trombones, and muted French horns and when, amid this tonal chaos, there suddenly rings out an incredibly daring B flat), Rimsky-Korsakov replied not without pride: "Not in a textbook perhaps, but nevertheless, it's superb. And I'm happy that I succeeded in writing it. What's more, my major thirds aren't so bad either." Inexhaustible artist!

The latest news—M. A. Vrubel has gone mad.

29 March

I was at the Siloti Concert. It was under the direction of Nikisch. They played Tchaikovsky's Fourth Symphony, Glazunov's *Overture solennelle,* a concerto by Rachmaninov, and three overtures: to Mozart's *Don Giovanni,* Mendelssohn's *Fingal's Cave,* and Wagner's *Tannhäuser.*

Sitting in the balcony above the stage, I was able to study Nikisch's movements. I saw Nikolai Andreyevich seated beside Felix Blumenfeld, listening very attentively to the whole program and only occasionally passing a remark about the performance. It will be interesting to learn what he thought.

As for me, I deeply admire Nikisch, even though I did not agree completely with the tempo in the Andante of Tchaikovsky's symphony. (It was too fast, I thought.) I was also not entirely satisfied with his performance of *Fingal's Cave.* On the other hand, the Mozart overture, the first, third, and fourth movements of the Symphony and the overture to *Tannhäuser* were played matchlessly.

8 April

Tonight *Kashchei the Immortal* was given at the Rimsky-Korsakovs' for the Stasovs and a few other guests, including the Blumenfeld brothers, Belsky, Lapshin, Bessel, Ossovsky, and Glazunov.

The music began at eleven o'clock and continued until one in the morning. Actually, the opera ended at twelve-fifteen, when, at the request of V. Stasov and Nadezhda Nikolayevna, Glazunov played his Second Sonata. As before I am completely indifferent to this work and, despite the opinion of most everyone else, I consider it lacking in inspiration.

Thanks to Felix Blumenfeld's lifeless playing, tonight's performance of *Kashchei* left absolutely no impression on me. Neither Stasov nor Bessel understood it at all, but they pretended they got something out of it. Alexander Konstantinovich, on the other hand, was so carried away with it that at supper he offered the following toast to Rimsky-Korsakov: "I drink to the one who killed Kashchei the Immortal, for, though a 'criminal,' he is deserving of the fullest mercy since, thanks to this 'villainy,' something new and great in art has come into being."

17 April

I spent the entire evening at the Rimsky-Korsakovs'. Fortunately, no one else was there, except Troitsky, and he spent most of the time with the young people. Since *Kashchei* is to be delivered to the printer tomorrow, we did not waste any time but began at once going through the first scene. What a wealth of magnificent music, what daring and original harmonies, what a world of beauty!

We talked about the fact that the appearance of *Kashchei* had produced no particular impression; that even after hearing it, Liadov, Glazunov, and Stasov had not felt it necessary to share this news with anyone. It was as if nothing had happened.

"That only goes to show that no one is greatly interested in my music," observed Rimsky-Korsakov. "But then, I got used to this long ago, back in 1894, when I was writing *Christmas Eve.*"

I related to Nikolai Andreyevich a conversation between Stasov and Timofeyev. In Stasov's opinion, there is absolutely nothing to be derived from listening to *Kashchei*. "I never heard anything like it. . . ."

"Perhaps I don't understand anything," Stasov ventured, but then he immediately corrected himself, adding, "One thing I do know and that is, that if I don't like something right away, it's a sure sign I'll never like it."

When Timofeyev suggested that perhaps Vladimir Vasilyevich had not delved into the work sufficiently, Stasov replied that this was not so.

Speaking further about Rimsky-Korsakov's operas, I told him that I have no special favorite, since I value each and every one of them. He himself believes they can be very useful to young, beginning opera composers, because they are written well and quite intelligently.

Our conversation turned to the subject of Tchaikovsky's songs. Upon my remarking that I find some twenty-five to thirty of them beautiful, Nikolai Andreyevich expressed surprise. "Oh," he said, "I think there are considerably fewer than that."

He then told me that he wants very much to write another large-scale Russian fantastic opera, and has already partially outlined the plot.

"And then," he said, "I'll be able to take a rest. I'm absolutely exhausted. I feel as though I'm playing the same role in music as an old husband with an insatiable wife."

We burst out laughing.

"This time," he continued, "I'd like to compose an opera not out of contrariness, but just for myself, without rushing."

During tea we talked about the wealth of talent to be found in *Prince Igor* and also about the fact that only the Petersburg composers know how to orchestrate well, that their orchestration always sounds noble.

"This is not so with the Muscovites," said Rimsky-Korsakov. "Somehow their orchestra always squeaks, even when the instrumentation itself seems exquisite (as in the case of Klenovsky and others). I was convinced of this once more when I heard Schumann's *Carnaval* in the orchestration of the Petersburgers and the Muscovites."

Tomorrow Rimsky-Korsakov will be at Glazunov's to look through the score of Glinka's *Life for the Tsar* with him and Liadov with a view to preparing a new, anniversary edition. They are going to make some revisions in the orchestration.

4 May

I was at the Second Russian Symphony Concert, which was given at the Taurida Palace under the direction of Nikisch. They performed Berlioz' overture to *Benvenuto Cellini*, Beethoven's Seventh Symphony, the Introduction to Arensky's *Nal and Damayanti*, the Introduction to Glazunov's ballet *Les ruses d'amour*, Borodin's *In Central Asia*, Rimsky-Korsakov's *Capriccio espagnol*, and Wagner's *Rienzi* overture.

Berlioz, Beethoven, Arensky, Glazunov, and Wagner were played excellently (especially Wagner). However, the performance of Borodin and Rimsky-Korsakov was far from ideal. For example, why Nikisch increased the tempo in the coda of *Central Asia* no one knows. Many of the tempi in the *Capriccio espagnol* were also taken too fast, which created a great deal of fire but for me, at least, no warmth.

9 May

Shortly after I arrived at Rimsky-Korsakov's tonight, Timofeyev appeared and we fell to discussing an article in *Novoe vremia* about *Ein Hel-*

denleben,[9] Strauss, Balakirev, the vile intrigues of Klenovsky and Smolen-sky, and the departure of Liadov and Sokolov from the Court Chapel. Then other guests began to arrive—N. I. Richter, Mitusov and his wife, Stasov, Glazunov, Belsky, and Mikhail Nikolayevich Rimsky-Korsakov and his wife.

The evening was very lively. They talked about Nikisch. Rimsky-Korsakov was highly pleased with his performance of *Capriccio espagnol,* not altogether satisfied with that of Borodin's *In Central Asia,* and enthusiastic about the way he conducted Tchaikovsky's fourth and fifth symphonies. Someone mentioned that at a supper at Contant's, Nikisch had called Khessin "der kleine Nikisch."

Glazunov went on at great length about Bruckner, his fawning upon Kapellmeister Hans Richter, and his request that Franz Josef forbid Han-slick to disparage his works. Someone else remarked that Wagner always assumed the pose of a genius when he knew someone was watching him through a chink in his study. In turn we learned the following about Brahms: according to Esipova, he loved to listen to his own works but could not stand it when young composers came to see him. Once, upon catching sight of such a person, he ran quickly down the stairs, only to meet the young man already at the entrance doors. To the latter's query, "Is this where the great Brahms lives?" he replied, "Upstairs, on the third floor," and slipped away.

They got into a discussion about capital punishment, whereupon Ni-kolai Andreyevich became terribly agitated. He declared that in his view, people (i.e., society) dare not kill anyone; it is contrary to our nature. Criminals must be punished, but they must not be put to death.

After tea Glazunov played his new, as yet unfinished Seventh Symphony.[10] It is a magnificent work. Besides this, he played his new *Ballade* for orchestra[11]—also unusually interesting, strong, and beautiful.

From further conversation I learned that on May 22 the entire Rimsky-Korsakov family is going to Heidelberg[12] to see Mikhail Nikolayevich, who is being sent on a mission by the University. Andrei Nikolayevich will be there too.

At about three o'clock, as Belsky and I came out on the Fontanka, the rising sun was already gilding the topmost cross of the Troitsky Cathedral. It was as light as day.

When I entered the Rimsky-Korsakovs' tonight, we embraced warmly. I reported on the performance of *The Tsar's Bride,* which had not gone particularly well.[13]

Nikolai Andreyevich told me that the orchestration of *The Stone Guest* will be completed in a day or two,[14] and that the vocal score and most of the full score of *Kashchei* are already finished.

Following this, I learned that after Heidelberg, the Rimsky-Korsakovs traveled for three weeks. They spent a week in Switzerland and then went to Munich and Dresden, where they heard a complete performance of *Götterdämmerung,* which they enjoyed tremendously.

Rimsky-Korsakov also told me that if Belsky will prepare what he wants and if it turns out well, he will disclose to me the subject of the new opera he is planning to write.

"It will be very fantastic or, as you would say, mysterious and even mystical," he said. "However, I'm tired of proofreading, composing, even of orchestrating. I feel rather weary, so this one will go relatively slowly, not as before."

Then, speaking of the fate of his operas, Nikolai Andreyevich said, "All my operas (after *Sadko*) have, I think, only temporary interest. Later on they will cease to be given altogether, and only *Snegurochka* will continue to be associated with my name."

By the way, Tchaikovsky envied Rimsky-Korsakov: "I read Korsakov's *Snegurochka* and I was amazed at his artistic ability and even, I am ashamed to confess, envied him." (*Zhizn' Petra Il'icha* [The Life of Peter Ilyich], part 14, p. 164)

Troitsky related an amusing conversation which took place in the smoking room of the Olympia Theater at a performance of Ivanov's *Zabava Putyatishny.*

"No," protested the person with whom Troitsky was conversing, "Ivanov has written better operas than this—*The Tsar's Bride,* for example."

1 October

Servilia was given its premiere tonight before a full house. The performance began a few minutes past eight and ended at eleven-forty-five. The opera was received enthusiastically. Rimsky-Korsakov was recalled very warmly fourteen times.

The cast included, among others, Markevich as Tigellinus, Morskoi—Trasea (very good), Kuza—Servilia (wonderful), Yershov—Valerius (good), Chuprynnikov—Montanus (good), Yakovlev—Aegnatius (so-so), Serebryakov—Soranus (good), and Nosilova—Locusta. The staging was under them supervision of O. O. Paleček. Felix Blumenfeld conducted. I felt there was much to be criticized in the latter's interpretation, but Rimsky-Korsakov was completely satisfied with it.

When the opera ended, a number of us went to the Rimsky-Korsakovs' for supper. I told the guests about an encounter I had had today with Stasov's grandniece, Natalya Pivovarova. She was incensed over the fact that Rimsky-Korsakov had written an "Italian" opera, to which I retorted sharply that, first of all, this opera could not have been written any other way and, secondly, by making such statements she only revealed her total lack of understanding of music.

They talked about the fact that some of the text of *Servilia* had been supplied by V. V. Belsky (Aegnatius: "Idet . . . boius', poslushny i budut dukhi"; the words of the finale of the opera "Molis' emu, v nem blagosti net mery," etc.)

Further, Rimsky-Korsakov told us about Kuza's ridiculous behaviour at the dress rehearsal. It seems that she wanted to know whether she would have a real spinning wheel (in act 3), and when Nikolai Andreyevich replied that he knew nothing about this—that it was the business of the stage manager—she flew into a rage and called him a "milksop."

"But today she suddenly seized hold of me and kissed me," he added with a laugh.

During supper Nadezhda Nikolayevna, who, by the way, does not care very much for *Servilia*, urged Nikolai Andreyevich in jest to take some lessons from Glazunov and write a symphony or suite.

Toward the end of supper, Rimsky-Korsakov raised a glass of champagne and thanked Felix Mikhailovich with all his heart for the way he conducted the opera.

"It was exactly as I wanted it," he said. "I didn't want it 'literally' but with 'un poco rubato.'

"You know," he continued, "I have a very high regard for Napravnik and the great service he renders but you, Felix Mikhailovich, are a man of today. Besides, you like me and this is what endears you to me as a person and as a conductor."

Glazunov quipped that at last, by writing an opera based on Roman life, Nikolai Andreyevich has finally justified his surname. ["Rimsky" is the Russian adjective "Roman."]

I learned that in a few days Rimsky-Korsakov is going to Moscow for a brief visit.

It is a long time since I have seen him so contented on the day of the first performance of one of his operas.

7 October

Despite the generally unfavorable reviews of Servilia,[15] the second performance was relatively well received by the subscription audience. Except for the part of the Old Man, in which Sharonov was replaced by Kastorsky, the cast remained the same.

12 October

I would have liked to borrow the score of Servilia to look through when I went to Rimsky-Korsakov's tonight, but it was at Bleichmann's. I learned that Kashchei is going to be published soon, as well as an Eastern song from Aivazovsky's album[16] and the "Galkin" variations,[17] which were played at the Russian Concerts.

We discussed Stasov's opinion of Servilia. What he likes best is the appearance of the apparition. After that, Nikolai Andreyevich told me that Belsky has already completed two scenes of the new opera and has promised to finish the third of the seven scenes soon (it will have three acts and a prologue-introduction). I heard also that Nikolai Andreyevich has no intention of going to Moscow; he started this rumour only so that people would think he is not in Petersburg, and thus he could avoid the curtain calls at the subscription performance of Servilia.

We read a poem about Servilia, published in Peterburgskii listok (6 October), no. 274.[18] Nikolai Andreyevich himself considers all of Servilia's role completely successful, and he is very glad that I liked the opera.

20 October

Today Nikolai Andreyevich confessed that he is writing an opera about the period of Tatar rule over Rus, that is, on the subject of *The Invisible City of Kitezh*.

We talked about Ivanov's impertinent and nasty little article in *Novoe vremia*,[19] and his jeering at an unfortunate misprint in Mey's *Servilia* having to do with a description of the stage set of the first act. (This misprint was repeated in the piano score of the opera.) "Tselyskaya Mountain" was written "Pelyskaya Mountain," which was of no importance whatsoever either to the set designer or to the composer, but sent Mr. Ivanov into a rage.[20]

Rimsky-Korsakov is planning to go to Moscow to hear Grechaninov's *Dobrynya*[21] and his own *Snegurochka* (at the Private Opera) and *Kashchei the Immortal*.

Finally, we got into a discussion about the music of Berlioz.

"I don't know another composer who appeals to me less," declared Rimsky-Korsakov, "despite the fact that he just fell short of being a literary genius and was an extraordinary poet. Something within him seethes and yet, with very little exception, his music is uncommonly ugly."

As we said good-bye, Rimsky-Korsakov apologized once again for saddling me with the task of compiling his biography.

25 October

I received the following letter from Nikolai Andreyevich:

Dear Vasily Vasilyevich!

I have rewritten[22] your biographical essay, partly because I find it too verbose and also because of a certain lyricism (for example: "Eleven whole years") and certain inaccurate statements (such as: "His acquaintance with Balakirev determined all his later work.") (!! ?! ?!!). I have again reduced the list of compositions and this is the one I am using. I am sending you both of them and I ask you to make a fair copy at my expense.

Thank you a thousand times for everything.

Yours, N. R.-K

24 October.

26 October

Because of the forthcoming performance of Zolotarev's symphony and the arrival of Nikisch in Petersburg, Nikolai Andreyevich has decided to postpone his trip to Moscow for a while.

"But you'll see," he said, smiling, "on November 9, I'll put on my frock coat and take my place in the first row as an Honorary Member of the Philharmonic Society to listen to Beethoven's Mass."[23]

We chatted about Findeisen and his offhanded praise and faultfinding; also about how he had asked Nikolai Andreyevich recently to send an autograph excerpt from Kashcheyevna's song (the one she sings while whetting her sword) for his journal, but Nikolai Andreyevich had not done so.

"From this alone," said Nikolai Andreyevich, "that of all of *Kashchei*, what Findeisen liked most was this little song, I realized how little he understood the opera."

28 November

I dropped in on the Rimsky-Korsakovs to find out whether Nikolai Andreyevich had gone to Moscow, and if not, whether he will be at *Servilia* tomorrow. He was not at home, so, after finding out from Vladimir Nikolayevich what I was to do, I set out for the florist's to order a wreath, which we planned to present to him tomorrow as a "protest" at the seventh performance of *Servilia*. [24] Those joining in the protest, besides my wife and me, were Vladimir and Rafail Belsky, Timofeyev, Lapshin, the Fried family, and also Parmen Petrovich, Sasha, and Volodya Shenshin.

29 November

The seventh and final performance of *Servilia* took place tonight. The theater was half full (the Directorate and "critics" have achieved their aim!).

Included in the cast were Serebryakov as Soranus, Karelin—Montanus, Yershov—Valerius, Smirnov—Aegnatius, Papayan—Servilia, and Tugarinova—Locusta. Yershov was unsure, Smirnov rather inexpressive, but Papayan was somewhat better than usual—even the audience demanded that she repeat her aria ("Tsvety moi"), but for some reason she did not do so.

Despite the poor attendance, the artists were called out three or four times after each act (seventeen times in all) and the composer six times. Cui was in the parterre with his daughter. Nadezhda Nikolayevna, on the other hand, preferred to go to hear Hofmann and appeared in the theater only at the very end.

Thus, I have heard eight performances of *Servilia* (that is, including the dress rehearsal), and each time my enthusiasm for it has increased.

30 November

Upon returning from the Conservatory (due to the overwhelming success of the violinist Jan Kubelik, the concert did not end until midnight), I found the following sad letter from Nikolai Andreyevich:

Dear Vasily Vasilyevich!

Thank you for the wreath, which adorned yesterday's Torricellian vacuum at the Marinsky Theater. The composer is fully justified, I think, in placing in *Novoe vremia* the following black-bordered announcement:

"It is with deep sorrow that I notify the most highly esteemed public of the death of my dear opera *Servilia*. It would be the height of stupidity for the Directorate to give *Servilia* again. It will also be stupid if they should take it into their heads to present it in Moscow." [25]

Yours,   N. R.-Korsakov

30 November 1902

P.S. If others joined you in presenting the wreath, please convey to them my appreciation.

N. R.-K.

7 December

I went to the first Russian Symphony Concert, which was under the direction of Liadov. They performed Taneyev's Symphony in C minor, Cui's *Suite miniature,* Balakirev's *Tamara,* and two movements from Borodin's unfinished Symphony in A minor.

The last two numbers were played fairly well, but the orchestra seemed terribly tired and, besides, they never pay much attention to Liadov.

Before the concert and during the intermission, I ran into Rimsky-Korsakov. He told me that tomorrow he is going to Moscow to hear *Kashchei,* as it is supposed to be given there on the twelfth.

"How is it that the newspapers reported that you had already left?" I asked.

"Apparently for the same reason that Ivanov's *Potemkin Holiday*[26] has turned out to be the best Russian opera," he replied with a chuckle.

I then told him that my review of *Kashchei the Immortal* will appear soon in *Izvestiia*[27] over the signature "Credo," and consequently, this review will have a certain bias.

"You know," I continued, "Goffe called it a poem!"

"Poème d'amour, wasn't it?" asked Rimsky-Korsakov, jokingly.

"No, Nikolai Andreyevich," I replied, "only Cantique d'amour."

29 December

This morning at Rimsky-Korsakov's, we talked about the Moscow performance of *Kashchei* and the enthusiastic reviews it received from the critics (Kruglikov and Engel).[28]

"I must send these reviews to Petrovsky," remarked Nikolai Andreyevich. "Let him see how the critics and public in Moscow feel about me!"

I reported on the performance of *Tsar Saltan* at the Conservatory with its terribly fast tempi and total lack of poetry.

"Did you notice that I wasn't at the performance?" asked Rimsky-Korsakov. "This was my way of demonstrating against Baskin. I'm sure the Director understood this very well."[29]

Then Rimsky-Korsakov showed me a very amusing and senseless article about d'Alheim's singing, which appeared in *Mir iskusstva* (no. 11, 1902).[30] The gist of it was that Petersburg criticism has acquired a new, very unsympathetic spokesman in the person of the musical failure, Mr. Nurok, who from the outset declared war on the Conservatory, Rimsky-Korsakov, and Glazunov. As if Messrs. Bernhard and Johansen actually teach their students anything!

Nikolai Andreyevich has a dream that someday some new patron of

Russian Music (Belyaev would not do for this!) will establish an opera theater like the Stanislavsky Theater, in which although there might not be a single Chaliapin, the entire company would be homogeneous and thoroughly respectable and its orchestra and chorus—first-rate.

"Then it might be possible to begin to acquaint our public with Russian operas!" he exclaimed.

I forgot to mention that Nikolai Andreyevich and I had a rather long discussion about Vladimir Solovyov and his extremely witty and caustic articles countering the Russian decadents and also Mr. Rozanov and his "special tribute to Pushkin." In a letter to the editor of *Vestnik Evropy*,[31] Solovyov wrote in part:

Mr. Rozanov points to the pagan Pythia, seated over a Delphic crevice, whence stupefying sulphuric vapors poured forth. The inspiration here issues from somewhere below. That (in the opinion of Mr. Rozanov) is the reason Pushkin is "expendable"; his poetry (alas! only the poetry!) was inspired too much from above—not from a crevice exuding suffocating sulphuric vapors, but from a place where there is free and radiant, abiding and external beauty.

CHAPTER 13

1903

5 January

I went to the amateur dramatics at the Rimsky-Korsakovs', which did not begin at eight o'clock, as set, but later, and, therefore, dragged on until one in the morning.

Three plays were given: Hauptmann's *Lonely People* and Shcheglov's *Women's Nonsense* and *Guest Star.*

Among those participating were Sofia Nikolayevna, Nadyusha Nikolayevna, and Vladimir Nikolayevich Rimsky-Korsakov, N. I. Richter, N. A. Mitusova, and V. P. Troitsky. There were at least thirty-five guests. Shcheglov's little plays were the best performed. All the programs were handwritten by Nikolai Andreyevich. (I have kept one for my collection of Rimsky-Korsakov's manuscripts.)

Today was the thirtieth anniversary of the first performance of *The Maid of Pskov.*

19 January

Nikolai Andreyevich was having lunch when I arrived at the Rimsky-Korsakovs' this afternoon.

"Oh, there are so many anniversaries these days," he said as I entered the dining room. "Espiova's, Arkhangelsky's, Slavina's,[1] and I have to be everywhere. It's awfully boring."

I read him a letter of Ivan Alexandrovich Klimenko,[2] in which, among other things, this close friend of Tchaikovsky expressed the hope that Rimsky-Korsakov would reorchestrate Schumann's symphonies, something which Tchaikovsky had wanted to do but had never realized.

Speaking then of Cui's latest songs (to words by Nekrasov), I asked Nikolai Andreyevich what he thinks of them, whereupon he replied curtly: "Not much! I don't even care much for the fairly good one of this set, the one to the words 'U liudei-to v domu.' It automatically calls to mind Borodin's setting of the same words with its glorious, purely Russian harmonies. I don't even want to listen to Cui's songs any longer.

"However," he added, "both of these songs have certain shortcomings. In Borodin's, the accompaniment is poor; in Cui's, in terms of harmony, the melodic figurations at the end are somewhat muddy."

Rimsky-Korsakov told me that Safonov performed the "musical pictures" from *Tsar Saltan* in Vienna and Prague, but that in the latter city it was poorly received, because there was no explanatory text accompanying the program and therefore, no one understood anything. The critics, hearing the oft-repeated fanfare, decided that the first number of these "pictures" was some kind of Russian military march.

At the end, we discussed Grechaninov's *Dobrynya Nikitich*. When I remarked that the music of this opera left me quite indifferent because of its total lack of originality—one continually hears either Borodin, Rimsky-Korsakov, Cui, Tchaikovsky, or someone else—Nikolai Andreyevich replied, "I, on the other hand, was so glad that the subject of the opera is Russian and the music, too, is Russian in a way, even though, of course, it's not original enough.

"In our country," he continued, "Russian subjects have not fared well somehow. It may even be my fault for having written so much that is based on them. Unfortunately, the public neither senses nor understands the profound beauty of these subjects."

26 January

Rimsky-Korsakov visited us from two-thirty until quarter to five. After tea we talked about the new version of Balakirev's *King Lear* Overture, which in Nikolai Andreyevich's opinion, is much worse than the original one.

"However," he said, "it may be simply that time has left an imprint on my present tastes. After all, at one time I liked this overture tremendously, but now for some reason I don't care for it at all."

Nikolai Andreyevich believes that in his youth an artist can and even should listen to everything and everyone but, after that, he must, so far as he is able, remove himself from everyone and everything and compose completely independently, listening only to the inner voice of his own creative feelings, his own artistic instinct.

"Take, for example, my 'revision' of *The Maid of Pskov,*" he said. "Isn't this in a way yielding to the insistence and advice of Glazunov? After all, *May Night* also has flaws, but I'm not even thinking of reworking it again."

After this, we talked about Nikolai Andreyevich's Third Symphony. He feels that it is no worse than the symphonies of Brahms, and yet, for some reason, it is almost never played. Next we turned to *Sheherazade.* This work Nikolai Andreyevich regards as the culmination of his development in orchestration, although, of course, he admits that, artistically and musically, it is inferior to *Mlada.* We also discussed his new version of *Antar.* In reply to my arguments and praise, Nikolai Andreyevich said that he will listen to this score again, attentively; only then will he tell me what he thinks of it.

Besides this, I learned that Belsky has already prepared the following texts for Rimsky-Korsakov's new opera: the Prologue, the second scene of act 2, and both scenes of act 3. (Act 1 and the first scene of act 2 have not yet been written.)

These days, Nikolai Andreyevich said, it seems to take him longer to compose and orchestrate, and this is "a sure sign of old age."

1 March

This morning I went to the dress rehearsal of the fourth Russian Symphony Concert. I listened to Cherepnin's *Allegro dramatique*[3] to words by the poet F. Tyutchev, sitting beside Nikolai Andreyevich. Much of it is very good; the sound is magnificent but, it seemed to me, excessively loud and cumbersome. In this work the composer employs the Korsakov tone–half-tone scale. As for Scriabin's *Rêverie,* it called to mind Pushkin's words: "Mechty, mechty, gde vasha sladost'?" (Daydreams, where is your sweetness?) Indeed, this was not a "daydream" but a kind of black melancholy.

Regarding the variations, composed by Artsybushev, Wihtol, Liadov, Rimsky-Korsakov, Sokolov, and Glazunov on a Russian theme drawn from Balakirev's Collection[4] (no. 28, "Uzh ty, pole moe, pole chistoe"—chosen by Nadezhda Nikolayevna), I remarked to Rimsky-Korsakov that although his variation no. 4 with its *bylina*-like character is not bad, "it will not bring him new laurels," and that the best variation is Sokolov's. This is partly because Rimsky-Korsakov, Liadov, and Glazunov wrote theirs in jest, while Sokolov took his task seriously. The same may be said of Wihtol's fairly good variation.

Today Nikolai Andreyevich seemed particularly pleased with Tchaikovsky's *Capriccio italien*. He even asked me to bring him the score this afternoon on my way to the bank.

Not much can be said about *Night on Mount Triglav*. It is brilliant, but it was played very poorly. Liadov did not even notice that in the "Infernal Kolo" the trumpet was off-pitch continuously, playing E flat instead of E natural. That's Liadov for you! What a conductor! But how carping, how strict he is with others!

During the intermission, Rimsky-Korsakov boasted to me that he had recently attended an exhibition of decadent paintings.[5]

"You know," he said, "sometimes I like to irritate myself, so I take myself off to look at this rubbish."

The concert itself took place tonight. I am coming to like Cherepnin's *Allegro* more and more. Korsakov's variation sounded spirited. Glazunov's statement of the original folk song was good, but his variation (no. 6) was colorless, and besides it sounded excessively cumbersome.

Following *Mlada* Rimsky-Korsakov was called out three times.

6 March

This morning I sent Naikolai Andreyevich a basket of hyacinths and a bunch of roses with a congratulatory message on his fifty-ninth birthday.

In the evening I went to his house. Among the other guests were Stasov, Glazunov, Felix Blumenfeld, Belsky and his wife, the Ossovskys, and Igor Stravinsky, who, on behalf of his parents, brought Nikolai Andreyevich a large portrait of his late father in the role of Pan Golova (from *May Night*).

The evening was very lively. Felix Blumenfeld played many of his own pieces as well as works by Chopin, Liszt, and Schumann. Stravinsky entertained us with very charming and witty musical jokes of his own invention. In my opinion Igor Feodorovich is a man of undoubted talent.

Tea was served, fruit and grapes, then supper. Before the guests arrived Rimsky-Korsakov and I had talked about the performance, in Prague, of *The Tsar's Bride* (it has already been given there four times), which the critics of that city did not fully approve of, considering it, in a formal sense, a step backward from *May Night*.

"This is absolutely untrue," remarked Rimsky-Korsakov. "Formally these two operas are identical."

In this connection Nikolai Andreyevich expressed the view that, in most cases, criticism lags behind art, since usually it only echoes the fashionable tastes of society. As an example he pointed to Glinka's *Ruslan*, which was given fifty-two performances its first season and fell into disfavor only later on, when the Italian company arrived in Petersburg.

"As you can see," concluded Rimsky-Korsakov, "Stasov was not entirely correct when he wrote at one time that *Ruslan and Ludmila* was a failure from the moment it made its appearance."[6]

Rimsky-Korsakov imparted nothing more about his latest opera.

During supper, Stasov, being the eldest present, proposed a toast to the health of Nikolai Andreyevich, "the youngest," that is, "the newborn," to which the latter replied, laughingly, that although being an infant, he should only be able to say "ooh," he nevertheless will venture to drink to the health of the dear guests who have honored him with their kindness and consideration. Then, in honor of Nikolai Andreyevich, the young people sang the "Hymn of the Berendeys" (from *Snegurochka*), with Sofia Nikolayevna singing both Lel's part and the soprano in the chorus.

27 March

Today Nikolai Andreyevich recounted to me the plot of his new opera *The Invisible City of Kitezh*. This work will consist of a Prologue and three acts—six scenes in all. The libretto is by Vladimir Ivanovich Belsky. It was drawn in part from Melnikov-Pechersky's well-known novel *In the Forests* and *On the Hills* and in part from *The Legend of St. Fevronia.*

Rimsky-Korsakov means to write this opera in a very Russian style and to orchestrate it as interestingly as possible, *à la Tristan.* The score will call for one less instrument than *Mlada* (four French horns instead of six; two tubas instead of one). When I remarked that the opera's last two scenes recall, somewhat, the mood of Nesterov's paintings, Rimsky-Korsakov concurred.

Besides this I learned that Nikolai Andreyevich is thinking of writing still another opera on a Russian subject, this time in collaboration with I. F. Tyumenev.[7]

"My only fear is that I won't live long enough to finish it," he said.

Further, Rimsky-Korsakov told me that Mussorgsky had contributed to the libretto of *The Maid of Pskov* (texts of the choruses "Iz-pod kholmika, pod zelenogo" and "Akh, dubrava, dubravushka") as did one Vladimir Vasilyevich Nikolsky, a student of Olga Shestakova (texts of the final chorus "Sovershilas' volia Bozhiia" and the five-measure duet between Olga and Mikhail Tucha in scene 1, act 3). However, the librettos of *May Night* and *Snegurochka* are entirely his own.

Then turning to the subject of Tchaikovsky's opera *Mazeppa,* Nikolai Andreyevich noted that after listening to some of it recently, he was stunned by the unevenness of the orchestration—it is neither thoroughly bad nor thoroughly good.

"I sat alongside Napravnik," he said, "and followed the old vocal score, and again I was amazed at how easily Peter Ilyich yielded to the advice of friends and other musicians."

Mazeppa had been cut a great deal at the urging of Napravnik. It had also been lengthened. For example, at the insistence of Korsov, a new aria had been composed, and so on.

Regarding Eduard Franzevich, Nikolai Andreyevich added, "Of course, you know, no one can ruin any music so completely and irrevocably as Napravnik, if he wants to."

Then Nikolai Andreyevich said that he is beginning to feel more and more alienated and lonely in the musical world.

"Judge for yourself," he said, "my best music always strives to be pictorial, to deal with themes drawn from the life of the folk. Meanwhile, today one senses a sharp turn toward symphonic music. (I'm not speaking now only about Richard Strauss and others like him.)

"However," he continued, "I'll write only for myself and as I think best, even if nobody wants this music. After all, you can't please everybody."

I forgot to say that the other day Rimsky-Korsakov played through his *Sadko* two evenings in a row, and he is still very pleased with it.

9 May

I spent this evening, from eight-thirty until one in the morning, at the Rimsky-Korsakovs'. I brought Nikolai Andreyevich the piano reduction and full score of his prelude-cantata.

Nadezhda Nikolayevna and Andrei left for Krapachukha yesterday; Sofia Nikolayevna and her husband will go there tomorrow. Rimsky-Korsakov will not go until the twentieth of this month, because he has to be in Petersburg for the Conservatory examinations.

Belsky arrived shortly after I did and Glazunov just before tea. Our far-reaching discussion touched on Koptyaev's curious new book;[8] Mr. Ivanov's malicious feuilletons; I. A. Klimenko's impassioned letter in his own defense to the editor of *Russkaia muzykal'naia gazeta;*[9] and Apukhtin's witty parody.[10] Besides this I learned that Liadov has begun to work seriously on certain numbers of Mussorgsky's unfinished opera *The Fair at Sorochintsy* and has already completed the introduction.[11]

During tea and afterward, there was a great deal of talk about the Moscow Art Theater, the frequently excessive realism of its productions, and the new method employed by Stanislavsky and Nemirovich-Danchenko (the persistent swatting of gnats in the first act of Chekhov's *Uncle Vanya;* the unbearable and fortuitous scraping and squeaking of the swing; to say nothing of the unfailing rumble of carriage wheels and tinkle of bells in the last scene, as though all Russian country houses always have a planked bridge at the exit, and all Russian landowners always hang little bells on the carriage shafts).

Second Visit to Krapachukha (19, 20, and 21 July 1903)

Having left Petersburg at eleven-thirty on the night of July 18, I arrived at Okulovka at seven in the morning. By the time I reached Krapachukha, it was nine-thirty. It was raining. After a warm greeting and embrace from Nikolai Andreyevich, I was shown to the study, where I freshened up and made myself comfortable.

19 July

I learned that Rimsky-Korsakov has written a new opera, *Pan Voyevoda* on a text by Tyumenev, and the full score is almost finished.

We spent almost the entire day strolling about. Nikolai Andreyevich told me that he had looked through Arensky's opera *A Dream on the Volga* and was truly delighted with much of it (Nedviga's tale, for example).

"They don't write this way anymore," he remarked. "It has about it the sense of something irretrievable."

Arensky later grew enamored of the "Rubinstein musical style," and his writing became very colorless. *A Dream on the Volga* was composed while he was still in Rimsky-Korsakov's class.

We talked about the idealization of the muzhik, the Russian peasant, in Russian music. He is a kind of "supermuzhik." Something has been lost.

We also spoke about Grechaninov's second *Liturgy* and the new liturgical style. Rimsky-Korsakov does not like it particularly, but he praised the Credo highly.

20 July

During the course of the day, Nikolai Andreyevich played Arensky's opera again. After that we talked about the long-windedness of his *Christmas Eve* (it seems like two operas in one) and *May Night* (the "Proso" chorus, the first game of raven, etc.). It is this that accounts for the relatively limited success of these operas. Regarding the fact that *Snegurochka* has not held its ground on the private stages in the provinces,

Nikolai Andreyevich expressed the view that apparently his music has become old-fashioned or that it may be too cerebral.

"You won't believe it," he said jokingly, "but although in everyday life I'm not particularly intelligent—perhaps I'm even simply stupid—when I'm composing, I become incredibly wise, and this is my shortcoming. For from this wisdom comes my objectivity, my eclecticism, and my way of thinking (undiscriminating—in the opinion of M. A. Goldenblum). I'm a kind of Russian Cherubini, and that's why the general public is very cold and indifferent to my music."

Rimsky-Korsakov plans to write *Kitezh* without rushing, endeavouring to do the very best he can. (What if it does not succeed?)

21 July

Before and after dinner Nikolai Andreyevich played *Pan Voyevoda*.[12] A great deal of it is excellent (a good half of act 1; the scene beside the road in act 2; much of act 3, with the song about the dying swan; and most of act 4). In places the music is unusually lovely, fresh, touching, and very tuneful. The opera is dedicated to the memory of Chopin.

Rimsky-Korsakov informed me that he has two more librettos (by Tyumenev[13]) from the days of Yaroslav the Wise and King Harold and one on the subject of Ilya Muromets, but that most likely he will not use them. He is tired and his memory is failing (he has grown old).

We talked about Glazunov, his goodness and credulousness; also about his conducting at Pavlovsk,[14] which is really beneath him. This summer Nikolai Andreyevich is yearning for Petersburg, for a good orchestra; he is looking forward to the fall. He has been rereading Turgenev's *On the Eve* and *Fathers and Sons* and is very enthusiastic about them.

After supper, at about nine-twenty, I made ready for my departure. The train left at eleven, and we had to be in time for it. Despite the rain, I started out; had it not been for Nikolai Andreyevich's raincoat, I would have been soaked to the skin. All the Rimsky-Korsakovs were exceedingly warm and kind to me.

21 September

"Since it's raining today, I came to you," said Rimsky-Korsakov, upon entering my room. He was in an excellent mood. He looked at the photographs on the walls and the piano, praising those I had taken myself. We read some short articles from a new music journal (with a vile trend), which unashamedly denied that Rimsky-Korsakov has any melodic gift.[15]

"And that's not all," remarked Rimsky-Korsakov smiling. "In *Mir iskusstva* some Mr. Nurok, the new 'Baskin,' came out flatly against instrumentation, finding both it and me (at the same time) totally superfluous phenomena in music."

From further conversation, I learned that Nikolai Andreyevich feels that, judging from his latest opera *Les barbares,* Saint-Saëns has completely written himself out; that this season all of Wagner's *Parsifal* is going to be given at the home of Count Sheremetyev (without scenery, of course), and that Siloti is going to play Rimsky-Korsakov's prelude-cantata *From Homer* at one of his concerts.[16]

In conclusion, Nikolai Andreyevich told me that *Kitezh* is progressing; that he is thinking of introducing domras and balalaikas into the scene of the wedding procession, and, with this in mind, he wants to work a bit with Andreyev.

In October, Paleček is being sent to Moscow to stage *Servilia* and the Moscow producer Vasilevsky is coming to Petersburg to stage *The Maid of Pskov* with Chaliapin.[17]

24 September

This evening at the Rimsky-Korsakovs' the conversation turned to the programs to be given at the Russian Musical Society's symphonic evenings. The first of the six concerts, under Khessin, will be dedicated to the memory of Tchaikovsky; another (not yet known which one) will be devoted entirely to the music of Berlioz (*Te Deum,* etc.),[18] and, finally, at the second one, Khessin will conduct the third act of Rimsky-Korsakov's *Mlada.*[19]

Nikolai Andreyevich has made considerable progress with *Kitezh.* All of the most important music has been written; only the end of the first scene of act 2 (the disappearance of the city) remains to be done. A rough copy of all of act 4 (both scenes) and the second half of act 3 have been completed.

In this opera, Rimsky-Korsakov has introduced, as a curiosity, a scale of the type [example 62].

Example 62   (Or this)

18 October

I was at the first Siloti concert. During the intermission, at the end of Liszt's *Faust* Symphony, I ran into Nikolai Andreyevich. When I asked him how he liked this work today, he replied: "I've never cared for this symphony particularly; it's frightfully long and boring. Even from the standpoint of orchestration it's not faultless."

9 November

When I arrived at the Rimsky-Korsakovs', I found that Nikolai Andreyevich had gone to the Belgian Quartet [20] and to Glazunov's for dinner. Nadezhda Nikolayevna, Andrei, and Volodya were playing trios. Later Igor Stravinsky came (with a terrible headache) and Sofia Nikolayevna with N. A. Mitusova. Finally, at nine-fifty, Nikolai Andreyevich returned. Although he was rather tired, he was in excellent spirits.

The conversation touched on various subjects. We learned that *Kitezh* is progressing slowly; that Nikolai Andreyevich is somewhat offended by the title "professor," since that is not what is most important about him; that he is hurt by the ceaseless jabs at his latest works (for example, *The Maid of Pskov* is considered "new" even today, but not *Servilia* or *The Tsar's Bride*).

"Meanwhile, I'm convinced that there's a great deal that's not only good but also new in these operas," said Nikolai Andreyevich.

"In general," he continued, "I've observed that my old friends like my *Snegurochka* and *Maid of Pskov* the best, while the younger people prefer *Sadko*. And that's understandable. A large factor in all this is the age at which someone first finds something to his liking. I'm certain that if these younger admirers of mine had lived earlier, they, too, would have preferred *Snegurochka,* because at the time they first heard it, they would have been more impressionable. The same works strike people differently at different ages."

We discussed the fact that although his operas are given, Nikisch conducts *Capriccio espagnol,* and Chaliapin sings *Prorok, Na kholmakh Gruzii,* and other songs, Rimsky-Korsakov enjoys only relatively limited popularity.

Speaking of the performances of *The Tsar's Bride,* he was very pleased with the one at the People's House, especially with the orchestra; he did not attend the performance at the Marinsky Theater. In his opinion *Vera Sheloga* should be given with *The Maid of Pskov.*

Rimsky-Korsakov is glad that Grigory Timofeyev is going to work on the new newspaper *Rus',* which is owned by Suvorin's son.[21] Apropos of music critics, he related the following incident which took place between M. M. Ivanov and the Technological Institute in connection with the Institute's seventy-fifth anniversary. As a former student, Ivanov proposed that he compose a cantata (or festive march) for the occasion. In fact, he had even invited some artist to sing. The technologists very adroitly extricated themselves from this situation, however, by replying that, since he was a former student, they had nothing against his participating in their jubilee, but they hesitated to accept his proposal since he is a "novovremenets"[22] and at the request of the students, this newspaper had been removed from their reading room and was no longer sent to them.

We spoke of the fact that Nikolai Andreyevich is really an opera composer, pointing out how relatively insignificant his writings for the piano are (except for the concerto) and how brilliant and rich in content his operas. We chatted about *Pan Voyevoda,* this sort of old-Polish *Tsar's Bride,* with its strongly "Chopinesque" music (stylistically, that is)—tender, gentle, and elegant.

16 December

Rimsky-Korsakov's *Snegurochka* was given tonight for the first time at the People's House. The sets were by A. Ya. Alexeyev, the conductor— I. P. Arkadyev. The opera began promptly at seven-thirty and, owing to the lengthy intermissions, did not end until eleven fifty-five. All of the "critical world" were there, as well as we, the regular attendants of the Belyaev Concerts, the entire Rimsky-Korsakov family, etc. The opera was given almost without cuts; even the scene with the trio between Kupava, Lel, and Snegurochka was performed.

On the whole, the performance went fairly well. The sets were good, especially that of the palace of the King of the Berendeys, which was done in the style of Vasnetsov. It enjoyed considerable success. In the course of the evening, the composer was called out fourteen times. I ran into him only in passing; he seemed very preoccupied.

CHAPTER 14

1904

3 January

I attended the sixth Symphonic Evening of the Russian Musical Society, under the direction of A. K. Khessin. The program consisted of *Night on Mount Triglav* (act 3 from the opera-ballet *Mlada* in a concert arrangement by Rimsky-Korsakov—first time), *Intermezzo* by Liadov, and Glazunov's suite *From the Middle Ages*[1] (first time),[2] Tchaikovsky's Violin Concerto (with Fidelman as soloist), and Napravnik's Funeral March (op. 42) and the Serenade from his String Quartet (op. 16).

After *Mlada,* the audience, with one voice, called for Nikolai Andreyevich. It is only a pity that this marvelous music was not given in full.

18 January

Nikolai Andreyevich visited me this afternoon. We discussed Mitrofan Petrovich Belyaev's sudden death;[3] his "Fridays," which, in keeping with his wishes, were continued even during his illness; his carefully thought-out and detailed will—so admirable for its meaning to Russian music; his designation of Rimsky-Korsakov, Liadov, and Glazunov as the first executors of his will.[4]

We also chatted about Stasov and his increasing senility.

"I'm of the opinion," observed Rimsky-Korsakov, "that everyone, especially an artist or public figure, ought to leave the scene when his time has come. Otherwise, there can be very undesirable results. Furthermore, I've recently come to believe that the most important quality a person possesses is his memory. Without it, he can be neither a scholar, composer, nor even a critic."

We got onto the subject of Alexei Alexeyevich Suvorin and his strange behavior with his *Rus'*, which, unwittingly perhaps, is playing into Ivanov's hands.

"Oh, beware," said Nikolai Andreyevich, "when these literary gentlemen who don't know anything and don't listen to anyone, take it upon themselves to run a music section.

"By the way," he continued, "have you read Ivanov's latest feuilleton?[5] No? What a curious thing! Ivanov has reached the point where he flatly denies that there's a single real Russian opera in Russia. Now, that's what is called going too far!"

Besides this, Rimsky-Korsakov told me that when Arensky's opera *Nal and Damayanti* was given in Moscow,[6] the composer declared categorically that neither Sobinov nor Chaliapin was to sing in it, since only when the audience's attention is not diverted by its idols can it listen attentively to the music.

"You know," added Rimsky-Korsakov, "I agree with him completely. Judge for yourself. Famous gentlemen usually sing only one or two performances of an opera. Then, under some pretext or other, they refuse to appear in it again. Meanwhile, the opera is given more than twice, and when the public learns that their favorites are not singing, they lose interest in it entirely."

On leaving, Nikolai Andreyevich asked me not to forget him, but he added that he is not usually at home on Mondays as that day is set aside for meetings on Belyaev matters. Also, he will not be at home on the days when Wagner's operas are given at the Marinsky Theater.

"You won't believe this," he said, "but I've become so forgetful that every year I listen to Wagner's last operas as if I were hearing them for the first time. In the beginning I found this music rather repellent, but then I got used to it, and now I'm beginning to like it immensely."

17 February

I spent this evening from eight-thirty until two in the morning at the Rimsky-Korsakovs'. At about ten-thirty N. I. Zabela appeared. The other guests were Stasov, Richter, Mitusov, Lapshin, Liadov, Glazunov, Troitsky, and Stravinsky.

First Richter played two of Liadov's *Variations on a Polish Song.* Then, with Glazunov as accompanist, Zabela sang arias and songs by Rimsky-Korsakov and songs by Rachmaninov, Strauss, and Grieg. Unfortunately, she was not in good voice tonight. This became apparent particularly in the lullaby from *Kashchei* and the aria from *Servilia.*

During tea I had a talk with Nikolai Andreyevich about the fact that undoubtedly the general public finds something artificial about even the most realistic type of opera, and thus, the loftier the work (musically), the more the average, unprepared listener dislikes it.

"The fact is that *The Maid of Pskov* wasn't any more successful than *Servilia,*" commented Rimsky-Korsakov. "Nevertheless, I know quite well that it's far from a poor opera."

At yesterday's concert of the Music Society, Nikolai Andreyevich conducted his march from *Tsar Saltan,* and the day after tomorrow, he is going to direct his short new piece, *At the Grave,* written in memory of Belyaev.[7]

After supper, young Stravinsky played his *Comic Little Songs* and Richter sang the famous (and senseless) gypsy song *Raspasha* and (to the horror of Nadezhda Nikolayevna) even played a "cakewalk," whereupon Mitusov and Stravinsky gave a very amusing demonstration of how it is supposed to be danced.

On the whole, the evening was very gay, interesting, and lively.

I forgot to mention that I learned from conversation with Nikolai Andreyevich that next year they are not going to give *Servilia* in Moscow but *Pan Voyevoda.* Thus, the question of presenting *Servilia* on the Moscow public stage still remains open.

6 March

Today was Nikolai Andreyevich's sixtieth birthday. His writing table was literally "loaded" with flowers. Besides me, the guests included Stasov, Artsybushev, Liadov, Glazunov, Cherepnin and his beautiful wife (née

Benois), the Blumenfeld brothers, Ossovsky and his wife, Lapshin, Belsky, Richter, the young Stravinsky, and members of the Rimsky-Korsakov family.

As always in such cases, the conversation was of a general nature and consequently not very interesting. On the other hand, there was a great deal of music. It began with Felix Blumenfeld and Glazunov playing a four-hand arrangement of Zolotarev's overture *Fête villageoise,* after which Felix Mikhailovich played Debussy's *Estampes* and a number of his own pieces.

At the request of the guests, Glazunov then played his Second Sonata. Sigismund Blumenfeld sang Rimsky-Korsakov's *Anchar,* accompanied by Glazunov, and, finally, Ossovsky, Lapshin, Mitusov, and Nikolai Andreyevich sang Borodin's comic *Serenade in Honor of a Lady by Four Cavaliers,*[8] which sent Stasov into raptures.

During supper the "young Korsakovs," led by Stravinsky, performed a very charming "cantata," composed by Igor Feodorovich especially for this day and dedicated to Nikolai Andreyevich.[9] (At the wishes of the audience, the "cantata" was repeated.) In addition, the "young amateur chorus" sang a quartet by Borodin.

31 March

I was at the Rimsky-Korsakovs', but I saw Nikolai Andreyevich no more than thirty minutes, because he did not return from Belskys' until eleven-thirty.

Our conversation was limited almost entirely to the terrible destruction of the battleship Petropavlovsk, the deaths of Admiral Makarov, the artist Vereshchagin,[10] and the Rimsky-Korsakovs' relative Mikhail Pavlovich Molas, Chief of Staff of the Pacific Squadron. We speculated on who would be named to replace Makarov—Rozhdestvensky or Skrydlov.

Finally, we turned to Stasov's enthusiastic review in *Novosti*[11] of the performance of the suite from *Christmas Eve* at the Belyaev concert.

Thus, it was many long years before Stasov understood how mistaken he was in regarding this opera a total failure, unworthy of his attention.[12]

6 April

I was at the Rimsky-Korsakovs' tonight from nine o'clock until two-thirty. Others there besides me were Stasov, Glazunov, Liadov, Felix Blumenfeld, N. I. Zabela, Mitusov, Richter, Stravinsky, and Belsky.

Before the music, Rimsky-Korsakov told me that he really has a strong dislike for the latest lyricists (Scriabin, etc.)

"They all turn themselves inside out," he said, "and inside there's nothing but muck, a kind of Limburger cheese—that's all."

Finally, the music began. First to be played were Scriabin's two poems (op. 12) and four preludes (op. 33). Following this, Zabela sang several songs by B. K. Yanovsky and arias and songs by Rimsky-Korsakov. She was in good voice.

During supper Nikolai Andreyevich talked at length with her about *The Tsar's Bride.* Among other things, he noted that Fried sings the role of Lyubasha too delicately, "in a somewhat foreign manner." We also chatted about Yermolenko—her superb voice (the best on the Imperial Stage, according to Felix Blumenfeld) but inadequate artistic development.

Speaking with Felix Mikhailovich, I learned that he does not like (or rather he does not know) Rimsky-Korsakov's latest songs—he finds nothing "of Korsakov" in them; also he considers abstract music (nonprogrammatic and nonvocal) superior to all other kinds of music.

23 April

Ossovsky and I arrived at the Rimsky-Korsakovs' together tonight. At first our conversation dealt mostly with the new Western composers, the music of retrogression, so to speak, and not of progress (Debussy's *Pelleas and Mélisande,* for example).

Before and after tea, Nikolai Andreyevich played through the first act of his *Kitezh.* This time he was relatively calm, and therefore he played fairly well. (Ossovsky helped out, at sight.) This work is first-class, deeply moving (I wept), with much that is new, especially in feeling. There's Korsinka for you!

During tea, there was talk about the new commission, which is engaged in reexamining and revaluating the Russian alphabet. One scholar (a foreigner) had even drawn up a plan for replacing the Cyrillic alphabet by the Latin but, fortunately, he was prevented in time from putting this stupid proposal into effect.

"This strikes me as a symptom of the beginning of the disintegration not only of an alphabet but of an entire people," remarked Rimsky-Korsakov.

Again I spent the evening at Zagorodny. Mikhail Nikolayevich Rimsky-Korsakov was also there. We got into a discussion about today's untalented geniuses of the West, citing as an example, the bad music of Wolf-Ferrari's *La vita nuova,* in which everything simple is very mediocre and everything complicated—"rubbish." For some reason, Ossovsky is mad about it.

"This is the state of musical creativity in the West nowadays," remarked Rimsky-Korsakov. "The music of these so-called geniuses is almost always, like Mussorgsky's *Marriage,* in a world of vague, morbid idealism. And this convinces me once more that we're living at the 'beginning' of the end."

This brought us to the subject of Scriabin, whose music, for all his enormous gifts, is always pervaded by a kind of a "one-and-a-half mood," (Rimsky-Korsakov's expression), a mood that is sick, disturbed.

"There's no happiness, no joy, no tranquility, no gaiety in it," observed Nikolai Andreyevich. "An exception, perhaps, is the first movement of the First Symphony, the music of which is really good."

Chatting thus, about this and that, we noted that the Tatars in *Kitezh* are "Slavonicized," that is, they are not as they actually might have been, but as they were perceived by the Russians and were pictured in folk songs about the "Tatar yoke."

Then we talked about the music evening which is to take place on May 8 at Pavlovsk under the direction of Edouard Colonne and Wilhelm Zemanek. Participating in the program of orchestral works, songs and arias by Rimsky-Korsakov will be the artists of the Imperial Theaters— E. V. Slatina, M. M. Chuprynnikov, and V. S. Sharonov. Mention of this called to mind Zabela, her dislike of all sopranos—Insarova, in particular—and also her overweening egotism.

After tea, when we returned to the study, Nikolai Andreyevich expressed his joy at the prospect that he is going to the country early this year.

"Otherwise, heaven only knows when I should see the blossoming foliage," he said. "Very likely the lindens are just beginning to bud. The lilies of the valley are already in full bloom, I'm sure. This summer I ought to be able to finish and orchestrate *Kitezh.* It's an enormous task."

Fourth Visit to Vechasha (August 21, 22, and 23, 1904)

21 August

Having left Petersburg on the one o'clock train, I arrived at Plyuss at six and at Vechasha at eight-thirty, in time for tea. When I entered, Rimsky-Korsakov was engaged in lively conversation with Semyon Kruglikov, who was standing beside the piano.

I learned that Stravinsky has been staying with them since August 11.

I shared a room with S. N. Kruglikov. We talked about Rimsky-Korsakov, his *Kitezh,* and its new style, which, according to Semyon Nikolayevich, Nadezhda Nikolayevna will never understand. We also discussed Klimenko (Tchaikovsky's friend), the Moscow critic Engel, and the Moscow Opera Company. On Kruglikov's advice, they are going to give *Servilia.*

I confided to Semyon Nikolayevich that I am writing reminiscences of Nikolai Andreyevich.

22 August

Kruglikov left for Moscow this morning. In the afternoon, Nikolai Andreyevich and Igor Fedorovich were occupied with the orchestration of *Kitezh* and also with writing the scenario in the orchestration of scene 1, act 3, which was completed only yesterday.

I took pictures of Vechasha, while everybody went for a walk in search of mushrooms. Nikolai Andreyevich played the second act of *Kitezh.* Wonder of wonders! I wept.

Rimsky-Korsakov believes he has repeated himself somewhat in the scene of the marketplace, but I was completely enraptured. For example, the modulations from A, B-flat, B, and C-sharp minor into C minor in the scene with the bear (how daring it is!); the rhythm of the *gusli* player's song (continuous alternation of 6/4 and 3/2); the moving scene of Fevronia's entrance, to say nothing of the scene of the "people's commotion" (chorus in 9/8 time, in groups of three) [example 63]. How fresh and new all this is!

Example 63

The manuscript of the opera is dated 1–21 August 1904.

After tea, Nadezhda Nikolayevna and Igor Stravinsky played Glazunov's Fifth Symphony (rather poorly). We argued with her about it (she does not like it).

23 August

This morning after tea, Nikolai Andreyevich and I walked on the upper path of the garden. Igor Feodorovich joined us, and we talked about Rimsky-Korsakov's extraordinary good fortune. Thanks to Azanchevsky's willingness to take a chance, though completely unprepared for the post, he was appointed professor of composition at the Conservatory and later, Inspector of Bands of the Navy Department.

"They literally pushed me into music!" said Nikolai Andreyevich.

In the afternoon, while Stravinsky was occupied with the instrumentation of the winds at the beginning of the polonaise from *Pan Voyevoda*, Nikolai Andreyevich and I strolled in the garden. On returning home, he decided to spend an hour looking through some of *Kitezh*, while I, after taking a photograph of him in his study, glanced through the piano reduction of *Voyevoda* and the manuscript of act 2 of *Kitezh*. At my request, Nikolai Andreyevich gave me his autograph from act 1, that is, four measures from Fevronia's "confession" [example 64]. He inscribed it: *"Legend of the Invisible City of Kitezh.* 23 August 1904. Vechasha. N. R.-Korsakov. (Must be performed tenderly, with feeling.)"

Example 64

Nikolai Andreyevich expressed the view that the Russian style (in music) will come to an end, for even it has its limits. Turning to his own operas, he observed that in them the music always embodies the text exactly and therefore, if the text happens to be weak, this is reflected in the quality of the music. He gave as an example the part of Lykov in *The Tsar's Bride*.

"I'm terribly amused," he said, "when they claim that I made a study of folk songs. Believe me, dear friend, this alleged 'study' consisted only in the fact that, thanks to a certain gift, it was easy for me to remember and assimilate what was most typical in the tunes—that's all."

The weather was wonderful. The young people were playing croquet in front of the house when the horses were brought. At four-fifteen I started for the station. They all gathered to see me off. The final farewell came from Rimsky-Korsakov. How kind and warmhearted he is!

I reached Petersburg just after midnight. On the whole, I was pleased with my visit.

17 September

No one was at home when I arrived at Zagorodny. However, shortly afterward Nikolai Andreyevich appeared with Igor Stravinsky.

Nikolai Andreyevich told me that he has already orchestrated the Intermezzo[13] and transcribed all three acts of *Kitezh;* also that he has made considerable progress with the scoring of the last scene. He told me, too, that he had first learned from the newspapers that he had been named "Honored Professor," since he did not receive official notification of it until today.

"They had to make the harpist Tsabel an 'Honored Professor,' " he said, "so they gave me the title at the same time. A high-sounding title, but what does it mean? Absolutely nothing! Today—Honored Professor; tomorrow—somebody doesn't like you—they hire and fire. In the end we're nothing but hirelings!"

When I asked him to show me the official document, he said, "Really, it's not worth it. Someday, after my death, you'll see it; I don't even remember where I put it." He never showed it to me.

To my remark that I will not rest until he is made a "Doctor of

Music,"[14] Nikolai Andreyevich replied facetiously that, even without this, he has been a "healer of musical ailments" all his life.

"That may be so," I replied, "but in that case the word 'healer' must be given its loftiest meaning, since you, Nikolai Andreyevich, have not only treated people, but at times have even resurrected 'the dead' (Mussorgsky, Borodin, Dargomyzhsky) and this, I dare say, can be done only by a 'healer' of a special order." We laughed.

2 October

I went to the dress rehearsal of *Pan Voyevoda*.[15] It began at eight-forty in the evening and lasted until one-twenty-five. On the whole, the opera had been reasonably well prepared, and, despite the fact that all last week they had two rehearsals a day, the artists sang well, without apparent fatigue.

The cast included, among others, Insarova, Aslanova, Bolshakov, Medvedev, and Antonovsky. V. I. Suk conducted. Quite a few people attended the rehearsal.

Rimsky-Korsakov was called out after act 3, and at the end of the opera, they played a fanfare for him. During the intermission, I saw him, Insarova, and Suk briefly. Nikolai Andreyevich expressed amazement at how quickly the company had learned their parts. He attributed this entirely to Suk's conducting experience. Yes, I thought, Felix Blumenfeld is surely no Suk.

Outstanding among the cast were Antonovsky as the Voyevoda, Insarova—Maria, and Aslanova—Yadviga. I will never forget Insarova's acting in the scene in which she sings the infinitely sad and poetic *Song of the Dying Swan*. It was very beautiful.

21 October

This afternoon Rimsky-Korsakov visited me from two o'clock until three-fifteen. Our conversation touched on various subjects—the music of Dukas (whose orchestration is wonderful but programmatic content stupid); the death of Laroche (who left nothing of value to the history of criticism except an article on Glinka); *Boris Godunov* and *Pan Voyevoda*; Timofeyev's departure from the newspaper *Rus'*; and Shestakova's opinion (or rather, Balakirev's) that Cui's *Ratcliff* is the best opera after *Ruslan.*

"There was a time when these words had meaning, but now they've lost it," said Nikolai Andreyevich. "Actually, not everything in *Ruslan* is first-rate (Farlaf's rondo, the duet between Finn and Ratmir, etc.). The same may be said about *A Life for the Tsar* (this perpetual mazurka, even in the forest). It is also not true that *The Paladin* is Dargomyzhsky's best song. In its day—yes, but now—no. Both Cui's *Smerkalos'* and Balakirev's *Song of the Golden Fish* are incomparably better."

We agreed that *Ruslan* was not the last word, for there are many things in *Snegurochka, Boris, Maid of Pskov,* and *Sadko* that Glinka never dreamed of. And this newness endows these operas with importance (even if they were not superior to *Ruslan*). Of course, this is something which neither Ludmila Ivanovna, Balakirev, nor Stasov will ever understand.

3 November

I went to the Conservatory for the fourth performance of *Pan Voyevoda.* It was under the direction of Suk and met with considerable success, even though Antonovsky (Pan Voyevoda) did not keep to the rhythm; Bolshakov (Chaplinsky) was rather coarse; Insarova (Maria) was not in "good form," as they say; and in the scene where Yadviga throws herself on the dead body of the Voyevoda, Aslanova cried out not on high C but on B, which completely ruined the effect.

All this notwithstanding, the audience applauded the artists enthusiastically.

20 November

After dinner at Princess O. A. Melikova's, I went to Zagorodny. Act 2 of *Kitezh* was played before tea; both scenes of act 3—after tea. In addition to me, Liadov, Ossovsky, Vladimir and Rafail Belsky, and the Troitskys were also there.

There is much in this opera that is superb, although, of course, from a first hearing, it was difficult to make out the third act. All three songs about the Tatar yoke were employed brilliantly, especially the first one.

The opera contains a great deal that is new harmonically. The wedding procession is magnificent as is also the young girls' glorification song. The final chorus at the end of scene 1, act 3, and the orchestral sound of the bells in scene 2 of this act are excellent.

Nikolai Andreyevich promised to play act 4 soon and, at that time, to repeat acts 2 and 3.

From glancing through the manuscript, I found that act 2 was begun on May 17, 1904, and completed on July 24; the wedding procession, ending with the bells, was dated June 13; the entire act was transcribed on July 29. Act 3 was begun August 1 and finished September 27, 1904.

Nikolai Andreyevich told me that he had been in Moscow from October 29 to November 2.[16] He showed me Sakhnovsky's review of *Servilia*.

On November 27, 1904, issue no. 347 of the newspaper *Rus'* carried the following notice:

The M. P. Belyaev Prizes

We, the Executors of M. P. Belyaev's estate—N. A. Rimsky-Korsakov, A. K. Liadov, and A. K. Glazunov—hereby give public notice that the late M. P. Belyaev bequeathed a sum of 75,000 rubles, the interest of which is to be awarded in the form of annual prizes to Russian composers for the published compositions which indicate the most talent. These prizes have been named by the benefactor the "Glinka Prizes," and they are to be awarded on November 27, the day of the first performance of both of Glinka's operas. The awarding of the prizes has been entrusted by the benefactor to us, as the Executors of the estate of the deceased and, subsequently, as the first members of the Trustees' Council for the Encouragement of Russian Composers and Musicians, upon confirmation of its charter.

The prizes are divided into five categories according to the type of musical composition, and the amounts to be awarded were fixed exactly by the benefactor in the draft charter of the Trustees' Council, the total amount of all the prizes not to exceed, annually, the sum of 3,000 rubles.

The first Glinka Prizes are to be awarded on November 27, 1904 to:

A. S. Arensky for his Piano Trio in D minor (op. 32)—500 rubles

S. M. Liapunov for his Piano Concerto in E-flat minor—500 rubles

S. V. Rachmaninov for his Second Piano Concerto in C minor—500 rubles

A. N. Scriabin for his Piano Sonata no. 3 (op. 23)—300 rubles

Also to A. N. Scriabin for his Piano Sonata no. 4 (op. 30)—200 rubles

S. I. Taneyev for his Symphony in C minor (op. 12)—1,000 rubles.

At this time we, the Executors of the M. P. Belyaev Estate, consider it our duty to state that during the period of our membership in the Trustees' Council, we will not present our own compositions for consideration for Glinka Prizes, renouncing the right to do so granted us by Paragraph 14 of the Charter.

N. RIMSKY-KORSAKOV, AN. LIADOV, A. GLAZUNOV.

19 December

In the afternoon I went to *Boris Godunov* (not with Chaliapin, with Sharonov). At the end of the Polish Act, I ran into Nikolai Andreyevich. He was very happy to see me, but he scolded me, very gently, for not having been to see him. I promised to visit him during the holidays.

CHAPTER 15

1905

1 January

I spent the evening from eight until one in the morning at the Rimsky-Korsakovs'. Belsky and Troitsky were also there. Nikolai Andreyevich seemed very pleased with our visit.

We got into a discussion about Ossovsky and his excessively harsh article about Cui and Liadov.[1] Then we talked about the works of Richard Strauss and Max Reger. According to Nikolai Andreyevich, Strauss' *Symphonia domestica* is "vertical nonsense," while Reger's Sonata is "horizontal nonsense."[2] We also talked about the extremely poor and colorless harmonization of some of Hugo Wolf's songs.

Before tea, Rimsky-Korsakov played the first scene of act 4 of *Kitezh* for us. What marvelous poetry, how inspired! However, he is not going to offer it for performance.

"It doesn't matter. They'll only do it badly," he said.

I borrowed the Moscow reviews of *Servilia*—two by Kashkin and one each by Kruglikov, Engel, and Sakhnovsky.[3]

Nikolai Andreyevich thanked us several times for visiting him.

"All my closest friends think I'm terribly busy," he remarked, "and as a result, no one ever comes to see me."

Following a suggestion by Belsky, the Rimsky-Korsakovs have decided to have "musical evenings" at their house on alternate Wednesdays.

Besides me, Troitsky, the Belsky brothers, Lapshin and several others attended the first of the Rimsky-Korsakovs' "Wednesdays."

During tea, there was a long discussion about Isadora Duncan,[4] and after that, about chords of "taste," chords of "color," and a scale of "moods," which led Nikolai Andreyevich to quip: "The next thing you know, to suit these theories, we'll have to consider a crawfish an octave derived from a lobster." Everyone laughed.

At our request, after tea, Rimsky-Korsakov played all of act 4 of *Kitezh*. What matchless poetry, what purity, what ineffable color! I wept. How far *Kitezh* is from the *Easter Overture!* As Lapshin put it, in this great work Nikolai Andreyevich "did not mean to raise the earth to the heavens, but to bring heaven itself down to earth and he succeeded superbly!" Indeed, we are all ecstatic over this opera.

Rimsky-Korsakov then played the first scene of act 3. Thus, our first "Wednesday" was a great success.

On my way home, I noticed that all the trees were covered with hoarfrost and they glistened like white coral.

19 January

The second "Wednesday" was also very interesting. The subject of Isadora Duncan came up again, and we laughed heartily at the theory of "the dance of the future," being propagated by her, and the curious trip which Mitusov made to Berlin for the sole purpose of making her acquaintance and once more attending her dance seances.

I told them about the workers' barricades, which have been erected on Line 5 of Vasilevsky Island, not far from our house. Rimsky-Korsakov confessed that of late he had become a "vivid red," but he asked me to stop talking about the shocking things that went on from January 9 to the 13, as all this upsets him terribly.[5]

After tea, at the request of Lapshin and myself, Nikolai Andreyevich played the second act of *Kitezh*. He also showed us the newly published score of the suite from *Pan Voyevoda* (op. 59).

Besides this, he told us that these days he seems to have completely forgotten how to express his thoughts. It is the same with letters; he would like to write one thing but ends up writing something else. He has become absentminded; at times he simply cannot concentrate. He begins to think of one thing and suddenly notices that he is thinking about something completely different. . . .

6 February

This afteroon Rimsky-Korsakov visited me from two to three, and despite the brevity of his visit, it was very lively and interesting.

First we discussed the performance of his *Snegurochka,* which was given for the first time in revival on January 29 at the People's House by the Association of Operatic Artists. The theater was filled; the artists were called out warmly several times after each act.

Because of the long intermissions, the performance dragged on until twelve-twenty-five. The sets and costumes, though not new, were good. The orchestra was far from impeccable either rhythmically or as regards sonority, despite all the efforts of the conductor, A. N. Sheffer. The same may be said also about the chorus. On the whole, the opera had not been prepared sufficiently. There were the usual cuts. Unfortunately, my review, which was supposed to have been published in *Nasha zhizn',* was not, because at the present moment, due to the political situation, the paper could not spare even the small space which would have been required.

Among various other things, Nikolai Andreyevich told me that *Kitezh* was finished on January 31, but if there are many people at his house next Wednesday, he is not going to play it.

"Incidentally," he added, "so far, the only thing Glazunov has praised in all of *Kitezh* is the Tatar."

"Oh well," I responded, "tastes vary. Take Mme Larina, your great admirer—she hates *Snegurochka.*"

Finally we talked about Nikolai Andreyevich's letter to the newspaper *Nashi dni* (published in no. 39), endorsing the resolution signed by twenty-nine Moscow composers and musicians, which had appeared in issue no. 37 of the same newspaper and which stated:

"Only art that is free is vital; only creativity that is free is joyful." To these wonderful words of our fellow artists we, musicians, wholeheartedly subscribe. The freedom of art cannot be limited by anything in the world except the inner wishes of the artist and the basic demands of society, if it wants to be truly powerful, truly holy, and able to respond to the deepest needs of the human soul. When life is bound hand and foot, art cannot be free, for feeling is only a part of life. When there is neither freedom of thought and conscience, nor freedom of speech and press in the land, when obstacles are erected to all the creative undertakings of the people, artistic creativity withers. Then the title "free artist" sounds like a bitter joke. We are not free artists, but, like all other Russian citizens, the disenfranchised victims of today's abnormal social conditions. It is our conviction that there is only one solution: Russia must at last embark on a road to radical reforms, the reforms set forth in the well-known eleven points of the resolution of the District Council, to which we, too, subscribe.

Signed, 2 February. A. T. Grechaninov, S. I. Taneyev, Yu. Engel, S. Rachmaninov, F. Chaliapin, S. Kruglikov, et al.

Rimsky-Korsakov responded to this appeal with the following open letter:

Being wholeheartedly in sympathy with the resolution of the Moscow composers and musicians, which appeared in no. 37 of Nashi dni, I ask you through your esteemed newspaper to add to it the signature of a Petersburg musician.

N. Rimsky-Korsakov

(Saturday, 5 February 1905).[6]

As he was leaving, Nikolai Andreyevich reminded me once more that he expects me without fail on Wednesday the ninth.

9 February

Before tea at the Rimsky-Korsakovs', Richter played Igor Stravinsky's F-sharp minor Sonata, which was dedicated to him. What talent this piece shows! Then Zabela sang Glazunov's Nereida, songs by Rimsky-Korsakov, and two excerpts from Tsar Saltan. She was accompanied by Glazunov. After tea Richter played Glazunov's Nocturne (D flat).

Nikolai Andreyevich reported to us on the second performance of M. M. Ivanov's opera Kashirskaia starina.[7] The opera had been well prepared, and, on the whole, it is better orchestrated than Solovyov's Ei, ukhnem.[8]

"I'm beginning to envy Ivanov's success," he remarked. "See what happens: the man writes a poor opera, but nevertheless, they produce it, and what's more, the theater is filled to overflowing."

Speaking of Scriabin, Rimsky-Korsakov praised my favorite first movement of his First Symphony highly. He finds Scriabin an impressive talent, but one capable of expressing only a very limited number of moods. And this is his shortcoming.

23 February

The third "Wednesday" at the Rimsky-Korsakovs' again was very successful. Troitsky, Mikhail Nikolayevich Rimsky-Korsakov and his wife, the Belsky brothers, Lapshin, N. Richter, and Felix Blumenfeld came, and, at about ten-thirty, in walked Glazunov and Ossovsky.

At first the conversation concerned politics and the bombing of Mukden. But soon, it turned to music and, before tea, Richter played the first act of *Kitezh* (with some help from Felix Mikhailovich and Nikolai Andreyevich). Then Blumenfeld played the second act with help from Richter and Glazunov. If we are to believe Felix Mikhailovich, he is enraptured with the first act; he even kissed Nikolai Andreyevich. Nadezhda Nikolayevna seemed very glad that he likes *Kitezh* even more than she does (in his words).

They discussed the disturbances at the Conservatory.

"Tomorrow the Council," said Nikolai Andreyevich, "and then what? The strikers will either whistle at us or, at best, they'll carry the most popular professors out of their classes. As you see, neither of these possibilities is particularly alluring."

I forgot to mention that before the guests arrived, Nikolai Andreyevich and I had a long talk about Chekhov. I think that as a person, Chekhov was very much like Rimsky-Korsakov; the same innate honesty and modesty, the same profoundly comic sense of the world around him.

9 March

The following is a letter sent by Rimsky-Korsakov to the Director of the St. Petersburg Conservatory, A. R. Bernhard. It was published in *Russkie vedomosti* and later reprinted in *Rus'* (no. 70, March 19, 1905):

My dear August Rudolfovich:

The movement which assumed the form of a strike of the students of the Higher Educational Institutions has also affected the St. Petersburg Conservatory, which, in terms of problems of musical education, is closely related to them. From the very outset of this movement, together with several of my colleagues, I made every effort by word and deed to temper this movement and ease the minds of those participating in it. When, despite this, the movement spread, the Conservatory was closed temporarily, until February 28. At the Art Council meeting of February 24, I was one of the twenty-seven teachers who voted in favor of closing the Conservatory until September 1. Nevertheless, by order of the Directorate of the St. Petersburg Branch of the Imperial Musical Society, the Conservatory proved to be closed only temporarily, until March 15.

In view of the possibility that disorders might erupt again with the reopening of the Conservatory, disorders amid which the normal course of studies would be inconceivable, I insisted once more that the Conservatory remain closed until September 1, as had been decided by the majority of votes of the Art Council. Now that the strike of the Higher Educational Institutions is an accomplished fact which the professors and the Government have to face, the Conservatory, at the behest of the Directorate of the Musical Society, has taken a position unlike that of all the other educational institutions and, contrary to the example of the others (despite the Art Council's resolution), has decided to reopen classes beginning March 16.

The consequences which were anticipated have come to pass: today, after eleven A.M. the Conservatory found itself surrounded by a cordon of foot and mounted police, who dispersed those students who tried, in vain, to enter the building. Admission to the Conservatory was by tickets, which had been distributed beforehand to students wishing to continue their studies. Only an insignificant number of such students (about ten) put in an appearance. This is how it was today, how it will be tomorrow, the day after tomorrow, etc. The striking students have been left to the mercy of the police, while those not on strike are protected by them. Is a regular course of instruction possible under such conditions? I find it impossible, as do many other teachers. The Conservatory authorities—the Director, the Inspectors, the Directorate of the Musical Society—look at it differently, unperturbed by events which make the Government itself stop to think.

Is any progress in the field of music possible at an institution where the resolutions of the Art Council have no meaning, at an institution where, under its Charter, the musical artists are subordinate to the Directorate—that is, to a group of amateurs and dilletantes—at an institution where, under the same Charter, the Director is not elected for a specified period but is an irremovable element, and finally—at an institution totally indifferent to the fate of its students in questions of education?

All the above regulations of the Charter and the actions of the administration of the Conservatory I find inexpedient, antiartistic, and callous from the moral point of view, and I consider it my duty to express my protest.

This letter was the spark that ignited the fire—and how brilliantly it burned!

23 March

Nikolai Andreyevich seemed terribly tired tonight. We talked about the disorders at the Conservatory and his dismissal from the faculty.

"They hired me and they've fired me," he remarked with a laugh. "You don't believe it? Take a look at today's *Rus.'* "[9]

In the section entitled *Stsena* (Stage) in *Rus'* (March 23, 1905), no. 74, appeared the following: "The Directorate of the St. Petersburg Branch of the Imperial Russian Musical Society has dismissed N. A. Rimsky-Korsakov from the faculty of the Conservatory." However incredible this may be, it is a fact.

This was followed by a postscript: "On March 19 Professor Bernhard resigned his position as Director of the St. Petersburg Conservatory."

Rimsky-Korsakov told me that his letter will appear tomorrow in *Rus'*. Also, on Sunday *Kashchei the Immortal* will be given at Mme. Komissarzhevskaya's Theater by students of the Conservatory under the direction of Glazunov. (What an interesting time this is!)

Open Letter to the Directorate of the St. Petersburg
Branch of the Imperial Russian Musical Society

In accordance with a resolution adopted by the Directorate at a meeting on March 19, 1905, and communicated to me officially, on the basis of Article 5 §14 of the Charter of the Conservatory and §55 of the Charter of the Russian Imperial Musical Society, I have been relieved of my duties as professor of the Conservatory, because I "publicly, in a sharp manner, and with a distortion of the facts, expressed a protest against the action of the Directorate aimed at reinstituting the studies which were suspended at the Conservatory. This clearly impedes the efforts of the Directorate to establish tranquility and restore the even tenor of educational life," and therefore the Directorate "considers my further activity as professor impossible."

If in my open letter to the Director of the Conservatory I made reference to the twenty-seven votes in favor of closing the Conservatory until September 1, and indeed, this period received a minority of the votes, and the majority were for closing the Conservatory "until passions shall have been calmed," the inexactness on my part obviously cannot be construed as a distortion of the facts, since it does not change the sense of my letter, and the phrase "passions shall have been calmed" indicates a period possibly even more remote than September 1. For it cannot be said that on March 15 passions were calmed. Therefore, I request the Directorate to show me which facts I distorted. Without this, the undeserved implication that I have been irresponsible will prove a not altogether honorable act on the part of the Directorate. My dismissal, over the heads of the Art Council, proves once more that I am correct in thinking that it is the Charter which gives rise to the abnormality in the relations between the Art Council, the Director of the Conservatory, and the Directorate.

I hereby resign my honorary membership in the St. Petersburg Branch.

N. Rimsky-Korsakov

P.S. Several hours before the meeting of the Directorate on March 19, which ordered my dismissal, I received a letter from a member of the Directorate, containing the following lines: "Would it not have been better if, instead of protesting, you had agreed, for the sake of calming the passions of the young people, to assume the reins of the administration in place of A. R. Bernhard?" Most likely, this member of the Directorate dissented, but he signed the resolution. In reply I refused.

(*Rus'* [March 24, 1905], no. 75)

27 March

On Sunday afternoon, March 27, I was at Mme Kommissarzhevskaya's Theater for the historic first performance of *Kashchei the Immortal,* given in honor of Rimsky-Korsakov by the students of the Conservatory with the help of Mme N. F. Lezhen and Glazunov directing.

Today's performance had a very special character: it was in the nature of a enormous political demonstration, the like of which I never saw before or since. Such was the nervous tension throughout that I left the theater with a headache. I confess that I would never attend such an event a second time, but I am happy that I did manage to see something of this sort at least once in my life.

Before *Kashchei* began, the overflow audience greeted Glazunov enthusiastically and presented him with three wreaths. At the end, Rimsky-Korsakov was given an ovation such as was probably never given to anyone anywhere. He was presented with seven wreaths from his students, bearing the inscriptions (in flowers): "To a fighter, from the Directors of Mme Kommissarzhevskaya's Theater," "From Admirers," "From the Editorial Board of *Teatral'naia Rossiia,*" etc. One of the ribbons read: "To a Great Artist and Citizen." Congratulatory telegrams were read from Glazunov, Liadov, I. E. Repin, Siloti, and others. V. V. Stasov delivered a very emotional speech, in which he hailed Nikolai Andreyevich's enormous contribution to Russian music and also pointed out that all great people always have enemies.

"But, like all truly great people, you, Nikolai Andreyevich," he said, turning to Rimsky-Korsakov, "have a great soul and therefore, the most fitting, wonderful words one can say to you about your enemies are those of the Christians: 'Forgive them for they know not what they do.' But, besides these great words, there are still others, spoken by a great man, our Pushkin: 'The hammer is so heavy that, in breaking the glass, it shatters the sword.' These words apply to you exactly."

This speech was greeted by bravos and deafening applause. Several other addresses were then read: from Conservatory students, the Union of Master Craftsmen, Russian Women, the Intelligentsia, the Engineers' Union, the Ukrainian Circle, Moscow Musicians, Lawyers, etc.

There is no telling how much longer these readings would have continued if, finally, Rimsky-Korsakov himself had not asked that the festivities be brought to a close in view of a threat to arrest the audience.

As Ossovsky put it so aptly in *Slovo* (March 28, 1905), no. 108,[10] Nikolai Andreyevich did not want this festive occasion in his honor to be linked in the public's mind with the memory of the "iron curtain," which was lowered, obviously on orders of the police, even as the reading of the addresses was beginning.

Shaken and terribly embarrassed, Rimsky-Korsakov said, bowing to the orchestra and the audience, "Thank you, gentlemen, thank you very much. Believe me, I did not deserve this."

The second part of this memorable musical morning did not take place. There was an announcement in the foyer that, due to circumstances beyond the managers' control, the concert could not be held, as it was necessary to prepare the hall for the evening performance. And even though, of course, everyone understood perfectly well the real reason for calling off this part of the program, there were no subsequent incidents.

In addition to Ossovsky's article in *Slovo,* the following periodicals published articles, reviews and even caricatures of Rimsky-Korsakov's *Kashchei: Rus',* no. 79 of 28 March (signed V. K., i.e., Kolomiitsev); *Syn otechestva,* nos. 34 and 35 of 28 and 29 March (Timofeyev); *Slovo,* no. 109 of 29 March (A. Ossovsky); *Novoe vremia,* no. 10440 and 10441 of 29 and 30 March (unsigned); *Peterburgskaia gazeta,* no. 79 of 29 March (signed R.). *Peterburgskii listok* no. 79 of 29 March published a caricature entitled: "A Colleague's Send-Off," showing Rimsky-Korsakov carrying away the top of the Conservatory and his scores, while the lower part of the building remains with all sorts of organ grinders, accordianists, and penny whistle players, and above this the inscription "They dismissed him." It also published an amusing poem entitled *Kashchei the Immortal,* signed with the pseudonym *Gusliar.* Further, no. 14 of the *Peterburgskii dnevnik teatra* of 5 April contained an article by Grigory Timofeyev and no. 15 of *Teatral'naia Rossiia* of 9 April—a charming caricature in which Rimsky-Korsakov was portrayed as Prince Igor, the Director—Kashchei, and public opinion— *Buria-bogatyr.*[11]

30 March

Tonight Rimsky-Korsakov gave me a detailed account of what has been going on at the Conservatory. It seems it all began because of the stupid escapade of some student named Manets[12] and the tactless behavior of Bernhard. Nikolai Andreyevich also told me that his dismissal notice was written by Kurochkin (most ungrammatically), signed by Klimchenko and Tur, and approved (without consultation with the Art Council) by Grand Duke Konstantin Konstantinovich "on his own responsibility." Thus, strictly speaking, Rimsky-Korsakov can bring a suit against the Central Board of Directors of the Russian Musical Society for its illegal action.

On Nikolai Andreyevich's writing table lay huge piles of press clippings, letters of support, greetings, and addresses. I looked at the wreaths he had received at the performance of *Kashchei:* one "From Admirers," a second from *Teatral'naia Rossiia,* a third "From Kommissarzhevskaya's Theater," a fourth "From loving and devoted Conservatory students" ("To dear Rimsky-Korsakov—a Great Artist and Man"), and the fifth from us (the Belskys, Alpers, Timofeyev, M. Yanova, and myself) inscribed "To a Great Artist and Citizen." The only ones who sent no messages of support were Cui and Balakirev (Rimsky-Korsakov did not expect anything from the latter since they are on bad terms) and, except for Morskoi, Butkevich, and Losev, there was no word from the artists of the Imperial Russian Opera.

Nikolai Andreyevich mentioned that he had been elected second vice-president at the Conference of Professors held on March 25,[13] and had occupied a place of honor along with Prince Trubetskoi (from Kiev) and Professor Vernadsky (from Moscow).

"They'll probably honor me again tomorrow," he said. "If only they'd stop, I could at least thank all of them at once through the press."

He hopes that they will not celebrate his fortieth aniversary.

"Otherwise I'll really run away," he added jokingly.

Rimsky-Korsakov will not return to the Conservatory under any circumstances unless K. K.[14] leaves, which, of course, is impossible.

As I said good-bye, I commented on the difference between the joyful tribute paid him in Moscow at *Saltan* and the gloomy, sinister mood of the festivities at Kommissarzhevskaya's Theater.

"Those were other times," he said smiling.

Letter to the Editor of the Newspaper *Rus'*

Dear Sir! Since it is impossible for me to thank individually all the academic, art, and musical societies, institutions and corporations, unions and other social groups, newspapers, students of institutions of higher learning, colleagues who teach at the Conservatory, its students, my students, and all the private individuals who have expressed their sympathy to me through protests, speeches, addresses, articles, wreaths, letters, telegrams, and those who sent greetings to me from Petersburg, Moscow, and other cities on the occasion of my dismissal by the Directorate of the I. R. Musical Society from the faculty of the Conservatory, I wish, through the press, to express to all my profound, heartfelt gratitude.

I ask the editors of other newspapers in Petersburg, Moscow, and the provinces to reprint this statement of mine in full.

N. Rimsky-Korsakov.

2 April 1905. [*Rus'* (April 3, 1905), no. 85]

Letter to the Editor of the Newspaper *Rus'*

Dear Sir! This evening's edition of *Birzhevye vedomosti* (no. 8757) published a conversation with the President of the S.-Petersburg Branch of the Imperial

Russian Musical Society, P. N. Cheremisinov, concerning recent events at the Conservatory, my dismissal, and the possibility of inviting me to return to the Conservatory. In his discussion of the movement, which took hold of the capital's institutions of higher learning, among them the Conservatory, Mr. Cheremisinov says that I "headed the movement of students at the Conservatory, who decided to strike, and that such a point of view can be called political." I consider these words of the President an explicit public denunciation of me, and I find it beneath me to attempt to justify myself. Further, in Mr. Cheremisinov's conversation, I read: "Rimsky-Korsakov would like to return to the Conservatory, and the Directorate would like to see him in his former post again." Perhaps the Directorate would like this, but where does Mr. Cheremisinov get the idea that I wish to return? Thus, to avoid any misunderstanding, I wish to state that I consider my return to the Conservatory an impossibility under existing regulations, and, after the conversation of the President published today, obviously expressing the views of the entire Directorate, I have no intention of having any dealings with the present membership of the Petersburg Directorate or of carrying on any negotiations with them.

N. Rimsky-Korsakov.

4 April 1905. [*Rus'* (April 5, 1905), no. 87]

19 April

This afternoon Nikolai Andreyevich told me that nothing could induce him to return to the Conservatory if they do not grant it "autonomous rights"; that beginning with the fall, he will give private lessons and also raise the question of his works being performed.

"Perhaps Siloti and I will set up a small private music school," he added. "For the time being, however, these are only plans."

I do not recall very well now how it came about, but somehow, in connection with the "paradise" in *Kitezh* or something else, our conservation turned to the subject of the philosopher-poet Vladimir Solovyov and his unshakable belief in the resurrection of Christ.

"I personally don't believe for a minute in the possibility of life after death," said Nikolai Andreyevich, "nor do I believe that in all the universe, only our earth was populated."

From further conversation, I learned that he is thinking of taking a rest from opera and writing something else, although, as luck would have it, he already has in mind a subject suited specifically to opera.

"But I'm so tired," he said, "that even such purely mechanical work as setting a cantata to Homer wears me out. It's a good thing we'll be going to Vechasha soon." (The Rimsky-Korsakovs are planning to move to the country at the beginning of May.)

Although in general Nikolai Andreyevich really does not like caricatures, he likes the one depicting him carrying the roof of the Conservatory on his head.

Finally, he told me that he almost always finds it difficult to write introductions to his operas. There are as many as six sketches in full score of an introduction to *Christmas Eve,* several versions of introductions to *Snegurochka* and *Servilia,* and numerous sketches of an introduction to *The Legend of the Invisible City of Kitezh.* Only the march which introduces act 1 of *Saltan* was written straightaway.

Rimsky-Korsakov went from me to Belsky. (Can it be that he went for new material for an opera?)

30 April

Liadov and Felix Blumenfeld were already at Rimsky-Korsakov's when Lapshin and I arrived. Shortly afterward the others appeared and the music began. Felix Mikhailovich played the first three acts of *Kitezh* before tea, and after tea—the fourth (with Igor Stravinsky helping out and Ossovsky and Nikolai Andreyevich singing).

Speaking about the music of a "church character," Nikolai Andreyevich quipped that he had written it especially for Kompaniesky, that the music of the "potion" is "medical music," that the very end of act 3 (where, instead of a final chord, there is a diminished fifth) was composed for Rebikov, and that the "cukoo of the fourth" in *Kitezh* was a "Vechasha cuckoo."

Someone mentioned that Marfa's aria from *The Tsar's Bride* was sung recently at Ernest's Restaurant and that tomorrow, at the opening of Pavlovsk, Morskoi is going to sing Levko's Serenade from *May Night.*

"But it was reported in the newspapers," said Rimsky-Korsakov, "that because of Kuza, my works and Bleichmann's have been forbidden."[15]

In connection with something or other, the conversation turned to Balakirev and his eccentric behavior. Someone said that "fewer and fewer people want to spend time with him," whereupon Nikolai Andreyevich retorted, not without some slight irritation, "Well, then, no one will ever beleaguer him."

The music ended shortly after one. Stasov seemed well pleased with the libretto of *Kitezh*, although he would have liked to comment on certain passages to Belsky. As for Liadov, he was excited about the first act (finding it "poetic as could be") and also enchanted by the moment where the "miracle occurs"[16] and the church bells begin to ring softly.

Tomorrow Nikolai Andreyevich will be at Belsky's and on Tuesday (May 3) he will probably go to Vechasha.

1 May

I ran into Nikolai Andreyevich again at the Belskys' today. They talked about new subjects for operas *(Nausicaä, Stenka Razin, Heaven and Earth)*.[17] During tea there was a lively argument about philosophy. When he was taking his leave, Nikolai Andreyevich asked Vladimir Ivanovich to bring him a scenario for *Nausicaä*.

Nikolai Andreyevich is tired of what is going on at the Conservatory. He feels that he has gotten old, that he is worn-out and decrepit. These were his last words to me on the staircase.

Upon learning that I was free and would be going home, he asked me to accompany him as far as the Nikolayevsky Bridge. I agreed, of course, and rode with him to his house. In the carriage, he confessed that to some degree he believes in "fate."

"When I became a professor at the Conservatory," he said, "my life assumed a new direction. I began to educate myself and to compose. My years at the Chapel developed in me a propensity for brilliant orchestration. During that period, I wrote *Capriccio espagnol, Sheherazade,* and finally *Mlada.* Soon after leaving the Chapel, I began to write my operas, one after the other. Now that they've expelled me from the Conservatory, what's going to happen?"

I suggested that he start writing his memoirs or critical articles about his operas *(Snegurochka, Kitezh,* or *The Maid of Pskov).*

"You're one of the few people, alas," continued Nikolai Andreyevich, "who understand that every musician must stop composing in time or else the inevitable will happen. For example, we were at the Molases' recently for a performance of *Mozart and Salieri* and some of *The Stone Guest,* and what do you think? Alexandra Nikolayevna sounded worse than ever, and the worst part of it was that she wasn't even aware of it. This is what I fear about myself, and yet I want very much to write—and to write something large-scale. You know, I'm even thinking of turning to new poets and composing something like *Mozart and Salieri* to the words of Maeterlinck; also of writing a number of songs to the poetry of Balmont, Grinevskaya, or even Rathaus and others."

I advised him not to be unfaithful to Pushkin, Lermontov, Count Alexei Tolstoi, and Mey, at which point he confessed that even in his school days, he had not been overly fond of Lermontov's poetry (wasn't this due to Balakirev's influence?).

Finally, Rimsky-Korsakov and I parted at the gates of his house. We embraced firmly. He invited me to Vechasha and asked me to write. It was by then quarter to one in the morning.

I forgot to mention: today Rimsky-Korsakov received an invitation to go to New York to teach composition under exceedingly advantageous conditions, but obviously he will not go there.

25 May

This evening, when I arrived at the Rimsky-Korsakovs', Nikolai Andreyevich was still sleeping, and, therefore, I spent some time with young Nadezhda Nikolayevna. She is a lovely person. Shortly afterward, Nikolai Andreyevich appeared. He greeted me very cordially, and when I remarked that I thought he had gone to Pavlovsk yesterday, where Glazunov had conducted his *Easter Overture,* he replied: "No, I won't be going to hear my works for a long time."

We talked about Suk's excellent performance of the suite from *Pan Voyevoda* at the opening of Sestroretsk.[18]

Further, we discussed Merezhkovsky's book *Peter and Alexis.*

"While reading it," said Rimsky-Korsakov, "though I never had felt any special tenderness toward Peter, I came to despise him for his incredible cruelty to his son. As I see it, Peter was a worse person even than Ivan the Terrible."

N. D. Mironov, who was also visiting Nikolai Andreyevich, tried to persuade him to go to the portrait exhibit at the Taurida Palace, organized by S. Diaghilev.[19]

"I'm afraid I won't understand anything about it and it won't interest me," remarked Rimsky-Korsakov. "For unlike Merezhkovsky, I'm not at all erudite, and I don't take pleasure in looking at lots of people I don't know."

Yesterday Nikolai Andreyevich had a visit from Belsky, who promised to return again on Saturday. Most likely nothing will come of *Nausicaä*. Nikolai Andreyevich is afraid that he will not be able to write anything this summer.

"In former years," he said, "by spring my head was bursting with all kinds of themes. But now, somehow, there's nothing, no plans at all."

(This was aside from his intention to orchestrate Borodin's song, *More,* and two of his own songs, *Zaklinanie* and *Nimfa*).[20]

"Oh, well," he added, "maybe I'll write something symphonic, with a program."

31 May

Rimsky-Korsakov told me that on Sunday (May 29) he went to the portrait exhibit at the Taurida Palace, but he did not find it very satisfying.

"In the first place," he said, "I don't care much for portrait painting and, secondly, I knew almost no one there, and if I had, being by nature a confirmed Social Democrat, I wouldn't have like them.

"When I entered Peter Hall," he continued, "I saw dozens of portraits of Peter the First, whom I've hated for many, many years, surrounded by all sorts of 'Sebastian Bachs,' sitting and standing in various poses. In Catherine Hall, everything was from *The Queen of Spades,* and in Alexander Hall—from *Eugene Onegin.* What's more, a great many of the portraits were simply bad.

"You know," he said suddenly, "a new critic made his appearance recently, a follower of Nurok. He has absolutely no use for Glazunov and me (Glazunov less than me). His name is Yanovsky. Remember—Zabela sang his strange songs. And here's why: he's a great admirer of Vrubel and other decadent artists. Meanwhile, everything about our music strikes him as old-fashioned and uninteresting. It's different in the West—there they have their d'Indys, Strausses, Faurés. Well, let Yanovsky praise this rubbish, but not denounce us, the old men. After all, we did a little something for music and it wasn't even all that bad."

"What do they want anyhow?" I asked jokingly. "Why, you've even written an impressionist opera of sorts—*Kashchei*."

"But the trouble is," replied Rimsky-Korsakov, "that despite the seemingly refined harmony, this work, alas, is completely healthy and not decadent."

At about half past six, Mme Siloti dropped in. She is an unusually pleasant and friendly woman. The conversation was about Safonov and his desire to be the Director of two conservatories at the same time.[21] This "Eagle of the Caucasus"[22] would like to make everyone knuckle under.

I stayed on for half an hour after Mme Siloti left. Then Rimsky-Korsakov and I bade good-bye for the summer (probably until July).

Fifth Visit to Vechasha (July 22, 23, 24, and 25, 1905)

22 July

It was half past six in the morning when I reached Vechasha, and everyone was still asleep. The morning was magnificent. I walked around the garden and took a photograph from the path in front of the balcony. Everything was as before, except that the garden has more flowers.

At eight-thirty Nikolai Andreyevich came out and greeted me. He was much improved and looked refreshed. He is taking iodine.

Before and after coffee, we had a long talk about Nikolai Andreyevich's new works and his "chronicle." The latter, which has been put aside for the time being, has been brought up to the year 1885.[23] However, according to Nikolai Andreyevich, there are some rather important gaps in it. He read to me the rough draft of his critical analysis of *Snegurochka*. It is interesting but somewhat too detailed. Incidentally, he is planning to write about the musical forms of his operas.[24]

After lunch, Nikolai Andreyevich set to work on his *Textbook of Orchestration* and almost finished the section on strings. Following a walk, he played his prelude-cantata *(From Homer)* from the proofs. Then we strolled in the garden again and talked about Pechersky's *In the Forests*. We are both enchanted with this magnificent, picturesque chronicle of the Zavolzhie.[25]

After dinner, Nikolai Andreyevich worked again and then we went to the lake to "see the sun off." We admired the sky and the clouds. Nikolai Andreyevich said that he has fallen in love with the beauty of the heavens and understands now why people have placed God there. We said good night at about ten-thirty, and Nikolai Andreyevich went to write letters.

I forgot to mention an incident which occurred with the peasants of Vladimir. It seems that they collected two rubles seventeen kopecks for the benefit of Rimsky-Korsakov. This so delighted Stasov that he wanted Rimsky-Korsakov or Glazunov to write a chorus based on their letter, which, he was certain, would soon be sung throughout all of Russia.[26] However, Nikolai Andreyevich donated the money, which had been offered to him through Ivanov-Razumnik, to the starving peasants of Tula Province, and thus the incident was closed.

23 July

I rose at six-thirty and took some pictures. Nikolai Andreyevich appeared at about eight-thirty. Our conversation touched on the importance and the immortality of composers and the works of Rimsky-Korsakov. I urged him to write an article on the forms of music drama, explaining the reason for what I called, in jest, the "fourteen styles" because of his fourteen operas. He began to look through *Snegurochka* for suitable examples of a doubled pizzicato and pizzicati in general. He pointed out to me certain details in the orchestration of *Sadko* (such as the dropping of the winds before the Princess' first reply) and the unsuccessful, extremely weak pizzicato in *Snegurochka* ("Pusti ee").

"This will have to be changed," he said, "at least during the performance."

He then proceeded to work on the harp and I went for a walk.

After breakfast Nikolai Andreyevich and young Nadezhda Nikolayevna went to Lyubensk, and he asked me to look through the score of *Kitezh* and select examples of the harp, which I did after going through three acts.

Nikolai Andreyevich did almost no work after dinner. We went for a walk along the Lyubensk road. It was beautiful. We watched the sunset and talked about a phenomenal pianist, Leopold Godowsky (whom Rimsky-Korsakov met at Glazunov's), and the way he tossed off the immensely difficult Chopin études.[27] Godowsky expressed a desire to make a transcription of the polonaise from *Christmas Eve,* so Nikolai Andreyevich gave him the score of the suite from this opera.

After tea, Rimsky-Korsakov went to work again, and I set off for the lake.

24 July

I rose rather late (at about seven-thirty). Everyone was still sleeping. It was a marvelous morning. Tea was served in the garden. How heavenly it is here! At quarter to nine Rimsky-Korsakov appeared, in a good mood. He made coffee. The he worked and I looked through act 4 of *Kitezh.* Between periods of rest and work, we strolled in the garden.

When Nikolai Andreyevich returned to his study, he continued to write about the harp, and I copied out examples of the percussion instruments. While going through *Snegurochka,* Nikolai Andreyevich apparently grew somewhat tired (he slept poorly last night) so he lay down for ten minutes. After that we went again to the lake. It was windy, but in general the weather was ideal.

Oh, if only I could stay here not for four days but for the whole summer and work with Nikolai Andreyevich, I could learn so much!

On returning from the lake, Nikolai Andreyevich told me that he already has in mind how he will begin his new composition. Besides this, he said that tomorrow he will finish the "percussion group" (which was begun on June 4), and after that, he will make a final revision of the section on the stringed instruments; only then will he consider how to set forth the general section of the textbook. He is thinking of calling it "A Textbook of Orchestration of Operatic Works." He is writing about the xylophone. When I entered the study, he read to me what he had written about the celeste; also his section on the bowed instruments.

At nine-thirty tea was served, after which everyone (except Volodya) went for a stroll. It was a perfect night: stars and a light breeze.

At present Rimsky-Korsakov would like more than anything else to hear his *Saltan* on the Imperial stage. Then let them withdraw it if they want to.

In these eleven years of intense creativity, Nikolai Andreyevich has grown weary. He has begun to forget a great deal (such as details of the death of his mother, whom he loved deeply). He remembers his early operas (the first *Maid of Pskov, May Night,* and *Snegurochka*) much better than *Tsar Saltan, Sadko, Servilia,* and *Kashchei.*

We said good night shortly before eleven o'clock. Rimsky-Korsakov had to write to Siloti and some others.

25 July

During a talk about the instrumental examples and their grouping, I learned that Glazunov prefers complex doubling of the timbres of the orchestra. This is understandable, since by nature he is a symphonist. On the other hand, Rimsky-Korsakov, being an opera composer, who has to portray not only the external but the intimate life of his heroes, favors using individual timbres.

After tea Nikolai Andreyevich withdrew to his study to work on the strings, while I sat on the balcony and jotted down these lines. He was occupied with his textbook from lunch until dinner, after which we walked to the pond beyond the vegetable garden. He admired the willows on the opposite bank of the overgrown little pond. We talked about hearing and Nikolai Andreyevich complained that he has noticed that with the years, his hearing has become somewhat impaired. Even though he still has a keen ear, he has difficulty catching what people are saying when many of them talk simultaneously. He has never been able to differentiate between the timbres of singers' voices, he said, unless there is something exceptional about them. Except for Anton Rubinstein, it is the same with pianists.

This is what happened once at Leonova's in Oranienbaum.

"Cui, Burenin, and I drove there together," said Nikolai Andreyevich. "In the evening Anton Grigorevich came. He played on a terrible piano, but how wonderfully he played. What a singing quality he produced!

"These days," he continued, "I can't tell the difference between similar notes on the clarinet and piccolo-clarinet. By the way, the upper register of the clarinet should always be doubled with the flute—only then will the beauty of tone be preserved. Otherwise it sounds sort of strident, hollow. In this sense, the piccolo clarinet is particularly unpleasant and shrill."

Before dinner Nikolai Andreyevich read to me his revised section on the strings. This part was set forth with extreme clarity and simplicity.

After dinner he played some dance music for his little granddaughter Irochka (a krakowiak, waltzes from *Faust* and *Der Freischütz,* and a chorus from *William Tell*).

At seven o'clock, after receiving the mail and reading the newspapers, Nikolai Andreyevich shut himself up again in his study. However, in ten minutes he came out into the garden. We talked about his operas—about the orchestration of the chromatic scale in the scene of Marfa's fainting spell (in *The Tsar's Bride*), which was unusually successful; about the "horn theme" in the first act of *Servilia,* which he considers a marvelous fanfare, and Servilia's aria ("Tsvety moi"), which he regards as his best aria. Further, we noted that judging from the fact that they sing, all the Korsakov "prophetic birds" (the Swan Princess in *Saltan,* Alkonost in *Kitezh*) must either possess perfect pitch or, at least, have taken the full course in solfège and finished the Conservatory. We agreed that from the vocal standpoint, *The Tsar's Bride, Servilia, Pan Voyevoda,* and *Kitezh* are the best written of his operas and *Kashchei the Immortal*—the most difficult. Finally, we spoke of the fact that although Rachmaninov is a wonderful musician, his *Covetous Knight* is totally lacking in melody, something which offends Nikolai Andreyevich.

Toward evening Nadezhda Nikolayevna (the younger), Nikolai Andreyevich, and I went to watch the sunset. I tried to take a picture of Rimsky-Korsakov in the orange light of the setting sun. It came out very well. At eight-thirty Nikolai Andreyevich went to write a letter[28] and I— to pack. It was a perfect evening, with a light, warm breeze and grasshoppers chirping. Vladimir Nikolayevich watered the vegetable garden and flowers. A nocturne, pure poetry! We sat on the porch, watching the falling stars.

Before my departure we all went once again to the lake. On our right—the orange reflection of the moon in the water.

From further conversation with Rimsky-Korsakov, I learned that after the question of setting up a higher school of music,[29] which he has been considering, had been settled in principle, the Directorate of Music made certain changes, insulting to the reputations of Rimsky-Korsakov, Glazunov, Liadov, and Siloti. For example, no decision was made with respect to inviting new teachers, and the name "Advanced Courses in Music" was changed simply to "Music School." The application was submitted to the Minister of Internal Affairs, the Ministry forwarded it to the Governor of the City, and then, the latter sent it to the Directorate of the Musical Society for consideration. All this had been extremely distasteful to Nikolai Andreyevich. In fact, he is literally incensed.

Besides all this, in his eagerness to open the school in September, Siloti has been too hasty. Rimsky-Korsakov found out that it cannot be opened until the program has been worked out in detail, and this may take at least until October 1—especially since Glazunov is still weak from tonsilitis and will not be able to give lectures for a long time. His illness led to complications and an abscess in his ear, and even though his eardrum has been pierced, it is almost impossible for him to hear music.

"What's more," added Rimsky-Korsakov, "I don't think much of the rooms at Shröder's."[30]

What a pity Belyaev is gone.

Shortly before midnight, I took leave of Nikolai Andreyevich and together with Troitsky, set off for Petersburg. It was quarter to seven when we arrived at the capital.

13 September

After work I went to Zagorodny. As it turned out, the Rimsky-Korsakovs had returned from the country on the tenth, as planned. When I entered the house, I found the young Stravinsky (brother of Igor Feodorovich) and some lady who had come on business.

Nikolai Andreyevich was in a wonderful mood. He gave me a pile of music—the manuscript score of excerpts from *Kitezh* and the published scores of the suite from *Christmas Eve* and Borodin's *Sleeping Princess* (in Rimsky-Korsakov's orchestration).[31] He mentioned, in passing, that if the Conservatory becomes autonomous, he will resume his post as professor.

Further, I learned that during the summer, besides writing the duet *Gornyi kliuch* as a vocal trio, Nikolai Andreyevich had also orchestrated *Pan, Pesn' pesnei,* and *Nimfa,* and that he is planning to do the same with the songs *Son v letniuiu noch'* and *Gornimi tikho letela dusha nebesami.*[32] I learned, too, that even though *Snegurochka* is his favorite opera, he believes that in the sense of their technical craftsmanship and as "teaching tools," so to speak, the scores of *The Tsar's Bride* and *Servilia* are more useful for his textbook of orchestration.

"By the way," he said, "you know, I don't particularly like the tuba—it's rather coarse, not like the trombone, which I find attractive."

As I was leaving, Rimsky-Korsakov informed me that the proposed "Siloti School" is not going through; the whole thing has collapsed.

18 September

Nikolai Andreyevich told me tonight that after attending rehearsals of *The Tsar's Bride* and *Tsar Saltan,* he has become thoroughly disenchanted with both operas. He finds them colorless and commonplace, except perhaps, for the beginning of the scene of Marfa's delirium, which actually is very good.

"Judging from the symptoms," I remarked jokingly, "I would say you're writing a new opera."

"No, dear friend, you're mistaken," he replied, "I'm not writing an opera. For the time being, there's only a subject—there's not even a libretto—and, if for no other reason, I have no possibility of composing anything."

On the subject of operatic style, Nikolai Andreyevich ventured the thought that perhaps the early Italian composers were right in presenting the public (which, as always, knows nothing and has no serious interest in anything) with a few fairly good musical numbers tacked onto a bad, simple libretto.

"Otherwise," he continued, "given the relatively complicated operatic writing of today, a conscientious (but unmusical) listener would probably have had to follow the example of a general I know, who had to attend every opera several times: once to look at the scenery; then to listen to the singers; a third time to follow the libretto carefully and try to make out the plot; a fourth time to listen attentively to the orchestra ('Surely this is also very interesting,' he said, 'but I can't take it all in at once.'); finally, a fifth time specially to enjoy the ensemble, etc.

"And you know," added Rimsky-Korsakov, "however ridiculous this may seem at first, such an attitude toward music is more admirable than the indifferent disdain of our subscription audiences."

19 September

Tonight the Association of Operatic Artists presented its first performance of *Tsar Saltan* at the People's House. It attracted a huge audience:[33]

even Baskin and Ivanov were there. Although, on the whole, the performance was only moderately good, the singers were called out enthusiastically and, at the end, they were given a ten-minute ovation. The audience called insistently for the composer, but Rimsky-Korsakov was not there, although his entire family was.

The next performance will take place on Saturday, September 24.

9 October

Rimsky-Korsakov visited me this afternoon after the christening of his granddaughter, Elena. He reported on his trip to Moscow for the performance of *Pan Voyevoda* at the Bolshoi Theater.[34]

"The orchestra played well," he said, "and the opera won considerable success, but the singers left much to be desired.

"You know," he continued, "Rachmaninov[35] is considering *Kitezh,* but Telyakovsky, whom I saw in Moscow, decided not to transport the Petersburg sets of *Sadko* there but to order their own for Moscow. Besides this, he plans to give *Kitezh* next season here, at the Marinsky Theater, though I myself would prefer that they give *Saltan* and *Kaschei the Immortal* on the Imperial stage first. I'll have to talk with the conductor about this."

Nikolai Andreyevich also went to the Solodovnikov Theater to hear *Sadko.* Sekar was poor; the cuts senseless, the performance slovenly. Pagani, or rather, "Poganyi-dirizher," ("vile conductor") directed.

Besides this, he told me that during his stay in Moscow, he heard thousands of workers singing *Dubinushka*[36] as they moved along Tversky Boulevard.

14 October

Tonight Rimsky-Korsakov and I discussed the Moscow reviews of *Pan Voyevoda*[37] and the general tendency of our critics toward disparaging criticism. The libretto in particular came in for harsh treatment; and in Rozenov's review, the music, too, despite some slight praise. It was stated, for example, that beginning with *Sadko,* Rimsky-Korsakov started to retrogress noticeably, striving more and more for form; that even the public had begun to understand this shortcoming. (As if *Snegurochka, Sadko,* and even *The Maid of Pskov* were lacking in form!) The charge was also made that in *Voyevoda,* Dzyuba is forever singing mazurkas and the Voyevoda, polonaises. This, too, is untrue, for in act 2 (the Scene of the Terror), Dzyuba has not a single measure in the style of a mazurka and the Voyevoda (in the aria and duet) not a measure in the style of a polonaise.

I forgot to mention that apropos of *The Maid of Pskov, Christmas Eve,* and Tchaikovsky's *Oprichnik* being banned from the stage of the Moscow People's House, Nikolai Andreyevich remarked, "Well, since there's already been such censorship of music, why not my *Saltan?* It's the worst of all of these. What with the frequent repetitions of the musical characterizations (and themes), its music (and consequently the subject) is much easier to understand than *Snegurochka.*"

8 November

After some delay, caused first by a strike by the ballet company and then for other, unknown reasons, the revival of *Snegurochka* finally took place tonight. It was a nonsubscription performance; the theater was almost filled.

The opera enjoyed a great success; the composer was called out ten times. The King of the Berendey's first cavatina, the Dance of the *Skomorokhi,* and Lel's third song had to be repeated.

Among the cast were: Markovich (Spring), Serebryakov (Grandfather Frost), Bolska (Snegurochka), Yershov (King of the Berendeys), Zbruyeva (Lel), Sharonov (Mizgir), and Bukhtoyarov (Bermyata). Zbruyeva was excellent; Yershov, Bolska, and Markovich—very good; Sharonov and Bukhtoyarov—fair. The rest of the cast were so-so. The opera was under the direction of Blumenfeld.

9 November

Tonight I attended the Rimsky-Korsakovs' second "Wednesday." Others there besides me were N. I. Richter and Igor and Gury Stravinsky. There was some talk about last night's performance of *Snegurochka,* with everyone agreeing that Yershov sang excellently, though he overacted somewhat, and that Zbruyeva was magnificent.

Before tea, Igor Stravinsky and N. I. Richter played Taneyev's First Symphony. After tea Richter played Scriabin's *Nocturne* in D flat (for the left hand) and a barcarolle and prelude by Rachmaninov. To my remark that these new things always contain sort of "morbid" chords, Nikolai Andreyevich replied: "And the new music will never be free of them."

Then Nadezhda Nikolayevna and Richter (or Igor Stravinsky?) played Grechaninov's *Fables* and Wagner's *Eine Faust Ouverture*.

The second half of the evening was less interesting to me—I scarcely had a chance to talk with Nikolai Andreyevich. He was in his study literally surrounded by his scores. I did learn, though, that at Siloti's first concert, on October 22, they played a fanfare for him after the suite from *Mlada* and he was called out five times; also that *Dubinushka* was not particularly successful at Siloti's second concert (on November 5),[38] but then how could it have been—this little march-like number without any special musical qualities?

Stasov is copying out the missing twenty pages of Mussorgsky's *Marriage;* evidently he would very much like Rimsky-Korsakov to orchestrate it. However, Nikolai Andreyevich does not care much about undertaking this task; he will do it only to please Vladimir Vasilyevich.[39]

11 November

The second performance of *Snegurochka,* like the first, was nonsubscription. This time the Marinsky Theater was filled. The opera began at seven-thirty-six and ended at eleven-forty-five. The choruses were sung unrhythmically (Oh, what a conductor—Felix Blumenfeld!), but even so, the opera again had a great success.

The composer was called out thirteen times. Some of the cast were new. Spring was sung by Fried (fairly good); Grandfather Frost—Filippov (better than Serebryakov), Snegurochka—Paskhalova (so-so), Bermyata—Grigorovich, Kupava—Kuznetsova-Benois. Those who evoked the warmest response were Kuznetsova-Benois, Yershov, and Zbruyeva.

23 November

At the Rimsky-Korsakovs' third "Wednesday," we got into a discussion about Scriabin, a great talent, who, despite his unusual pungency, is an impeccable harmonist and, unlike Reger and Strauss, does not write rubbish. Of course, he has strayed off somewhere and will never come back.[40] His music contains almost no consonances (not a single little art-less note), only enharmonic modulations and, therefore, though it is very good, it is monotonous.

We talked about Dukas and his *Sorcerer's Apprentice.*

"In terms of orchestration." remarked Nikolai Andreyevich, "I think he outshines all of us and, surprisingly, his music is relatively free of rubbish."

Someone mentioned the first meeting held at M. V. Yanova's for the purpose of setting up a Russian section of the International Musical Society. Those attending were N. D. Bernstein, S. K. Bulich, Zaremba, Timofeyev, and I. (What nonsense!)

After tea, Felix Blumenfeld played some of his own pieces. On the whole, they were very boring. I looked at photographs.

Rimsky-Korsakov has been asked to arrange a concert for the benefit of the victims of the strike.

4 December

Tonight I went to the Hall of the Tenishevsky School for the benefit concert arranged by Rimsky-Korsakov. The entire proceeds from this evening are to go to the families of needy workers.

For some reason neither Rimsky-Korsakov's *Pesn' pesnei* nor the duet from Rubinstein's *Maccabees* was performed. Instead, the artists sang many things not listed on the program (about freedom, prisoners, and shackles). Rimsky-Korsakov was given an ovation after his *Vostochnyi romans* (sung excellently by Tartakov). It was the same at the end of the concert, when Rimsky-Korsakov, Felix Blumenfeld, Verzhbilovich, Siloti, Kuznetsova-Benois, and Sharonov were called out three times. Although Yershov had been announced, for some reason he did not appear. Those who sang best were Bolska, Tartakov, and Kuznestova-Benois; Sharonov and Kuznetsova-Benois enjoyed the greatest success. During the concert they took up a collection. In addition to *Vostochnyi romans* the works of Rimsky-Korsakov performed were: Levko's song from *May Night* (Morskoi), *Hebrew Song* (Petrenko), and *Zvonche zhavoronka pen'e* (Bolska).

At the end of the concert, the young people broke out into their famous workers' *Marseillaise* and *Warszawianka.*

14 December

This evening at the Rimsky-Korsakovs' I learned that the benefit concert arranged by Nikolai Andreyevich had realized fifteen hundred rubles (after expenses).

We discussed conservatory matters: the all but unanimous selection of Glazunov as Director (only one negative vote, obviously his own); the resignation of Cheremisinov and Taneyev as members of the Directorate and their election as honorary members of the Russian Musical Society, with Cheremisinov occupying the former "Korsakov chair."[41] At the present time the Art Council is drawing up a new charter for the Conservatory and classes will probably begin after the holidays.

"You know," said Rimsky-Korsakov, suddenly, "some day I'm going to let you rummage around in my cupboard; there's something there that will interest you. But I warn you in advance, in days to come, these reminiscences about me will not be anywhere near as interesting as you think."

Our conversation turned to Mussorgsky's *Marriage* and Nadezhda Nikolayevna promised to let me know when it will be given at their house. Then Nikolai Andreyevich told me that at his request the concert of his works, proposed by Glazunov, is not going to take place; that in general he is opposed to any kind of celebration whatever of the fortieth anniversary of his composing career. He implored me, if I should hear anything about this, to frustrate such plans, since at a moment like this, when such terrible things are taking place in Moscow, he would find festivities of any sort intolerable.

When tea was served, besides the Rimsky-Korsakovs and myself, there were Belsky, Lapshin, Troitsky, Mironov, Nadezhda Nikolayevna, Gury and Igor Stravinsky, Yekaterina Nosenko (the latter's fiancée), Glazunov, Volodya, and Richter.

After tea Richter played Max Reger's *Improvisations* and Glazunov his own Eighth Symphony. Nikolai Andreyevich has already heard this symphony three times, and therefore he has come to know it thoroughly.

19 December

After the bank, I went to Nikolai Andreyevich to congratulate him on the fortieth anniversary of his career. When I rang, he was in the drawing room, giving a lesson to students from the Conservatory, and Igor Stravinsky was awaiting his turn. After Stravinsky's lesson on orchestration, some of which I sat in on, we had dinner.

Earlier in the day, the entire Rimsky-Korsakov family had gone to a rehearsal of *Mozart and Salieri*[42] and *Pagliacci* (with Chaliapin).

We talked about Glazunov's Eighth Symphony. Rimsky-Korsakov and I share the same opinion of it—that the second movement is the best and, after that, the first movement. I was right in thinking that there is no trio in the scherzo; it is simply a kind of rondo.

Rimsky-Korsakov gave me (and also Igor Feodorovich) a photograph of himself, mine with the following amusing inscription: "To dear Vasily Vasilyevich Yastrebtsev, from his devoted forty-year-old composer. N. R-K. 19 December 1905."

At exactly eight o'clock we left—Rimsky-Korsakov for a meeting on Belyaev matters and I for home. When we bade good-bye, Nikolai Andreyevich thanked me again and again for my attentiveness and solicitude and promised to let me know when *The Marriage* will be given at their home.

CHAPTER 16

1906

3 January

In the afternoon, while I was at the bank, I received a postcard from Rimsky-Korsakov, which read:[1]

Vasily Vasilyevich!

Example 65

V   den' Va- si- li- ia u- god-   ni- ka (on   kho- da- tai bed- nykh brazh- ni- kov)

I thought you would visit us and I would wish you Happy New Year, but this didn't happen. Belated greetings. I beg you to come on Wednesday evening January 4. There will be a "Marriage," however, no one else's but Mussorgsky-Gogol's.

N. R-K.   2 January 1906

4 January

I was at the Rimsky-Korsakovs' "Wednesday" from eight until two-thirty. Among the many other guests (thirty-five in all) were Stasov, Chaliapin, Glazunov, the four Blumenfelds, Bessel, the Belskys, the Ossovskys, Gury and Igor Stravinsky, the latter's fiancée, the Troitskys, Sandulenko, Richter, and the young Rimsky-Korsakovs.

The evening began with Mussorgsky's *Marriage,* with Sigismund Blumenfeld, A. P. Sandulenko, Gury Stravinsky, and S. N. Troitskaya in the singing roles and Nadezhda Nikolayevna as accompanist. This strange work of Mussorgsky's contains some talented moments, but, on the whole, as music, it is weak and boring.

The second number to be performed was Rachmaninov's *Covetous Knight.* Participating in it were Chaliapin, Ossovsky, Sandulenko, and Sigismund and Felix Blumenfeld (who accompanied). In the opinion of Chaliapin, this opera is not based on the text of Pushkin's play but rather on the overall moods of its various scenes and, from this point of view, despite its unquestioned talent, it is full of incongruities and shortcomings.

Feodor Ivanovich does not like it when composers use musical ideas from their earlier works in new ones.

"For example," he said, "in *The Covetous Knight,* in the scene of the old Baron's monologue, Rachmaninov incorporated almost all the music from one of the movements of his piano suite.

"It seems to me," he continued, "that in such cases, when composing his new works, a composer not only does not grow rich but, on the contrary, he sort of steals a twenty kopek piece from himself." (We laughed.)

Before tea, when we were in Nikolai Andreyevich's study, he showed us his manuscript of Borodin's *More* and told us that he had given a great deal of thought to how best to orchestrate the fugue of the accompaniment in this ballad. He thinks he has succeeded.

Stasov began speaking about Cui and his strange relationship to the current political life of Russia.

"Actually there's nothing particularly surprising about this," he said. "All his life this man has been willing to bow and scrape before anyone in power. In this sense, César Antonovich has always been a most worthless, most unprincipled person."

Felix Blumenfeld told us that the last time Chaliapin was so wonderful as Salieri that not only he but even Napravnik wept.

This evening at the Rimsky-Korsakovs', we talked at length about *Kitezh,* noting that it is really not for the public; that the beginning of it is constructed à la Bülow, that is, what Fevronia sings and the introduction ("Pokhvala pustyne") are almost identical, musically. As a consequence, the listener hears the same music twice in a row and thus he can, to some degree, get to know it immediately.[2] Finally, we observed that Fevronia's part contains a great many new and very subtle harmonies, and that her theme (in 5/8), which is counterposed to her principal melody and sort of grew out of it,[3] is strikingly fresh.

"It isn't more than fifteen or fifteen and a half years old," I said jokingly. We laughed.

Nikolai Andreyevich seems to have lost interest in the textbook of orchestration.

"And do you know why?" he asked. "I bought the score of Wagner's *Die Meistersinger* and, on looking through it, I saw that it's possible to orchestrate completely differently from the way I do and with wonderful results. Therefore, there's no use writing the textbook.

"Besides," he continued, "I keep asking myself whether one really ought to teach those who can't do anything without instruction. After all, I'd already written *Sadko, Antar,* and *The Maid of Pskov* when I set to work on fugues."[4]

Generally speaking Nikolai Andreyevich would like very much to leave the Conservatory.

"I'm bored with the Conservatory and bored with the students," he said. "And the reason is that so very few of them are gifted."

After tea, while Nadezhda Nikolayevna and Richter played a symphony by Bruckner (dedicated to God!?), Nikolai Andreyevich and I sat in his study, discussing the latest German and French music. In his opinion, even in music with a complicated texture, one now and then comes across something that is fairly good. On the other hand, these new Western composers absolutely cannot write simple music—they do not know how to. What's more, they have completely forgotten how to write a melody.

"Meanwhile," observed Rimsky-Korsakov, "music consists and must consist of contrasts between simplicity and complexity (complexity in music is very good), of clarity and the most intricate, devilish tricks in harmony and counterpoint, should the need arise. However, the music of the Strausses, d'Indys, Rebikovs, and company is nothing but cheerless pretentiousness."

Further, Nikolai Andreyevich told me that he gave the piano score of *Kitezh* to E. M. Petrovsky and Igor Stravinsky (who, by the way, was married today and has gone to Imatra); also that in a letter to him, Petrovsky called the musical types in that opera not characters but icons, which of course, is partly true.

Finally, we talked about the fact that Fevronia is a "Slavic Parsifal," but a wise Parsifal, not lifeless and foolish like Wagner's. In this connection, we recalled that earlier, in the scene of Servilia's death, one sensed that same idealistic mood which makes *Kitezh* so great.

In his analysis of *Servilia* (unpublished, unfortunately), Timofeyev characterized this mood wonderfully:

The entire scene of Servilia's death, with its extraordinarily graceful, inspired music, profound and sincere feeling, which corresponds fully to the dramatic situation, moves the listener to tears and transports him together with Servilia to some other world, a world better than this one. This scene bears some resemblance to that of Snegurochka's melting away, to the transformation of Princess Volkhova into the Volkhov river in *Sadko*, to Marfa's death in *The Tsar's Bride*. Here we find the same eternally feminine principle which lures mankind to the world of fantasy:

> Das ewig Weibliche
> Zieht uns hinan.

15 January

This afternoon Rimsky-Korsakov paid me a visit. He told me, among other things, that because of Chaliapin, for whom they are continually giving *Ruslan,* and because of their total preoccupation with *Rogneda,*[5] (in connection with Kamenskaya's forthcoming twenty-seventh anniversary), *Sadko* is not going to be given until next year. He also reported that the Solodovnikov Theater was burned down.

Chatting further, Nikolai Andreyevich mentioned that Napravnik often ruins new works when conducting them, simply because he does not like them.

1 February

Again there were many people at the Rimsky-Korsakovs' "Wednesday," eighteen in all. They talked about Wagner and Wagnerism.

"When it comes to Russian composers, it's quite a different matter," said Rimsky-Korsakov. "What could possibly be more original than Mussorgsky's 'Inn Scene.' Yet our public is quite indifferent to it. Recently I heard Chaliapin sing it at the Stasovs' and I was struck once again by its extraordinary originality."

Then, still speaking of Mussorgsky, Nikolai Andreyevich remarked jokingly that all his life he has been a kind of editor in chief of other people's works.

Besides this, he told us that the fate of *Kitezh* is being decided today. And indeed, during tea, a note arrived from Felix Blumenfeld with the news that the production of *Kitezh* has definitely been approved and also that *Sadko* will be given in the spring. Everyone was overjoyed.

After that we got into a lengthy discussion about politics and the K-D party,[6] and I made it clear that while I am wholeheartedly in accord with this party, any new false progression or fresh and original modulation means more to me than politics.

After tea Sandulenko sang a number of Rimsky-Korsakov's songs. Richter concluded the musical program with Schumann's *Kreisleriana*. How fine this music is, in spite of its excessive length!

9 February

This afternoon I received the following letter from Rimsky-Korsakov:

My very dear k——d Vasily Vasilyevich,

On Friday there will be a gathering at our house—this time not a musical. Ivanov (Razumnik),[7] a friend of my son Andrei, whom you do not know, is going to give a talk or lecture about the peasants of Vladimir Province—their development, views, opinions, etc. Along with this there will be a collection ad libitum in the dining room for the unemployed. If you are interested, please come at 8:30.

Yours,   N. R-Korsakov, 8 February 1906.

15 February

It was exactly twenty years ago today that I saw Nikolai Andreyevich for the first time at Anton Rubinstein's seventh historical concert. How long ago that was, yet how recently!

Tonight there were quite a few guests at Zagorodny for the musical evening—nineteen in all. Before tea, I chatted with Nikolai Andreyevich about his textbook of orchestration, and he informed me that he is thinking of arranging it according to a new and different plan, that is, combining the various instruments and entire orchestral groups.

Besides this, he drew my attention to the fact that Wagner notwithstanding, in his works the cellos almost never play in the middle and lowest registers, the bassoon relatively seldom plays above,[8] and that, on the whole, especially of late he has begun to avoid the extreme registers (the highest and lowest).[9] Finally, in terms of instrumental capriciousness, Nikolai Andreyevich regards *Snegurochka* as the richest of all; in terms of craftsmanship—*Sheherazade, Mlada, Kitezh,* and, to some extent, *Christmas Eve.*

After that we talked about the death of Anton Stepanovich Arensky on February 12 and his burial in the Alexander Nevsky cemetery on the sixteenth.

"The man burned himself out," said Rimsky-Korsakov, "but he was not lacking in talent. You know, Mme. Siloti (a former pupil of his) saw him just before his death. She went to live in Finland expressly for this purpose."

After tea, Zabela sang songs by Rimsky-Korsakov and Felix Blumenfeld played many of his own things.

There was talk again about Wagner. Blumenfeld literally worships *Tristan*. As for Nikolai Andreyevich, although he, too, likes this opera very much, he prefers *Die Walküre* (act 1). On the whole, he feels that *Das Rheingold* sounds quite unsatisfactory compared with the rest of the operas of this cycle, especially *Götterdämmerung*.

I forgot to mention that before tea, speaking about Tchaikovsky's charming *Cradle Song* ("Spi, ditia moe, spi, usni"),[10] dedicated to Nadezhda Nikolayevna, Nikolai Andreyevich remarked: "What is saddest of all is that now such music will no longer be written; somehow they've forgotten the art completely—and how beautiful it was!"

26 February

Today, when I dropped in on Belsky's "at home," I found young Nadezhda Nikolayevna, Nikolai Andreyevich, and the Troitskys there. Everything would have been fine had it not been for a strange incident involving Rimsky-Korsakov. (Even now I cannot fully understand it.) The conversation turned to the second Belyaev concert. When Rimsky-Korsakov announced that they are thinking of including in the program Wihtol's *Feast of Ligo* and Vyshnegradsky's *Vision of St. Anthony*, Vladimir Ivanovich remarked jestingly: "Well, these *are* family affairs." Scarcely had he managed to complete the sentence, when Nikolai Andreyevich flew into a rage and smashed his cigarette holder. (I myself had also had some doubts about the advisability of presenting such unimportant works as those of Vyshnegradsky at the Russian Symphony Concerts, especially since there are so few of these concerts.) With this he proposed that we denounce their decision in the newspapers and not go to the concert. We were dumfounded by this scene. By way of excusing ourselves, we replied that so far as we personally were concerned, it is better not to listen to any music than to listen to bad music. Fortunately, by the time tea was served, everything had calmed down. It is a long time since I have seen Nikolai Andreyevich so agitated, irritated, and resentful.

During tea we talked about the coming State Duma. As Rimsky-Korsakov sees it, the only thing the people can do is to boycott the elections, which are encumbered by restrictions. I totally disagreed.

Besides this, Belsky told us that he has already written eight pages of verse for Rimsky-Korsakov's new opera,[11] and he began to tease me, saying that the whole thing is going to take place in the land of the Naiads; that if I wished, I could easily guess but that for now he can say nothing more about this subject; he hasn't the right.

1 March

Tonight, at the Rimsky-Korsakovs', Nadezhda Nikolayevna and Richter played Scriabin's First Symphony, and Sandulenko sang songs from Max Reger's *Schlichte Weisen,* Sergei Taneyev's song cycle *Ostrovok,* and a number of songs by one Olenine from a cycle entitled *Osen'.* Richter accompanied. Nikolai Andreyevich did not care much for the Reger songs nor those of Olenine but he highly praised Taneyev's cycle.

Just before tea Nikolai Andreyevich told me that although he is captivated by a new subject,[12] he does not know what will come of it. Further, since it is drawn from the Bible, before the Flood, there is one detail which is hardly suitable for the stage.

"By the way, how would you suggest that they be dressed?" he asked with a chuckle. "They all walked around naked in those days, you know."

Then he added, "A fine subject, indeed."

During tea we argued about decadent paintings, Malyavin and his "everlasting red peasant women."[13]

"Evolution, no doubt," remarked Rimsky-Korsakov with a smile. "First they painted pictures of various madonnas; then beauties of all kinds; now they're painting only ugly mugs."

We turned to the subject of the Belyaev concerts, agreeing that, despite the wishes of Belyaev himself, in the future some evenings will have to be devoted to vocal music, since with so many songs being written these days, it would be a great mistake not to present them.

6 March

Thirty-three people came to the Rimsky-Korsakov's tonight to celebrate Nikolai Andreyevich's sixty-second birthday. He received a great many flowers, and Stasov presented him with the latest volume of his collected works.[14]

The conversation turned to politics, Peter Struve's brilliant articles, the vile execution of Lieutenant Schmidt, the workers' boycott of the Duma, etc.

The music began. First Igor Stravinsky played his *Conductor and Tarantula*. After that, Zabela sang a group of Rimsky-Koraskov's songs and, with Sigismund Blumenfeld, the duet and Maria's song from Cui's *William Ratcliff*. Then Sigismund Blumenfeld sang songs by Mussorgsky and Rimsky-Korsakov. Following this, at Stasov's request, Ossovsky, the Blumenfelds, and Nikolai Andreyevich performed Borodin's *Serenade in Honor of a Lady by Four Cavaliers* three times in succession. Tonight Zabela's voice sounded quite good and therefore the singing afforded great artistic enjoyment. To conclude, Felix Blumenfeld and Glazunov played (four hands) the second and third movements from Rimsky-Korsakov's *Antar* and the Scherzo from Borodin's First Symphony.

At two o'clock in the morning we sat down at the table. There were toasts to Nikolai Andreyevich's health and many speeches. The most amusing was Sigismund Blumenfeld's: "You know, gentlemen, I'm finally convinced that, like Mendelssohn, Rimsky-Korsakov was no stranger to sentimentality for, when installing electricity, in his heart of hearts, he really felt sorry for the kerosene." We all burst out laughing.

After supper, when most of the guests had left, Richter (with Felix Blumenfeld accompanying) gave an imitation of a dance by Isadora Duncan. He rushed about wildly to the sounds of a Beethoven Andante, bent down and whirled around in the ludicrous manner of Litvin,[15] after she had drunk the love potion in the first act of *Tristan and Isolde*. Finally, again with Felix Mikhailovich accompanying, Mitusov gave a very clever imitation of a French chansonette singing a fashionable "cakewalk." On the whole, this was an extraordinarily interesting and lively evening.

Incidentally, Maria Nikolayevna Insarova was supposed to have come, but she sent a letter saying that she was ill. I can just imagine what it would be like if she and Zabela were to find themselves at the Rimsky-Korsakovs' at the same time!

23 March

Having read in the newspapers that "Petersburg elected all 160 candidates of the Party of the People's Freedom,"[16] Nikolai Andreyevich sent me the following amusing postcard:

Vasil. Island, Line 5, 34, K.D. Vasily Vasilyevich Yastrebtsev. [Example 66.] 22 March 1906.[17]

Example 66

Po- be di- khom, po-sra-mi-khom, pre-re- ko-khom, pre-re-   ko-khom i pre-pre-khom

I received this note on the morning of March 23.

26 March

Nikolai Andreyevich paid me a visit this afternoon. He was in an excellent mood. At present he is orchestrating and revising cuts he had made in *Boris Godunov* (except for the chiming clock; he has some doubts about whether it is worthwhile working on it.) He has already finished the orchestration of Pimen's Tale and the scene between Dmitri and the Jesuit.

5 April

In the course of talking with Rimsky-Korsakov at his "Wednesday," I learned the following about his work on *Boris Godunov:*

The supplementary scenes which were omitted from the 1896 edition have already been completed and the orchestral manuscript is dated thus:

(1) Scene between Boris and the Tsarevich Feodor ("Chto takoe, ai kysh" and "Popinka"—17–19 March 1906;

(2) Pimen's tale about the Tsars ("Ne setui, brat")—21–22 March;

(3) excerpt from the scene at the fountain between the Pretender and Rangoni ("Net, net otveta")—23–27 March;

(4) excerpt from the scene at the fountain after the Polonaise ("Iezuit lukavyi krepko szhal menia v kogtiakh svoikh prokliatykh")—30–31 March; and finally

(5) "The chiming clock" ("Uf, tiazhelo, dai dukh perevedu. Chto eto tam, v uglu")—31 March to 1 April 1906.

Rimsky-Korsakov has decided to send an autograph of a choral excerpt from *The Tsar's Bride* for the publication being undertaken for the benefit of the unemployed by the Committee of the Trade Unions.[18]

"I think the words of the chorus will be most appropriate to the present moment," he said.[19]

7 May

Rimsky-Korsakov visited me again this afternoon. Nadezhda Nikolayevna and Andrei have already gone to Nauheim,[20] but because of the Conservatory and Volodya's State examinations, Nikolai Andreyevich cannot go to Italy before May 20. He insisted (in jest, of course) that he is writing Mussorgsky's opera *The Marriage,* but he added that when the piano score is published, he intends to put in, here and there, Mussorgsky's own "diacritical marks."

Today Nikolai Andreyevich looked very strong and healthy. He said that at the present moment he is not composing because, as he put it, he "cannot come up with anything" and to repeat the old in a new way is not worthwhile; what is more, he does not wish to. He has put aside his textbook of orchestration until the production of *Kitezh* at the Marinsky Theater. After that, he said, he would like very much to hear *Tsar Saltan* on the Imperial stage.

Finally, chatting about Glazunov, specifically his anthem (to words by N. A. Sokolov),[21] Nikolai Andreyevich remarked, "Evidentally it's impossible to write a truly national anthem, since even someone as gifted as Alexander Konstantinovich has not been able to write anything out of the ordinary."

May 11

As planned, I was at the Rimsky-Korsakovs' tonight from quarter to eight until eleven. Of the family, only Volodya and Troitsky were there.

Nikolai Andreyevich told me that Mussorgsky's *Marriage* is moving ahead, but he does not expect the new version to be better than the old. He admitted that he is very tired and has grown so lazy that he does not even answer all the letters he receives. The political disorders have exhausted him to the point where he has even lost interest in music. He is also sick to death of the Conservatory and its petty squabbles, and he is seriously considering leaving it once and for all. For now what he wants more than anything is to go abroad, to get as far away as possible from all this turmoil, these Trepovykhs, Durnovos, Stishinskys, and co.

Finally, we talked about the diploma Nikolai Andreyevich has received from Stockholm[22] (which none of us could read) and also about Tikhvin, where I intend to go this summer.

"You know, the last time I was in Tikhvin," he said, "was for my father's funeral. He died March 19, 1862, and I haven't been there since then. I can imagine how everything has changed.

"It would be interesting," he continued, "to see whether the former names of parts of the city—Romanikha, Vypolzov, etc.—have been preserved; whether the corridors in the upper part of the monastery wall along which I used to love to run as a child are still intact; whether my father's grave still exists in Tikhvin."

After tea we left together—Rimsky-Korsakov for Glazunov's, I for home.

When we bade good-bye, Nikolai Andreyevich asked me to visit him before he leaves.

22 May

I was at the Rimsky-Korsakovs' from eight o'clock until midnight. They are leaving for Lago di Garda (Italy) on the twenty-fifth or twenty-sixth.

Our conversation touched briefly on politics but soon turned to music. Rimsky-Korsakov believes that music has reached an impasse temporarily but that we can still expect something. This will come, however, only from people reared on the traditions of the period which saw the flowering of Russian music (that is, the Russian music of the past forty to forty-five years). In his opinion, we can expect nothing from the others.

Further, we talked about Rimsky-Korsakov's liberalism.

"While I was sailing on the clipper *Almaz,*" he began, "that is to say, during the years 1862–65, one of the naval cadets from the navigation school named P. A. Mordovin gave me my first taste for reading and when, in the winter of 1862–63, we anchored for four months on the Thames, not far from London, he wanted to introduce me to Herzen, whom he had visited (anyone who wished to could visit the famous publicist). But at the time I wasn't sufficiently developed, and therefore I declined this opportunity. Actually, I didn't have much interest in politics *per se,* and besides I regarded Herzen, compared to me, as too great a 'general' in the field of liberalism.

"As for my lack of faith," he went on, "the story of that is still simpler. My spiritual turning point occurred while I was still in the Navy, without any suffering and almost without any outside influences—by itself, so to speak. The only thing that troubled me was whether my lack of faith was bad or criminal. However, when I learned that Balakirev, Cui, and Stasov—good people—didn't believe in the church's God, my mind was finally put at ease.

"By the way," he added, "you know that after the loss of her daughter, Ludmilla Shestakova also became a nonbeliever."

During tea, Rimsky-Korsakov told me that this summer he would like to orchestrate several of Mussorgsky's songs—*Gopak, Po griby,* and *Kolybel'naia smerti*—and also his own *Anchar* and *Son v letniuiu noch'*.[23]

Besides that, I learned that the vocal score of Dargomyzhsky's *Stone Guest* has already been published and Mussorgsky's *Marriage* has been given to the printer.

After this, Rimsky-Korsakov told me that although, at the request of the priest Lisitsyn, he had joined other composers of sacred music[24] in signing a statement concerning the abolition of the censorship of sacred music, when he actually looked through the compositions of this Lisitsyn, he found them so bad that he suddenly had a terrible desire to ban them.

"The fact is that there are quite a few gentlemen like Lisitsyn," he said. "There are even worse people, but what can we do about them? And so, while in theory one can be vehemently opposed to all censorship, in practice you can want to preserve it, at least when it comes to sacred music."

Rimsky-Korsakov would like to take up his reminiscences once again; there are gaps in the account of the years 1867–72 and 1884–90 as well as in all of the most recent period. After that he will set to work on a diary,[25] as objective as possible, of course, like his "chronicle."

At the end Nikolai Andreyevich reminisced about the first performance of *Kashchei* and the political demonstration he had witnessed on that memorable day, March 27, 1905.

"How unpleasant it is to receive praise you don't deserve," he said. "If only I could have forseen the consequences of my letter to Bernhard—how they would exaggerate its importance—I never would have written it."

Nikolai Andreyevich's parting words to me were: "I would be very grateful and glad if you would come to see me off."

He promised to let me know the day and hour of his departure.[26]

5 September

I dropped in on the Rimsky-Korsakovs'. They had returned on September 2 and on the third, Nikolai Andreyevich went to Stasov's "for Chaliapin," who sang and recited a great deal.

Nikolai Andreyevich talked at length about Riva and Lago di Garda. In Vienna, he heard *Die Meistersinger, Die Walküre, Das Rheingold,* and *Siegfried.* All of the performances went perfectly smoothly; the orchestra was marvelous, he said. He plans to give me part of the orchestral manuscript of

Servilia[27] as a memento of Rome (where he did not go). He told me that he had taken down some Italian songs, which he had heard, but that he has not yet orchestrated *Kashchei.*[28] He did, however, complete the score of his song *Son v letniuiu noch'* (on July 8 [New Style]).

Then Nikolai Andreyevich permitted me a glimpse of his chronicle—from a distance.

"There's even something about you in it,"[29] he said, smiling. "You'll read it after my death. For the time being, not even Nadezhda Nikolayevna has seen it. It's better that way. I'm thinking now of starting a diary."

17 September

When I went to the Rimsky-Korsakovs' this afternoon to congratulate Nadezhda Nikolayevna (the elder), Nadezhda Nikolayevna (the younger), and Sofia Nikolayevna on their name day, I found a number of other guests there. Stasov arrived just as I was leaving. I managed only to shake his hand. This proved to be the last handshake as I never saw him alive again: he died on October 10.

I learned that my article on *Kashchei the Immortal* has been included in Cheshikhin's *History of Russian Opera.*[30]

We spoke briefly about yesterday's *Sadko.*[31] In Nikolai Andreyevich's view Rostovsky (Sadko) has a marvelous voice but he has no understanding of the role and the character he portrays.

11 October

I went to the memorial service for Vladimir Vasilyevich Stasov. Besides me, those attending included Rimsky-Korsakov, N. P. Molas, P. I. Veinberg, the sculptor Ginsburg, Dmitri Stasov, A. V. Vereshchagin, the Blumenfelds, Grigory Timofeyev, and Antokolsky.

Our illustrious "moguchii-bogatyr" ("mighty warrior") lay as though he were alive. His body was removed to the Alexander Nevsky cemetery, where he is to be buried on October 13.

After the service many of us went to Zagorodny.

"It's empty, somehow, without Stasov," remarked Nikolai Andreyevich.

When we went into the study, he showed me the score of *Dubinushka,* which he had just finished today.[32] It was dated "11 October 1906" and bore the postscript: "On 10 October at 10:15 V. Vas. Stasov died."

There was a great deal of music tonight. First Berson, Nadezhda Nikolayevna (the younger), and S. N. Troitskaya sang Rimsky-Korsakov's trio *Strekozy.* Nadezhda Nikolayevna (the elder) accompanied. After that, Zabela sang several songs by M. Steinberg, accompanied by the composer.[33]

Regarding these songs Nikolai Andreyevich observed: "Very skillful and at the same time absolutely concise, which makes them very dear to me. Take note, Vasily Vasilyevich. This is important, very important." Steinberg and Richter then played the former's *Variations* (op. 2).

After tea Zabela sang, in memory of Stasov, his favorite Rimsky-Korsakov song, *Ne penitsia more,* and also *Nimfa.* These were followed by many other songs, including Tchaikovsky's *Kolybel'naia* and Nikolai Andreyevich's *O chem v tishi nochei,* which Igor Stravinsky accompanied.

Besides this, as a joke, Nadezhda Nikolayevna (the younger), Troitskaya, and Nikolai Andreyevich sang, twice in succession, the popular Neapolitan song *Funiculi.*[34]

13 October

I went to the Alexander Nevsky Monastery for the funeral of Vladimir Vasilyevich Stasov. Almost every distinguished mind and talent in Petersburg was there.

The wife of Dmitri Vasilyevich Stasov, Poliksena Stepanovna Stasova, delivered a wonderful, wise, and heartfelt eulogy. Many people cried, I among them. The sculptor Ginsburg spoke at the graveside, as did the music critic Timofeyev.

In our farewell to Stasov, I, along with many others, kissed his cold hand, asleep forever. Leaving the church, I was a pallbearer, but yielded this honor to Balakirev for a while since he, too, wanted to carry the coffin. The grave was adorned with a very effective gonfalon made in the form of a star.

Thus, in this sorrowful way, at the grave of this mighty old man, was marked the fifteenth anniversary of my friendship with Nikolai Andreyevich Rimsky-Korsakov.

At tonight's "musical evening," there was a discussion about Mahler's Fifth Symphony,[35] and it was generally agreed that it is very bad and utterly devoid of genius despite the opinion of the critic Mr. Kolomiitsev.

Nikolai Andreyevich presented me with the new, revised piano score of *The Stone Guest* with the following inscription: "To dear Vasily Vasilyevich Yastrebtsev the regenerated *Stone Guest* from the unregenerate N. Rimsky-Korsakov. 1 November 1906."

After tea, Zabela, Sandulenko, and Sigismund Blumenfeld performed the first act of *Kitezh*. Later, while strolling with Nikolai Andreyevich in the drawing room, I jokingly told him that I had finally found in him, in the words of Salieri, "my enemy!" It was not bad enough that he has written fourteen operas—during the summer he also finished his "chronicle," and with this book, he has completely undermined any future interest there might be in my reminiscences of him. However, I am magnanimous, I added with a smile, and I greet this blow joyously.

I will even say I am happy that such a truthful book has been written.

Before the other guests arrived for this "Wednesday," we talked about Nikolai Andreyevich's new opera, *The Golden Cockerel*. He seems to be terribly pleased that he is composing again, even though many things prevent him from concentrating as he should.

"Now it's as though the book on orchestration never existed," he said.

In further conversation, he expressed surprise that not a single critic praised Krushevsky's performance of Tchaikovsky's Sixth Symphony.[36]

"That's what is meant by bias," he remarked.

He is enraptured with Tchaikovsky's *Francesca*, except for the whirlwind before the *fortissimo* (which he finds rather weak) and the identical scoring of the repeat (which somewhat displeases him, particularly since it was due most likely to the composer's laziness).

Before tea, Richter and Igor Stravinsky played Tchaikovsky's Third Symphony. During tea there was a discussion about whether Borodin had really intended to write an opera on Mey's drama *The Tsar's Bride* and whether he had written any of it. In his biography of the composer, Stasov[37] states that Borodin started such an opera, at the suggestion of

Balakirev, and had composed several first-rate scenes and choruses, the most outstanding being a chorus of the reveling *oprichniki.*

"That's absolutely untrue," said Rimsky-Korsakov. "Borodin never had any finished numbers for *The Tsar's Bride.* He may have played a few measures for Stasov—I don't know anything about that. But I do know one thing—Vladimir Vasilyevich was inclined to consider something finished on the basis of chords he liked or even simply a composer's intention to do it."

After tea, Richter performed some of Arensky's *Variations,* Wihtol's *Berceuse,* and other things. As I was leaving, he and Igor Stravinsky began to play Tchaikovsky's *Voyevoda.*

24 November

I went to the dress rehearsal of the first Russian Symphony Concert,[38] which will be dedicated to the memory of V. V. Stasov. Among those attending, along with the musical youth, were Rimsky-Korsakov, Glazunov, Siloti, and Dmitri Stasov. I heard Glazunov's new prelude "In Memory of Stasov" for the first time.[39] It is a kind of "graveside sob" based on the theme "With Holy Repose." A very interesting and profound piece.

At the end I was invited to the Rimsky-Korsakovs' for Sunday, the twenty-sixth, to hear Chaliapin sing *The Stone Guest.*

When Nikolai Andreyevich bade me good-bye, he said that after hearing the way they played his *Sheherazade* today, he would like to blow his brains out. Noting my bewilderment, he added (not without bitterness), "Then, at least, after my death, perhaps they will play my music with greater respect. Now they always play me carelessly, probably thinking they can take liberties with me, since all of them know me and my character extremely well and know, too, that I won't carp at them. Is it really fair of the members of the orchestra to treat me this way? Don't I deserve better?"

26 November

I was at the Rimsky-Korsakovs' "for Chaliapan" from eight-thirty until four-thirty in the morning. What a wonderful evening!

We had just about decided that Chaliapin was going to let us down, when suddenly at about eleven o'clock, the bell rang and in walked the culprit and the music began.

Feodor Ivanovich sang "in every voice": bass, baritone, tenor, and soprano. He began with the first two scenes of act 1 and continued with part of act 2 (scene with the statue) from Dargomyzhsky's *Stone Guest*, which he had learned for V. V. Stasov. After that came Rimsky-Korsakov's *Mozart and Salieri*, in which he sang both Mozart and Salieri, and finally, Mussorgsky's *Po griby*. Felix Blumenfeld accompanied throughout, and wonderfully. Despite earnest entreaties from Poliksena Stepanovna Stasova and N. F. Pivovarova for *Gopak* and *Seminarist,* Chaliapin flatly refused to sing them.

After a brief rest, he wanted to sing the second scene of the third act of *The Maid of Pskov,* but because Zabela was not quite sure of Olga's part, he did not. What a terrible pity!

On the whole, tonight Feodor Ivanovich was as simple, warm, and affable as could be. As he was leaving, he urged Rimsky-Korsakov to write an opera on the subject of *Oedipus Rex.*

8 December

I went to the dress rehearsal of the second Russian Symphony Concert. They "messed up" Glazunov's Eighth Symphony and played Borodin's *Central Asia* and Steinberg's *Variations* poorly. Only Glazunov's charming violin concerto was given a truly elegant performance (by the violinist Alexander Schmüller).

During the interval I ran into Nikolai Andreyevich. I asked him what he thought of Max Reger,[40] and he replied: "Nothing at all. His fugues are better than his other things, but in our day the ability to write fugues more or less well doesn't indicate a real gift for composition but just the opposite. All in all, I cannot understand what there is to like about this composer."

13 December

The Rimsky-Korsakovs' "Wednesday" went on from about eight-thirty until two o'clock. Before the music, Rimsky-Korsakov returned to me the concluding pages of *Kashchei* with the inscription: "To dear Vasily Vasilyevich Yastrebtsev: the end of the very likely mortal music of *Kashchei the Immortal* as a token of remembrance of the certainly mortal composer Rimsky-Korsakov. 13 December 1906."

Besides this he also gave me the orchestral manuscripts of *Anchar, Gopak,* and *Po griby.* Then we talked about Steinberg's *Rusalka,* which he believes to be magnificent. During my entire acquaintance with Nikolai Andreyevich I have never heard him praise any of the young composers so highly. I was not only very glad but also surprised.

"Moreover," he added, "in addition to being gifted, Maximilian Osseyevich is also a very charming and honorable person."

In the course of the evening, Zimbalist and Richter played Glazunov's Violin Concerto, Zabela sang several of Rimsky-Korsakov's songs, Taneyev played pieces by his idol, Arensky, and Richter concluded with all twenty-two of Rachmaninov's very long *Variations on a Theme by Chopin.*

After Taneyev finished the Arensky pieces, Nadezhda Nikolayevna argued rather heatedly with him about what she considers a lack of originality in Anton Stepanovich's music. While Sergei Ivanovich did not offer any strong defense of Arensky, he insisted that she is wrong, that Arensky's piano pieces are astonishingly fresh and good.

Besides this, I learned that Napravnik had visited the Rimsky-Korsakovs today. This called to mind what Napravnik had said when the staging of *Sadko* was proposed: "It's impossible to put on all of Rimsky-Korsakov's operas—he keeps on composing them year in and year out."

"There you have it," said Nikolai Andreyevich. "No wonder there's not a single one of my operas in the repertoire. To all of them, my operas are only a necessary evil."

Talking of the Korsakov "Chronicle," I urged Nikolai Andreyevich not to procrastinate but to keep a diary and record in it his impressions during the creative process.

I forgot to mention that when I arrived, Rimsky-Korsakov permitted me a glimpse of the orchestral manuscript of part of act 1 of *The Golden Cockerel.* With this, he confided to me that he is beginning again to fear death, as he always does when he is composing something.

"To die suddenly without finishing what you have undertaken would be awfully stupid and lamentable," he added.

Yesterday's orchestral run-through of *Kitezh* drove Nikolai Andreyevich into total despair. First of all, they played extremely carelessly; secondly, the bells sounded abominable—an octave higher and out of tune.[41] Thirdly, the balalaikas were scarcely audible, even though there were twenty-four of them. And what sound they did produce was extremely poor and thin.

"On the other hand, the violins, which entered after them *pizzicato,* sounded regal to me," said Nikolai Andreyevich.

"This is how it is with people," he continued. "You meet them somewhere on a ship or in the country—they're pleasant enough—but then you see them in a more intellectual setting, and they're colorless somehow. The same can be said of balalaikas. They sound good only in Andreyev's orchestra, not in the orchestra of the Marinsky Theater.

"By the way," he continued, "I deeply resent the orchestra players' attitude toward *Kitezh,* and consequently also toward me. Just imagine, at one of the first rehearsals during the 'birds' (in act 1), someone started to whistle and sing along, mimicking both me (my voice, that is) and my music. I became so angry that I wanted to leave the theater and never attend another rehearsal. I don't think that in the course of my entire career, I've ever done anything really bad or reprehensible with regard to music—anything that should cause the gentlemen artists of the Russian Opera to greet a new work of mine, in my declining years, with such hostility and undue familiarity—I'll even say impertinence.

"Of course this could have been nothing more than a childish prank on their part, but was it only that? However that may be, I've always thought—mistakenly, of course—that in view of my past artistic activity, I have the right to expect if not interest, then at least great respect for my works."

Nikolai Andreyevich would like to destroy his book on orchestration. He feels that no one will have any use or need of it.

"Consider for a moment," he said. "Why expatiate on the best way to orchestrate this or that music, when there's no such thing as a 'normal orchestra,' unvarying and obligatory for all theaters, with a minimum complement of instruments beyond whose limits we get negative results? I'll give you an example: In scene 2 of *Sadko,* when the swans are depicted as swimming, the violas are combined with the English horn. Now, in the Marinsky Theater, the violas predominate, but in the People's House, it's the English horn. There the violas are almost completely inaudible; it's as though they weren't even playing. From this you can draw only one conclusion: whatever orchestra you have, there has to be a special orchestration adapted to that orchestra, otherwise it won't sound as it should."

Turning to another subject, Nikolai Andreyevich told me that today, after listening to the first two acts of Tchaikovsky's *Cherevichki,* he was convinced once again how little this music suits the subject. Tchaikovsky's Solokha (at the very beginning of the opera) is a kind of lovely winter idyll, like Grandfather Frost in his *Snegurochka.* The chorus of the *rusalki* (in the ice hole), while charming musically, in no way corresponds to the generally accepted Slavic conception of *rusalki*—and the fault is entirely that of the librettist, the poet Polonsky. Finally, Vakula's beautiful, graceful aria, however good as music, is altogether alien to Gogol and the poetry of the Dikanka stories.

During tea our conversation turned to the subject of *The Golden Cockerel,* which, Nikolai Andreyevich said, is moving along. He is continuing to orchestrate the first act, which was begun on December 10. There is a great deal of caustic humor, even, perhaps, sarcasm in the portrayal of the characters of this fable. The music can be characterized by the words of Berlioz' Mephistopheles: "La bestialité dans toute sa candeur."

Siloti's name came up. They will never be close friends, said Nikolai Andreyevich, because they are people of "different parishes." Alexander Ilyich likes publicity, likes to have his activities talked about.

"I, on the other hand, am not at all interested in that," said Rimsky-Korsakov. "Take, for example, the committee for the celebration of Glazunov's anniversary. Isn't this a kind of publicity? And isn't the organization rather cumbersome for the purpose it's supposed to serve? It's all Siloti's doing."

I was the only guest at Nikolai Andreyevich's tonight, and he seemed pleased that I was observing this traditional annual visit on the nineteenth of December. Just before I left, he maintained again that he is growing old, that he has lost interest in many things, among them politics; that he forgets a great deal—in short, he is becoming increasingly "old and stupid."

"What's going to happen when my real old age comes?" he asked.

We laughed.

CHAPTER 17

1907

13 January

I attended the third Russian Symphony Concert. Except for one number, it was under the direction of N. N. Cherepnin. The program consisted of the introduction to Cui's opera *Le flibustier* and the introduction to his children's opera *The Snow Giant* (the latter a premiere played from the manuscript), W. I. Maliszewski's Second Symphony (also a premiere, conducted by the composer), the first scene from act 4 of N. N. Cherepnin's tragedy *Macbeth,* Rimsky-Korsakov's songs *Nimfa* and *Son v letniuiu noch',* given their premiere in the composer's setting with orchestra (sung by Zabela), and N. V. Artsybushev's Suite in D major (also a premiere played from the manuscript).

After the first two numbers, Cui came out for a bow. Zabela sang *Nimfa* so perfectly that it had to be repeated. Nikolai Andreyevich was recalled twice.

17 January

This afternoon, during my absence, a card arrived from Nikolai Andreyevich with the following message: "[Example 67.] 16 Jan. 1907 N. R.-K."

Example 67

Gde ty, gde ty?

At eight-thirty I went to the Rimsky-Korsakovs'. There were many people, among them the two Stravinsky brothers, N. I. Richter, Zherebtsova and her husband, Mlle Berson, the violinist Zimbalist, and the artist Nikolai Dmitryevich Kuznetsov and his wife.

There was also a great deal of music. Before tea Zherebtsova sang songs by Glazunov and Rimsky-Korsakov, and her husband (N. V. Andreyev) sang Grechaninov's *Stepiu idu ia unyloi* and the first aria from Rimsky-Korsakov's *Sadko*.

After tea Zherebtsova sang all three of Lel's songs from *Snegurochka,* accompanied by Richter, who then performed an étude by Moszkowski, Felix Blumenfeld's Étude in E-flat minor, and Scriabin's Étude in D-flat (for left hand).

Conversing about this and that with Nikolai Andreyevich I learned that he does not care much for the poetry of Fet; he has forbidden the sale of his *Son v letniuiu noch';*[1] he thinks *Nimfa* sounds perfect with the orchestration; *Kitezh* will not be given before February 2; the bells now sound tolerable but the balalaikas have been eliminated from act 2, to the great chagrin of V. V. Andreyev.

At the present time Nikolai Andreyevich is writing the second act of *The Golden Cockerel.* Half of the first act has already been orchestrated.

"I'm sure you'll approve of my *Cockerel,*" he said, "especially Dodon's Sleep."

After this, he talked about Glazunov's Second Symphony. In his opinion the worst parts of it are the Finale and some of the Andante. On the whole, however, he much prefers it to Glazunov's Third Symphony.

"By the way," he continued, "you know, I've already written a greeting piece for Alexander Konstantinovich's anniversary celebration."[2]

The talk about Glazunov led imperceptibly to the subject of Nikolai Andreyevich's work, and he admitted that these days he is doing relatively little composing, as something is always interfering—theater rehearsals, concerts, or chance visitors.

During tea, I sat beside Kuznetsov and had a long talk with him about painting, music (which he loves very much), and his wife, M. N. Kuznetsova-Benois. Nikolai Andreyevich related two amusing anecdotes: one about a cabman, who drove him to the Conservatory, and the other about the French Ambassador. As they were passing the statue of Glinka, Nikolai Andreyevich asked the driver if he knew to whom this monument had been erected. To this the cabman replied, "Of course. This monument was erected to Prince Kholmsky in gratitude for his having laid down his life for the Tsar."

"As you can see," added Rimsky-Korsakov smiling, "this cabman was obviously literate. But what would you say about Bompard? My student, the Argentinian Ambassador Garcia-Mansilia, recently related to me a very amusing conservation he had had with the French Ambassador, Bompard, at one of his receptions. According to Bompard, he is an admirer of mine and likes my music, even though he finds it somewhat old-fashioned. When Garcia-Mansilia took issue with him, saying that, on the contrary, not only have I always been in step with the times, but I'm something of a daring innovator, Bompard began to insist in all seriousness that he's mistaken, that he's obviously confused me with someone else since he, Bompard, knows for a fact that I've been dead for 60 years."(!?)

31 January

This time at the Korsakovs', the music dragged somewhat. Before all the guests arrived, Nadezhda Nikolayevna read through pieces by Debussy and Sibelius. She was followed by Richter, who played Glazunov's *Prelude* in D-flat (op. 25), and a very graceful étude by Liadov (which I did not know). Finally, Zabela sang Maria's song from Cui's *Ratcliff,* Servilia's aria, and Rimsky-Korsakov's *Nimfa.*

Nikolai Andreyevich complained to me again that he is not making any progress with *The Golden Cockerel* because of all the concerts, anniversaries, and rehearsals. Besides this, we argued about Chaliapin and singers in general.

"Since *The Demon* is not especially good," he said, "no Chaliapin is going to make me like it.[3]

"And I'll go even further," he continued, "his enormous talent only points up more forcefully the defects of such music."

Speaking then about the music of *Kitezh,* Nikolai Andreyevich said, "Obviously I'd like the *Legend* to find favor, but if I were to know that it would appeal to everyone without exception, I'd be very distressed, for when a new work is greeted with such universal success, this only indicates that there's something wrong with it."

7 February

The Legend of the Invisible City of Kitezh and the Maiden Fevronia received its first performance (nonsubscription) at the Marinsky Theater on Wednesday, February 7, 1907. The sets of act 1 and scene 1 of act 4 were from sketches by K. A. Korovin and Baron N. A. Klodt; acts 2 and 3 and scene 2 of act 4—from sketches by A. M. Vasnetsov. The costumes were designed by K. A. Korovin; the mise en scène—by the regisseur V. P. Shkafer. The opera was conducted by Felix Blumenfeld.

The performance began at five after eight and ended at twelve-twenty. The choruses were sung poorly; the bells were almost inaudible. Included in the cast were: Filippov as Prince Yury (magnificent); Labinsky—Prince Vsevolod (so-so), Kuznetsova-Benois—Fevronia (good, beautiful, but cold), Yershov—Grishka Kuterma (excellent but a bit too cynical), Sharonov— Feodor Poyarok (so-so), Kastorsky—the *gusli* player (very good), Zabela—Siry (worse than at the rehearsal), and Zbruyeva—Alkonost (good).

Beginning with the first act, the composer was called for insistently, but he did not come out; only the singers took bows. However, Rimsky-Korsakov took nine curtain calls later and he was presented with two wreaths. The opera enjoyed a great success but, as they say, today's was "his public."

11 February

I went to Richter's concert at the Tenshivesky School. Among other things, he played Schumann's *Kreisleriana* and pieces by Grieg, Liadov, Glazunov, Balakirev, Wihtol, Felix Blumenfeld, Scriabin, and Rachmaninov. On the whole, this talented pianist had considerable success.

During the intermission I went to the artist's room, where I saw Rimsky-Korsakov. We talked about the critics' derogatory reviews of *Kitezh* (Kolomiitsev, Nesterov, and others).[4] With this, Siloti remarked, turning to Rimsky-Korsakov, "I asked Kolomiitsev why he wanted to make a fool of himself three times?"

Again today Ossovsky's behavior struck me as somewhat two-faced. On the one hand, he was indigant at the critics for their senseless reviews; on the other, he himself expressed no opinion whatever about *Kitezh*. He even "gossiped" about Timofeyev, telling Nikolai Andreyevich that he could not understand why he (Timofeyev) had felt it necessary to become friendly with Messrs. Ivanov, Baskin, etc.

Speaking with Rimsky-Korsakov about his health, I learned that he has begun to take "lily of the valley" (Convallaria) drops. When I expressed concern about the condition of his heart, he replied jestingly: "All sorts of 'grasses' are good for mankind. By the way, have you noticed that thus far Ossovsky has written nothing about *Kitezh?* This is not accidental."

16 February

I went to *Kitezh* again. The cast was somewhat different: Cherkasskaya was Fevronia (voice good but acting poor), Bolshakov—Prince Vsevolod (better than Labinsky; singing and acting more noble), Davydov—Grishka Kuterma (although he tried he was extremely bad and colorless), Smirnov—Poyarok (so-so but at times off-key), Fried—Otrok (well trained but, unfortunately, her voice is far from what it was), Losev—*gusli* player (fair, but much worse than Kastorsky), Sazonova and Petrenko—Siry and Alkonost (so-so). The performance began at seven-thirty-five and ended at eleven-thirty-five. The theater was completely sold out.

The choruses of act 2 were sung extraordinarily poorly. Given such performances it should come as no surprise if the opera is dropped. By the way, tonight, the bells were sufficiently audible at all times, but they were played horrendously!

In the course of the evening, Rimsky Korsakov was recalled six times.

27 February

After tea tonight, Nikolai Andreyevich and I had a long talk about *Kitezh,* in the course of which he expressed his thoughts about it. First of all, he considers acts 1 and 4 his best; he is very pleased with the part of Fevronia. On the whole, he considers the orchestration good, but he has definitely decided to eliminate the balalaikas and domras in the new edition of the score, as they are totally inaudible. Also, the new score will call for five-valve tubas instead of four-valve.

Following this we discussed the singers' dislike of the opera, and Nikolai Andreyevich told me that the February 19 performance had been cancelled because of the illness of Cherkasskaya and the "feigned" illness of Kuznetsova-Benois, who did not want to sing in it.

"How little these people understand great art," I remarked.

"On the other hand, I'm pleased about Cui," he said, and he handed me a letter César Antonovich had sent him the day after the premiere. It read: "Dear Nikolai Andreyevich! Yesterday I could understand a great deal, and it goes without saying this crowned my enjoyment. An original and remarkably integrated work. All praise to you! Yours, C. Cui. 8 Febr."

In conclusion, I learned that little progress has been made with *The Golden Cockerel* and also that in May, Nikisch is going to perform the following of Rimsky-Korsakov's works in Paris: the suite form *Christmas Eve*, Lel's first two songs from *Snegurochka,* the suite from *Saltan,* act 3 of *Mlada* (in concert arrangement), and the underwater kingdom of *Sadko*. In all likelihood, Rimsky-Korsakov will not go there ("he doesn't feel like it"), even though Diaghilev has been urging him to.[5]

The time had come to leave, and we had already started to say good-bye, when suddenly Nikolai Andreyevich remembered the wreath he had received at the premiere of *Kitezh* and began to excuse himself and to thank me (and through me, the others who had joined in presenting it).

"See, *you* brought me a wreath for my opera," he said jokingly, "but the gentlemen of the press—Kolomiitsev, Nesterov, and Petrovsky—I didn't please at all."[6]

3 March

I was at the Marinsky Theater for the thirtieth performance of *Sadko* (nonsubscription). The theater was filled to overflowing. The Rimsky-Korsakovs were seated in a second tier box.

Felix Blumenfeld conducted and, therefore, the dances and songs of the *skomorkhi* were extraordinarily fast. The opera was given with the usual cuts. When will we ever hear the finale of *Sadko* in its entirety?

The sets for scenes 5 and 6 were excellent. Included in the cast were Yershov as Sadko (good), Markovich—Lyubava (also good), Zbruyeva—Nezhata (fairly good), Bukhtoyarov and Ugrinovich—Duda and Sopiel, Serebryakov—Viking Guest (rather course), Chuprynnikov—Indian Guest (good), Tartakov—Venetian Guest (good), Filippov—Sea King (fair), Paskhalova—Princess Volkhova (quite tolerable), and Losev—the Apparition (not bad).

Today, for the first time, the bell in the scene at Sadko's house sounded perfect. How beautiful it was!

11 March

Tonight at the Rimsky-Korsakovs' a quartet composed of Volodya and Andrei Nikolayevich Rimsky-Korsakov, M. O. Steinberg, and Naum Ilyich Sheinin performed works by Borodin, Haydn, Cherepnin, and Beethoven. Besides this, Steinberg played his new F-major *Procession,* written in honor of Glazunov's jubilee.

We talked about *Sadko* and Nikolai Andreyevich offered the following opinions about it: he likes the transition to scene 6; the chorus in honor of Nikola; the passage, in scene 3, when Sadko recalls the Sea Princess; Volkhova the Beautiful (violin solo); the song of the Indian Guest; the end of the Lullaby, etc., but he finds the gusli player's song in the first scene too thickly orchestrated and considers this an undeniable flaw in the *bylina.* Besides this, he prides himself on the fact that he was able to incorporate church music in an opera.

In all this time Liadov has not said a single word about *Kitezh.* This distresses Nikolai Andreyevich.

During tea we talked about the fact that Rachmaninov is highly overrated as a composer; also that Rimsky-Korsakov recently attended a rehearsal of Wagner's *Die Walküre* and this time he liked it very, very much.

I forgot to mention that he has already played some of *The Golden Cockerel* (music of the "fog" from scene 2) for Belsky.

"When I show you these diminished seventh chords over augmented triads (despite the seeming unbelievability of this combination)," he said, "I think you'll also like them, since I know that you're a great admirer of my music."

He laughed.

"By the way," he continued, "when you listen to *The Golden Cockerel,* note how increasingly thick the orchestration becomes with each act and that the Astrologer is the 'Someone in Gray,' as it were, of this opera-fable."

We were already in the entrance hall when Rimsky-Korsakov informed me that his eyes are deteriorating noticeably. Sometimes, for no apparent reason (after a long rest, for example) he sees a sort of green halo around a light (a candle or lamp)—a mixture of F-sharp major, E minor, and E major.

Besides this, I learned that Nikolai Andreyevich is not keeping a diary.[7] He cannot manage it somehow; he is too busy with other things. What a terrible pity!

8 April

I was at the Rimsky-Korsakov's for another quartet evening. Besides me there were Zimbalist, Sheinin, Igor Stravinsky, and Steinberg. First they played the first movement of Steinberg's Quartet no. 1 (in A). The music is charming, though the beginning of the coda is somewhat "cerebral" (perhaps Maximilian Osseyevich is still reworking this place). This was followed by Glazunov's *Suite* for string quartet (op. 35) with the "Orientale" and "Mistico."[8] During the "Orientale," Nikolai Andreyevich remarked jestingly that in this number "the East is everywhere," as Kuzma Prutkov would say, and it is the most Eastern of all Eastern music. Following the *Suite,* they played Franz Schubert's Quartet in A minor and, finally, Glazunov's Quartet no. 5.

During tea there was a discussion about last night's party at the Conservatory, at which everyone got drunk and most of them drank to "Brüderschaft." In fact, Verzhbilovich was so "tipsy" that he went around kissing the students' hands. Nikolai Andreyevich was outraged by this story.

"Before, there was no autonomy," he said, "and there wasn't any drunkeness at the Conservatory. They received autonomy and they've turned the Conservatory into a saloon. How disgusting! And worst of all—rumors of this unfortunate incident can reach the press, and then there won't be any way to counter their attacks on the Conservatory, because it's the absolute truth. I must confess, sadly, that evidently our young Russian students are still too immature for real freedom. And how immature they are!"

After tea we went into the drawing room, where the conversation about the senseless goings-on at the Conservatory continued.

"The reason for all this," explained Nikolai Andreyevich, "is that Glazunov literally became exhausted and let everything get out of hand. It will be interesting to see who will be able to put things right again. This is the way the young people have expressed their appreciation to Alexander Konstantinovich for his extreme kindness and tolerance and also, since he is in no particular need of money, for having renounced forever his Director's salary for the benefit of poor Conservatory students. Who but Glazunov would have done that? No one, of course."

The Rimsky-Korsakovs are going to Paris on April 27–28 and will return between May 20 and 25.

18 April

This evening the Rimsky-Korsakovs had a special gathering for the performance of *The Golden Cockerel*. Besides me there were Mikhail Rimsky-Korsakov, V. I. Belsky, M. Steinberg, and Igor Stravinsky, to whom Nikolai Andreyevich presented the orchestral manuscript of the "Musical Pictures" from *Tsar Saltan* on the occasion of his (Stravinsky's) works having been performed.[9]

Steinberg played the first act of the opera. It lasted fifty or fifty-five minutes. Particularly good are: the Introduction, the "entrance of the astrologer" (juxtaposition of the tonalities: E and F major, C and D-flat major, A-flat and A major, etc.), the housekeeper Amelfa, the very beginning of whose theme is borrowed partly from a folk song (see Balakirev's collection, no. 33, "Kak po lugu, po luzhochku"), the ravishingly harmonized "parrot," and finally, the gorgeous music of Dodon's sleep, representing a kind of lullaby of official Oblomovshchina.[10] Also very interesting is the fancifully exquisite characterization of the Queen of Shemakhan and the extremely daring (harmonically) "cockerel."

"Well, dear friend," said Nikolai Andreyevich, when we were finally alone. "What do you think? Is it worth going on?"

"Very much so," I replied.

But at this point Igor Feodorovich came in and the conversation was broken off.

27 May

This afternoon I received a postcard from Nikolai Andreyevich: "Dear Vasily Vasilevich, where are you? I am here, that is, in Petersburg. Yours, N. R.-K. 26 May 1907."

Accordingly, this evening I went to Zagorodny, Liadov was there. Later Sofia Nikolayevna dropped in.

They talked about Paris[11] and the Russian Concerts,[12] which were given May 16/3, 19/6, 23/10, 26/13, and 30/17.[13] I congratulated Rimsky-Korsakov on his glittering success. And indeed, according to him, he and Chaliapin enjoyed the greatest success; Borodin and Mussorgsky—less; Glinka and Tchaikovsky—the least of all.

"The concerts were long," said Rimsky-Korsakov, "and therefore, unfortunately, Tchaikovsky's Fourth Symphony and Liadov's folk songs (for orchestra) had to be dropped. Actually, in view of their brevity, the songs could have been played in their entirety at the second concert.

"You know," he continued, "in Paris, the director of the theater[14] is at the same time the chief regisseur. He's always appointed from among the former artists, which can only prove beneficial to the enterprise. It's not like this in our country, where people totally unrelated to music are often appointed to the directorship of the theaters."

Rimsky-Korsakov also reported to me that Saint-Saëns, Bourgault-Ducourdray, and others have no use whatsoever for the music of Richard Strauss. They call him the "arrogant calf."

"And so," he said, "we Russian composers were looked upon as some sort of Mozarts compared with Strauss, Debussy, and Dukas. Incidentally, the latter two have an interesting way of orchestrating. And this is their undeniable virtue."

Further, Nikolai Andreyevich told me that he had been introduced to Richard Strauss at Colonne's, but he had exchanged scarcely a word with him.

"There wasn't anything to talk about," he said. "They say that after the first concert, after hearing the first act of *Ruslan,* the first act of *Prince*

Igor, and the suite from *Christmas Eve,* Strauss remarked: 'This is all very well, but unfortunately, we are no longer children.'

"In the opinion of these gentlemen," added Rimsky-Korsakov, "Mozart is one thing and they—another. Two poles of art."

Besides this, we chatted about Scriabin and the two recitals and seven special music-choreographic evenings and other mysteries conceived by him.[15]

"Isn't he really going out of his mind from religio-erotic madness?" asked Nikolai Andreyevich. "All this preaching of his about a physical and spiritual union with the godhead is as unintelligible as his idea of creating a temple of art in India, right on the banks of the sacred Ganges. Doesn't all this really border on madness?

"I also heard his *Poem of Ecstasy,*" he continued, "on the piano, it's true. It may be very powerful, but all the same, it's a kind of musical V-I!"

Rimsky-Korsakov then told us that while in Paris he went neither to the Russian colony, where he was supposed to meet Skrydlov, nor to the reception at the home of Grand Duke Paul Alexandrovich, to which he also was invited (and where Chaliapin sang his *Prorok*), nor to Grand Duchess Maria Pavlovna's box. After this, Taneyev, who had been playing up to the Rimsky-Korsakovs all this time, suddenly grew cold to them.

"On the other hand," he said, "I did go to Saint-Saëns', Colonne's, and other's, and during the visit to Paris I gave out a lot of autographs.

"Just imagine," he continued, "from conversation with the French I learned that Berlioz has largely 'had his day' there. The only thing they still go to is *The Damnation of Faust,* and the only when it's performed by first-class musicians."

Finally, Rimsky-Korsakov said that in the fifth act of *Khovanshchina,* despite the great fascination with his name, Chaliapin had a very dubious success.

"By the way," he said suddenly, "did you know that Glazunov received two doctorates of music simultaneously; one from Cambridge University and the other from Oxford?"

During tea we talked about the dacha in Lyubensk (Bukharova's estate) near Vechasha, where the Rimsky-Korsakovs are going this year (they have invited me).

Shortly before I left, Nikolai Andreyevich informed me that he has almost decided definitely to leave the Conservatory, for he finds the non-sensical goings-on there extremely irritating and distressing.

"Then, at least, I won't see all this," he said. "And I'll be better off."

Besides this, he said that somehow he has fallen behind with *The Cockerel,* and therefore the first thing he is going to do when he arrives at the dacha will be to score act 2. But he will not go any further with the writing of the opera until his heart is really in it.

Visit to Lyubensk (28–30 August 1907)

28 August

Andrei Rimsky-Korsakov and I left Petersburg this afternoon at five after four and arrived at Plyuss at ten in the evening. From there we drove in a troika to Lyubensk. It was dark; stars glittered only rarely here and there.

The Rimsky-Korsakovs, who had been expecting their son Vladimir, too, were slightly diappointed at first that he had not come, but their mood soon changed to one of pleasure at seeing Andrei and me.

After tea Nikolai Andreyevich informed me that he will definitely finish *The Golden Cockerel* tomorrow, since all that remains is to make a fair copy of two pages and double the voices in the score here and there. We talked about the new beginning of the opera and the major importance of act 2 (in a musical sense).

We said good night at quarter past twelve but I did not fall asleep until two o'clock. I had been given Nikolai Andreyevich's study. There, on the writing table, lay the orchestral score of *The Golden Cockerel,* so, having been granted permission by Nikolai Andreyevich, before going to sleep, I went through it noting down the chronology of its composition.

29 August

I awoke at about six o'clock but did not get up until quarter to seven. It was a gray morning, but by eight o'clock it began to clear up a bit. At quarter to nine the sun came out, and Nikolai Andreyevich appeared. We went into the dining room and drank coffee.

We talked about Diaghilev, and Nikolai Andreyevich told me that next spring (1908) he would like to give *Sadko* in Paris (with cuts). Of *Boris Godunov,* he will present only the Coronation scene; the Inn scene; the scene at the fountain and that of Boris' death (omitting scene 1); the scene with Pimen; the act at Marina's castle and the scene in the forest near Kromy. He is afraid that otherwise the French will not appreciate these works, since they do not like long operas.

"You see," said Rimsky-Korsakov, "later on, when people will be even more high-strung, long operas like *Sadko* and *Ruslan* will be given on two evenings. As a matter of fact, in the future they will cease to perform works in their entirety but will make orchestral arrangements of the best of the music, adapting their arrangements to the public's taste and demands, as Liszt did with his piano transcriptions of the great masters."

After this we went into the garden. Vechasha,[16] Lake Pesno, and the village of Andromer were clearly visible. The Lyubensk garden itself is charming, with its many beautiful avenues, wonderful, ancient oaks, sixteen of which form something like an arbor; near the house, huge, majestic ash trees; bushes of white acacia; entire avenues of lilacs, asters, fragrant sweet peas, nasturtiums, pansies; in front of a round pond, an enormous bed of tobacco plant; an avenue of birch trees; and, finally, not far from the house, to the left, a small linden-lined avenue, thick with acacia, which I liked terribly and from this time was called "my" garden. All this was extraordinarily beautiful.

Thus, Rimsky-Korsakov is a land-owner(!), proprietor of twenty *desiatiny*[17] of land (nine for farming and eleven for a garden). I congratulated him with all my heart on this marvelous purchase.[18] Walking through "my" avenue, we talked about literary pornography and the reasons for it; also about the fact that these days, composers like Glazunov and Scriabin receive up to two thousand rubles and more for their symphonies, almost as much as is paid for a whole opera. We agreed that this is not normal.

At ten-thirty, Rimsky-Korsakov set about completing *The Golden Cockerel.* He had only to finish writing the last twenty-six measures. I strolled about the garden again, this time with Andrei, and then we were shown two small cannons ("Dodon's cannons," we called them) which had belonged at one time to the former owners, the Bukharovs.

At noon we sat down to lunch. Shortly afterward Nikolai Andreyevich appeared. He had just finished *The Cockerel.* At Nadezhda Nikolayevna's suggestion we greeted him with loud applause. The only one who at first refused to join us was their charming three-year-old granddaughter, Irisha (the Troitsky's little daughter), but after we explained to her in comprehensible language what was going on, she joyfully joined in.

After lunch Nikolai Andreyevich played through all of act 3 of the opera twice. The music is surprisingly interesting and original, with a great deal that is extraordinarily daring (for example, the procession of the "truly Eastern people"; the episode at the Astrolger's words: "I poprobuiu zhenit'sia"; the moment when King Dodon kills the Astrologer; and finally, when the Cockerel pecks Dodon's head).

When I remarked that, judging from this opera, Nikolai Andreyevich is truly a master of harmony, he replied jokingly: "This is as it must be. A composer must be in full command of his tonal forces, otherwise they will master him. Bear in mind that like a composer without knowledge, so music—especially daring harmonies—is no good at all without clear part writing, since when harmonies are complicated and tricky, part writing is everything."

From further conversation, I learned that Rimsky-Korsakov has not served as a "Belyaev executor" since May 1 (1907); that he had named to replace him N. V. Artsybushev, a man of "business," a jurist by profession, and, according to Nikolai Andreyevich, a fine musician. Also, he does not know when his new opera will be published (not by Jurgenson?) because the "Belyaev people" have no money.

Speaking then about *The Golden Cockerel,* Rimsky-Korsakov said that he is tired of bizarre harmony and the so-called "newest style" in general; that he composed this opera as, at one time he had *Kashchei the Immortal,* almost solely, to show that "he could do it, too," but now he would like to write an opera expressly for the voice, though, of course, with a sumptuous orchestral accompaniment. In addition, he wants to compile a short textbook of orchestration and also to write a number of articles on the subject of descriptive music and operatic forms and styles.

Finally, Rimsky-Korsakov read to me letters from Telyakovsky and Felix Blumenfeld, informing him that next season they plan to give *Kitezh* ten times.

We said good night at quarter to twelve. I looked through some of the score again, read the text of acts 2 and 3, and also copied off the following notes made by Nikolai Andreyevich. "Records of the voices of nature": midges hum in the key of F sharp; bees, in B; beetles, in D; bumblebees in C or C sharp (see examples 68 and 69).

Example 68

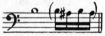

Example 69

30 August

I rose at seven-thirty. The morning was cool but sunny. Everyone was still asleep. At nine o'clock Nikolai Andreyevich came out. We talked about the daring harmonies in the third act of *The Golden Cockerel*. How audacious it all is and at the same time how profoundly logical!

After coffee, Nikolai Andreyevich played all of act 2 of *The Golden Cockerel*. There are many splendid things in it.

"I wanted this act to be the most interesting," he said, "and I think I've succeeded.

"Isn't that so?" he asked half-jokingly. "Music can be very good, even without false profundities." We laughed.

Nikolai Andreyevich is obviously pleased with the music of the tale of the Queen of Shemakhan ("Mezhdu morem i nebom visit ostrovok"), with its comical "siskin" (on the bassoons) and minor thirds at the words "Gromche, tishe. Dal'she, blizhe." As for the theme, which had been played by Mussorgsky and borrowed by Rimsky-Korsakov in the scene of Dodon's dance, first of all, it has been altered somewhat chromatically and secondly, there will be an annotation about it in the piano reduction.

In the afternoon, Rimsky-Korsakov played his very interesting and beautiful altered version of the introduction to the first act of *The Golden Cockerel*. So far as I can judge, there will be a great deal of music for the clarinet and celesta in this opera, with the part of the Queen of Shemakhan predominating (in a purely musical sense and in scope as well) even though Pushkin devoted only a few words to her ("Vdrug shater raspakhnulsia, i devitsa—Shemakhanskaia tsaritsa, vsia siiaia, kak zaria, tikho vstretila tsaria"). One can only marvel, I said, at Belsky's talent; at how skillfully and cleverly he was able to extend the walls of even such highly artistic works as those of Pushkin; how, from the poet's single fleeting (brilliant, it's true) detail, he created the charming, richly hued, capricious character of the Queen of Shemakhan.

While walking through the garden, Nikolai Andreyevich started talking about how in his heart of hearts he often feels that he is a "confirmed kuchkist"; that he is profoundly imbued with the precepts of *Boris Godunov* and *The Stone Guest*. Also, he prides himself on the fact that he had not believed there is only one true operatic form but had offered in his music a number of different solutions to this complicated artistic problem.

"In a certain sense Saint-Saëns and even Massenet are 'kuchkists,' " he continued. "What's more, Tchaikovsky's *Queen of Spades* also conforms to the principles of the 'kuchka.' And these principles are the following: (1) an intelligible and interesting libretto, (2) artistic truth, and (3) intelligent utilization of all the rich resources of today's orchestra and harmony, while at the same time giving primary importance (predominance) to the voice."

On another subject, I learned that Nikolai Andreyevich has declined the title Doctor of Music, offered him by the British (though, of course, he thanked them for wanting to honor him).

"I personally find such titles as 'Councillor of State' and even 'Professor' slightly offensive," he said. "If there's anything good about me, it's only that I am 'I', Nikolai Andreyevich Rimsky-Korsakov, not that I hold this or that title, even if it were a scientific one. Every title, essentially, is nothing more than an empty phrase."

After that, Nikolai Andreyevich told me that at Glazunov's request and not wanting to upset him, he plans to remain at the Conservatory for another two years or so, but then he will leave.

Before dinner we sat outside the gates to the estate for a long time, admiring the view. Nikolai Andreyevich wants very much, he said, if only once more in his life, to visit Tikhvin, where he has not been since his childhood.

Our conversation turned again to *The Golden Cockerel*. He is very glad that I like it. We talked about the second half of act 2, noting that it is something like the enchanted, fairytale kingdom of the Peri in *Antar;* that the chorus "Tvoi vernye kholopy" in act 3, based on a Russian folk theme (see Rimksy-Korsakov's collection, no. 21: "Vkrug kusta, kusta, rakitova kustika"), is a *lubok*[19] perfectly embodied in sounds; that the harmonies of the final chorus are strikingly original, as are those at the beginning of act 2 at the words, "Mesiatsa bagrovy shchit," to say nothing of the "harmonies of the fog" (pp. 96–97 of the piano score). Finally, we agreed that an author must absolutely love his heroes.

Nikolai Andreyevich told me that he will not be returning to Petersburg until around September 10.[20]

On our way to the house, as we passed the "Korsakov" ash tree, Nikolai Andreyevich said, "Just look at this wonderful tree; it's positively fresh. Its leaves aren't yellow yet, but it has only to sense the approach of the frost and suddenly, at once, its leaves will fall."

The train left at six-thirty and therefore they served me dinner at four o'clock. Rimsky-Korsakov kept me company at the table, while Nadezhda Nikolayevna paced the room. Saying good-bye to me, Nikolai Andreyevich embraced me warmly and thanked me for having visited him. As a memento he presented me with four pages of the manuscript of *The Golden Cockerel.* I was very pleased with my visit to Lyubensk.

31 August

Upon returning from Lyubensk, I went to the fifth performance of *The Legend of the Invisible City of Kitezh.* The cast included the following: Filippov—Prince Yury (worse than usual), Labinsky—Young Prince Vsevolod (rather bad), Cherkasskaya—Fevronia (so-so), Davydov—Grishka (poor and colorless), Sharonov—Feodor (passable), Markevich—Otrok (excellent), Losev—the *gusli* player (not bad), Zabela—Sirin (did not hold the high notes), and Petrenko—Alkonost (tolerable). Shkafer is not yet in Petersburg, and therefore the directing side left much to be desired.

The performance ended exactly at midnight. The theater was not full; the opera scored only a moderate success.[21] The performance was lifeless; the choruses at times sang abominably. Although the bells were audible, they were played out of tune and not in their proper place. For some reason Blumenfeld accelerated the tempi terribly in the bell scene. Besides this, the "pipe of paradise" was played by a tromba piccola[22]—the effect was not bad but certainly not ideal.[23]

23 September

Learning by post that the Rimsky-Korsakovs had returned from Lyubensk, I went to Zagorodny this evening. Steinberg was also there.

The piano reduction of *The Golden Cockerel* has been completed. Act 2 is dated 10 September, and act 3—13 September. As we see, the last act was transcribed by Rimsky-Korsakov in three days. What colossal speed! The introduction now begins with the Cockerel's theme of the first type—"Tsarstvui, lezha na boku."[24]

Tonight Nikolai Andreyevich looked tired, rather pale and his face seemed drawn. Before and after tea, Steinberg played the second and third acts of the opera. When he came to the "music of the fog" (act 2), Rimsky-Korsakov remarked that "this is a sop to decadence"; that when playing it on the piano, it is necessary to use a soft pedal and that perhaps he will revise this passage.

During tea we talked about Serov's *Judith*, which, in Rimsky-Korsakov's opinion, except for a few brief "musical oases," is so crude, inept, and trite (including even Holofernes) as to be worthy of Mikhail Ivanov. Exceptions, perhaps are the Chorus of the Odalisques, some of the March, and Vagao's song "Lublu tebia, mesiats."

"I don't imagine anyone would dispute the fact that the 'Borodin dances' (from *Igor*) utterly destroyed their prototype," remarked Nikolai Andreyevich. (It appears that he knows *Judith* very well and remembers it in every detail.)

Finally, Nikolai Andreyevich does not think that the tromba piccola is good enough for the part of the "pipe of paradise" in *Kitezh,* so as soon as Belsky has heard it, he is going to take it out.

22 October

Steinberg called for me at about half past seven and we went to the Rimsky-Korsakovs'. First Steinberg and Nikolai Andreyevich looked through the beginning of the Finale of the former's quartet. Then Volodya and

Steinberg played a violin sonata by Mozart, and Nikolai Andreyevich and I went into the study. I leafed quickly through Rimsky-Korsakov's new Italian song for orchestra (op. 63), which was finished on October 19 of this year and is based on Denza's *Funiculi*. I also looked through the orchestral manuscript of Mussorgsky's *Lullaby* ("Spi, usni, krestianskii syn"), which Rimsky-Korsakov had revised somewhat and orchestrated in Riva on June 17, 1906.

We got into a discussion about operatic styles, a rather sore subject for Rimsky-Korsakov since he has been reproached many times because till now he has not been able to settle upon and work out one of his own.

"But what if I simply don't want to?" he asked. "I've never believed nor do I now that there's only one true operatic form. Considering how many subjects there are in the world, there ought to be as many (almost) forms suited to them."

Further, I learned that the singer Zbruyeva would like to set up a society in Petersburg like Kerzin's in Moscow to acquaint singers with the song literature of earlier and contemporary composers, for, generally speaking, the repertoire of our singers is extremely limited and tasteless.

During tea we talked about the "dirty tricks" of our so-called critics, about the resignation of M. D. Nesterov and N. D. Bernstein from the newspaper *Tovarishch* and also about the formation of a Union of Writers on Music,[25] where, for some reason, Grigory Nikolayevich Timofeyev turned up.

After tea Steinberg played the second act of *The Golden Cockerel*. What a world of the new and original! Besides this, he and Nikolai Andreyevich played (four hands) the frivolous (as Nikolai Andreyevich calls it) *Neapolitan Song*. Pleasant music but nothing more.

31 October

I was at the Rimsky-Korsakov's first "Wednesday" of the season from eight-thirty until one-fifteen. The guests included Zabela-Vrubel, the Stravinsky brothers, Steinberg, K. O. Berson, Ossovsky, and Belsky. A conversation arose about Mahler and his (ungifted and) tasteless symphony with its extremely coarse and cumbersome orchestration. "Evidently he was contemplating the universe," remarked Rimsky-Korsakov jokingly.

"You simply can't imagine," he continued, turning to me (I had not heard this symphony), "what kind of a work it is. It's sort of a pretentious improvisation on paper, in which the composer himself doesn't know what his next measure will be. It's a pity, really, for him as a musician. In truth, he's a house painter.[26] Far worse than Richard Strauss."

After that, someone mentioned that the Solodovnikov Theater in Moscow had burned down yesterday and with it all the scenery, costumes, and orchestral instruments.

Nikolai Andreyevich told us that he signed a contract with Diaghilev.

"You know," he said, "next May they're going to give *Boris Godunov* at the Grand Opéra with Russian singers, and in October (1908)—the first, second, fourth, fifth, and sixth scenes of *Sadko,* in French. As for *Snegurochka* at the Opéra comique, they're having some difficulty with it. Bessel is asking fifteen thousand francs for the production rights, forgetting that at present a Wagner cult has developed among the French like the Brahms cult among the Germans."

During tea, Nikolai Andreyevich related an incident that had occurred recently with the singer Yershov.

"The other day I was at the Marinsky Theater on some business," he said, "and, as I came out from backstage, I unexpectedly ran into Yershov. We had hardly managed to exchange greetings, when suddenly, for no apparent reason, he mumbled, as he passed by: 'You know, Nikolai Andreyevich, you write awkwardly for the voice. You'd do better if, when composing opera, you'd consult us singers!' "

After this there was a discussion about the outrageously complicated orchestration of Balakirev's *Islamey,* made by some harpsichordist named Casella.[27] Seemingly, it met with the approval of Balakirev, even though it calls for brasses, which runs counter to the character of Eastern music.

"This kind of instrumentation is alien to me," observed Nikolai Andreyevich. "I myself would have done it much more simply."

After tea, Igor Stravinsky and Steinberg played Grieg's *Norwegian Dances* and Nadezhda Nikolayevna (the younger) sang Balakirev's *Pustynia* and Stravinsky's *Pastorale,* which he had dedicated to her on October 29, the day he composed it. (An original song but with strange harmonies.) Next, Stravinsky presented his new song "Zvony, stony, perezvony"[28] (to words by Gorodetsky). It has beautiful music in the middle but a very strange beginning. It automatically called to mind the following anecdote about the poet Apukhtin:

"Mama," asked the child upon seeing the incredibly corpulent figure of the poet, "is that a man or just pretending?"

Surely one could ask the same thing about the orgy of sounds at the beginning of Stravinsky's song. "Is that music or just pretending?"

Nadezhda Nikolayevna also sang four of Rimsky-Korsakov's "sea-songs" and, finally, Zabela sang two songs by Steinberg—*Lesnye travy* and *Poslednii luch*. After listening to them, Rimsky-Korsakov turned to me and commented, "They're delicate, elegant, and at the same time daring, aren't they? Not like Rachmaninov."

Zabela remarked that Steinberg's songs are particularly easy to sing, unusually grateful for the voice, to which Nikolai Andreyevich replied, jestingly, "Not like mine." We all burst out laughing.

From conversation with Maximilian Osseyevich, I learned that the purchase of Lyubensk has not yet been finalized. How long everything takes here in Russia!

By the way, I also learned that *The Golden Cockerel* is going to be given on the Imperial stage next season.[29]

4 November

I was at the Rimsky-Korsakov's for their second quartet evening. The players were Mestechkin (first violin), Volodya (second violin), M. Steinberg (viola), and Andrei (cello). They played Beethoven's Second Quartet, a quartet by Grieg, and Glazunov's Quartet no. 4.

Nikolai Andreyevich and I had a talk about Sibelius' Third Symphony.[30] He rather liked the first and second movements.

"It sounds different, somehow, not like our music, and this is good," he said. "Therefore, there's no need for me to write the textbook of orchestration.

"And yet," he added, "maybe this originality is purely superficial and no more remarkable than it is that from the day he's born, the French peasant speaks French, not Russian. Who knows?

"Take Grieg," he continued, "he's pretty monotonous, yet he's original and therefore good. I'm beginning to value originality in a composer. I myself am writing now as I did before, and that's not good. If my *Cockerel* could have made its appearance in the eighties, it would have been contemporary. I really think I'm living too long. Art is moving in a different direction, and something else is needed now.

"Besides," he concluded, "I know perfectly well that my *Snegurochka* is worth more than all my other operas, since when I composed it, I wasn't straining after anything. Then there followed, as you know, a rather protracted lull—from 1882 until 1894 (I don't count *Mlada*)—and it wasn't until *Christmas Eve* that I came alive again for creative work."

From further conversation I learned that Nikolai Andreyevich has composed two passages to be inserted in scene 2 at the Paris production of *Boris Godunov*. For them he has used the themes of the "glorification" and the "bells" (the manuscript is dated 14 September 1907).

In Rimsky-Korsakov's opinion, Igor Stravinsky's talent has not yet become sufficiently defined. For example, in the fourth movement of his First Symphony, he is still imitating Glazunov too much, and in his new songs (to words by Gorodetsky) he has embraced modernism too zealously.

11 November

After dinner at Fried's, I went to Rimsky-Korsakov's for another evening of quartets. Following one of Beethoven's "Razumovsky" quartets (op. 59), they played Smetana's quartet "From My Life," and Glazunov's so-called Slavic quartet.

When the music ended, Nikolai Andreyevich told us that at yesterday's Shröder concert,[31] Nezhdanova sang Oxana's first aria from *Christmas Eve* without the third clarinet and he has written Shroeder about this.

"This aria of mine was orchestrated elegantly," he said, "but owing to the absence of the third clarinet, the accompaniment sounded empty and ugly in places."

There was a great deal of talk about Steinberg. According to Rimsky-Korsakov, like Glazunov, he has never written like a student.

"Maximilian Osseyevich has enormous talent," he said. "There's nothing to fear about his future as a composer."

After this he reported that both insertions for *Boris Godunov* had been orchestrated by November 7 and sent to the printer; also that *Russkaia muzykal'naia gazeta* (no. 45) has published his views on the question of the simplified score.[32]

The conversation turned to the subject of the latest music of Messrs. Strauss, Reger, and others of that kind. Nikolai Andreyevich believes that their music represents nothing more than a "shaking of the foundations for the sake of shaking them." Steinberg, on the contrary, thinks that Reger, at least, is sincere. They could not compose anything simple and beautiful, so they threw themselves into "shaking the foundations"; they had no other way out. Rimsky-Korsakov offered the thought that while there are two aspects to every creative act—one, spontaneous (harmony from melody), the other, cerebral (music from harmony)—what is truly valuable in art is the artist's gift for spontaneity.

I learned that Rimsky-Korsakov's unpublished mazurka for violin[33] is based on three Polish folk songs which had been sung by his mother, who had heard them when her husband, Andrei Petrovich, was a retired Civil Governor. Later, they were incorporated in part in the mazurka in the opera *Pan Voyevoda* (episodes in G and D-flat major).

I forgot to mention that, speaking of "newness" in music, Nikolai Andreyevich said: "Take the beginning of Mendelssohn's overture to *A Midsummer Night's Dream.* Seemingly there's nothing special about it, yet how fresh and new it is to this day. Really, true novelty in music does not consist in harmony but in something special, something accessible only to genius, and that is spontaneous inspiration—a certain creative naiveté—not a quest for something unprecedented.

"I don't think," he concluded, "that even Strauss' veneration of Mozart is sincere. It may just be the result of an overweening egotism. It goes like this—there was the great Mozart; now another genius, superior to Mozart has appeared, and that is Richard Strauss. Thus, to Strauss, Mozart is simply a stage in the development of German music, the summit of which is now occupied by Strauss himself."

27 November

I went with Steinberg to the first rehearsal of the Siloti concert. Also there were Ossovsky, Igor Stravinsky, Belsky, Nadezhda Nikolayevna (the younger), and Mme Siloti. At about ten o'clock Rimsky-Korsakov, Liadov, and Glazunov appeared.

They rehearsed Liszt's *Mazeppa,* Liadov's *Pro starinu,* Nikolai Andreyev-ich's *Funiculi,*[34] and Glazunov's Fourth Symphony. The gallop and episode with trills (in the march) from *Mazeppa* are excellent. By the way, the beginning of the gallop undoubtedly inspired Tchaikovsky when he wrote the gallop for *Voyevoda* and Rimsky-Korsakov when composing the "scene of the people's wrath" in act 1 of *Servilia.*

Liadov spoke rather disparagingly about his ballad *Pro starinu;* it really did not merit such disfavor. As for *Funiculi,* despite some pleasant epi-sodes, there is nothing noteworthy about it. What is more, it did not sound particularly effective. As it turned out later, this distressed Nikolai Andreyevich very much and caused him to reflect painfully on whether he is too old for composing and no longer fit for it. Such a conclusion was premature, to say the least, since at that very time he was writing his brilliant *Golden Cockerel.* Besides, the orchestra's read-through of his little Neapolitan song was rather rough and slovenly (*fortissimo* through-out). They went through the piece twice, and each time it took only three or three and half minutes.

We talked about Cherepnin's *Pavillon d'Armide,*[35] which Rimsky-Korsa-kov likes very much (even though it contains little that is original). Also, Nikolai Andreyevich said he is quite dissatisfied with his *Funiculi.* He is going to revise it later on, but for the time being he is not permitting it to be performed. Belsky and I left after the first movement of Glazu-nov's symphony (which, incidentally, Rimsky-Korsakov appeared very taken with today).

When I met Nikolai Andreyevich at the rehearsal, he gave me the issue of Findeisen's *Russkaia muzykal'naia gazeta* (November 25, 1907), no. 47, containing his article entitled "A Plan for Reorganizing the Program of the Theory of Music and Practical Composition at the Conservatory."[36]

30 November

I went to the twelfth performance of *Kitezh.* It was nonsubscription, but even so, the theater was full. Despite the poor performance, the opera enjoyed a remarkable success. Rimsky-Korsakov was called out seven times.

Today the tromba piccola was not used for the "pipe of paradise." Serebryakov had learned the role of Burundai and he sang it rather well.

Yershov was magnificent as Grishka almost throughout. Cherkasskaya was also good as Fevronia, although she did not fare well in the first act. In the second act the chorus was almost on pitch, but in the second scene of the third act, it was unusually off-key.

Cherepnin conducted.

5 December

Counting the Rimsky-Korsakovs, there were seventeen people at their "musical evening," among them, Steinberg, Igor Stravinsky and his wife, Lapshin, the two Cherepnins, and K. Berson.

We congratulated Nikolai Andreyevich on having been awarded two Belyaev prizes simultaneously: 1,000 rubles for *Kashchei the Immortal* and 700 rubles for *Mozart and Salieri.*[37]

Bessel visited Rimsky-Korsakov recently and declared elatedly that he did not permit the value of Russian music to fall, that they are going to pay as much for *Snegurochka* as for Wagner's operas—15,000 francs. He also said that *Saltan* is going to be given this season on the Imperial stage after all.

Besides this there was a discussion about our wretched critics—Nesterov, Kolomiitsev, Bernstein, and Koptyaev—and their morally vile activity, which is so harmful to music.

In connection with my parallel examples from *Boris* (Mussorgsky and Rimsky-Korsakov), for which Nikolai Andreyevich suggested that I must, without fail, supply suitable annotations, we recalled a witty note written on the margin of an old piano arrangement of the opera (which belonged to Rimsky-Korsakov). In the scene between Boris and Shuisky, at the latter's words: "Ne smert' strashna, strashna tvoia nemilost' " occurs the following, in Nikolai Andreyevich's hand:

> "Open the balcony"—he is undone,
> Carried off into a swamp of false notes. . . .[38]

This note I had come across quite by chance while copying out examples from the old *Boris.*

After tea, Cherepnin and Steinberg played the suite from the former's *Pavillon d'Armide.* Then Berson sang some of Schumann's songs and, finally, at our request and with Nikolai Andreyevich's approval, Steinberg played several excerpts from *The Golden Cockerel* (the introduction, the scene with Amelfa, the scene with the parrot, and Dodon's "sleep" music). When the music ended, they commented on the fact that in this opera, Nikolai Andreyevich had shown, with extraordinary clarity, that sometimes the tratic can be comic and the comic—tragic.

Besides this, they chatted about Charpentier's *Louise*, which, in Rimsky-Korsakov's view, is a very weak and mediocre opera. (Incidentally, the French are mad about it.)

Well, the Rimsky-Korsakovs have a telephone!

13 December

After dinner at Fried's, I went to the Rimsky-Korsakovs' for their quartet evening. They played Beethoven's Quartet op. 59, no. 2, a quartet by Grechaninov, one by Glière, and Haydn's "Emperor Quartet." Those who performed this time were: Mestechkin, Vladimir and Andrei Rimsky-Korsakov, and M. Steinberg.

I saw a letter from the Permanent Secretary of the Paris Academy of Fine Arts (dated November 30/17, 1907), informing Rimsky-Korsakov that he had been elected a corresponding member of the Academy to fill the place of Edvard Grieg, who had died on September 4.[39]

We talked about *Snegurochka* and Rimsky-Korsakov told me that Bessel has received 10,000 francs for the rights to the production (and the music) in Paris, of which 1,000 were given to the translators (Mme Halperine and Lalo); also that a percentage of the receipts from each performance,[40] should the French choose to pay it, would be divided equally between the librettist and the composer.

"I think," said Nikolai Andreyevich, "that if *Snegurochka* fails in Paris, the interest in Russian music in general and mine in particular will simply die out forever. This is especially so since at the moment the French have a very lively interest in Russian art."

Besides this, I learned that originally Rimsky-Korsakov had received a total of 1,500 rubles in royalties for *Snegurochka,* but later he had paid Bessel as his share of the cost of printing the score the sum of 700–800 rubles. Thus, Rimsky-Korsakov's net recompense for this brilliant opera was only 700–800 rubles. (What outrageous exploitation!!) I learned further that *Tsar Saltan* is not going to be produced because Arensky's *Nal and Damyanti* is going to be presented on January 15, 1908, and they will not have time to learn the Korsakov opera.

Rimsky-Korsakov would like to make some revisions in the orchestration of his violin mazurka since it was scored originally for the orchestra of the Court Chapel. He also wants to orchestrate Mussorgsky's *Marriage.*

"If Cui wished," he said, "I would with great pleasure reorchestrate his *Ratcliff,* even though I have strong doubts about the future of this opera."

We discussed the situation at the Conservatory, where unpleasantnesses of various kinds have arisen again (between Glazunov and Miklashevsky). Nikolai Andreyevich is finally convinced that the Conservatory is not yet mature enough for autonomy.

During tea, we talked about the fact that Nikolai Andreyevich's petition for payment of at least part of the author's fee for his orchestration of *Boris Godunov*[41] had been rejected because there are no provisions in the law for authorship of this kind.

Finally, Rimsky-Korsakov asked me not to tell anyone that *Antar* will be given in a new orchestration.[42] "I'm interested to see whether the critics will notice this," he said.

25 December

I spent the afternoon from three-thirty until five o'clock at the Rimsky-Korsakovs'. The other guests were the two Stravinskys, their mother, and Steinberg.

Nikolai Andreyevich looked all right, but when Mme Stravinskaya asked how he felt, he replied: "I've been feeling ill in the mornings—some sort of asthma, so now I drink lily of the valley."

In response to my season's greetings, he squeezed my hand, then very affectionately put his arm around my shoulder and patted my head.

There was a great deal of talk about Balakirev, his caprices, and his dislike for Sergei Ivanovich Taneyev.

"As far as I know," said Rimsky-Korsakov, "this dislike arose from an incident which occured between them at a concert given by Balakirev in Smolensk during the unveiling there of a monument to Glinka."

After that, apropos of young Nadezhda Nikolayevna's performance of

Igor Stravinsky's songs *Vesna* and *Pastorale,* he commented: "I'm still of the same opinion as before about the first of these things, that is, I simply cannot understand what pleasure anyone can derive from composing music to poems like Sergei Gorodetsky's: 'Zvony, stony, perezvony.' To me all this modern, decadent, impressionist lyricism with its wretched, empty, meaningless content and pseudo-Russian folk language is nothing but 'haze and fog.' "

I told Rimsky-Korsakov about the following amusing, utterly French announcement which appeared in the journal *Le Guide musical* (no. 52, 2 December 1907, p. 831):

Toujours très actif, malgré son grand âge, le compositeur russe Rimsky-Korsak-off vient de terminer un opera: 'Zolotoi Pietouchok,' qui sera représenté au cours de cette année à l'opéra de Saint-Pétersbourg sous sa direction.

I do not recall now in what connection it was but, speaking about *Tsar Saltan,* Nadezhda Nikolayevna told me that the theme of the old man's tale ("klich zaklikali po lesu temnomu") is a modified version of the cry of a peddler in a St. Petersburg courtyard [example 70].

Example 70

"O- gur- chi- ki   ze- le- nye,   re- dis- ka   mo-   lo-   daia!"

"By the way," interjected Rimsky-Korsakov, "I never told you, did I, that the melodic and rhythmic scheme of the Call of the Heralds from *Snegurochka* was drawn from the folk? No? Then listen. In Tikhvin, in the days of my childhood, the street tradesmen would shout and praise their wares with this little motif:

Example 71

"Sa-   a- ai- ki,   bul- ki! Kren- de- li   kho- ro- shi- e!"

"And at the harvest time, the monks of the Tikhvin Monastery would walk through the streets of the city, alone or in pairs, calling the people together to lend them a hand with this tune [example 72].

Example 72

"Te- tush- ki,ma-mush-ki,de-vi-tsy kras- ny- e!   Po- di-   te po-

grab'- te,   sen- tsa dlia bozh'ei ma-te-ri!"

"So you see, even then there was something just like the music of the Heralds. The customs were certainly simple in those days, weren't they?" We laughed.

30 December

When I dropped in on Nikolai Andreyevich this evening, I found that he is still not completely well. Steinberg also was there.

Today Nikolai Andreyevich and Nadezhda Nikolayevna talked at length about Mussorgsky—first, about his song *Noch'* (on an altered text by Pushkin).

"This song," said Nikolai Andreyevich, "Mussorgsky wrote in 1864 (before *Salammbô, The Marriage,* and *Boris Godunov*), at a time when he still believed in beauty. A glorious thing. I must orchestrate it and also *Serenada smerti.*"[43]

Further, they told me that Mussorgsky lived in the home of Opochinin's brother in the Engineers' Palace;[44] then, for almost a year (1871–72) with Nikolai Andreyevich and after the Rimsky-Korsakovs' marriage—in the same house as they did—Morozov's on Shpalernaya (this was completely by chance).

"We used to hear him play his *Boris,*" said Nadezhda Nikolayevna. "At that time, he grew somewhat cold toward us. The Molases absolutely 'worshipped' him. They even began to gossip about Nikolai Andreyevich, claiming that he didn't like Mussorgsky's music, etc. As a result, Modest Petrovich began to visit us less and less."

"Generally speaking," added Nikolai Andreyevich, "at the end of his days, when he was very poor and living in one, small room, always going about in his worn, greasy coat, he still tried to play the dandy. He liked, suddenly, without rhyme or reason, to interrupt a conversation with some recherché French phrase, muttering it through his teeth. By then that was all that remained of Mussorgsky's former elegance.

"His last years were spent at the house of Terty Ivanovich Filippov, where he often played the piano," continued Nikolai Andreyevich. "He also spent some time at Leonova's. Once when he as at the Filippovs', he got so drunk that he collapsed in a fit and they immediately took him to the hospital. It was in that hospital that Repin painted his famous portrait of Mussorgsky. He remained in the hospital for several weeks. Now and again his speech became confused. He died of adiposis of the heart. What a sad story! What a pitiful, I'd even say tragic end."

Rimsky-Korsakov added that he has revised Mussorgsky's song *S Nianei* (from *The Nursery*) replacing all the 7/4, 3/4, 6/4, 5/4, and 4/4 meter markings with a 2/3 marking.

I forgot to mention that when, in 1874–75, Rimsky-Korsakov was making a serious study of counterpoint and fugue, Mussorgsky grew very cool to him.

"He also didn't like my *May Night,*" said Nikolai Andreyevich, "because, in his view, the recitatives were bad. But actually, there are almost no recitatives in that opera."

Finally, we talked about the evening at the "Contemporaries"[45] and about Igor Stravinsky's song *Vesna* ("Zvony, stony, perezvony").

"The middle of this song is very good and expressive in some places," said Nikolai Andreyevich, "but the beginning is frenetic and harmonically senseless."

"It would be better," I remarked, "if today's young musicians (as Dr. I. I. Lazarev said to Steinberg) would try harder to write not so much for the 'Contemporaries' as for posterity."

Rimsky-Korsakov liked this witticism very much.

After tea, Steinberg played his latest song *Zabytoe,* to words by Balmont. (The manuscript was dated 28–29 December 1907). Nikolai Andreyevich liked the music very much but he thought little of the text. Maximilian Osseyevich also played the Gavotte and Polka from his *Ballet Suite.*

Today Nikolai Andreyevich did not look too bad but now and then he coughed quite hard. According to Nadezhda Nikolayevna he has become irritable of late. Despite a certain discomfort he refuses to go to the doctor. On the whole he was exceedingly kind and friendly toward us.

CHAPTER 18

1908

1 January

Rimsky-Korsakov rang me on the telephone twice today: the first time at eleven o'clock, when I was not at home, and the second time, around one o'clock to wish "Vasilii velikii" (Basil the Great) a happy name day and "ditto" (his word) for the New Year. Then he remarked, with a chuckle, "Isn't the telephone really a mysterious, even mystical thing? Here we are four versts from each other and we're talking."

In the afternoon, at about two o'clock, just as we had sat down to our *blini,* in walked Misha Korsakov to invite us to their *yelka* (New Year's party).

2 January

Nikolai Andreyevich and I spoke again on the telephone. I told him that I would be at his house this evening and also that I would like to write to *Rech'* regarding Valter's stupid article in their New Year's issue.[1] He approved of both proposals.

I spent from quarter past eight until midnight at the Rimsky-Korsakovs'. Everyone was there, including Steinberg. They showed us a charming bouquet of lillies, which Nikolai Andreyevich had received from Mme Siloti yesterday.

At my request, Volodya Rimsky-Korsakov played the violin mazurka on three Polish songs ("Souvenir de trois chants polonaises"), written by Rimsky-Korsakov in Nezhgovitsy in August 1889, finished and orchestrated in Petersburg on November 28, 1893. It was agreed that this mazurka ought to be published, even though the first and third themes were used subsequently in *Pan Voyevoda*. Here are all three themes of the violin mazurka [examples 73, 74, and 75].

Example 73

First theme

Example 74

Second theme

Example 75

Third theme

As we can see, they are not entirely folk themes but were composed in the folk style.

We fell to talking about leitmotivs and how they had found their way into Russian music as early as Cui's *Ratcliff* and *Boris Godunov*. Rimsky-Korsakov holds the view that the idea of the leitmotiv came not so much through Wagner as it did through Berlioz and his *Symphonie fantastique;* that it was already in the air and Wagner himself might not have hit upon it himself had it not been for Berlioz.

"Sometime I'll have to ask César Antonovich Cui about this," concluded Nikolai Andreyevich. "He knows more about it."

Speaking about the current trend in music, I said that I foresee a kind of new "Renaissance era" in this field since the Strausses, Regers, Scriabins, and co. who now write in this style have nowhere to go. Consequently, I suggested, the new generation of composers is going to begin to write in the style of the composers of the eighteenth and nineteenth centuries.

"And this is what I think," said Rimsky-Korsakov. "They'll revive something still simpler and begin again with song."

After this, he told me that he has just finished reading Andreyev's *Darkness* and he does not like it at all.

"It's a disgusting thing from beginning to end," he said, "nothing but stench and filth. On the other hand, I'm reading Chekhov with great pleasure, and I'm coming to like him more and more."

In conclusion, I learned that Rimsky-Korsakov has sketched out the orchestration of Mussorgsky's song *Noch'* but that somehow he has forgotten how to make a fair copy straightaway, even though he has thought through the plan of the orchestration in detail.

"You orchestrate something," he said. "You think you've done it fairly well, and then, suddenly, you're plagued with doubts, and you begin to alter and revise. I repeat, I used to orchestrate faster and better."

9 January

Among the other guests at the Rimsky-Korsakovs' tonight were Bukharova, N. V. Artsybushev, Zabela, the Stravinsky brothers, Belsky, Richter, Steinberg, K. O. Berson, Felix Blumenfeld, and Siloti and his wife.

In a discussion about the French, Rimsky-Korsakov expressed a general dislike for them, although he considers Saint-Saëns' *Samson et Dalila* the best contemporary opera in the West (after Wagner, of course).

Suddenly he turned to me and said: "You know, I almost telephoned you the other day to complain about the fact that my *Pan Voyevoda* is not being given anywhere. After playing through the second act, I'm convinced that it's not as bad as many people think. In any case, it's better than all those Zazas, Salomes, and other such things that are being performed everywhere."

There was a great deal of music both before and after tea. Felix Blumenfeld played the Introduction, Wedding Procession, and all of act 2 of *The Golden Cockerel;* Zabela sang songs by Gnessin, Steinberg, Spendiarov, and Rachmaninov, among them the latter's *Lilacs,* whose last page Rimsky-Korsakov considers the best thing Rachmaninov ever wrote. Finally, Nadezhda Nikolayevna (the younger) sang two arias from Saint-Saëns' *Samson et Dalila,* and Berson sang an aria by Scarlatti and two songs by Strauss. At the end we all joined in a "mock ovation" (concocted by Gury Stravinsky, of course) to Berson for her performance of the Strauss.

15 January

Besides me, Mestechkin and Steinberg came to the Rimsky-Korsakovs' for the quartet evening. This time they played Beethoven's Quartet op.

59, no. 3, N. Sokolov's Third Quartet, a quartet by Glinka, one by Mozart, and the first movement of a quartet by V. Zolotarev.

When I arrived, Rimsky-Korsakov looked rather tired and somewhat drawn, but later on he brightened up and appeared perfectly well. He told me that he has lost interest in his textbook of orchestration; also that at one time he had thought of taking a number of examples from Glazunov.

"My orchestration is somewhat more transparent and more pictorial than Alexander Konstantinovich's," he said, "but it offers almost no examples of 'brilliant symphonic tutti.' Meanwhile, in Glazunov there are as many examples of just this kind of instrumentational writing as you'd want, for, generally speaking, his orchestration is thicker and more vivid than mine."

We noted that nowadays there is a trend—they are beginning to perform Rimsky-Korsakov's operas everywhere with entire scenes and even entire acts omitted. Thus, in Kiev (at Brykin's) they gave *Snegurochka* without the first act; in Moscow (on the Imperial Stage) they omitted the fantastic scene in *Christmas Eve;* and at one of the holiday matinee performances at Zimin's, *Saltan* was given without the symphonic interludes (March, The Sea, and The Three Wonders). They even cut out the first scene of the last act. What a dirty trick!

"By the way, consider this," said Rimsky-Korsakov, "despite the fact that my operas have become the vogue in Paris, not a single one is being given in Petersburg. It's also interesting that the 'official stage,' which doesn't find it necessary to celebrate my anniversary, for some reason wanted to celebrate the anniversary of Solovyov's opera *Cordelia,* which is not even performed.

"This is typical of our Imperial Theater," he concluded.

We talked about Igor Stravinsky's symphony,[2] noting that while the first movement contains some very beautiful harmonic and instrumental episodes, on the whole the orchestration is excessively heavy. This symphony is going to be performed by the Court Orchestra on Tuesday, January 22.

In conclusion, I mentioned to Nikolai Andreyevich my desire to publish a biography of him as a separate brochure. He offered to write to Jurgenson and did so then and there. Here is the text of the letter:

S. P.burg. 15. 1. 1908
Dear Boris Petrovich,[3]

I am writing to you this time about a matter unrelated to *The Golden Cockerel*.

In 1900, on the occasion of my thirty-fifth anniversary, *Russkaia muzykal'naia gazeta* (Findeisen's) published a biography of me written by my close friend, V. V. Yastrebtsev. The author is now thinking of augmenting and somewhat revising it. (Incidentally, it contains a complete and detailed list of all my compositions). Would your firm be interested in publishing this work if it does not exceed a single written page?

Should you feel so inclined, the author will write to you and clarify his terms. If you reply affirmatively, I will so inform him.

Sincerely yours,   N. R.-Korsakov.

I sent this letter on the morning of January 16. I wonder what will come of it?[4]

21 January

I went to an "at home" at Vladimir Ivanovich Belsky's. Rimsky-Korsakov was there. I told him that I have already received a reply from Jurgenson. We talked about the unsuccessful French translation of *Boris Godunov* made by Michel Delines. Then Nikolai Andreyevich told me that Breitkopf & Härtel has commissioned a vocal score of *Snegurochka* with a French text; also that during his stay in Paris, the barman at the Opéra refused to accept any money from him for lemonade since, in his opinion, Nikolai Andreyevich is the Russian Gounod. Incidentally, it is rumored that the sets for the Paris production of *Snegurochka* were painted by Roerich and that Mamontov went there to produce the opera.

Later, speaking about Isadora Duncan, Nikolai Andreyevich said that on principle he will not go to see her, for he absolutely cannot help listening to music and most attentively, whenever it is played, even in the Bolshoi Moskovsky tavern. And this is Beethoven, Chopin!

"I'd just like to know what legs and rhythmic movement have to do with it," he added.

During tea we talked about Timofeyev's article in *Rech'*.[5]

"Everything would have been fine, if it hadn't been for his unfair attacks on Siloti," said Nikolai Andreyevich. "Just imagine, this time Alexander Ilyich went out of his way to give *Antar* a decent performance.

I even went back to thank him. And then Timofeyev berated him. One must not be so biased against an artist."

Someone asked Rimsky-Korsakov which societies have made him an honorary member.

"I really don't know," he replied. "It seems to me I'm a member of some Moscow Pushkin society, the Academic Union, and something else. But it doesn't matter—I don't go to meetings anyhow."[6]

Today Rimsky-Korsakov was very lively and he looked excellent. We left together and he gave me a lift to the corner of Line 5 and Bolshoi Prospekt. When we said good-bye, I promised to bring him Balakirev's second collection.[7] It turned out that he did not know anything about it.

23 January

When I arrived for the Rimsky-Korsakovs' "Wednesday" Nikolai Andreyevich was still resting (he had gone to bed late last night, as he went to the Stravinskys', following the Court Orchestra's performance of Igor Stravinsky's works.)[8]

In addition to me, the other guests were Zabela, I. I. Lapshin, the Stravinsky brothers, S. Belyaev, A. Spendiarov, and Maximilian Steinberg.

There was a great deal of singing. Zabela, Nadezhda Nikolayevna (the younger), and Gury Stravinsky performed songs by Tchaikovsky, Igor Stravinsky, Rimsky-Korsakov, Spendiarov, Gnessin, Steinberg, and Borodin.

In the course of the evening the conversation touched on news of the day, musical and nonmusical. Lapshin suggested that I make a study of the new harmonies which Rimsky-Korsakov had introduced into contemporary music.

"By the way," I said, turning to Nikolai Andreyevich, "what kind of harmony is this in act 2 of *The Golden Cockerel*? What is it called?" [Example 76.]

Example 76

After considering for a moment, Rimsky-Korsakov replied: "I really don't know exactly what chord it is. All I know is that it has three resolutions: F minor, C-sharp minor, and A minor."

During tea, the Rimsky-Korsakovs told us that they had attended the dress rehearsal of Arensky's opera *Nal and Damayanti,* but they did not like it very much.

"There are a few fairly good places," remarked Nikolai Andreyevich, "but all the rest is extraordinarily colorless and boring."

When we returned to the drawing room, Nikolai Andreyevich began to urge Spendiarov to write an opera sometime, "Eastern without fail."

"You're a man of the East by birth," he said. "You have the East in your blood, as they say, and by virtue of this you can do something authentic, really valuable in the field of music.

"This is not the case with me," he added. "My East is rather cerebral, intellectual."

Just before we left, Rimsky-Korsakov sat at the piano and played some musical parodies and jokes, which Borodin had once made up; a parody on the March and beginning of the Scene at the Black Rock from Cui's *Ratcliff;* a caricature of Rimsky-Korsakov's song *Iuzhnaia noch'* and a frenzied "gallop" on a theme from *The Maid of Pskov.*[9]

30 January

Nikolai Andreyevich told me tonight that he received an invitation from von Bool, Comptroller of the Moscow Imperial Opera, to go to Moscow for the dress rehearsal of *Kitezh* on February 9.[10] (The performance is scheduled for February 12.)

"I replied that maybe I'll come," he said, "only not just for the dress rehearsal but earlier, as otherwise the trip will make no sense whatsoever."

Yesterday Nikolai Andreyevich listened to some of *Saltan,* and he is terribly pleased with it.

"It's devilishly good," he said smiling, "but our Directorate is stupid; they don't give *Tsar Saltan*—they give Arnesky's unsuccessful *Nal and Damayanti.*"

During tea the conversation touched on Borodin and his striking musical originality, whereupon Rimsky-Korsakov remarked: "It's different with me. He didn't have any 'stolen goods.' "

He believes that had it not been for Borodin's cholera and sudden death, he might have contributed a great deal more to music.

In conclusion, I asked Nikolai Andreyevich about Ivan the Terrible's theme, in *The Maid of Pskov*. He derived it, he said, from the singing of the monks in the Tikhvin Monastery of Our Lady and from znamenny chant of the type [shown in example 77].[11] This motif from the theme of

Example 77

"Bog ot-   tsa   mo- e-   go
I   pro- sla-   vlu e-   go"

Ivan the Terrible, and also from the folk tune *Slava* (in minor) [is shown in example 78],

Example 78

4 February

Today my wife and I went to the People's House for the dress rehearsal of *Tsar Saltan,* which is being given by the management of Kirikov and Zimmerman. With the exception of Militrissa and Guidon, the performers were more or less satisfactory. Zelyony conducted—energetically and intelligently.

Speaking of the introduction to the opera, Nikolai Andreyevich commented, not without humor: "Now, this is truly Russian music, isn't it!"

"By the way," he added, seriously now, "this scene contains quite a number of the so-called Mixolydian modes." He is obviously highly pleased with this scene.

We discussed at length the harmonic and rhythmic features of this opera.

Thus, each time the lullaby of the seven nurses is sung, it is sung a half-tone lower (in C, B, and B-flat major); in the scene between the Skomorokh and the Old Man, the Skomorokh always puts his questions in the same key (E flat), while the Old Man always replies in different tonalities, and the first notes of his reply form a kind of scale (G, A, B flat, C, D, E flat, F, G); in the scene with Guidon, Militrissa always ends her phrase on a different note (the first time before B on E; the second time on F sharp; the third time on G); in the scene where the merchants describe the wonders to Saltan, the Tsar always expresses his amazement in the same F-sharp major, but when he sees them with his own eyes, his rejoinders are expressed in a structural theme which rises continually by half-tones. The same may be said about the "trumpet signals": before each new wonder, the trumpet plays a half-tone higher (C, D-flat, and D major).

As for the special features of the rhythms in *Saltan*, first let me draw attention to the fact that in the scene in which the people glorify the Prince Guidon ("S krepkii dub tebe povyrasti," etc.) from act 1 on, two independent five-beat rhythms are combined successively; music in 5/8 (groupings of 2/8 and 3/8) and music in 5/4 (groupings of 3/4 and 2/4). Further, the theme of the Swan Queen is set in various rhythmic patterns: in 5/4 (in Babarikha's tale), in 2/2–3/2 (in the scene between Guidon and the Swan), and in 3/4 (in the scene in which the Swan is transformed into a Princess); in 4/4 (in the introduction to scene 1 of act 4); in 9/8 (in the love duet between Guidon and the Swan); and finally in 3/4 with the continuation of this theme in 4/4 (in the musical interlude The Three Wonders). In addition, let me point out the seven-beat (A major) Chorus of the Young Girls ("Chto tak rano, rano, solntse krasno") from scene 1 of act 4 (groupings of 3/4 and 4/4 equal 7/4).

In the evening I was at the Rimsky-Korsakovs' for their quartet playing. When I entered Nikolai Andreyevich was still sleeping but he came out shortly afterward. He was very affectionate today. He gave me the score of the suite from *The Golden Cockerel* with the following inscription: "To dear Vasily Vasilyevich Yastrebtsev from his loving N. Rimsky-Korsakov. 4 Feb. 1908."

He told me that the French would like him to recommend a conductor who is familiar with *Snegurochka*, so that the opera might be prepared properly for performance in Paris. They had sought this advice from Vinogradsky, but he was unable to suggest anyone.

"Isn't it strange," said Rimsky-Korsakov, "that it never entered their heads to approach me personally and ask me to conduct it."

By the way, *Tsar Saltan* has already been given in Kiev.

Tonight they played Borodin's marvelous Quartet no. 2.

13 February

Again I went to the Rimsky-Korsakovs' "Wednesday." The other guests included Insarova, the two Spendiarovs, Steinberg, and K. O. Berson. Tonight the music did not go so well somehow. Berson sang an aria by Mozart and fairly well (German music seems suited to her). She was accompanied by Steinberg. Then, with her mother accompanying, Nadezhda Nikolayevna the younger sang a number of her father's songs. Finally, Insarova sang arias from *The Tsar's Bride* and *Sadko*. Again Steinberg accompanied.

Rimsky-Korsakov and I had a long talk about the Conservatory.

"You know," he said, "I definitely plan to leave it and get three or four private students instead, since all these members of the directorate are on friendly terms with Alexander Konstantinovich, and his work as administrator is totally worthless. He's too weak to be the Director, and thus he unwittingly falls under the influence of all sorts of Iretskayas and Conservatory Black Hundreds of that ilk. As a result, all his good intentions come to nought.

"This is a pity," he went on, "because the work suffers. Take today, for example. I should have attended a meeting of the Art Council but I didn't go—it's very painful to see all this and realize there's nothing you can do about it."

16 February

We all (the Lazarevs, my wife, and I) went to the second Belyaev concert. It was directed by Felix Blumenfeld. The program consisted of Borodin's First Symphony; Stravinsky's suite *Faun and Shepherdess* (first performance); the Introduction and Wedding March from Rimsky-Korsakov's *Golden Cockerel* (first performance); Mussorgsky's songs *Spi, usni, krestianskii syn, Po griby,* and *Gopak,* as orchestrated by Rimsky-Korsakov (also the first time), and Glazunov's *The Sea.* The soloist in both the Stravinsky and Mussorgsky works was E. F. Petrenko.

Because of Blumenfeld, both *Po griby* and *Gopak* were "messed up," as they say. The audience liked *The Sea* and called Alexander Konstantinovich out twice. The Introduction to *The Golden Cockerel* was played badly, but the Wedding March met with tumultuous applause, and Rimsky-Korsakov was recalled three times.

In conclusion let me say that, despite the considerable influence that Rimsky-Korsakov's *Mlada,* Tchaikovsky's overture to *The Tempest,* and Wagner (in general) had on the music of Stravinsky's suite, it contains quite a few interesting details. The voice part is not without awkwardness à la Mussorgsky, but on the whole, this work shows talent. In some places it is very beautiful, and most important—it is young (although thanks to this it is also uneven). Stravinsky was called out.

Of Borodin's symphony I can say only that it was played quite acceptably and not without élan. Marvelous music!

21 February

Tonight I found Rimsky-Korsakov looking excellent. He read to me a letter from S. Belanovsky about the first Moscow performance of *Kitezh,* which took place on February 15. Owing to the tribute to Salina,[12] it lasted until twelve-forty-five. Through Belanovsky, Suk invited Rimsky-Korsakov to come for the second performance scheduled for the second week of Lent. On the whole, wrote Belanovsky, the opera went tolerably well, though the choruses, particularly in the folk scene of act 2, were extremely stylized and because of this, utterly lifeless.

"Judge for yourself," he wrote. "In act 2, where the infuriated Tatars attack the people of Kitezh, the people stand absolutely motionless."

During tea we got into a discussion about the dubious necessity of orchestrating songs. One can agree fully with Rimsky-Korsakov about this. For while a song gains in sonority, owing to a certain heaviness in orchestration, it loses a great deal of its intimacy. And for such a subtle musical genre as this, the latter may be even more important than the former.

While on the subject of songs, Nikolai Andreyevich expressed the thought that in Mussorgsky's *Spi, usni,* the "angels" are depicted exactly as they appear in old, "poor" ikons, where, instead of a gold nimbus, the face of the angel was adorned with a "radiance" of gold foil.

"The old grandmother, rocking her grandchild to sleep, never saw the other angels," said Nikolai Andreyevich.

I mentioned to him that I intend to write an article some time in the future about the use of folk songs in his music, provided, of course, that he would not object.

"I have no fears of such a study," he replied. "After all, then you'd have to reproach Glinka and Mussorgsky for lacking a gift for melodic invention."

Finally, apropos of Karatygin's review of *The Golden Cockerel* in no. 242 of *Stolichnaia pochta* (February 20, 1983)[13] stating that in the Introduction to this opera, Rimsky-Korsakov, with purely Straussian audacity, introduces a complicated chromatic melody and chromatic scales in thirds on an original pedal point—a full chord of the ninth, Nikolai Andreyevich said: "I've never been noted for any cowardice when it comes to new harmonies; all I've done in my compositions is to keep them within the bounds of common sense."

On the whole, Rimsky-Korsakov likes Karatygin's style of writing.

"Yes," he said, "times have changed a great deal. These days, after *Kashchei,* the 'moderns' approve of me, but there was a time when Mr. Nurok called me, in print, an 'old-fashioned professor,' 'harmful' to the Conservatory. How unfair and undeserved all that was!"

23 February
Just before one o'clock, Nikolai Andreyevich phoned to tell me that another piano composition of two pages had turned up in his house. It was printed in an Armenian album[14] and appears to be a song with an Eastern coloring. Upon learning that I had sent my article to Moscow yesterday, he assured me that this little piece could easily be inserted when the proofs are corrected.

27 February
At around five-thirty Nikolai Andreyevich phoned to tell me that the drama censor had scribbled all over his *Golden Cockerel.* First, the libretto

was returned "clean," but then, the very next day (probably because of some adverse criticism), the censor requested it again, and this was the result: the Prologue, Epilogue, and many of Pushkin's words were crossed out ("Tsarstvui, lezha na boku," "Zhdem pogroma s iuga, gliad', a s vostoka lezet rat," etc.)

At the same time, much crueler things were left in.

"What fools!" exclaimed Rimsky-Korsakov. "I'm certain they really don't know Pushkin's tale at all."

At around seven-thirty Steinberg called for me and we went together to Zagorodny. Only a few others came to this "Wednesday"—Igor Stravinsky, N. I. Richter, and Sofia Nikolayevna. At Rimsky-Korsakov's request, Steinberg played his First Symphony. He mentioned that he has already written the first movement of his second. Nikolai Andreyevich was overjoyed at this news.

Rimsky-Korsakov showed me the Armenian album he had referred to a few days earlier. It is called *Artsunkner* (meaning "Tears") and was published under the editorship of Isabella Gria-Berberian and Yegish A. Bagdasarian. Listed as no. 3 was the so-called *Song* (Andantino), which Nikolai Andreyevich had composed in 1901.

I learned that this afternoon Belsky had been at the Rimsky-Korsakovs', and they decided to go together to have a talk with Belgard about the stupid incident with the libretto.

They got onto the subject of a new symphonic poem by Gnessin, based on Shelley's *Prometheus Unbound*,[15] and this led to the following exchange:

Rimsky-Korsakov: "I'm not particularly elated over this work."

Steinberg: "And I was sure you'd be pleased with it, since it was written for you, that is, partly in accord with your taste."

Rimsky-Korsakov was astonished. Lowering his voice, as if half-sadly, half-jokingly he replied: "What do you mean, for *me?* So this is what I've come to! Evidently he composed both for himself—more complicated—and for me—simpler."

We laughed.

During tea, Nikolai Andreyevich, told us that he had rejected Suk's suggestion regarding the desirability of cuts in *Kitezh,* even though Suk had tried his best to persuade him to agree to them so as to ensure this "excellent opera" (Suk's words) the best possible success.

After tea, Richter played a great deal—a Scriabin sonata, a mazurka in

C-sharp minor by Chopin, a novelette by Schumann, and several pieces by Grieg.

Tonight Stravinsky presented Nikolai Andreyevich with a wonderful daguerreotype of Robert Schumann.

29 February

At about ten-thirty I was at Zagorodny, arriving just in time for tea. Nikolai Andreyevich told me that he and Belsky had gone to see Telyakovsky about *The Golden Cockerel*. This whole stupid incident with the censor was entirely Telyakovsky's fault, since it was he who wanted Belgard to take a closer look at the text. Otherwise, he said, Hershelman (in Moscow) might forbid it. This time the censor "overdid" it; finding nothing to "censor" on the first reading, on the second—he crossed out many lines, mostly Pushkin's!

"However," concluded Rimsky-Korsakov, "perhaps all this will be straightened out somehow."

After tea, Steinberg played the first movement of his Second Symphony. Nikolai Andreyevich did not understand it immediately. (It is far from simple.) He found the style very "modernistic," sort of "Scriabinesque," very complicated, though at the same time elegant. He suggested that there might be more contrast in the second theme, at least in orchestration. Evidently, on this first hearing, what he liked least was the underlying principle of the music.

6 March

Among those who came to celebrate Rimsky-Korsakov's sixty-fourth birthday were Steinberg, Glazunov, Liadov, Belsky, the three Stravinskys, Misha Rimsky-Korsakov and his wife, Artsybushev, and Lapshin. Nikolai Andreyevich received a great many flowers. The drawing room and study called to mind the corresponding scene in act 4 of *Kitezh*.[16]

While Igor Stravinsky and Steinberg played Glazunov's Eighth Symphony and Nadezhda Nikolayevna (the younger) sang an aria from Saint-Saëns' *Samson et Dalila*, Nikolai Andreyevich and I talked about Engel's interesting review of *Kitezh,* in which he simultaneously lauded the opera and pointed out the undeniable boredom of certain scenes.[17]

We also discussed Lipayev's biography of Nikolai Andreyevich, which was published in *Muzykal'nyi truzhenik,*[18] in which the critic, in his desire to lavish the highest praise on the orchestration of the composer of *Snegurochka,* wrote: "Rimsky-Korsakov's Achilles heel is his amazing orchestration."

"Now, you see, this is the kind of critics we have in our country," said Rimsky-Korsakov with a smile.

From conversation with Belsky, we learned that, according to Telyakovsky, the censor has restored some of the cuts in *The Golden Cockerel.*

We went into the dining room.

During tea, Nikolai Andreyevich confided to me, in a low voice so the others might not hear, that his heart has grown weak, that the shortness of breath he has been experiencing indicates more eloquently than words that his body is, to some degree, worn out.

"You know," he continued, "in my youth, my heart was perfectly healthy. I used to swim around the ship two and a half times. In the 1880s I couldn't swim more than six or eight meters. And starting in the 1890s I finally had to stop swimming altogether. It was then that my sclerosis began to become acute.

"As you see," he concluded, "everything is proceeding normally; it's all moving toward a single end."

When we returned to the study, Liadov (who was the "hit" of the evening, as they say) started to talk about wanting terribly to write a small opera on some clever little Russian folk tale. But this he would do, he said, only if Belsky wrote the libretto with the beautiful, typically Russian expressions and turns of speech of which he (Vladimir Ivanovich) is such a master.

"You'll laugh at me," continued Anatoly Konstantinovich, "but I'm in love with folk song refrains like 'Rozan, moi rozan, vinograd zelenyi'— senseless but nevertheless moving. What's more, I literally adore the names of certain railroad stations, like 'Malaya Vishera,' 'Spirovo,' etc. They're just like a bouquet, exuding the fragrance of ancient Russia, Russia from time immemorial."

At the end Liadov insisted that compared with contemporary artists, Nikolai Andreyevich is a kind of fossilized "icthyosaurus" or "plesiosaurus."

"Nowadays we're surrounded by grains of sand and pottery shards.

There are no longer any gigantic mountains and vast landscapes," he said. On the whole, this was a delightful and lively evening.

8 March

We all went to the third Russian Symphony concert. The program consisted of Steinberg's Symphony in D (premiere), Scriabin's Piano Concerto in F-sharp minor, I. I. Wihtol's Overture to the Latvian fairy tale *Spriditis* (premiere), Liadov's *Variations for Piano on a Theme by Glinka,* and Glazunov's dramatic overture *The Song of Destiny* (premiere). Both Scriabin's Piano Concerto and Liadov's *Variations* were played by V. I. Scriabina.

Before the concert I met Nikolai Andreyevich and I walked with him in the lower foyer. He struck me as worried or not quite well. He was unusually serious and greeted me rather coldly. As it turned out, this morning he had some difficulty breathing and this evidently upset him. His sclerosis is acting up again, and so he is taking more convallaria and iodine.

The concert began at about quarter to nine. At the end of his symphony, Steinberg was called out twice. Dmitri Stasov liked it, but Cui did not seem to care for it particularly. The orchestra did not applaud, but on the whole, the symphony scored a success with the audience. Evidently, Cui liked Liadov's *Variations* very much for, at the end, he shook Anatoly Konstantinovich's hand vigorously. As for Scriabina, she was applauded enthusiastically and after the *Variations,* she played, as an encore, two of her husband's études.

After the concert I went to the Rimsky-Korsakovs'. There were about thirty guests. It was a very gay evening with lots of laughter. The Stravinsky brothers made up a story based on the names of singers, composers, and conductors. At first, Nikolai Andreyevich was horrified at this nonsense, but afterward he was drawn into it and, together with Liadov he also made up something to the pleasure of all the guests.

Before supper Zabela sang the A-major music from the second act of *The Golden Cockerel,* accompanied by Blumenfeld. (However, it was too high for her and thus, in my opinion at least, her singing was not fully satisfying from an artistic point of view.) Then V. I. Scriabina played three of her husband's études.

As usual there were many toasts. No sooner was the champagne served than Felix Blumenfeld stood up and announced that he was drinking to the health of the engaged couple—Maximilian Osseyevich Steinberg and Nadezhda Nikolayevna. After that we drank to the health of Nikolai Andreyevich and with this, he passed among the guests with a glass in his hand, thanking each one individually. We also drank to Nadezhda Nikolayevna the elder, Liadov, Blumenfeld, Glazunov, Wihtol, et al. There were two amusing toasts—one by N. I. Richter (at the request of the young people) in elegantly affected French, and the other by S. S. Mitusov, who said that only here, at the Rimsky-Korsakovs', and specifically thanks to Nikolai Andreyevich does he every year have a chance to indulge in "twaddle" to his heart's content. Hearing these two toasts, we all laughed until we cried.

Tonight we were at the Rimsky-Korsakovs' from quarter to twelve until four-thirty in the morning. By the time Steinberg and I reached the island, the church bells were ringing for early mass.

14 March

I went to *Die Walküre*. In the intermission before act 3 I saw Nikolai Andreyevich in the distance, talking animatedly with Stravinsky. Could I have imagined then that this was the last time in his life that Rimsky-Korsakov would hear the brilliant, endlessly beautiful and poetic magic fire music?

19 March

I was at the Rimsky-Korsakovs' from eight-fifteen until one-thirty. Zabela, Richter, Sandulenko, and Maximilian Steinberg were also there. (Volodya had gone to Lyubensk.)

Speaking with Rimsky-Korsakov, I learned that *The Golden Cockerel* has already been printed and even stitched, but it is being held up because of Bilibin (the cover is not ready). Further, he told me that the other day, the committee[19] rejected M. Ivanov's opera *Woe from Wit;* that the artist V. Serov drew a pencil portrait of him for S. Diaghilev but it came out very badly; and that N. N. Cherepnin came to say good-bye today— he is leaving for Paris tomorrow to conduct *Snegurochka.*

Looking through the latest number of Findeisen's *Russkaia muzykal'naia gazeta* (of March 16, 1908), I came across a sharp comment, written in pencil by Rimsky-Korsakov, objecting to Findeisen's undeservedly derogatory review of Steinberg's symphony.[20]

We also talked about the "armored"[21] sound of Wagner's orchestration. Nikolai Andreyevich expressed deep disappointment in *Das Rheingold*. "The music is terribly coarse in some places," he said. "I prefer something a little more subtle."

Tonight Zabela sang Liapunov's charming *Nachtstück*[22] (which Rimsky-Korsakov likes very much) and two songs by Nikolai Andreyevich. Richter played a scherzo by Glière, a sonata (op. 7) by Grieg, *Isoldens Liebestod* by Wagner-Liszt, and a number of excerpts from *Tristan* and *Die Walküre*.

Apropos of the music of *Isoldens Liebestod,* Nikolai Andreyevich remarked: "In my opinion the beginning and end of this scene are brilliant but in the middle, Wagner gets confused somehow."

Finally, Sandulenko sang two songs—Spendiarov's *Pesn' Gafiza* and *Tol'ko vstrechu ulybku tvoiu,*[23] both of which Rimsky-Korsakov approved heartily.

Before tea we talked at length about the power and importance of publicity. Nikolai Andreyevich is strongly opposed to it.

25 March

At exactly eight-thirty I was at Zagorodny. Nikolai Andreyevich seemed listless, as if he were not quite well. When I entered, Nadezhda Nikolayevna and Steinberg were playing the *Sinfonietta.*[24] Following that, they played Rimsky-Korsakov's Third Symphony.

Nikolai Andreyevich and I had a long talk about Mikhail Fabianovich Gnessin. Nikolai Andreyevich would like to invite him to visit them.[25]

"You know," said Nikolai Andreyevich, "I agree completely with Anton Grigoryevich Rubinstein that a composer must possess a certain simplicity and naïveté."

"And in my opinion," I countered, "the times are different now; you can't find whole, integrated personalities. Life and its problems have become more complex."

Before tea Steinberg played a new prelude by Gnessin. Everyone liked it very much.

"A beautiful thing," commented Rimsky-Korsakov, "and even less affected than usual. And this makes me happy."

Speaking further about Gnessin, Nikolai Andreyevich expressed the thought that he does not deny that Mikhail Fabianovich has a rather original creative gift and overall talent, but he is worried about one thing: whether he will follow the "proper path." When I told him that Gnessin loves his works; that he has already made a study of *Christmas Eve* and is now studying *Mlada;* that I had lent Gnessin my own score, as I do not think it right to refuse music to talented and interested people like Steinberg and Gnessin, Nikolai Andreyevich approved of what I had done. At the same time he said with great surprise, "But except for *Kashchei* and a few other things, my works must seem sort of childish to Gnessin."

Shortly after midnight, Volodya returned from Lyubensk. He began to unpack. This occasioned much laughter. Nikolai Andreyevich became cheerful. However, when Volodya reported that the Bukharova estate and consequently their farmstead is being advertised, Nikolai Andreyevich became terribly agitated.[26]

29 March

I went to hear *Siegfried.* During the first intermission I dropped in on the box where the Rimsky-Korsakovs and Stravinsky were sitting. They were all in raptures over the opera's brilliant first act.

As I was leaving, I ran into Nikolai Andreyevich in the corridor. He had just arrived at the theater and was still in his fur coat and cap. It seems he had not felt quite well—he felt exhausted all day—and had decided to lie down after dinner. He did so and slept until eight o'clock.

6 April

This afternoon, after a visit to Belsky, Rimsky-Korsakov came to see me. He stayed from four-fifteen until five-thirty. (As it turned out subsequently, this was his last visit to me.) He was in an excellent mood. We chatted about this and that: Melgunov's curious musical theories[27] with their extremely artificial unit of rhythm—"mora"; Steinberg's marvelous memory; Gnessin's charming *Snezhinki* (which I adore); my little cactus. ("I suspect this cactus has its own god living in it," remarked

Nikolai Andreyevich.) I showed him the drawings of my little ten-year-old son Vasya. He looked them over very intently and even praised them.

"I assure you," he said, "your Vasya's childish sketches would be among the best pictures at the 'Venok' exhibit."[28]

The conversation turned to Wagner's *Ring.* Nikolai Andreyevich expressed the view that, even though it contains many totally unnecessary and tedious passages which only serve to mar it, it is a major work. Meanwhile, thanks to its formlessness, this tetralogy could easily be cut. Besides this, a great deal of the superfluous, pseudo-profound philosophy ought to be "sifted out." Nikolai Andreyevich also feels that despite the many contrasts, the *Ring* contains little genuine, fine music. Even the magnificent, dazzling orchestration, for all its undeniable, enormous merits, is too heavy and cumbersome. The sound is almost continually "armored" with brass.

"You know," said Nikolai Andreyevich, "so far as I'm concerned, the best music Wagner wrote for the *Ring* occurs in the scene in which the sword is forged (act 1 of *Siegfried*) and that in which Siegfried plunges through the flames (act 3 of the same opera). The music of these brilliant scenes has absolutely no equal in all contemporary operatic literature."

He then showed me two letters he had received from Cherepnin (dated April 9 and 12 New Style) containing a detailed description of the Paris production of *Snegurochka.* Nikolai Nikolayevich reported that the opera was given many rehearsals and the singers knew their parts perfectly. However, the performer of Spring is poor and will be replaced. The Wood Sprite, a contralto, will also be replaced—by a tenor. Furthermore, because of the Parisians' passion for dance, there is a great deal of ballet in the opera (the *maîtresse de ballet* is an unlikable, fat lady with an enormous hat). They dance in the scene of The Farewell to Butterweek and during Lel's second and third songs. Cherepnin hopes to be able to change some of this, but it will not be without a struggle.

In addition, Nikolai Nikolayevich wrote that, following an idea of the art director, for some reason or other, the scenery in the Prologue was suddenly changed from a winter scene into a spring landscape. This, however, will be discarded.

Cherepnin will not be conducting, but a local conductor named Rühlmann. Otherwise it would have been necessary to obtain special permission from the Ministry of Fine Arts. In general, according to Cherepnin, they treat him like a god and comply with all his wishes.

One thing that is delaying the staging of the opera is the chorus. They still have not learned their parts and, besides this, they refuse to sing more than one hour a day. On the other hand, the staging of the Ballet of the Birds is perfect. Never has Cherepnin seen such little ballet dancers. The heralds are also excellent. The Chorus of the Flowers, sung by nine choristers, sounded marvelous in the hall.

"I don't know what kind of stage sets they will have," said Nikolai Andreyevich. "All I know is that they won't be Roerich's or Mamontov's. And that's a pity."

Today Dr. I. I. Lazarev finally came to see Rimsky-Korsakov. This was their first and last meeting. To me Nikolai Andreyevich did not look bad, but in Lazarev's opinion he is not well.

"To me as a doctor," he said, "his sallow complexion and shortness of breath while conversing are bad symptoms. He must have an entire summer of rest and not be permitted any kind of strenuous work."

At first I refused to believe the doctor, but unfortunately he was right; within five days, Nikolai Andreyevich suffered his first severe attack of angina pectoris.

I forgot to mention that when I suggested to Rimsky-Korsakov that he probably had a good reason for going to Belsky's, that usually such spring visits presage a "fall harvest," he began most seriously to deny any possibility of such a thing, pointing out that by now he is too old.

And so—until Wednesday, April 9.

9 April

Besides Steinberg and me, there were quite a few guests at the Rimsky-Korsakovs' tonight—Gnessin, N. I. Richter, Mikhail Nikolayevich, Sofia Nikolayevna, and Berson. They talked about Maeterlinck and Wagner, and Nikolai Andreyevich said again that he had never liked the Funeral March from *Götterdämmerung*.

Richter and Steinberg played Dargomyzhsky's *Finnish Fantasy* (in which augmented triads were used alongside other harmonies for the first time in Russian music); Rimsky-Korsakov's Symphony no. 1 (in Nikolai Andreyevich's view, what is most interesting about it is the second movement and also the fact that one is aware of the influence of Glinka and here and there, of "Balakirevian" measures); and excerpts from *The Golden Cockerel,* the piano reduction of which is to come out this week.

During tea, Nikolai Andreyevich read to us a third letter from Cherepnin (dated April 20/7). Apparently by now Nikolai Nikolayevich is somewhat disillusioned. He reported, among other things, that Mme Carré is a Parisian Kuznetsova, and the conductor is mortally afraid of her; that the "skomorokhi" and a good third of the dances are executed in a stately manner, but by the time of the performance this will be changed; the choristers sing below pitch and in the chorus in 11/4 they are unsure of themselves; in the *khorovod* they move with too much speed and bustle (they are also trying to rectify this); the *gusli* players are poor. On the other hand, the Chorus of the Flowers[29] is going perfectly; there will never be such a charming production of this scene in our country.

11 April

Upon learning that Nikolai Andreyevich is not well, toward evening I went to Zagorodny, where I stayed from seven-thirty until ten-thirty. How could I have imagined yesterday, seeing him so hale and hearty, that such misfortune would befall him?

From young Nadezhda Nikolayevna, I learned that Nikolai Andreyevich had gone to bed rather late last night (at around two-thirty), and at four-thirty he suddenly had a severe attack of asthma. Dr. Borodulin and Dr. Spengler were summoned. By five-thirty both of them were there, and Nikolai Andreyevich soon began to feel better. It has been established that he is suffering from cardiac asthma (angina pectoris). This is a terrible thing to have to accept, but it is a fact.

Nikolai Andreyevich felt weak all throughout the day; he kept dozing. But this did not prevent him from drinking tea and eating dinner in the dining room. In the afternoon at his request, they sent for Liadov.

Nadezhda Nikolayevna told me that all during this recent period, Nikolai Andreyevich has not been taking care of himself. On Sunday (the sixth) he went to Belsky's—on the fourth floor; to me—on the third floor. On Monday (the seventh) he was at Cui's—on the fifth floor. On Wednesday (the ninth), he went to bed at three in the morning, and on Thursday (that is, yesterday, the tenth)—at around two-thirty, after a discussion with Steinberg about the textbook of orchestration, which went on until one-forty-five. He wants to go to Lyubensk as soon as possible.

When Rimsky-Korsakov awoke, we went into his study and I gave him his medicine. Most of the time he was lying down, even though he claimed he was feeing fairly well. His only complaint was that he felt as if he had been given a good beating.

I read a third letter from Cherepnin (dated 16/3 April). While I was reading it, Nikolai Andreyevich closed his eyes and seemed to doze off. Noting this, Nadezhda Nikolayevna started to suggest that we go into the drawing room for a while, when evidently Nikolai Andreyevich guessed what we were about to do and, without opening his eyes said softly: "I'm sleeping, but my heart is a light sleeper." We stayed.

We talked about an enthusiastic article about *Kitezh* which appeared in *Golos Moskvy* over the pseudonym "Mizgir."[30] (Could that be the same "Mizgir" whose ecstatic articles I happened upon once in *Permskii vestnik?*)

"It suits your taste perfectly," said Rimsky-Korsakov, smiling.

Today for the first time since I have known the Rimsky-Korsakovs, I saw his daughter Nadezhda Nikolayevna seated beside her father on the divan, holding his head in her arms and caressing him. He asked them to write to Andrei about what happened but not to frighten him, putting it all in the past tense. "Such-and-such happened . . ."

Shortly before I left, Rimsky-Korsakov and I fell to talking about those "half-believers," who, while not having a deep belief in God, observe the rituals and go to church.

"I don't understand them at all," said Rimsky-Korsakov. "As I see it, either you really believe, take communion and go to church, or you don't believe, in which case you neither go to church nor fast. Otherwise it's just some extraordinary nonsense—a meaningless compromise between dead belief and lack of belief."

When we said good-bye, Rimsky-Korsakov thanked me for my attentiveness and asked me not to forget him.

"Come to see me tomorrow and the day after," he said. "As often as you can."

12 April

This evening I again dropped in on the Rimsky-Korsakovs'. Although Nikolai Andreyevich appeared strong, at times he was still rather listless. I gave him a lacquer tray with a picture by Bilibin of Tsar Saltan's three sisters walking toward a hut. He seemed very pleased with it.

Steinberg was also there and Gury Stravinsky had come in the afternoon with a bouquet of flowers. After dinner Maximillian Osseyevich played excerpts from Igor Stravinsky's *The Bees*.

I stayed with them through dinner. On the whole, I felt depressed. I left just as young Nadezhda Nikolayevna, Steinberg, and Volodya and Nikolai Andreyevich were settling down to paint eggs. Rimsky-Korsakov thanked me very much for my kind attention to him. Meanwhile (I do not know why), I felt empty and lonely inside. . . .

When I reached the street, I met Nadezhda Nikolayevna (the elder). We talked about Nikolai Andreyevich and his illness. She was obviously extremely upset.

13 April

I was at Zagorodny again from eight o'clock until midnight. Rimsky-Korsakov had a wonderful night. Besides me, Mikhail Nikolayevich and his wife, Sofia Nikolayevna, Steinberg, and Liadov were also there. The latter had come, he said, first, to inquire about Rimsky-Korsakov and secondly, to tell him how delighted he is with *The Golden Cockerel*. It was clear that this made Rimsky-Korsakov very happy, and he embraced Liadov firmly.

"You know," said Liadov, "it is so peaceful, so quiet in the scene where Dodon is lulled to sleep (in act 2) that it seems you can hear a fly flying and beating its wings against the glass."

Then, over protests from Rimsky-Korsakov, Liadov insisted that he (Rimsky-Korsakov) is a decadent and this is very good. There is a great deal of beauty in decadence, he maintained, and, furthermore, we must approach everything new and unknown not with prejudice but with love.

Anatoly Konstantinovich then read to us some extremely witty aphorisms of Oscar Wilde. I recall one which struck me particularly: "Every great man has his disciples, but it is always a Judas who writes his biography."(!) So, then, *I* am Rimsky-Korsakov's Judas (what a fine title!)

During tea they talked about our miserable critics: Nesterov, Kolomiitsev, Valter, Bernstein, and also about Goldenblum and the celebration of his twenty-fifth anniversary which is to take place tomorrow.[31]

"I must send him a telegram," said Nikolai Andreyevich. "Otherwise he'll be offended."

As Nadezhda Nikolayevna sees it, such "semi-artists" could do very well without jubilees. Cruel but true.

The discussion turned to *Russkaia muzykal'naia gazeta*. For some reason Liadov started to attack Findeisen but then stopped and said: "But I know that you, Nikolai Andreyevich, adore him and always take his part."

"Nothing of the kind," retorted Rimsky-Korsakov. "I simply appreciate the fact that now and then he'll publish some of Glinka's letters [32] and other things of that kind, and that's good."

I forgot to mention that before tea, Steinberg and Nadezhda Nikolayevna played the *Easter Overture* and, after tea, all four pieces from Scriabin's op. 51 [33] and the first movement of Steinberg's Second Symphony.

They started to talk about Belsky and Gnessin, whereupon Liadov turned to Steinberg and asked, in all seriousness, if he did not find him (Gnessin) a bit mad. The question was put so amusingly and Steinberg replied so properly that he did not think so, that we all burst out laughing. (What a comical fellow Liadov is!)

Generally speaking, Anatoly Konstantinovich was the "star" of the evening. He suggested that it would be a good idea if Belsky drew up a libretto based on Pushkin's *Tale of the Dead Princess*.

"Those were better times," he said, "the days of Pushkin, when there were Arina Rodionovnas,[34] who recited the folk prayer every night about curbing Tsar Ivan the Terrible."

Liadov then told us a bit about the childhood of the famous writer Andersen, whose father, though a shoemaker by trade, was a profound dreamer at heart, etc. With this Rimsky-Korsakov remarked that Anatoly Konstantinovich had obviously read a great deal.

'Oh, but you—" retorted Liadov, "how much you've written!"

Turning to the subject of the Conservatory, Anatoly Konstantinovich said that in a certain sense he agrees with Stasov that entry to that institution should be made as difficult as possible, otherwise what you get is absolute rubbish.

From further conversation, it became clear to me that Liadov does not care much for Rachmaninov's music. In his opinion, it is lacking in elegance. Besides, most of it tends to be morose, like the composer himself.

"Rachmaninov owes a great deal of his fame to Siloti," said Anatoly Konstantinovich, "and also to the fact that he's an excellent conductor and gifted pianist."

I forgot to mention, Nikolai Andreyevich has never seen a motion picture.

I was at the Rimsky-Korsakovs' tonight from six o'clock until quarter to nine. N. I. Richter and Steinberg were also there. When I entered, young Nadezhda Nikolayevna was singing something from Verdi's *Aida* (accompanied by Steinberg), and Nikolai Andreyevich was taking a nap. However, within a quarter of an hour, he came into the drawing room.

First, Rimsky-Korsakov expressed a desire to read Ibsen—he must buy a complete set of his works, he said. Then he told us that last night Cherepnin had dropped in to report about *Snegurochka,* and that Belsky had been there today, as well as Felix Blumenfeld, who is going to Paris.[35]

We chatted about Taneyev, who is very arrogant toward subordinates but extremely kind, courteous, even saccharine toward musicians who play his music.

During dinner, Nikolai Andreyevich received a check for four hundred sixty francs from Paris.

"This means that this season they've taken in a hundred and fifty rubles for my music alone," he remarked jokingly.

After dinner Richter played all of the second act of *The Cockerel.* While he was playing, Nikolai Andreyevich and I sat on the divan in the drawing room exchanging our impressions. Nikolai Andreyevich pointed out to me the orchestration of the music in A major (canonic imitation in the cello, oboe solo above, etc.). This time (that is, in act 2) he had his fill of the key of A, he said. He prides himself on the fact that his works contain a great deal of modulation.

Again today he drew my attention to the harmonization of the phrase [shown in example 79] and the minor thirds in the part of the Queen of Shemakhan at the words: "Gromche . . . tishe . . . dal'she . . . blizhe" [example 80].

"I think it came out fairly well," he said.

But at this point he became uneasy. He felt hot. He removed his jacket. However, he continued to sit in the drawing room for a full half hour, talking about *The Golden Cockerel.* He pointed out that this "tale of

Example 79

Voz- dukh stal ka- koi- to p'ia- nyi, vlazh- nyi, i gus-

toi i pria- nyi kak dur-man noch- nykh tsve- tov.

kak ig- ra

Example 80

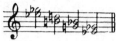

a Queen and Her Kingdom" is orchestrated very subtly and that he him-self is pleased with it.

At about quarter to nine Rimsky-Korsakov apparently wanted to lie down. Without a word he rose quietly from the divan and went into his study. Walking through the drawing room, I saw him first go up to the window and then, after standing there briefly, slowly make his way to the divan. (It was dark in the study.) He was lying down when I went into say good-bye. His last words were, "Drop in on us, dear friend." I promised to come tomorrow.

I already had my coat on when Richter, at my request, began to play the D-flat major music from the first act of *The Cockerel.* What inspired peace! After listening to these wondrous sounds, I left.

On leaving, I closed the study door carefully and with this, I was suddenly overcome by a feeling of extraordinary terror and sadness. For a long time my head was filled with the theme of the brilliant lullaby from *The Cockerel,* and my heart was tormented by its sound.

There was something unusual, something special about tonight's visit to Rimsky-Korsakov. An unforgettable, prophetic evening. It was the eve of the second severe attack of angina pectoris.

16 April

I was at the Rimsky-Korsakovs' from two o'clock until three-fifteen, but I did not see Nikolai Andreyevich. The doctors have advised that no one be admitted. I learned that last night, after I left, Nikolai Andreyevich slept for about three quarters of an hour, after which he had a severe coughing spell (the beginning of an asthmatic attack), which made him very irritable. He went to bed at midnight. At four o'clock he had an-other severe asthmatic attack. Neither nitroglycerin, hot water, nor mus-tard plasters gave him any relief. At five o'clock Dr. Servirog came and at five-twenty he gave Nikolai Andreyevich an injection of morphine and the pain subsided almost immediately. Nikolai Andreyevich did not leave his bedroom all day; he either lay in bed or sat beside it in an armchair.

Besides me, Mikhail Nikolayevich and his wife, Elena Georgiyevna, So-fia Nikolayevna, and Steinberg were there. (Andrei Nikolayevich did not leave for Lyubensk, as planned.) Elena Georgiyevna hinted to me in passing that this year Nikolai Andreyevich had some sort of family trouble which had upset and worried him terribly.

From further conversations I learned that the first asthmatic attack had occured in the summer of 1906, in Italy, but after that they seemed to have ceased completely and were not noted again until December 1907.

In the opinion of Dr. Borodulin, such a close succession of attacks as the present ones—all within five days—is not a good sign. For the present, the chief remedy is complete rest. Nikolai Andreyevich must not think about anything—the Conservatory, lessons; everything must be put aside. He must go to the countryside and follow a very rigid regimen. He is also forbidden coffee. How difficult this will be for his peace of mind. How difficult it will be for him to accustom himself to the idea that he is, in fact, near death! They have even taken away his coffee, his favorite drink, for which he would often say a special prayer after dinner: "Thank you, God, for having created coffee."

Today I returned to Vasilyevsky Island with Steinberg. On the way he recounted to me how yesterday Felix Blumenfeld, sprawled out on the divan with an air of great importance and the score of *Prince Igor* in his hand, had discussed with Nikolai Andreyevich the cuts he proposed to make, while Nikolai Andreyevich stood the whole time bending over him, looking through the music. (Considerate people, these Belyaevites, I must say!)

Meanwhile, Nikolai Andreyevich is very anxious that the proofs of act 2 of *The Golden Cockerel* be sent to Moscow as soon as possible, and that mention should be made of the harp (where two should play—where one).

At eight o'clock in the evening, Maximilian Osseyevich phoned to tell me that in the afternoon, after we left, there was fear of another attack, and Servirog was summoned but fortunately, no attack occured. Nikolai Andreyevich cannot lie down because of difficulty in breathing, and therefore he sits in the armchair almost all day.

At ten-thirty Steinberg phoned again to say that Nikolai Andreyevich is holding his own and has quieted down somewhat, but that he has difficulty swallowing (because of a kind of spasm in his throat). Therefore, it has been decided that Steinberg should spend the night there. He promised to phone me again tomorrow morning.

What is going to happen? It is awful to contemplate.

---

17 April

Shortly after ten o'clock this morning, Maxmilian Osseyevich telephoned to report that Rimsky-Korsakov had spent a relatively quiet night. At present he is sitting in the armchair. I promised to drop in on him after work.

I arrived at the Rimsky-Korsakovs' at about four-thirty and stayed until five-fifteen. I learned that they would like to call in Professor Sirotinin but that Nikolai Andreyevich has objected. In Dr. Borodulin's opinion, his condition is very serious and for the time being, they cannot even think of going abroad or to the country.

"We have to find a way somehow to put him right," he said. "There's no doubt that the aorta is very dilated. In short, it is the usual angina pectoris, though of a somewhat different type from M. M. Koryakin's. Nikolai Andreyevich must still remain in his bedroom tomorrow. Then maybe the day after tomorrow he can be moved to his study.

"You know," added Dr. Borodulin, "despite his serious illness, Nikolai Andreyevich wants to look at proofs. What am I to do with him?"

18 April

This morning before work, I learned from young Nadezhda Nikolayevna by telephone that Nikolai Andreyevich had spent a rather quiet night. He slept in bed until three-thirty and then dozed, now in the armchair, then in bed again. In the morning he drank cocoa, with obvious relish. Today they are awaiting a reply from Dr. Sirotinin.

Thank God—only how long will this improvement last?

At six o'clock Steinberg dropped in on me. He told me that yesterday Liadov and Glazunov had visited Rimsky-Korsakov; also that toward evening, Servirog had noticed that his feet were slightly swollen, but that this morning the swelling was down almost completely, at least in one foot. Nikolai Andreyevich's voice was normal. He was even joking.

At around ten in the evening, Maximilian Osseyevich telephoned from the Rimsky-Korsakovs' to tell me that Dr. Sirotinin had been there at four o'clock this afternoon, had confirmed the diagnosis, but at the same time had found kidney damage. After the consultation, Rimsky Korsakov's mood was so-so.

Both *Rech'* and *Slovo* have reported on Rimsky-Korsakov's illness.[36]

20 April

Andrei telephoned to say that Rimsky-Korsakov had a fairly good night, even though he had not slept very much. The edema has almost completely disappeared, but he became slightly upset when he saw in the French edition of *Snegurochka* that the role of the Wood Sprite is sung by a mezzo-soprano. Nonrelatives are still not permitted to visit him.

In the afternoon I saw Steinberg, who told me that Belsky had dropped in yesterday but, like Glazunov and Liadov, he had not been permitted to see Nikolai Andreyevich. Dr. Borodulin stayed with him for five hours yesterday and Servirog two and a half hours.

Sirotinin, as before, insists that Rimsky-Korsakov has a kidney stone. He has already been permitted to walk by himself from the bed to the armchair and back and even to look at proofs a little at a time. (They are kept hidden from him, however, otherwise he would immediately overtire himself.)

During the day Nikolai Andreyevich plays rams [a card game] (at least he did yesterday). Even though he is feeling relatively better, by evening he is tired and becomes anxious, fearful of an attack. Besides this, the pain in his back persists. All this time he has not smoked and does not even want to, but this has also made him somewhat depressed.

26 April

I learned, by telephone, that Nikolai Andreyevich is feeling completely well. As before he is going over the proofs little by little; he looks excellent and even seems to have gained weight. Evidently Glazunov's visit of yesterday did not harm him in the least.

Further, Nadezhda Nikolayevna the younger asked me to tell Belsky that on Sunday, Nikolai Andreyevich will receive the two of us—one at one o'clock, the other at four. She also said that Liadov, Mikhail Nikolayevich, and Steinberg had been there today.

And so, until tomorrow.

27 April

When I arrived at the Rimsky-Korsakovs' this afternoon, Nikolai Andreyevich was sitting in the dining room in a dressing gown. At first he struck me as sad, preoccupied. However, this mood soon passed and we began to speak calmly about his health.

"The swelling in my feet is still not down completely though it is slight," he said. "All this is the result of a weak heart."

He is not coughing anymore. He has given up smoking once and for all and, as proof of this, he gave me a thousand cigarettes he had just received. The doctor is keeping him at home for a while before permitting him to move to the country because of the stairs there. During this illness, he said, he has realized for the first time the enormous importance of rest to the restoration of health.

Speaking further, I learned that *Snegurochka* is going to be given in Paris on April 28 and *Boris Godunov* on May 6,[37] and that Diaghilev and Blumenfeld are exceedingly pleased with Nikolai Andreyevich's insertions. I learned, too, that today Nikolai Andreyevich worked on selecting musical examples for his textbook of orchestration from the works of Glazunov.

I left at ten minutes to five, after dear Nikolai Andreyevich and I embraced warmly, and he asked me to visit him again.

"Reflective, silent sat before us Rimsky."[38] This was our first meeting since Nikolai Andreyevich's second attack of angina pectoris.

30 April

After work (at around four-thirty) I dropped in at Zagorodny where I found Olga Blumenfeld, Steinberg, and Dr. Borodulin. Later Mikhail Nikolayevich, Sofia Nikolayevna, and N. I. Richter also came.

Dr. Borodulin left at about five o'clock. His last words were: "Our patient is improving, improving." I went into the dining room, where Nikolai Andreyevich was sitting. He was wearing his many-colored "Shemakhan" dressing gown; he looked extremely well and was in an excellent mood. He greeted me at the door with the words: "Well, you see, thanks to my illness I'm following a rather strict regimen."

He showed me the French translation of the libretto of *Snegurochka* (made by Halperine and Lalo) and the Breitkopf piano reduction of the opera, both of which carried a protrait of him and a facsimile.

Snegurochka is going to be given in Paris May 22/9 without the capricious Mme Marguerite Carré. This Nikolai Andreyevich learned from Cui, who visited him yesterday and was extremely kind, begged him never to climb the stairs and to let him (César Antonovich) know if he needs him, saying that if so, he will come immediately.

In addition, César Antonovich sent Rimsky-Korsakov a letter with the clipping from Le Figaro.

Further, Nikolai Andreyevich told me that he is thinking of taking his textbook of orchestration with him this summer and really working on it—and also Mussorgsky's Marriage. I suggested that he spend some time on orchestrating Cui's William Ratcliff and begin with act 3 since he had already orchestrated part of it. To waste time and effort on Mussorgsky's Marriage, which has no future, would really be a thankless task.

While we were talking, Nikolai Andreyevich was brought a dry English biscuit (orange), which he ate instead of smoking.

"You know," he said, smiling, "my ideal at the present moment would be not to smell any cigarette smoke before going away.

"This summer," he continued, "the only thing I can conceive of is a chance to smell makhorka [39] and I don't suppose that will tempt me."

Nikolai Andreyevich is still suffering from backaches.

"Just to think," he said, "two weeks have already passed since the second attack. To me this time has seemed unusually short somehow. The days have gone by quickly."

Upon learning from me that I have already received the proofs of my article,[40] Nikolai Andreyevich asked me to bring them to him, as he would like to keep them for a little while (I was extremely flattered).

I did not leave until eight o'clock. Nikolai Andreyevich's last words were: "Come to see me."

I forgot to mention that while the doctor was with Nikolai Andreyevich, Nadezhda Nikolayevna (the elder) asked me whether she should show him Mme Halperine's letter about the possible nonpayment of an author's fee for Snegurochka and Mr. Gaugnat's letter of reply, which was enclosed.

"I don't want these letters to upset him," she said, "But there isn't the slightest possibility of concealing them from him as he's obviously awaiting word and is wondering why it has taken Mme Halperine so long to reply."

We decided not to show them to him for the time being but to wait a day or two.

4 May

I spent almost the entire day (from four-thirty until quarter to twelve) at the Rimsky-Korsakovs'. We talked about the *Textbook of Orchestration.*

"As soon as I've collected enough examples, I'm going to begin to write again," he said. "You can't imagine how difficult it is to delineate the sections. Meanwhile, there will be four principal ones: Melody, Harmony, Figuration, and Counterpoint. Just judge for yourself. In which section would you put the phrase [in example 81] (the shepherd's accompaniment) from *Snegurochka?*

Example 81

"What is it? Is it harmonic figuration on the 6/4 chord, or should it be considered melody? There are dozens of such cases."

Then he said that one general rule must always be borne in mind: a melody in octaves should always be scored for instruments of the same timbre; otherwise the octaves will not sound good.

"And yet," he continued, "a melody in octaves given to the top register of the flutes and the bottom register of the oboes and violins does not sound bad. On the other hand, a pedal point can be given to instruments of a different timbre than the chords (this is even better), since it is a note foreign to the harmony."

Nikolai Andreyevich drew my attention to the fact that only two of his works end in a key different from that in which they begin, namely, the overture to *May Night* (which begins in E and ends in C) and the overture to *Vera Sheloga* (which begins in B-flat major and ends in D minor and where this B-flat major seems to be the sustained VI step of D minor).

During dinner Nikolai Andreyevich told me that he has been taking iodine for about eighteen years. At first he took two drops twice a day; now he takes five drops three times a day with milk.

"What is most surprising about all this," he remarked, "is that my body adapted itself to this medicine and tolerates it excellently. Usually iodine causes a skin rash and even blisters."

When it came time to say good-bye, I moved solemnly toward Rimsky-Korsakov, kissed his brow, and said, "And now accept this kiss from me—the kiss of Judas, according to Oscar Wilde, for I am your future biographer and, in the opinion of that writer, the biography of a great man is always written by a Judas."

"Don't believe him, my dear friend," he replied, kissing me a second time. "They're all fools."

What a wonderful old man, the most honest person in the world!

6 May

On the day of the first performance of *Boris Godunov* in Paris, I was at the Rimsky-Korsakovs' from three-thirty until midnight. Glazunov telephoned from the Conservatory to say that the Art Council had decided, by a large majority, to award M. Steinberg the small gold medal and the so-called Mikhailov Prize of twelve hundred rubles for travel abroad. We were all overjoyed by this news and congratulated the laureate.

A part of my visit I spent in Rimsky-Korsakov's study looking through the new edition of Mussorgsky's songs (with French text).[41] I noticed that *S Nianei* (from *The Nursery*) was given in two versions: in its original form and under the same number with the notation "bis" in a free musical treatment by Rimsky-Korsakov.

Nikolai Andreyevich told me that he is not making any progress on his textbook of orchestration.

"I began this work thirty years ago," he said, "and nothing came of it. I took it up again about five years ago, again without result. The same thing happened three years ago, in the summer of 1905. Finally, I've started working on it again, but somehow it's not coming out as I'd like. And that's because it's really a terribly difficult task."

In the afternoon, Dr. Borodulin came and he confirmed that the swelling in Nikolai Andreyevich's feet is completely gone. This made Nikolai Andreyevich very happy. V. Suk also dropped in with the score of *Kitezh*, having corrected all the misprints.

I forgot to mention that when we were congratulating Steinberg, he told Nikolai Andreyevich that, after hearing the Scherzo from his First Symphony at the rehearsal for the graduation exercises, Cherepnin said to him: "Talent is talent, it follows its own course. But Rimsky-Korsakov has given you truly sound instruction, and for this, embrace him for me."

To this Rimsky-Korsakov countered, "And I'm of the opinion that just as only a person himself can fall asleep, so only a person himself can learn music. I've taught a great many people during my lifetime, but that hasn't brought forth many real musicians."

Before tea, Rimsky-Korsakov improvised a bit on the piano on the theme of my little Orlov Whitsun song. Afterward he talked about the Baptistry in the city of Pisa and its unique acoustics. It seems that beneath the dome of this old chapel, the faintest chord resounds for an extraordinary length of time and, as it does, the tones become ever more tender, more transparent and bewitching.

"For beauty, I've never heard anything anywhere like these crystal-clear sounds, slowly dying away," he said.

8 May

Today Rimsky-Korsakov received two telegrams from Paris: one from Felix Blumenfeld about the success of *Boris* and the dress rehearsal of *Snegurochka;* the other from Carré congratulating him on the enormous success of *Snegurochka.* I also read an enthusiastic review of *The Golden Cockerel* by some "Mizgir."[42]

In addition, Nikolai Andreyevich informed me that, as evident from a letter from von Bool, *The Golden Cockerel* has not been included in the repertoire of the coming season of the Moscow Imperial Theater and, in all likelihood, it will be presented next year at the Marinsky Theater in Petersburg.

"Mr. Telyakovsky is responsible for all this," remarked Rimsky-Korsakov.

9 May

Liadov and Belsky were just leaving as I entered the Rimsky-Korsakov's this afternoon. However, during my visit several others came, mostly relatives. Timofeyev and some others were not admitted, as Nikolai Andreyevich was tired. Today he received a great many flowers and several congratulatory telegrams (from N. I. Richter, Lapshin, etc.).

Before dinner, while Nikolai Andreyevich took a ten-minute nap, I looked through the proofs of the third act of *The Golden Cockerel* and also made a copy of a rather nasty review in *Novoe vremia* of the Paris performance of *Boris*. Here is what appeared in no. 11549 of this newspaper (of May 8/21, 1908):

Boris Godunov was given here before an overflow audience. Among those present were the President of the Republic Fallières, Ministers, and the aristocracy. During the performance there was frequent applause, but no feeling of excitement; at times the audience was obviously bored, not understanding a word. They did not like the music, but were impressed by the choruses and the cast. The connoisseurs maintain that as a work of art the overall conception was a failure. Some favorable comments were heard among the audience, however. (The usual "avant-garde"—ours and yours.)

At six-thirty Nadezhda Nikolayevna the younger and Steinberg returned from the Commencement exercises, and shortly before seven we sat down to dinner. We looked at Maximilian Osseyevich's certificate bearing the citation: "This small gold medal is herewith awarded' for exceptional and versatile compositional talent." Then we drank to Nikolai Andreyevich's health and to Maximilian Osseyevich and his brilliant achievement.

There was talk about Glazunov and the fact that he is positively in love with "his" Conservatory; in Alexander Konstantinovich's opinion even the poor Conservatory orchestra (with its six violins) is good, since the first violin section is composed entirely of straight-A students; and the horn player is a "miracle" because not once during the entire Commencement exercises did he go off-pitch! Well, every snipe praises his own bog!

After dinner we persuaded Nikolai Andreyevich to take a rest, and he slept from eight-fifteen until nine-fifteen. Scarcely had he gone to lie down when Glazunov appeared, and Steinberg and I kept him occupied for a good hour talking about the Conservatory. At eleven-fifteen the three of us left.

On the whole, today's visit left me feeling somewhat sad.

11 May

I was at the Rimsky-Korsakovs' from four-fifteen until quarter to eight. Steinberg was also there. Volodya had returned from Lyubensk, and Andrei went there. The repairs on the house have not yet been completed, and this is delaying their moving until the latter part of May.

Speaking of yesterday's performance of *Snegurochka* at the People's House, I reported to Rimsky-Korsakov that the theater was filled to capacity, and the opera met with considerable success. However (except for the exceedingly slow tempo in the scene of Kupava's complaint) on the whole the tempi were too fast, and the chorus, as usual, overacted. As for the singers, Tomars (Berendey) was the best. Zelyony conducted.

After dinner, Nikolai Andreyevich read to me a letter he had received from Felix Blumenfeld in Paris (dated 21/8 May), reporting that there had been a rehearsal of *Boris Godunov* on 17/4 May; the first performance had taken place on 19/6 and the second on 21/8; also that on 20/7 he (Blumenfeld) had attended a rehearsal of *Snegurochka,* at which acts 3 and 4 had been given without intermission, and that the fairytale enchantment of the Paris staging of the Chorus of the Flowers had literally taken his breath away.

Furthermore, Felix Mikhailovich wrote that Camille Bellaigue still regards the music of *Snegurochka* extremely favorably and teases his Parisian fellow-critics unmercifully, contending that they are not sufficiently sensitive to the great beauty of this remarkable opera because of the current vogue of Richard Strauss.

Despite this praise, Nikolai Andreyevich said he is absolutely certain that (as is generally the case with Russian operas) *Snegurochka* will never become part of the standard repertoire in Paris. They will give it a few times, to amuse themselves, and then take it off.

"As you know," he said, "I've no faith in the musicality of the French. To them fashion is everything."

"By the way, I wouldn't be surprised if Telyakovsky put on *The Cockerel* next year instead of *Tsar Saltan.* Golovin certainly won't have the scenery for *Saltan* ready in time, and Korovin could quickly prepare what's needed for *The Cockerel.* I'm almost certain that none of this stupid hullabaloo over censorship of the opera would have occurred if it had not been for Korovin's tactless, though well-intentioned 'whopper.' 'No,' he told Telyakovsky, 'our Hershelman in Moscow won't pass such a libretto. This is not Petersburg. No! Serov and I roared with laughter when we read this cock-and-bull story. To be sure, everyone got *his* in *The Cockerel.* And how cleverly it was done!'

"Of course," concluded Nikolai Andreyevich, "this entire monologue is my own invention, but I could swear that such a conversation actually took place between Korovin and Telyakovsky."

When we said good-bye, Nikolai Andreyevich thanked me for my visit. I told him that I will come again on Tuesday night (the thirteenth) at ten-fifteen, after I have seen my wife off to the country.

13 May

After seeing my wife off to Grigorovo, I went to the Rimsky-Korsakovs'. I found Steinberg, Misha Nikolayevich, and N. I. Richter already there.

I brought with me the second proof of my article, which I received yesterday and had already corrected. Nikolai Andreyevich wanted to look through it and make some notations on it. (I can imagine what will be left that is mine!)

I learned that Cui had visited the Rimsky-Korsakovs this afternoon, that the proofs of the Breitkopf edition of *Boris Godunov* with French and German texts had arrived, and also that *Novoe vremia* published highly enthusiastic reviews of the Paris productions of *Snegurochka* and *Boris Godunov*.[43]

Tonight Rimsky-Korsakov made a fairly good impression on me.

16 May

After the bank, I dropped in on Rimsky-Korsakov. When I entered, Alexander Nikolayevich Purgold was there. Nikolai Andreyevich was telling him about his illness. He ended by saying that now he is an invalid in the full sense of the word.

After Alexander Nikolayevich left, I told Nikolai Andreyevich that I had mentioned in my article about him that he has, among his unpublished manuscripts, the first movement of a Quintet in B flat for piano, flute, clarinet, French horn, and bassoon written in 1876. Besides this, I learned that the Public Library has uncovered the manuscript of Mussorgsky's song *Noch'* with the complete Pushkin text.

We read an article from *Novoe vremia* about the Paris reviews of *Snegurochka* (which was given on May 9, 12, 15, and 16).[44] The French admit that they do not understand anything about Russian music, since until now they have considered the East—*Slavianshchina*.[45] Most of the French critics share a great enthusiasm for the Dance of the Skomorokhi with its voluptuous rhythmic pattern which, in their exalted wisdom, deals a death blow to counterpoint, fugue, and sonata form.

"What nonsense," said Nikolai Andreyevich. "It's precisely this 'Skomorokhi' which adheres to the 'sonata form'—the second theme appears first in the dominant and then (after the development) moves to the tonic."

Asked by Nadezhda Nikolayevna whether the French reviews of Snegurochka were good, Rimsky-Korsakov replied, in jest, "It depends upon where. Where they praise, they're good; where they disparage, they're obviously foolish."

We laughed. Finally, Nikolai Andreyevich launched an attack on literature.

"It's all deception," he said, "the poetry of the word. It's not so with music where, even admitting that the feelings and moods expressed are deceptive, the tonal edifice itself is immutable."

I took issue with this, but Rimsky-Korsakov stood his ground firmly.

He is taking all his orchestral scores to Lyubensk; he feels he may need them for his textbook of orchestration.

18 May

Steinberg and I were at the Rimsky-Korsakovs' tonight from seven-thirty until twelve-thirty. We talked about Glazunov and how engrossed he is in his Conservatory. These days he talks of nothing else—not about music, his own compositions, the Paris performances, or even The Cockerel (a copy of which Nikolai Andreyevich gave him as a gift). On the other hand, he told Nikolai Andreyevich about his great joy—that they had finally managed to connect a drainpipe from the Conservatory directly to Ekaterinovka.

"Now, I ask you," remarked Nikolai Andreyevich, "what has all this to do with me?"

He is really annoyed with Alexander Konstantinovich for having removed himself from music.

Today Nikolai Andreyevich unearthed his critical analysis of Snegurochka, and this led to a minor incident between us. Just as I was about to look at it, he asked, "And what right have you to read it?"

"Because you yourself once read it to me," I replied.

He seemed to have regained his calm, but then he became somewhat agitated again, rose from the divan (I was sitting at his desk), snatched the manuscript I was reading, and said with some irritation, "Even though you criticized this work severely, I'm going to continue it, but I won't show it to you."

With this strange outburst, the matter was closed.

Somehow we got onto the subject of Yakovlev, who, once, when talking with Nikolai Andreyevich about the nondramatic subjects of his operas, began with great earnestness to urge him, at least once in his life to write an opera on a realistic libretto, not a fairy tale.

"A lot these gentlemen understand about music, I must say—all these Valters, Figners, and their ilk," commented Rimsky-Korsakov.

He expressed a fear that he will not get anything done this summer. I suggested that he try to set down his views on operatic forms, but he replied that he is thinking of going on with his "chronicle," since he has not kept up the "diary" (since 1906) as he had intended, and now it is too late to take it up again—too much has been forgotten and the rest of his impressions have already lost their sharpness.

"I really should describe the Paris concerts," he concluded, "and the swinish behavior of the management and singers during the production and rehearsals of *Kitezh*."

From further conversation, I learned that Glazunov had visited the Rimsky-Korsakovs during the day; also that Nikolai Andreyevich had spoken on the telephone with Telyakovsky, who informed him that *Snegurochka* is going to be given in the fall, but for the time being, he knows nothing about plans for Rimsky-Korsakov's latest operas. They may stage *Tsar Saltan,* perhaps even *The Golden Cockerel.* Telyakovsky also told Nikolai Andreyevich that he probably would not like certain features of the Paris production of *Snegurochka* (the French are sorely lacking in simplicity), but there were some highly successful moments, and these ought to be adopted.

During my visit Rimsky-Korsakov tried twice to get some rest; the first time he dozed off for a few minutes; then he slept for about half an hour.

After tea, we moved to the drawing room where Nikolai Andreyevich and Steinberg sat at the piano for more than half an hour, discussing a single F sharp in the first movement of Steinberg's Second Symphony.

Finally they decided to change the harmonization somewhat to make it conform to this episode.

"But don't take me too seriously," said Rimsky-Korsakov. "Perhaps all this is routine, and I'm simply too old to judge."

While our maestros were engrossed in the ill-fated F sharp, Nadezhda Nikolayevna confided to me that there is a possibility that they may have to remain in Lyubensk until the fall, because of Nikolai Andreyevich.

Finally, we talked about Nikolai Andreyevich's deep longing for Lyubensk, for the countryside.

"However," he said, not without bitterness, "even there I'll probably be walking . . . to the nearest bench. How difficult and boring all this is."

On parting, Nikolai Andreyevich asked me not to forget him and to look in on them again before their departure.

20 May

I was at the Rimsky-Korsakovs' from seven-fifteen until quarter to eleven on the evening before their departure for Lyubensk. When I ran the doorbell, Nikolai Andreyevich had just laid down to rest, so Volodya and I tiptoed past his room. Volodya told me that shortly before I arrived, Dr. Servirog had been there and had taught them how to administer hypodermic injections. The doctor had found the state of Nikolai Andreyevich's health quite satisfactory but he prescribed rest, as before. The Rimsky-Korsakovs may have to remain in Lyubensk for the winter, Volodya said, since in the city it would be absolutely impossible to protect his father from needless worries, all sorts of rehearsals, which interested him, and upsetting visits.

Rimsky-Korsakov awoke around nine o'clock and Volodya, Steinberg, and I went into his study. I gave Nikolai Andreyevich a brief summary of Mark Twin's *Adam's Diary*. He appeared to be interested in it and decided to read it. I also promised to give him Count Salias' novel *In Moscow* this summer (a famous work from the time of Catherine II set against the background of the plague).

"You know," remarked Nikoali Andreyevich, "like you, in literature I prefer the small forms, although, of course, I'm also mad about Tolstoy's *War and Peace*. But that's an exception.

"I have a tremendous desire to read something wholesome, not decadent," he continued. "I'm bored with these ungifted poseurs. They all lie and put on airs."

Rimsky-Korsakov said again today that for him the time seems to be passing unusually quickly. And this, he concluded, is because his soul seems empty; he does not have enough stimulation.

At around four-thirty the doorbell rang and in walked Glazunov. They fell to discussing the Conservatory and Siloti. According to Alexander Konstantinovich, the rich and well-known Van-der-Pals has refused to subsidize the Siloti concerts because he is displeased with Alexander Ilyich.

Glazunov then asked Nikolai Andreyevich what he plans to work on this summer.

"Why, I'm going to write a potpourri," replied Nikolai Andreyevich in all seriousness.

He was referring to the idea he had of compiling a large orchestral suite from *The Golden Cockerel,* since he has no hope of the opera being produced on the Imperial Stage in the near future.

The conversation turned to Balakirev who, it seems, has finished his second symphony.[46]

Alexander Konstantinovich would like to reorchestrate Balakirev's *Islamey,*[47] even though it has already been scored by a certain Casella. With this purpose in mind he has even thought of an excellent modulation for the transition to D major, since the beginning of the piece had to be transposed to E-flat major.

"But do you really have the right to do that?" asked Nikolai Andreyevich. "After all, it will be a sort of new, not entirely Balakirevian *Islamey.*"

"You'll see," replied Alexander Konstantinovich. "It will be fine."

After tea, Glazunov, Steinberg, and I rose to leave (tomorrow everyone has to get up early). In parting, Nikolai Andreyevich and I embraced heartily three times. I promised to go to the station to see him off. He was obviously touched.

21 May

I was at the Warsaw Station at exactly eight-thirty this morning. Nikolai Andreyevich, Nadezhda Nikolayevna, Nadya, Steinberg, and I sat in the waiting room for about a quarter of an hour. Between Rimsky-Korsakov and me was Rex, his favorite dog, whom he held on a leash and kept patting while talking with me. To my remark that I personally prefer bronze dogs to living ones, Nikolai Andreyevich retorted: "But what a marvelous soul they have, the real dogs. And it's this soul that the bronze dogs just don't have." And he gently patted Rex, who was wagging his tail.

When it came time to board the train, fate seemed to favor Nikolai Andreyevich. First of all, the car in which he was to ride, stopped just opposite the exit; secondly, due to the fact that some important general with a plume was traveling in the same car, a ramp covered with red cloth had been placed between the station platform and the car vestibule, thus sparing Nikolai Andreyevich not only excessive walking but also the necessity of climbing the steps into the car. As we see, even generals can be of use sometimes!

On the whole, Nikolai Andreyevich was in an excellent frame of mind, even though he had become so upset and angered by Leonid Andreyev's *The Seven Who Were Hanged,* which he skimmed through after we left last night, that he had to take a bromide.

Promptly at nine o'clock the train started to move. Before I left the car, we embraced heartily four times and I asked Rimsky-Korsakov to let me know how his trip to Lyubensk had been, which of course, he promised to do. He urged me to visit him in Lyubensk, especially for the wedding.[48] Alas, I could not hear his final words just before the train pulled out, as it was impossible to open the windows. The third bell sounded. As the train receded, Nikolai Andreyevich kept blowing kisses to Steinberg and me, and as long as we could see him, he was holding his hat above his head.

23 May

When I telephoned Lyubensk today, I learned from Andrei that Nikolai Andreyevich had another attack during the night of May 21. This one, however, was not especially severe. Evidently the trip and walking in the garden had tired him. He was given an injection of morphine, and shortly afterward the attack subsided. They summoned a local doctor, who determined that the heart was dilated and advised that Rimky-Korsakov be taken abroad. As of this moment he is quite weak and staying in bed, but his voice is normal. Poor, poor maestro!

According to Andrei, on arriving at Lyubensk, Nikolai Andreyevich looked very well, felt strong and, when he retired he was certain that he was not going to have another attack today.

The attack began at two o'clock in the morning. When he coughed up phlegm (for the first time during his illness), it was somewhat discolored with blood.

30 May

This morning I spoke on the telephone again, this time with Volodya. Although he did not have any detailed information, he assumed that Nikolai Andreyevich is better, since he flatly refused to have a doctor in attendance for the summer or even to have Servirog visit them.

2 June

The last news about Rimsky-Korsakov which I had from Lyubensk I received from Steinberg on Whitmonday, in a letter dated 31 May.

Here is what Maximilian Osseyevich wrote: "Nikolai Andreyevich is feeling fine. He keeps himself occupied, sits on the balcony. We are thinking of permitting him to go down into the garden tomorrow. The weather yesterday and today was marvelous. Everyone sends regards."

How could I have imagined that only a week later I would receive the following fateful telegram from Lyubensk: "Nikolai Andreyevich passed away during the night. Steinberg."[49]

This telegram was sent on June 8 at nine-nineteen. I received it on Monday, June 9, at the Grigorov's estate, where I had arrived from Petersburg the day before. I was deeply shocked.

10 June

Thus, Rimsky-Korsakov died on Saturday night, June 7, 1908. On Tuesday, June 10, his body was brought from Lyubensk to Petersburg. The train of the Warsaw Railroad bearing the oak casket, in which rested the remains of this great man, arrived at three-forty in the afternoon.

The memorial and funeral services were held at the Conservatory. On Wednesday, June 11 (the Feast of St. John, according to the new calendar), Rimsky-Korsakov was laid to rest in the cemetery of the Novodevichy Monastery.[50]

On June 17, 1908, in its issue no. 143, the newspaper *Rech'* carried the following letter:

Permit us through your newspaper to express our deepest gratitude to the St. Petersburg Conservatory and its Director, the city of St. Petersburg, the University of St. Petersburg, the Imperial Russian Musical Society and its branches, the Court Choir, the Court Orchestra and the other musical institutions of Russia, and also the artists, friends, acquaintances, and pupils of Nikolai Andreyevich Rimsky-Korsakov who have paid their respects to the memory of the deceased and expressed their sympathy for our great sorrow.

The Rimsky-Korsakov Family
Other newspapers please copy.

The same issue of *Rech'* reported that on June 16, nine days after the death of N. A. Rimsky-Korsakov, a memorial service for the deceased was celebrated in the Karamzin Church of the Novodevichy Monastery. Almost no one except members of the family attended.

I will conclude my reminiscences with a letter I received from Steinberg and statements by Karatygin and Glazunov.

Lyubensk, 23 June 1908

My dear Vasily Vasilyevich,

I received your letter today. I have been meaning to write you for several days, but somehow I have not been able to do it. I am in such a state of depression that I have no desire to do anything. It is empty and lonely here without Nikolai Andreyevich. Besides, for almost two weeks it has been raining continuously, from morning until night, and we have almost forgotten what the sun looks like.

I still cannot get used to the idea that Nikolai Andreyevich is no more and will never be again.

The last days before his death I was with him almost constantly; now I feel completely orphaned. The death of my own father was far less painful to me than this senseless and cruel catastrophe.

I do not want to give you in a letter the details of Nikolai Andreyevich's death; it is much too difficult to write about. At our very first meeting I will tell you about his last minutes, which I witnessed. For now I will describe to you only in a general way what happened after my last letter to you, when it was still warm, bright, joyful, and cozy here.

I think it was June 2 when we permitted Nikolai Andreyevich to go down into the garden. He strolled about slowly, rested fifteen seconds on each step coming up and felt wonderful. Our wedding was on the fourth. Nikolai Andreyevich did not come to the church but remained at home with Sonya. He was in very good spirits and upon our return from church he threw oats at us, asked about the ceremony in church, chuckled at the priest—in a word, he was in an excellent mood. During those days, Nikolai Andreyevich walked down to the garden two or three times a day, assuring us that he was not a bit tired when we tried to protest.

During the following three days, Nikolai Andreyevich was somewhat out of sorts, the reason being two unpleasant letters he received: the first, from Telyakovsky, with news that *The Cockerel* is not going to be staged at all because of censorship problems. *Saltan* also seemed to be canceled, although the letter made no clear reference to this.

The second letter was from Paris. The Society of Composers[51] refused to accept Nikolai Andreyevich as a member and consequently to pay him any royalties for *Snegurochka*.

It is difficult to say which piece of news upset Nikolai Andreyevich more. It was impossible to tell from his outward appearance.

On Saturday (the seventh), despite our protests, Nikolai Andreyevich walked a great deal and did not even count how many times he went down to the garden.

In the evening he came to us and asked me to go outside the gate to watch the sunset. We sat together on the bench for a long time. Nikolai Andreyevich talked about his voyages. At ten o'clock we went to have tea. Nikolai Andreyevich played the piano for a while (standing); then he talked for a long time about various things—the Conservatory, moving to the new apartment. At eleven-thirty Nadya and I went to our room.[52] We were awakened at two o'clock, immediately after the onset of the attack. At around quarter past, after morphine, Nikolai Andreyevich seemed somewhat better, but then suddenly he lost the power of speech, and at about two-thirty (a bit earlier, to be exact) death followed due to heart failure. The doctor did not arrive until six o'clock. All that remained for him to do was to sign the death certificate.

I do not feel like writing about myself now. I will write some other time. . . .

Do not forget us. Write. It will bring great joy to your devoted and loving

M. Steinberg.

I will conclude with the words of V. G. Karatygin and A. K. Glazunov. Karatygin said: "With the death of Rimsky-Korsakov an entire epoch in the life of the new Russian music has ended." [53]

Glazunov spoke truly when, over Nikolai Andreyevich's grave on the day of his funeral at the Novodevichy Monastery on Wednesday, June 11, he said:

"We have lost someone the like of whom there never was before and may never be again. Nikolai Andreyevich was a great genius, with an inquiring mind and a lofty soul. He always strove for the highest ideal."

NOTES

1. *Russkaia muzykal'naia gazeta* (1895), no. 2, col. 314.

1. 1886–1891

1. During the 1885–86 season, Anton Rubinstein gave a series of seven recitals covering the history of piano music from the sixteenth century to the present. These recitals were presented in St. Petersburg, Moscow, Berlin, Leipzig, Paris, London, and Vienna. Besides this, Rubinstein also gave a set of three shorter recitals in Dresden and Brussels.

2. The Russian Symphony Concerts were founded in Petersburg in 1885 by Mitrofan Belyaev, a wealthy businessman and champion of Russian music, for the purpose of propagating native works. Rimsky-Korsakov was the principal conductor of these concerts from their inception on October 15, 1886, until the 1900–1 season.

In the mid-1880s Belyaev also brought together a group of the leading Russian musicians, headed by Rimsky-Korsakov and linked "by heredity" with the "Mighty Handful," who met at his house on Fridays to play string quartets and other chamber music and to acquaint themselves with the latest compositions of their fellow members and other contemporary works.

During the 1887–88 season there were five Russian Symphony Concerts—on October 24 and 31; November 7 and 21; and December 5, 1887. The program of the first concert, in memory of Borodin, included, besides the works mentioned, premieres of the Overture to *Prince Igor;* two movements from the unfinished Symphony in A minor; and the songs *Dlia beregov otchizny dal'noi* and *Arabskaia melodiia.*

3. During the 1889–90 season there were six Russian Symphony Concerts—on October 22, November 11 and 25, and December 10, 1889; and January 20 and February 18, 1890. (Trans.)

4. The Symphonic Suite *Antar* (originally called Symphony no. 2) based on O. I. Senkovsky's tale of the same name, was composed in 1868. It was published in 1880, revised in 1897 and again

in 1903. [See Gerald Abraham, *Slavonic and Romantic Music* (London: Faber and Faber, 1968), pp. 198–201. (Trans.)]

5. After Borodin's death, the Finale to act 4 of the collective opera-ballet *Mlada,* which had been allotted to Borodin, was orchestrated by Rimsky-Korsakov. It was this version which was given its première at the Russian Symphony Concert. (Trans.)

6. *The Inn Mazurka* for orchestra (op. 19, 1887).

7. Balakirev's *Islamey,* Oriental fantasy for piano (1869), was performed by Felix Blumenfeld.

8. Symphonic poem *Sadko,* composed 1867, rescored in 1892.

9. Overture-Fantasy *Hamlet,* after Shakespeare (op. 67, 1888); first performed on November 12, 1888, at the third Symphonic Evening of the Russian Musical Society in St. Petersburg. The Concert Fantasy for Piano (op. 56, 1884) was played by Felix Blumenfeld.

10. The Russian Musical Society was founded in the spring of 1859 for the purpose of raising the level of music in Russia (according to its prime mover, Anton Rubinstein). It presented its first concert on November 28 of that year. (Trans.)

11. During the years 1887–1889 the Russian Musical Society was under the direction of Leopold Auer. Judging from subsequent entries of Yastrebtsev, the meeting with Rimsky-Korsakov described here occurred in 1888.

12. *Snegurochka* (Snow Maiden), an opera in four acts and prologue (1881). Libretto drawn from A. N. Ostrovsky's play of the same name.

13. *Vakula the Smith*—opera by Nikolai Solovyov based on Gogol's story "Christmas Eve"; composed in 1875 and first performed January 12, 1880, by the St. Petersburg Musical and Dramatic Society. It was submitted to an opera competition which had been set up in 1873 by the Russian Musical Society in memory of the late Alexander Serov. The libretto was written by Polonsky originally for Serov, but the latter died before it could be set to music.

14. The twenty-fifth anniversary of Tchaikovsky's debut as a composer was celebrated at the St. Petersburg Conservatory on December 3, 1890.

15. A testimonial drawn up by Stasov and written in Slavonic script, followed by facsimile signatures of the subscribers (preserved in the GITIM, N. A. and A. N. Rimsky-Korsakov Archives). In honor of the occasion, Stasov also wrote an article entitled "Nikolai Andreevich Rimskii-Korsakov," which appeared in *Severnyi vestnik* (1890), no. 12. It was published separately the same year and republished in V. V. Stasov, *Izbrannye sochineniia v trekh tomakh* (Selected works in three volumes) (Moscow, 1952), 3:366.

16. December 19—it was on this date, in 1865, that Rimsky-Korsakov's First Symphony received its premiere, at a Free Music School concert with Balakirev conducting. (V.V. Ya.)

17. The concert, under the direction of Rimsky-Korsakov and Glazunov, took place on the day of this entry. [*Mlada,* an opera-ballet in four acts, plot by S. A. Gedeonov, libretto by Rimsky-Korsakov, was composed in 1889–1890. The entire opera was first performed at the Marinsky Theater on October 20, 1892. (Trans.)]

18. *The Kremlin*—Symphonic Suite in three movements by Glazunov (op. 30, 1891). This performance, its first, was conducted by the composer.

19. Reference to the spring examinations in opera performance in which the Conservatory students—singers, instrumentalists, conductors—took part. (The last named received their training in the composition class.) On March 17, excerpts from Cui's *Captive of the Caucasus,* Rimsky-Korsakov's *Snegurochka,* and Solovyov's *Vakula the Smith* were given in the very small and uncomfortable hall of the old Conservatory building.

20. A play on the Russian proverb: Morning is wiser than evening. (Trans.)

21. From 1883 to 1894 Rimsky-Korsakov served as Assistant director to the Court Chapel,

where he introduced order into the system of instruction and, after devoting special attention to the instrumental classes, organized a symphony orchestra of Chapel students.

22. In 1891 Liadov taught a required course in harmony at the St. Petersburg Conservatory.

23. *Skazka (Fairy Tale,* originally entitled *Baba Yaga)* op. 29, 1880. In the program of this work Rimsky-Korsakov quoted lines from the Prologue to Pushkin's *Ruslan and Ludmila.* Later, when composing *Sheherazade* (Op. 35, 1888), Rimsky-Korsakov took for his literary basis *Arabian Nights.* Yastrebtsev was seeking to establish to what extent the composer intended these works to be taken literally, i.e., as a musical retelling of the literary texts. For more on this see Nikolai Andreyevich Rimsky-Korsakov, *My Musical Life,* Judah A. Joffe, trans. (New York: Vienna House, 1972). (Trans.)

24. The number of the Rimsky-Korsakovs' apartment at the Court Chapel on Bol'shaia Koniushennaia St., no. 11.

25. *100 russkikh narodnykh pesen* (100 Russian folk songs), op. 24, 1877.

26. *Sbornik russkikh narodnykh pesen. Tekst i melodii sobral i muzyku aranzhiroval dlia fortep'iano i semistrunnoi gitary Mikhail Stakhovich* (A Collection of Russian Folk Songs. Text and melodies collected and music arranged for pianoforte and seven-stringed guitar by Mikhail Stakhovich) (*Teatr* 1–4) (St. Petersburg, 1851, 1852, 1854).

27. *Russkie narodnye pesni, sobrannye N. A. L'vovym (100). Napevy zapisal i garmonizoval Ivan Pratsch* (Russian folk songs, compiled by N. A. L'vov [100]. Tunes taken down and harmonized by Ivan Prach), 1790; 2nd ed., 1806 (150 songs); 3rd ed., 1815; 4th ed., 1955.

28. *Sbornik russkikh narodnykh pesen, sostavlennyi Balakirevym* (Collection of Russian folk songs, compiled by Balakirev) (1866). No. 9 is "A my proso seiali," a *khorovod* song.

29. Rimsky-Korsakov's collection contains still another millet sowing melody: pt. II, no. 48— "A my sechu chistili." It is one of the spring *khorovod* (round dance) songs of Saratov Province, Kuznetsk District, village of Evlashev. This variant was used for a chorus in *May Night.* (V. V. Ya.)

30. On 23 January 1892, Rimsky-Korsakov, replying once more to Yastrebtsev's request for an explanation of the program of *Skazka,* stated: "I believe that this overture has in it everything that each person perceives in it." This attempt to endow *Skazka* and *Sheherazade* with a meaning not intended by the composer is referred to yet again in Yastrebtsev's entries of 18 March and 20 April 1893. Again Rimsky-Korsakov denies that these works represent a literal depiction, musically, of the works on which they are based. (Trans.)

31. A rough draft of the beginning and coda of Borodin's *Ei Ukhnem* is preserved in the N. A. Rimsky-Korsakov Archives (nos. 110 *a, b, v*—in the manuscript division of the G.P.B.).

32. Rimsky-Korsakov entertained the idea of writing a textbook of orchestration over a period of many years. The first sketches of it, relating to general questions of acoustics, a classification of wind instruments, a detailed description of their construction, etc. date to 1873–74. During 1891–1893 he again turned to the textbook. The sketches made then were preserved in the composer's notebooks; the unfinished preface was published in St. Petersburg in 1911 in the collection titled *N. A. Rimskii-Korsakov, Muzykal'nye stat'i: zametki* (N. A. Rimsky-Korsakov, Articles and notes on music) (1869–1907). Rimsky-Korsakov destroyed most of the manuscript and stopped working on the project. In 1905 he wrote the first six chapters, which form the basis of the published book. However, work on it was once again interrupted by the composition of *The Golden Cockerel.* In the summer of 1908, in Lyubensk, Rimsky-Korsakov began the final reworking of the material and the rewriting of the first chapter. This chapter was finished on June 7, the eve of the composer's death.

Osnovy orkestrovki (Principles of orchestration, 2 vols.) was first published in 1913 under the editorship of Maximilian Steinberg.

33. The schism which occurred in the Russian church in the seventeenth century as a result of reforms introduced by the Patriarch Nikon. (Trans.)

34. The first Russian Symphony Concert of the 1891–92 season took place on November 30, 1891. The second and final one was held on January 25, 1892. Both were under the direction of Rimsky-Korsakov.

35. This work in the orchestration by Rimsky-Korsakov's student Tushmalov was performed, from manuscript, for the first time at the November 30 concert.

2. 1892

1. *Tristan, the Ring, Ruslan, Snegurochka, Igor, Boris, Maid of Pskov,* and *Stone Guest.* (V.V. Ya.)

2. Rimsky-Korsakov made the first orchestration of Dargomyzhsky's *Stone Guest,* which had been left unfinished at the author's death (1869), in 1870. The opera received its premiere at the Marinsky Theater on February 16, 1872. Later, Rimsky-Korsakov became dissatisfied with the orchestration and revised it: the first scene in 1897, and the remainder in 1902. Yastrebtsev is in error here. The symphonic poem *Sadko* was written in 1867, that is, three years before the orchestration of *The Stone Guest.*

3. That is, Balakirev's circle. (V. V. Ya.)

4. *William Ratcliff*—opera in three acts, after Heine's tragedy of the same name, written by Cui in 1861–68, first performed at the Marinsky Theater on February 14, 1869.

5. *The Stone Guest* was given at the Purgolds' on January 26; *William Ratcliff* at the Molases' on February 14. (Trans.)

6. A concert given by the Court Chapel for members of the royal family.

7. This arrangement was made by Rimsky-Korsakov (on behalf of Balakirev) for Alexander III, an amateur woodwind player. Its location is unknown. A rough draft of Yastrebtsev's reminiscences of Balakirev contains the following entry for February 4, 1892: "Regarding Chopin's Polonaise in A (arranged for woodwinds by Rimsky-Korsakov—for the Tsar) Balakirev said: 'Just listen to how exciting it sounds.' " (Yastrebtsev's unpublished reminiscences of M. A. Balakirev. GITIM, N. A. and A. N. Rimsky-Korsakov Archives, Yastrebtsev Fund.)

8. Rimsky-Korsakov began his revision of Mussorgsky's *Boris Godunov* in 1889, with the rescoring of the Polonaise. In 1891–92 he reorchestrated the entire Coronation Scene. He continued working on the opera and completed his revision of it in May 1896. The major work was done in the period from December 1895 to May 1896.

9. This is what I called Wagner's orchestra, which is constructed in threes and sixes instead of pairs and fours. (V. V. Ya.)

10. This is what Rimsky-Korsakov jestingly called Kashchei's music from the third act of *Mlada,* which I was absolutely mad about. (V. V. Ya.)

11. This concert, under Napravnik, was the second of three given during Lent by the Directorate of the Imperial Theaters. The other two took place on March 2 and 5. (Trans.)

12. Incidental music to Alexei Tolstoi's dramatic poem *Don Juan* (op. 54, 1891) for soloists, chorus, orchestra, and reciter.

13. This refers to the all-European quartet competition set up in 1891 by the St. Petersburg Chamber Society, with the prize money donated by Belyaev. From the 134 quartets submitted, the first prize went to the Czech violinist and composer Miroslav Weber; the second to Sokolov, for his Quartet no. 2.

14. In the article "Episody iz zhizni russkikh artistov i kompozitorov" (Episodes from the life of Russian artists and composers) by P. S. M-v, published in *Voskresnyi listok muzyki i ob'iavlenii*

(1879), no. 9, it was claimed that A. N. Verstovsky had won the opera *Askold's Tomb* from A. E. Varlamov in a card game. This report was pure fabrication.

15. Here Rimsky-Korsakov recalls his articles on Napravnik's opera *Nizhegorodtsy* (The People of Nizhegorod), published in *S.-Peterburgskie vedomosti* (January 3, 1869), no. 3, and Cui's *Ratcliff,* published in the same paper (February 21, 1869), no. 52. Both articles were republished in Rimsky-Korsakov's *Muzykal'nye stat'i i zametki* (Articles and notes on music). In view of the forthcoming production of *Ratcliff* at the Marinsky Theater under the direction of Napravnik, Cui, not wishing to jeopardize his relations with the conductor, refused to write the review of his opera (which the Balakirev circle did not much like) and prevailed upon Rimsky-Korsakov to do it.

16. The third version of *The Maid of Pskov,* made in 1891–92, was essentially a return to the first version of the opera. [Hardly. See Gerald Abraham, *Slavonic and Romantic* Music (London: Faber and Faber, 1968), p. 203: "Finally (1898) the prologue was largely rewritten as an indepdent one-act opera: *Boyarinya Vera Sheloga.*" Trans.]

17. Tchaikovsky's *Romeo and Juliet,* composed in 1869; second version, 1870; third version, 1880. The orchestral suite from *The Nutcracker* (1892) was performed for the first time in St. Petersburg at the Russian Musical Society concert on March 7, 1892, under the composer's direction.

18. "Toward new shores"—slogan used by Mussorgsky in a letter to V. V. Stasov dated 18 October 1872. "The artistic representation of beauty alone, in its material sense," wrote Mussorgsky, "is crude childishness—art in its infancy. The subtlest traits in man's nature and in the masses of humanity, persistent prying into these little-known regions and conquering them—this is the true mission of the artist. Toward new shores! Fearlessly through storms, shoals, and treacherous rocks, toward new shores!" M. P. Mussorgsky, *Pis'ma i dokumenty* (Letters and documents) (Moscow-Leningrad, 1932).

19. The new Russian school of music—a progressive trend in Russian music during the 1860s and 1870s, known as the "Balakirev circle" or *"moguchaia kuch'ka"* ("Mighty Handful"). The first to be associated with it were Balakirev, Borodin, Mussorgsky, Rimsky-Korsakov, and Cui. Later it attracted composers of the younger generation, such as Glazunov, Liadov, and others, who formed what was called the "Belyaev circle."

20. The symphonic poem *Sadko* was rescored in 1892 for a new edition to be published by Jurgenson. It received its premiere on January 16, 1893, at the second Russian Musical Society concert under the direction of Glazunov.

21. In all there were ten rehearsals. The performance itself took place at the Molases' on November 22. (Trans.)

22. The public performance of cantatas written by students who had completed the course in composition.

23. Cui was a contributor to the Moscow journal *Artist* (1887–95), the editor of whose music section was Semyon Kruglikov, a critic and close friend of Rimsky-Korsakov.

24. The Rimsky-Korsakov family spent the summer of 1892 (as they had in 1888, 1889, and 1890) at Nezhogovitsy, the estate of Glinka-Mavrin, 18 kilometers from Luga on Lake Cheremenetskoye.

25. Ivan Kupala—"John the Bather"—popular epithet of John the Baptist or the name of the festival in his honor celebrating the summer solstice. "Kupala"—St. John's Eve; also called "Festival of Kupana." For more on this see: Y. M. Sokolov, *Russian Folklore,* Catherine Ruth Smith, trans. (New York: Macmillan, 1950). (Trans.)

26. The so-called new *Mlada,* the opera-ballet composed in 1890 by Rimsky-Korsakov, had its premiere under the direction of Napravnik at the Marinsky Theater on October 20, 1892. It succeeded by some twenty years the "old" Mlada, on which Borodin, Mussorgsky, Cui, and

Rimsky-Korsakov had collaborated (1871–1872). This latter work, left uncompleted, had been based on a scenario by S. A. Gedeonov, then Director of the Imperial Theaters.

27. Appearance of Cleopatra in scene 2, act 3.

28. Balakirev's symphonic poem based on a work by Lermontov (1884).

29. *Kolo*—a fast Slavonic round dance.

30. Unison tenor chorus in scene 3, act 3.

31. *Redowa*—a fast Czech dance in 3/4 time in scene 3, act 1.

32. In scene 2, act 2.

33. *Mlada* had six performances—the last one on January 29, 1893, after which it was dropped from the repertoire. (Trans.)

34. Juliusz Słowacki's tragedy about the struggles between the legendary Slavonic tribes the Weneds and the Lekhites, the cruelty of the conquerors, and selfless feats of Lilla Weneda. The work is full of the gloomy and fantastic, of sharp romantic contrasts. The Rimsky-Korsakov Archives (located in the G.P.B., no. 180, 6) contain a scenario of a tragedy titled *Lilla Weneda* copied in an unknown hand and dated 17 December 1892.

35. *Bylina*—Russian epic song. (Trans.)

36. *Sadko*—opera-*bylina*. Libretto by Nikolai Andreyevich Rimsky-Korsakov (with the collaboration of Stasov, Shtrup, and Belsky). The idea of writing this opera occupied Rimsky-Korsakov over a period of many years. See N. A. Rimsky-Korsakov, *Letopis' moei muzykal'noi zhizni* ("My Musical Life") (Moscow, 1955), p. 196.

37. The third concert of the season on November 21, 1892.

38. The subject of *Sadko* was drawn from a folk epic. The best-known record of it was made by A. F. Hilferding from the narrator A. P. Sorokin. A. F. Hilferding, *Onezhskie byliny* (Onega Byliny), vols. 1–3 (St. Petersburg, 1873). According to Findeisen's plan, the opera was to comprise four acts and a prologue.

39. Yevpaty Kolovrat—hero of the popular Ryazan tale of the time of the invasion of Baty, who defeated the Tatars, in Suzdal. The story is included in the *Povest' o prikhode Batyevoi rati na Riazan'* (Tale of the arrival of Baty's host in Ryazan). Preserved in the Rimsky-Korsakov Archives (G.P.G., no. 180, *kk*) is a manuscript scenario of an opera in four acts and prologue titled *Evpatii Kolovrat* (after Mey).

40. Preserved in the Rimsky-Korsakov Archives (G.P.B., no. 180, *sh*) is a manuscript scenario of an opera titled *David and Saul* and a separate sheet with a note in Rimsky-Korsakov's hand giving the name of the opera and a brief summary of the prologue, six scenes, and an epilogue, dated 26 March 1891.

41. *The Mines of Falun*—tale by E.T.A. Hoffmann, from *The Serapion Brothers*. *Nal and Damayanti*—poem ("Indian Tale") by V. A. Zhukovsky, reworking of one of the episodes of the Indian epic *Mahabharata* (after the German translation by F. Rückert). *The Beautiful Mélusine* (Provençal legend)—medieval tale of the love of the beautiful nymph for the knight Raymond; known in many versions in German literature. *The Hussites*—the heroic struggle of the Czech patriots, followers of Jan Hus, for the freedom of their homeland inspired many of the world's poets and romantic writers. The present reference is not to a specific literary work.

42. Preserved in the Rimsky-Korsakov Archives (G.P.B., no. 180, *ia*) is a manuscript libretto by P. A. Viskovaty, *Katerina,* opera in five acts (after Gogol's story "The Terrible Vengeance").

43. The idea for an opera based on Byron's mystery *Heaven and Earth* continued to occupy Rimsky-Korsakov in 1898–99 and, later, in 1905–6. A number of sketches, jotted down in 1906, are extant in the composer's notebooks. The opera, however, was never realized.

3. 1893

1. *Snegurochka* (Snow Maiden) had its first Moscow performance at the Bolshoi Theater on January 26, 1893.

2. *Switezianka*—cantata for soprano, tenor, chorus, and orchestra (op. 44). Text by A. Mickiewicz as translated by L. A. Mey. Reworked in 1897 from a song on the same text composed by Rimsky-Korsakov in 1867.

3. The reference here is to Balakirev's *Song of the Golden Fish,* a setting of Lermontov's poem *Mtsyri* (1860).

4. N. F. Solovyov, Professor at the Petersburg Conservatory.

5. Moguchaia kuchka ("Mighty Handful")—otherwise known as "The Five," or the Russian national school. (Trans.)

6. The subject of the discussion was the extreme formalist system of musical aesthetics of the Viennese critic Hanslick, set forth in 1854 in his *Vom Musikalisch-Schönen,* first translated into Russian by M. M. Ivanov (1885) and again by Hanslick's ardent champion H. A. Laroche (1895). Hanslick, an opponent of Wagner and admirer of Brahms, looked upon Russian music with contempt.

7. Reference to L. A. Sacchetti, Professor at the St. Petersburg Conservatory, and his essay "Ob otnoshenii muzyki k tekstu" (On the relation of music to text), read before the Neophilological Society on December 4, 1892, and at the Petersburg Conservatory on February 18, 1893. It was later published in Sacchetti's book, *Iz oblasti estetiki i muzyki* (From the field of aesthetics and music) (St. Petersburg: L. Turygina, pub., 1896), pp. 96–111.

8. N. F. Solovyov.

9. No. 26 (p. 50). Khorovodnaia (music for a Russian round dance)—"Stoi, moi milyi khorovod, ostanovis'," Nizhegorod Province, Arzamas District.

10. In answer to an article by Stasov on the third exhibit of the pictures of M. M. Antokolsky (*Novosti* [February 16, 1893], no. 46), the reactionary journalist A. A. Diakov, a contributor to Suvorin's *Novoe vremia* (and not V. P. Burenin, as Yastrebtsev erroneously asserts), wrote a libelous satire (under the pseudonym "A Citizen") called "Gospodin Stasov i kritika iskusstva" (Mr. Stasov and art criticism), *Novoe vremia* (February 21, 1893).

11. Unfortunately this book was not destined to be published; it was burned.

12. Since Rimsky-Korsakov goes into this matter in his autobiography, I have taken the liberty of omitting the passages in Yastrebtsev dealing with them. See Rimsky-Korsakov, *My Musical Life,* p. 246, regarding *Skazka,* and pp. 292–294, for *Sheherazade.* (Trans.)

13. At that time Repin was painting Rimsky-Korsakov's portrait. (V. V. Ya.)

14. Rimsky-Korsakov had heard Leoncavallo's *Pagliacci* in Moscow in 1892. *Pagliacci* received its first performance in St. Petersburg on November 23, 1898, at the Marinsky Theater.

15. *Cavalleria rusticana* received its first performance in St. Petersburg on January 18, 1893, at the Marinsky Theater.

16. Stasov's article, "Nikolai Andreevich Rimskii-Korsakov (po povodu 25-letnego iubileia)" (Nikolai Andreyevich Rimsky-Korsakov [on the occasion of his 25th anniversary]), appeared in *Severnyi vestnik* (1890), no. 11. It was reprinted in the 3-volume edition of Stasov's works (Moscow, 1952, 3:366).

17. This article was published in *Vestnik Evropy* (May–June, 1891).

18. Following his graduation from the Naval Academy as a midshipman (April 8, 1862), Rimsky-Korsakov was assigned to the clipper *Almaz* for a practice cruise. For details regarding this voyage, which lasted from October 20, 1862, to May 21, 1865, see Rimsky-Korsakov's *My Musical Life.*

19. Glazunov had not yet composed his magnificent Fourth, Fifth, and Sixth symphonies nor

had he written *Raymonda* and therefore one could naturally have come to this conclusion. (V. V. Ya.)

20. The introductions to both the first and fifth scenes in *Sadko* are in E-flat major; only the introduction to the submarine kingdom (sixth scene) is in E major. (V. V. Ya.)

21. For several years between 1862 and 1896, the St. Petersburg Conservatory occupied the private home of Demidov (at the corner of Demidov Lane and the Moika Canal); then for many years it was housed in the building of the Ministry of Internal Affairs (on what is now Zodchi Rossi Street). The location was crowded and poorly suited for musical activities. On January 13, 1888, Anton Rubinstein submitted a report to Tsar Alexander III outlining the necessity for a new location for the Conservatory. As a consequence, in 1889 the Conservatory was given the building of the Bolshoi Theater for its permanent use, with the right to do any reconstruction required by its particular needs. The alterations, based on plans drawn by the architect V. V. Nikol, were begun in April 1891 and completed in 1896 at a cost of 1.9 million rubles.

22. Although the book was not realized, fragments of Rimsky-Korsakov's writings on the subject of musical aesthetics were published in the posthumous collection *Muzykal'nye stat'i i zametki* (Articles and notes on music), published under the editorial supervision of N. N. Rimskaya-Korsakova with an introductory chapter by M. F. Gnesin. (Trans.)

23. Kuzma Prutkov—joint pseudonym of A. K. Tolstoi and his two cousins Zhemchuzhnikov. Under this pseudonym they published satirical, humorous, and nonsense verse and prose from 1853 to 1863. (Trans.)

24. The two letters written by Serov to his sister S. N. Dyutur (dated Simferopol, October 31 and November 28, 1845) were published by Findeisen in the journal *Russkaia starina* of March 1893, under the title "Novye materialy dlia biografii Aleksandra Nikolaevicha Serova" (New materials for a biography of Alexander Nikolayevich Serov), pp. 616–624.

25. Cf. entries: 15 August 1895; 11 February 1896; 17 March 1899. (Trans.)

26. "Nikolai Andreevich Rimskii-Korsakov, Kratkii ocherk zhizni i tvorchestva" (Nikolai Andreyevich Rimsky-Korsakov, a brief sketch of his life and work). Written to commemorate the twenty-fifth anniversary of Rimsky-Korsakov's musical activity (December 19, 1865—first performance of Rimsky-Korsakov's Symphony no. 1 at a concert of the Free Music School, conducted by Balakirev). The article was published for the first time in *Severnyi vestnik* (1890), no. 11; reprinted in V. V. Stasov, *Izbrannye sochineniia,* (Moscow, 1952), 3:366. Yastrebtsev gives an inaccurate title to Stasov's second article. It was originally titled "Dvadtsat' piat' let russkogo iskusstva" (Twenty-five years of Russian art) and included within it a section "Nasha muzyka" (Our Music). It was first published in *Vestnik Evropy,* November and December 1882; February, June, and October 1883. Reprinted in V. V. Stasov, *Izbrannye sochineniia v trekh tomakh* (Selected works in three volumes) (Moscow, 1952), 2:522.

27. *Peterburgskaia gazeta* of April 29, 1893, published an interview with Anton Rubinstein. Referring to Rubinstein's intention to leave the country permanently, the author of the article quoted him as saying: "Only there is it possible at present to find a real musical life. . . . There they love music, they worship it, they treasure it. Of course, I'm speaking exclusively about Germany; France, England, Italy don't count. . . . And Russia? Here, for a population of a hundred million, there are only two opera houses—in Petersburg and Moscow; in Germany for thirty million people there are a hundred of them."

28. Tchaikovsky was on his way to London.

29. Tchaikovsky had attended the premiere of this opera on May 16, 1863, and after it, he had written out, from memory, Judith's aria "Ia odenus' v visson."

30. In a subsequent entry, on 15 September 1893, we find that Tchaikovsky changed his mind and consented to conduct "three or even four concerts." (Trans.)

31. Tchaikovsky was awarded the degree of Doctor of Music *honoris causa* on June 1, 1893.

32. This part of the 9 September 1893 entry has been omitted since the account given by Rimsky-Korsakov is to be found in English in Rimsky-Korsakov's *My Musical Life;* M. D. Calvocoressi and Gerald Abraham, *Masters of Russian Music* (New York: Tudor, 1944); and Edward Garden, *Balakirev* (London: Faber and Faber, 1967). (Trans.)

33. Rimsky-Korsakov's statement about Balakirev's complete seclusion in 1872–73, quoted here in Yastrebtsev, is not altogether accurate. During these years Balakirev continued, albeit rarely, to visit Shestakova, D. V. Stasov, and I. V. Bessel, and met with Mussorgsky. See Mussorgsky, *Pis'ma i dokumenty* (Letters and documents) (Moscow–Leningrad, 1932), pp. 236–237.

34. The first sketches of Balakirev's C Major Symphony date to 1864. Apparently the composer did not work on it again until the summer of 1893, when he returned to the composition of the first and second movements.

35. Rimsky-Korsakov had begun to work on his autobiography on August 30, 1876; the last entry is dated August 22, 1906. The young Balakirev and the period of the 1860s are presented in chapters 3, 4, 6, and 7. A detailed chronology of the writing of the autobiography is appended to the edition published in Moscow in 1955.

36. In view of his expected retirement from the Court Chapel, in the fall of 1893 Rimsky-Korsakov and his family moved to an apartment at Zagorodny Prospekt, 28, where they remained until the composer's death. (Trans.)

37. The September 12, 1893, edition of *Peterburgskaia gazeta* includes an interview entitled "U E. F. Napravnika" (At E. F. Napravnik's), which deals with the projected reforms of the opera theater's charter. In the article Napravnik touches upon questions of the state of the opera theater, the organization of musical education in Russia, the preparation of opera singers, and the creative direction of Russian composers.

38. The name of the German composer Friedrich Wilhelm Kücken was a derogatory epithet for saccharine German music.

39. The manuscript of this unpublished work, dating to approximately 1879, is preserved in the GITIM, N. A. and A. N. Rimsky-Korsakov Archives.

40. Findeisen's journal *Russkaia muzykal'naia gazeta* began publication in 1894. Yastrebtsev contributed several articles to it.

41. At Yastrebtsev's request Rimsky-Korsakov consented to be his witness. The wedding took place on October 17. (Trans.)

42. "To dear and most kind Vasily Vasilyevich Yastrebtsev as a remembrance from the composer, N. Rimsky-Korsakov. 9–10 May 1893. St. Petersburg."

43. From 1868, when the Directors of the Russian Musical Society appointed him a professor at the St. Petersburg Conservatory, Auer served as teacher, conductor, soloist and head of the Russian Musical Society's quartet. His jubilee at the Conservatory was celebrated on September 1, 1893.

44. Borodin suffered a mild attack of cholera at the end of June 1885. This was not, however, the cause of his death on February 15, 1887. (Trans.)

45. *Khleb-sol'*—literally "bread-salt," a Russian expression of greeting. (Trans.)

46. I learned subsequently that Nikolai Andreyevich had come by several times to inquire of my mother which scores I did not have and finally decided on these. (V. V. Ya.)

47. According to the playbill, the first performance of *Khovanshchina* took place not on October 27, as Yastrebtsev writes, but on October 29, 1893, in Kononov's Hall. (See the collection of playbills of the St. Petersburg Imperial Theaters for 1893).

48. The subsequent performances went better. (V. V. Ya.)

49. Actually *Khovanshchina* was given its premiere by an amateur group, the Petersburg Music

and Dramatic Society, in Kononov's Hall on February 9, 1886. Yastrebtsev gives no indication either here or in his entry of 31 October 1893, where the opera is mentioned again, under whose auspices it was presented, who performed it, etc. on this occasion. (Trans.)

50. This Russian Symphony Concert, consisting entirely of works by Tchaikovsky, took place on November 20, 1893, under the direction of Rimsky-Korsakov.

51. On December 17, 1888.

52. This concert was given, under Rimsky-Korsakov's direction, on November 27, 1879. (Trans.)

53. Reference to performance (then being proposed in St. Petersburg) by the Pollini Company under the direction of Mahler.

54. Rimsky-Korsakov evidently heard this opera at the Marinsky Theater on November 4, 1893.

55. Rimsky-Korsakov submitted his resignation from the Court Chapel on November 3, 1893. Among the reasons he gave for resigning were: strained relations with Balakirev, his direct superior; the reigning atmosphere in the Chapel of informers and sycophants; severe nervous exhaustion; and, finally, the possibility, after ten years of service, of receiving a pension. After Rimsky-Korsakov's retirement, the position of Assistant Director of the Court Chapel was filled by S. M. Liapunov (from 1894 through 1902).

56. Rimsky-Korsakov had conceived the idea of compiling a manual of harmony long before this. Indeed, in the summer and fall of 1884 he wrote such a manual, based on his own pedagogical experience and discussions with Liadov about methods of teaching a harmony course at the Conservatory. He returned to this work in 1893. "At the beginning of my stay in Yalta," he writes in his autobiography, "I made some progress on the orchestration of *The Maid of Pskov* and was about to begin compiling a textbook of forms and one of the theory of harmony; but instead of simple, practical textbooks, some sort of philosophical daydreams took over." (*Letopis' moei muzykal'noi zhizni*, pp. 192–193.) *Prakticheskii uchebnik garmonii* (The practical manual of harmony) was published in 1884 (in lithograph) and in 1886 (printed). The seventeenth edition, revised and amplified by Maximilian Steinberg, was published in 1949.

57. With this concert, Rimsky-Korsakov resumed the conductorship of the Russian Symphony Concerts. During the 1893–94 season, there were three in all. The others were given on December 18, 1893, and January 22, 1894. (Trans.)

58. This article, which appeared in the *Teatral'naia gazeta* (November 3, 1893), no. 23, was called "Musorgskii i ego 'Khovanshchina'" (Mussorgsky and his *Khovanshchina*). In it Laroche accused Rimsky-Korsakov of "a mania for perfection," thanks to which Mussorgsky's "outrageous" work was staged.

59. This was a public concert given by the St. Petersburg branch of the Russian Musical Society under the direction of Nikolai Galkin.

60. *Intermezzo symphonique in modo classico*—composed in 1861 as a piece for piano. This intermezzo was reworked and orchestrated by the composer in 1867. The question of the correlation between Russian and West European elements in this *Intermezzo* was resolved correctly by Stasov: "It . . . was called *Intermezzo symphonique in modo classico* by the composer himself and this is justified in fact by its general mold and even by its main theme, rather in the style of Bach. But it is worth nothing that, for all its external classicism and Europeanism, this composition has within it content imbued with the Russian national character." *Sobranie statei V. V. Stasova o Musorgskom i ego proizvedeniiakh* (Collected articles of V. V. Stasov on Mussorgsky and his works) (Moscow, 1922), p. 12.

61. Song by Mussorgsky on his own text: "Akh, ty p'ianaia teteria" (Oh, you drunken sot) ("From the adventures of Pakhomych") composed in 1867 and dedicated to a friend of the composer, Vladimir Vasilyevich Nikolsky, professor of literature at the Alexandrovsky Lycée in St. Petersburg. "Pakhomych" was the nickname of Nikolsky. The song was not published until 1926.

62. This is inaccurate. The second quartet evening of the Russian Musical Society took place on Thursday November 11, 1893, and, consequently, this could not have kept Rimsky-Korsakov from attending the performance on Sunday of *Boris Godunov* at the Molas home.

63. *Khovanshchina*—literally, the "Khovansky group," the young Tsar Peter's contemptuous epithet for the party opposed to change; in this case, those who opposed Rimsky-Korsakov's changes in the score. (Trans.)

64. Taneyev's operatic trilogy on a libretto by A. A. Vinkstern after Aeschylus' *Orestes* (1887–1893). Its premiere took place at the Marinsky Theater on October 17, 1895.

65. Serenade for violoncello and piano (op. 37, 1893), published by Belyaev. A mazurka on three Polish folk themes for violin and orchestra was composed in 1888 but it remained in manuscript. In 1949 it was published in the composer's arrangement for violin and piano.

66. V. V. Stasov became personally acquainted with Tolstoy at the end of the 1870s. The two established a lasting friendship and correspondence which continued until Stasov's death. Stasov was always a welcome guest at Yasnaya Polyana, and he visited the author there in 1880, 1891, 1892, 1899, 1902, 1903, and 1904. See Vl. Karenin, *Vladimir Stasov* (Leningrad, 1927), 2:576–577; and I. Ginzburg, "Stasov u Tolstogo" (Stasov at Tolstoy's) in the collection *Nezabvennomu Vladimiru Vasil'evichu Stasovu* (To the unforgettable V. V. Stasov) (St. Petersburg), pp. 26–34.

4. 1894

1. V. V. Stasov's seventieth birthday and the fiftieth anniversary of his official activity were celebrated on January 2, 1894. Addresses from "the older and younger generations of musicians" were given in his honor. The first of these was read by Rimsky-Korsakov (see *Russkaia muzykal'naia gazeta* [1894], no. 2, p. 41).

2. This was Rubinstein's last concert in Russia. It was given at the Assembly Hall of the Nobility as a benefit and consisted entirely of his works.

3. Dmitry V. Grigorovich (1822–1899) played a major role in the discovery of Chekhov. (V. V. Ya.)

4. The third Russian Symphony Concert on January 22, 1894, marked the tenth anniversary of Rimsky-Korsakov's directorship of these concerts. It occasioned several speeches, the presentation of wreaths, etc. See *Peterburgskii listok* (January 23, 1894); *Chestvovanie N. A. Rimskogo-Korsakova;* and also *Peterburgskaia gazeta* (January 24, 1894). The last carried an article and feuilleton (both unsigned) in which the authors derided the Russian Symphony Concerts, Rimsky-Korsakov's jubilee, and Stasov's congratulatory address; see "Teatral'noe ekho" (Theatrical echo) and "Momental'ny snimok" (Instant snapshot).

5. The Rimsky-Korsakovs went to Odessa on the twenty-eighth, not on the twenty-seventh as stated here. Also, there were three not two concerts. They were given at the Odessa Municipal Theater under the auspices of the Odessa branch of the Russian Musical Society. The first was dedicated to the memory of Tchaikovsky; the second consisted entirely of works by Rimsky-Korsakov; the third (a benefit for the orchestra) presented works by both Tchaikovsky and Rimsky-Korsakov.

6. This symphony, dedicated to Anton Rubinstein, was finished on December 4, 1893. (Trans.)

7. In 1868, at Cui's request, Rimsky-Korsakov orchestrated the wedding chorus and the scene of the blessing from *William Ratcliff,* for the opera's premiere, which took place at the Marinsky Theater on February 14, 1869. But the opera as a whole was not rescored. [In an entry dated 7 February 1894, which has been omitted, Yastrebtsev reports that "Nikolai Andreyevich is at present orchestrating the Entr'acte and Introduction to *William Ratcliff.*" This obviously refers to the Introduction and Entr'acte to act 3, the manuscript of which (in Rimsky-Korsakov's orchestration)

is preserved in the N. A. and A. N. Rimsky-Korsakov Archives (GITIM). It is dated 8 February 1894, Odessa (Fund A, no. 312). (Trans.)]

8. V. P. Pogozhev held the post of business manager of the St. Petersburg Imperial Theaters, the same as that held by P. M. Pchelnikov in Moscow.

9. Grand Duke Sergei Alexandrovich, Governor General of Moscow.

10. *Dubrovsky*—opera by Napravnik after Pushkin's novel of the same name, with libretto by M. I. Tchaikovsky (op. 58, 1894); first performed on January 3, 1895, at the Marinsky Theater.

11. *Tushintsy*—opera by P. I. Blaramberg after Ostrovsky's dramatic chronicle *Tushino;* performed for the first time on January 24, 1895, in Moscow.

12. A polemic developed between Stasov and Burenin in the pages of the newspapers *Novosti* and *Novoe vremia* in connection with an article by Repin entitled "Pis'ma ob iskusstve" (Letters about art), which had been published in *Teatral'naia gazeta* (October 31, 1894), no. 22. [The date "October 31, 1894" seems a misprint, as this entry is dated "22 February 1894." (Trans.)] Burenin subjected this article to scathing criticism, accused its author of "phenomenal ignorance," and declared that artists should not be allowed into print ("Beware when an artist begins to write articles"), meaning in this case Vereshchagin, Antokolsky, and Repin. Stasov came forward in Repin's defense, demonstrating Burenin's ignorance in questions of art and championing the right of artists to write for the press. See *Novoe vremia* (January 28 and February 18, 1894) and *Novosti i birzhevaia gazeta* (February 6 and 22, 1894).

13. V. G. Karatygin has communicated to us a variant of the same excerpt from the Dance of the Persian Girls, in manuscript, which belonged to Countess Olga Andreyevna Golenishcheva-Kutuzova. It is dated 1876.

14. *Molokane*—one of a group of Christian sects which dissented from the official Russian Orthodox Church. Considered inimical to the Tsarist state, it was vigorously persecuted during the nineteenth century. (Trans.)

15. This theme was communicated to Mussorgsky by the singer Lyubov Karmalina, who recorded it in the Northern Caucasus.

16. The parallel drawn by Yastrebtsev between the original of *Khovanshchina* and the revised version of Rimsky-Korsakov, denying the significance of Mussorgsky's music in its own right, bears witness to Yastrebtsev's extremely narrow musical horizon.

17. Laroche's feuilleton "G. Suvorin i muzyka" (Mr. Suvorin and music), *Novosti* (February 18, 1894), 1st ed., no. 49, was devoted to an exposé of the publisher of *Novoe vremia*. With skillfully selected examples, Laroche proves Suvorin's lack of a musical ear, taste, and feeling.

18. This untitled piece (Moderato, E major) had been written by Chopin in an album belonging to Count S. D. Sheremetyev's mother (the former Princess Vyazemskaya) in Paris in 1843. Late in 1893 Count Sheremetyev told Rimsky-Korsakov that he had come across it while rummaging through his mother's albums. Not being a musician, he showed it to Balakirev, who authenticated it, said it was a complete little piece and had never been published. In 1894 the count published

it in a lithograph edition. A copy of this lithograph is preserved in the Balakirev Archives in the Manuscript Division of the G.P.B. [Published in 1910, the piece is listed as no. 151 in Maurice J. E. Brown's *Chopin: An Index of His Works in Chronological Order,* 2d. ed. rev. (London: Macmillan, 1972). (Trans.)]

19. In a later entry, dated 21 March 1894, Yastrebtsev reports that the entire scene has been finished and amounts to 101 pp. (Entry omitted—Trans.)

20. Untitled article signed "E. P-sky" (E. M. Petrovsky) with an epigraph taken from a notice in the corridor of the Marinsky Theater: "The Directorate of the Imperial Theaters strictly forbids any public display of disapproval of the artists in the Imperial Theaters." (*Russkaia muzykal'naia gazeta* [March 1894], no. 3.) In the article Petrovsky protests the exclusion of Russian classical operas from the repertoire.

21. This refers to the performance of works by members of the Balakirev circle at the homes of Dargomyzhsky, the Purgolds, Shestakova, the Stasovs, and Rimsky-Korsakov at the end of the 1860s and beginning of the 1870s, in which Nadezhda Nikolayevna Purgold (Mme. Rimsky-Korsakov) always participated as accompanist.

22. *Fantasia on Serbian Themes* for orchestra (op. 6), 1867.

23. *Paraphrases on a Constant Theme* ("Chopsticks")—a collective composition by Borodin, Cui, Rimsky-Korsakov, N. Shcherbachev, and Liadov consisting of 24 variations, finale, and 15 little pieces for piano four hands (published 1879).

24. This was one of several rehearsals for a performance which took place at the Molases' on April 10. Except for Koryakin, a basso from the Marinsky Theater, the cast was composed of amateurs. Gabrilovich and Khessin accompanied. (Trans.)

25. Berlioz' *Damnation of Faust* was given on March 27, 1894, in the Assembly Hall of the Nobility under the direction of the Paris conductor Edouard Colonne and with the noted tenor Ernest Van Dyck.

26. Kruglikov's article "Viliam Ratklif. Opera Ts. A. Kyui. (K 25-letiiu ego pervogo predstavleniia)" (William Ratcliff. An opera by C. A. Cui. [On the 25th anniversary of its first performance]) was published in the journal *Artist* (February 1894), no. 34, p. 161. Characterizing Cui's music, the author points to its kinship with that of Schumann. "Mr. Cui," writes Kruglikov, "is one of the most eminent Schumannists of our time. . . . It would be more correct to call him the Russian Schumann, thus better to express the concept of an affinity of nature rather than of imitation."

27. In his autobiography, Rimsky-Korsakov states that he burned "all these sketches" on January 21, 1894, that is, about two months before this entry of Yastrebtsev, "as being worthless." Rimsky-Korsakov, *My Musical Life,* p. 338. (Trans.)

28. The response to Rimsky-Korsakov's urging Yastrebtsev to write a monograph on harmony. (Trans.)

29. The theory of *podgoloski* (independent contrapuntal voice parts) was first elaborated by Yu. N. Melgunov in his work *Russkie pesni, neposredstvenno s golosov naroda zapisannye* (Russian songs, recorded directly as sung by the people), published in two parts: part 1, 1879; part 2, 1885. In the foreword the author speaks of the polyphonic nature of Russian folk songs, meaning the independence and equality of all the choral voice parts.

30. *Troitskie* songs—songs for Trinity Sunday; *rusal'nye*—songs for the Sunday before Whitsun; *vesnianki*—folk songs celebrating the vernal equinox. (Trans.)

31. *Bytovye* songs—songs pertaining to everyday life (e.g., lamentations and funeral laments). (Trans.)

32. *216 malorossiiskikh narodnykh pesen* (216 Little Russian Folk Songs, Recorded by A. I. Rubets). Published in 1871.

---

33. This statement clearly shows Rimsky-Korsakov's underestimation of the outstanding role of Lysenko in the development of Ukrainian music.

34. *Angelo,* opera by Cui based on Victor Hugo's play (1876).

35. The new opera was *Christmas Eve,* which was begun in the spring of 1894. For more on this see Rimsky-Korsakov, *Letopis' moei muzykal'noi zhizni,* p. 195.

36. The idea of composing an opera on the biblical subject of King Saul, following a plan for the libretto by V. I. Belsky, was never realized although Rimsky-Korsakov returned to it repeatedly.

37. In 1891 Rimsky-Korsakov contemplated writing an opera to be called *Zoryusha,* based on V. I. Dahl's play *Noch' na rasput'e* (Night at the crossroads). He did not give up this idea until the fall of 1906. During 1889–90 Liadov had also worked on an opera on the same subject with a scenario drawn up by Stasov and himself. The rough drafts of his *Zoryusha* have been preserved.

38. Liadov subsequently used portions of the music he had written for an opera on this subject in his symphonic poems *Kikimora* and *The Enchanted Lake.* (Trans.)

39. On another occasion, apropos of tone color, Nikolai Andreyevich stated: "Every tonality, key, and chord, at least for me personally, is to be found only in nature, in the color of the clouds and in the strikingly beautiful, shimmering streams of light and luminous rays of the Aurora Borealis. That's where the real C sharp is and B, A flat, and everything that you want." (Entry of 25 April 1894, omitted—Trans.)

40. In the nocturnal scene of the *rusalki* from the third act of *May Night,* this tonality is used to depict the golden reflection of the moon on the surface of the water. (V. V. Ya.)

41. Snegurochka's plaint, Voislava's lament (from *Mlada*), the song of the dying swan (from *Pan Voyevoda*). (V. V. Ya.)

42. The Rimsky-Korsakovs spent the summers of 1894, 1895, 1898, 1899, 1904, and 1905 at Vechasha. It was there that Rimsky-Korsakov composed *Christmas Eve, Sadko, The Tsar's Bride,* and *The Tale of Tsar Saltan* and completed *The Legend of the Invisible City of Kitezh.*

43. Yastrebtsev lived at Troitsky Prospect, no. 24 (now Rubinstein St.).

44. *Christmas Eve,* based on a story of the same name by Gogol. (Trans.)

45. *Kolyada*—originally pagan rituals and cermonies connected with the "birth of the sun" after the winter solstice; later the name applied to Christmas festivities and the custom of carol singing; *Kolyady* or *kolyadki*—the Christmas songs (carols) themselves. *Ovsen*—originally the first day of spring, March 1. (Trans.)

46. Reference to Tchaikovsky's *Vakula the Smith,* which was awarded the first prize in a competition (in 1875). Revised and renamed *Cherevichki* (The Little Shoes) in 1885.

47. *Cordelia* (1885) and *Vakula the Smith* (1875)—operas by Solovyov.

48. *Baba Yaga*—symphonic poem, op. 56, 1905. As the program for this work Liadov selected an episode from the Russian fairy tale *Vasilisa the Beautiful,* from A. N. Afanasyev's collection of folk tales.

49. On 9 May, Rimsky-Korsakov asked Yastrebtsev: "Just tell me why, in your study of aesthetics, you give special attention only to harmony and orchestration and say nothing about rhythm, which, in terms of its variety, is really the richest element of music?" (Trans.)

50. The program of the first summer concert at the Pavlovsk Station on May 20 included, besides the works mentioned, Schumann's *Manfred* Overture and Vieuxtemps' Violin Concerto no. 5. Galkin conducted.

51. *Chopiniana* (op. 46) and *Valse de concert* (op. 47) were published in 1894 (M. P. Belyaev, Leipzig). A copy of the latter, inscribed to Rimsky-Korsakov and dated 20 May 1894, is preserved in the GITIM, N. A. and A. N. Rimsky-Korsakov Archives.

52. The Rimsky-Korsakovs left for Vechasha on the morning of May 26. (Trans.)

---

53. According to legend, there were miraculous flowers which were thought to bloom on St. John's Night. It was a custom among the peasants to search for such flowers, most often that of the fern. (Trans.)

54. *Revue Wagnérienne*—journal published in Paris, 1885–88.

55. These letters appeared in *Russkaia muzykal'naia gazeta* in 1894–1895. They were published separately by Findeisen in 1896.

56. Schumann's thoughts on music were set forth in the brochure *Zhiznennye pravila i sovety molodym muzykantam* (Rules of life and advice to young musicians), translated by P. I. Tchaikovsky, 4th ed., 1895, and in the article "Iz zapisnoi knizhki maestro Raro, Florestana, i Eizebia" (From the notebook of Maestros Rareau, Florestan, and Eusebius), translated by I. Korzukhin —*Russkaia muzykal'naia gazeta* (1894), no. 7.

57. According to Rimsky-Korsakov's autobiography, shortly before he went to Vechasha, Findeisen urged him to write an opera on the subject of *Sadko* and proposed a plan for the libretto. It was this plan to which Yastrebtsev refers here. However, the following summer (1895), V. I. Belsky evinced a strong interest in the opera and he subsequently became Rimsky-Korsakov's collaborator on the libretto. See Rimsky-Korsakov, *My Musical Life,* pp. 345, 353–356. (Trans.)

58. As, for example, in Mussorgsky's attempt to depict "butting" in his song *The He-Goat*, which once sent Stasov into raptures. (V. V. Ya.)

59. The article "Tematizm opery 'Snegurochka' N. A. Rimskogo-Korsakova" (Thematic scheme of N. A. Rimsky-Korsakov's opera *Snegurochka*) (April 1894), no. 4.

60. See entry of 14 October 1892. (V. V. Ya.)

61. *Belorusskie narodnye pesni* (Belorussian folk songs) (1874) of the collector and folklorist P. V. Shein.

62. Collection of P. N. Rybnikov—*Pesni . . . narodnye byliny, stariny i pobyval'shchiny* (Songs . . . popular byliny of olden days and events) (1909–10), 3 vols, A. E. Gruzinsky, ed. Kirsha Danilov—presumed compiler of a manuscript collection (mid-eighteenth century) of *byliny,* historical songs, and satirical verses. Appended to the collection were musical transcriptions of folk tunes. The collection was published first in 1804, without the music; it was republished in 1818 with the music, under the title *Drevnie rossiiskie stikhotvoreniia* (Ancient Russian poems). The latest edition, edited by S. K. Shambinago, appeared in 1938. Reference here is to *Pesni, sobrannye P. V. Kireevskim* (Songs, collected by P. V. Kireyevsky).

63. Laroche's work *M. I. Glinka i ego znachenie v istorii muzyki* (M. I. Glinka and his significance in the history of music) was published in *Russkii vestnik* in 1867–68 and republished in *Sobranie muzykal'no-kriticheskikh statei* (Collected articles of music criticism) (Moscow, 1913), 1:1–162.

64. Masha, the Rimsky-Korsakovs' sixth child, born in January 1888, died and was buried in Yalta in August 1893. (Trans.)

65. A. N. Molas.

66. Lombroso's *Genius and Insanity* (1872) was published in Russian in 1885 by the publisher Pavlenkov.

67. The opera had its premiere on January 9, 1880, at the Marinsky Theater. It met with considerable success. (Trans.)

68. October 16, 1894, marked the twenty-fifth anniversary of the founding of the publishing firm of V. Bessel and Co. by the brothers V. V. and I. V. Bessel. In terms of the quantity and quality of the works published, this firm was one of the outstanding publishing houses in Russia. It published many of the major works of Russian composers, among them Dargomyzhsky, Rimsky-Korsakov, Mussorgsky, Borodin, Tchaikovsky, Cui, Glazunov, and Anton Rubinstein. In addition, V. V. Bessel brought out two music journals—*Muzykal'ny listok* (1872–1877) and *Muzykal'noe obozrenie* (1885–1889).

69. Rimsky-Korsakov considered Gluck a poor musician and disliked his music. Eloquent testimony to this is the omission of Pushkin's lines about Gluck in Rimsky-Korsakov's opera *Mozart and Salieri.*

70. These articles appeared in the journal *Istoricheskii vestnik* (June–July 1894).

71. For similar reasons, Rimsky-Korsakov disliked Repin's portrait of Mussorgsky.

72. This article was written on the occasion of the first performance of Wagner's *Lohengrin* at the Marinsky Theater on October 4, 1868, in *S.-Peterburgskie vedomosti* (1868), no. 278. The article was dedicated to Rimsky-Korsakov.

73. Serov's views on Glinka's *Ruslan and Ludmila* are to be found in many articles. They are expressed most fully in a long article, " 'Ruslan' i ruslanisty" (*Ruslan* and the Ruslanists), which appears both in A. N. Serov, *Kriticheskie stat'i* (Critical articles) (St. Petersburg, 1895), 4:1667, and *Izbrannye stat'i* (Selected articles) (Moscow-Leningrad, 1950), 1:193. Rubinstein's comments on *Ruslan and Ludmila* are included in his book *Muzyka i ee predstaviteli. Razgovor o muzyke* (Music and its representatives. A conversation about music).

74. This opera was given four performances in April 1895 under the auspices of the Music Society, mainly on the initiative of Shtrup. (Trans.)

75. Although Rimsky-Korsakov revised and completed many other of Mussorgsky's works, of *The Fair at Sorochintsy,* he rewrote and rescued only the Dream Intermezzo, which became the orchestral piece entitled *Night on Bald Mountain.* (Trans.)

76. This article (*Artist* [1894], no. 42), written in connection with the revival of *May Night* at the Marinsky Theater, contains Cui's usual praise and carping criticism of Rimsky-Korsakov.

77. Here Yastrebtsev cites several more examples of Rimsky-Korsakov's achievements as a melodist, humorist, etc. (Trans.)

78. Balakirev was the director of the Court Chapel during 1883–94.

79. M. M. Ivanov's article, "Anton Grigor'evich Rubinshtein (po povody ego konchiny 8-go noiabria 1894 goda)" (Anton Grigoryevich Rubinstein [On the occasion of his death, November 8, 1894]), was published in *Novoe vremia* (November 14, 1894), no. 6722. In this article, the author pointed to Rubinstein's creative originality and artistic independence, adding: "If Rubinstein had possessed a more brilliant gift for orchestration such as that of Rimsky-Korsakov, his genius for composition would have revealed itself clearly even to the most stupid listener."

80. For a memorial concert in honor of Rubinstein, held on December 3. (Trans.)

81. Rimsky-Korsakov means by this himself, Borodin, Mussorgsky, Balakirev and Cui. (V. V. Ya.)

82. Krylov's fable *Svin'ia pod dubom* (The pig under the oak) tells of a pig which, having eaten up all the acorns from an oak, dug at the roots of the tree until the tree died.

83. Rimsky-Korsakov had a strong dislike for Laroche and his musical views. Therefore, the establishment (in the early 1890s) of friendly relations beween Laroche and a group of Petersburg composers (particularly Liadov and Glazunov) provoked his displeasure and a certain anxiety. Rimsky-Korsakov considered Taneyev a musician of a conservative bent, close to Laroche in his convictions. However, in the second half of the 1890s, he moved away from this view. Noting Taneyev's relationship to the Petersburg musicians, Rimsky-Korsakov wrote: "This change coincided with the beginning of a new period in his compositional work, a period when, while still preserving his astonishing contrapuntal technique, he became freer and was guided by the ideals of contemporary music." *(Letopis' moei muzykal'noi zhizni,* p. 215.) Rimsky-Korsakov thought highly of Taneyev's mature works, such as the opera *Oresteia* and Symphony in C minor.

84. Symphony no. 3, an aria from the first scene of the opera *Moses, Don Quixote,* Piano Concerto no. 4 (played by N. Lavrov), the song *Prince Rostislav* and the *Persian Songs* (sung by M. Dolina), and Eastern and Italian dances from the ballet *The Vine.* (V. V. Ya.)

85. The problem with the censor arose from the fact that the Empress Catherine II (the Great) was included among the dramatis personae of *Christmas Eve*. For more on this, see Rimsky-Korsakov, *My Musical Life,* pp. 350–352. (Trans.)

5. 1895

1. Arensky's visit was evidently connected with the post of Director of the Court Chapel, left vacant by the departure of Balakirev and Rimsky-Korsakov's refusal to take it. Arensky served in this capacity from 1895 to 1901.

2. The first performance of *Snegurochka* in Kiev took place on January 23, 1895.

3. Rachmaninov's *Aleko* was given its premiere in Kiev on October 18, 1893, under the composer's direction. The production, hastily executed, was very poorly prepared. See *Artist* (Moscow, 1893), no. 32, p. 179.

4. On another occasion it was noted that the best places in Napravnik's *Dubrovsky* were taken directly from Tchaikovsky or Borodin. (Trans.)

5. "Grozen tsar' idiot," "Udarili v zastenia," and "Zakliuchitel'nyi." (V. V. Ya.)

6. This article, titled "Chaikovskii kak dramaticheskii kompozitor" (Tchaikovsky as a dramatic composer), *Ezhegodnik Imp. Teatrov* (1893–94), vol. 1, contained a number of attacks upon the composers of the young Russian school.

7. Though now an old woman, this celebrated folk tale narrator and wailer from Olonets Guberniya was said to remember about 19,000 lines of wedding, funeral, and recruiting laments. Rimsky-Korsakov had heard her in Solyanoi Gorodok (a lecture-concert on January 8, in the exhibition hall opposite the Summer Garden). (V. V. Ya.) After hearing her at the Nizhny Novgorod Fair in 1896, Gorky described his impressions in a sketch entitled *The Wailer*. At that time Fedosova was in her nineties. (Trans.)

8. Safonov conducted the Russian Musical Society's third concert of the season on January 21. (Trans.)

9. The Kiev production of the *Snegurochka* occasioned a series of articles by L. Goncharov, a great admirer of Rimsky-Korsakov's music, which appeared in the Kiev journal *Zhizn' i iskusstvo,* 1895. These articles were largely critical notes aimed at the performers, the artist, and the producer. (Trans.)

10. Glazunov's *Coronation Cantata* for soprano, mezzo-soprano, tenor, bass, chorus, and orchestra, to words by V. A. Krylov (op. 56, 1895) was performed on May 14, 1896, at the Granovitaya Palata in Moscow.

11. The fourth and final concert of the 1894–95 season, which took place on February 4, 1895. (Trans.)

12. This article, "Muzykal'nyi kritik osobogo roda" (A music critic of a special sort), *Russkaia muzykal'naia gazeta* (1895), no. 1, dealt with V. S. Baskin's recently published book on Tchaikovsky, *Russkie kompozitory. P. I Chaikovskii. Ocherk ego deiatel'nosti* (Russian composers. P. I. Tchaikovsky. A survey of his activity) (L. F. Marks, pub.), which Ossovsky subjected to devastating criticism.

13. See note 6. (Trans.)

14. Laroche's two-part article entitled "Otkrytoe pis'mo N. N. Figneru" (An open letter to N. N. Figner), appeared in *Novosti* (February 17 and 19, 1895), nos. 47 and 49. It produces a strange impression. Along with some valuable ideas about the aesthetics of opera in general and Tchaikovsky in particular, it is full of contradictions.

15. On February 16, 1895, Glazunov was awarded third prize for his Quartet no. 4 in A minor.

16. In 1894 and 1895, *Russkaia muzykal'naia gazeta* published a series of critical articles, reviews, and translations by Ossovsky.

17. Balakirev's Symphony no. 1 in C was begun in 1862 and not finished until 1898.

18. The young composers F. S. Akimenko, V. A. Zolotarev, S. A. Barmotin. et al., who studied at the Chapel under the auspices of Balakirev.

19. It was Yastrebtsev's custom to drop in on Rimsky-Korsakov on Mondays, on which day they usually served *kisel'*, a kind of fruit gelatin, for dessert. It is this to which Rimsky-Korsakov is referring here. (Trans.)

20. *Nal and Damayanti*—this opera (in three acts and six scenes) took its subject from the Indian epic *Mahabharata* in a poetic treatment by Zhukovsky. The libretto was by M. I. Tchaikovsky. "Greek Rhythms" is a cycle of six pieces for piano entitled *Essais sur des rythmes oubliés* (op. ?8), in which Arensky used ancient Greek poetic meters. *Basso ostinato* is from *Six Morceaux* for piano (op. 5, no. 5).

21. Familiar diminutive for the name Herman.

22. Actually, Laroche did not write an opera on the subject of Alfred de Musset's comedy, *Carmosine*. He collected money for it in advance but finished only the overture. This was performed once in an orchestration by Tchaikovsky and under his direction at a Russian Musical Society concert on October 16, 1893. This was during Tchaikovsky's final visit to St. Petersburg. The overture had no success.

23. Schubert's C major Symphony was performed on March 4, 1895, under Napravnik at the sixth symphonic evening of the Russian Musical Society.

24. V. S. Baskin, *Russkie kompozitory. M. P. Mussorgskii. Ocherk muzykal'noi deiatel'nosti* (Russian composers. M. P. Mussorgsky. A survey of his musical activity) (Moscow: Jurgenson, 1887).

25. The squabble between Laroche and Ivanov originated in 1895 in the pages of *Novosti* and *Novoe vremia*. Laroche, in his article "Konstert pod upravleniem M. M. Ivanova v Dvorianskom sobranii" (A concert under the direction of M. M. Ivanov at the Assembly Hall of the Nobility), sharply criticized and ridiculed Ivanov as composer, conductor, and critic. Ivanov replied with an equally scathing article, in which he maintained that Laroche had turned from "a man who had once shown promise" into "a windbag who could write on both sides of a question." See *Novosti i birzhevaia gazeta* (March 22, 1895) and *Novoe vremia* (March 17, 1895).

26. The opera had three additional performances—on April 7, 13, and 16. (Trans.)

27. Balakirev's collection, no. 21. (V. V. Ya.)

28. The article by Vaksel, signed "V. P.," appeared in the *Journal de St. Petersbourg* (April 9, 1895), no. 94, under the title "Reprise de la 'Pskovitaine' de M. Rimsky-Korsakow."

29. Lel's song and choruses from *Snegurochka*, the women's choruses from *The Maid of Pskov*, etc. See *Nov'* (1885) 2(8):670, "Myzukal'naia khronika." Although the article is unsigned, it undoubtedly belongs to the pen of Ivanov. (V. V. Ya.)

30. A facsimile autograph of Rimsky-Korsakov was printed in *Russkaia muzykal'naia gazeta* (1895), nos. 5 and 6, as an illustration to an article by Yastrebtsev entitled "Neskol'ko slov o vtoroi i tretei redaktsiiakh 'Pskovitianki' i narodnykh temakh, vziatykh Rimskim-Korsakovym v etu operu" (A few words about the second and third versions of the *The Maid of Pskov* and the folk themes borrowed by Rimsky-Korsakov in this opera).

31. Alexander III (1881–94). (Trans.)

32. Setting of the "Cherubim," a Russian Orthodox hymn. (Trans.)

33. "Otkrytoe pis'mo N. N. Figneru" (An Open Letter to N. N. Figner) was written by Laroche in reply to an invitation to participate in the work of a commission formed "for the drawing up of rules and regulations for a competition for best opera." In his letter, Laroche refused to participate because of a dislike, on principle, for competitions and a conviction that "it is useless and even harmful to pay court to composers." In his opinion what Russian composers need rather than monetary encouragement is "brutally frank" criticism, for in Russia "not too little but too

much," is written. The creative output of Russian composers, in comparison with West European musicians, "finds immediate acceptance." The Russian public, asserts Laroche, was unfair only to Anton Rubinstein, in stubbornly ignoring his music. See *Novosti i birzhevaia gazeta* (February 17 and 19, 1895).

34. *Feramors*—opera in three acts based on Rodenberg's text of *Lalla Rookh* by Thomas Moore (1863); first performed in Dresden in 1863, and in Petersburg on April 24, 1884, at the Musical and Dramatic Society.

35. August Rudolfovich Bernhard—a student of Rimsky-Korsakov, who became a professor and finally Director of the Petersburg Conservatory from 1898 to 1905. (Trans.)

36. Glazunov's Fifth Symphony (op. 55, 1895), on which the composer worked from April to October of 1895.

37. *Variations on a Russian Theme for String Quartet.* Collective composition by Artsybushev, Scriabin, Glazunov, Rimsky-Korsakov, Liadov, Wihtol, Blumenfeld, Winkler, Sokolov, and Ewald.

38. In a review of Turygina's *Rukovodstvo k istorii muzyki* (Handbook of music history) (St. Petersburg, 1895), Ivanov criticized in particular the author's appended list of "excellent works" on the history of music, saying that it contains everything "from Elise Polko's romantic gibberish about Paganini to worthless articles by Porfiry Trifonov." At the conclusion of his article, apropos of a concert given on behalf of the ailing D. M. Leonova, at which selections from Solovyov's *Cordelia* and Rimsky-Korsakov's *Snegurochka* were performed, Ivanov asked: "Why don't they return them to the place in the Marinsky Theater which they occupied so honorably?"

39. " 'Pskovitianka'—opera N. A. Rimskogo-Korsakova. Postanovka ee v novoi redaktsii na stsene Tanaevskogo teatra Obshchestvom muzykal'nykh sobranii" (*Maid of Pskov*—opera by N. A. Rimsky-Korsakov. Its first performance in a new version on the stage of the Panayevsky Theater by the Musical Society), *Russkaia muzykal'naia gazeta* (1895), nos. 5 and 6.

40. An article under the heading "Pridvornaia pevcheskaia kapella" (The Court Chapel), *Novoe vremia* (May 19 and 20, 1895), nos. 6903 and 6904, contained complaints about the decline of performances in the Chapel and the worldly character of its instruction. The same complaints were repeated in the article, "Pevcheskaia kapella i ee zadachi" (The Court Chapel and its problems), *Novoe vremia* (October 23, 1895), no. 7059.

41. Serov's remarks about the *Fantasia on Serbian Themes* appeared in a review titled "Vtoroi i tretii kontserty Russkogo muzykal'nogo obshchestva" (The second and third concerts of the Russian Musical Society). See A. N. Serov, *Kriticheskie stat'i* (Critical articles) (St. Petersburg, 1895), 4:1835.

42. Alexander Serov died in 1871. The review referred to here was republished in an 1895 edition of his critical articles. First published in the journal *Muzyka i teatr* (under the heading "Khronika"), the excerpt reads:

> Not having had as yet an opportunity to acquaint myself with the score of this charming orchestral piece, I will not write a detailed analysis of it. Let me state here only that the freshness and clarity of its coloring, its masterful orchestration and the working out of the Serbian melodies in this "fantasia" indicate that this burgeoning young composer is the possessor of an enormous talent. In this piece he comes exceedingly close to the brilliant lezghinka from *Ruslan*—with a richer palette, perhaps, and a spirit of something new, charming.
>
> We have a right to expect a very great deal from one who begins so incredibly brilliantly as Mr. Rimsky-Korsakov, if only—but here one gets into ideals of art, a subject which has no place in "notes in brief." Alexander Serov. (V. V. Ya.)

43. Georgi Ottonovich Deutsch (1857–91), conductor, student of Rimsky-Korsakov, and member of the Belyaev Circle.

44. Max von Erdmannsdörffer, a German conductor, directed the Imperial Musical Society in

Moscow from 1882 to 1889 and the St. Petersburg branch of the Russian Musical Society from 1895 to 1897. (Trans.)

45. *The Barber of Baghdad*—this idea of a comic opera was never realized. In his "Vospominaniia o N. A. Rimskom-Korsakove" (Reminiscences of N. A. Rimsky-Korsakov), I. F. Tyumenev quotes Rimsky-Korsakov as follows: "In addition to a Russian one I plan to write another opera, but it will be short, in one act, on a subject from *Thousand and One Nights*. There's a story there about a Baghdad barber that is extremely funny. This barber, a great chatterbox, talks incessantly about his acquaintances, about his brothers, showing how this one sings, that one dances, etc. I've already selected a librettist for this opera. You probably know the poet Velichko and remember how well he expressed the oriental element. He's the one I've been thinking of asking." *Muzykal'-noe nasledstvo: Rimskii-Korsakov. Issledovaniia, materialy, pis'ma* (A musical legacy: Rimsky-Korsakov. Research, materials, and letters) (Moscow, 1954), 2:208. Sketches of themes for this opera were found in Rimsky-Korsakov's notebook with the note *"The Barber of Baghdad,* October 1895." The libretto of the opera was published in an article by A. A. Gozenpud, "Neosushchestvlennyi opernyi zamysel" (An unrealized operatic idea), *Ibid.,* p. 255.

46. According to the original plan of the opera, the dancing in the underwater realm was to have been interrupted by the appearance of St. Nicholas of Mozhaisk, Protector of Novgorod. However, the censor did not permit this, so this character was changed subsequently to Starchish-chii Moguchii-bogatyr'. (Trans.)

47. Song to words by I. I. Kozlov (1832).

48. *Slava, a Christmas Carol for Chorus and Orchestra,* op. 21. In 1876 Rimsky-Korsakov made a sketch for an eight-voice fugue on the Russian song *Slava* for double chorus and orchestra. Finding it somewhat dry, he dropped it, but took it up again in 1879–80. It was published by A. Büttner under the title given. The orchestral score bears the date 1880; the vocal score—1879. (Trans.)

49. The premiere of the opera was scheduled to take place on November 21. (Trans.)

50. They took her to represent Catherine II. (Trans.)

51. See Rimsky-Korsakov, *Letopis' moei muzykal'noi zhizni,* p. 202.

52. In 1852 Turgenev was arrested and banished to his estate in the village of Spasskoye-Lutovinovo, Orlov Province, for having published an obituary of Gogol in *Moskovskie vedomosti.*

53. The premiere of *Christmas Eve* had been set for November 21, 1895, as a benefit for O. O. Paleček, on the occasion of his twenty-fifth anniversary as basso, producer, and professor of opera at the St. Petersburg Conservatory. The performance took place on November 28.

54. After having granted permission for the performance of *Christmas Eve* with the appearance of the Tsaritsa as a character, under the influence of Grand Duke Vladimir Alexandrovich, Nicho-·las II went back on his word. "I considered my case lost," wrote Rimsky-Korsakov in *My Musical Life,* "since according to reports, the Emperor was in complete accord with Vladimir Alexandrov-ich and had rescinded his permission for producing my opera. Vsevolozhsky, eager to save Pale-ček's benefit performance and his production, suggested that I replace the Tsaritsa (mezzo-so-prano) with a Most Serene Highness (baritone). . . . While this struck me as sad and absurd, I did not want any trouble, so I agreed. Vsevolozhsky began to pull strings—through whom, I do not know—but he obtained permission from the Tsar to give *Christmas Eve* with a Most Serene Highness instead of the Tsaritsa." (*Letopis' moei muzykal'noi zhizni,* p. 202.)

55. This symphonic poem was performed at the sixth symphonic evening of the Russian Mu-sical Society on November 25, 1895.

56. In his autobiography, Rimsky-Korsakov states that "not one member of the Imperial family attended any of the performances," adding that "and after that, Vsevolozhsky's attitude towards me and my compositions underwent a profound change." *My Musical Life,* p. 359. (Trans.)

57. Regarding this, Rimsky-Korsakov wrote in his autobiography: "I did not attend the first

performance, but stayed at home with my wife. I wanted at least in this way to show my displeasure at everything that had happened. My children were at the theater. The opera was fairly successful. Yastrebtsev brought me a wreath." *(Letopis' moei muzykal'noi zhizni,* p. 202.)

58. Solovyov's article, untitled and signed simply "N. S.," was published in the newspaper *Svet* in the column "Teatr i muzyka." Here Solovyov sees *Christmas Eve* as a "blaspheme" because on the "holy" night "the stars dance a ballet," the Christmas star appears "in the guise of a beautiful woman," and the Church Clerk's romantic outpourings to Solokha sound like "the reverential chanting of the monasteries."

59. According to Yastrebtsev, the sixth performance of the opera, on December 12, and the seventh, on December 26, were very successful. Incidentally, Rimsky-Korsakov states, on p. 359 of *My Musical Life,* that after the premiere, the opera was given only four more times. This makes a total of five performances as against Yastrebtsev's eight. For Yastrebtsev's report on the eighth performance see 9 January 1896. (Trans.)

60. In an article entitled "Novaia opera N. A. Rimskogo-Korsakova" (A new opera by Rimsky-Korsakov) *Novosti* (December 10, 1895), no. 340, Laroche, while acknowledging Rimsky-Korsakov as an impeccable composer, finds his score very poor melodically and the opera considerably poorer in musical content than *Snegurochka* and *May Night.* The best parts, according to him, are the genre scenes and the choruses, in which the folk element has been worked out with the true taste, tact, and understanding, which never abandon Rimsky-Korsakov in such cases. Least successful, in Laroche's view, is the comic side. Overall the music of the opera, "like the blue sky over the deserts and oases, stretches impeccable instrumentation, this marvelous Korsakov orchestra."

61. Arensky's *Variations for Orchestra* (op. 33, no. 3) was performed on December 16, 1895, at a Russian Musical Society concert.

62. "Humperdincks"—admirers of Humperdinck, the German composer of the Wagnerian school, headed by Laroche. In Russia *Hänsel and Gretel* enjoyed a certain popularity. It was given its Petersburg premiere at the Panayevsky Theater on January 2, 1896, and was performed again at the Marinsky Theater on October 24, 1897, under Napravnik.

63. Rimsky-Korsakov's First Symphony was given its premiere on December 19, 1865, at the first concert of the Free Music School, with Balakirev conducting.

64. Kashkin's article, " 'Noch' pered Rozhdestvom,' Byl'-koliadka po povesti N. V. Gogolia. Opera v 4 deistviiakh N. A. Rimskogo-Korsakova" (*Christmas Eve,* A Christmas tale after the story by N. V. Gogol, an opera in 4 acts by N. A. Rimsky-Korsakov), was published in *Russkie vedomosti* (December 18, 1895), no. 349.

65. This refers to a concert of the St. Petersburg Philharmonic Society under the direction of Yulii Bleichmann, their conductor from 1895 to 1897.

6. 1896

1. In 1895–96, Belyaev, captivated by Scriabin's talent, organized a concert tour abroad at his own expense. Scriabin's performance of his own piano works met with great success in Paris, Berlin, Brussels, Amsterdam, and other European cities. Belyaev accompanied the performer everywhere.

2. In early 1896, Josef Hofmann made several concert appearances in Petersburg. Besides performing with the Russian Musical Society (twice), the St. Petersburg Philharmonic Society, and for philanthropic societies, he also gave four solo recitals.

3. Cui subsequently concurred with Rimsky-Korsakov on this matter, and the score was published without Cui's corrections (V. V. Ya.)

4. This article, entitled "Noch' pered Rozhdestvom" (Christmas Eve), was published in *Russkaia muzykal'naia gazeta* (1896), no. 1.

5. This letter, addressed to Rimsky-Korsakov, is dated Shilovo, 15 August 1868. (Trans.)

6. Yastrebtsev here equates the two reactionary critics, Solovyov and M. V. Stanislavsky (contributor to the newspaper *S.-Peterburgskii vedomosti*), with the characters of *Das Rheingold:* the short Solovyov to the dwarf Mime; Stanislavsky to the giant Fafner.

7. Cui's article " 'Verter,' liricheskaia drama Massne. Pervyi Russkii simfonicheskii kontsert (Rimskii-Korsakov, Borodin, Rakhmaninov, Ippolitov-Ivanov)" (*Werther,* a lyric drama by Massenet. First Russian symphonic concert [Rimsky-Korsakov, Borodin, Rachmaninov, Ippolitov-Ivanov]), was published in *Novosti i birzhevaia gazeta* (January 22, 1896), no. 22, under the heading "Muzykal'nye zametki, (Musical notes). Cui wrote: "On the whole, Rimsky-Korsakov's Third Symphony is an outstanding work—a harmonious union of inspiration and technique, form and content." See C. A. Cui, *Izbrannye stat'i,* (Selected articles), (Leningrad, 1952), p. 451.

8. *Hänsel and Gretel* was given its Russian premiere on January 2, 1896, at the Panayevsky Theater. Rimsky-Korsakov attended one of the subsequent performances, probably on January 12.

9. The American soprano, Sibyl Sanderson, for whom Massenet had written the title role. (Trans.)

10. Cui's "Ocherk razvitiia russkogo romansa" (A survey of the development of the Russian romance) was published as separate articles in the journal *Arist* (1895), nos. 45–46, and then in the newspaper *Nedelia* (1895), nos. 25–31. In 1896 Findeisen published it in the form of a book entitled *Russkii romans* (St. Petersburg). Excerpts from the latter were republished in C. A. Cui, *Izbrannye stat'i,* p. 439.

11. The 120th exhibition of the paintings of I. K. Aivazovsky, at which eighty of the artist's paintings were displayed, opened on December 28, 1895. Almost simultaneously, works by Vereshchagin, devoted to the theme of Napoleon's invasion of Russia, were also put on view. For reviews of these exhibits see *Novosti* (January 15, 1896), no. 15—L. E. Obolensky, "120-ia vystavka kartin I. K. Aivazovskogo" (The 120th exhibition of paintings by I. K. Aivazovsky)—and *Novosti* (January 11, 1896), no. 11—"Na vystavke kartin V. V. Vereshchagina" (At the exhibition of the paintings of V. V. Vereshchagin).

12. Of the operas listed the following were given during the 1896–97 season: Boito's *Mefistofele* (December, January, and February), Leoncavallo's *Pagliacci* (December, January, and February), Saint-Saëns' *Samson et Dalila* (premiere—November 19), Massenet's *Esclarmonde* (February), and Minkus' ballet *Mlada* (September, October, November, December, February, and April).

13. Rimsky-Korsakov was then scoring act 2 of *Boris.* (V. V. Ya.)

14. Solovyov's patronymic—Feopemtovich. (Trans.)

15. Actually, Rimsky-Korsakov completed the orchestration of the scene between Boris and Shuisky not on the 12 but on the day of this entry, 11 February 1896. (V. V. Ya.)

16. In his youth Solovyov wrote this piece on themes taken from *The Maid of Pskov.* It was published but has never been located and is presumed to have been destroyed by the composer. (Trans.)

17. Borodin's humor expressed itself in musical jokes such as this. Few of them were ever published.

18. Nadezhda Nikolayevna ought also to doubt the musicality of Glinka and Schumann, since they, too, admired Berlioz. (V. V. Ya.)

19. See entry of 4 February 1896. (Trans.)

20. Vladimir Ivanovich Belsky collaborated with Rimsky-Korsakov on the libretto of *Sadko.* (Trans.)

21. This song was retained.

---

22. In the aria following Golo's recitative one already hears the sounds of the love duet from Wagner's *Tristan and Isolde* and in the final scene of act 1—the future "motive of fate" from the *Nibelung's Ring*. (V. V. Ya.)

23. Schumann's *Genoveva* was given its first performance in Russia on April 1, 1896, at the Mikhailovsky Theater. This performance was put on by the Music Society with the assistance of Count Sheremetyev's orchestra under the direction of Goldenblum.

24. Cui's article "Genoveva, opera Roberta Shumana" (*Genoveva*, opera by Robert Schumann) was published in *Novosti i birzhevaia gazeta* (April 3, 1896), no. 91, under the heading "Teatr i muzyka" (Theater and music). The article was reprinted in C. A. Cui, *Izbrannye stat'i*, p. 452.

25. Ivanov's unsigned article on the performance of Schumann's *Genoveva* appeared in *Novoe vremia* on April 3, 1896. According to the author, this opera "does not stand up to the most lenient criticism either as opera music or as music taken on its own merits." Solovyov, on the contrary, approved the Music Society's choice of *Genoveva*; see "Pervoe predstavlenie opery 'Genoveva' " (First performance of the opera *Genoveva*), *Birzhevye vedomosti*, April 3, 1896.

26. Refers to Cui's sharply negative review of Tchaikovsky's graduation cantata, based on Schiller's *Ode to Joy*. *S.-Peterburgskie vedomosti* (March 24, 1866), no. 82.

27. See *Concerte, Komponisten, und Virtuosen*, 1886, pp. 175–296. (V. V. Ya.)

28. These rehearsals were in preparation for the Music Society's presentation of *Boris Godunov*. The opera was given four performances—on November 28 and 29 and December 3 and 4, 1896. The first was under the direction of Rimsky-Korsakov, the remaining three—under Goldenblum. (Trans.)

29. Introduced into the opera by Rimsky-Korsakov. This was not in Borodin. (V. V. Ya.)

30. The last 19 pages were orchestrated partly by Borodin, or rather, with his agreement by Rimsky-Korsakov.

31. On May 16 the Rimsky-Korsakovs moved to a house on the estate of Baron Tiesenhausen at Smerdovitsy, where they remained for the summer. (Trans.)

32. *Obikhod*—a collection of hymns of the Orthodox Church.

33. "To starina slavna, to i deianie."

34. August 19, 1896.

35. See the Czech newspapers *Národní Listy* (nos. 242 and 248), review by the critic Borecký; *Narodni Politika* and simply *Politika* (no. 242), article by Emanuel Ghvála; *Dalibor* (from 7/19 September), notes by Karel Knittl, professor at the Prague Conservatory; further, *Svêtozor* (no. 45), an article by F. K. Hejda and, finally, *Hlas Národa* (no. 242), a critical article by V. Novotný. (V. V. Ya.)

36. In actual fact, Rimsky-Korsakov had little knowledge of or interest in the compositions of Smetana.

37. The French writer Pierre d'Alheim's book *Moussorgsky* was published in Paris in 1896. That same year together with his wife, the singer Marie Olenine, he gave seven concert-lectures of the composer's songs in that same city, which aroused great enthusiasm. From then on until 1900, they presented numerous concerts of Mussorgsky's works in France and Belgium. These concerts, too, met with increasing success. So far as is known, Rimsky-Korsakov never met the d'Alheims. (Trans.)

38. The new building of the Conservatory, reconstructed during the years 1891–1896 from the Imperial Bolshoi Theater (Opera), was opened on November 12, 1896.

39. The estimable lecturer, most likely, had no idea of the simple fact that *Khovanshchina*, which he praised so highly, had also been reworked by Rimsky-Korsakov. Consequently, the naive Pierre d'Alheim never knew Mussorgsky's own version of the opera. (V. V. Ya.)

40. *Snegurochka* was given its first performance in Kharkov on October 11, 1896.

41. The concerts in memory of Tchaikovsky took place on November 9 and 10, 1896, in the Assembly Hall of the Nobility. The first was under the direction of Nikisch, the second, of Napravnik. The programs consisted entirely of the works of Tchaikovsky.

42. The celebration of Rimsky-Korsakov's anniversary on October 25, 1896, was attended by representatives of the Board of Directors of the Russian Musical Society, and professors, teachers, and students of the Conservatory. Congratulatory addresses were given by Cui and the Director of the Conservatory, Johansen.

43. "Svet moi, Savishna, iasnyi moi sokol, lubi menia, bezumnogo." "Iasnyi moi sokol," literally "my bright falcon," is a folk idiom usually rendered as "my darling." (Trans.)

44. Some, for example, were so carried away with Mussorgsky, that they called him a "giant," a "genius," and almost the equal of Beethoven. (V. V. Ya.)

45. The original Varlaaam, Koryakin, had to be replaced because of illness. (Trans.)

46. This performance of Boris Godunov in Rimsky-Korsakov's version was given in the Large Hall of the Conservatory. On November 29 and December 3 and 4 it was directed by Goldenblum. The cast varied somewhat at each performance.

47. M. Ivanov. " 'Tristan i Izol'da,' muzykal'naia drama v 3 deistviiah Vagnera" (Tristan and Isolde, a musical drama in three acts by Wagner). Novoe vremia (November 4 and 18, 1896).

48. V. Stasov, "Dirizherskaia palochka Rimskogo-Korsakova" (Rimsky-Korsakov's baton), Novosti (December 1, 1896). This article was devoted to the first performance of Boris Godunov in Rimsky-Korsakov's orchestration. The performance was viewed as a "major event," and Rimsky-Korsakov's orchestration was considered a "great service" to his deceased friend.

49. Rimsky-Korsakov attended the performance of Saint-Saëns' Samson et Dalila at the Marinsky Theater on December 2, 1896. The premiere took place on November 19.

50. Entry of 5 February 1896. (Trans.)

51. Thus, for example, the final scene bears the note: 28 December 1895. (V. V. Ya.)

7. 1897

1. See entries of 24 November and 1 December 1892. (V. V. Ya.)

2. The Theater Committee of the Directorate of the Imperial Theaters, which chose the operas to be performed.

3. H. Riemann, "N. Rimsky-Korsakow, 'Schecherazade,' " op. 35," Der Musikführer, Frankfurt am Main: Bechhold.

4. Modern numbering, 102. (Trans.)

5. The revised version of 1897, not the one falsely described in some editions as Nouvelle rédaction (1897): see Gerald Abraham, Slavonic and Romantic Music (London: Faber and Faber, 1968), pp. 199–201.(Trans.).

6. The final page carries the same note, except that there it reads not simply "village of Shilovo," but "8 July/68 izba [peasant hut] in Shilovo." A similar note is found also preceding Scene 3 (with the Matchmaker): "2/68 July. Izba in Shilovo." (V. V. Ya.)

7. This refers to the first song, "S Nianei" (With Nanny), from Mussorgsky's Nursery, in Rimsky-Korsakov's version. On the manuscript, alongside of the title, is a postscript, in Rimsky-Korsakov's hand: "A simplified retelling." (See N. A. Rimsky-Korsakov Archives, G.P.B., no. 60.) [The Russian niania and her role having been so different from that of a British "nanny" or American "nurse," I prefer to retain the Russian name for her, pronounced exactly as transliterated. (Trans.)]

8. Following the performance of Christmas Eve in 1895, Rimsky-Korsakov's operas were not

performed at the Marinsky Theater for three years. They were revived only on December 15, 1898, with the production of *Snegurochka*.

9. Of the operas listed, those given during the 1896–97 season were *Don Giovanni, The Oprichnik,* and *Hänsel and Gretel*. The first two were revivals. *Don Giovanni* opened on September 2, 1896, and *The Oprichnik* on January 22, 1897. The premiere of *Hänsel and Gretel* took place on October 24, 1897.

10. *The Sleeping Princess,* a tale for voice and piano to words by Borodin. 1867. Dedicated to Rimsky-Korsakov. (Trans.)

11. Glazunov's Sixth Symphony (op. 58, 1896) was given its premiere at this concert on February 9, 1897, under the composer's direction.

12. Taneyev was the soloist in this *Andante and Finale for Piano and Orchestra,* a version, made by him, of materials which Tchaikovsky sketched in 1892 for a contemplated symphony in E flat but left unscored. It was published in 1897 as op. 79.

13. The work referred to here is the one performed by Taneyev on February 9. (Trans.)

14. See entry of 13 February 1895. (V. V. Ya.)

15. In *Georgian Song* one notes also the harmony which later occurs in the scene of Olga in the forest (in *The Maid of Pskov*) and seems to depict the luring sounds of the thicket. (V. V. Ya.)

16. The rhythmic background on the small drum. (V. V. Ya.)

17. At the beginning of The Joy of Revenge. (V. V. Ya.)

18. See entries of 14 and 20 November 1897. (V. V. Ya.)

19. For a list of these songs, see entry of 15 June 1897.

20. The cantata *Switezianka* for tenor, soprano, chorus, and orchestra was a reworking of a song composed originally in 1867, on a text by Mey (after Mickiewicz). See entry of 14 February 1893. (Trans.)

21. In English known as *Pan,* op. 47, no. 1 (Trans.)

22. In a subsequent entry (dated 8 September), Rimsky-Korsakov informed Yastrebtsev that, besides the two duets and *Switezianka,* since the spring he had written in all thirty-four songs as well as an opera in two scenes entitled *Mozart and Salieri* (after Pushkin). (Trans.)

23. Yastrebtsev obviously means the last twelve, the "London" symphonies, nos. 93–104. (Trans.)

24. This mazurka, as is known, was sketched by Chopin shortly before his death, but because of his extreme weakness, he was not able to try it out on the piano (V. V. Ya.)

25. *The Banquet* (op. 5, no. 3, 1867), story for voice with piano accompaniment to text by Kol'tsov. First published in 1868 by Johansen in St. Petersburg. Reprinted in 1908 by Belyaev in Leipzig with a French translation by I. Sergennois.

26. The symphonic suite *Antar* (originally named Second Symphony) was composed in 1868. It was revised and rescored twice—in 1875 and again in 1897. It was the final version which was played at this concert. (Trans.)

27. The musical evening referred to here took place on December 20. In addition to *Mozart and Salieri* they performed excerpts from *Sadko* and songs by Rimsky-Korsakov. (Entry omitted—Trans.)

28. Cui's four-act opera *The Saracen* (1896–1898) was given its premiere at the Marinsky Theater on November 2, 1899.

29. The Solodovnikov Theater was the home of a private opera company in Moscow subsidized by S. I. Mamontov, a wealthy patron of the arts. The first performance of *Sadko* was given there on December 26, 1897. (Trans.)

8. 1898

1. The third Russian Symphony Concert took place on January 10, 1898, under the direction of Rimsky-Korsakov.

2. The third and fourth performances of *Sadko* by Mamontov's Private Russian Opera took place at the Solodovnikov Theater on December 30, 1897, and January 3, 1898. See N. A. Rimsky-Korsakov, *Letopis' moei muzykal'noi zhizni* ("My Musical Life") (Moscow, 1955), p. 209.

3. From the members of the Private Russian Opera. (V. V. Ya.)

4. *Gornyi kliuch* ("Otkuda ty, o kliuch podgornyi")—duet for soprano (or tenor) and mezzo-soprano (or baritone) (op. 52, no. 1, 1897) to words by A. Maikov.

5. Rimsky-Korsakov's proposed visit to Moscow took place in the fall. The composer directed the Russian Symphony Concert on October 17.

6. The program consisted of Glazunov's Second Symphony, Tchaikovsky's Overture to *The Tempest*, Rimsky-Korsakov's Piano Concerto in C-sharp minor, the Persian Dances from Mussorgsky's *Khovanshchina* (Rimsky-Korsakov), and Glinka's *Kamarinskaya*. (V. V. Ya.)

7. This meeting took place on January 3, 1898, in Yasnaya Polyana.

8. I first heard about this meeting from A. N. Pypin, who, in turn, had been told about it by the sculptor I. Ya. Ginsburg, who had also been at the Tolstoys' that evening. (V. V. Ya.)

9. P. Veinberg's article " 'Sadko,' opera-bylina N. A. Rimskogo-Korsakova (Po povodu postanovki ee na stsene Chastnoi russkoi opery)" (*Sadko*, an opera-*bylina* by N. A. Rimsky-Korsakov [On the occasion of its performance by the Private Russian Opera]) appeared over the signature "V" in *Moskovskie vedomosti* (1897), no. 356. N. Kashkin's article " 'Sadko'—opera-bylina v semi kartinakh N. A. Rimskogo-Korsakova na stsene Chastnoi russkoi opery v teatre Solodovnikova" (*Sadko*—opera-*bylina* in seven scenes by N. A. Rimsky-Korsakov as performed by the Private Russian Opera at the Solodovnikov Theater) was carried by *Russkie vedomosti* (1898), no. 7, over the signature of N. K-in.

10. See entry of 29 December 1897.

11. "Catholic" means "universal" and, consequently, according to the Orthodox religion, is not inconsistent with the true feelings of the wife of a Novgorod merchant. (V. V. Ya.)

12. That is, St. Nicholas' theme (see entry of 23 August 1896). (V. V. Ya.)

13. Tolstoy's wife assured the Rimsky-Korsakovs that Lev Nikolayevich actually not only worships Beethoven but even values beauty very highly and that his hatred for them is purely philosophical. (V. V. Ya.)

14. Handel's aria—most likely Almirena's aria "Lascia ch'io pianga" (Largo) from act 2, scene 4 of the opera *Rinaldo*. [Although the Soviet editors have identified the aria as above, it was more likely "Ombra mai fu," the famous Largo from *Xerxes* (Trans.)]

15. Tolstoy attended a performance of Wagner's *Siegfried* (on April 18 or 29, 1896) during the period when he was working on the essay *What Is Art?* Chapter 13 is given over to an analysis of the opera and an explanation of the reasons for its success. Tolstoy perceived *Siegfried* as an antiartistic work, the skillful fabrication of a "limited, opinionated German, with bad taste and style, who has the most fallacious conceptions of poetry, and who, in the crassest and most primitive manner, wishes to transmit to me these false and mistaken conceptions of his." After act 1 he "fled the theater with a feeling of revulsion."

16. "1898. January. Tolstoy's visit with V. V. Stasov, V. V. Matte, I. Ya. Ginsburg, N. A. Rimsky-Korsakov, S. I. Taneyev. Tolstoy's argument with Rimsky-Korsakov about art. Tolstoy rejected all of Rimsky-Korsakov's artistic and musical views and, when saying good-bye, said to him, 'Today I have seen gloom.' " N. Gusev, *Letopis' zhizni i tvorchestva L. N. Tolstogo* (Chronicle of the life and work of Leo Tolstoy) (Moscow-Leningrad, 1936), diary for January 4.

17. *Muzykal'nye fel'etony i zametki Petra Il'icha Chaikovskogo (1868–1876)* (Articles and notes on music by Peter Ilyich Tchaikovsky [1868–1876]). With a portrait, an autobiographical description of a trip abroad in 1888, and preface by H. A. Laroche. (Moscow, 1898). Reprinted as P. I. Tchaikovsky, *Muzykal'no-criticheskie stat'i* (Articles on music) (Moscow, 1953).

18. "Po povody 'Serbskoi fantazii' g. Rimskogo-Korsakova" (On Mr. Rimsky-Korsakov's *Fantasia on Serbian Themes*), *Sovremennaia letopis'* (1868), no. 8.

19. That is, the rehearsal of *The Maid of Pskov* performed in St. Petersburg by the Moscow Private Russian Opera.

20. Zagorodny prospekt, house 28, apt. 39—the Rimsky-Korsakovs' apartment.

21. Despite the somewhat ironic and deliberately oversimplified account of the content of *Sadko*, in his article Cui pointed out its originality, profound artistic importance, and the craftsmanship of its composition. " 'Sadko,' opera-bylina Rimskogo-Korsakova" (*Sadko*, an opera-*bylina* by Rimsky-Korsakov), *Novosti i birzhevaia gazeta* (1898), no. 64, in the section *Teatr i muzyka* (Theater and music).

22. Reference to Ivan the Terrible's aria "Vot obelil ia Pskov," dedicated to Chaliapin. It was published separately in 1898. The copy presented to Chaliapin bears the inscription in the composer's hand: "To the amazing, extraordinary performer of Ivan the Terrible, F. I. Chaliapin."

23. Mitrofan Petrovich Beylaev, founder of the music publishing firm that bore his name and of the Russian Symphonic Concerts; benefactor of the annual Glinka Prizes. Savva Ivanovich Mamontov, patron and head of the Mamontov Private Russian Opera of Moscow. (Trans.)

24. The cycle *U more* (By the Sea) op. 46, composed in 1897 to words by A. K. Tolstoi, contains five songs: *Drobitsia, i pleshchet, i bryzzhet volna; Ne penitsia more, ne pleshchet volna; Kolyshetsia more, volna za volnoi; Ne ver' mne, drug; Vzdymaiutsia volny, kak gory.*

25. This concert on April 11, 1898, in the Assembly Hall of the Nobility was followed by a celebration in honor of the thirty-fifth anniversary of Balakirev's association with the Free Music School's concerts; see *Russkaia muzykal'naia gazeta* (1898), no. 5–6.

26. This was Balakirev's last appearance as a conductor. (Trans.)

27. In his article "Moskovskaia russkaia chastnaia opera. 'Sadko' " (The Moscow Russian Private Opera, *Sadko*), Petrovsky refused to render a final judgment of the opera because of its complexity and contradictions. He limited himself to a few comments about the work as a whole, describing his first impression of the performance.

28. Reference to the production of *Mozart and Salieri* by the Moscow Private Opera Company. The opera was not given its premiere until November 25, 1898.

29. Two ariosos for bass and orchestra to words by Pushkin (op. 49, 1897, published 1898): *Anchar* (The Upas Tree), dedicated to F. Stravinsky, and *Prorok* (The Prophet), dedicated to V. V. Stasov.

30. *Boyarina Vera Sheloga*—musico-dramatic prologue to the opera *The Maid of Pskov*. At the end of the autograph score there is a note: "N. R.-K. 7 Apr. 98." The original version of this prologue was written in 1877; the overture to it in 1881. The final version dates to 1898. [It became the separate, one-act opera *Boyarina Vera Sheloga*. (Trans.)]

31. In the entry of 27 April (omitted) Rimsky-Korsakov mentioned to Yastrebtsev that he had begun a new opera on April 15. He did not divulge the subject, but it was *The Tsar's Bride.* (Trans.)

32. Rimsky-Korsakov's symphonic picture *Sadko* (1867).

33. See entries of 9 February and 11 April 1900.

34. In due course *May Night* was also translated into German.

35. The opera "which begins immediately with a fast overture" is *The Tsar's Bride;* by a "thoroughly decadent opera" Rimsky-Korsakov apparently meant *The Tale of Tsar Saltan.*

---

36. Altogether the Rimsky-Korsakovs spent six summers in Vechasha—1894, 1895, 1898, 1899, 1904, and 1905. (Trans.)

37. *Noch'* (Night) ("Moi golos dlia tebia i laskovyi i tomnyi")—fantasy for voice and piano, words by Pushkin, dedicated to N. Opochinina. It was orchestrated by Mussorgsky in 1868 and revised in 1871. Pushkin's text was adapted freely.

38. Ilya Feodorovich Tyumenev collaborated on two of Rimsky-Korsakov's operas, writing some additional scenes for *The Tsar's Bride* (at Rimsky-Korsakov's request) and (on commission from the composer) an original libretto for *Pan Voyevoda*. (Trans.)

39. For a long time it has been the custom at the Marinsky Theater (introduced by Napravnik) to sew together the pages of a score which had been cut. In most cases, the cuts were made arbitrarily, by the conductor. We have only to recall the utterly absurd cuts in the third act of *Prince Igor* and in the scene of the *rusalki* from *May Night*. (V. V. Ya.)

40. The revival of Rimsky-Korsakov's *Snegurochka* at the Marinsky Theater did not take place on November 6 but on December 15, 1898.

41. The Russian Symphony Concert directed by Rimsky-Korsakov was highly successful. See *Russkaia muzykal'naia gazeta* (1898), no. 11, article by I. Lipayev.

42. Rimsky-Korsakov and Mamontov had had a temporary falling out due to the latter's intransigence during the preparation of operatic productions and disagreements over the choice of performers.

43. Due to differences between Koptayev and its sponsor, this newspaper ceased publication after only three issues. (V. V. Ya.)

44. This interview, entitled "Beseda s P. I. Chaikovskim" (conversation with P. I. Tchaikovsky), was published in the journal *Peterburgskaia zhizn'* (1892), no. 2, over the signature "G. B." In it Tchaikovsky highly praised the musical activity of Rimsky-Korsakov, calling him the "finest adornment of the new Russian school." (P. I. Tchaikovsky. *Muzykal'no-kriticheskie stati*, p. 367).

45. The article "Po povodu 'Serbskoi fantazii' g. Rimskogo-Korsakova" (On Mr. Rimsky-Korsakov's *Fantasia on Serbian Themes*), *Sovremennaia letopis'* (1868), no. 8, was reprinted in Tchaikovsky's book *Muzykal'nye fel'etony i zametki;* included in the new edition, P. I. Tchaikovsky, *Muzykal'no-kriticheskie stat'i*, pp. 25–27.

46. *Christmas Eve* received its Moscow premiere at the Bolshoi Theater on October 27, 1898.

47. In his article "Novaia russkaia muzyka s kul'turnoi tochki zreniia," A. Koptyaev tried to characterize the New Russian School in the light of the development of European culture. Comparing the creativity of the composers of this school with that of the representatives of the new French and German schools of music, Koptyaev noted that the Russian composers are more talented (no. 1, p. 203).

48. Raoul Pugno played the Grieg Piano Concerto at the concert of the Russian Musical Society on November 14, 1898.

49. *Mozart and Salieri* was given its premiere by the Moscow Private Russian Opera with V. Shkafer as Mozart and Chaliapin as Salieri.

50. *Boris Godunov* was performed on December 7, 1898, not on November 30.

51. The first Russian Symphony Concert of the 1898–99 season took place on December 5, 1898. Scriabin played the prelude referred to here and also his Piano Concerto in F-sharp minor. The orchestra was under the direction of Rimsky-Korsakov.

52. The program of the second Russian Symphony Concert included the first performance of excerpts from the prologue to Rimsky-Korsakov's *Maid of Pskov (Vera Sheloga)* under the direction of the composer.

53. The first and second Russian Symphony Concerts (on December 5 and 19, 1898) were reviewed in *Novosti i birzhevaia gazeta* and *Novosti dnia*. In these reviews Yastrebtsev detected the views of Cui, Ivanov, and Bloch, contributors to the newspapers mentioned.

54. This was the first performance of a Rimsky-Korsakov opera at the Marinsky Theater since the premiere of *Christmas Eve*, which was held on December 10, 1895. (Trans.)

55. Reference to the costumes and sets designed for the original production of *Snegurochka* in 1882. (V. V. Ya.)

56. Rimsky-Korsakov made his first public appearance as a composer on December 19, 1865, when his E-flat minor Symphony, op. 1, was played together with Mozart's *Requiem* at a concert of the Free Music School, conducted by Balakirev. (Trans.)

57. All works designated by asterisks were being performed for the first time. (V. V. Ya.)

58. See entry of 15 December 1898. (V. V. Ya.)

59. Reporting on the second Russian Symphony Concert, at which Zabela sang the role of Vera Sheloga, M. Ivanov expressed surprise that "the composer, conducting the orchestra himself, could be satisfied with such a flaccid, colorless performance which, far from lending support to the composition, slaughtered it." *Novoe vremia,* (1898), no. 8197, in the section *Teatr i muzyka* (Theater and music).

In a letter to Yastrebtsev, Zabela wrote, "My visit to St. Petersburg was very enjoyable, except that I had the imprudence to read the review in *Novoe vremia,* which, I must confess, shattered me. I have never before read such cruel, harsh, downright destructive criticism. Was the performance really that bad? What can Ivanov have against me? Note that the success wasn't even mentioned. This is very, very painful to me and there's no way to counteract the harm such a review is certain to cause." (Undated letter, preserved in the G.P.B. V. V. Yastrebstev Fund.)

60. See note 53. (Trans.)

9. 1899

1. This I learned from Nadezhda Nikolayevna; Rimsky-Korsakov himself almost never spoke of such things. (V. V. Ya.)

2. This refers to Lipayev's articles " 'Motsart i Sal'eri.' Opera N. Rimskogo-Korsakova, v Moskve" (*Mozart and Salieri.* Opera by N. Rimsky-Korsakov, in Moscow) and " 'Boiarina Vera Sheloga.' Muzykal'no-dramaticheskii prolog N. Rimskogo-Korsakova, v Moskve" (*Boyarina Vera Sheloga.* Musico-dramatic prologue by N. Rimsky-Korsakov, in Moscow), *Russkaia muzykal'naia gazeta* (1899), nos. 1 and 2.

3. V. V. Stasov, "Moi adres publike" (My address to the public), *Novosti i birzhevaia gazeta* (1899), no. 43; reprinted in V. V. Stasov, *Izbrannye sochinenia* (Selected works) (Moscow, 1952), 3:264. This article was written on the occasion of an exhibition of works by V. Vasnetsov in St. Petersburg in early 1899.

4. The praise of our musical papers notwithstanding. (V. V. Ya.)

5. Conductor of the Italian Opera. (V. V. Ya.)

6. Hans Richter conducted the seventh symphonic evening of the Russian Musical Society on January 22 and 23, 1899, at the hall of the St. Petersburg Conservatory. The soloist was the cellist Abbiate.

7. Evidently Richter attended the performance of Napravnik's opera *Dubrovsky* at the Bolshoi Theater in Moscow on January 1, 1899.

8. The exhibition of paintings by V. Vasnetsov opened at the Academy of Art on February 4, 1899.

9. Glazunov studied with Rimsky-Korsakov from 1879 to 1881.

10. The total number of performances of this opera since its premiere in 1882. (V. V. Ya.)

11. Rimsky-Korsakov's fifty-fifth birthday.

12. In this article entitled "Iz moikh vospominanii o P. I. Chaikovskom" (From my reminiscences of P. I. Tchaikovsky), Yastrebtsev gives an account of three meetings with the composer

(the meeting at the Rimsky-Korsakovs' was recorded in these *Reminiscences* on 9 May 1893). Accompanying the article was an editorial disclaimer regarding the controversial nature of the author's (Yastrebstev's) judgments. These judgments, which were given at the end of the article, infuriated Stasov.

"As a composer," writes Yastrebtsev,

Tchaikovsky was unquestionably one of the most gifted spokesmen of his time. The contemporaneity of his music, it seems to me, constitutes the principal reason, perhaps even the secret of his enormous popularity. Indeed, at a time when Mussorgsky and Dargomyzhsky were wedded to an extreme, not always artistic naturalism and genre; when Borodin was immersed in a prehistoric period with its alluring epic remoteness; when Rimsky-Korsakov—this undeniably greatest of contemporary musician-artists—had withdrawn into his own strikingly individual pagan, fantastic or, more correctly, "phantasmal world," full of the richest, almost inaccessible beauty and poetry; and at time when César Cui with his amazingly ingenious *William Ratcliff* flew away to Scotland (a place alien to us), Tchaikovsky was totally imbued with the spirit of the time, and with all the intensity and passion of his profoundly sensitive and impressionable nature responded to its call. And so, embodying in sounds an image of the past—the days of our grandfathers and great-grandfathers—he always remained true to himself and, perhaps, without even realizing it himself, portrayed only us ourselves with our unresolved doubts, our sorrows and joys.

13. Towards Lent of 1899, Mamontov's Private Russian Opera paid its second visit to St. Petersburg. This time, in addition to *Sadko,* the company presented *The Maid of Pskov, Boris Godunov,* and the Petersburg premieres of *Boyarina Vera Sheloga* and *Mozart and Salieri.* (Trans.)

14. Reference to the first performance in St. Petersburg by the Moscow Private Russian Opera, in the Large Hall of the Conservatory.

15. Cui's articles were published in *Novosti i birzhevaia gazeta* in the section *Teatr i muzyka* (Theater and music) (March 9 and 12, 1899), nos. 67 and 70. They were entitled "Moskovskaia Chastnaia russkaia opera. 'Boris Godunov' Mussorgskogo" and "Moskovskaia Chastnaia opera. 'Motsart i Salieri' A. S. Pushkina i N. A. Rimskogo-Korsakova" (Moscow Private Russian Opera. *Boris Godunov* by Mussorgsky and Moscow Private Opera. *Mozart and Salieri* by A. S. Pushkin and N. A. Rimsky-Korsakov).

In the article about *Boris Godunov,* while acknowledging Rimsky-Korsakov's mastery of harmony and orchestration, Cui expressed a preference for the original opera and stated a desire to see it produced at the Marinsky Theater in its original form. Rimsky-Korsakov replied to this article in a letter to the editor of *Novosti i birzhevaia gazeta* (March 12, 1899), no. 70, in which he quoted the text of the foreword to the opera *Boris Godunov* and stated the motives which had prompted him to undertake to edit and orchestrate it.

16. The opera *The Tsar's Bride* was completed on November 25, 1898. It was given its first performance on October 22, 1899, by the Moscow Private Russian Opera. The overture was performed for the first time on March 20, 1899 at the fourth Russian Symphony Concert under the direction of Rimsky-Korsakov.

17. See note 15.

18. Petrovsky wrote: "Before us . . . two artists . . . Pushkin and Korsakov, the first of whom totally devoured the second. . . . The chosen subject has, in this instance, proven beyond his creative powers, and the music applied to Pushkin's text, while retaining the charm and the beautiful outlines of the text, merely skims its surface, without plumbing its depths. We repeat, *Mozart and Salieri* is an unsuccessful step in a new direction by a major talent." *Russkaia muzykal'naia gazeta* (March 20, 1899) no. 12, in the section *Opera i kontserty* (Opera and Concerts).

19. A "run-through" of *The Tsar's Bride* by amateur singers, except for Zabela. (Trans.)

20. *Russkaia muzykal'naia gazeta* (1899), no. 12, carried an unsigned article on Rimsky-Korsakov's *Mozart and Salieri.* Angered by this article and the evaluation of the opera, Stasov sent Findeisen a "scathing" letter, in which he spoke his mind with his customary bluntness:

I (and several others as well) am highly indignant over this article. It's a pity that it is unsigned; whoever wrote it is clearly incapable of understanding music and writing about it. . . . The anonymous author (evidently E. M. Petrovksy) considers Rimsky-Korsakov's opera an unsuccessful *step in a new direction by a major artist*. I, on the other hand, believe this article by an anonymous writer to be an unsuccessful step *in the old direction* by some minor and untalented person—that is, in a direction which becomes him like a saddle does a cow." (Letter of 22 March 1899.)

Replying to Stasov's letter, Findeisen, after expressing his own negative reaction to Rimsky-Korsakov's opera ("I, too, did not like *Mozart and Salieri*"), went on to defend the author of the article, saying that he had as much right to express his opinion openly as Stasov did. "But, all the same," he wrote, "I have to defend the latter (Stasov), this upright soul who loves Rimsky-Korsakov; although he (the author) may be groping in the dark, this can pass." (G.P.B., N. F. Findeisen fund.)

21. "Moskovskaia Chastnaia russkaia opera. 'Kniaz' Igor' Borodina" (Moscow Private Russian Opera. *Prince Igor* by Borodin), in the section *Teatr i muzyka* (Theater and music).

22. *Snegurochka*—music to A. N. Ostrovsky's spring tale in four acts (op. 12, 1873).

23. As a rule, Nikolai Andreyevich did not use the familiar *ty* ("thou"). I believe that, aside from his relatives, there were only three persons he addressed thus, that is, Iretsky, Prince Myshetsky, and his former music teacher and friend, Kanille. (V. V. Ya.)

24. In the spring of 1899, at the request of S. Mamontov, Rimsky-Korsakov orchestrated the arioso for bass *Prorok,* which Chaliapin was scheduled to sing at the Pushkin evening in Moscow. This work subsequently entered the concert repertoire of the great artist.

25. Widow of Karl Yulevich Davydov, cellist, composer, conductor, and from 1876 to 1887 Director of the Petersburg Conservatory. (Trans.)

26. This conversation about Nikisch was occasioned by the fact that he was currently conducting the Berlin Philharmonic Orchestra in several concerts in St. Petersburg. The programs, presented on April 19, 20, 28, and 29, 1899, included works by Beethoven, Brahms, Berlioz, Wagner, Weber, Liszt, Tchaikovsky, Schumann, and Strauss.

27. She declared that anyone who did not like Nikisch was a personal enemy of hers! (V. V. Ya.)

28. *St.-Petersburger Zeitung* (March 23, 1899), no. 82, and (April 23, 1899), no. 113.

29. M. Ivanov. "Pushkin v muzyke—opery i kantaty na ego suzhety" (Pushkin in music—operas and cantatas on his plots).

30. "I've grown old and mischievous; you'd better keep an eye on me." The miller's aria from Dargomyzhsky's *Rusalka.* (Trans.)

31. Nikolai Ivanovich Richter, pianist and teacher, not Hans Richter, the conductor. (Trans.)

32. *Song of Oleg the Wise* (Pushkin) for tenor, bass, male chorus, and orchestra, op. 58. (Trans.)

33. The suite *Pictures from The Tale of Tsar Saltan,* which was derived from the orchestral introductions to the first, second, and fourth acts of the opera.

34. See entry of 17 December 1901. (V. V. Ya.)

35. During the summer of 1899, Rimsky-Korsakov worked on the opera *The Tale of Tsar Saltan* and the cantata *Song of Oleg the Wise.* The latter was finished in September.

36. Rimsky-Korsakov did not realize this intention; *Prince Kholmsky* was published under the joint editorship of Rimsky-Korsakov and Glazunov but not until 1902.

37. *The Poet,* op. 45, no. 5.

38. See entry of 12 April 1898, note 24. (Trans.)

39. Vsev. Cheshikhin. " 'Parsifal,' drama-misteria Rikharda Vagnera (kriticheskii etiud)" (*Parsifal,* drama-mystery by Richard Wagner [critical study]), *Russkaia muzykal'naia gazeta* (1899), nos. 27–28. The articles and essays of Ye. Petrovsky and N. Findeisen on the operas of Wagner (*Lohengrin,*

Tristan and Isolde, Tannhäuser, etc.) were carried in nos. 11, 15–17, 31–39, and 42 of *Russkaia muzykal'naia gazeta* for 1899.

40. In his unsigned reviews of Wagner's opera *Tristan and Isolde* (*Russkaia muzykal'naia gazeta* [1899], nos. 15–17), E. Petrovsky called Blumenfeld's conducting "smooth," but "dull and lifeless," adding that "it would be crass flattery to call a gifted pianist a gifted conductor."

41. "Novye sochineniia N. A. Rimskogo-Korsakova. 4 romansa dlia tenora, op. 55; 2 romansa dlia soprano, op. 56; Izd. M. P. Beliaeva v Leipzige" (New works by N. A. Rimsky-Korsakov: 4 songs for tenor, op. 55; 2 songs for soprano, op. 56; M. P. Belyaev Publishers, Leipzig), *Russkaia muzykal'naia gazeta* (1899), nos. 21–22.

42. Prince Sergei Mikhailovich Volkonsky, the newly appointed Director of Imperial Theaters. He retained this post until 1901, when he was succeeded by Vladimir Arkadyevich Telyakovsky. (Trans.)

43. Prince A. A. Tsereteli was impressario of the Kharkov Private Opera Company. (Trans.)

44. Rimsky-Korsakov was in Moscow for the premiere of *The Tsar's Bride* on October 22, 1899. It was given by the Association of Russian Private Opera, formerly the Mamontov Company whose head, S. I. Mamontov, was declared insolvent by the fall of 1899. (Trans.)

45. The Moscow critics, in the persons of Kashkin and others, considered *The Tsar's Bride* a "remarkable major work, certain to enjoy wide popularity" and "destined to exert a considerable influence on composers of future generations" (*Moskovskie vedomosti* [1899], nos. 291–294, 296). E. Rozenov's article " 'Tsarskaia nevsta' v Chastnoi opere" (*The Tsar's Bride* at the Private Opera) pointed to the new style of the opera, saying that Rimsky-Korsakov "has given up his former style of writing and in many respects has returned to the methods of the old operatic school, allowing the lyrical mood to entirely overshadow dramatic truth and musical form to predominate over free dramatic characterization." Summing up his analysis of the work, Rozenov wrote: "Thus, *The Tsar's Bride,* while on the one hand, a superb example of the contemporary operatic technique, on the other hand, proves to be a step toward a conscious renunciation by the composer of the cherished principles of the New Russian School. To what new course our beloved composer's 'renunciation' will lead, only the future will tell. In any case, the opera has already made a strong impression on the public." *Novosti dnia* (October 25, 1899), no. 5897.

46. *The Tale of Tsar Saltan* was published by Bessel in 1900.

47. Reference to V. I. Safonov's dismissal of G. E. Konius from the Moscow Conservatory.

48. The appearance of Timofeyev's book, *Frederik Shopen* (Frédéric Chopin), gave rise to a polemic in the pages of the St. Petersburg newspapers between V. Stasov and M. Ivanov, who had written a tactless review of it. M. Ivanov: (1) "Kak ne sleduet pisat' " (How not to write) and (2) " 'Saratsin," opera v 4-kh deistviiakh S. Kui—g. Stasov v myshelovke" (*The Saracen,* opera in 4 acts by C. Cui—Mr. Stasov in a mousetrap), *Novoe vremia* (1899), nos. 8499 and 8513. V. Stasov: (1) "Nepozvolitel'naia statia" (Impermissible article) and (2) "Uvertiki i perevertki g. Ivanova" (Mr. Ivanov's twists and turns), *Novosti i birzhevaia gazeta* (1899), nos. 302 and 314.

49. See note 16.

50. Suvorin, censuring Russian music critics for their hostility toward the new compositions of Russian composers, drew attention to an article by Bellaigue, filled with sincere enthusiasm for Rimsky-Korsakov, his music and, in particular, *Snegurochka. Novoe vremia* (1899), no. 8512, *Malen'kie pis'ma.* (Brief letters), CCCLVI.

51. For reviews of the performance of excerpts from *The Tale of Tsar Saltan* see: *Russkaia muzykal'naia gazeta* (1899), no. 50, N. Findeisen; *Severnyi kur'er* (December 6, 1899), in the section *Teatr i muzyka* (Theater and music), E. Bormann; *Syn otechestva* (December 6, 1899), Veimarn; *Rossiia,* (December 6, 1899), Solovyov; *S.-Peterburgskie vedomosti* (December 6, 1899), Koptyaev.

52. *Song of Oleg the Wise*—cantata for tenor, bass, male chorus, and orchestra (op. 58, 1899).

53. *Rossiia* (1899), no. 236, review by N. Solovyov in the section *Teatr i muzyka* (Theater and music).

54. From the song cycle *Songs and Dances of Death*. (Trans.)

55. Lykov's aria "Tucha nenastnaia mimo promchalasia" (act 3, scene 3). Regarding the composition of this aria, Rimsky-Korsakov writes the following: "Sekar-Rozhansky, who sang the role of Lykov, asked me to write an aria for him, indicating a moment for it in act 3. I had never composed an aria for anyone, but this time I had to agree with him, since his remark about the inappropriate brevity and incompleteness of Lykov's role was really true." *Letopis' moei muzykal'noi zhizni*, p. 215.

56. In Iv. Shcheglov's (Leontiev's) comedy *Turusy na kolesakh* (Nonsense) the editor is a worldly-wise man, incapable of losing patience. The action takes place in his waiting room. The authors who come to the editorial office demand an advance and are incensed when their manuscripts are rejected. The secretary tries to calm them down. In particularly scandalous cases, the editor himself pacifies the callers.

57. *Myl'nyi puzyr'* (lit. soap bubble—a show-off)—the newspaper mentioned in the comedy *Turusy na kolesakh*.

58. *The Tsar's Bride* was performed on December 22, 1899, by A. Tsereteli's Kharkov Private Opera. A review of it, signed "Do-diez," appeared in *Uzhnyi Krai* (1899), no. 6524; the other one referred to, titled " 'Tsarskaia nevesta' " *(The Tsar's Bride)* and signed "K. B.," was carried by *Kharkovskie gub. vedomosti* (1899), no. 337.

10. 1900

1. Rimsky-Korsakov's songs were to have been performed at the Kerzin Society of Lovers of Russian Music, a Moscow organization which was in existence from 1896 until 1912 under the leadership of its founders, Arkady Mikhailovich Kerzin and his wife, Maria Semyonova.

2. Rimsky-Korsakov was invited to Brussels to conduct a concert of Russian music at the Théâtre de la Monnaie. The invitation was extended to him by D'Auost, organizer of Les Concerts populaires de Bruxelles.

3. Piano duet arrangements of Balakirev's collection *30 pesen russkogo naroda dlia odnogo golosa s akkompanementom fortep'iano* (30 songs of the Russian people for voice and piano.) (St. Petersburg, 1900), based on material collected by Deutsch and Istomin in 1886.

4. *The Tale of Tsar Saltan* (with scenery by M. Vrubel) was given in Moscow by the company of the Solodovnikov Theater on November 3, 1900. Rimsky-Korsakov went there for the premiere of the opera.

5. *The Saracen* (1896–98), based on Alexandre Dumas' *Charles VII ches ses grands vassaux*, received its premiere at the Marinsky Theater on November 2, 1899. (Trans.)

6. See entries of 27 January and 10 February 1897. (V. V. Ya.)

7. The first performance of *Sadko* at the Marinsky Theater took place on January 26, 1901. The Rimsky-Korsakov archives contain a petition with 33 pages of signatures from the public to Prince Volkonsky, Director of the Imperial Theaters, requesting that *Sadko* be given during the 1900–01 season. Apparently, this petition was never presented, since the matter of the operas to be performed had already been decided.

8. Wagner's *Die Walküre* was performed at the Marinsky Theater on November 24, 27, and 30 and December 8, 13, and 21, 1900; and on January 1 and February 2 and 9, 1901.

9. This collection consists of settings from the liturgy of St. John Chrysostom: two *Cherubic Hymns*, *The Creed*, *Mercy of Peace*, *We Praise Thee*, *It Is Truly Meet*, *Our Father*, and a Communion hymn, *Praise the Lord from the Heavens*. (V. V. Ya.)

10. Choral dance celebrating the festival of Kupala (eve of St. John the Baptist's Day). (Trans.)

11. Apropos of this, *Novoe vremia* reported:

The other day, the Academy of St. Cecilia in Rome gave one of its regular concerts, at which the conductor was V. Safonov. In view of this, the program consisted entirely of Russian works, played for the first time in Rome. Included were Tchaikovsky's Symphony no. 4, the Andante from a string quarter by Rubinstein, Rimsky-Korsakov's *Sheherazade,* Glazunov's *Spring,* and Scriabin's *Élègie.* The conductor scored a wonderful success; the Rome newspapers spoke in glowing terms of his talent. As for the works themselves, those which fared best were Rubinstein's Andante and the finale of Tchaikovsky's symphony. The audience did not like Scriabin's *Élègie.* Glazunov's *Spring* created a somewhat better impression. As for *Sheherazade,* during its performance, the electricity suddenly failed. The lights could not be restored, so the concert ended and Rimsky-Korsakov's work remained unfinished. The concert was attended by Queen Margherite, who invited Safonov to her box and conversed amicably with him about his impressions of Italy and Russian music. *Novoe vremia* (1900), no. 8577, in the section *Teatr i muzyka* (Theater and music).

12. On March 4 the following newspapers carried reports and reviews of the first performance of *The Tsar's Bride* on March 2 by the Kharkov Opera at the Panayevsky Theater: *Novoe vremia,* no. 8627, untitled article signed "V"; *Syn otechestva,* no. 63, "Otkrytie sezona khar'kovskoi opernoi truppoi" (Opening of the Kharkov Opera season), signed "P. V." (P. Veimarn); *Birzhevye vedomosti,* no. 62, untitled article by N. Solovyov; *Rossiia,* no. 308, untitled article by N. Solovyov; *Peterburgskie vedomosti,* no. 62, "Novaia opera N. A. Rimskogo-Korsakova 'Tsarskaia nevesta' " (N. A. Rimsky-Korsakov's new opera, *The Tsar's Bride*) by A. Koptyaev; *Severnyi kur'er,* no. 121, "Gastroli Khar'kovskoi Russkoi opery" (Guest performances by the Kharkov Russian Opera), by E. N. Bormann; *Novosti i birzhevaia gazeta,* no. 63, in the section *Teatr i muzyka* (Theater and music), "Debut Khar'kovskoi opery, 'Tsarskaia nevesta' N. A. Rimskogo-Korsakova" (Debut of the Kharkov Opera, *The Tsar's Bride* by N. A. Rimsky-Korsakov) by C. Cui.

13. Les Concerts populaires de Bruxelles were under the direction of their founder, Adolphe Samuel (1865–72); then Henri Vieuxtemps (1872–73); and after that, Joseph Dupont (1873–99). (V. V. Ya.)

14. On the initiative of the wealthy art patron d'Auost. (V. V. Ya.)

15. The Concert Colonne, at which Berlioz' *Requiem* was performed, took place at the Marinsky Theater on March 5, 1900.

16. By "Russian" and "French oboes" Rimsky-Korsakov had in mind only the Russian and French oboists' style of playing, not the instruments.

17. In his entry of 21 March 1900 (omitted), Yastrebtsev reports that according to *Russkaia muzykal'naia gazeta, The Tsar's Bride* also met with great success in Saratov, where, because of local interest, it had to be given several times. "Saratov (ot nashego korrespondenta 'Inkognito')" (Saratov [from our correspondent, "Incognito"]), *Russkaia muzykal'naia gazeta* (1900), no. 12. (Trans.)

18. Glazunov's *Intermezzo romantico* for orchestra (op. 69) was completed on February 28, 1900, and was given its first performance at the fourth Russian Symphony Concert under the direction of Rimsky-Korsakov.

19. Originally composed in 1867, *The Destruction of Sennacherib,* a choral setting of Byron's poem, was orchestrated partially by Rimsky-Korsakov in 1874. The *Overture on Three Russian Themes* (op. 28, 1866) was revised and reorchestrated in 1879–80.

20. For a report of the Tchaikovsky festival in Leipzig, see *Russkaia muzykal'naia gazeta* (1900), no. 12.

21. See entry of 15 May 1900. (V. V. Ya.)

22. Rimsky-Korsakov and his family spent the summer of 1900 in Germany and Switzerland.

23. Bulich's article on Russian music gives a one-sided estimate of Rimsky-Korsakov's work, assigning the most importance to his earlier compositions. In particular, he anticipated his own

unsympathetic evaluation of *Sadko* with the general observation: "From the beginning of the 1880s a period of decline set in in Russian opera." Such critical evaluations incurred the composer's displeasure.

24. Following its performances in Petersburg, Tsereteli's Kharkov Private Opera went to Moscow.

25. *Kriuk* (znamenny)—a neume used in Russian liturgical music of the eleventh–eighteenth centuries.

26. In *Snegurochka* (one of Spring's themes); *Mlada* (the fantastic *kolo* and in the scene depicting night on Mount Triglav); *Switezianka* (main phrase of "Svitezy burlivoi"); *Oleg the Wise;* the song *Redeet oblakov letuchaia griada;* the opera *Sadko* ("Slava novgoroda'); the first movement of Rimsky-Korsakov's Quartet, op. 12 (main theme); and finally, in *Tsar Saltan* (scene of the appearance of the fantastic city of Ledenets), etc., etc. (V. V. Ya.)

27. In 1886 Albert Payne began to publish full scores in a small, "pocket-size" format. In 1892 his entire edition was acquired by the publishing house of Ernst Eulenburg, Leipzig.

28. G. N. Timofeyev. "Dve novye russkie opery. I. 'Tsarskaia nevesta' Rimskogo-Korsakova," (Two new Russian operas. I. *The Tsar's Bride* by Rimsky-Korsakov), *Russkii vestnik* (July 1900), pp. 180–196.

29. *Asya*—opera by Ippolitov-Ivanov after Turgenev's story of the same name (1900). It was given its premiere by the Moscow Private Opera on September 28, 1900.

30. Reference to Verdi's *Quatro Pezzi sacri: Stabat Mater, Te Deum, Ave Maria, Laudi alla Vergine,* 1889.

31. Yastrebtsev went to Moscow for the premiere of *Tsar Saltan* at the Solodovnikov Theater on October 21, 1900. It was performed by an independent opera company formed from the personnel of the Mamontov Opera after S. I. Mamontov was declared insolvent (fall 1899). In his entry of the following day (22 October), Yastrebtsev reports that the entire Moscow press—*Kur'er* (no. 293), *Russkie vedomosti* (no. 294), *Moskovskie vedomosti* (no. 292), and *Russkii listok* (no. 292)—gave *Tsar Saltan* an enthusiastic reception. (Trans.)

32. M. Ivanov. " 'Skazka o tsare Saltane,' opera N. Rimskogo-Korsakova. Pervaia postanovska v Moskovskoi Chastnoi opere" (*The Tale of Tsar Saltan,* opera by N. Rimsky-Korsakov. First performance by the Moscow Private Opera).

33. Glinka's music to Kukolnik's tragedy *Prince Daniil Dmitrievich Kholmsky* was written in the period between September 19 and October 15, 1840. Obviously, the reference here is to the overture, which was begun on September 19 and completed on September 26.

34. At the time, Rimsky-Korsakov was working on the opera *Servilia.*

35. Symphony no. 1 in C (1898).

36. The performance of Camille Saint-Saëns' *Danse macabre* at the Russian Musical Society concert on November 15, 1875, elicited a caustic remark from Mussorgsky; see M. P. Mussorgsky, *Pis'ma i dokumenty* (Letters and documents) (Moscow-Leningrad: Muzgiz, 1932), pp. 331–332.

37. This was the first of many celebrations on the thirty-fifth anniversary of Rimsky-Korsakov's musical career. The others took place on December 11, 16, 17, 19, 25, and 28, 1900, and January 21 and 26, 1901. There were nine tributes in all. Those on December 19 and 28 were held in Moscow. (V. V. Ya.)

38. In response to public demand, the Procession of the Princes was performed twice, as was Liadov's *Intermezzo.* (V. V. Ya.)

39. The Fourth Symphony represents a kind of "renaissance" in Glazunov's creativity. The Scherzo is a musical illustration, as it were, for Bëklin's famous painting *Diana's Chase.* Let me note, by the way, that today the public insistently demanded that the Scherzo be repeated, but for some reason Anatoly Konstantinovich remained firm and did not repeat it. (V. V. Ya.)

40. Rimsky-Korsakov actually made his debut on December 18, 1865, with his first Symphony (in E-flat minor). (Trans.)

41. Rimsky-Korsakov wrote, apropos of the celebrations of the thirty-fifth anniversary of his composing career: "I called my anniversary 'chronic,' like a lingering disease." *Letopis' moei muzykal'noi zhizni,* pp. 221–222.

42. In other words, you become the hero of a topical, satirical, "variety" piece in *Obozrenie Peterburga* or the hero of a feuilleton by the well-known feuilletonist Doroshevich.

43. The concert of the Russian Musical Society in Moscow took place on December 23, 1900.

44. The Petersburg Society of Music Teachers and Other Workers in the Field of Music was founded in 1899 with the aim of rendering creative and material aid to its members. The Society had a mediatory bureau, chorus, vocal and string quartets. The tribute to Rimsky-Korsakov took place at the fifth musical meeting of this Society on December 17, 1900.

45. This refers to the first annual symphony concert for the benefit of deaf-mutes, organized by M. Dolina. Participants were the orchestra of the Imperial Theaters under the direction of H. Zumpe, M. Dolina, A. Arensky, K. Burian (tenor), E. Ondříček (violin), and R. Pugno (piano). The concert took place on December 9, 1900.

46. This refers to the article by Yastrebtsev, which was published in the issue of *Russkaia muzykal'naia gazeta* dedicated to Rimsky-Korsakov's thirty-fifth anniversary (1900), no. 51: "N. A. Rimskii-Korsakov. Ego biografia. Ego znachenie v istorii russkoi muzyki. Spisok proizvedenii Rimskogo-Korsakova" (N. A. Rimsky-Korsakov. His biography. His significance in the history of Russian music. List of Rimksy-Korsakov's works).

47. N. F. Findeisen.

48. E. Bormann. "K 35-letiu N. A. Rimskogo-Korsakova" (For the thirty-fifth anniversary of Rimsky-Korsakov). The author highly praised the work of Rimsky-Korsakov as an artist, humanist, composer, teacher, who created his own school, and as the editor of works by Borodin, Dargomyzhsky, and Mussorgsky.

49. The fanfares were selected from the *Capriccio espagnol, Snegurochka, Tsar Saltan, May Night, Mlada,* and *Sadko.*
[The idea of replacing the usual flourish with fanfares from the works of Rimsky-Korskaov, as well as the selection of the fanfares, came from N. F. Findeisen. (V. V. Ya.)]

50. Both articles were mine. (V. V. Ya.)

51. P. P. Gnedich's *Goriashchie pis'ma* (Alexandrovsky Theater, 1886) is a salon trifle. The hero is a naval officer, which may have led to its performance at the Rimsky-Korsakovs'. V. V. Bilibin's *Prilichiia* is a farce in the same vein (Alexandrovsky Theater, 1895). Kuzma Prutkov's *Oprometchivyi turka, ili Priatno li byt' vnukom? Estestvenno-razgovornoe predstavlenie* is a one-act satire with a prologue, which ridicules a man of letters (A. Grigoryev) and an opinionated musician.

52. Dedicated to Nikolai Andreyevich. (V. V. Ya.)

53. Yastrebtsev does not identify this newspaper. On December 27, Rimsky-Korsakov addressed another letter of gratitude to *Novoe vremia* for the numerous letters and telegrams received from many cities and additional societies, institutions, and individuals during his absence from St. Petersburg. (Trans.)

54. "I vse lish' svet da blesk kholodnyi, i net tepla."

55. A kind of variant of the riddle which the Swan Princess poses to Tsar Saltan in the last act of that opera: "Razgadai zagadku, Tsar', vsekh mudreishyi gosudar'" (Solve the riddle, Tsar, wisest ruler of them all)—the line reads "Solve the riddle, kind sir." (Trans.)

11. 1901

1. V. Gutor's article "N. A. Rimskii-Korsakov. K 35-letiu ego muzykal'noi deiatel'nosti" (N. A. Rimsky-Korsakov. On the 35th anniversary of his musical activity) was published in the Kishinev newspaper *Bessarabets* of 19 December 1900 (no. 328). It contained a brief account of Rimsky-Korsakov's life and works and a report of the tributes to him in Petersburg and Moscow.

2. The tributes to Rimsky-Korsakov continued. On the afternoon of January 21 there was a student concert at the St. Petersburg Conservatory directed by Galkin, followed by a dinner given by Nikolai Andreyevich's colleagues. On the evening of the same day the Music Society devoted its entire program to works by Rimsky-Korsakov and presented him with the customary wreath. (Trans.)

3. This article was entitled "K benefisu orkestra Marinskogo teatra" (A benefit for the Marinsky Theater orchestra). It was written in connection with the performance of the opera *Sadko* for the benefit of the orchestra of the Imperial Theaters (26 January 1901).

4. The Gramen family, a vocal and instrumental ensemble which performed in restaurants.

5. Reporting on the third performance of *Sadko* on February 6, Yastrebtsev states that despite Napravnik's ridiculous cuts and listless tempi, the opera won an enormous success with the public. (Trans.)

6. Insarova. (V. V. Ya.)

7. Theme drawn from the Chorus of the Novgorodians, act 1 of *Sadko*. (V. V. Ya.)

8. A literary and artistic society, headed by A. Suvorin, publisher of *Novoe vremia*. Suvorin rented the Maly Theater (now the Gorky Bolshoi Theater of Drama), where they regularly staged plays.

9. Mendelssohn's incidental music to Racine's tragedy *Athalie* was performed at the concert of the Russian Musical Society on February 24, 1901, under the direction of Napravnik.

10. In this article N. Kashkin, pointing out that the music of *Mozart and Salieri* opens new paths to the illustration of text, wrote: "Rimsky-Korsakov worked out his technique mainly through instrumental composition, which does not tolerate formlessness, and therefore, having adopted Dargomyzhsky's style, he avoided his mistakes. *Mozart and Salieri* represents a masterful experiment in unifying text and music, thereby giving them equal expression." See N. Kashkin's article "Znachenie poezii Pushkina v russkoi muzyke" (The significance of Pushkin's poetry in Russian music) in *Zhizn'*, pp. 143–145.

11. Piano Sonata no. 1 in B-flat minor (op. 74, 1901).

12. Arensky was the Director of the Chapel Choir and Liapunov was his assistant.

13. The article "Teoria i praktika i obiazatelnaia teoria v russkoi konservatorii" (Theory and practice and obligatory theory in the Russian conservatory) was published in N. A. Rimsky-Korsakov, *Muzykal'nye stat'i i zametki (1869–1907)* (Articles and notes on music [1869–1907]) (St. Petersburg, 1911). The introductory section of the article was written in 1892.

14. Two newspaper articles, 1869: " 'Nizhegorodtsy' E. Napravnika," (E. Napravnik's *Nizhegorodtsy*) and " 'Viliam Ratklif' C. Cui" (C. Cui's *William Ractcliff*). *(Ibid.)*

15. The Sextet in A mentioned here was one of two chamber works which Rimsky-Korsakov wrote in 1876 for a competition held by the Russian Musical Society. It received honorable mention. The second work submitted was a quintet in B flat for piano and wind instruments. It was not even considered for a prize. Both works were published posthumously. (Trans.)

16. In the most recent list of Rimsky-Korsakov's works, op. 19 designates the fifteen Russian folk songs published by Jurgenson, although in that edition the opus number is not given. (V. V. Ya.)

17. *Russkaia muzykal'naia gazeta* reported:

The audience of La Scala does not readily acclaim the artists who appear there. It is especially hard on young and unknown singers. But this evening was a real triumph for a Russian artist, whom the audience recalled with fervent enthusiasm and thunderous ovations. The profound impression created by Chaliapin is fully understandable. He is a wonderful singer and superb actor, and, in addition, he has a truly Dantean pronunciation, an amazing accomplishment for an artist for whom Italian is not his native tongue. Unsigned. "Torzhestvo g. Chaliapina v Italii (Mr. Chaliapin's triumph in Italy), *Russkaia muzykal'naia gazeta* (1901), no. 12.

18. Patsyuk's chords from *Christmas Eve.* I once remarked to Rimsky-Korsakov that they created a "mysterious, even mystical" mood, to which he retorted jestingly that this is somewhat tautological, since the word *mystique* and the word mysterious come from the same root. (V. V. Ya.)

19. This melody is Marfa's final phrase from the last act of *The Tsar's Bride,* at her words: "Pridi zhe zavtra, Vania." (V. V. Ya.)

20. The String Quartet in G major was composed in September 1897. The score was included in the *Polnoe sobranie sochinenii N. A. Rimskogo-Korsakova* (complete works), vol. 27.

21. See entry of 22 May 1898, (V. V. Ya.)

22. *The Bride of Messina*—cantata by A. K. Liadov after Schiller (1878).

23. For N. Galkin's tenth anniversary, Rimsky-Korsakov, Glazunov, Liadov, Wihtol, Sokolov, and Artsybushev wrote and dedicated to him an orchestral suite (theme and variations), which was played for the first time at a concert in Pavlovsk on July 4, 1901.

24. The Trio in C minor for piano, violin, and cello was not published. The opera *Nausicaä,* based on an episode from Homer's *Odyssey,* was not realized. The Rimsky-Korsakov Archives in the G.P.B. contain a libretto for the opera. Some rough sketches for it are also to be found in one of the composer's notebooks. [The trio was published in Moscow, 1970. Trans.]

25. Vasily Vailyevich Andreyev (1861–1918), virtuoso balalaika player, conductor, and founder of an orchestra composed of Russian folk instruments. (Trans.)

26. To hear Liadov play through *Servilia.* (Trans.)

27. Arcadia—a garden located in Novaia Derevnia with an open-air and indoor theater. Russian operas were given in the indoor theater by the Association of Operatic Artists under the management of M. K. Maksakov.

28. Rimsky-Korsakov's letter, to which Tchaikovsky was responding, was evidently lost, but the sense of it can be reconstructed in part from Peter Ilyich's letter to von Meck, which follows. (V. V. Ya.)

29. This letter is dated "San Remo, 24 December 1877." (Trans.)

30. Alina Andreyevna Yastrebtseva died on July 5, 1901.

31. M. Tchaikovsky. *Zhizn' P. I. Chaikovskogo v 3-kh tomakh* (The life of P. I. Tchaikovsky in three volumes) (Moscow: Jurgenson, 1900–02).

32. Prelude-cantata *From Homer* for three female voices, female chorus, and orchestra (op. 60, 1901).

33. Reference to an article entitled "Paralel'nye primery iz 'Borisa Godunova,' 'Khovanshchiny,' i 'Salambo' Mussorgskogo v redaktsii Rimskogo-Korsakova (kritika bez slov), sostoiashchei iz notnykh vyderzhek" (Parallel examples from *Boris Godunov, Khovanshchina,* and *Salammbô* by Mussorgsky edited by Rimsky-Korsakov [criticism without words], consisting of excerpts in notes). The preface to this article was published by Yastrebtsev in the weekly *Muzyka* (1913), no. 135, and in *Russkaia molva* (1913), no. 174.

34. Rubinstein refused to play Tchaikovsky's First Piano Concerto, ridiculing both the composition and the composer. The concerto was dedicated to Hans von Bülow, who gave it its first performance.

35. Rimsky-Korsakov went to Moscow on October 2, 1901, for the production of *The Maid of Pskov.* The first performance took place at the Bolshoi Theater on October 10, 1901. (Trans.)

36. The anonymous author of the review of the Public Concert given by A. Siloti and A. Verzhbilovich on October 6, 1901, at the Assembly Hall of the Nobility found Glazunov's Sonata op. 74 devoid of artistic unity and poorly suited to the piano. *Russkaia muzykal'naia gazeta* (1901), no. 41.

37. Bogomir Bogomirovich Korsov (1845–1929)—a bass-baritone at the Marinsky Theater. (Trans.)

38. Tchaikovsky wrote Mazeppa's "inserted arioso" "O Maria, Maria" to words by V. Kondaurov, with the direction "For performance as desired in scene 2, act 2, between nos. 10 and 11."

39. This was the first performance of *The Tsar's Bride* at the Marinsky Theater. (Trans.)

40. Sheremetyev's fifty-first public concert took place on November 4, 1901. Of the works of Rimsky-Korsakov, they played the suite from *The Tale of Tsar Saltan, Fantasia on Two Russian Themes,* and the Chorus of the Maidens from Dargomyzhsky's opera *Rogdana* as orchestrated by Rimsky-Korsakov.

41. The reference here is to an article by V. V. Stasov entitled *"Iskusstvo XIX veka"* (Nineteenth-century art), which was first published in 1901 in a special edition of the journal *Niva—XIX vek.* Specifically, Yastrebtsev and Rimsky-Korsakov are speaking of the following passage from the article:

> In the very last years of the nineteenth century, Rimsky-Korsakov created two operas, diametrically opposite in style: *Mozart and Salieri* in 1898; *The Tsar's Bride* in 1899. [The dates of composition given by Stasov are incorrect—they should have been 1897 and 1898.] They are as antithetical as the two cardinal poles—the zenith and the nadir. The first embodies the modern progressive trend, the style of Dargomyzhsky's *Stone Guest,* with its rejection of all the old traditional forms, its free approximation of the intonations of the human voice; the second represents a return (albeit highly skillful and talented) to the conventional forms of earlier opera with arias, duets, etc. It is as if Rimsky-Korsakov were saying to the approaching century: "Here is the new, there is the old. It is possible to be talented both in chains and free of chains. Choose the one you want." I believe the twentieth century will choose the one free of rusty chains. At least *Mozart and Salieri* demonstrates the enormous superiority of truth, inspiration, creativity (in the amazing characterization of the artistic martyr Salieri), and beauty. The marvelous recitative of Mozart himself before the performance of the excerpt from the *Requiem* is the finest recitative created by Rimsky-Korsakov thus far. In terms of its profound, poetic spirit and mood, it is strikingly close to the spirit of the music which opens the *Requiem.* V. V. Stasov, *Izbrannye sochineniia v 3 tt.* (Selected works in three volumes), vol. 3: *Iskusstvo* (Art) (Moscow, 1952), p. 736.

42. Evidently Rimsky-Korsakov attended the rehearsal of Wagner's *Lohengrin* on November 10. The premiere of the opera at the Marinsky Theater took place on November 13, 1901.

43. Rimsky-Korsakov did not realize this intention to compile a textbook of orchestration from his own compositions until later. In his autobiography he states: "I finally set about realizing an idea of long standing—to write a textbook of orchestration with examples drawn exclusively from my own compositions." The manuscript of this textbook is dated 4 July 1905. The first thought of writing a textbook of orchestration and the first sketches for it date to 1873.

44. *The Maid of Pskov* was performed at the Bolshoi Theater; the premiere took place on October 10, 1901. S. Kruglikov's article "Pskovitianka" *(Maid of Pskov)* was published after repeated performances in two issues of the newspaper *Novosti dnia* (October 22, 1901), no. 6595, and (October 26) no. 6598. The article presented a history of the opera's composition, a musical analysis of it, and an evaluation of its performance.

45. *Paraphrases*—eight variations and six pieces for piano on a constant and unchanging theme ("Tati-tati") by Cui, Borodin, Liadov, and Rimsky-Korsakov. [Actually *Paraphrases* consists of twenty-four variations and fourteen pieces. The theme on which it is based in the well-known Chopsticks. (Trans.)]

46. "I am familiar with the Variations by R.-Korsakov and Co.," wrote P. I. Tchaikovsky to Mme von Meck on November 18, 1879. "The work is original in its way and displayed remarkable

talent for harmony on the part of its authors, but I do not like it. As a jest it is too heavy and difficult to swallow, with all those persistent and endless repetitions of the theme. As an artistic creation it amounts to nothing. It is not surprising that, for their own amusement, a few talented people should have set themselves the task of inventing all kinds of variations on a trivial and commonplace theme. What is surprising is that these amateurish trifles should be published and advertised. Only amateurs can imagine that each and every piquant chord is worthy of being given to the public. As for Liszt, he replies with exaggerated praise of everything sent to him for his august inspection. He is, by nature, a kind man; indeed, he is one of the few famous artists who has never been touched by petty jealousy (Wagner and, to some degree, Anton Rubinstein owe their success to him; he also did a great deal for Berlioz); but he is too much of a Jesuit to be truthful and sincere.

"Returning to the Variations themselves, I must say that unfortunately this piquant musical curiosity, while revealing the great gifts of the composers, is one-sided, that is, concerned only with harmony. If you should come across it, take a look at Borodin's *Requiem*. That is a remarkably successful caprice."

47. *Snegurochka*—music to A. N. Ostrovsky's spring tale in 4 acts for soloists, chorus, and orchestra (op. 12, 1873).

48. They went to Moscow to attend a special concert given by the Russian Musical Society for the benefit of widows and orphans of Moscow musicians and artists, at which Rimsky-Korsakov conducted a concert performance of the third act of his *Mlada*. (Trans.)

49. Chaliapin's concert repertoire included a ballad by Keneman, *Kak korol' shel na voinu*, to words by M. M. Konopnicka (op. 7, no. 6, 1901).

50. The Red Dacha was located in Shevelov Park near Petersburg.

51. Iola Ignatyevna Tornagni.

52. The theater used only for the Imperial family and guests. (Trans.)

12. 1902

1. *Poème lyrique* for large orchestra (op. 12, 1887).

2. Liszt's symphonic poems ("Symphonische Dichtung"). (V. V. Ya.)

3. This conversation about Mahler was undoubtedly occasioned by his visit to St. Petersburg. The first concert which he conducted took place on March 5, 1902, with a program consisting of Beethoven's Third Symphony, Mozart's G minor Symphony, and the Introduction to the Death of Isolde from Wagner's *Tristan and Isolde*. The second and third concerts were held on March 9 and 14, 1902. On this visit Mahler did not conduct any of his own works.

4. Felix Blumenfeld joined the Marinsky Theater in 1895 as a coach and assistant to Napravnik. In 1898 he was named third conductor.

5. Sofia Malozemova, a pupil of Anton Rubinstein, succeeded in realizing the great pianist's desire to hear Schumann's *Carnaval* (one of his best loved works and one he performed especially successfully) in orchestrated and theatrical form—with dances, costumes, and scenery. The work was orchestrated in 1902 by a group of composers—Glazunov, Klenovsky, Petrov, Rimsky-Korsakov, Kalafati, Cherepnin, Liadov, Winkler, Wihtol, Sokolov, and Arensky. Rimsky-Korsakov scored no. 6, *Florestan,* and no. 18, *Promenade*. The first performance was given on April 20, 1902, in a production by the ballet master N. Legat in the Great Hall of the Conservatory, at a concert in memory of Anton Rubinstein, and on July 23, 1903, in a concert performance under the direction of Glazunov at the seventh Russian Musical Evening (at the Pavlovsk Station). The score of *Carnaval* in this orchestration was published in 1956 by Muzgiz (the State Music Publishing House), edited by I. Jordan and G. Kirkor.

6. Subsequently I learned that Rimsky-Korsakov's older daughter, Sofia Nikolayevna, played a very active role in drawing up the text. (V. V. Ya.)

7. N. Rimsky-Korsakov. *Prakticheskii uchebnik garmonii* (Practical textbook of harmony) (1884); first lithograph edition, 1885; first printed edition, St. Petersburg: Büttner 1886. This textbook was revised repeatedly. [*Practical Manual of Harmony,* translated from the 12th Russian edition by Joseph Achron, 5th ed. (New York: Carl Fischer, 1930).]

8. This concert by the Great Russian Orchestra under the direction of V. Andreyev took place on April 4, 1902. The program consisted of folk songs and works by Cui, Tchaikovsky, Rimsky-Korsakov, Dargomyzhsky, Yuferov, and Andreyev. See entry of 8 April.

9. In the May 9, 1902, issue of the newspaper *Novoe vremia* in the section *Teatr i muzyka* (Theater and music), head of the Court Orchestra K. Shtakelberg reported that a second performance of Strauss' *Ein Heldenleben* would be given on May 11. It had been performed for the first time by the Court Orchestra on April 30, 1902, at an orchestral evening under the auspices of *Muzykal'nye novosti. Ein Heldenleben* evoked contradictory opinions.

10. Glazunov's Seventh Symphony *(Pastoral),* op. 77, was finished on July 4, 1902.

11. Glazunov's *Ballade* for orchestra (op. 78, 1902).

12. The Rimsky-Korsakovs left Petersburg on May 23, 1902, to spend the summer abroad. Nikolai Andreyevich returned home on September 1. (Trans.)

13. Reference to the thirteetnh performance of this opera, which Yastrebtsev attended on September 10. (Entry omitted—Trans.)

14. Rimsky-Korsakov began work on the orchestration of Dargomyzhsky's *Stone Guest* in 1897 (scene 1). Most of the work on it was done during the summer and fall of 1902. The autograph score of scenes 2–4 bears the following dates in the composer's hand: "18–21 July 1902 Villa Ogotava," "4–17 August 1902 Heidelberg. Villa Ogotava. N. R.-K.," and "19 September 1902. S.-P-Burg."

15. The presentation of *Servilia* called forth a number of articles and reviews in various Petersburg newspapers (*Petersburgskie vedomosti,* no. 270; *Novosti i birzhevaia gazeta,* no. 272; *Peterburgskaia gazeta,* nos. 269–271, etc.) In the main, criticism centered on the fact that the composer had chosen a subject alien to him and thus had pursued a false path.

16. Rimsky-Korsakov's Eastern song was published under the title *Pesen'ka* (Song) for piano (1901) in an Armenian album *V pamiat I. K. Aivazovskogo* (In memory of I. K. Aivazovsky) (publisher D. Okriants, 1903). The album consists of three sections, the first of which contains two articles, "Pes'nia i romansy v XIX v." (The song in the nineteenth century), an essay by Bagdasarian, and "Vospominaniia ob armianskoi muzyke" (Reminiscences of Armenian music), by K. Ovsenian. The second section is devoted to painting. The music section contains songs and short piano pieces by Cui, Rimsky-Korsakov, Kazachenko, S. Taneyev, Tigranov, Spendiarov, Bagdasariants. Most of them are arrangements of folk songs and dances—Armenian, Tatar, etc.

17. Galkin variations—orchestral variations, composed by Rimsky-Korsakov, Glazunov, Liadov, Withol, and Sokolov for the tenth anniversary of N. Galkin's conductorship of the concerts at Pavlovsk (20 June 1901).

18. In the section *Listki iz 'Alboma svistunov'* (Pages from the *Hecklers' Album*), the newspaper *Peterburgskii listok* published a satirical poem about *Servilia* signed "Kuk," entitled: "V tsarstve kontrapunkta. Servilia, ili Chem tebya ya ogorchila" (libretto opernogo antrakta s prologom i epilogom) (In the kingdom of counterpoint: *Servilia,* or, How did I sadden thee? [a libretto for an opera entracte with prologue and epilogue]).

19. Reference to M. Ivanov's article " 'Servilia,' opera v piati deistviakh, muzyka N. A. Rimskogo-Korsakova (pervoe predstavlenie 1 oktiabria na Marinskoi stsene)" (*Servilia,* opera in five acts, music by N. A. Rimsky-Korsakov [first performance 1 October at the Marinksy Theater]),

Novoe vremia, (1902), no. 9552. The author subscribes to the general opinion of Rimsky-Korsakov's new opera expressed in the pages of the Petersburg press. M. Ivanov rebukes both Mey and Rimsky-Korsakov for having turned to a classical world foreign to them and contends that this accounts for the composer's creative failure. Ivanov also refers in passing to an error in the libretto and the piano reduction.

20. Interestingly, Ivanov's article, in its turn, contains rather ridiculous misprints (such as the young girls from "Kupala" instead of "Kupava"), but neither Ivanov, Ostrovsky, nor the readers perished, for everyone understood full well that the fault lay with the typesetter and not with the author. (V. V. Ya.)

21. *Dobrynya Nikitich*—opera by A. Grechaninov (1902); first performed on October 27, 1903, at the Bolshoi Theater in Moscow.

22. Nikolai Andreyevich's original essay is preserved in my general collection of Rimsky-Korsakov's autographs. (V. V. Ya.)

Yastrebtsev's essay, "N. A. Rimskii-Korsakov (1865-1900). Ego biografiia—Ego znachenie v istorii russkoi muzyki—Spisok ego sochinenii" (N. A. Rimsky-Korsakov, his biography, his significance in the history of Russian music, a list of his works) (St. Petersburg, 1901).

Yastrebtsev's archives contain a copy with Rimsky-Korsakov's notes in the text and comments on the margins. In 1908 the article was published in a revised version in a brochure by P. Jurgenson.

23. On November 9, 1902, the St. Petersburg Philharmonic Society marked its centennial with a concert at which Beethoven's *Missa solemnis* was performed under the direction of Nikisch.

24. The seventh performance of the opera *Servilia* was its last in St. Petersburg. The presentation of the wreath to Rimsky-Korsakov by his friends, as a "protest," was obviously occasioned by the cold reception the opera was given by the St. Petersburg press and public.

25. *Servilia* was given at the Solodovnikov Theater in Moscow on November 2, 1904. It was received more favorably there by both the critics and the public than it was in St. Petersburg and met with success.

26. *Potemkin Holiday,* opera by M. Ivanov (1888). In 1901 Lyubimov's Private Opera rehearsed the opera, but it was not performed.

27. See *Izvestiia peterburgskogo Obshchestva muzykal'nykh sobranii* (December 1902).

28. *Kashchei the Immortal* was given its first performance at the Solodovnikov Theater on December 12, 1902.

29. The opera *The Tale of Tsar Saltan* was given at the Conservatory in 1902 by the Private Russian Opera. In his autobiography, Rimsky-Korsakov writes apropos of this: "However, since the principal, though unofficial director of repertory was Baskin, music critic of *Peterburgskaia gazeta,* I attended neither the rehearsals nor the performance of *Saltan.* They say it was quite poor." (*Letopis' moei muzykal'noi zhizni,* p. 226.)

30. Andrei Bely. "Pevitsa (Posle kontserta Oleninoi-d'Algeim v. Moskve)." (Singer [after a concert by Olenine-d'Alheim in Moscow]).

31. The article referred to here is an example of Vl. Solovyov's "witty, caustic" articles against Russian decadence. The decadent journal *Mir iskusstva* (1899), nos. 13–14, published an article entitled "Zametka o Pushkine" (Remark on Pushkin), in which the author Vasily Rozanov declared Pushkin to be an "empty, obscene poet who no longer has anything to say to future generations," because "he is too rigid, too serious" and "as blind as old Homer." Indignant at the tone and content of this article, Solovyov rebuked Rozanov in this letter to the editor entitled "Osoboe chestvovanie Pushkina" (Special tribute to Pushkin), *Vestnik Evropy* (1899), 7; 432.

13. 1903

1. On the January 18 the thirty-fifth anniversary of A. Esipova's career was marked at the Eighth Symphonic Evening of the Russian Musical Society; on January 19, A. Arkhangelsky's twentieth anniversary; and on January 29, M. Slavina's twenty-fifth anniversary was celebrated at the Marinsky Theater.

2. This letter of Tchaikovsky's friend, the architect I. Klimenko, published in *Grazhdanin* (1903), no. 8, gave rise to further controversy. A contributor to *Russkaia muzyikal'naia gazeta* placed the following note in no. 12 of March 23, 1903, based on a careless reading of Klimenko's letter: "In *Grazhdanin* one Mr. Klimenko puts forth the utterly ridiculous idea (allegedly fostered by Tchaikovsky) that all four symphonies of Schumann should be rescored for string orchestra and what is more, he proposes that this absurdity be carried out by N. Rimsky-Korsakov." Klimenko angrily refuted this statement (in *Russkaia muzyikal'naia gazeta,* no. 25/26), maintaining that what he had written had to do with rescoring the symphonies for full orchestra and that Rimsky-Korsakov was in complete sympathy with Tchaikovsky's idea. The editors of *Russkaia muzykal'naia gazeta* replied to Klimenko with the following comment: "From whomever it originated, the idea of rescoring Schumann's symphonies is stupid. The creative work of such an artist as Schumann must remain untouched and does not need correcting."

3. *Allegro dramatique*—dramatic fantasy (op. 17), performed for the first time in 1903.

4. *Variations on a Russian Theme* (without opus no., 1901). See note 23, 1901.

5. On February 14, the journal *Mir iskusstva* opened its fifth art exhibition in the halls of the Society for the Encouragement of the Arts, presenting works by Serov, Pasternak, Bakst, Korovin, Benois, Roerich, Malyavin, Lanseray, et al.

6. Regarding *Ruslan,* V. V. Stasov wrote:

Of course, such a thing could only have seemed strange and displeasing to everyone. This opera made every listener uneasy about his customary habits and sympathies. It was really and truly distressing, for it alienated them from themselves. As a consequence, they all turned their backs on it, and when, the following year, the Italians arrived, they dropped it and all Russian operas and replaced them with the "Sonnambulas," "Puritanis," "Lucias," and other dreary rubbish. Then all the Russians sighed a sigh of relief, as if a disgusting, hundred-pound stone had fallen from their breasts. V. V. Stasov, *Izbrannye sochineniia* (Selected works) (Moscow: Iskusstvo, 1952), 3:720.

7. This was the opera *Pan Voyevoda* on a libretto by I. Tyumenev (1902–3).

8. A. Koptyaev. *Muzyka i kul'tura. Sbornik muzykal'no-istoricheskikh i muzykal'no-kriticheskikh statei* (Music and culture. Collected articles on music history and criticism) (Jurgenson, 1903).

9. See note 2.

10. Among A. Apukhtin's poems are a number of parodies and epigrams connected with the names of Russian composers. It is difficult to establish precisely which parody was being discussed here. Possibly it was the poem entitled "Pevets vo stane russkikh kompozitorov" (A singer in the camp of Russian composers), in which Apukhtin mentions Stasov, Rimsky-Korsakov, Cui, Afanasyev, Kashperova, Santis, Borodin, Rubinstein, Laroche, Tchaikovsky, and Napravnik. A. N. Apukhtin. *Sochinenia* (Works) (1907), pp. 300–303.

11. *The Fair at Sorochintsy*—unfinished comic opera by Mussorgsky on the theme of Gogol's story of the same name (1874–1881). After Mussorgsky's death, at Rimsky-Korsakov's suggestion, Liadov agreed to finish the opera and to edit it for publication. Liadov confined himself to editing and orchestrating separate numbers from the opera, which was published by V. Bessel and Co. in 1904.

12. While playing the first act, which Nadezhda Nikolayevna knew, and wanting to proceed

further with what she had not heard, Nikolai Andreyevich decided to call her. But it turned out that she had a headache and was taking a rest. Nikolai Andreyevich carefully tiptoed out of her room and, at his suggestion, we went into the garden. Rimsky-Korsakov's exceptional consideration of his wife, with whom he has lived thirty-one years, touched me deeply. (V. V. Ya.)

13. In 1901–1902, Rimsky-Korsakov and I. Tyumenev drew up librettos for three operas: *Harold, Yaroslav,* and *Ilya Muromets.* None of them was realized.

14. Glazunov frequently conducted the concerts at the Pavlovsk Station.

15. In January 1903, a weekly journal of theater and music, *Sovremennyi teatr i muzyka,* began publication in Petersburg under the editorship of N. N. Bronevsky. It consisted of a music section made up of piano compositions, mostly of exceedingly doubtful quality, and brief articles. Issue nos. 1–2 included an amateurish and provocative article by some "Homo Quidam" entitled "Koechto o muzyke voobshche i sovremennoi russkoi muzyke v chastnosti" (Something about music in general and contemporary Russian music in particular). This article was directed against the members of the Belyaev circle and the Russian Symphony Concerts. In it Glazunov was characterized as a "skilled musical technician"; Rimsky-Korsakov was called a person with an ability to veil "scarcity of thought and poverty of melodic creativity in a brilliant shroud at times amounting to decadence"; Liadov, it was said, is a "composer not one of whose works is distinguished by originality and individuality." Articles of this kind were also published in other numbers of this journal (see, for example, the review in no. 5 of the third Russian Symphony Concert, entitled "Vzgliad i nechto (Po povodu 3-go kontserta kruzhka sovremennykh Betgovenov") (A glance and something else [The third concert of the circle of modern Beethovens]). For criticism of the journal see: *Russkaia muzykal'naia gazeta* (1903), no. 11, section *Bibliografia* (Bibliography).

16. Reference to A. Sheremetyev's Popular Symphony Concerts and A. Siloti's symphony concerts. The prelude-cantata *From Homer* was given at Siloti's third subscription concert on January 15, 1903.

17. The new production of *The Maid of Pskov,* with the prologue *Boyarina Vera Sheloga,* was presented at the Marinsky Theater on October 28, 1903.

18. The concert in memory of Tchaikovsky took place on October 25, 1903. O. Gabrilovich was the soloist in the First Piano Concerto and Nina Fried presented songs. The concert marking the centenary of Berlioz' birth was held on December 6, 1903. Both concerts were under the direction of A. Khessin.

19. Act 3 of *Mlada*—"Night on Mount Triglav"—was performed at the Russian Musical Society concert on January 3, 1904.

20. The Belgian Quartet performed on November 7, 1903, at a quartet evening of the Russian Musical Society. The program consisted of works by Mozart, Schumann, and Tchaikovsky.

21. Alexei Alexeyevich Suvorin, son of Alexei Sergeyevich Suvorin, founder and publisher of *Novoe vremia.* (Trans.)

22. "Novovremenets"—literally a "New Times-er," that is, someone attached to the newspaper *Novoe vremia.* (Trans.)

14. 1904

1. Yastrebtsev is mistaken here. The work he calls *Intermezzo* was Liadov's *Inn Mazurka,* which had its premiere in St. Petersburg on December 5, 1887. Glazunov's suite *From the Middle Ages* was given its first performance on December 21, 1902, at the second Russian Symphony Concert under the composer's direction.

2. That is, first performance at a concert of the Russian Musical Society. This does not mean that these works had never been played in Petersburg before. (V. V. Ya.)

3. Reference to M. P. Belyaev's death on December 28, 1903, and the events connected with it.

4. See entry of 20 November 1904—"The M. P. Belyaev Prizes."

5. The article referred to is "35-letie smerti A. Dargomyzhskogo—20-letnii iubilei artista G. Donskogo" (Thirty-fifth anniversary of the death of A. Dargomyzhsky—Twentieth anniversary of the artist G. Donskoy), *Novoe vremia* (1904), no. 10006. However, it does not lead to the conclusion drawn by Rimsky-Korsakov.

6. Arensky's opera *Nal and Damayanti* was given its premiere on January 9, 1904, at the Bolshoi Theater in Moscow.

7. *At the Grave*—prelude (op. 61, 1904). In it Rimsky-Korsakov used funeral themes from the *Obikhod* (church service) and sounds of a funeral bell (knell) heard in Tikhvin in his childhood.

8. *Serenade in Honor of a Lady by Four Cavaliers*—a humorous quartet for four men's voices.

9. Regarding Stravinsky's "cantata," Rimsky-Korsakov wrote in his diary: "During supper, while the champagne was being poured, singing broke out in the drawing room. It turned out that Igor had composed a congratulatory chorus in my honor. It was fairly good. It was sung by Sonya, Nadya, Ossovsky, Stepan, Lapshin, and Volodya." (*Letopis' moei muzykal'noi zhizni*, p. 241.)

10. The battle painter V. Vereshchagin and Admiral S. Makarov went down with the battleship *Petropavlovsk* when it was sunk on April 13, (N. S.) 1904, by a Japanese torpedo in the harbor of Port Arthur. Vice Admiral Z. P. Rozhdestvensky was named Admiral of the Pacific Squadron.

11. Reference to Stasov's article "Tost trem russkim muzykantam—N. A. Rimskomu-Korsakovu, A. K. Liadovu, i A. K. Glazunovu" (A toast to three Russian musicians—N. A. Rimsky-Korsakov, A. K. Liadov, and A. K. Glazunov), which was written apropos of the Russian Symphony Concerts conducted by these three composers. *Novosti i birzhevaia gazeta* (1904), no. 80.

12. After hearing the opera *Christmas Eve* at the home of the Rimsky-Korsakovs, V. Stasov wrote to D. Stasov (on 27 November 1898): "What can I say about this opera? I regret that it was written and will be presented on the stage. They will give it two or three times and after that, they will drop it." *Muzykal'noe nasledstvo. Rimskii-Korsakov* (Musical heritage: Rimsky-Korsakov), vol. 1. M. O. Ianovskii, *Stasov i Rimskii-Korsakov* (Strasov and Rimsky-Korsakov) (Moscow: AN SSSR, 1953), p. 374.

13. "Intermezzo" is the title given to the music played between scenes 1 and 2 of the third act of *Kitezh*, that is, The Battle of Kerzhenets.

14. When, in the summer of 1907, Glazunov was in England to receive the degree of Doctor of Music from Oxford and Cambridge universities, he was charged with finding out from Rimsky-Korsakov how he would feel about accepting a doctor's degree from these universities. In a letter to Glazunov dated 20 June 1907, Rimsky-Korsakov declined. The main reason for declining was his belief that honorary titles are not becoming to composers in general and to him in particular.

15. *Pan Voyevoda* was performed by A. Tsereteli's company in the Great Hall of the Petersburg Conservatory.

16. Rimsky-Korsakov went to Moscow to attend a performance of *Servilia* by a private opera company at Solodovnikov's Theatr. (Trans.)

15. 1905

1. Reference to two reviews by Ossovsky: "Sesar Kui, 25 prelud dlia fortepiano, soch. 64" (César Cui, 25 preludes for piano, op. 64) (Jurgenson, Moscow, 1904) and "Mademuazel' Fifi,' opera S. Kui," (*Mademoiselle Fifi*, opera by C. Cui). The author sharply criticizes the works named and Cui's music in general (*Slovo*, 1904, no. 28; 1905, no. 30). In a brief review of A. Liadov's republished *Intermezzo pour l'orchestre* (C major), Ossovsky, while acknowledging Liadov's originality

and brilliant instrumental writing, accuses the composer of "wasting his talent on trifles"; maintains that "lack of will, indolence and a kind of corroding skepticism" are cutting the root of his creative powers; that in the sphere of music he "behaves like a *barin,*" composes "out of purely feminine caprice"; "took it into his head—did it. Now I can but I don't want to—I simply don't want to." Referring in passing to Glinka, Ossovsky ended his review with the words: "great artists have also always been great workers, but our Russian gentry of music belong to a different time and place." (*Izvestiia Peterburgskogo Obshchestva muzykal'nykh sobranii,* 1904, June, July, August, *Bibliografia,* pp. 34–35.)

2. R. Strauss' *Symphonia domestica* was played for the first time at a concert of the Russian Musical Society on December 4, 1904, under the direction of M. Fiedler. Reger's Sonata in C major for Violin and Piano was performed by E. Nalbandian and A. Medem at a concert of the Evenings of Contemporary Music.

3. The Moscow press responded with a number of articles on the performance of *Servilia* at the Solodovnikov Theater on November 2, 1904.

The newspaper *Moskovskie vedomosti* carried two articles by N. Kashkin: " 'Servilia,' opera N. A. Rimskogo-Korsakova" (*Servilia,* opera by N. A. Rimsky-Korsakov) (1904, no. 303) and " 'Servilia' N. A. Rimskogo-Korsakova na stsene teatra Solodovnikova" (N. A. Rimsky-Kovakov's *Servilia* at the Soldovnikov Theater) (1904, no. 310). *Novosti dnia* (1904, nos. 7693 and 7699) published two articles by S. Kruglikov, both entitled "Servilia." *Russkie vedomosti* (1904, no. 325) carried an article by Yu. Engel entitled " 'Servilia' Rimskogo-Korsakova."

Unlike the Petersburg newspapers, the Moscow press was favorably inclined toward Rimsky-Korsakov's new opera, viewing it as an interesting creative experiment.

4. Isadora Duncan's first appearance in Petersburg evoked a protest in the press from a number of musicians. See "Prof. L. Auer, A. Siloti, i . . . g-zha Dunkan" (Prof. L. Auer, A. Siloti, and . . . Mrs. Duncan), *Russkaia muzykal'naia gazeta* (1905), no. 5; "Miss Duncan," signed "Double Sharp", *Slovo* (1905), no. 15; "Isidora Duncan," by A. B-n, *Slovo* (1905), no. 18; etc.

5. Sunday, January 9, 1905, marked the culmination of a long period of political ferment in Russia. On that day, workers marched to the square in front of the Winter Palace for a peaceful demonstration. There they were stopped by Tsarist troops and, when they refused to disperse, they were fired upon. Some 130 of them were killed and several hundred more were wounded. Unrest broke out among the students at the university and the conservatory. Shocked by these events, particularly by "Bloody Sunday" (as it came to be known), many members of the intelligentsia rallied to the support of the workers and rebellious youth. On February 2, 1905, the Moscow newspaper *Nashi dni* published a resolution protesting the government's interference in artistic matters. On February 5, Rimsky-Korsakov joined his fellow musicians with an open letter to *Nashi dni* endorsing the resolution. (Trans.)

6. The letter was also signed by R. M. Glière, A. B. Goldenweiser, K. N. Igumnov, L. V. Nikolayev, A. D. Kastalsky, A. N. Koreshchenko, G. L. Katuar, E. E. Linyova, L. V. Sobinov, and others. The addition of Rimsky-Korsakov's name was greeted with great joy in Moscow. The statement of the Russian musicians and Rimsky-Korsakov was also published in the newspaper *Russkaia muzykal'naia gazeta* (1905), no. 7.

7. *Kashirskaya starina* ("Gordynia") was given its premiere at the St. Petersburg Conservatory in January 1905.

8. N. F. Solovyov's orchestral overture on the song *Ei, ukhnem* was played at the ninth Symphonic Evening of the Russian Musical Society.

9. The dismissal of Rimsky-Korsakov from the Conservatory evoked a wide response from the Petersburg and Moscow press. A number of indignant articles were published in *Russkaia muzykal'naia gazeta* (see nos. 13–15, 1905).

10. Reference to an article by Ossovsky entitled "Prazdnik russkogo kompozitora (A Russian composer's fête), devoted to the performance of *Kashchei* and the acclaim Rimsky-Korsakov received in an atmosphere of great excitement.

11. A character in *Kashchei*. (Trans.)

12. The Conservatory students demanded that the Director expel the unregistered student Manets, a soldier in a musical detachment, who participated in the shooting of workers on January 9 and cynically boasted about it to friends. However, the Directors sided with him and took repressive measures against the students.

13. The Conference of Professors took place in Petersburg during March 25–28, 1905. Those participating in the first meeting were members of the Union and representatives of the universities and other institutions of higher learning. The Petersburg group gave a report on a draft for the organization of a union. The work of the Conference was divided into three sections: one dealing with academic problems, another with general questions, and the third with organizational and financial matters. The meetings on March 27 and 28 were given over to a discussion of the reports of the sections and to approving the draft of the constitution.

At the first meeting, Rimsky-Korsakov was presented with a testimonial on his dismissal from the Conservatory, signed by the teachers of the institutions of higher learning.

14. K. K. —Grand Duke Konstantin Konstantinovich Romanov, Vice-President of the Russian Musical Society.

15. The newspaper report that the works of Rimsky-Korsakov and Bleichmann (husband of the singer E. I. Kuza) were banned because of Kuza cannot be located. However, it is known that at the time there was an unpublished government order forbidding the performance of Rimsky-Korsakov's music. Also known was the following incident involving Kuza, which occurred in Petersburg on January 10, 1905. As reported in *Pervaia russkaia revoliutsiia i teatr* (Moscow, 1956), p. 143: "As she was riding on the Nevsky past a company of soldiers, the artist shouted loudly: "I congratulate you on your first victory: you have fired at your own brothers.' "

16. At the end of this entry, there is a postscript in pencil in Yastrebtsev's hand: "Liadov on the 'decadent' harmonies (in 'the miracle')." Rimsky-Korsakov categorically denied that there is anything decadent about them.

17. Rimsky-Korsakov's plan to write operas based on *Nausicaä, Stenka Razin,* and *Heaven and Earth* was never realized.

The idea of using a subject drawn from Homer, specifically the episode of *Nausicaä,* occurred to him in 1894, during his stay in Odessa. In the winter of 1901, he and Belsky discussed and worked out the plot of the opera. In the summer of that year Rimsky-Korsakov wrote a prelude-cantata, which was meant to serve as the introduction to *Nausicaä. (Letopis' moei muzykal'noi zhizni,* p. 223.)

In 1905 together with Belsky Rimsky-Korsakov worked out the plots of the operas *Heaven and Earth* and *Stenka Razin.*

Rimsky-Korsakov first mentioned Byron's mystery *Heaven and Earth* as a possible theme for an opera during the years 1898–99. In 1905 he turned to this theme for a second time. By then Belsky had drawn up the libretto of the opera, and Rimsky-Korsakov had made sketches of the music. But work on the opera itself progressed with difficulty and soon came to a halt. Abstractness, mysticism, symbolism, and the unreal images of the mystery were alien to Rimsky-Korsakov. The libertto and sketches of the opera are preserved in the composer's notebooks.

Rimsky-Korsakov had the intention of writing an opera on the subject of *Razin* in 1905. The first sketches, based on the folk songs *Ei, ukhnem, Vniz po matushke po Volge,* and *Dubinushka* date to the fall of 1905. These sketches represent all of the work done on the new opera.

18. The summer concert season at Sestroretsk opened on May 15, 1905.

19. This historic art exhibit of Russian portraits, organized by L. Bakst, I. Bilibin, and S. Diaghilev for the benefit of the widows and orphans of soldiers killed in battle, opened on March 7, 1905, at the Taurida Palace. It consisted of works drawn from State and private collections. In all about 3,000 portraits by Russian artists were shown. The exhibit aroused great interest. Many articles and essays were devoted to it (see *Peterburgskie vedomosti, Slovo, Rus'*, etc.), and a special catalogue was issued.

20. Borodin's song *More* (The Sea) was orchestrated by Rimsky-Korsakov and published by Jurgenson. *Zaklinanie* (Evocation) was never orchestrated. Rimsky-Korsakov's *Nimfa* (The nymph) was orchestrated in the summer of 1905 and published by Belyaev in 1908.

21. After A. R. Bernhard's departure, the Directorship of the Petersburg Conservatory was offered to V. I. Safonov, Director of the Moscow Conservatory. The negotiations ended inconclusively. Because of the protracted delay in naming a Director, a committee composed of the older professors of the Petersburg Conservatory was set up, consisting of L. Auer, N. Solovyov, V. Tolstoy, and S. Gabel. The interim committee (whose membership was changed) governed the Conservatory until Glazunov was chosen Director in December 1905.

22. The "Eagle of the Caucasus"—nickname of V. Safonov, obviously because he was born in the Northern Caucasus.

23. By "Nikolai Andreyevich's new works" Yastrebtsev could have meant work on the score of the opera *The Legend of the Invisible City of Kitezh,* which was being prepared for publication; orchestration of the song *Nimfa* (The nymph) and the rewriting of the duet *Gornyi kliuch* (The mountain spring) as a vocal trio; writing of the analysis of the opera *Snegurochka* (from June 27 to July 3); various chapters for the textbook of orchestration, which were begun July 4, 1905; chapter 13 (1881–82) of the "chronicle," i.e., *Letopis' moei muzykal'noi zhizni* ("My Musical Life"), which was also finished in June 1905.

"Quite upset by the incident at the Conservatory, I could not turn to anything for a long time. After trying my hand at an article containing an analysis of my *Snegurochka,* I finally turned to carrying out an idea of long standing—to write a textbook of orchestration with illustrations culled exclusively from my own compositions. This labour consumed the entire summer," wrote Rimsky-Korsakov in *My Musical Life* (pp. 141–415).

Principles of Orchestration with Examples Drawn from His Own Works was published posthumously under the editorship of Maximilian Steinberg. (Berlin—Moscow—St. Petersburg: Rossiiskoe muzykal'noe izdatel'stvo, 1913; 2nd ed., Moscow—Leningrad, 1946.)

24. The composer's analysis of *Snegurochka* is part of Rimsky-Korsakov's writings of musical criticism, devoted to an analysis of his operas. The plan, apparently written in the early 1900s (and going as far as *Servilia*), has been preserved. It bears the title: "Raznye stat'i i mysli o moikh sobsvennykh operakh" (Various articles and thoughts on my own operas). Rimsky-Korsakov worked on the analysis of *Snegurochka* at the end of June and beginning of July 1905. It goes as far as the middle of the prologue.

25. *In the Forests*—novel by Andrei Pechersky (pseudonym of P. I. Melnikov) describing the life of a community of Old Believers who lived "beyond the Volga" (Zavolzhie). (Trans.)

26. The letter of the peasants of the Yurevsky District of Vladimir Province, responding to Rimsky-Korsakov's dismissal from the conservatory, was published in the newspaper *Syn otechestva* of July 6, 1905. In a letter to N. N. Rimskaya-Korsakova regarding this (Vechasha, 10 July 1905) Nikolai Andreyevich wrote: "I have received a letter from Stasov. He is all excited about the peasants' letter to me, which was printed in *Syn otechestva,* and he would like me to set it to music (!!?) . . ."

27. Leopold Godowsky made his first appearance in St. Petersburg on February 12, 1905, at a concert of the Russian Musical Society. At a Clavierabend on October 13, he performed Chopin's

twenty-four études. The press drew attention to his staggering technique, soft touch, and also "lack of fire." Glazunov dedicated his First Piano Concerto to him.

28. This summer he carried on a wide correspondence. He wrote to relatives abroad, E. P. Glazunova, Liadov, Siloti, Kruglikov, V. V. Stasov, me, and others. He sent off two or three letters with every post. (V. V. Ya.)

29. After Rimsky-Korsakov's dismissal from the Conservatory, Siloti conceived the idea of setting up a school for advanced musical studies free of bureaucratic control. The idea appealed to Rimsky-Korsakov, Glazunov, and Liadov. They decided to offer courses in specialized subjects, which would exceed the level of requirements of the Conservatory. The opening of the school was announced in *Peterburgskie vedomosti* (1905), no. 103, and *Rus'* (1905) no. 109. The May issue of *Russkaia muzykal'naia gazeta* (1905) nos. 19–20, carried the following announcement in the section *Raznye izvestiia* (Various news): "A plan has been projected for the opening of a school of advanced courses in music in St. Petersburg, beginning in the fall. The founders—N. A. Rimsky-Korsakov, A. K. Glazunov, A. I. Siloti, and A. K. Liadov have already presented the required application. Subjects offered will include an advanced course in piano and theory of composition. For the course in piano, theory will be required; for the course in theory, piano will be required (elementary courses in piano and theory will not be given). The courses will be conducted on the premises of K. Shröder (Nevsky Prospect, corner of Sadovaya). The fee will be 150 rubles for the year."

The application was approved, but the school was never opened. By the fall of 1905, the initiators of the project lost interest in it. At the same time, the Conservatory gradually began to return to its normal academic life.

30. "Shröder's Premises," consisting of a hall and a number of rooms adjoining it, is used right up to the present time for concerts and theatrical purposes. Chamber music concerts and performances by the puppet theater under the direction of Demmeni have been presented there. It has long been the home of the Leningrad Banch of the All-Russian Theatrical Society.

31. Borodin's *Sleeping Princess* in Rimsky-Korsakov's orchestration was published by Jurgenson in 1903.

32. After Rimsky-Korsakov's death, a copy of this song with an indication of the principal instruments was found. M. Steinberg reconstructed the full score of the work according to the sketch. (V. V. Ya.)

33. The performance of *Tsar Saltan* on October 19, 1905, opened the operatic season at the People's House. It was presented by the impressarios Kabanov and Yakovlev.

34. The opera *Pan Voyevoda* was given its first performance at Moscow's Bolshoi Theater on September 27, 1905, under the direction of Rachmaninov. [Rimsky-Korsakov went to Moscow for this performance on September 22. (Trans.)]

35. Rachmaninov conducted opera at the Bolshoi Theater from 1904 to 1906. (Trans.)

36. This folk song, *the* revolutionary song of Russia whose singing was forbidden for years, was arranged by Rimsky-Korsakov for chorus and orchestra in 1905. Not satisfied with this arrangement, the composer expanded and reorchestrated it the following year. (Trans.)

37. During the first days of October, following the premiere of *Pan Voyevoda,* the Moscow newspapers carried a number of articles about it: N. Kashkin, " 'Pan Voevoda.' Opera N. A. Rimskogo-Korsakova" (*Pan Voyevoda,* opera by N. A. Rimsky-Korsakov), *Moskovskie vedomosti* (1905), nos. 264 and 265; E. Rozenov, " 'Pan Voevoda' Rimskogo-Korsakova" (Rimsky-Korsakov's *Pan Voyevoda*), *Novosti dnia* (1905), no. 8014; S. Kruglikov, "Pan Voevoda" (*Pan Voyevoda*), *Russkoe slovo* (1905), no. 264; and Yu. Engel, " 'Pan Voevoda' Rimskogo-Korsakova" (Rimsky-Korsakov's *Pan Voyevoda*), *Russkie vedomosti* (1905), no. 264.

All articles were as one in their criticism of the libretto. However, this was not the case with regard to the music. E. Rozenov saw the new opera as a "strange turning point," which could not be explained "solely by a temporary decline in the composer's creative powers; rather it reflected a certain artistic tendency, which held his former bold and free inspiration in thrall." This tendency, in Rozenov's view, consists in the fact that "Rimsky-Korsakov, a true poet-colorist and strict adherent of pure musical form, has decided, evidently, to use his creativity to give a decisive rebuff to the contemporary ultrarealistic trend of the stage, which has begun to make itself felt in operative productions." In *Pan Voyevoda* Rozenov sees the appearance of a "reactionary" direction in the work of Rimsky-Korsakov.

N. Kashkin expressed himself more guardedly. "In making the acquaintance of a new work by N. A. Rimsky-Korsakov, you can always be sure that you will find an abundance of tonal beauty, rich harmonies, and technical mastery. All this applies fully to the music of *Pan Voyevoda*." In the final analysis, Kashkin nevertheless finds the opera a failure because of the libretto. Engel's opinion is very close to that of Kashkin.

Kruglikov hears in the music of *Pan Voyevoda* "something of an infusion of the music of Chopin," "a loving understanding of the essence of the Chopinesque style."

38. According to Rimsky-Korsakov, *Dubinushka*—folk song for orchestra and chorus *ad libitum* (op. 62, 1906)—was written "under the influence and on the occasion of the revolutionary disturbances of 1905." Added to this was V. Stasov's request that Rimsky-Korsakov write a folk chorus, which could become the anthem of the revolutionaries, for "now is no longer the time for *God Save the Tsar!*" *Dubinushka* was finished on October 11, 1905, and on November 5 it was performed (from the manuscript) at Siloti's second concert.

Performed, too, at this concert (also from the manuscript) was Glazunov's arrangement for chorus and orchestra of the boatman's song *Ei, ukhnem,* likewise inspired by the revolutionary events of 1905.

In a letter to his brother dated 20 October 1905, V. V. Stasov wrote: "The day before yesterday Siloti rushed to Glazunov and said: 'I *have to* begin several concerts with the 'anthem,' but I *don't want to.* "I want to begin with something else. Do me a great favor, Sasha. Write immediately the boatman's chorus *Ei, ukhnem* for orchestra.' Glazunov did it—yesterday, for full orchestra, and today they played it."

After hearing Glazunov's new work, Siloti and Rimsky-Korsakov advised him to "add an ending full of power and invincible passion." Glazunov dedicated the piece to Siloti. Rimsky-Korsakov evaluated the two works as follows: "To the same degree that Glazunov's piece turned out magnificent, my *Dubinushka* proved, though loud, brief and insignificant." (*Letopis' moei muzykal'noi zhizni,* p. 233.) Excerpt from Stasov's letter quoted from the book *Muzykal'noe nasledstvo. Rimskii-Korsakov* (Musical heritage. Rimsky-Korsakov), vol. 1: M. O. Yankovsky, *Stasov i Rimskii-Korsakov.* (Stasov and Rimsky-Korsakov) (Moscow: AN SSSR, 1953), p. 401.

39. The manuscript of Mussorgsky's *Marriage* was kept in the Public Library, concealed from outsiders by Stasov. Rimsky-Korsakov knew of its existence but was not acquainted with the music. It was given its first performance on January 4, 1906, at the home of the Rimsky-Korsakovs. (See Yastrebtsev entry of 4 January 1906 and *Letopis' moei muzykal'noi zhizni,* p. 234.)

The Marriage, as edited by Rimsky-Korsakov, was published by Bessel in 1908.

40. Scriabin was then living in Switzerland. (Trans.)

41. See Rimsky-Korsakov's open letter to the newspaper *Rus'.*

42. The opera *Mozart and Salieri* was given its premiere at the Marinsky Theater on December 20, 1905.

16. 1906

1. See act 2 of *The Legend of the Invisible City of Kitezh.* (V. V. Ya.)

2. As is known, in order to give the audience a better understanding of a new work, Hans von

Bülow often performed the same symphony twice at one concert. After playing some new and original piece, he would even announce: "Since you, ladies and gentlemen, have only just heard this work for the first time and obviously do not understand it very well, I am going to play it for you again." (V. V. Ya.)

3. *Kitezh,* act 2, fig. 106. (V. V. Ya.)

4. Here Rimsky-Korsakov is obviously referring to his symphonic poem *Sadko,* composed originally in 1867; to the symphonic suite *Antar,* composed originally in 1868; and to his first opera, *The Maid of Pskov,* composed originally in 1868–72. All three of these early works were subsequently revised. (Trans.)

5. The farewell benefit for Maria Danilovna Kamenskaya, who sang the role of Rogneda in Serov's opera of the same name, took place at the Marinsky Theater on February 10, 1906.

6. The "Cadet," or Constitutional Democratic Party, a liberal political party. (Trans.)

7. The literary critic and publicist Ivanov-Razumnik. Yastrebtsev was unable to attend because of illness, but in a reply on February 12, he promised to contribute. (Trans.)

8. Recall the scene of Kupava's complaint to the King of the Berendeys from *Snegurochka* and the wonderful bassoon solo in Vera Sheloga's tale. (V. V. Ya.)

9. But what of the birds of paradise in scene 2, act 4 of *Kitezh* which trill on A? (V. V. Ya.)

10. No. 1 of *Six Songs* (op. 16, 1872).

11. The new opera was *The Golden Cockerel* to a libretto by Belsky.

12. The "new subject" refers to an unrealized opera *Heaven and Earth,* which Rimsky-Korsakov himself sometimes called *Heaven and Earth* and at other times *Earth and Heaven.*

13. Philip Andreyevich Malyavin's painting *The Whirlwind* (bright swirling dresses of a women's *khorovod*), which caused a sensation. The artist repeated the motif of this painting many times.

14. Vol. 4 of V. V. Stasov's *Sobranie sochinenii* (collected works) (St. Petersburg, 1906).

15. Felia Vasilyevna Litvin (Litvinova)—soprano of the Marinsky Theater, irreplaceable performer of the female roles in the Wagnerian repertoire. Her outward appearance, poses, and gestures in these roles lent themselves to parody.

16. *Rech',* no. 28. (V. V. Ya.)

17. Chorus of the Raskolkini; see end of act 2 and beginning of act 3 of *Khovanshchina* with its amusing text by Mussorgsky himself. (V. V. Ya.)

18. The Federation of Trade Unions, formed in 1905.

19. As they watch the Oprichniki, the people sing: "There they go! Someone is going to get it, poor fellow! They'll have his head! They call themselves the Tsar's servants, but they're worse than mad dogs." (V. V. Ya.)

20. They went to Nauheim so that Andrei could take the cure for his rheumatism. (Trans.)

21. *Izbrannikam russkogo naroda* (To the chosen of the Russian people) ("Vam, izbrannikam naroda, Rus' chelom b'et do zemli")—anthem for chorus, words by N. Sokolov (1906). First published in the newspaper *Dvadtsatyi vek* (April 27, 1906), no. 30, the day of the opening of the State Duma.

22. The Rimsky-Korsakov archives in the I.T.M.K. contain the diploma of the Royal Swedish Academy of Music, awarded to the composer on April 26, 1906.

23. The Mussorgsky works named and also Rimsky-Korsakov's *Anchar* and *Son v letniuiu noch'* were orchestrated in Riva in the summer of 1906.

24. Grechaninov, Lisitsyn, Kompaneisky, Kastalsky, et al. (V. V. Ya.)

25. Rimsky-Korsakov finished chapters 9–11 (1868–70) and 19–21 (1883–92) of his "chronicle" in the summer of 1906 in Riva and Florence. The final chapter (28, 1905–06) was written on August 22. It ended with the words: *"The Chronicle of My Musical Life* has been completed. It is without order, is not equally detailed throughout, is written in a poor style, often even extremely dry; on the other hand, to compensate for this, it contains *nothing but the truth* and this will afford

it interest." [The English edition ends with the further comment: "On my arrival in St. Petersburg, perhaps, my long yearned for idea—of writing a diary—will be realized. Whether this idea will last long—who knows? . . . " *My Musical Life,* p. 424. (Trans.)]

26. Rimsky-Korsakov left Petersburg for Italy with his son Volodya and daughter Nadezhda on May 24 and returned on September 2. (Trans.)

27. As it turned out, this part of the score consisted of three acts of the opera: 2, 4, and 5. I subsequently gave it to my friend, V. N. Kupriyanov, and after his death it was sold to the Leningrad Conservatory. (V. V. Ya.)

28. Rimsky-Korsakov worked on *Kashchei* during the summer of 1906 (in Riva), adding the offstage chorus.

29. Chapter 21 of Rimsky-Korsakov's *Letopis'* ends with these lines about Yastrebtsev: "My acquaintance with V. V. Yastrebtsev, a great admirer of mine, dates approximately to this time. Having made my acquaintance at a concert, he gradually began to visit me more and more frequently, recording (as it turned out subsequently) his conversations with me, the ideas I expressed, and so on, in the form of reminiscences. Since he had all of my works in full score in his library and had collected my autographs, he knew every note in them almost by heart, at least every interesting harmony. He painstakingly recorded the time of the beginning and completion of each of my works. In the company of my acquaintances, constant and passing, he was an ardent advocate of my works and my defender against every kind of critical attack. During the first years of our friendship, he was also a fervent admirer of Berlioz. Later this passion cooled considerably and gave way to a worship of Wagner." *Letopis' moei muzykal'noi zhizni,* pp. 176–177.

30. V. Cheshikhin: *Istoriia russkoi opery s 1674 po 1903* (History of Russian opera from 1674 to 1903) (St. Petersburg: Jurgenson, 1905).

31. The Russian Opera Society presented *Sadko* at the People's House on September 16. (Trans.)

32. This was the second version of the folk song. (Trans.)

33. Four songs for high soprano and piano (1905–1906): *Zacharovannyi grot* (The Enchanted Grotto), words by Balmont (1905); *Ia zhdal tebia* (I Waited for You), words by Apukhtin (1906); *Fialka* (The Violet), words by N. N. (1905); *Kolybel'naia* ("Lipy dushistye") (Lullaby) words by Balmont (1906).

34. *Funiculi*—in 1907 Rimsky-Korsakov made an orchestral version of this Neapolitan folk song, but it was unsuccessful and was not published. [It was published in Moscow, 1966. (Trans.)]

35. Reference to Mahler's Fifth Symphony performed at Shroeder's second concert under the composer's direction.

36. On November 11, 1906, the orchestra of the Imperial Russian opera presented a concert in memory of Tchaikovsky at the Assembly Hall of the Nobility. This concert was to have been under the direction of Napravnik, but due to his illness, it was conducted by Krushevsky, Assistant Conductor of the Marinsky Theater.

37. In his work *Alexander Porfiryevich Borodin,* Stasov wrote: "Simultaneously with his first songs, Borodin began work on the subject of Mey's drama, *The Tsar's Bride,* which was suggested to him by Balakirev. He wrote several first-rate scenes and choruses (the most outstanding being a chorus of reveling oprichniki), but he soon lost interest in the subject and dropped the opera and asked me to suggest another subject, also Russian. I proposed various others, but for a long time he could not decide on which one." V. V. Stasov, *Izbrannye sochinenia* (Collected works), 3 vols., 3:350. As seen from Yastrebtsev's text, Rimsky-Korsakov flatly denied that Borodin had composed an opera *The Tsar's Bride.*

38. This concert, dedicated to the memory of Stasov, took place on November 25 under the baton of Felix Blumenfeld. The remainder of the program consisted of Balakirev's *King Lear* Overture, *Sheherazade,* Tchaikovsky's fantasy *The Tempest,* Liadov's *Baba Yaga,* the Introduction (Dawn

over the Moskva River) and Entr'acte (Prince Golitsyn's Flight into Exile) from *Khovanshchina* (Mussorgsky–Rimsky-Korsakov), and Glazunov's *Cortège solennel* (op. 50), composed in 1894 on the occasion of the fiftieth anniversary of V. V. Stasov's career. (Entry omitted—Trans.)

39. *Two Preludes for Orchestra* (op. 85), no. 1 "In Memory of V. Stasov" (1906).

40. At the Siloti concert on December 2, 1906, Max Reger conducted his own *Serenade* and, with Siloti, played his *Variations and Fugue on a Theme by Beethoven* for two pianos.

41. On December 20, upon learning from me about this unpleasantness with the bells, G. N. Timofeyev informed Rimsky-Korsakov by letter that the firm of Červený and Co. in Kiev has a section given over to triangular bells in all keys and with exact intonation. "Perhaps these bells will set the tune to rights," wrote Grigory Timofeyev.

[These are the so-called laminated bells sometimes used by a symphony orchestra in place of the usual church bells. (Trans.)]

17. 1907

1. Rimsky-Korsakov found the sound of *Son v letniuiu noch'* (Summer Night's Dream) in his setting with orchestra unsatisfactory and intended to destroy the score. However, it was published in 1910 under the editorship of M. Steinberg.

2. Rimsky-Korsakov composed *Zdravitsa dlia iubileinogo chestvovaniia A. K. Glazunova* (Hail to A. K. Glazunov on his anniversary) on December 31, 1906. It was given its first performance on January 27, 1907, the day of the celebration of the composer's twenty-fifth anniversary, at a concert conducted by Rimsky-Korsakov and Siloti. *Russkaia muzykal'naia gazeta* devoted a special issue to Glazunov: (January 7, 1907), no 1.

3. It has been said that, through his performance, Chaliapin can make you fall in love with anything. (V. V. Ya.)

4. In his review of *The Legend of the Invisible City of Kitezh*, Kolomiitsev offered Rimsky-Korsakov the following advice:"Cut out the Second Act . . . and combine the Third and Fourth. In this way all that will remain will be the scene of Fevronia's death and the appearance of the ghost; from the concluding scene make a short apotheosis." *Rus'* (1907), no. 44. However, on the whole the tone of the first reviews of the opera was quite favorable.

5. To Diaghilev goes the credit for organizing the so-called "Russian seasons abroad (symphony concerts in 1907, operatic performances beginning with the year 1908, ballet—beginning with 1909). Major Russian artists participated in these "seasons." They demonstrated the richness of Russian classical music and the high level of its performance. The cycle of "five Russian symphonic concerts" took place in Paris in May of 1907 (the 16, 19, 23, 26, and 30). The concerts were under the direction of A. Nikisch, C. Chevillard, F. Blumenfeld, Rimsky-Korsakov, Glazunov, and Rachmaninov. The participating soloists were Litvin, Chaliapin, Hofmann; artists of the Imperial opera—Zbruyeva, Petrenko, Cherkasskaya, Smirnov, Kastorsky, and Filippov; and the chorus and orchestra of the Lamoureux Concerts. The programs of the concerts presented works by Glinka, Rimsky-Korsakov, Tchaikovsky, Borodin, Mussorgsky, Scriabin, Glazunov, Rachmaninov, Balakirev, Liapunov, Cui, and Taneyev. At the invitation of Diaghilev, Rimsky-Korsakov went to Paris on April 28, 1907.

6. The critics named devoted long articles to Rimsky-Korsakov's *Kitezh*. In one of them, entitled "Pervoe predstavlenie novoi opery Rimskogo-Korsakova 'Skazanie o nevidimom grade Kitezhe i deve Fevronii' " (First performance of Rimsky-Korsakov's new opera *The Legend of the Invisible City of Kitezh and the Maiden Fevronia*), M. Nesterov begins his analysis of the opera with a criticism of the libretto, stating that the "librettist succeeded only in depicting a few lifeless, boring, almost unconnected scenes." In his overall evaluation Nesterov writes: "As a musical work *The Legend of*

the Invisible City of Kitezh is interesting in the sense that it clearly shows how difficult it is in our day for a very gifted composer to stay on the thorny path of an artist. With his *Kitezh* Rimsky-Korsakov has finally moved into the camp of the musician-technicians. Dazzling orchestral colors, an abundance of fascinating harmonic details, and subtle tonal patterns—these are the virtues of the music of *Kitezh*. Listening to the opera only confirms the cold rational craftsmanship of its excellent technique. There is as little 'music passing from heart to heart' in this work as there is novelty in its thematic material." Of the entire opera Nesterov singles out only the third scene; see *Tovarishch'* (1907), no. 188.

V. Kolomiitsev does not lag behind Nesterov in his denunciation of the opera. In an article entitled " 'Skazanie' Rimskogo-Korsakova" (Rimsky-Korsakov's *Legend*), *Rus'* (1907), no. 40, pp. 42–44, he gives the orchestral sound its due. "This music is as transparent as a mountain stream," he writes. "It is very beautiful to the ear. It is made up throughout of enchanting details and subtle forms, in places 'decked out' (if one can say that) in brilliant tonal colors. . . . However, for great music drama, written on a lofty subject, the superficial tonal aspect alone is not enough. Lacking vivid outbursts and powerful emotional ferment, being without fervor or even sincere religious feeling, it seems cold and cerebral for all its craftsmanship. There is very, very little 'music of the spirit' here, as little as there is novelty in this score."

E. Petrovsky's article "Skazanie o nevidimom grade Kitezhe i deve Fevronii" *(The Legend of the City of Kitezh and the Maiden Fevronia), Russkaia muzykal'naia gazeta* (1907), nos. 7, 8, and 11, might have offended Rimsky-Korsakov with its tone and the wit which is customary for this writer. But, on the whole, it is exceedingly favorable. The author calls the work the "nearest to the folk of all of Korsakov's operas" and he concludes: "We repeat, the opera is beautiful, and in its last two acts, it will most likely prove to be one of the composer's best and most important works."

7. There is a break in the entries in Rimsky-Korsakov's diary from March 9, 1904, to November 28, 1907.

8. Suite for String Quartet (op. 35, 1889). "Orientale" is the third movement; "Mistico" is one of the variations of the fourth movement.

9. On April 14–16, 1907. (V. V. Ya.)

10. *Oblomovshchina*—"Oblomovism," inertness, apathy, as typified by the hero of Goncharov's novel *Oblomov*. (Trans.)

11. The Rimsky-Korsakovs went to Paris on April 28 and returned on May 24. (V. V. Ya.)

12. The following works of Rimsky-Korsakov were performed at the five "Russian historic concerts": the Suite from *Christmas Eve*, the Introduction and Lel's first two songs from *Snegurochka*, and act 3 of *Mlada* (all these under the composer's direction); and the Suite from *Tsar Saltan* and Introduction and "Scene of the Underwater Kingdom" from *Sadko* (directed by Nikisch).

13. Here Yastrebtsev gives both the Old and New Style dates. (Trans.)

14. Brussan and Carré. (V. V. Ya.)

15. *Mystère*—an unrealized work of Scriabin. The plan of it combined Christian-apocalyptic elements with motifs of ancient Hindu religious doctrines.

16. The estate where the Rimsky-Korsakovs spent many years and which I visited more than once. It was here that *Christmas Eve, Sadko,* and many other works were composed. (V. V. Ya.)

17. One *desiatina* equals 2.7 acres. (Trans.)

18. On 14 October 1907 Yastrebtsev reports that a deed of purchase of Lyubensk was being drawn up in the names of Andrei, Vladimir, and Nadezhda Nikolayevna (the elder). (Entry omitted—Trans.)

19. A *lubok* is a primitive Russian woodcut, folk art very popular with the common people during this period. (Trans.)

20. Actually, Rimsky-Korsakov was in Petersburg from September 2 until the sixth. On Sep-

tember 4 he was backstage at the performance of his *Kitezh*. He did not return to the city for good, however, until September 19. (V. V. Ya.)

21. According to Yastrebtsev, the opera did not fare any better at the performance of September 4, under N. N. Cherepnin. (Trans.)

22. At first Rimsky-Korsakov rejected the tromba piccola (alto trumpet in F), but later, out of kindness toward Belsky, he introduced it temporarily instead of a flute.

23. Belsky insisted on this instrument. (V. V. Ya.)

24. Before this, the introduction began with the Cockerel's fanfare of the second type—"Beregis', bud' nacheku." (V. V. Ya.)

25. The Union of Writers on Music was organized in 1907, with a Board consisting of S. Bulich (president), N. Kompaneisky (vice-president), M. Nesterov (secretary), and N. Bernstein (librarian).

According to the constitution, which was adopted March 27, 1907, the purpose of the Union was to unite musical writers. The Union was granted the right to hold private and public meetings, present concerts, performances, lectures, symposiums; to publish musical works, books, and journals on music; and to have its own library and mutual aid fund.

26. A play on the Russian word *maliar* (house painter). The conversation here concerns Mahler's Second Symphony, which was performed at Shroeder's first Symphonic Concert.

27. Alfredo Casella—Italian pianist, conductor, and composer. (Trans.)

28. This was the song *Vesna* (Spring). (Trans.)

29. Because of censorship problems, this opera did not receive its premiere on the Imperial stage. It was presented for the first time at the Solodovnikov Theater in Moscow, on October 7, 1909, after the composer's death. (Trans.)

30. Sibelius' Third Symphony was performed at Siloti's concert on November 3, 1907, under the direction of the composer.

31. Shroeder's third concert under the direction of Oskar Fried.

32. *Russkaia muzykal'naia gazeta* (1907), nos. 34–35, initiated a discussion of the question of the simplified score, which had been raised by the German musicians Weingartner and Schillings, the theoretician Capellen, and others. The Russian musicians who joined the discussion in the pages of the newspaper were A. Siloti, A. Vinogradsky, A. Grechaninov, V. Cheshikhin, E. Napravnik, A. Glazunov, V. Suk, I. Slatin, and N. Rimsky-Korsakov (see nos. 37, 40, and 45).

Glazunov supported the idea of retaining the full score, claiming that the difficulty of reading it arises not from the necessity of transposing a certain number of instruments into the key of their real sonority, but from the difficulty of grasping with the eyes more than three musical systems (no. 40).

Rimsky-Korsakov, joining Glazunov, developed his position (no. 45).

33. *Mazurka on Three Polish Folk Themes* for violin and orchestra was composed in the summer of 1888. It was first published in the composer's arrangement for violin and piano in a supplement to the journal *Sovetskaia muzyka* (1949), no. 11.

34. *Funiculi*—Rimsky-Korsakov's Neapolitan song, finished on October 11, 1907, was played twice at the rehearsal but was not performed at the Siloti concert on December 1, 1907. The score is preserved in the G.P.B. (Rimsky-Korsakov archives).

35. *Pavillon d'Armide*—ballet by N. Cherepnin after a scenario by Alexander Benois. It was performed for the first time on November 25, 1907, at the Marinsky Theater. Dances from the ballet were given their first performance (from the manuscript) at A. Siloti's fifth subscription concert on December 13, 1903.

36. Rimsky-Korsakov's plan carried the following weighty epigraph: "The striving for musical creativity must be *selfless*. By *selflessness* I mean not only a disinterest in monetary gains but also the absence of a pursuit of special status, diplomas, etc."

37. He received these awards on November 27, 1907. (V. V. Ya.)

38. "Open the balcony"—a phrase from Dargomyzhsky's *Stone Guest;* "he" (i. e., Mussorgsky) has been carried off into a swamp of false notes. See entry of 30 June 1897. (V. V. Ya.)

39. The Russian composers elected previously were Tchaikovsky and Cui. (V. V. Ya.)

40. Amounting to 15 percent, I think. (V. V. Ya.)

41. Especially since Mussorgsky did not leave his own rights to any heir. (V. V. Ya.)

42. Third version.

43. Rimsky-Korsakov finished the orchestration of Mussorgsky's song *Noch'* (Night) on January 4, 1908. He worked on the orchestration of *Serenada* (Serenade) (no. 3 of the cycle *Songs and Dances of Death*) in 1908, but it remained unfinished. (It was subsequently completed by M. Steinberg.)

44. Mussorgsky lived in an apartment with Alexander Opochinin and his sister Nadezhda in the Engineers' Palace from 1868 until 1871. (Opochinin was head of the Archives of the Engineering Department.)

45. The thirty-ninth evening of the Society for Contemporary Music was held on December 27. The first half of the concert was devoted to works by Russian composers: Rachmaninov, *Prelude* and *Vostochnyi tanets* (Eastern Dance); Steinberg, *Posledniaia zvezda* (The Last Star); Gnessin, *Snezhinki* (Snow Flakes); I. Stravinsky *Pastorale* and *Vesna* (Spring); Karatygin, *Kolokol'chiki zveniat* (The Little Bells Are Ringing); Senilov, *Vozvrashchenie* (The Return) and *Krugi* (Circles); Winkler, *Prelude* and *Caprice;* the second half presented *Epitalam* by the French composer Gros and Fantasy and Fugue on a Theme by Bach by the American composer Middleschulte.

18. 1908

1. In the opinion of V. Valter Rimsky-Korsakov's opera *The Invisible City of Kitezh* was a failure. "The major flaw in Rimsky-Korsakov's creativity," he wrote, "is his coldness. Rimsky-Korsakov is a great master so long as he reproduces in sound natural phenomena, the external life of man, everyday occurrences. But when it comes to the intimate side of the life of the human soul, when it becomes necessary to embody human suffering in sound, Rimsky-Korsakov's talent immediately grows weak. This weakness becomes especially apparent at those intense moments when it is necessary to convey mystical terror and mystical rapture." *Rech'* (1908), no. 1.

2. First Symphony (op. 1, 1905–07).

3. Son of Peter Ivanovich Jurgenson. (V. V. Ya.)

4. The brochure was published by the firm of P. Jurgenson after the comopser's death. It was entitled: *V. Iastrebtsev. Nikolai Andreevich Rimskii-Korsakov. Ocherk ego zhizni i deiatel'nosti. Polnyi spisok sochinenii. S prilozheniem portreta i faksimilei* (V. Yastrebtsev. Nikolai Andreyevich Rimsky-Korsakov. Survey of his life and work. Complete list of compositions. With appended portrait and facsimiles).

5. The article was "Kontserty A. Siloti," *Rech'* (1908), no. 17. G. Timofeyev criticized A. Siloti as a conductor (erratic tempi, lack of passion during the performance of *Antar*) and as a pianist, accompanying P. Casals. ("He all but destroyed the soloist.")

6. Actually, Rimsky-Korsakov was an honorary member of more than fourteen Russian and foreign societies. (V. V. Ya.)

7. *30 Songs of the Russian People* (1900).

8. I. Stravinsky's suite for orchestra and mezzo-soprano *Faun and Shepherdess* (op. 2, 1907) and First Symphony (op. 1, 1905–07) were performed on January 22, at the Court Orchestra's twenty-first evening of "Musical Novelties."

9. In the words of Ekaterina Borodina (the composer's wife):

A perpetual punster in life, Alexander Porfiryevich liked to pun and parody in music. He composed many musical jokes. None of them was published, of course, but in his circle he enjoyed amusing his friends with a "quadrille" on motifs from Rimsky-Korsakov's *Maid of Pskov*, a waltz on Varlaam's song "Vot edet on" from *Boris Gudunov;* a lancer constructed on church modes; a parody of Rimsky-Korsakov's song *Iuzhnaia noch'*, in which, leaving the melody unaltered, he so chanted the text and accompaniment that all the charm and poetry of the original was replaced, for fun, by the most rollicking banality. V. V. Stasov. *Izbrannye sochineniia* (Collected works), 3 vols, 3:359–360.

10. The first Moscow performance of *The Legend of the Invisible City of Kitezh and the Maiden Fevronia* took place on February 15, 1908. The composer attended neither the rehearsals nor the premiere.

11. If we permit the voice a bit more flexibility, we will have something very close to Ivan's theme.

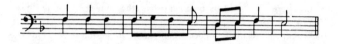

12. The first performance of *Kitezh* was timed to coincide with the farewell benefit for N. Salina, who performed the role of Fevronia.

13. In this article V. Karatygin pointed out the defects in Glazunov's *The Sea* and praised Borodin's First Symphony. He devoted his major attention to the excerpts from *The Golden Cockerel*. *Stolichnaia pochta* (February 20, 1908), no. 242.

14. This piano piece (1901) was published in an art and music album titled *V pamiat' professora I. K. Aivazovskogo* (In memory of Professor I. K. Aivazovsky) (St. Petersburg: D. Okryants, 1903).

15. In the original this work is called *After Shelley (To Prometheus Unbound)*, symphonic fragment, 1906–1908.

16. The scene in which the forest is turned into a garden of paradise.

17. In an article entitled "Skazanie o nevidimom grade Kitezhe i deve Fevronii" (The Legend of the Invisible City of Kitezh and the Maiden Fevronia), Yu. Engel points out the innovatory character of the opera and underscores the beauty of the music.

18. I. V. Lipayev. "N. A. Rimskii-Korsakov. Ocherk ego muzykal'noi deiatel'nosti" (N. A. Rimsky-Korsakov. Survey of his musical activity), *Muzykal'nyi truzhenik* (1908), nos. 1, 4, 9, 12–13, 16–17.

19. Opera Committee of the Marinsky Theater.

20. "As the symphony," writes Findeisen, "they played a raw (student) composition by M. O. Steinberg, called 'Symphony in D major, op. 3.' What one notes primarily in this exceedingly immature work is the strong influence of the music of Glazunov." *Russkaia muzykal'naia gazeta* (1908), no. 11.

21. My expression. (V. V. Ya.)

22. *Nachtstück*—song to words by A. Khomyakov from the cycle *Romances* (op. 14, no. 3, 1901).

23. *Tol'ko vstrechu ulybku tvoiu*, song no. 3, and *Pesn' Gafiza*, song no. 4 from op. 13—*Chetyre romansa dlia vysokovo golosa* (Four songs for high voice, 1906).

24. Most likely they were performing Rimsky-Korsakov's *Sinfonietta on Russian Themes* (op. 31, 1884).

25. Gnessin visited the Rimsky-Korsakovs for the first time on March 28, 1908. (V. V. Ya.)

26. The Rimsky-Korsakovs had actually paid everything, but since the bank had not yet received notification from the old notary about the transfer of part of the Bukharova estate to them,

when the list was compiled for publication, "their" farmstead was listed among those for sale. (V. V. Ya.)

27. Rimsky-Korsakov did not subscribe to Yu. Melgunov's schematic and contrived theories, although he acknowledged that there were elements of polyphony, created by independent subordinate voices in the Russian folk song.

28. *Venok*—(wreath or garland) name given to the decadent exhibition of the New Society of Artists held in Petersburg in the middle of March. Among the artists represented were Yakovlev, Naumov, Masyutin, and Malyutin. The public reception of it was negative. In a review signed O. Bazankur it was described as follows: "Several young people who never completed their artistic or general education . . . decided that at the present time of reappraisal of values it is appropriate for them to present themselves as innovators and seekers. . . . For this nothing seemed required except impertinence." "Vystavka 'Venok' " (The Venok Exhibition), *Peterburgskie vedomosti* (1908), no. 70.

29. In Paris this chorus was sung by nine choristers, the number of spring flowers Ostrovsky glorifies. (V. V. Ya.)

30. This article, entitled "Skazanie o nevidimom grade Kitezhe i deve Fevronii" (Legend of the Invisible City of Kitezh and the Maiden Fevronia), contains an enthusiastic account of the text and music of *Kitezh*. *Golos Moskvy* (1908), nos. 57 and 84.

31. The twenty-fifth anniversary of M. Goldenblum's career was celebrated on April 14, 1908. Congratulatory messages were sent to him by Rimsky-Korsakov, Glazunov, Napravnik, Auer, Nikisch, Liadov, et al. The celebration was concluded with a concert, at which Dolina, Tartakov, and Bukhtoyarov sang songs by the honoree; see *Russkaia muzykal'naia gazeta* (1908), nos. 14 and 17.

32. Reference to the letters of Glinka published by N. Findeisen in *Russkaia muzykal'naia gazeta* (1907), nos. 5–6, in connection with the fiftieth anniversary of the composer's death. Included were excerpts from unpublished letters to his sister L. Shestakova.

33. The first piece was played by Steinberg and Liadov. (V. V. Ya.)

34. Arina Rodionovna Yakoleva—Pushkin's *niania*. (Trans.)

35. Felix Blumenfeld went to Paris to conduct *Boris Godunov* at the Paris Opera.

36. The newspaper *Rech'* (no. 92) published the following report: "The composer N. A. Rimsky-Korsakov has been taken seriously ill. On the night of April 11 he suffered a heart attack. This was followed by a more severe attack on the night of April 16. The doctor in attendance diagnosed the illness as asthma. He has prescribed complete rest but, not feeling weak, the ever energetic and active N. A. Rimsky-Korsakov finds this enforced inactivity somewhat burdensome."

The newspaper *Slovo* (No. 345) carried a brief report stating that Rimsky-Korsakov has been ill for two weeks, he has asthma and has suffered two heart attacks.

37. The dates given are Old Style. The Russians followed the Julian, or Old Style, calendar until 1918, when the Soviet government adopted the Gregorian, or New Style, calendar. In this entry, Yastrebtsev uses only the Old Style dates, while in his entry of 30 April, he uses both.

According to the entry of 29 April (omitted), the Paris newspaper *Le Figaro* reported that due to the illness of Mme Carré, *Snegurochka* had been postponed for a week or two or even until the next season. (Trans.)

38. Variant of the words of the old monk Pimen in *Boris Godunov:* "Zadumchiv, tikh, sidel pred nami Groznyi" (Reflective, silent sat before us Tsar Ivan the Terrible). (V. V. Ya.)

39. A kind of shag. (Trans.)

40. Evidently they had forgotten to tell him about this the day before, even though I telephoned them especially. (V. V. Ya.)

41. In 1908 the firm of Bessel & Co. in St. Petersburg published a number of songs by Mus-

sorgsky in a new edition under the editorship of Rimsky-Korsakov, with French translations of the texts made by M. Calvocoressi and German by A. Bernhard. Included were the songs of the cycle *Bez solntsa* (Sunless), *Videnie* (Vision), *Gopak, (Gornimi tikho letela dusha nebesami* (Softly the Spirit Flew up to Heaven); the cycle *Detskaia* (The Nursery; with French translation by M. Delines and German by A. Bernhard); *Detskaia pesenka* (Child's Song), *Kallistrat, Klassik* (The Classicist), *Ne bozhiim gromom gore udarilo* (Not Like Thunder from Heaven), *Noch' (Night)*, *Ozornik* (The Urchin); the cycle *Pesni i pliaski smerti* (Songs and Dances of Death); *Mephistofeles' Song* (The Song of the Flea) (with French text by M. Calvocoressi and Goethe's original German text); and *Strannik* (The Wanderer). Besides this in 1908 Bessel also published separately the song *S Nianei*, no. 1 from the cycle *Detskaia* (The Nursery) freely adapted by Rimsky-Korsakov.

42. This article, entitled "Novaia opera Rimskogo-Korsakova" (A new opera by Rimsky-Korsakov) and signed "Mizgir," gives an extended report on the publication of the vocal score of *The Golden Cockerel*. The author points out the link between Rimsky-Korsakov's latest opera and the present day. He states in part:

"One of the most renowned sons of the Russian land, the greatest of our living artists after Leo Tolstoy, Rimsky-Korsakov has responded to the period of stagnation of the past decade with an amazing creation, one might say a work of genius. He has not only enriched art with a new form of opera—an artistic satire—but he has immortalized in musical images this dark epoch of Russian history, from whose oppressive legacy we have not even now taken leave." *Golos Moskvy* (1908), no. 98.

43. The Paris productions of Rimsky-Korsakov's *Snegurchka* and Mussorgsky's *Boris Godunov* were discussed in an article by I. Yakovlev entitled " 'Boris Godunov' v Bolshoi opere" (*Boris Godunov* at the Bolshoi Opera), *Novoe vremia* (1908), no. 11552.

A second article by Yakovlev entitled " 'Snegurochka' v Opera Komik" (*Snegurochka* at the Opera Comique) was devoted to the dress rehearsal of the opera. *Novoe vremia* (May 13, 1908), no. 11554.

On May 15, in an article entitled "Parizhskaia pechat' o 'Borise' i 'Snegurochke' " (The Paris press on *Boris* and *Snegurochka*), signed K. A., it was reported that "the reviews of the Paris newspapers, even if not detailed, were very favorable to both operas. They were perhaps even more enthusiastic about Mussorgsky than about Mr. Korsakov." *Novoe vremia* (May 15, 1908), no. 11556.

44. *Novoe vremia* (1908), no. 11557, in the section *Teatr i muzyka* (Theater and music).

45. *Slavianshchina*—literally, the Slavs' domain, derogatory. (Trans.)

46. Balakirev dedicated his second symphony to Ulybyshev, in honor of the fiftieth anniversary of his death. It was performed for the first time on March 2, 1909, in Moscow under the direction of E. Cooper.

47. Balakirev's *Islamey* in Casella's orchestration was published by Jurgenson in 1908; in Liapunov's orchestration, in 1916.

48. The wedding of M. O. Steinberg and Nadezhda Nikolayevna Rimsky-Korsakova, which took place on June 4/17, 1908. (Trans.)

49. On the night of the fifth, Nikolai Andreyevich had suffered another mild attack. (V. V. Ya.)

50. Rimsky-Korsakov was buried in the Novodevichy Cemetery. In the summer of 1936 his remains were removed to the Necropolis of the Alexander Nevsky Monastery.

51. Société des compositeurs de musique. (Trans.)

52. During the night there was a sudden, brief but violent thunderstorm at Lyubensk. (V. V. Ya.)

53. See *Ezhegodnik imperatorskikh teatrov* for 1909, p. 69. (V. V. Ya.)

RIMSKY-KORSAKOV'S WORKS

This list gives opus number, Russian title, English title or translation, date of composition, city and year of publication, city and date of first performance whenever applicable.

Moscow first performances at the Solodovnikov Theater; St. Petersburg first performances at the Marinsky Theater unless otherwise stated.

OPERAS

Pskovitianka (The Maid of Pskov), opera in four acts. Libretto by Rimsky-Korsakov, after L. A. Mey.

First version composed 1868–72. Published St. Petersburg, 1872. First performance St. Petersburg, January 17, 1873.

Second version composed 1876–77. Not published, not performed.

Third version composed 1891–92. Published St. Petersburg, 1892. First performance Panayevsky Theater, St. Petersburg, April 18, 1895. New aria, act 3, composed 1898.

Mlada, opera-ballet in four acts in collaboration with Borodin, Cui, Mussorgsky, and Minkus. Libretto by V. A. Krylov. Composed 1872. Unfinished.

Maiskaia noch' (May Night), opera in three acts. Libretto by Rimsky-Korsakov after Gogol. Composed 1878–79. Published Leipzig, 1893. First performance St. Petersburg, January 21, 1880.

Snegurochka (Snow Maiden), opera in four acts and a prologue. Libretto by Rimsky-Korsakov after A. N. Ostrovsky.

First version composed 1880–81. Published St. Petersburg, 1881. First performance St. Petersburg, February 10, 1882.

Second version composed c. 1895. Published St. Petersburg, 1898. Not performed.

Mlada, opera-ballet in four acts. Libretto by Rimsky-Korsakov after Krylov. Composed 1889–90. Published Leipzig, 1891. First performance St. Petersburg, November 1, 1892.

Noch' pered Rozhdestvom (Christmas Eve), opera in four acts. Libretto by Rimsky-Korsakov after Gogol. Composed 1894–95. Published Leipzig, 1895. First performance St. Petersburg, December 10, 1895.

Sadko, opera in seven scenes. Libretto by Rimsky-Korsakov and V. I. Belsky. Composed 1894–96. Published Leipzig, 1897. First performance Moscow, January 7, 1898.

Bagdadskii borodobrei (The Barber of Baghdad), opera in one act, sketches. Libretto by Rimsky-Korsakov. Composed 1895. [See note 45, chapter 5. Trans.]

539

Op. 48, *Motsart i Sal'ieri* (Mozart and Salieri), opera in one act, two scenes. Text by Pushkin. Composed 1897. Published Leipzig, 1898. First performance Moscow, December 7, 1898.

Op. 54, *Boyarina Vera Sheloga* (revision of prologue to second version of opera *Pskovitianka,* with additional new material, 1876–77), opera in one act. Libretto by Rimsky-Korsakov after L. A. Mey. Composed 1898. Published St. Petersburg, 1898. First performance Moscow, December 27, 1898.

Tsarskaia nevesta (The Tsar's Bride), opera in four acts. Libretto by Rimsky-Korsakov and I. F. Tyumenev after L. A. Mey. Composed 1898. Published Leipzig, 1899. First performance Moscow, November 3, 1899. New aria, act 3 composed 1899.

Skazka o Tsare Saltane, o syne ego slavnom i moguchem bogatyre kniaze Gvidone Saltanoviche i o prekrasnoi tsarevne lebedi (The Tale of Tsar Saltan, of His Son, the Famed and Mighty Hero, Prince Guidon Saltanovich, and of the Beautiful Swan Princess), opera in four acts and a prologue. Libretto by Belsky after Pushkin. Composed 1899–1900. Published St. Petersburg, 1900. First performance Moscow, November 3, 1900.

Serviliia (Servilia), opera in five acts. Libretto by Rimsky-Korsakov after L. A. Mey. Composed 1900–1. Published St. Petersburg, 1900. First performance St. Petersburg, October 14, 1902.

Kashchei bessmertnyi (Kashchei the Immortal), opera in one act. Libretto by Rimsky-Korsakov after E. M. Petrovsky. Composed 1901–2. Published St. Petersburg, 1902. First performance Moscow, December 25, 1902. Conclusion rewritten 1906.

Pan Voevoda (Pan Voyevoda), opera in four acts. Libretto by Tyumenev. Composed 1902–3. Published St. Petersburg, 1904. First performance St. Petersburg Conservatory, October 16, 1904.

Skazanie o nevidimom grade Kitezhe i deve Fevronii (The Legend of the Invisible City of Kitezh and the Maiden Fevronia), opera in four acts. Libretto by Belsky. Composed 1903–5. Published Leipzig, 1906. First performance St. Petersburg, February 20, 1907.

Zolotoi petushok (The Golden Cockerel), opera in three acts. Libretto by Belsky after Pushkin. Composed 1906–7. Published Moscow, 1908. First performance Moscow, October 7, 1909.

Sten'ka Razin (Stenka Razin), opera, sketches. Libretto by Belsky. Composed 1905. Not published.

Zemlia i nebo (Heaven and Earth), opera, sketches. Libretto by Belsky after Byron. Composed 1905. Not published.

CHORAL WORKS

Op. 13. Two three-part choruses for female voices unaccompanied. Words by Lermontov.
1. *Tuchki nebesnye* (Clouds in the sky).
2. *Nochevala tuchka zolotaia* (The golden cloud had slept). Composed 1875. Published Leipzig, 1875.

Op. 14. Four variations and fughetta on a Russian folk song, *Nadoeli nochi* (Tired am I of the nights), four-part chorus for female voices with piano or harmonium ad lib. Composed 1875. Published Leipzig, 1875.

Op. 16. Six choruses unaccompanied. Published St. Petersburg, 1876.
1. *Na severe dikom* (In the wild North). Mixed voices. Composed 1875.
2. *Bakkhicheskaia pesn'* (Bacchic song). Male voices. Composed 1875.
3. *Staraia pesnia: Iz lesov dremuchikh severnykh* (Old song: From the dense northern forests). Mixed voices. Composed 1876.
4. *Mesiats plyvet i tikh i spokoen* (The moon floats peacefully). Mixed voices. Composed 1876.
5. *Posledniaia tucha razseiannoi buri* (The last cloud of the storm). Female voices. Composed 1876.
6. *Molitva: Vladyko dnei moikh* (Prayer: Ruler of my days). Mixed voices. Composed 1875.

Op. 18. Two choruses for mixed voices unaccompanied. Composed 1876. Published St. Petersburg, 1876.

1. *Pred raspiat'iem* (Before the Cross).
2. *Tatarskii polon* (The Tatar Captivity).

Op. 23. Four three-part choruses for male voices with piano ad lib.

1. *Krest'ianskaia pirushka* (The peasant feast).
2. *Voron k voronu letit* (Raven flies to raven).
3. *Plenivshis' rozoi solovei* (Enslaved by the rose, the nightingale). Words by Koltsov.
4. *Daite bokal* (Give me the goblet). Composed 1876. Published Leipzig, 1876.

Op. 20. *Stikh ob Aleksee Bozh'em cheloveke* (Verse about Alexei, the man of God). Traditional words. Arranged for mixed chorus and orchestra. Composed 1878. Published Leipzig, c. 1880.

Op. 19. Fifteen Russian folk songs arranged for mixed voices unaccompanied 1879. Published Moscow, 1879.

1. *Iz za lesu, lesu temnogo* (From the forest, the dark forest).
2. *Kak pri vechere* (At evening).
3. *A i gusto na bereze list'ia* (The leaves are thick on the birch tree).
4. *Zelena grusha vo sadu* (The green pear tree in the garden).
5. *Kak za rechkoi* (Across the river).
6. *Vo luziakh* (In the meadows).
7. *Chto vilis'-to moi rusy kudri?* (Why were my light brown curls so wavy?).
8. *Podui, podui nepogodushka* (Begone, begone bad weather).
9. *Akh, talan-li moi* (Oh, my good fortune).
10. *Ty vzoidi solntse krasnoe* (Rise, red sun).
11. *Vzoidi, ty, solntse, ni nizko, vysoko* (Rise, O sun, not low but high).
12. *Ai, vo pol lipen'ka* (In the field there is a lime tree).
13. *Zapletisia pleten'* (Plait the wattle fencing).
14. *Posmotrite-ka, dobrye liudi* (Just see, good people).
15. *So v'iunom ia khozhu* (With a youth I walk).

Op. 21. *Slava* (Gloria). Traditional word.. Arranged for mixed chorus and orchestra. Composed 1879–80. Published St. Petersburg, 1880.

Tebe Boga khvalim (We praise Thee, O God). Greek chant. Arranged for double chorus. Composed, 1883. Published St. Petersburg, 1883.

Op. 22. *Liturgiia sv. Ioanna Zlatousta* (Eight settings from the liturgy of St. John Chrysostom). Liturgical text. Arranged for mixed chorus 1883. Published St. Petersburg, 1884.

1, 2. *Kheruvimy* (Cherubic hymns).
3. *Veruiu* (The Creed).
4. *Milost' mira* (Mercy of peace).
5. *Tebe poem* (We praise Thee).
6. *Dostoino est'* (It is truly meet).
7. *Otche nash* (Our Father).
8. *Khvalite Gospoda s nebes* (Praise the Lord from the Heavens).

Op. 22b. *Tserkovnoe pesnopenie* (Liturgical text). Arranged for mixed chorus 1884. Published St. Petersburg, 1886.

1. *Kheruvimskaia pesnia* (Cherubic Song).
2. *Da molchit vsiakaia plot'* (Let all mortal flesh keep silent).
3. *Voskresnyi prichastnyi stikh* (Sunday Communion hymn).
4. *Se zhenikh griadet* (See the bridegroom cometh).
5. *Chertog tvoi vizhdu, Spase Moi* (I enter Thy mansion, my Saviour)

6. *Psalm: Na rekakh Vavilonskikh* (By the waters of Babylon).

Op. 44. *Switezianka,* cantata for soprano, tenor, mixed chorus, and orchestra. Words by L. A. Mey after Mickiewicz. (Rewording of song on the same text, op. 7, no. 3, composed 1867.) Composed 1897. Published Leipzig, 1898.

Op. 58. *Pesn' o veshchem Olege* (Song of Oleg the Wise), scored for tenor, bass, male chorus, and orchestra. Words by Pushkin. Composed 1899. Published St. Petersburg, 1901.

Op. 60. *Iz Gomera (From Homer),* prelude-cantata for soprano, mezzo-soprano, contralto, female chorus, and orchestra. Text from *The Odyssey.* Composed 1901. Published Leipzig, 1905.

Op. 62. *Dubinushka* (The little oak stick). Folk song. Arranged for chorus and orchestra, 1905. Published Moscow, 1966. Expanded and rescored, 1906. Published Leipzig, 1907.

ORCHESTRAL WORKS

Op. 1. Symphony no. 1 in E-flat minor.
First version composed 1861–65. Published Moscow, 1953.
Revised and reorchestrated, in E minor, 1884. Published St. Petersburg, 1885.

Op. 28. *Overture on Russian Themes.*
First version composed 1866. Published Moscow, 1954.
Revised and reorchestrated, 1879–80. Published Leipzig, 1886.

Op. 6. *Fantasia on Serbian Themes.*
First version composed 1867. Published Moscow, 1870.
Reorchestrated, 1888. Published Moscow, 1895.

Op. 5. *Sadko.*
First version composed 1867. Title: *Epizod iz bylini o Sadko* (Episode from the legend of Sadko). Published Moscow, 1951.
Second version composed 1869. Title: *Muzykal'naia kartina—Sadko* (Musical Picture—Sadko). Published Moscow, 1870.
Third version composed 1892. Title: same as the seond. Published Moscow, 1892.

Symphony in B minor. Sketches only; part of second subject used in Mizgir's aria, *O liubi menia, liubi,* in *Snegurochka.* Composed 1866–69. Published Moscow, 1970.

Op. 9. Symphony no. 2 *Antar.*
First version composed 1868.
Second version composed 1875. Revised 1903, St. Petersburg, 1903. Published St. Petersburg, 1880.
Third version composed 1897 (described as Symphonic Suite). Published St. Petersburg, 1913.

Op. 32. Symphony no. 3 in C major.
First version composed 1866–73. Scherzo composed 1866, trio 1870, other movements 1873. Published Moscow, 1959.
Second version composed 1886. Published Leipzig, 1888.

Pskovitianka (The Maid of Pskov), incidental music to Mey's play.
First version composed 1877.
Second version composed 1882. Published Moscow, 1951.

Concerto for trombone and military band in B-flat major. Composed 1877. Published Moscow, 1950.

Variations for oboe and military band in G minor, based on Glinka's song *Chto krasotka molodaia?* (Why do you cry, young beauty?). Composed 1878. Published Moscow, 1950.

Concertstück for clarinet and military band in E-flat major. Composed 1878. Published Moscow, 1950.

Op. 29. *Skazka* (Fairy Tale). Original title: *Baba-Yaga*. Composed 1879–80. Published Leipzig, 1886.

Op. 31. Sinfonietta on Russian Themes in A minor. (Based on the first three movements of the String Quartet on Russian themes, 1878–79). Composed 1880–84. Published Leipzig, 1887.

Op. 30. Concerto for piano and orchestra in C-sharp minor. Composed 1882–83. Published Leipzig, 1886.

Symphony no. 4. Piano sketches for scherzo, in D minor. Composed 1884. Published Moscow, 1970.

Op. 33. Fantasia on two Russian themes for violin. Composed 1886–87. Published Leipzig, 1887.

Op. 34. *Kaprichchio na ispanskie temi* (*Capriccio espagnol*). Based on projected Fantasia on Spanish themes, for violin and orchestra. Composed 1887. Published Leipzig, 1888.

Malorossiiskaia fantazia (Little Russian fantasia). Piano sketches only. Composed 1887. Published Moscow, 1970.

Op. 35. *Sheherazade*, symphonic suite. Composed 1888. Published Leipzig, 1889.

Mazurka on three Polish themes for violin and orchestra (*Souvenir de trois chants polonaises*). Composed 1888. First and third themes used later in mazurka in *Pan Voyevoda*. Arranged for violin and piano 1893. First published in this arrangement Moscow, 1949. See under chamber music.

Op. 36. *Svetlyi prazdnik* (Easter Overture, called also Russian Easter Overture). Based on liturgical themes. Composed 1888. Published Leipzig, 1890.

Variation no. 4 in A major (for variations on a Russian theme, *Uzh ty pole moe* [My meadow], in collaboration with Artsybushev, Wihtol, Liadov, Sokolov, and Glazunov). Composed 1901. Published Leipzig, 1903.

Noch' na gore Triglav (Night on Mount Triglav). Orchestral arrangement of act 3 of opera *Mlada*. Composed 1899–1901.

Op. 37. Serenade. Composed 1903. (Orchestral arrangement of Serenade for cello and piano, 1893). See under chamber music.

Op. 57. *Skazka o Tsare Saltane* (The Tale of Tsar Saltan). Musical pictures. Suite from the opera. Composed 1900. Published Leipzig, 1904.

Op. 59. *Pan Voyevoda*. Suite from the opera. Composed 1903. Published Leipzig, 1904.

Mlada. Suite from the opera. Composed 1903. Published Leipzig, 1904.

Noch' pered Rozhdestvom (Christmas Eve). Suite from the opera. (Chorus ad lib.) Composed 1903. Published Leipzig, 1904.

Op. 61. *Nad mogiloi* (At the Grave). In memory of M. P. Belyaev. Composed 1904. Published Leipzig, 1905.

Zdravitsa dlia iubileinogo chestvovania A. K. Glazunova (Hail to A. K. Glazunov on his anniversary). For Glazunov's jubilee, 1907. Composed 1907. Published Moscow, 1966.

Op. 63. *Neapolitanskaia pesen'ka* (Neapolitan song). Arrangement of Denza: *Funiculi, Funicula*. Composed 1907. Published Moscow, 1966.

Zolotoi petushok (The Golden Cockerel). Concert arrangement of introduction and wedding march from the opera. Composed 1907.

Skazka o rybake i o rybke (Tale of the fisherman and the fish). Symphonic poem. After Pushkin. Sketches only. Composed 1907.

CHAMBER MUSIC

Op. 12. String Quartet in F major. Composed 1875. Published Moscow, c. 1875.

String Sextet in A major, for two violins, two violas, and two cellos. Composed 1876. Published Moscow, 1912.

Quintet in B-flat major, for flute, clarinet, horn, bassoon, and piano. Composed 1876. Published Leipzig, 1911.

String Quartet on Russian Themes.

    1. *V pole* (In the field).

    2. *Na devichnike* (At the wedding-eve party).

    3. *V khorovode* (In a khorovod).

    4. *U monastyria* (At the monastery). Composed 1878–79. Published Moscow, 1955. First three movements used later in *Sinfonietta,* op. 31; last movement arranged for piano four hands as *V tserkvi* (In church). See under piano works.

Four Variations on a Chorale for string quartet, in G minor. Composed 1885. Published Moscow, 1955.

String Quartet *B-A-F.* Composed 1886. Published Leipzig, 1887. First movement only (remainder by Liadov, Glazunov, and Borodin); arranged for piano four hands. See under piano works.

String Quartet *Jour de fête.* Composed 1887. Published Leipzig, 1889. Finale only; remainder by Glazunov and Liadov.

Nocturne in F major for four horns. Composed c. 1888. Published Moscow, 1955.

Two Duets in F major for two horns. Composed ?1883–94. Published Moscow, 1955.

Canzonetta and Tarantella for two clarinets. Composed ?1883–94. Published Moscow, 1955.

Serenade for cello and piano. Composed 1893. Published Leipzig, 1895. Orchestrated in 1903 as op. 37.

Mazurka on three Polish themes for violin and piano. 1893. Arrangement of work for violin and orchestra, composed in 1888. Published Moscow, 1949. See under orchestral works.

String Quartet in G Major. Composed 1897. Published Moscow, 1955.

Trio in C minor for violin, cello, and piano. Composed 1897. Published Moscow, 1970.

Theme and variation No. 4 in G major for string quartet. (For Variations on a Russian Theme, *Nadoeli nochi nadoshuchili,* in collaboration with Artsybushev, Scriabin, Glazunov, Liadov, Wihtol, Blumenfeld, Ewald, Winkler, and Sokolov.) Composed 1898. Published Leipzig, 1899.

Allegro in B-flat major for string quartet. Composed 1899. Published Leipzig, 1899. (For the collective quartet *Les vendredis;* collaborators Glazunov, Artsybushev, Sokolov, Liadov, Wihtol, Osten-Sacken, Blumenfeld, Borodin, and Kopylov.)

PIANO WORKS

Overture. Composed 1855. Unfinished.

Allegro in D minor. Composed 1859–60.

Variations on a Russian Theme. Composed 1859–60.

Nocturne in D minor. Composed 1860.

Funeral March in D minor. Composed 1860.

Scherzo in C minor for piano four hands. Composed 1860.

Op. 17. Six fugues in D minor, F major, C major, E major, A major, and C minor. Composed 1875. Published St. Petersburg, c. 1875.

Four-part fugue in C major. Composed 1875. Arranged for piano four hands, 1875. Published Moscow, 1951.

Three four-part fugues in C major, E minor, and G minor. Composed 1875. Published Moscow, 1951. Nos. 2 and 3 are double fugues; no. 3 on B-A-C-H.

Six three-part fugues in G major, F major, E major, A major, D minor, and D major. Composed 1875. Published Moscow, 1951.

Three fughettas on Russian themes. Four-part, G minor and D minor; Three-part, G minor. Composed 1875. Published Moscow, 1951.

Op. 15. Three pieces: *Valse, Romance,* and *Fugue.* Composed 1875–76. Published St. Petersburg, c. 1880.

Op. 11. Four pieces: *Impromptu, Novellette, Scherzino,* and *Etude.* Composed 1876–77. Published St. Petersburg, 1878.

Op. 10. Six variations on B-A-C-H: *Valse, Intermezzo, Scherzo, Nocturne, Prelude,* and *Fugue.* Composed 1878. Published St. Petersburg, 1878.

Chopsticks paraphrases. Composed 1878. Published St. Petersburg, 1880. Variations nos. 1, 2, 6, 11–13, 16, 19 and *Berceuse, Fughetta on B-A-C-H, Tarantella, Minuet, Carillon,* and *Grotesque March;* remainder by Borodin, Cui, Liadov, Liszt, and Shcherbachev.

V tserkvi (In church), for piano four hands. Composed 1879. Published Moscow, 1966. Arrangement of last movement of string quartet on Russian themes.

Variations on a theme by Misha, for piano four hands. Composed ?1878–79. Published Moscow, 1959. Theme by Rimsky-Korsakov's eldest son, Mikhail.

Shutka kadril' (Joke Quadrille). Composed 1885. Published Leipzig, 1891. Figure 6 (finale) only; remainder by Artsybushev, Wihtol, Liadov, Sokolov, and Glazunov.

String quartet *B-A-F,* arranged for piano four hands. Composed 1886. Published Moscow, 1966. First movement only.

Op. 38. Prelude-impromptu, Mazurka. Composed 1894. Published St. Petersburg, 1896. For Bessel's twenty-fifth jubilee album; in collaboration with Artsybushev, Cui, Glazunov, Liadov, and Sokolov.

Allegretto in C major. Composed 1895. Published Moscow, 1959.

Prelude in G major. Composed 1896. Published Moscow, 1959.

Fugal intermezzo for piano four hands. Composed 1897. Intended for *Mozart and Salieri.*

Variation no. 1 in A major. Composed 1899. Published Leipzig, 1900. For Variations on a Russian theme; in collaboration with Winkler, Blumenfeld, Sokolov, Wihtol, Liadov, Glazunov.

Pesen'ka (Song). Composed 1901. Published St. Petersburg, 1903. In the Dorian mode; melody later included as no. 3 in the Armenian collection *Artsunker* (Tears) (St. Petersburg, 1907).

SONGS

Duet, *Babochka* (The Butterfly). Words, anonymous. Composed 1855.

Vykhodi ko mne, sin'ora (Come out to me, Signora). Words, anonymous. Composed 1861.

V krovi gorit (My blood burns). Words by Pushkin. Composed 1865.

Op. 2. Four songs. Published St. Petersburg, 1866.

1. *Shchekoiu k shcheke ty moei prilozhis'* (Lean thy cheek to mine). Words by Heine; translated by M. Mikhailov. Composed 1865.

2. *Plenivshis' rozoi, solovei* (Enslaved by the rose, the nightingale). Words by A. Kol'tsov. Composed 1866.

3. *Baiu, baiushki, baiu* (Lullaby). Words by L. A. Mey. Composed 1866. (Used later in the second version of *The Maid of Pskov* and in *Boyarina Vera Sheloga*).

4. *Iz slez moikh* (From my tears). Words by Heine; translated by Mikhailov. Composed 1866.

Op. 3. Four songs. Composed 1866. Published 1866.

1. *El' i pal'ma* (The pine and the palm). Words by Heine; translated by Mikhailov. Orchestrated 1888. Published in this arrangement Leipzig, 1891.

2. *Iuzhnaia noch'* (Southern night). Words by N. Shcherbina.

3. *Nochevala tuchka zolotaia* (The golden cloud had slept). Words by Lermontov.

4. *Na kholmakh Gruzii* (On the hills of Georgia). Words by Pushkin.

Op. 4. Four songs. Composed 1866. Published St. Petersburg, 1866.

1. *Chto v imeni tebe moem?* (What is my name to thee?) Words by Pushkin.

2. *Gonets* (The messenger). Words by Heine; translated by Mikhailov.

3. *V temnoi roshche zamolk solovei* (In the dark grove the nightingale is silent). Words by I. Nikitin.

4. *Tikho vecher dogoraet* (Quietly evening falls). Words by A. Fet. Nos. 3 and 4 orchestrated 1891. Published Moscow, 1922.

Op. 7. (Originally Op. 5). Four songs. Composed 1867. Published St. Petersburg, 1867.

1. *Moi golos dlia tebia i laskovyi, i tomnyi* (My voice for thee is sweet and languid). Words by Pushkin.

2. *Evreiskaia pesnia* (Hebrew Song). Words by Mey.

3. *Switezianka.* Words by Mickiewicz, translated by L. A. Mey. (Used later in choral setting, op. 44).

4. *Kak nebesa, tvoi vzor blistaet* (The glance is radiant as the heavens). Words by Lermontov.

Op. 8. Six songs. Published Moscow, 1970.

1. *Gde ty, tam mysl' moia letaet* (Where thou are, my thought flies to thee). Composed 1870.

2. *Noch'* (Night). Words by Pleshcheev. Composed 1868. Orchestrated 1891. Published Moscow, 1922.

3. *Taina* (The Secret). After Chamisso. Composed 1868.

4. *Vstan', soidi!* (Arise, come down!). Words by Mey. Composed 1870.

5. *V tsarstvo rozy i vina* (In the kingdom of roses and wine). Words by Fet. Composed 1870.

6. *Doride [Ia veru, ia lubim]* (I believe I am loved). Words by Pushkin. Composed 1870.

Op. 25. Two songs. Words by Heine, translated by Mikhailov. Published St. Petersburg, 1876.

1. *K moei pesne* (To my song). Composed 1870.

2. *Kogda gliazhu tebe v glaza* (When I gaze into thy eyes). Composed 1876.

Op. 26. Four songs. Composed 1882. Published, St. Petersburg, 1882.

1. *V poryve nezhnosti serdechnoi* (In moment to delight devoted). Words by Byron, translated by Kozlov.

2. *Zaklinanie* (Evocation). Words by Pushkin.

3. *Dlia beregov otchizny dal'noi* (For the shores of thy far native land). Words by Pushkin.

4. *Pesnia Zuleiki* (Zuleika's song). Words by Byron, translated by Kozlov.

Op. 27. Four songs. Composed 1883. Published St. Petersburg, 1883.

1. *Gornimi tikho letela dusha nebesami* (Softly the spirit flew up to Heaven). Words by A. K. Tolstoi.

2. *Ekho* (The echo). Words by F. Coppée, translated by S. Andreyevsky.

3. *Ty i vy* (Thou and you). Words by Pushkin.

4. *Prosti! Ne pomni dnei paden'ia* (Forgive! Remember not these tearful days). Words by N. Nekrasov.

Op. 39. Four songs. Words by A. K. Tolstoi. Composed 1897. Published Leipzig, 1897.

1. *O, esli b ty mogla* (Oh, if thou couldst for one moment).

2. *Zapad gasnet v dali bledno-rozovoi* (The west dies out in the pale-rose distance).

3. *Na nivy zheltye niskhodit tishina* (Silence descends on the golden cornfields).

4. *Usni, pechal'nyi drug* (Sleep, my sad friend).

Op. 40. Four songs. Composed 1897. Published Leipzig, 1897.

1. *Kogda volnuetsia zhelteiushchaia niva* (When the golden cornfield waves). Words by Lermontov.

2. *Po nebu polunochi* (Across the midnight sky). Words by Lermontov.

3. *O chem v tishi nochoi* (Of what I dream in the quiet night). Words by Maikov.

4. *Ia v grote zhdal tebia v urochnyi chas* (I waited for thee in the grotto at the appointed hour). Words by Maikov.

Op. 41. Four songs. Composed 1897. Published Leipzig, 1897.

1. *Nespiashchikh solntse* (Sun of the sleepless). Words by A. K. Tolstoi after Byron.

2. *Mne grustno* (I am unhappy). Words by Lermontov.

3. *Lublu tebia, mesiats* (I love thee, moon). Words by Maikov.

4. *Posmotri v svoi vertograd* (Look in thy garden). Words by Maikov.

Op. 42. Four songs. Composed 1897. Published Leipzig, 1897.

1. *Shopot, robkoe dykhan'e* (A whisper, a gentle breath). Words by Fet.

2. *Ia prishol k tebe s privetom* (I have come to greet thee). Words by Fet.

3. *Redeet oblakov letuchaia griada* (The clouds begin to scatter). Words by Pushkin.

4. *Moia balovnitsa* (My spoiled darling). Words by Mickiewicz, translated by Mey.

Op. 43. *Vesnoi* (In spring). Composed 1897. Published Leipzig, 1898.

1. *Zvonche zhavoronka pen'e* (The lark sings louder). Words by A. K. Tolstoi.

2. *Ne veter, veia s vysoty* (Not the wind, blowing from the heights). Words by A. K. Tolstoi.

3. *Svezh i dushist tvoi roskoshnyi venok* (Cool and fragrant is thy garland). Words by Fet.

4. *To bylo rannei vesnoi* (It was in early spring). Words by A. K. Tolstoi.

Op. 45. *Poetu* (To the Poet). Published Leipzig, 1898.

1. *Ekho* (The Echo). Words by Pushkin. Composed 1897.

2. *Iskusstvo* (Art). Words by Maikov. Composed 1897.

3. *Oktava* (The Octave). Words by Maikov. Composed 1897.

4. *Somnenie* (Doubt). Words by Maikov. Composed 1897.

5. *Poet* (The Poet). Words by Pushkin. Composed 1898. [According to Yastrebtsev, *Poet* was written in the summer of 1899. (Trans.)]

Op. 46. *U moria* (By the sea). Words by A. K. Tolstoi. Composed 1897. Published Leipzig, 1898.

1. *Drobitsia, i pleshchet, i bryzzhet volna* (The waves rise up).

2. *Ne penitsia more* (The sea does not foam).

3. *Kolyshetsia more* (The sea is tossing).

4. *Ne ver' mne, drug* (Do not believe me, friend).

5. *Vzdymaiutsia volny* (The waves rise up).

Op. 47. Two duets for mezzo-soprano and baritone or soprano and tenor. Composed 1897. Published Leipzig, 1898. Orchestrated 1905. Published 1906.

1. *Pan*. Words by Maikov.

2. *Pesn' pesnei* (The song of songs). Words by L. A. Mey.

Op. 49. Two songs for bass. Words by Pushkin. Published Leipzig, 1898.

1. *Anchar* (The upas tree). Composed 1882. Revised 1897. Orchestrated 1906. Published Leipzig, 1907.

2. *Prorok* (The prophet). Composed 1897. Orchestrated with male voices ad lib, 1899. Published Leipzig, 1899.

Op. 50. Four songs. Words by Maikov, after modern Greek poems. Published Leipzig, 1898.

1. *Deva i solntse* (The maiden and the sun).

2. *Pevets* (The singer).

3. *Tikho more goluboe* (Quiet is the blue sea). Above three composed 1897.

4. *Eshche ia poln, o drug moi milyi* (I am still filled, dear friend). Composed 1898.

Op. 51. Five songs. Words by Pushkin. Composed 1897. Published Leipzig, 1898.

1. *Medlitel'no vlekutsia dni moi* (Slowly drag my days).

2. *Ne poi, krasavitsa, pri mne* (Do not sing to me, o lovely one).

3. *Tsvetok zasokhshyi* (Withered flower).

4. *Krasavitsa* (The beauty).

5. *Nenastnyi den' potukh* (The rainy day has waned).

Op. 52. Two duets, for soprano and mezzo-soprano or tenor and baritone. Words by Maikov. Published Leipzig, 1898.

1. *Gornyi kliuch* (The mountain spring). Composed 1897. Arranged as trio for soprano, mezzo-soprano, and contralto with orchestral accompaniment. Op. 52b. 1905. Published Leipzig, 1906.

2. *Angel i demon* (Angel and demon). For soprano and baritone or tenor and mezzo-soprano. Composed 1898.

Op. 53. *Strekozy* (Dragonflies). For two sopranos and mezzo-soprano. Words by A. K. Tolstoi. Composed 1897. Published Leipzig, 1898. Orchestrated with female voices ad lib, 1897. Published Leipzig, 1898.

Op. 55. Four songs for tenor. Published Leipzig, 1898.

1. *Probuzhdenie* (Awakening). Words by Pushkin. Composed 1897.

2. *Grechanke* (To a Grecian girl). Words by Pushkin. Composed 1898.

3. *Snovidenie* (The dream). Words by Pushkin. Composed 1898.

4. *Ia umer ot schast'ia* (I died from happiness). Words by L. Uhland, translated by Zhukovsky. Composed 1898.

Op. 56. Two songs for soprano. Words by Maikov. Composed 1898. Published Leipzig, 1899.

1. *Nimfa* (The nymph). Orchestrated 1905. Published Leipzig, 1908.

2. *Son v letniuiu noch'* (Summer night's dream). Orchestrated 1906. Published under editorship of M. Steinberg, 1910.

FOLK SONG COLLECTIONS

Sorok narodnykh pesen (Forty folk songs). Compiled 1875 with T. I. Filippov. Published Moscow, 1882.

Op. 24. *Sbornik 100 russkikh narodnikh pesen* (Collection of 100 Russian folk songs). Compiled 1875–76. Published St. Petersburg, 1877.

WORK ON COMPOSITIONS BY OTHERS

Borodin: final chorus of *Prince Igor*, orchestrated 1879; prologue and act 1, scene 1, revised 1885 whole opera completed and orchestrated with Glazunov, 1887–88.

—Nocturne from String Quartet no. 2, arranged for solo violin and orchestra, 1887.

—Finale to act 4 of collective *Mlada*, orchestrated 1890.

—Song *The Sleeping Princess*, orchestrated 1897.

—Song *The Sea*, orchestrated 1906.

Cui: Wedding chorus and "blessing scene" from *William Ratcliff*, orchestrated 1868. Introduction and Entr'acte to act 3, 1894.

Dargomyzhsky: *The Stone Guest*, orchestrated 1869; scene 1 reorchestrated 1897; remainder reorchestrated and some passages rewritten, 1902.

—Chorus of Maidens from *Rogdana*, orchestrated 1873.

Glinka: *A Life for the Tsar* and *Ruslan and Ludmila*, edited with Balakirev and Liadov, 1878–81.

—Music for stage band in *Ruslan and Ludmila*, 1878.

—Excerpts from operas, arranged for string quartet, 1884.

—Incidental music to *Prince Kholmsky*. Edited with Glazunov, 1902.

Handel: seven numbers from *Samson*, orchestrated 1875–76.

Mussorgsky: second version of trio from *The Destruction of Sennacherib*, orchestrated 1874; complete work orchestrated later.

—Persian dances from *Khovanshchina*, edited and orchestrated 1879; whole opera rewritten, completed, and orchestrated 1881–83.

—Miscellaneous orchestral and choral works, songs, etc., edited and orchestrated 1881–83.

—Dream Intermezzo from *The Fair at Sorochintsy* rewritten and rescored for orchestra as *Night on Bald Mountain*, 1886.

—Polonaise from *Boris Godunov*, reorchestrated 1888; coronation scene, reorchestrated 1892; whole opera cut, rewritten, and reorchestrated, 1892–96; rewritten and reorchestrated with cuts restored, 1906; two additional passages composed for the coronation scene for Diaghilev's Paris production, 1907.

—Song *The Field Marshal*, orchestrated 1899.

—*The Marriage*, revised and partly orchestrated, 1906.

—Songs *Hopak*, *Gathering Mushrooms*, and *Peasant Lullaby*, orchestrated 1906.

—Song *S nianei* (*With Nurse* from *The Nursery*) free musical rendering, 1908.

—Songs *Night* and *The Field Marshal* and part of *Serenade* (from *Songs and Dances of Death*), orchestrated 1908.

Schubert: March for the Coronation of Nicholas I, orchestrated 1868.

Schumann: "Florestan" (no. 6) and "Promenade" (no. 18) from *Carnaval*, orchestrated 1902.

TRANSCRIPTIONS FOR MILITARY BAND (1873–83)

Beethoven: Overture to *Egmont*.

Mendelssohn: Nocturne and Wedding March from *A Midsummer Night's Dream*.

Leopold de Meyer: Berlioz' version of *March marocaine*.

Meyerbeer: Coronation March from *Le Prophète*.

—Isabella's aria from *Robert le Diable;* clarinet, military band.

—Conspiracy scene from *Les Huguenots*.

Schubert: March in B minor.

Wagner: Prelude to *Lohengrin*.

WRITINGS

Dnevnik 1904–07 (Diary 1904–7; fragments only), A. V. Ossovsky and V. N. Rimsky-Korsakov, eds. (Moscow, 1955).

Letopis' moei muzykal'noi zhizni (Chronicle of my musical life) (St. Petersburg, 1909; French translation, 1914; English translation as *My Musical Life*, 1923, 1942, 1972).

Muzykal'no-kriticheskie stat'i (Articles on music criticism), N. V. Shelkov, ed. (Moscow, 1963).

Muzykal'nye stat'i i zametki 1869–1907 (Articles and notes on music 1869–1907), N. Rimskaya-Korsakova, ed. (St. Petersburg, 1911).

Osnovy orkestrovki (Principles of orchestration), M. O. Steinberg, ed. (St. Petersburg, 1913, 2d ed., 1946; French translation, 1914; German translation, 1922; English translation, 1922, 2d ed., 1964).

Polnoe sobranie sochinenii: literaturnye proizvedeniia i perepiska (Complete edition of compositons: literary works and correspondence) (Moscow, 1955–).

Prakticheskii uchebnik garmonii (Practical textbook of harmony) (1884); first lithograph edition, 1885; first printed edition, St. Petersburg: Buttner, 1886. This textbook was revised repeatedly. *Prac-*

tical Manual of Harmony, translated from 13th Russian edition by J. Achron, 5th ed. New York: Carl Fischer, 1930.

Razbor "Snegurochki" (An analysis of *Snegurochka*), V. V. Protopopov, ed. (Moscow, 1960).

Stat'i i materialy po voprosam istorii muzyki i estetiki (Articles and materials on the history of music and aesthetics), N. V. Shelkov, ed. (Moscow, 1963).

Uchebnik garmonii (Textbook of harmony) (St. Petersburg, 1884–85, 2/1886 as *Prakticheskii uchebnik garmonii,* 19/1949; German translation, 1895; French translation, 1910; English translation, 1930).

Vystupleniia v pechati (Miscellaneous articles and letters), N. V. Shelkov, ed. (Moscow, 1963).

INDEX

Abbiate, Louis (1866–1933) (cellist), 507n6

Abraham, Gerald (1904–) (eminent English writer on music): *Slavonic and Romantic Music*, 480n4, 483n16, 502n5

Achron, Joseph (1886–1943) (violinist, comp.), 519n7

Adikayevsky, Vasily Semyonovich (chief censor), 132

Aeschylus: *Orestes*, 489n64

Afanasyev, Alexander Nikolayevich (1826–1871) (Russian folklorist), 492n48

Afanasyev, Nikolai Yakovlevich (1821–1898) (violinist, comp.), 521n10

Aivazovsky, Ivan Konstantinovich (1817–1900) (painter), 143, 318, 500n11, 519n16, 535n14

Akhsharumovs (sister and brother-in-law of N. N. Rimskaya-Korsakova), 189

Akimenko, Feodor Stepanovich (1876–1945) (comp., pianist), 255, 496n18

Albert, Eugène d' (1864–1932) (pianist, comp.): *Gernot*, 210

Alexander III (1845–1894), Tsar, 116, 142, 286, 482n7, 486n21, 496n31

Alexandra Iosifovna, Grand Duchess, 272

Alexeyev, A. Ya. (Director of the Association of Operatic Artists), 335

Alheim, Pierre d' (1862–1922) (writer), 159, 160, 161–62, 501nn37,39

Alpers, Vladimir Mikhailovich (1863–1921) (comp., pianist, music critic), 360

Altani, Ippolit Karlovich (1846–1919) (cond.), 26, 105

Amadeus (Broadway show), xiii

Andersen, Hans Christian (1805–1875), 455

Andreyev, Leonid Nikolayevich (1871–1919) (writer, dramatist): *Darkness*, 432; *Seven Who Were Hanged, The*, 474

Andreyev, Nikolai Vasilyevich (tenor), 401

Andreyev, Vasily Vasilyevich (1861–1918) (balalaika virtuoso; cond.; founder of Great Russian Orchestra), 286, 311, 333, 398, 401, 516n25, 519n8

Annenkov, Vasily Vasilyevich (tenor), 277

Antokolsky, Mark Matveyevich (1834–1902) (sculptor), 29–30, 60, 95, 392, 485n10, 490n12

Antonovsky, Alexander Petrovich (b. 1864) (bass), 293, 346, 347

Apukhtin, Alexei Nikolayevich (1841–1893) (poet), 330, 420, 521n10, 530n33

Arabian Nights, 31, 127, 481n23

Arakcheyev, Count Alexei Andreyevich (1769–1834) (favorite of Tsars Paul I and Alexander I), 41

Arensky, Anton Stepanovich (1861–1906) (comp., Director of Court Chapel, 1895–1901), 104, 110, 114, 274, 281, 286, 384, 397, 495n1,

Arensky, Anton Stephanovich (*continued*)
514n45, 515n12, 518n5; *Basso ostinato* (from *Six Morceaux* for piano, op. 5), 112, 496n20; *Dream on the Volga, A,* 331; *Essais sur des rhythmes oubliés,* op. 28, 112, 496n20; *Nal and Damayanti,* 112, 314, 338, 425–26, 437, 496n20, 523n6; Piano Trio in D minor (op. 32), 348; Symphony no. 2, 215; *Variations for Orchestra* (op. 33, no. 3), 134, 395, 499n61

Arkadyev, Ivan Petrovich (1872–1946) (cond., violinist, comp.), 335

Arkhangelsky, Alexander Andreyevich (1846–1924) (cond.), 325, 521n1

Artsybushev, Nikolai Vasilyevich (1859–1937) (comp.), 307, 327, 339, 413, 433, 444, 497n37, 516n23; Suite in D major, 400

Aslanova (soprano), 346, 347

Auer, Leopold Semyonovich (1845–1930) (violinist, cond., professor at SP Conservatory), 3, 45, 52, 83, 152, 163, 480n11, 487n43, 524n4, 526n21, 536n31

Azanchevsky, Mikhail Pavlovich (1839–1881) (pianist, comp., director of SP Conservatory), 344

Bach, Johann Sebastian (1685–1750), 13, 14, 57, 116, 126, 174

Bach, Konstantin von (cond.), 300

Bagdasarian, Yegish A. (editor), 443, 519n16

Bakst, Lev Samoilovich (1866–1924) (painter), 521n5, 526n19

Balakirev, Mily Alexeyevich (1837–1910) (pianist, comp., cond., leader of the New Russian School ["Mighty Handful"], xi, 5, 14, 22, 23–24, 32, 35–36, 37, 46, 47–48, 55–56, 61, 66, 74, 78, 83–85, 98, 100, 105, 111, 112, 120, 124, 127–28, 136, 144, 146–47, 159, 161, 165, 168, 190, 192, 204, 206, 222–23, 231, 241, 249, 281, 286, 291, 295, 303–4, 306, 315, 360, 364, 390, 393, 395, 403, 426, 451, 480n16, 482n7, 483n19, 486n26, 487nn33,35, 488n55, 490n18, 494nn78,81, 495n1, 499n63, 505nn25,26, 507n56, 530n37, 531n5, 537n46; Bacarolle, 183; *Collection of Russian Folk Songs,* 29, 285, 306, 327, 408, 436, 496n27, 511n3; *Georgian Song,* 83, 182–83, 503n15; influence on R-K, 182–84; *Islamey,* 2, 3, 100, 419, 473, 480n7, 537n47;

King Lear Overture, 182, 226, 325–26, 530n38; *Ne penitsia more,* 125; *Pustynia,* 429; *Rus',* 192; Scherzo in B minor, 2; *Slyshu li golos tvoi,* 198; song cycle: *Dream* (no. 20), 183; *Song of the Golden Fish,* 27, 100, 183, 347, 485n3; songs: *Pridi ko mne, Pesnia Selima, Pesnia zolotoi rybki,* 156; Symphony no. 1, 48, 110, 111–12, 204, 243, 268, 487n34, 496nn17,18; 513n35; Symphony no. 2, 48, 473; *Tamara,* 74, 100, 182–83, 213, 245, 321; *Thirty Songs of the Russian People,* 511n3; *Vzoshel na nebo mesiats iasnyi,* 145

Balakirev Circle, *see* "Mighty Handful" *(Moguchaia Kuchka)*

Balbanova (contralto), 206

Balmont, Konstantin Dmitriyevich (1867–1942) (poet), 364, 429, 503n33

Barmotin, Semyon Alexeyevich (1877–?) (student of Balakirev and R-K), 496n18

Bartsal, Anton Ivanovich (1847–1927) (tenor), 271, 291, 297

Baskin, Vladimir Sergeyevich (1855–1919) (music critic), 49, 53, 108, 113, 141, 153, 163, 333, 373, 404, 495n12, 496n24, 520n29

Bazankur, O. (art critic), 536n28

Bedlevich, Anton Kazimirovich (bass), 201, 227

Beethoven, Ludwig von (1770–1827), 14, 17, 39, 42, 85–86, 88–89, 124, 156, 173–74, 187, 198, 226, 236, 280, 300, 306, 387, 406, 425, 435, 502n44, 504n13, 509n26; *Egmont* Overture, 230, 307; *Leonore* Overture no. 3, 181; *Missa solemnis* (Mass in D major), 45, 320; Piano Concerto no. 4, 244; Piano Sonata ("Les Adieux"), 32; Quartet op. 59, no. 2, 425; Quartet op. 59, no. 3, 433–34; "Razumovsky" quartet (op. 59), 421; *Ruins of Athens,* 2; Second Quartet, 420; Symphony no. 3 *(Eroica),* 128, 193, 518n3; Symphony no. 4, 20, 217, 314; Symphony no. 6 *(Pastoral),* 31; Symphony no. 7, 20, 217, 314; Symphony no. 9, 5, 7, 46, 224

Bellaigue, Camille (1858–1930) (music critic), 243, 468, 510n50

Belanovsky, Sergei Petrovich (hotel mgr.), 441

Belgard, A. V. (Director of Publications in Censorship Office), 443, 444

Belgian Quartet, 334, 522n20

Belinsky, Vissarion Grigoryevich (1811–1848) (lit. critic), 156

Bellini, Vincenzo (1801–1835) (comp.), 290, 305

Belskaya, Agrippina Konstantinova (wife of V. Belsky), 257, 278

Belsky, Rafail Ivanovich (1868–?) (brother of V. I. Belsky), 31, 320

Belsky, Vladimir Ivanovich (1866–1946) (lawyer, mathematician, librettist of several R-K operas), xi, 31, 54, 149, 152, 208, 209, 236, 238, 240, 242, 267, 281, 284, 285, 287, 307, 310, 316, 317, 318, 320, 326, 329, 347, 351, 354, 362, 363, 365, 385, 406, 408, 415, 417, 422, 423, 435–36, 444, 449, 451, 452, 455, 456, 484n36, 492n36, 493n57, 500n20, 525n17, 529n11, 533nn22,23; at R-K, 205–6, 225, 257, 258, 283, 288, 307, 311, 312, 315, 330, 340–41, 350, 377, 418, 433, 443, 444, 445, 461, 466

Belskys, 31, 139, 158, 191, 203, 257, 274, 279, 281, 327, 347, 351, 354, 360, 380

Bely, Andrei (1880–1934) (writer), 520n30

Belyaev, Mitrofan Petrovich (1836–1904) (founder of music publishing firm of M. P. Belyaev in Leipzig, the RSC, benefactor of M. P. Belyaev Prizes [Glinka Prizes], 6, 60, 66, 105, 108, 117, 118, 126, 128, 138, 143, 155, 178, 181, 194, 206, 212, 235, 241, 242, 259, 265, 270, 274, 304, 323, 338, 371, 378, 413, 479n2, 482n13, 489n65, 492n51, 503n25, 505n23, 510n41, 526n20; death of, 337, 523n3; at R-K, 29, 47, 66, 99, 191, 206, 225, 258, 307, 436

Belyaev circle. see "Mighty Handful" (Moguchaia Kuchka)

Belyaev Prizes (Glinka Prizes), 348–49, 424, 505n23, 523n4

Benois, Alexander Nikolayevich (1870–1960) (painter, scenic designer, art critic), 521n5, 533n35

Benois, Maria Albertovna (wife of N. N. Cherepnin), 340

Benois-Efron, Mafia Karlovna (1861–1909) (pianist, professor at SP Conservatory), 286

Berlioz, Hector (1803–1869), x, xi, 5, 8, 22, 27, 33, 34, 36, 37, 39, 83, 86, 90, 94, 147, 156, 161, 188, 265, 319, 399, 500n18, 509n26, 518n46, 530n29; Benvenuto Cellini, 314; Damnation of Faust, The, 14, 67, 116, 146, 193, 410; Dance of the Nubians, 14, 48; Enfance du Christ, L', 255; Flight into Egypt, The, 14; Harold in Italy, 14, 193; Rákóczy March, 181; Requiem,

254, 512n15; Roman Carnival overture, 14, 68; Romeo and Juliet, 264; Symphonie fantastique, 50, 264, 300, 432; Te Deum, 333; Troyens, Les, 146; Tuba Mirum, 39; Waltz of the Sylphs, 14

Bernhard, August Rudolfovich (1852–1908) (music theorist, professor and director of SP Conservatory; translator of librettos of Glinka, R-K, Tchaikovsky operas into German), 116–17, 207, 210, 283, 286, 322, 354–56, 359, 391, 497n35, 526n21, 537n41

Bernstein, Nikolai Davidovich (1876–1938) (music critic), 376, 418, 424, 454, 533n25

Berson, Kazimira Osipovna (Gets) (chamber singer), 393, 401, 418, 424, 433, 440, 451

Bessel, Ivan Vasilyevich (brother of V. V. Bessel), 487n3, 493n68

Bessel, Vasily Vasilyevich (1843–1907) (founder and owner of SP music publishing firm, V. Bessel and Co.), 45, 88, 92, 96, 105, 144, 165, 209, 223, 242, 274, 283, 285, 312, 380, 419, 424–25, 493n68

Bessel and Co., 493n68, 521n11, 536n41

Bilibin, Ivan Yakovlevich (1876–1942) (painter), 447, 453, 526n19

Bilibin, Victor Victorovich (1859–?) (writer): Prilichia (The Proprieties), 274, 514n51

Bizet, Georges (1838–1875), 35; Carmen, 289

Blaramberg, Pavel Ivanovich (1841–1907) (comp.), Tushintsy, 62, 490n11; Wave, The, 172–73

Bleichmann, Yuly Ivanovich (1868–1909) (comp., cond.), 136, 138, 318, 499n65, 525n15

Bloch, Grigory Anatolyevich (1867–?) (music critic), 141, 213, 218, 506n53

Blumenfeld, Felix Mikhailovich (1863–1931) (pianist, cond., comp.), 98, 99, 101, 107, 120, 139, 145, 181–82, 191, 202, 204, 210, 214, 215, 220, 224, 226, 239, 274, 299, 306, 307–8, 312, 317–18, 328, 340, 346, 374, 375, 376, 383, 384, 392, 396, 403, 405, 413, 416, 433, 440–41, 459, 462, 466, 468, 480nn7,9, 497n37, 510n40, 518n4, 530n38, 531n5; Étude in E-flat minor, 401; at R-K, 203, 225, 226, 258, 281, 307–8, 311, 312, 327–28, 340–41, 354, 362, 380, 386–87, 446, 447, 456, 536n35; songs, 206

Blumenfeld, Olga (daughter of Felix Blumenfeld), 462

Blumenfeld, Sigismund Mikhailovich (1852–1920) (comp., singer, accompanist), 120, 139, 191, 202, 203, 205–6, 274, 307–8, 312, 340, 380, 386–87, 392, 395

Böcklin, Arnold (1827–1901) (Swiss painter): Diana's Chase, 513n39

Boito, Arrigo (1842–1901) (comp.), 35, 47, 94; Mefistofele, 143, 166, 282

Bolshakov, Nikolai Arkadyevich (1874–1958) (tenor), 346, 347, 404

Bolska (pseud., née Skompska, married name Brokhotskaya), Adelaida Yulianovna (1864–1930) (lyric soprano), 277–78, 292, 293, 374, 376

Bompard, Louis Maurice (1845–1935) (French ambassador to Russia), 402

Borecký (Czech music critic), 501n35

Bormann, Emil (1864–?) (music critic), 232–33, 234, 253, 272–3, 510n51, 512n12, 514n35

Borodin, Alexander Porfiryevich (1833–1887), 2–3, 13–14, 38, 41, 42, 46, 52, 53, 74, 86, 101, 106, 116–19, 136, 146, 154, 156, 159, 161, 180, 222, 240, 308, 325, 340, 346, 394–95, 406, 409, 436–38, 479n2, 483n19, 487n44, 493n68, 494n81, 495n4, 500n17, 501nn29,30, 508n12, 514n48, 521n10, 530n37, 531n5; Arabskaia Melody, 479n2; Dlia beregov otchizny dal'noi, 479n2; Ei ukhnem, 481n31; Mlada (collective), 3, 119, 480n5, 483n26, 484n26; More, 365, 380, 526n20; On the Steppes of Central Asia (In Central Asia), 192, 218, 314, 315, 396; Overture to Prince Igor, 141, 479n2; Paraphrases, 491n23, 517n45; Petite Suite, 80; Polovtsian March from Prince Igor, 3; Prince Igor, 5–6, 38, 42, 121, 141, 143, 149, 153, 154, 155, 216, 229–30, 257, 275, 314, 417, 482n1, 509n21; Quartet no. 2, 440; Requiem, 518n46; Scherzo in B minor, 2; Serenade in Honor of a Lady by Four Cavaliers, 340, 386, 538n8; Sleeping Princess, 177–78, 371, 503n10, 527n31; Symphony no. 1, 52, 265, 386, 440, 441, 535n13; Symphony no. 2, 3, 74, 217, 218; Symphony no. 3 (unfinished), 256, 321, 479n2

Borodina (née Protopopova), Yekaterina Sergeyevna (1832–1887) (pianist, wife of A. Borodin), 180, 534n9

Borodulin, Vasily Mikhailovich (R-K's doctor), 452, 459, 460, 461, 462, 465

Borovka, Yosif Alexandrovich (1853–c. 1920) (pianist, professor at SP Conservatory), 106

Boswell, James (1740–1795), ix

Bourgault-Ducoudray, Louis Albert (1840–1910) (French comp.), 161, 409

Bouyer, Raymond (French music critic), 161

Brahms, Johannes (1833–1897), 45, 92, 222, 304, 315, 326, 419, 485n6, 509n26; German Requiem, 223, 272

Brayer, Jules de (French music critic), 161

Breitkopf & Härtel (German book and music publishing firm), 435, 462, 469

Breuning, Stephan von (1774–1827) (friend of Beethoven), 173–74

Brockhaus Encyclopedic Dictionary, 261

Bronevsky, N. N. (editor of SP journal), 522n15

Brown, Maurice J. E. (1906–1975): Chopin: An Index of His Works in Chronological Order, 491n18

Bruckner, Anton (1824–1896), 315, 381; Mass in D minor, 210

Bruneau, Alfred (1857–1934) (French comp.), 162; Messidor, 209

Brussan (director of Opéra-Comique, Paris), 532n14

Brykin, Stepan Vasilyevich (1862–1912) (Kiev impresario), 434

Bukharova, A. V. (owner of Lyubensk estate), 410, 412, 433, 449, 535n26

Bukhtoyarov, Dmitri Ivanovich (operatic bass), 258, 374, 406, 536n31

Bulich, Sergei Konstantinovich (1859–1921) (music historian, president of Union of Writers on Music), 140, 261, 299, 376, 512n23, 533n25

Bülow, Hans von (1830–1894), 22, 46, 220, 381, 516n34, 528n2

Burenin, Victor Petrovich (pseud. "Count Alexis Zhasminov") (1841–1926) (lit. & art critic), 29, 63, 369, 485n10, 490n12

Burian, Karl (1870–1924) (tenor), 514n45

Butkevich, Maria Yakovlevna (mezzo-soprano), 212, 360

Büttner, A. (1780–1833) (founder of SP music publishing firm), 498n48, 519n7

Byron, George Gordon (1788–1824): Cain, 25, 84; Destruction of Sennacherib, The, 512n19; Heaven and Earth, 25, 157, 484n43, 525n17

Calvocoressi, Michel D. (1877–1944) (eminent French musicologist), 537n41; *Masters of Russian Music,* 487n32

Capellen, Georg (1869–1934) (music critic & theorist), 533n32

Carré, Albert (1852–1938) (director of Opéra-Comique), 466, 532n14

Carré, Marguerite (coloratura soprano), 452, 462, 536n37

Casals, Pablo (1876–1973), 534n5

Casella, Alfredo (1883–1947) (pianist, cond., comp.), 419, 473, 533n27, 537n47

Catherine II (1729–1796), Empress of Russia, 30, 236, 495n85

Cellini, Benvenuto (1500–1571), 30

Censors, *see under* Rimsky-Korsakov, Nikolai Andreyevich

Červený and Co. (inventor and manufacturer of brass instruments), 531n41

Chaliapin, Feodor Ivanovich (1873–1938) (bass), 195, 196, 201–3, 205, 210, 216, 226–30, 233, 259, 282, 291, 296–99, 323, 333, 335, 338, 349, 353, 378, 379–80, 382–83, 391, 395–96, 402–3, 409–10, 505n22, 506n49, 509n24, 516n17, 518n49, 531nn3,5

Chamberlain, Houston Stewart (1855–1927) (writer), 82

Charpentier, Gustave (1860–1956) (comp.): *Louise,* 295, 425

Chechott, Viktor Antonovich (1846–1917) (music critic), 299

Chekhov, Anton Pavlovich (1860–1904), 354, 432, 489n3; *Bear, The,* 245; *Uncle Vanya,* 330

Cheremisinov, Peter Nikolayevich (president, board of directors, SP branch of Russian Musical Society), 272, 361, 377

Cherepnin, Nikolai Nikolayevich (1873–1945) (comp., cond.), 143, 274, 400, 406, 424, 447, 450–51, 452, 453, 456, 518n5, 533n21; *Allegro dramatique* (op. 17), 326, 327, 521n3; *Macbeth,* 400; *Night,* 256; *Old Song,* 256; *Pavillon d'Armide* (ballet), 423, 424, 535n35

Cherepnins, 339–40, 424

Cherkasskaya, Marianna Borisovna (dramatic soprano), 404, 405, 416, 424, 531n5

Chernenko, Maria Dmitriyevna (mezzo-soprano), 201, 206

Cherubini, Luigi (1760–1842), 332

Cheshikhin, Vsevolod Yevgrafovich (b. 1865) (music critic), 239, 533n32; *History of Russian Opera,* 392, 530n30

Chevillard, Camille (1859–1923) (comp., cond.), 250, 531n5

Chopin, Frédéric (1810–1849), 34, 83, 86, 90, 156, 198, 280, 290–91, 304, 308, 328, 332, 367, 435; Ballade no. 4 (F minor), 190; *Berceuse,* 120; Études, 2, 89, 151, 190; Mazurka in C-sharp minor, 444; Mazurka in F minor, 190, 503n24; Moderato in E major ("Albumblatt"), 66, 490–91n18; Nocturne in E flat, 198; Piano Sonata in B-flat minor; 223 *Polonaise-Fantaisie,* 190; Polonaise in A, 17; Preludes, 190, 526n27; *Rondo à la Mazur,* 23

Chuprynnikov, Mitrofan Mikhailovich (1866–1918) (tenor), 91, 132, 145, 224, 226, 242, 258, 317, 342, 406

Chuprynnikovs, 147, 225, 281

Colonne, Édouard (1838–1910) (cond.), 77, 222, 224, 342, 409, 410, 491n25

Cooper, Emil Albertovich (1877–1960) (cond.), 537n46

Critics, *see under* Rimsky-Korsakov, Nikolai Andreyevich

Cui, César Antonovich (1835–1918), 6, 8, 19–20, 22, 32, 33, 35, 41, 49, 56, 63–64, 66, 86, 95–97, 105–6, 108, 114, 116, 127, 136–37, 141–42, 144, 147, 148, 152, 156, 159, 163, 189, 192, 201–2, 213, 223, 227–30, 249–50, 253, 257, 261, 278, 281, 300, 321, 325, 350, 360, 369, 380, 390, 405, 432, 446, 452, 462–63, 469, 480n21, 483nn19,23,26, 489n7, 493n68, 494nn76,81, 499n3, 501nn24,26, 502n42, 505n21, 506n53, 508n15, 512n12, 517n45, 519nn8,16, 521n10, 531n4, 534n39; *Angelo,* 70, 206; *Captive of the Caucasus,* 5, 8, 480n19; "French style" of, 34; Introduction to *Le Flibustier,* 400; *Mlada,* 483n26; *Mademoiselle Fifi,* 523n1; *Paraphrases,* 491n23; 517n45; *Peterburgskie vedomosti,* 86; Polonaise in C, 2; Quartet, 34; 25 Preludes for Piano, 523n1; *Saracen, The,* 193, 250, 503n28, 510n48; 511n5; Scherzo in B flat, 2; *Smerkalos',* 347; *Snow Giant, The* (children's opera), 400; songs, 141, 325; *Suite miniature,* 321; *William Ratcliff,* 17, 19, 63, 67, 74, 117–18, 139, 150, 210, 230, 282, 347, 386, 402, 426, 432, 437, 463, 482n4, 483n15, 489n7, 491n26, 515n14

Dahl, Vladimir Ivanovich (pseud. "Kazak Lugansky") (1801–1872) (writer): *Noch' na rasput'e*, 492n37

Danilov, Kirsha (1722–1790) (folklorist), 87, 493n62

Dargomyzhsky, Alexander Sergeyevich (1813–1869), 16, 17, 20, 46, 58, 97, 156, 191, 308, 346, 363, 491n21, 493n68, 508n12, 514n48, 515n10, 517n40, 519n8, 523n5; *Finnish Fantasy*, 451; *Kazachok*, 162, 249; *Old Corporal, The (Staryi Kapral)*, 203; *Paladin, The* (song), 347; *Rogdana* (opera), 517n40; *Rusalka*, 97, 509n30; *Stone Guest, The*, 16, 17, 27, 46, 58, 97, 103, 145, 173, 187, 192, 193, 254, 261, 316, 363, 391, 394, 395, 396, 415, 482nn2,5, 519n4, 534n38

D'Auost (Belgian musician, organizer of Les Concerts populaires de Bruxelles), 511n2, 512n14

David, Félicien (1810–1876) (comp.): *Désert, Le*, 166; *Lalla Rookh*, 177

Davidov, Alexei Augustovich (1867–?) (student), 160

Davydov, Alexander Mikhailovich (1872–1944) (tenor), 277, 278, 404, 416

Davydov, Karl Yulyevich (1838–1889) (cellist, comp., cond.), 40, 509n25

Davydova, M. (widow of Karl Yulyevich Davydov), 231, 509n25

Debussy, Claude (1862–1918), 402, 409; *Estampes*, 340; *Pelleas and Mélisande*, 341

Delines, Michel (French music critic, translator), 160, 435, 537n41

Demidov (owner of house which served as premises of SP Conservatory 1862–1896), 486n21

Deutsch, Georgi Ottonovich (1857–1891) (cond., student of R-K), 7, 63, 125, 497n43, 511n3

Diaghilev, Sergei Pavlovich (1872–1929), 90, 364, 405, 411–12, 419, 447, 462, 526n19, 531n5

Diakov, A. A. (music critic), 485n10

Dianin, Alexander Pavlovich (1851–1918) (chemist, student and friend of Borodin), 54, 145, 180, 191

Dianins, 163

d'Indy, Vincent (1851–1931), 91, 187, 188, 200, 204, 208, 253, 365, 382; *Petite sonate*, 91; *Wallenstein*, 91

Dolina (married name Gorlenko, née Sayushkina), Maria Ivanova (1869–1919) (contralto), 92, 101, 214, 242, 271, 272, 278, 494n84, 514n45, 536n31

Donizetti, Gaetano (1797–1848), 290, 305; *Lucia di Lammermoor*, 47

Donskoy, Laurenty Dmitriyevich (1858–1917) (tenor), 296, 523n5

Doroshevich, Vlas Mikhailovich (1864–1920) (drama critic), 271, 514n42

Dreyfus, Alfred (1859–1935), 236

Dukas, Paul (1865–1935), 346, 409; *Sorcerer's Apprentice, The*, 376

Dulova, Maria Andreyevna (soprano), 242

Dumas, Alexandre (Dumas père) (1802–1870): *Charles VII chez ses grands vassaux*, 193, 511n5

Duncan, Isadora (1878–1927), 351, 387, 435, 524n4

Dupont, Joseph (1838–1899) (cond.), 253, 512n13

Durnovo, Pavel Nikolayevich (1830–1903) (statesman), 389

Dyutur, Sofia Nikolayevna (sister of A. N. Serov), 82, 486n24

Dvořák, Antonin (1841–1904), 158

Elizaveta Mavrikiyevna, Grand Duchess, 132

Engel, Yuly Dmitriyevich (1868–1927) (music critic), 322, 343, 350, 353, 444, 528n37, 535n17

Erdmannsdörffer, Max von (1848–1905) (German cond. of Russian Musical Society), 126, 128, 181

Esipova, Anna Nikolayevna (1851–1914) (pianist), 92, 315, 325

Esposito, Michael (1855–1929) (Italian cond. of the Moscow Private Russian Opera), 160, 194, 201, 203

Eulenberg, Ernst (1847–1926) (German music publisher), 513n27

Ewald, Victor Vladimirovich (1860–1935) (comp.), 497n37

Fauré, Gabriel-Urbain (1845–1924) (comp.), 200, 208, 365

Fedosova, Arina Andreyevna (1820–1899) (folktale narrator), 106–7, 495n17

Feodorov (bass), 256

Fet (Shenshin), Afanasy Afanasyevich (1820–1892) (poet), 137, 185, 188, 401

Fidelman, R. A. (violinist), 337

Fiedler, Max (1859–1939) (German cond.), 524n2

Figner, Nikolai Nikolayevich (1857–1918) (tenor), 216, 255, 471, 495n14, 496n33

Filippov, Ivan Filippovich (bass), 375, 403, 406, 416, 531n5

Filippov, Terty Ivanovich (1826–1899) (State Inspector, amateur singer, collector of folksongs), 60, 156, 204, 429

Findeisen, Nikolai Feodorovich (1868–1928) (music historian, critic), 24, 25, 43, 50, 60, 66, 82, 83, 87, 110, 116, 118, 165, 177, 211, 219, 225, 228, 239, 272, 273, 282, 320, 435, 448, 455, 484n38, 486n24, 487n40, 493nn55,57, 500n10, 509nn20,39, 510n51, 514nn47,49, 535n20, 536n32; "Plan for Reorganizing the Program of the Theory of Music . . . at the Conservatory, A," 423

Fontainas, André (French music critic), 161

Franck, César (1822–1890), 161, 208; Symphonic Variations, 244

Fried, Nina Alexandrovna (1864–?) (mezzo-soprano), 5, 24, 139, 147, 191, 214, 223, 242, 257, 278, 291, 341, 375, 404, 421, 425, 522n18

Fried, Oskar (1871–1941) (German cond., comp.), 533n31

Frieds, 139, 320

Funiculi-Funicula (Luigi Denza), 393, 418, 530n34

Gabel, Stanislav Ivanovich (1849–1924) (bass), 22, 526n21

Gabrilovich, Ossip (Salomonovich) (1878–1936) (pianist, cond., comp.), 193, 491n24, 522n18

Galkin, Nikolai Vladimirovich (1850–1906) (cond.), 22, 40, 56, 181, 285, 488n59, 492n50, 515n2, 516n23

"Galkin" variations (Variations on a Russian Theme for String Quartet), 318, 497n37, 516n23, 519n17

Garcia-Mansilia (Argentinian ambassador), 402

Gedeonov, Stepan Alexandrovich (1861–1878) (lit. historian, Director of the Imperial Theaters), 119, 484n26

Georges, Alexandre (1850–1938) (comp.), 161

Ghvala, Emanuel (1851–1924) (Czech music critic, comp.), 501n35

Gilson, Paul (1865–1942), (Belgian comp.), 91, 291

Ginsburg, Ilya Yakovlevich (1859–1939) (sculptor), 198, 392, 393, 489n66, 504nn8,16

Giordano, Umberto (1867–1948): Andrea Chenier, 177

Gladkaya (married name Kedrova), Sofia Nikolayevna (1875–?) (soprano), 210, 293

Glazunov, Alexander Konstantinovich (1865–1936), xiv, 6, 7, 45, 46, 49, 60, 71, 78–79, 83–84, 100–1, 110, 117, 136, 138, 141, 143, 148, 154–55, 157, 163, 177, 179–80, 182, 192, 222, 224, 226, 233–34, 250, 252, 261, 265, 268, 274, 278, 280–81, 283–85, 290, 299, 307, 310, 313–14, 317–18, 322, 326–27, 332, 334, 337, 352, 357–58, 364–65, 367, 369–71, 389, 399, 401, 403, 406, 410, 412, 421–22, 434, 465, 478, 480n17, 483nn19,20, 493n68, 494n83, 495n15, 497n37, 507n9, 509n36, 516n23, 518n5, 519n17, 522n15, 523nn11,14, 527nn28,29, 531nn2,5, 533n32, 535n20, 536n31; American March, 37; arrangement of Volga boatman's song Ei, ukhuem, 528n38; Ballade for orchestra, 315, 519n11; Belyaev Prizes, 348–49; Chopiniana (op. 46), 80; Coronation Cantata, 107, 139, 495n10; Cortège solonnel, 531n38; on death of R-K, 476, 478; Director of Conservatory, 377, 408, 415, 426, 440, 467, 470, 526n21; Forest, The, 37, 265; From the Middle Ages suite, 337, 522n1; Intermezzo Lirico (Intermezzo romantico for orchestra [op. 69]), 256, 512n18; Kremlin, The, 7, 37, 480n18; Muza (song), 191; Nereida (song), 226, 353; Nocturne (D flat), 353; Overture solonnelle, 312; overture The Song of Destiny, 446; Piano Concerto no. 1, 527n27; Piano Sonata no. 1 in B-flat minor (op. 74), 282, 292, 515n11, 517n36; Poème lyrique, 303; Prelude in D flat (op. 25), 402; Quartet no. 4 in A minor, 420, 495n15; Quartet no. 5, 407; Raymonda (ballet), 191, 199, 210, 247, 249, 486n19; at R-K, 24, 26, 29, 44–46, 47, 67, 99, 139, 147, 191, 201, 203, 225, 258–59, 247, 249, 281–82, 306, 307, 308, 311, 312, 315, 327, 330, 339, 340–41, 354, 380, 386, 444, 447, 460, 461, 473; Ruses d'amour (ballet), 230, 314; Scènes de ballet, op. 52, 102, 141; Sea, The, 37, 227, 265, 441, 535n13; Seasons, The, 222, 226, 230; Second Overture on Greek Themes, 3;

Glazunov, Alexander Konstantinovich (*cont*)
Slavic quartet, 421; Sonata no. 2 in E, 307, 310, 340; *Stenka Razin*, 37, 265; *Suite* for String Quartet (op. 35), 407; Symphony no. 1, 222, 275; Symphony no. 2, 312, 401, 504n6; Symphony no. 3, 37, 401; Symphony no. 4, 61, 265, 270, 423, 485n19; Symphony no. 5 (op. 55), 117, 185, 213, 265, 344, 485n19; Symphony no. 6, 178, 185, 244, 265, 485n19; Symphony no. 7 (*Pastoral*), 315; Symphony no. 8, 377, 378, 396, 444; *Two Preludes for Orchestra* (op. 85), no. 1, "In Memory of Stasov," 395; *Valse de concert* (op. 47), 80; *Variations on a Russian Theme for String Quartet*, 117; violin concerto, 396, 397
Glière, Reinhold Moritsovich (1874–1956) (comp., cond.), 425, 448, 524n6
Glinka, Mikhail Ivanovich (1804–1857), 17, 33, 36, 41, 42, 46, 61, 66, 78, 87, 93, 94–5, 97, 147, 156, 182, 238, 240, 254, 261, 290, 299, 346, 402, 409, 426, 434, 442, 451, 455, 493n73, 500n18, 513n33, 524n1, 531n5, 536n32; *Barcarolle*, 2; *Gulf of Finland, The*, 295–96; *Karaminskaya*, 504n6; *Life for the Tsar, A*, 131, 230, 314, 347; *Prince Kholmsky*, 236–37, 267, 509n36, 513n33; *Ruslan and Ludmilla*, 5, 33, 34, 46, 94, 95, 96, 116, 131, 139, 181, 189, 200, 220, 230, 249, 250, 258, 262, 300, 328, 347, 382, 409, 412, 482n1, 494n73, 521n6; *Slavsia* (from *A Life for the Tsar*), 33, 69; *Souvenir d'une mazurka*, 2; *Tarantella*, 2; *Venetian Night*, 127
Glinka Prizes, *see* Belyaev Prizes
Gluck, Christoph Willibald (1714–1787), 14, 93, 130, 182; *Iphigénie en Tauride*, 271; *Orpheus*, 212, 227
Gnedich, Peter Petrovich (1885–1928) (novelist, dramatist, critic), *Goriashchie pis'ma* (Burned Letters), 274, 514n51
Gnessin, Mikhail Fabianovich (1883–1957) (comp., teacher), 433, 436, 448–49, 451, 455, 486n22, 535n25; *Snezhinki* (Snow Flakes), 449, 534n45; symphonic poem, 443, 535n15
Godowsky, Leopold (1870–1938) (pianist), 367–68, 526n27
Goethe, Johann Wolfgang von (1749–1832), 77, 85, 136–37, 225, 537n41
Goffe, Vladislav Ivanovich (pianist), 322

Gogol, Nikolai Vasilyevich (1809–1852), 129, 132, 133, 246, 399; "Christmas Eve," 480n13; *Christmas Eve*, 492n44, 498n53, 499n64, Dikahka stories, 399; *Fair at Sorochintsy, The*, 521n11; *Marriage, The*, 175; "Terrible Vengeance, The," 16, 25, 484n42
Goldenblum, Moriz Arnoldovich (1862–1919) (cond.), 160, 164, 165, 332, 454, 501nn23,28, 502n46, 536n31
Goldstein, Mikhail Yulyevich (1853–1905) (chemist, student, and friend of Borodin), 180
Golenishcheva-Kutuzova, Countess Olga Andreyevna, 490n13
Golovin, Alexander Yakovlevich (1863–1930) (painter, scenic designer), 468
Goncharov, Ivan Alexandrovich (1812–1891) (novelist): *Oblomov*, 532n10
Goncharov, Ivan Konstantinovich (1866–1910) (baritone), 92
Goncharov, L. (music critic), 495n9
Gorky, Maxim (1868–1936): *Wailer, The*, 495n7
Gorodetsky, Sergei Mitrofanivich (b. 1884) (poet), 420, 421; "Zvony, stony, perezvony," 427
Gounod, Charles (1818–1893), 435; *Faust*, 131, 289, 370; *Romeo and Juliet*, 54
Gramen ensemble (instrumental and vocal ensemble), 278, 515n4
Great Russian Orchestra, *see* Andreyev, Vasily Vasilyevich
Grechaninov, Alexander Tikhonovich (1864–1956) (comp.), 353, 425, 529n24, 533n32; *Dobrynya Nikitch*, 319, 325, 520n21; *Elegy for Orchestra*, 215; *Fables*, 375; *Liturgy* (second), 331; *Stepiu idu ia unyloi*, 401; Symphony in B minor, 106
Grieg, Edvard (1843–1907), 13, 36, 304, 339, 403, 420–21, 425, 444; *Norwegian Dances*, 419; Piano Concerto, 506n48; Piano Sonata (op. 7), 448
Grigorovich, Dmitri Vasilyevich (1822–1899) (writer), 60, 489n3
Grigorovich, Ivan Stakhiyevich (bass), 375
Grigoryev, Apollon Alexandrovich (1822–1864) (poet, drama critic), 514n51
Grinevskaya, Isabella (1854–?) (poet), 364
Grosz, Albert (1873–?) (comp.): *Epitalam*, 534n45

Gruzinsky, A. E. (folklorist; ed. Songs Collected by P. N. Rybnikov), 493n62

Gutor, Vasily Petrovich (1864–1947) (cellist), 277, 515n1

Halperine, Mme (translator), 425, 462, 463

Handel, George Friedrich (1685–1759): *Aria,* 198; *Rinaldo, Xerxes,* 504n14

Hanslick, Eduard (1825–1904) (Austrian music critic), 28, 32, 92, 134, 152–53, 315, 485n6; *Vom Musikalisch-Schonen* (Beautiful in Music, The), 92, 485n6

Hauptmann, Gerhard (1862–1946) (dramatist): *Lonely People,* 324

Haydn, (Franz) Joseph (1732–1809), 39, 189, 236, 406; Concerto for Cello no. 2, 275; *Creation, The,* 45; "Emperor Quartet," 425; "London" symphonies nos. 93–104, 189, 503n23; Symphony no. 12 (102) in B flat, 174, 181

Heine, Heinrich (1797–1856): *William Ratcliff,* 482n4

Hershelman, Sergei Konstantinovich (1853–1910) (assistant to director of Imperial Theaters), 143–44, 444, 468

Herzen, Alexander Ivanovich (1812–1870) (writer), 390

Hildebrand, Franz Nikolayevich (1852–1898) (violist), 106

Hilferding, Alexander Fedorovich (1831–1872) (folklorist): *Onega Byliny,* 484n38

Hoffmann, Ernst Theodor Amadeus (1776–1822) (novelist, comp., artist): *Mines of Falun, The,* 25

Hofmann, Josef (1876–1957) (pianist), 134, 139, 321, 531n5

Homer, 525n17; *Odyssey,* 516n24

Hugo, Victor (1802–1885): *Angelo, Tyran de Padoue,* 492n34

Humperdinck, Engelbert (1854–1921): *Hänsel and Gretel,* 135, 141, 177, 499n62, 503n9

Ibsen, Henrik (1828–1906), 456; *Heroes of the North,* 25

Ilina (married name Kobeliatskaya), Lidia Dmitrievna (mezzo-soprano), 161, 163–64

Inozemtsev, P. I. (tenor), 210

Insarova (Miklashevskaya), Maria Nikolayevna (1868–?) (soprano), 247, 256, 262, 278, 279, 281, 342, 346, 347, 387, 440

Ippolitov-Ivanov, Mikhail Mikhailovich (1859–1935) (comp., cond.), 266; *Asya,* 265, 513n29; *Caucasian Sketches,* 141

Iretsky, Konstantin Alexandrovich (friend of R-K), 230, 509n23

Iretskaya, Natalya Alexandrovna (1845–1922) (soprano), 230, 440

Istomin, Feodor Mikhailovich (1856–?) (ethnographer), 511n3

Ivanov, Mikhail Mikhailovich (1849–1927) (music critic, comp.), 46, 47, 98, 105–6, 113, 114, 117, 134, 152, 163, 164, 218, 223, 225, 234, 268, 319, 330, 335, 338, 373, 404, 485n6, 494n79, 496n25, 497n38, 502n47, 506n53, 507n59, 509n29, 510n48, 519n19, 520n20; *Kashirskaia starina,* 353–54, 524n7; *Potemkin Holiday,* 322, 520n26; *Woe from Wit* (opera), 447; *Zabava Putyatishna,* 282, 316

Ivanov-Razumnik, Ivan Vasilyevich (1878–?) (writer), 367, 383, 529n7

Jacobs, Edouard (1851–1925) (cellist), 275

Joachim, Joseph (1831–1907) (violinist), 83

Johansen, Yuly Ivanovich (Julius) (1826–1904) (director of SP Conservatory 1891–1897), x, 4, 5, 8, 22, 28, 45, 88, 163, 284, 322, 502n42, 503n25

Johnson, Samuel, ix, xii

Joly, Charles (French music critic), 294

Jordan, I. (music editor, wife of G. Kirkor), 518n5

Jurgenson, Boris Petrovich (1868–1935) (son of P. I. Jurgenson; music publisher), 534n3

Jurgenson, Peter Ivanovich (1836–1904) (founder and head of music publishing firm in Moscow), 21, 126, 308, 413, 434–35, 515n16, 521n8, 526n20, 527n31, 536n4, 537n47

Kabanov (opera impressario), 527n33

Kalafati, Vasily Pavlovich (1869–1942) (comp.), 235, 518n5; *Adagio,* 303; *Scherzo,* 303

Kalinovsky, Anton Augustovich (friend of V. Belsky): *In Commemoration of Rimsky-Korsakov's Thirty-Fifth Anniversary,* 273

Kamenskaya, Maria Danilovna (1852–1925) (mezzo-soprano), 132, 164, 382, 529n5

Kampionsky, Oscar Isaakovich (1869–1917) (baritone), 247, 256–57

Kanille, Feodor Andreyevich (1836–1900) (pianist, R-K.'s teacher), 78, 117, 128, 509n23

Karatygin, Vyacheslav Gavrilovich (1875–1925) (music critic, comp.), 442, 476, 478, 490n13; *Kolokoi' chiki zveniat*, 534n45, 535n13

Karelin, Vasily Lvovich (tenor), 320

Karenin, Vladimir, *see* Komarova-Stasova, Varvara Dmitriyevna

Karklin, Y. Y. (1867–1960) (tenor), 163, 201, 228, 229

Karmalina (née Belenitsyna), Lyubov Ivanovna (1836–1903) (amateur singer), 490n15

Karsayev, P. A. (music critic), 292

Kashkin, Nikolai Dmitriyevich (1839–1920) (music critic), 129, 135, 178, 194, 196–97, 242, 281, 350, 524n3, 528n37

Kashperova, Leokadia Alexandrovna (1870–?) (pianist, comp.), 521n10

Kastalsky, Alexander Dmitriyevich (1856–1926) (comp., pedagogue), 524n6, 529n24

Kastorsky, Vladimir Ivanovich (1871–1948) (bass), 318, 403, 404, 531n5

Katuar, Georgy Lvovich (1861–1926) (comp., musicologist), 524n6

Kazachenko, Georgy Alexeyevich (1858–1938) (comp., cond.), 6, 272, 519n16

Kedrov, Nikolai Nikolayevich (baritone), 163

Keneman, Feodor Feodorovich (1873–1937) (pianist, cond., comp.), 296, 298; *Kak korol' shel na voinu*, 518n49

Kerzin, Arkady Mikhailovich (1857–1914) (lawyer, organizer of Kerzin Society), 418, 511n1

Kerzin, Maria Semyonovna (c. 1865–1926) (pianist), 249, 511n1

Kerzin Society of Lovers of Russian Music, 266, 292, 296, 418, 511n1

Khessin, Alexander Borisovich (1869–1955) (cond.), 235, 258, 295, 300, 301, 303, 306–7, 315, 333, 337, 491n24, 522n18

Khomyakov, Alexei Stepanovich (1804–1860) (poet), 535n22

Kireyevsky, Peter Vasilyevich (1808–1856) (folklorist), 87, 493n62

Kirikov, M. F. (opera impressario), 438

Kirkor, Georgy Vasilyevich (1910–?) (comp.), 518n5

Klementovich (tenor), 268

Klenovsky, Nikolai Semenovich (1857–1915) (cond., comp.), 307, 314, 315, 518n5

Klimchenko, A. M. (member of Directorate of Russian Musical Society, 359

Klimenko, Ivan Alexandrovich (architect, friend of Tchaikovsky), 325, 330, 343, 521n2

Klimov, Nikolai Stepanovich (bass), 92

Klodt (Klodt von Yurgensburg), Mikhail Petrovich (1835–1914) (painter), 403

Kolomiitsev, Victor Pavlovich (1863–1936) (music critic), 359, 394, 404, 405, 424, 454, 531n4, 532n6

Kol'tsov, Alexei Vasilyevich (1809–1842) (poet), 503n25

Komarova-Stasova, Varvara Dmitriyevna (pseud. Vladimir Karenin) (1862–1943) (writer, musicologist), 489n66

Komissarzhevskaya, Vera Fedorovna (1864–1910) (actress), 356, 357, 358, 360

Kompaniyesky, Nikolai Ivanovich (1849–1910) (musicologist), 362, 529n24, 533n25

Kondaurov, V. A., 517n38

Kondratyev, Gennady Petrovich (1834–1905) (baritone, chief producer at Marinsky Theater), 5, 63, 128, 176

Konius, Georgy Eduardovich (1862–1933) (comp.), 243; *From Childhood*, 59

Konopnicka, Maria M. (1842–1910) (poet), 518n49

Konstantin Konstantinovich, Grand Duke (1858–1915) (vice-president of Russian Musical Society), 132, 272, 359, 360, 525n14

Konstantin Nikolayevich, Grand Duke (1827–1892), 124, 136

Koptyaev, Alexander Petrovich (1868–1941) (critic, comp.), 144, 210, 212, 238, 253, 305, 330, 424, 506nn43,47, 521n8; "New Russian Music from a Cultural Point of View," 211

Kopylov, Alexander Alexandrovich (1854–1911) (comp.), 66

Koreshchenko, Arseny Nikolayevich (1870–1921) (comp., cond., critic), 524n6

Korolenko, Vladimir Galaktionovich (1853–1921) (writer), 189

Korovin, Konstantin Alexandrovich (1861–1939) (painter), 201, 403, 468, 521n5

Korsov, Bogomir Bogomirovich (1845–1929) (bass-baritone), 292, 329, 517n37

Koryalin, Mikhail Mikhailovich (1850–1897) (bass), 67, 92, 101, 132, 143, 460, 491n24, 502n45

Kotlyarevsky, Nestor Alexandrovich (1863–1925) (literary historian), 14

Kozakovskaya, Adelaida Georgiyevna (soprano), 214, 224, 257

Kozlov, Ivan Ivanovich (1779–1840) (poet), 498n47

Kravchenko, Mikhail Stepanovich (1858–1917) (tenor), 278, 293

Kravetsky, Ya. L. (producer), 266

Kruglikov, Semyon Nikolayevich (1851–1910) (music critic, friend of R-K), 67, 129, 204, 211, 295, 296, 322, 343, 350, 353, 483n23, 517n4, 524n3, 527nn28, 37, 528n37

Krushevsky, Eduard Andreyevich (1857–1916) (cond.), 22, 45, 93, 139, 307, 394, 530n36

Krylov, Ivan Andreyevich (1769–1844) (eminent Russian fabulist), 100, 495n10

Krylov, Victor Alexandrovich (pseud. Victor Alexandrov) (1838–1906) (poet, dramatist), 495n10

Kubelik, Jan (1880–1940) (violinist), 321

Kücken, Friedrich Wilhelm (1810–1882) (German comp.), 50, 487n38

Kupriyanov, Vladimir Nikolayevich (friend of Yastrebtsev), 530n27

Kurochkin, Vasily Stepanovich (1831–1875) (poet, translator, journalist), 359

Kuza (married name Bleichmann), Yevfrosinia Ivanovna (1868–1910) (dramatic soprano), 317, 525n15

Kuzma (Kozma) Prutkov (literary pseud. of Alexei Tolstoy and Alexei, Vladimir, and Alexander Zhemchuznikov), 91, 407, 486n23; Hasty Turk, The, 274, 514n51

Kuznetson, Nikolai Dmitriyevich (1850–1920) (artist), 63, 401, 402

Kuznetsova-Benois, Mariya Nikolayevna (1880–1966) (lyrico-dramatic soprano, wife of A. N. Benois), 375, 376, 402, 403, 405

Labinsky, Andrei Markovich (1871–1941) (tenor), 403, 416

Lalo, Pierre (1866–1943) (music critic), 425, 462

Landowska, Wanda (1877–1959) (Polish pianist, harpsichordist): "Lullaby," "At the Source," "Autumn Night," "En Valsant," 190

Lanseray, Yevgeny Yevgenyevich [or Lenseré, Eugene] (1875–1946) (painter), 521n5

Lapshin, Ivan Ivanovich (1870–1952) (professor), 31, 162, 203, 208, 209, 320, 362, 424, 436, 466; at R-K, 274, 312, 339, 340, 351, 354, 362, 377, 444, 523n9

Larina (pseud.), Anna Dmitriyevna (lyric soprano), 163, 203–4, 352

Laroche, Herman Augustovich (1845–1904) (music critic), 19, 56, 66, 79, 87, 92, 101, 106, 109–10, 112–14, 116, 119–20, 128, 134, 136–37, 141, 163, 165, 173, 177, 182, 199, 222, 238, 260, 271, 278, 282, 299, 485n6, 490n17, 493n63, 494n83, 495n14, 496nn12,25,33, 499nn60,62, 505n17, 521n10; Carmosine, 113; death of, 346

Laube, Julius (cond.), 38

Lavrov, Nikolai Stepanovich (1861–1927) (pianist), 7, 120, 141, 147, 225, 257, 274, 494n84

Lazarev, Dr. Isaac Ilyich (friend of Yastrebtsev, nephew of M. M. Antokolsky), 429, 440, 451

Lebedeva, Yekaterina Nikolayevna (student of R-K), 116

Legat, Nikolai Gustavovich (1869–1937) (ballet dancer), 518n5

Lenepveu, Charles (1840–1910) (comp.): Deuil d'avril, 139

Lentovsky, Mikhail Valentinovich (1843–1906) (actor), 266

Lenz, Wilhelm von (1809–1883) (Russian writer on music), 124

Leoncavallo, Ruggiero (1858–1919) (comp.), 33, 47, 229, 278; Pagliacci, 34–35, 143, 378, 485n14

Leonova, Darya Mikhailovna (1829–1896) (contralto), 429, 497n38

Lermontov, Mikhail Yuryevich (1814–1841) (poet), 34, 139, 185, 246, 364, 484n28; Mtsyri, 485n3

Levi, Hermann (1839–1900) (cond.), 253

Lezhen, (Mme) N. F. (student), 357

Liadov, Anatoly Konstantinovich (1855–1914), xiv, 7, 8, 33–34, 46, 60, 71–72, 83, 93, 98, 100, 120, 127, 141, 154, 163, 168, 182, 222, 241, 252, 260–61, 265, 270, 274, 278, 280–81, 283, 285, 303, 310, 313–315, 321–22, 327,

Liadov, Anatoly Konstantinovich (*continued*)
330, 350, 358, 370, 402–3, 406, 422–23, 481n22, 483n19, 492n37, 494n83, 497n37, 505n23, 516nn23,26, 518n5, 519n17, 525n16, 521nn4,11,15, 523n4, 525n16, 527nn28,29, 536n31; *Baba Yaga* (symphonic poem), 79, 492n48, 530n38; Belyaev Prizes, 348–49; *Bride of Messina, The* (cantata), 67, 248, 516n22; *Children's Songs,* 307; *Enchanted Lake, The,* 492n38, Etude in A flat, 2; *Inn Mazurka, The,* 3, 480n6, 522n1; Intermezzo (for piano), 2; *Intermezzo pour l'orchestre,* 270, 337, 523n1; *Kikimora,* 492n38; *Musical Snuffbox, A,* 192; *Paraphrases,* 67, 491n23, 517n45; *Procession,* 67; *Pro Starinu,* 423; at R-K, 29, 47, 66–67, 99, 112, 147, 191–92, 203, 225, 257–58, 274, 281, 287–88, 307, 311, 339–41, 347, 362–63, 409, 444–47, 454–55, 460–61, 466; *35 Russian Folk Songs,* 306; *Scherzo,* 108; *Songs,* 308; *Variations for Piano on a Theme by Glinka,* 446; *Variations on a Polish Song,* 339

Liapunov, Sergei Mikhailovich (1859–1924) comp., pianist, 55, 78, 168, 281, 303, 515n12, 531n5, 537n47; *Ballade* for orchestra, 204; *Nachtstück,* 448; Piano Concerto in E-flat minor, 348; *Solemn Overture on Russian Themes,* 204

Lipayev, Ivan Vasilyevich (1865–1942) (musicologist, critic), 267, 445, 507n2, 535n18

Lippacher, Clément (comp.), 162

Lishin, Grigory Andreyevich (1854–1888) (comp.), 2, 28

Lisitsyn, Mikhail Alexandrovich (1871–1918) (comp.), 391, 529n24

Liszt, Franz (1811–1886), 9, 36, 37, 39, 43, 45, 78, 89, 100, 120, 145, 147, 150, 156, 166, 187, 257, 305, 328, 509n26, 518nn2,46; *"Ce qu'on entend sur la montagne,"* 41, 43; *Christus,* 300, 311; *Concerto pathétique,* 223; *Dante* Symphony (Magnificat), 43; "Dichtungen" ("Symphonishche Dichtung"), 305, 518n2; *Faust* Symphony, 43, 136, 334; *Festklänge,* 131; *Hungaria* (symphonic poem), 23, 43, 45; Hungarian Rhapsody no. 2, 259; Hungarian Rhapsody no. 8, 280; *Hunnenschlacht* (symphonic poem), 43, 45, 307; *Ideale, Die,* 43; *Isoldens Liebestod* (Wagner-Liszt), 448; *Mazeppa,* 43, 45, 423; *Mephisto Waltz,* 17, 41, 43, 111, 187, 225, 275–76; *Nächtliche Zug, Der,* 43; *Offertorium,* 43;

Orpheus (symphonic poem), 43, 281; *Préludes, Les* (symphonic poem), 43; *Prometheus,* 204; *St. Elizabeth,* 43, 183, 292; *Tasso,* 43, 45, 244

Litvin (Litvinova), Felia Vasilyevna (1861–1936) (soprano), 387, 529n15, 531n5

Livshits, B. O. (violinist), 300

Lombroso, Cesare (1835–1909) (criminologist), 91; *Genius and Insanity,* 493n66

Losev, Vladimir Ivanovich (bass), 360, 404, 406, 416

Lunacharsky, Mikhail Vasilyevich (1862–1929) (bass baritone), 163, 165, 228, 229

L'vov, Nikolai Alexandrovich (1751–1803) (folklorist), 481n27

Maeterlinck, Maurice (1862–1949) (poet, playwright), 364, 451

Mahabharata (Indian epic), 484n41, 496n20

Mahler, Gustav (1860–1911), 306, 307, 418–19, 488n53, 518n3; Symphony no. 2, 418–19, 533n26; Symphony no. 5, 394, 530n35

Maiboroda, Vladimir Yakovlevich (1854–1917) (bass), 214, 258

Maikov, Apollon Nikolayevich (1821–1897) (poet), 185, 188, 189, 195, 208, 239

Makarov, Stepan Osipovich (1848–1904) (admiral), 340, 523n10

Maksakov, Maximilian Karlovich (1869–1936) (baritone), 287, 5162n27

Maliotin, Sergei Vasilyevich (1859–1937) (painter), 536n28

Maliszewski, Witold (1873–1939) (Polish comp.): Symphony no. 2, 400

Malozemova, Sofia Alexandrovna (1845–1908) (pianist, professor at SP Conservatory), 165, 286, 308, 518n5

Malyavin, Philip Andreyevich (1869–1939?) (painter), 386, 521n5; *Whirlwind, The,* 529n13

Malyutin, Sergei Vasilyevich (1859–1937) (painter), 201, 536n28

Mamontov, Savva Ivanovich (1841–1919) (patron of arts, founder of Mamontov's Private Russian Opera Co. [also known as Moscow Private Russian Opera and Moscow Opera Co.], 159, 195, 199, 202, 206, 210, 216, 225, 228, 233, 435, 451, 503n29, 505n23, 506n42, 509n24, 510n44, 513n31; private opera company, 206, 231, 504n2, 505n23, 508n13, 510n44, 513n31

INDEX

Manets (student at SP Conservatory), 359, 525n12

Margherite, Queen of Italy, 512n11

Maria Feodorovna, Empress (widow· of Alexander III), 279

Maria Pavlovna, Grand Duchess, 410

Markevich, Nikolai (bass), 317, 416

Markovich, Maria Eduardovna (mezzo-soprano), 281, 374, 406

Marschner, Henrich (1795–1861) (comp., cond.), 260

Mascagni, Pietro (1863–1945) (comp.), 229; *Cavalleria rusticana*, 35, 94, 485n15

Massenet, Jules (1842–1912), 415, 500n9; *Esclarmonde*, 142, 143; *Navarraise, La*, 143; *Roi de Lahore, Le*, 166

Masyutin (painter), 536n28

Matte, Vasily Vasilyevich (1856–1917) (artist), 504n16

Maximovskaya (mezzo-soprano), 215

Meck, Nadezhda Filoretovna von (1831–1894) (patron of Tchaikovsky), 288, 517n46

Medem, Alexander Davydovich (pianist, comp.), 524n2

Medvedev, Mikhail Efimovich (1858–1917) (dramatic tenor), 346

Melgunov, Yuly Nikolayevich (1846–1893) (pianist), 69, 449, 491n29, 536n27

Melikova, Princess Olga Alexandrovna (sister of N. A. Fried), 347

Melnikov, Pavel Ivanovich (pseud. Andrei Pechersky) (1819–1883) (writer): *In the Forests*, 329, 366, 526n25; *On the Hills*, 329

Mendelssohn, Felix (1809–1847), 39, 44, 255, 387; *Athalie*, 280; *Hebrides, The* (or *Fingal's Cave*), 80, 280, 312; *Lieder ohne Worte*, 80; *Lorelei*, 19; *Midsummer Night's Dream, A*, 80, 103, 230, 280, 422; Symphony no. 4, 80

Merezhkovsky, Dmitri Sergeyevich (1865–1941) (writer): *Peter and Alexis*, 364

Mestechkin, Yakov Markovich (violinist), 420, 425, 433–34

Mey, Lev Alexandrovich (1822–1862) (poet), 185, 189, 209, 283, 319, 364, 394, 485n2, 503nn20, 37

Meyerbeer, Giacomo (1791–1864) (comp.), 143, 152, 153, 182; *Hugenots, Les*, 98, 131

Michelangelo Buonarroti, 30

Mickiewicz, Adam (1798–1855) (Polish poet), 185, 485n2, 503n20

Middleschulte, Wilhelm (1863–1943) (German organist): Fantasy and Fugue on a Theme by Bach, 534n45

"Mighty Handful" (*Moguchaia kuchka;* Balakirev circle, Belyaev circle), 83, 86, 172, 213, 288, 306, 415, 479n2, 483nn15,19, 485n5, 491n21, 497n43, 522n15

Mikhail Nikolayevich, Grand Duke (1847–1909) (son of Tsar Alexander II), 128, 129

Mikhailova, Maria Alexandrovna (1892–1913) (lyric soprano), 139, 257

Miklashevsky, Alexander Mikhailovich (1870–c. 1935) (pianist), 426

Minkus, Léon (Aloisius Ludwig) (1827–1890) (comp.): *Mlada* (ballet), 143, 144

Mironov, Nikolai Dmitreyevich (friend of Andrei R-K), 225, 283, 364, 377

Mitusov, Stepan Stepanovich (friend of Andrei and Vladimir R-K), 225, 245, 268–69, 280, 308, 315, 339, 340–41, 387, 447

Mitusova (née Davidova), Nina Alexandrovna (wife of S. Mitusov), 315, 324, 334

Molas (née Purgold), Alexandra Nikolayevna (1844–1929) (mezzo-soprano, sister of Nadezhda Nikolayevna R-K), 41, 57, 90, 147, 363, 493n65

Molas, Mikhail Pavlovich (d. March 31, 1904) (chief of staff, Pacific Squadron), 340

Molas, Nikolai Pavlovich (husband of Alexandra Nikolayevna Purgold), 57, 90, 392

Molases (Alexandra and Nikolai), 20, 21, 22, 53, 58, 64, 67, 101, 159, 163, 175, 281, 363, 428, 482n5, 483n21, 489n62, 491n24

Moore, Thomas (1779–1852) (Irish poet): *Lalla Rookh*, 497n34

Mordovin, Pavel Alexandrovich (1842–1907) (writer), 390

Morozov (owner of house in which R-Ks had apt.), 428

Morskoi, Gavril Alexeyevich (1862–1915) (lyric tenor), 163, 164, 165, 203, 212, 214, 244, 277, 293, 317, 360, 376

Moscow Opera Company, 271, 343; *see also* Mamontov, S. I.

Moscow Private Opera, 205, 513n29; *see also* Mamontov, S. I.

Moscow Private Russian Opera, 292, 505nn19,23,28, 506n49, 508nn14, 16; *see also* Mamontov, S. I.

Moszkowski, Moritz (1854–1925) (pianist), 401

Mottl, Felix (1856–1911) (cond., comp.), 253, 258, 300

Mozart, Wolfgang Amadeus (1756–1791), 14, 182, 236, 261, 294, 410, 418, 422, 434, 440, 522n20; *Don Giovanni*, 93, 130, 143, 177, 199, 200, 262, 312, 503n9; G minor Symphony, 518n3; *Magic Flute, The*, 280; *Requiem*, 227, 507n56, 517n41

Mravina, Yevgenia Konstantinovna (1864–1914) (lyric-coloratura soprano), 101, 128, 132, 214

Mrozovskaya, Elena (photographer), 250

Muck, Karl (1859–1940) (cond.), 300

Musset, Alfred de: *Carmosine*, 496n22

Mussorgsky, Modest Petrovich (1839–1881), 14, 20, 41–42, 49, 83, 97, 101, 103, 113, 119, 127, 136, 153, 156, 159, 161–63, 175–76, 187–88, 191, 268, 290, 329, 346, 386, 409, 414, 428–29, 442, 483nn18,19,26, 490nn15,16, 493n68, 494nn71,81, 496n24, 502n44, 508n12, 513n36, 514n48, 531n5, 534nn42,44; *Akh, ty p'ianaia teteria* (Oh, you drunken sot), 488n61; *Banquet, The*, 190–91, 503n25; *Bez solntsa* (Sunless, song cycle), 537n41; *Boris Godunov*, 7, 20, 21, 42, 44, 56, 57, 58, 66, 73, 134, 135, 142–45, 147–48, 161–66, 168–71, 203, 206, 212, 227–28, 292, 296, 299, 424, 428, 432, 435, 462, 467–68, 482nn1,8, 489n62, 502n46,48, 506n50, 508n15, 513n36, 535n9, 536n35, 537n43; *Child's Song*, 537n41; Dance of the Persian Girls (from *Khovanshchina*), 65, 504n6; *Destruction of Sennacherib, The*, 150, 256; *Fair at Sorochintsy, The*, 96, 130, 131, 330; *Field Marshal, The*, 245; *Gopak*, 390, 396, 441, 537n41; *He-Goat, The*, 493n58; *Hebrew Song*, 83; "Inn Scene" (from *Boris Godunov*), 383; *Intermezzo symphonique in modo classico*, 57, 192; *Kallistrat*, 115, 537n41; *Khovanshchina*, 42, 53, 54, 55, 56–57, 58, 65, 146, 296, 501n39, 504n6, 529n17, 531n38; *Lullaby* (Spi, usni, krestianki syn), 418, 440–41, 442; *Lullaby (Kolybel'naia smerti)*, 390; *Marriage, The*, 254, 342, 375, 377, 378, 379, 380, 381, 388, 389, 426, 428, 463; *Mephistofeles' Song* (Song of the Flea), 537n41; *Night on Bald Mountain*, 31; *Noch' (Night)*, 208, 428, 432–33, 469, 537n41; *Not Like Thunder from Heaven*, 537n41; *Nursery, The* (song cycle), 57, 58, 304, 429, 465, 537n41; *Oedipus*, 150; *Pictures from an Exhibition*, "The Catacombs," 15; *Po griby (Gathering Mushrooms)*, 390, 396, 441; *Raek (The*

Peepshow), 191; *Salammbô*, 58, 428; *Savishna*, 57, 161; *Seminarist, The*, 140, 307, 396; *Serenada smerti, (Serenade)*, 428, 534n43; *S Nianei (With Nanny)*, 429, 465, 502n7, 537n41; *Softly the Spirit up to Heaven*, 537n41; *Songs and Dances of Death* (song cycle), 511n54, 537n41; songs with French text, 465, 534n43, 537n41; *Sunless* (song cycle), 537n41; *Trepak*, 203; *Urchin, The*, 537n41; *Vision, The*, 537n41; *Wanderer, The*, 537n41

Mutin, Nikolai Vasilyevich (1868–1909) (bass), 201, 266

Myshetsky, Prince, 509n23

Nalbandian, Eunice Romanovich (1871–1942) (violinist), 524n2

Napravnik, Eduard Frantsevich (1839–1916) (cond., comp.), 6, 19, 22, 38, 40, 49, 63, 77, 98, 101, 108, 110, 113, 128, 135, 139, 172–74, 190, 209–10, 223, 271, 278, 293, 300–1, 317, 329, 380, 382, 397, 482n11, 483n26, 487n37, 499n62, 502n41, 506n39, 515nn5,9, 518n4, 521n10, 530n36, 533n32, 536n31; *Don Juan*, 18, 49; *Dubrovsky*, 62, 107–8, 220, 490n10, 495n4, 507n7; *Funeral March* (op. 42), 337; *Nizhegorodtsy*, 19, 282, 483n15, 515n14; Serenade from String Quartet (op. 16), 337

Naumov (painter), 536n28

Negrin-Shmidt (soprano), 196

Nekrasov, Ilya Vasilayevich (1862–1905) (folklorist, comp.), 80, 325

Nemirovich-Danchenko, Vladimir Ivanovich (1858–1943) (director, producer, founder with Stanislavsky of the Moscow Art Theater), 330

Nesterov, Mikhail Vasilyevidh (1862–1942) (painter), 329

Nesterov, M. D. (critic), 404, 405, 418, 424, 454, 531n6, 532n6, 533n25

New Russian School, 20, 27, 47, 73, 99–100, 101, 185, 249, 260, 506n47, 510n45

Nezhdanova, Antonia Vasilyevna (1873–1950) (lyric soprano), 421

Nicholas II (1868–1918) (Emperor of Russia and Tsar), 40, 130, 142, 143, 144, 176, 177, 250, 279, 498n54

Nikisch, Arthur (1855–1922) (cond.), 162, 166, 231, 232, 233, 234, 235, 258, 299, 300, 305, 311, 312, 314 315, 320, 335, 405, 502n41, 509n27, 520n23, 531n5, 532n12, 536n31

Nikol, V. V. (architect), 486n21

Nikolayev, Leonid Vladimirovich (1878–1942) (pianist, pedagogue), 524n6

Nikolsky, Vladimir Vasilyevich (1836–1883) (professor of literature), 329, 488n61

Nizhegorod Exhibition, 159

Nolle, Nikolai Mikhailovich (amateur singer), 205–6

Nosenko, Yekaterina Gavrilovna, see Stravinskaya, Yekaterina Gavrilovna

Nosilova, Yulia Nikolayevna (soprano), 128, 160, 163, 164, 165, 224, 293, 317

Novotný, Vaclav (1849–1924) (Czech music critic), 501n35

Nurok, Alfred Pavlovich (music critic), 322, 333, 365, 442

Offenbach, Jacques (1819–1880): La Grande-Duchesse de Geroldstein, 20

Oleg the Prophet (tale), 25

Okryants, D. (publisher of Armenian journal "In Memory of Prof I. K. Aivozovsky"), 535n14

Olenine, Alexander Alexeyevich (1865–1944) (comp.): Osen', 385

Olenine-d'Alheim, Marie Alexeyevna (1869–1970) (mezzo-soprano), 296, 299, 304, 322, 510n37, 520n30

Ondříček, Emanuel (1882–1958) (violinist), 514n44

Opochinin, Alexander Petrovich (1805–1887) (friend of Mussorgsky), 428, 534n44

Opochinina, Nadezhda Petrovna (1821–1874) (sister of A. Opochinin), 506n37, 534n44

Ossovsky, Alexander Vyacheslavovich (1871–1957) (musicologist), 108, 110, 267, 272, 280, 312, 341, 347, 350, 354, 358, 359, 362, 386, 404, 418, 422, 495nn12,15, 523nn1,9, 524n1, 525n10

Ossovskys, 327, 340, 380

Ostrovsky, Alexander Nikolayevich (1823–1886) (dramatist), 219, 520n20, 536n29; Snegurochka, 16, 230, 509n22, 518n47; Tushino, 490n11; Vasilisa Melentyeva, 267

Ovsenian, K. (author), 519n16

Paderewski, Ignace Jan (1860–1941), 223, 291

Paganini, D. (opera cond.), 373

Paganini, Niccolo (1782–1840), 137, 497n38

Paleček, Josef Josefovich (Osip Osipovich) (1842–1915) (bass), 129, 132, 160, 161, 317, 333, 498nn53,54

Palestrina, Giovanni de (1526?–1594), 68, 254

Papayan, Nadezhda Amvrosyevna (1868–1906) (soprano), 320–21

Paskhalova, Aleutina Mikhailovna (1878–1953) (lyrico-coloratura soprano), 202, 203, 375, 406

Pasternak, Leonid Osipovich (1862–1945) (painter), 521n5

Paul Alexandrovich, Grand Duke, 410

Paul Mavrikiyevich, Prince, 132

Pavlenkov (publisher), 493n66

Payne, Albert (1842–1921) (German music publisher), 264, 513n27

Pchelnikov, P. M. (business manager, Moscow Imperial Theaters), 62, 177

Pechersky, see Melnikov

Peter, I, Tsar, 364, 489n63

Petersen, Pavel Leontyevich (1831–1895) (pianist), 24–25, 45, 46

Petrenko, Elisabeta Fedorovna (1880–1952) (mezzo-soprano), 376, 404, 416, 441, 531n5

Petrov, Vasily Rodionovich (1875–1937) (baritone), 201, 518n5

Petrovsky, Yvgeny Maximovich (1873–1918) (music critic), 66, 110, 140, 205, 211, 228, 238–40, 273, 309, 322, 382, 405, 491n20, 505n27, 508n18, 509nn20,39, 532n6

Piltz, Mariya Vladislavovna (mezzo-soprano), 128

Pivovarova, Natalya Feodorovna (grandniece of V. Stasov), 317, 396

Pobedonostev, Konstantin Petrovich (1827–1907) (chief procurator of the Synod), 130, 270

Podesti (cond. of Italian Opera Co.), 220

Pogozhev, Vladimir Petrovich (1851–?) (business manager, Petersburg Imperial Theaters), 101, 143, 490n8

Polko, Elise (1822–1899) (German singer), 497n38

Pollini, Bernhard (German impressario) (1838–1897): company of, 488n53

Polonsky, Yakov Petrovich (1819–1898) (poet), 399, 480n13

Polovtsev (director Adm. Dept., Alexander III's cabinet), 103

Pratsch (Prač), Ivan (Jan Bogumir), (?–1818) (folklorist), 12, 481n26

Private Russian Opera, 504n2, 508n13, 520n29; see also Mamontov, S. I.

Prokofiev, Sergei (1891–1953), xiv

Puccini, Giacomo (1858–1924), 177; *Bohème, La,* 220, 229

Pugno, Raoul (1852–1914) (French pianist), 212, 506n48, 514n45

Purgold, Alexander Nikolayevich (brother of N. N. R-K) 206, 469, 491n21

Purgolds (family of N. N. R-K), 482n5, 491n21

Pushkin, Alexander Sergeyevich (1799–1837), x, 29, 31, 34, 185–86, 188–89, 191, 208, 230, 233, 235, 236–38, 240, 246, 268, 289, 323, 326–27, 358, 364, 380, 414–15, 428, 443–44, 455, 469, 481n23, 490n10, 494n69, 503n22, 505n29, 508nn15,18, 509nn24,29,32, 520n31

Pypin, Alexander Nikolayevich (1833–1904) (folklorist), 190, 231, 504n8

"Pypin group," 146–47

Pypins (house of), 14, 128, 190

Rachmaninov, Sergei Vasilyevich (1873–1943) (pianist, comp.), 312, 339, 353, 373, 375, 403, 406, 420, 455, 527nn34,35, 531n5; *Aleko,* 105, 495n3; *Covetous Knight,* 370, 380; *Lilacs,* 433; Prelude, 534n45; Piano Concerto no. 2 in C minor, 348; *Rock, The* (fantasy), 141; *Variations on a Theme by Chopin,* 397; *Vostochnyi tanets,* 534n45

Racine, Jean Baptiste (1639–1699): *Athalie,* 280, 515n9

Raphael Santi (1483–1520), 30

Rathaus, Daniil Maximovich (1869–?) (poet), 364

Rebikov, Vladimir Ivanovich (1866–1920) (comp.), 382

Reger, Max (1873–1916) (comp.), 375, 396, 422, 432; *Improvisations,* 377; *Schlichte Weisen,* 385; *Serenade,* 531n40; Sonata in C for Violin and Piano, 350, 524n2; *Variations and Fugue on a Theme by Beethoven,* 531n40

Repin, Ilya Efimovich (1844–1930) (painter), 32, 63, 95, 206, 358, 429, 485n13, 490n12

Richter, Hans (1843–1916) (cond.), 220, 223, 224, 225, 231, 253, 299, 300, 315

Richter, Mikhail Ivanovich (brother of N. I. Richter), 225, 245

Richter, Nicholas Ivanovich (1879–1943) (pianist, teacher), 235, 237, 245, 279, 280, 315, 324, 339, 340–41, 353, 377, 380, 381, 383, 385, 387, 393, 394, 397, 402, 403, 443, 447,

466; at R-K, 354, 374–75, 401, 443–44, 447, 451, 456, 458, 462, 469

Riemann, Hugo (1849–1919) (German musicologist), 173

Rimskaya-Korsakova, Elena Georgiyevna (wife of Mikhail Nikolayevich R-K), 444, 458–59

Rimskaya-Korsakova, Maria Nikolayevna (Masha) (1888–1893) (daughter of R-K), 47, 493n64

Rimskaya-Korsakova, Nadezhda Nikolayevna (née Purgold) (1848–1919) (pianist, wife of R-K), 2, 8, 27, 50, 52, 53, 54, 55–56, 61, 63, 66–67, 76, 81–83, 84, 86–87, 88, 89, 91, 97, 99, 104–5, 106, 107, 114–15, 116, 121, 122, 125, 128, 141, 146, 163, 168, 173, 175, 186, 198, 200, 222–23, 226, 228, 231–32, 233, 234, 235, 243, 245, 247, 248, 249, 252, 263, 271, 273, 281, 283, 286–87, 291, 296, 297, 298, 299, 312, 317, 321, 324, 330, 334, 339, 343, 344, 354, 375, 377, 380, 381, 384, 385, 388, 392, 393, 397, 402, 412–13, 416, 420, 427, 428, 447, 448, 452, 453, 454–55, 463, 470, 472, 473–74, 486n22, 491n21, 507n1, 521n12, 526n26, 532n18

Rimskaya-Korsakova, Nadezhda Nikolayevna (Nadya) (1884–?) (youngest daughter of R-K), 81, 122, 324, 340, 343, 364, 367, 370, 392, 393, 419, 422, 426–27, 433, 436, 440, 444, 452, 453, 454, 455, 456, 460, 461, 467, 473, 523n9, 530n26; marries M. O. Steinberg, 537n48

Rimskaya-Korsakova, Sofia Nikolayevna (Sonya) (1875–1948) (eldest daughter of R-K wife of V. P. Trotsky), 125, 139, 164, 203, 226, 229, 231, 245, 247, 257, 280, 324, 328, 330, 334, 340, 380, 393, 392, 409, 443, 451, 454, 458, 462, 477, 519n6, 523n9, 530n26

Rimskaya-Korsakova, Sofia Vasilyevna (1802–1890) (mother of R-K), 12

Rimsky-Korsakov, Andrei Nikolayevich (Andryusha) (1878–1940) (second son of R-K), 35, 44, 53, 81, 89, 107, 122, 189, 245, 260, 296, 297, 298, 330, 334, 383, 388, 406, 411, 420, 425, 453, 461, 474–75, 529n20, 532n18

Rimsky-Korsakov, Mikhail Nikolayevich (Misha) (1873–1951) (eldest son of R-K), 50, 195, 283, 307, 315, 342, 354, 408, 430, 444, 451, 454, 458–59, 461, 462, 469

Rimsky-Korsakov, Nikolai Andreyevich: amateur theatricals, 245–47, 324; and/at the Conservatory, 4, 8–9, 22, 55–56, 161, 260, 344, 363, 381, 389, 407, 411, 426, 440, 502n42, 526n23; as conductor, 3, 6, 15, 62, 99–100, 101, 106, 144, 159, 163, 195, 196, 202–3, 210, 213, 265, 270, 271, 272, 275, 488nn50, 52, 57, 489n4, 501n28, 504nn1,5, 506nn41,51, 508n16, 531nn2,5, 532n12; autobiography (also referred to as "Chronicle," *My Musical Life*, reminiscences), xiv, 48, 125, 366, 391, 392, 394, 397, 471, 487n35, 526n23, 529n25, 530n29; Belyaev Prizes ("Glinka Prizes"), 348–49, 424, 505n23, 523n4; bells, orchestral reproduction of, 38; benefit concert for strike victims; 376–77; biography of: 445, 535n18; censorship problems: 48, 103, 127, 129, 130, 132, 374, 391, 442–45, 468, 477, 498n46, 533n29; death of, 475–78; diary, 391, 397, 407–8, 471, 532n7; dismissal from the Conservatory, 356–61, 363; dream of opera theater, 322–23; family history, 81; folk elements in the works of (songs, motives, themes in folk style), 11–13, 23–24, 29, 31, 70, 84, 115–16, 123, 156–57, 234, 268–70, 285, 309, 329–30, 345, 422, 427–28, 431–32, 438, 442, 484n38, 525n17, 533n33; folksong collection, 11, 241, 269, 416; honorary degrees, memberships, awards, 47, 271, 273, 280, 320, 345–46, 357, 360, 389, 415, 425, 436; influence of Balakirev on, 48, 182–85; interest in religious rites and ceremonies, 81, 124; key-color relationships, 31–32, 40, 50–51, 72–73, 74–75; musical anniversaries, 5, 6–7, 134–35, 161, 215, 270–71, 272–76, 277, 299, 360, 377–78, 435, 513n37, musical autographs, 7, 31, 111, 248, 249, 275–76, 284, 295, 302, 344, 388, 397, 439; musical evenings, 138, 139, 141–43, 145–46, 147, 191–92, 193, 203–4, 205–6, 228, 229–30, 256–57, 281, 339, 340, 350–51, 352, 354, 374, 375–76, 379–80, 383, 384, 388, 395–96, 396–97, 402–3, 418–20, 424–5, 436–37, 443–44; in navy, 37, 51, 188, 205, 390; on art, 32–33, 36–37, 212, 352–53; on conductors, conducting, 21–22, 166, 232; on critics and criticism, 21, 22, 27, 29–30, 32, 66, 97–98, 114, 122, 133, 153, 177–78, 185, 194, 213, 244, 246, 253, 262, 306, 322, 325, 328, 335, 365, 373–74, 404, 405, 418, 424, 445, 448,

455; on death, 174, 397; on friendship; 85; on genius: 156, 246; on melody, harmony, rhythm, 29, 34, 55, 68–69, 73–74, 89, 94, 113, 187–88, 220–21, 237–38, 244, 251, 334, 343, 406, 413, 418, 436–37, 438–39, 442, 456–57, 464, 488n56; on his operas, 94, 121, 130–31, 289–90, 294, 298–99, 305, 316, 329–30, 345, 362, 370, 384, 403, 406–7, 421, 434; on orchestration, 17–18, 20, 30–31, 34–35, 38–40, 41, 61, 88–89, 90, 93–94, 96–97, 106, 113, 127, 151, 193, 200, 220, 228, 245, 289, 326, 329, 398–99, 405, 407, 434, 441, 456–59, 464; on the public, 261, 398; plan for opening a new music school, 361, 370–71, 372, 527n29; politics of, xi–xii, 351, 365, 385, 390, 524n5; portraits of, 204, 206, 247, 248, 249; quartet evenings, 406–8, 420, 421, 425–26, 433–35, 439–40; resignation from Court Chapel, 55, 61; sacred music, 250–51, 257, 511n9; sun worship, pantheism, 70, 71–72, 76

—works: chamber music: *Mazurka on Three Polish Folk Themes* (for violin and piano), 422, 431–32, 533n33; Quintet in B flat, 469, 515n15; Serenade for cello and piano, 489n65; Sextet in A, 282, 515n15; String Quartet in F, 254–55; String Quartet in G, 282, 283–84; Trio in C minor for violin, cello and piano, 285, 516n24

—works; choral: *Collection of Sacred Music* (op. 22), 250–51, 511n9; Dubinushka (folk song), 375, 393, 527n36, 528n38; *Nochevala tuchka zolotaia*, 284; Prelude-cantata *From Homer*, 289, 330, 333, 366, 516n32, 522n16; settings of sacred music used at Court (op. 22b), 257; *Slava*, 127, 273, 298n48; *Song of Oleg the Wise*, 235, 240, 244–45, 286, 289, 509nn32,35; *Switezianka*, 27, 188, 191, 212, 213, 485n2, 503n20; *Tuchki nebesnye*, 284

—works: folk song collection: *100 Russian Folk Songs*, 11, 241, 269, 416

—works: operas:

—*Boyarina Vera Sheloga*, 210, 215, 219, 227, 297, 335, 464, 508n13, 522n17; Lullaby, 232–33, 241; overture, 295

—*Christmas Eve*, xii, 82, 83, 87–88, 91–93, 98–99, 101, 103–5, 106, 108, 110–11, 113, 117, 121, 123, 127, 128–29, 130–36, 139–40,

Rimsky-Korsakov, Nikolai A. (*continued*)
142, 144, 147, 149, 168, 173–4, 176, 200, 210–11, 213, 219, 259, 261, 276–77, 289, 313, 331, 340, 362, 368, 371, 374, 384, 421, 434, 449, 492nn35,42,44, 502n8, 507n54, 516n18; polonnaise, 368; *Suite* from, 405, 410, 532nn12,14
—*Golden Cockerel, The,* xi, xiii, 394, 397, 399, 401, 402, 405, 406–7, 408, 411, 412–16, 417, 418, 420, 421, 423, 425, 433, 435, 436–37, 439, 442–43, 444, 445, 446, 447, 451, 454, 456–58, 459, 466, 468, 470, 471, 473, 477, 481n32, 529n11; Introduction and Wedding March, 440, 441
—*Kashchei the Immortal,* 309–10, 311, 312, 313, 316, 318, 319, 320, 322, 339, 356, 357–59, 365, 369, 370, 373, 391, 392, 397, 413, 424, 442, 449; libretto, 309
—*Legend of the Invisible City of Kitezh, The,* xi, xiii, 319, 328–29, 332, 333, 334, 341, 342, 343–44, 345, 347–48, 350, 351, 352, 354, 361, 362, 363, 367, 368, 370, 371, 373, 381, 382, 383, 384, 389, 394, 398, 401, 403, 404–5, 406, 413, 416–17, 423–24, 437, 441, 443, 444, 453, 471, 492n42, 526n23, 529n9, 533n20, 534n1, 535n10; libretto, 329
—*Maid of Pskov, The,* xi, 19, 29, 31, 38, 44–45, 62, 63, 67, 71, 79, 88, 96, 106, 113, 114–15, 116, 118–19, 122, 131, 152, 172, 177, 182, 188, 195, 199–203, 208–9, 216, 219, 225, 227–28, 231, 233, 242, 249, 257, 259, 261, 274, 277, 291–92, 296–97, 324, 326, 333–34, 335, 339, 347, 363, 369, 373–74, 381, 396, 437, 438, 500n16, 508n13, 526n35, 522n17, 529n4, 535n9; Chorus of the Maidens, 31; libretto, 329; Overture, 76, 295; Prologue; 205, 208, 209, 505n30
—*May Night,* 23, 30, 31, 51, 56, 58, 63, 67, 68–70, 71, 85, 87–88, 90, 91–92, 97, 104–5, 107, 109, 118, 125, 143, 145, 151, 158, 183, 199, 202, 212, 234, 242, 277, 301, 307, 326, 328, 331, 369, 376, 429, 492n40, 494n76, 499n60, 514n49; act 3, 48, 63, 68, 70; libretto, 329; overture, 464
—*Mlada,* 23, 24, 32, 39–40, 62, 71, 83, 97, 121, 142, 150–51, 176, 183, 185, 193, 222, 251, 255, 264, 277, 285, 289, 303, 326–27, 329, 337, 363, 375, 384, 421, 441, 449, 480n17,

483n26, 514n49; act 2, 23–24, 68; act 3 ("Egypt"), 5, 7, 19, 20, 23, 24, 29, 31, 38, 40, 73, 74, 141, 194, 298, 333, 522n19, 532n72; "The Birds," 31; concert arrangement, 405; Introduction, 76; "Kashchei's music," 482n10; "Lithuanian dance," 23; "new" (opera-ballet), 483n26; Procession of the Princes, 270
—*Mozart and Salieri,* xiii, 191–93, 199, 205, 209–10, 212, 213, 216, 219, 226–29, 232–34, 259, 267, 281, 285, 287, 293, 297, 299, 363–64, 378, 396, 424, 493n69, 503nn22,27, 508n13
—*Pan Voyevoda,* 331, 332, 335, 339, 344, 346, 347, 351, 364, 370, 373–74, 422, 431, 433, 506n38, 521n7; Song of the Dying Swan, 346; Suite from, 364
—*Sadko,* xi, 95, 105, 107, 116, 122–23, 130–31, 139, 144, 145, 149, 155–58, 159, 172–74, 176–77, 181–82, 186, 188, 190, 192–202, 205–7, 209–10, 216, 219–20, 226, 230–31, 233, 237–39, 242, 250, 257, 259, 262–65, 267, 271, 275, 277–80, 285–86, 288–90, 316, 330, 334, 347, 367, 373, 382–83, 392, 397–98, 401, 405–6, 412, 419, 440, 484nn36,38, 492n42, 503n27, 505nn21,27, 514n49, 532nn12,16; *Bylina o Volkhe Vseslav'eviche,* 125–26; Findeisen's plan of, 24, 25, 82, 493n57; Lel's song, 62; libretto, 87, 104, 118, 120–21, 127; "Procession of the Sea Monsters," 281; Song of the Viking, 229; Song of the Viking Guest, 203; Wedding Rite, 281
—*Servilia,* 283, 284–86, 287, 299, 305, 308, 316–17, 318, 320–21, 333, 334, 339, 343, 348, 350, 362, 369, 370, 371, 382, 392, 423, 513n34, 516n26, 526n24
—*Snegeurochka* 4, 5, 8, 9, 10, 11–13, 18, 19, 23, 26, 32, 38, 56, 62, 69–71, 80, 83–84, 94, 98, 105, 108, 111, 117, 131, 143, 159–60, 166–67, 193, 202–3, 207, 209–10, 213–14, 216, 219–20, 224–25, 230, 234, 242–44, 257–58, 261–62, 264, 271, 275, 277, 290, 298, 308, 316, 319, 331–32, 334–36, 347, 352, 362, 363, 366, 367, 368, 369, 371, 373, 374, 375, 384, 401, 405, 419, 421, 424, 425, 427–28, 434, 435, 439, 445, 447, 450–51, 456, 461, 462–63, 464, 466, 468, 469–70, 471, 477, 480n19, 497n38, 499n60, 503n8, 514n49, 526n23, 532n12; Ballet of the Birds, 96–97, 451; Chorus of

the Flowers, 31, 96–97, 107, 451, 452, 453; Dance of the Skomorokhi, 237; "Hymn of the Berendeys," 328; Kiev performance, 107; "Kiss scene," 74; Libretto, 329; March of the Berendeys, 31, 51; rights to, 105; Suite from, 102, 220

—Tale of Tsar Saltan, The, xi, 240–41, 242, 243, 244, 249, 250–52, 255, 257–59, 261–63, 265–70, 274, 276, 281, 285–86, 293, 299, 322, 339, 353, 360, 362, 368–70, 372–74, 389, 424–27, 434, 437–40, 468, 471, 477, 492n42, 509n35; libretto, 240, 262; Suite from, 271–72, 325, 408, 405, 517n40, 532n12

—Tsar's Bride, The, 216, 218, 220–22, 225–29, 235, 241–243, 245, 247, 253, 255–56, 258–59, 261–62, 264–65, 267, 271, 280, 285, 287, 289, 291–94, 298–99, 303–4, 311, 316, 328, 334–35, 341, 345, 362, 370–72, 382, 388, 440, 492n42

—works; orchestral: Antar, 3, 7, 17, 29, 41, 52, 62, 74, 77, 109, 140, 174, 183, 185, 188, 192–93, 220, 250, 253, 326, 381, 386, 416, 426, 435–36, 479n4, 503n26, 534n5; At the Grave, prelude, 339; Capriccio espagnol, xiii, 62, 109, 141, 253, 277, 307, 314, 315, 335, 363, 514n49; Easter Overture, xiii, 7, 38, 41, 77, 81, 116, 253, 291, 351, 364, 455; Fantasia on Serbian Themes, 67, 124, 200, 253; Fantasia on Two Russian Themes, 517n40; Funiculi, Funicula, 393, 423, 530n34, 533n34; Mazurka on three Polish songs ("Souvenir de trois chants polonaises"), 431, 533n33; Night on Mount Triglav, 327, 337; Overture on Three Russian Themes, 256; Piano Concerto in C-sharp minor, 3, 7, 120; Sadko, 3, 16–17, 21, 27, 28–29, 41, 93, 126, 150, 152–53, 207, 253, 270, 276, 277, 381; Sheherazade, xiii, 10, 13, 31, 39, 41, 45, 103, 109, 160, 173, 183, 186, 211, 220, 249, 251–52, 253, 326, 363, 384, 395, 481n23, 530n38; Sinfonietta, 139, 265; Skazka, x, 10, 13, 29, 31, 41, 93, 150, 220, 253, 262, 275, 303; Symphony no. 1, 7, 16–17, 40, 62, 67, 78, 277, 451, 499n63, 507n56, 514n40; Symphony no. 3, 40, 140–41, 210, 326, 448

—works: piano: Étude, 2; Novellette, 2; Paraphrases (on a theme by Nikhail Nikolayevich R-K), 50; Paraphrases ("Chopsticks," collective work), 295, 517n45, 517–18n46; Pesen'ka, 318, 443, 519n16, 535n14, Waltz, 2

—works: songs: Anchar, 157, 185, 189, 191, 205, 209, 229, 340, 397; Angel i Demon (duet), 229; books of (opus. nos. 3, 4, 7), 118; Chto v imenitebe moem, 139, 238; Doride, 236–37; Drobitsia, i pleshchet, i bryzzhet volna, 189, 505n24; Ekho, 189; El' i pal'ma, 241; Eshche ia poln, drug moi milyi, 226, 283; Gonets, 229, Gornimy tikho letela dusha nebesami, 371; Gornyi kliuch (duet), 195, 226, 371, 526n23; Grechanka, 208; Hebrew Song, 376; Ia umer ot schast'ia, 208; Iuzhnaia noch', 183, 241, 437; Kolyshetsia more, volna za volnoi, 505n24; Lullaby from Vera Sheloga, 241; Mezh tremia moriami bashnia, 189; Na kholmakh Gruzii, 141, 236–37, 241, 335; Ne penitsia more, 188, 206, 393, 505n24; Ne ver' mne, drug, 505n24; Ne veter, veia s vysoty, 188; Nenastnyi den' potukh, 189, 284; Nespiashchikh solntse, 206; Nimfa, 208, 215, 216, 226, 239, 283, 365, 371, 393, 400, 401, 402, 526n20; Noch', 67, 139; O chem v tishi nochei, 206, 283, 393; Oktava, 188; On spit, velikii Pan, 67, 188; Pan (duet), 189, 191, 280, 371; Pesnia Zuleiki, 139; Pesn' pesnei (Song of Songs) (duet), 189, 280, 371, 376; Poet, 235; Probuzhdenie, 188; Prorok, 189, 191, 205, 209, 229, 230, 233, 335, 410, 509n24; Redeet oblakov letuchaia griada, 186; "Sea-songs," 420; Snovedenia, 208; Son v letniuiu noch', 216, 239–40, 371, 392, 400, 401; 531n1; Srezal sebe ia trostnik, 188; Strekozy (trio), 393; Svezh i dushist troi roskoshnyi venok, 188; Taina, 139; Tikho, tikho more goluboe, 189, 226; Tikho vecher dogoraet, 24–25, 67, 139; U more (song cycle), 204; 505n24; V temnoi roshche zamolik solovei (song), 67; Vostochniaia pesnia, 271; Vostochnyi romans, 141, 241, 376; Vzdymaiutsia volny, kakgovy, 505n24; Zaklinanie, 365; Zvonche zhavoronka pen'e, 188, 376

—works: work on compositions by others:

—Borodin: More (The Sea) (song), 365, 380, 526n20; Prince Igor, 3, 18, 38, 149, 153–55, 459; Sleeping Princess, The (song), 177–78, 371

—Cui: William Ratcliff, 61, 63, 67, 139

—Dargomyzhsky: The Stone Guest, 16, 145, 316, 519n14

—Mussorgsky: Boris Godunov, 7, 17–18, 38,

Rimsky-Korsakov, Nikolai A. (*continued*)
56–58, 61, 66, 67, 75, 134, 135, 138, 142, 143, 144–45, 147, 148, 149, 153, 156, 160, 165, 166, 168–71, 177, 206, 227, 228, 296, 299, 387–88, 424, 426, 462, 465, 466, 467, 468, 469, 482n8, 491n19, 508n13, 535n9, 536n41; *Destruction of Sennacherib, The,* 512n19; *Fair at Sorochintsy, The,* 130–31; 494n75; *Field Marshal, The* (from song cycle, *The Songs and Dances of Death*), 245; *Gopak* (song), 390, 397, 441; *Intermezzo,* 192; *Khovanshchina,* 38, 44, 54, 55, 56–58, 65, 296, 501n39, 531n38; *Kolybel'naia smerti,* 390, 397; *Marriage, The,* 15, 388, 389, 391, 463; *Night on Bald Mountain,* 38, 494n75; *Noch'* (song), 428, 432–33; *Nursery, The* (song cycle), 58, 190; *Po Griby* (song), 390, 397, 441; *S Nianei* (from *The Nursery*), 429, 465; *Serenada smerti* (from *Songs and Dances of Death*), 428, 534n43; *Spi, usni, krestianskii syn* (song), 418, 440–41
—Schumann: *Florestan* (from *Carnaval*), 308, 518n5; *Promenade* (from *Carnaval*), 518n5
—writings: articles on teaching music theory, 282, 515n13; autobiography *(My Musical Life),* see under main entry; critical analysis of *Snegurochka,* 366; critical articles, 19, 526n24; *Muzkal'nye stat'i i zametki* (Articles and notes on music), 483n15, 486n22, 515n13; notes on aesthetics, 59; *On Poetic Images in Music* (unrealized), 41; *Textbook of Harmony,* 311, 519n7; textbook of orchestration, 366, 368, 369, 389, 394, 398–99, 413, 420, 434, 452, 462, 463, 464, 465, 470, 526n23; *Treatise on Orchestration,* 14, 481n32
Rimsky-Korsakov, Peter Voinovich (1861–?) (nephew of R-K), 43
Rimsky-Korsakov, Vladimir Nikolayevich (Volodya) (1882–?) (youngest son of R-K), 81, 122, 245, 246, 280, 324, 334, 340, 368, 377, 388, 389, 406, 417–18, 420, 425, 431, 447, 449, 454, 467, 472, 475, 523n9, 530n26, 532n18
Rogova, Alexandra Kapitonovna (the R-Ks' dressmaker), 245
Romer, Feodor Emilyevich (1838–1906) (journalist), 249, 280
Rossini, Gioacchino (1792–1868): *Barber of Seville,* 104, 130

Rostovsky, Nikolai Abramovich (tenor), 392
Rostovtseva, Alexandia Emelyanova (1872–?) (mezzo-soprano), 206, 226, 266
Rozanov, Vasily Vasilyevich (1856–1919) (critic), 323, 520n31
Rozenov, Emile Karlovich (1861–1935) (pianist, comp.), 242, 373, 510n45, 527n37, 528n37
Rozhdestvensky, Z. P. (Vice-Admiral), 340, 523n10
Rubets, Alexander Ivanovich (1837–1913) (collector of Ukrainian folksongs), 70, 127; *216 Little Russian Folk Songs,* 84, 491n32
Rubinstein, Anton Grigoryevich (1829–1894) (pianist, comp., founder of SP Conservatory and its director 1862–1867 and 1887–1891), 1, 5, 7, 8, 22, 44, 46, 60, 66, 78, 84, 101, 106, 190, 231, 286, 287, 299, 369, 384, 448, 480n10, 486nn21,27, 489nn2,6, 493n68, 494nn73,79,80, 497n33, 518nn5,46, 521n10; *Azra,* 100, 494n84; death of, 97; *Demon, The,* 100, 301, 402; *Don Quixote,* 100, 494n84, *Feramors,* 116, 497n34; *Maccabees, The,* 100, 376; Melody no. 1, 2; *Moses,* 494n84, *Persian Songs,* 100, 139, 141, 494n84; Piano Concerts no. 4, 494n84; Piano Sonata no. 2—Theme and Variations, 2; Piano Sonata no. 3, 2; Piano Sonata no. 4—Scherzo, 2; *Prince Rostislav,* (song), 494n84; songs, 141; *Slykhali l' vy,* 206; *Soirées de Saint-Petersbourg,* 2; Symphony no. 3, 99; *Tower of Babel, The,* 100, *Vine, The,* 494n84
Rubinstein, Nikolai Grigoryevich (1835–1881) (pianist, cond., founder of Moscow Conservatory and its director 1886–1881); *Feuillet d'album,* 2; *Waltz in A flat,* 2, 36, 290, 516n34
Rückert, Friedrich (1788–1866) (German orientalist and poet; trans. of *Mahabhrata*), 484n41
Rühlmann, Franz (1868–1948) (cond.), 450
Runge, Alexandra Karlovna (1868–?) (soprano), 91–92
Russian Musical Society, 2–5, 45, 46, 47, 53, 93, 107, 110, 126, 131, 212, 217, 223, 244–45, 271, 273, 275, 300, 480nn10,11,13, 483nn17,20, 487n43, 488n57, 495n8, 496n22, 497n41, 499nn2,61, 507n6, 513n36, 514n43, 515n15, 518n48, 522nn2,19,20, 524n2, 526n27; Board of Directors, 502n42; Central Board of

Directors, 359, 360–61; concerts, 3–4, 24–25, 45, 53, 212, 483nn17,20, 496n22, 499n61, 513n36; Directorate, 371, 377; Moscow branch, 272; Odessa branch, 62; quartet evenings, 52, 58; St. Petersburg Branch, 272, 488n59, 498n44; Symphonic Evenings, 272, 275, 280, 300, 333, 337, 480n9, 496n23, 498n55, 521n1, 524n8

Russian Opera Society, 530n31

Russian Private Opera Company, 194, 249

Russian Symphony Concerts, 2–3, 7, 15, 46, 47, 53, 54, 60, 63, 93, 96, 102, 108, 140–41, 146, 178, 192, 195, 212–13, 215, 217–18, 220, 227–28, 240, 241, 243, 244, 254, 256, 265, 270, 303–4, 314, 321, 326, 335, 340, 385, 386, 395, 396, 400, 440–41, 446–47, 479nn2,3, 480n5, 482n34, 488nn50,57, 489n4, 504nn1,5, 506nn41,51,52,53, 507n54, 508n16, 512n18, 522nn1,15, 523n11; rehearsals, 60–61; R-K conducting, 99–100, 106, 110

Rybnikov, Pavel Nikolayevich (1832–1885) (folklorist), 87, 485n7

Sacchetti, Liberius Antonovich (1852–1916) (music historian), 28; *Iz oblasti estetiki i muzyki,* 485n7; "Ob otnoshenii muzyki k tekstu," 485n7

Safonov, Nikolai Matveyevich (1865–?) (tenor), 153

Safonov, Vasily Ilyich (1852–1918) (pianist, cond.), 107, 193, 212, 240, 243, 251–52, 271, 272, 286, 298, 307, 325, 366, 495n8, 510n47, 512n11, 526nn21,22

St. Petersburg Conservatory, x, 4, 22, 40–41, 42, 44–45, 159, 162, 285–86, 298, 322, 354–57, 359–61, 363, 371, 377, 389, 407–8, 426, 440, 455, 476, 485n7, 486n21, 497n35, 509n25, 515n2, 526n21, 527n29; Glinka and Rubinstein museums, x; Large Hall, 241

Saint-Saëns, Camille (1835–1921), 89, 162, 253, 268, 406, 409, 410, 415; *Barbares, Les,* 295, 333; *Caprice arabe,* 281; *Danse macabre,* 268, 513n36; *Oratorio de Noël,* 273; *Peut-être,* 139; *Phaëton,* 281; *Rouet d'Omphale, Le,* 281; *Samson et Dalila,* 143, 164, 223, 433, 444, 502n49; Violin Concerto no, 3, 300

Sakhnovsky, Yury Sergeyevich (1866–1930) (comp.), 296, 298, 348, 350

Salias, Count Eugène (Salias) de Tournemir (1840–1908) (writer): *In Moscow,* 472

Salina, Nadezhda Vasilyevna (1864–1956) (soprano), 325, 441, 535n12

Samuel, Adolphe (Belgian comp.; founder and dir. of Les Concerts populaires de Bruxelles), 512n13

Samus, Vasily Maximovich (1852–1903) (baritone), 163

Sanderson, Sibyl (1865–1903) (soprano), 142

Sandulenko, Alexander Prokofyevich (amateur singer), 380, 383, 385, 394, 447, 448

Santis, Mikhail Ludvigovich (1826–1880) (pianist), 521n10

Sazonova, Alexandra Feodorovna (soprano), 404

Scarlatti, Alessandro (1659–1725), 433

Schiller, Johann Christoph Friedrich von (1759–1805), 516n22; *Ode to Joy,* 501n26

Schillings, Max von (1868–1933) (comp., cond.), 208, 533n32; *Ingwelde,* 210, 211, 271

Schindler, Anton (1795–1864) (violinist, cond., early biographer of Beethoven), ix

Schmidt, Peter Petrovich (lieut. of Black Sea Fleet), 386

Schmüller, Alexander (1880–1933) (violinist), 396

Schopenhauer, Arthur (1788–1860), 304

Schubert, Franz (1797–1828), 21, 38, 210, 255, 304; "Auf dem Wasser zu singen," 196; Symphony no. 9 in C major, 113, 496n23; Quartet in A minor, 407

Schuch, Ernst von (1846–1914) (cond. of Dresden Opera), 220

Schumann, Robert (1810–1856), 17, 27, 33, 45, 67–68, 82, 89, 147, 156, 210, 225, 291, 325, 328, 424, 444, 491n26, 493n56, 500n18, 509n26, 521n2, 522n20; *Andante,* 281; *Carnaval,* 223, 308, 314, 518n5; *Dichterliebe,* 304; *Florestan,* 308; *Genoveva,* 149–52, 501nn23,24,25; *Kreisleriana,* 383, 403; *Manfred* Overture, 492n50; *Paradies und die Peri, Das,* 93; "Vogel als Prophet," 2, 262

Schütt, Eduard (1865–1933) (student), 92

Scriabin, Alexander Nikolayevich (1872–1915), 111, 113, 138, 185, 299, 304, 341, 342, 354, 375–76, 401, 403, 410, 412, 432, 443, 497n37, 499n1, 528n40, *Élègie,* 531n4; 512n11, 531n5; Étude in D-sharp minor, 112, Étude in G-

Sciabin, Alexander Nikolayevich (*continued*) sharp minor, 112; Etude in D-flat (for left hand), 401; Four Preludes, op. 33, 341; *Mystère,* 532n15; *Nocturne* in D flat, 374–75; Piano Concerto in F-sharp minor, 446, 506n51; Piano Sonata no. 3 (op. 23), 348; Piano Sonata no. 4 (op. 30), 348; *Poem of Ecstasy,* 410; Poems (op. 12), 341; Prelude in E minor, 212; *Rêverie,* 326–27; Symphony no. 1, 265, 290, 342, 354, 385; Symphony no. 2, 303–4

Scriabina, Vera Ivanovna (1875–1920) (pianist, wife of A. Scriabin), 298, 446

Scado, Pierre (1806–1864) (French music critic), 27

Sekar-Rozhansky, Anton Vladislavovich (1863–1925) (tenor), 196, 201, 216, 226, 245, 266, 373, 511n55

Selyuk-Raznatovskaya, Serafima Frolovna (mezzo-soprano), 201

Semenov, Benjamin Petrovich (folklorist), 25

Semenovs, 31

Sementkovsky, Rostaslav Ivanovich (1846–?) (journalist): "Ideals of Art, The," 95

Senilov, Vladimir Alexeyevich (1875–1918) (comp.): *Krugi,* 534n45; *Vozrashchenie,* 534n45

Senkovsky, Osip Ivanovich (1800–1858) (writer): *Antar,* 479n4

Serebryakov, Konstantin Terentyevich (1852–1919) (bass), 214, 242, 278, 292, 317, 320, 374, 375, 406, 423–24

Sergei Alexandrovich, Grand Duke (Gov. Gen. of Moscow), 62

Sergei Mikhailovich, Grand Duke, 273

Sergennois, I. (French translator), 503n25

Serov, Alexander Nikolayevich (1820–1871) (comp., music critic), 14, 43, 46, 66, 82, 96, 124–25, 468, 480n13, 486n24, 494n73, 521n5; *Judith,* 46, 417; *Power of the Fiend, The,* 43, 241; *Rogneda,* 382

Serov, Valentin Alexandrovich (1865–1911) (painter, son of A. N. Serov), 204, 206, 247, 447

Serova, Valentina Semenovna (1846–1924) (comp., wife of A. Serov), 301

Servirog, Alexander Alexandrovich (R-K's doctor), 458, 459, 461, 472, 475

Sgambati, Giovanni (1841–1914) (pianist, comp.), 94

Shambinago, Sergei Konstantinovich (1871–1948) (lit. historian), 493n62

Sharonov, Vasily Semyonovich (1867–1929) (bass baritone), 244–45, 275, 318, 342, 349, 376, 403, 416

Shashalskaya (mezzo-soprano), 268

Shcheglov, Ivan Leontievich (pseud. of J. L. Leontiev) (1856–1911) (humorist): *Guest Star,* 324; *Nonsense,* 245, 246, 511nn56,57; *Women's Nonsense,* 324

Shcherbachev, Nikolai Vladimirovich (1853–?) (comp., pianist), *Paraphrases,* 491n23

Sheffer, Alexander Nikolayevich (comp.), 80, 352

Shein, Pavel Vasilyevich (1826–1900) (folklorist) 84; *Belorusskie narodnye pesni,* 493n61

Sheinin, Naum Ilyich (violinist), 406, 407

Shelley, Percy Bysshe (1792–1822): *Prometheus Unbound,* 443

Shenshins (Parmen Petrovich, Sasha, and Volodya, relatives of Yastrebtsev), 320

Sheremetyev, Count Alexander Dmitriyevich (1859–1931) (amateur musician), 160, 293, 333, 501n23, 517n40, 522n16

Sheremetyev, Count Sergei Dmitriyevich (1844–1918) (director of Court Chapel), 66, 273, 490n18, 522n16

Shestakova, Ludmila Ivanova (1816–1906) (sister of M. I. Glinka), 48, 60, 66, 91, 93, 114, 125, 141, 165, 233, 346–47, 390, 491n21, 536n32

Shestakova, Olga (daughter of L. Shestakova), 329

Shevelev, Nikolai Artemyevich (1874–1929) (baritone), 266

Shkafer, Vasily Petrovich (1867–1937) (tenor), 226–27, 266, 403, 416, 506n49

Shostakovich, Dmitri, xiv

Shröder, Karl (?–1889) (owner of piano factory in Petersburg; also of hall where musical and other events were held), 371, 421, 527nn29,30, 530n35, 533nn26,31

Shtakelberg, Konstantin Karlovich (head of court orchestra), 519n8

Shtrup, Nikolai Martynovich (1871–1915) (friend of Yastrebtsev), 25, 29, 31, 35, 53, 58, 59, 68, 71, 104, 115, 128, 190, 208; at R-K, 50, 76, 79, 96, 99, 117, 120, 158, 191, 205–6, 484n36, 494n74

Sibelius, Jean (1865–1957), 402; Symphony no. 3, 420, 533*n*30

Siloti, Alexander Ilyich (1863–1945) (pianist and cond.), 230, 259, 312, 333, 334, 358, 361, 369, 370, 371, 375, 376, 395, 399, 404, 422, 433, 435, 455, 473, 517*n*36, 522*n*16, 527*nn*28,29, 528*n*38, 531*nn*2,40, 533*nn*30,32,34,35, 534*n*5

Siloti (née Tretyakova), Vera Pavlovna (1866–1942) (wife of A. Siloti), 366, 422, 430, 433

Sinitsyna, Serafima Andreyevich (?–1920) (mezzo-soprano), 296

Sinkiewicz, Henrik (1846–1916) (writer), 84

Sirotinin (R-K's doctor), 460, 461

Skrydlov, Nikolai Illarionovich (1844–1925) (classmate of R-K), 340, 410

Slatin, Ilya Ilyich (1845–1931) (pianist, cond.), 533*n*32

Slatina, Elena Viktorovna (soprano), 342

Slavina, Marina Alexandrovna (1858–1951) (mezzo-soprano), 91, 92, 128–29, 224, 257, 293, 325, 521*n*1

Słowacki, Juliusz (1808–1849) (poet), Lilla Weneda, 24, 25, 172

Smetana, Bedřich (1824–1884), 158, 501*n*36; quartet "From My Life," 421

Smirnov, Alexander Vasilyevich (1870–1942) (baritone), 224, 258, 320, 404, 531*n*5

Smolensky, Stepan Vasilyevich (1848–1909) (musicologist, director of the Synod School), 286, 315

Sobinov, Leonid Vitalyevich (1872–1936) (lyric tenor), 296, 299, 338, 524*n*6

Sokolov, I. Ya. (bass), 201

Sokolov, Nikolai Alexandrovich (1859–1922) (comp. professor at SP Conservatory) 8, 19, 45, 66, 71, 99, 307–8, 315, 327, 389, 497*n*37, 516*n*23, 518*n*5, 519*n*17, 529*n*21; at R-K, 29, 66, 112; Quartet no. 2, 482*n*13; Quartet no. 3, 434

Sokolov, Yury M. (Russian folklorist): Russian Folklore, 483*n*26

Sokolovs (relatives of R-K), 88

Sokolovskaya, Alina Alexandrovna (soprano), 114

Solovyov, Nikolai Feopemptovich (1846–1916) (critic, comp., professor at SP Conservatory), 22, 27, 28, 40, 45, 46, 47, 49, 77, 98, 105–6, 114, 133, 141, 144, 152, 163, 225, 235, 245, 253, 268, 307, 485*nn*4,8, 499*n*58,

500*nn*6,14,16, 510*n*51, 511*n*53, 512*n*12, 520*n*31, 526*n*21; Cordelia, 77, 117, 434, 492*n*47, 497*n*38; Ei, ukhnem, 353; Klin Klinom, 145 524*n*8; Vakula the Smith, 5, 8, 77, 480*nn*13,19, 492*n*47

Solovyov, Vladimir Sergeyevich (1853–1900) (professor), 323, 361

Sorokin, A. P. (narrator of byliny), 484*n*38

Spendiarov, Alexander Afanasyevich (1871–1928) (comp., cond.), 244, 257, 433, 436, 437, 440, 519*n*16; Pesn' Gafiza, 448; Tol'ko vstrechu ulybku tvoiu, 448

Spengler, Dr. Alexander Eduardovich (1855–1941) (Glazunovs' family doctor), 206, 225, 452

Spohr, Ludwig (1784–1859) (violinist), 260

Stakhovich, Mikhail Alexandrovich (1819–1858) (collector and publisher of folk songs): A Collection of Russian Folk Songs, 269, 481*n*26

Stanislavsky, M. V. (art and music critic, journalist), 141, 500*n*6

Stanislavsky, Konstantin Sergeyevich (family name Alexeyev) (1863–1938) (director, producer), 330

Stanislavsky Theater, 323

Stasov, Dmitri Vasilyevich (1828–1918) (lawyer, one of the founders of the Russian Musical Society and SP Conservatory; brother of V. V. Stasov), 70, 124, 392, 395, 446, 487*n*33, 523*n*12

Stasov, Vladimir Vasilyevich (1824–1906) (art and music critic, ideologist of the "Mighty Handful," major figure in cultural life of nineteenth-century Russia), 3, 5, 6–7, 21, 29, 32, 33, 35, 41–42, 44, 45, 53, 56, 57, 59, 63, 69, 71, 91, 93, 103, 105, 108, 124, 138, 141, 164, 175, 177, 182, 190–91, 193, 197–98, 200, 214, 219, 222, 228–29, 243, 245, 255, 260, 270, 278, 287, 293, 299, 307–308, 310, 313, 318, 328, 340, 347, 358, 367, 375, 386, 390, 395–96, 396, 455, 480*n*15, 483*n*18, 484*n*36, 485*nn*10,16, 486*n*26, 488*n*60, 489*nn*1,66, 492*n*37, 493*n*58, 502*n*48, 504*n*16, 505*n*29, 507*n*3, 509*n*20, 510*n*48, 517*n*41, 521*nn*6,10, 523*nn*10,12, 526*n*26, 527*n*28, 528*nn*38,39, 529*n*14, 530*nn*37, 38, 531*n*38, 535*n*9, celebration honoring, 60; death of, 392, 393; "Nikolai Andreyevich Rimskii-Korsakov," 480*n*16; at R-K, 99, 111–12, 125–26, 191–92, 201, 203, 225, 256–57, 279, 281, 307–8, 312, 315,

Stasov, Vladimir Vasilyevich (*continued*)
327, 339, 340–41, 363, 379–80, 386, 392
Stasova, Poliksena Stepanovna (1839–1918) (wife of D. V. Stasov), 393, 396
Stasovs, 53, 163, 383, 491*n*21
Steinberg, Lev Petrovich (1870–1945) (cond.), 80
Steinberg, Maximilian Oseyevich (1883–1946) (comp., pedagogue, son-in-law of R-K), x, xiv, 406, 407, 408, 417–21, 424–26, 428, 430, 433–34, 436, 440, 444, 447, 449, 451–52, 454–55, 456, 459–61, 465, 467, 473–77, 481*n*32, 526*n*23, 527*n*32, 531*n*1, 534*n*43, 536*n*33; *Ballet Suite:* Gavotte and Polka, 429; *Fialka* (The Violet), 530*n*33; *Ia zhdal tebia* (I Waited for You), 530*n*33; *Kolybel'naia* (Lullaby), 530*n*33; *Lesnye travy,* 420; married R-K's daughter Nadezhda Nikolayevna, 537*n*48; *Posledniaia zvezda* (Last Star, The), 534*n*45; *Poslednii luch* (Last Ray, The), 420; *Procession* in F major, 406; Quartet no. 1 (in A), 407; at R-K, 448, 456, 458, 462, 469, 470; *Rusalka,* 397; Symphony no. 1, 443, 448, 465, 535*n*20; Symphony no. 2, 444, 446, 455, 471–72; *Variations* (op. 2), 393, 396; *Zabytoe* (Forgotten), 429; *Zacharovannyi grot* (Enchanted Grotto), 530*n*33
Stoyanovsky, Nikolai Ivanovich (1820–1900) (v.-pres. of Russian Musical Society), 163
Strakhova, N. I. (contralto), 201, 226, 266
Strauss, Richard (1864–1949), 188, 204, 208, 233, 237, 253–54, 281, 291, 300–1, 315, 330, 339, 365, 375, 382, 409–10, 419, 422, 432–33, 468, 509*n*26; *Also sprach Zarathustra,* 200, 209, 254; *Don Juan,* 233; *Don Quixote,* 305; *Ein Heldenleben,* 303, 304–5, 314–15, 519*n*9; *Guntram,* 209; *Symphonia domestica,* 350, 524*n*2; *Till Eulenspiegel,* 148
Stravinskaya, Anna Kirillovna (mother of Igor and Gury Stravinsky), 426
Stravinskaya, Yekaterina Gavrilovna (Igor Stravinsky's wife), 377–80, 382, 424, 444
Stravinsky, Feodor Ignatyevich (1843–1902) (bass), 132, 163, 164, 165, 207, 505*n*29
Stravinsky, Gury Feodorovich (brother of Igor Stravinsky), 371, 374, 377, 380, 433, 436, 444, 454
Stravinsky, Igor Feodorovich (1882–1971), 327–28, 334, 340, 343–44, 345, 362, 374–75, 377,

378, 380, 382, 393, 394–95, 407, 408–9, 419, 422, 424, 436, 441, 443–44, 449, 523*n*9; *Bees, The,* 454; *Comic Little Songs,* 339; *Conductor and Tarantula,* 386; *Faun and Shepherdess,* 440, 441, 534*n*8; Piano Sonata in F-sharp minor, 353; *Pastorale,* 419, 427, 534*n*45; Symphony no. 1, 421, 434, 534*n*8; song *Vesna* (Spring) ("Zvony, stony, perezvony"), 419–20, 427, 429, 434*n*45
Stravinsky brothers, 401, 418, 426, 433, 436, 444, 446
Struve, Peter Bernhardovich (1870–1944) (economist), 386
Suk, Vása (1861–1933) (violinist), 216, 255, 260, 346, 347, 364, 441, 443, 465, 533*n*32
Sukhomlina, M. P. (Antarova) (mezzo-soprano), 160, 163
Suvorin, Alexei Alexeyevich (son of A. S. Suvorin), 249, 338, 522*n*21
Suvorin, Alexei Sergeyevich, (1834–1912) (journalist), 66, 243, 280, 485*n*10, 490*n*17, 510*n*50, 515*n*8
Swert, Jules de (1843–1891) (cellist): Cello Concerto no. 1, 272

Taneyev, Alexander Sergeyevich (1850–1918) (comp.), 410, 456; Symphony no. 1, 46, 377
Taneyev, Sergei Ivanovich (1856–1915) (comp., pianist, pedagogue), 101, 222, 290, 353, 377, 397, 410, 426, 456, 494*n*83, 503*nn*12,13, 504*n*16, 519*n*16, 531*n*5; *Nocturne,* 300; *Oresteia,* 58–59, 62, 178, 210, 249, 256, 303, 489*n*64, 494*n*83; *Ostrovok,* 385; *Russian Song,* 300; Symphony no. 1 in C minor, 321, 348, 374, 494*n*83
Tartakov, Joachim Viktor Viktorovich (baritone), 271, 376, 406, 536*n*31
Tchaikovsky, Modest Ilyich (1850–1916) (librettist, brother of P. I. Tchaikovsky), 101, 200; *Reminiscences (The Life of P. I. Tchaikovsky),* 289, 516*n*31; librettist of Arensky's *Nal and Damayanti,* 496*n*20; librettist of Napravnik's *Dubrovsky,* 490*n*10
Tchaikovsky, Peter Ilyich (1840–1893), 3, 6, 19, 23, 24, 45, 52, 58, 66, 76, 85, 88, 93–94, 97–98, 105, 109–10, 112–13, 136, 160–62, 180, 187–88, 199, 200, 211, 225–26, 240, 258, 268, 281, 287–88, 291–92, 295, 313, 316, 325, 333, 436, 480*n*14, 486*nn*28,29,30, 487*n*31, 488*n*50, 489*n*5, 493*nn*56,68, 495*nn*4,6,12,14, 496*n*22,

502n41, 506nn44, 45, 507n12, 508n12, 509n26, 512n20, 516n28, 517n46, 519n8, 521nn2,10, 522n20, 530n36, 531n5, 534n39; *Andante and Finale* (op. 79), 179, 210, 503n12; articles and notes on music (1868–76), 505n17; *Capriccio italien,* 327; *Cherevichki* (see *Vakula the Smith*), 77, 399, 492n46; Concert Fantasy for Piano, 3, 480n9; as conductor, 46–47, 49; *Cradle Song,* 384; death of, 53; *Enchantress, The,* 53, 182; *Eugene Onegin,* 4, 16, 27, 109, 126, 150, 152, 365; *Francesca da Rimini,* 54, 55, 160, 394; graduation cantata, 501n26; *Kolybel'naia,* 393; *Manfred,* 166; *Mazeppa,* 329; memorial concert for, 54; *Nutcracker, The,* 19, 46, 62, 126, 181, 483n17; "O Maria, Maria" (arioso from *The Oprichnik*), 517n38; *Oprichnik, The,* 142–43, 177, 292, 374, 503n9; Overture—Fantasy *Hamlet,* 3, 480n9; Piano Concerto no. 1 in B-flat minor, 193, 290, 516n34, 522n318; song *Pogodi* (Wait) (op. 16, no. 2), 289; *Queen of Spades, The,* 77, 117, 150, 365; 415; *Romance,* 2; *Romeo and Juliet* Overture, 19, 74, 152, 160, 223, 308, 483n17; Scherzo à la russe, 2; Second Suite, 227; *Sleeping Beauty, The,* 27, 46, 181; *Snegurochka* (Incidental music to Ostrovsky's *Snow Maiden*), 230, 295, 399; *Song Without Words,* 2; Symphony no. 3, 255, 394; Symphony no. 4, 55, 235, 271, 312, 315, 409, 512n11; Symphony no. 5, 45, 160, 232, 315; Symphony no. 6, 53 160, 166, 225, 253, 394; *Tempest, The,* 54, 308, 441, 504n6, 530n38; unfinished piano concerto (*Andante and Finale for Piano and Orchestra,* op. 79), 179, 210, 503n12; *Vakula the Smith* (rev. and renamed *Cherevichki*), 492n46; Violin Concerto, 337; *Voyevoda, The* (symphonic ballad), 270, 395, 423; *Waltz,* 2

Telyakovsky, Vladimir Arkadyevich (1861–1951) (director of Moscow State Theaters), 259, 305, 373, 413, 444, 445, 466, 468, 471, 477, 510n42

Thomson, César (1857–1931) (violinist), 83

Tiesenhausen, Baron, 501n31

Tigranian (Tigranov), Nikolai Fadeyevich (1856–1951) (comp.), 519n16

Timoteyev, Andrei Alexandrovich (tenor), 164

Timofeyev, Grigory Nikolayevich (1861–1919) (music critic), 128–29, 139, 206, 225–26, 243, 264, 313, 320, 335, 346, 359, 360, 376, 382, 392, 393, 404, 418, 435–36, 466, 510n48, 513n28, 531n41; at R-K, 139, 206, 210, 225, 226, 314–15

Tolstoi, Alexei Konstantinovich, Count (1817–1875), xii, 139, 185, 188, 189, 364, 486n23, 505n24; *Don Juan,* 482n12; *Tsar Feodor Ionnovich,* 267

Tolstoy, Leo Nikolayevich, Count (1828–1910) 34, 196–99, 246, 281, 291, 489n66, 504nn13,15,16, 537n42; *Anna Karenina,* 59, 197, 198; *Boyhood,* 198; *Childhood,* 198; *Confession,* 118; *War and Peace,* 59, 197, 198, 472; *What Is Art,* 206, 504nn13,15,16

Tolstoy, Victor Pavlovich (1843–1907) (pianist), 526n21

Tolstaya, Sofia Andreyevna (1842–1919) (wife of Leo Nikolayevich Tolstoy), 178, 197, 504n13

Tolstoys, 197–99

Tomars, Joseph Semenovich (1867–1934) (tenor), 468

Tornagni, Iola Ignatyevna (wife of Chaliapin), 298, 518n51

Trepov Dmitri Feodorovich (1855–1906) (Gov. Gen. of SP), 389

Trifonov, Porfiry Alexeyevich (1844–1896) (music critic), 34, 35, 59, 66, 87, 99, 114, 117, 128, 497n38; death of, 156; at R-K, 33, 76, 79, 99

Triganov, Nikolai Fadeyevich (1856–1951) (comp.), 519n16

Troitskaya, Sofia Nikolayevna (1875–1948) *see* Rimskaya-Korsakova, Sofia Nikolayevna

Troitsky, Vladimir Petrovich (lawyer), 245, 279, 283, 313, 316, 324, 330, 339, 350, 351, 354, 377, 389

Troitskys, 347, 380, 385

Trubetskoi, Prince Sergei Nikolayevich (1862–1905) (professor), 360

Truffi, Joseph Antonovich (1850–1925) (cond.), 216

Tsabel, Albert Gentrikhovich (1835–1910) (harpist), 345

Tsereteli, A. A., Prince (impresario, manager of the Kharkov Private Opera Co.), 216, 241, 256, 510n43, 511n58, 513n24, 523n15

Tsvetkova, Elena Yakovlevna (1872–1929) (soprano), 159, 227, 266

Tugarinova, Claudia Alexeyevna (contralto), 320

Tur, Vladimir Antonovich (?–1907) (business manager, SP Conservatory), 45, 359

Turgenev, Ivan Sergeyevich (1818–1883), 34, 129, 160, 246, 489n52; *Asya,* 513n29; *Fathers and Sons,* 332; *On the Eve,* 332

Turygina, L.: *Rukovodstvo k istorii muzyki* (Handbook of music history), 497n38

Tushmalov, Mikhail Mikhailovich (?–1896) (student of R-K), 15, 482n35

Twain, Mark (1835–1910): *Adam's Diary,* 472

Tyumnev, Ilya Feodorovich (1855–1927) (novelist librettist), 209, 230–31, 329, 331, 332, 498n45, 521n7, 522n13

Tyutchev, Feodor Ivanovich (1803–1873) (poet), 326

Udine, Jean d' (1870–1938) (French writer on music), 250

Ugrinovich, Grigory Petrovich (d. 1918) (tenor), 92, 132, 139, 214, 406

Uland, Ludwig (1787–1862) (poet), 208

Ulybyshev, Alexander Dmitriyevich (1794–1858) (writer on music), 537n46

Usatov, Dmitry Andreyevich (1847–1913) (tenor), 298

Vaksel, Platon Lvovich (1844–1919) (music critic), 115, 496n28

Valter, Victor Grigoyevich (1865–1935) (violinist, music critic), 93, 282, 430, 454, 471, 534n1

Van-der-Pals (student of M. O. Steinberg; patron of Siloti concerts), 473

Van Dyck, Ernest (1861–1923) (tenor), 491n25

Vardot, Mme (mezzo-soprano), 163

Varlamov, Alexander Yegorovich (1801–1848) (comp.), 19, 483n14

Varlikh, Mme (soprano, student at SP Conservatory), 163, 164

Varzar (tenor, student at SP Conservatory), 163, 164

Vasilevsky, Romuald Viktorovich (1853–1919) (producer), 333

Vasnetsov, Apollinary Mikhailovich (1856–1933) (painter), 218, 250, 403, 507n8

Vasnetsov, Viktor Mikhailovich (brother of A. M. Vasnetsov), 214, 222, 507n3

Veimarn, Pavel Platonovich (1857–1901) (music critic), 114, 253, 510n51, 512n12

Veinberg, Peter Isayevich (1830–1908) (historian), 194, 196, 392, 504n9

Veinberg, Yevgeny Petrovich (critic), 194

Velichko, Vasily Lvovich (pseud. of V. Voronetsky) (1860–1903) (poet and journalist), 498n45

Verdi, Giuseppe (1813–1901), 47, 153, 166, 265–66; *Aida,* 456; "Donna e mobile, La," 266; *Otello,* 94; *Quatro Pezzi sacri: Stabat Mater, Te Deum, Ave Maria, Laudi alla Vergine,* 513n30; works, 265

Vereshchagin, Alexander Vasilyevich (1850–1909) (brother of V. V. Vereshchagin; general, writer), 392

Vereshchagin, Vasily Vasilyevich (1842–1904) (painter of battle scenes), 143, 340, 490n12

Veretinnikova, A. I. (soprano), 266

Vernadsky, Vladimir Ivanovich (1863–1945) (professor), 360

Verstovsky, Alexei Nikolayevich (1799–1862) (comp.): *Askold's Tomb,* 19, 483n14

Verzhbilovich, Alexander Valeryanovich (1850–1911) (cello virtuoso), 306, 376, 407, 517n36

Vieuxtemps, Henri (1820–1881) (violinist, comp.), 512n13; Violin Concerto no. 5, 492n50

Vinkstern, A. A. (librettist of S. I. Taneyev's *Oresteia*), 489n64

Vinogradsky, Alexander Nikolayevich (1856–1912) (cond.), 439, 533n32

Viskovaty, P. A.: *Katerina* (libretto for proposed R-K opera, unrealized), 484n42

Vladimir Alexandrovich, Grand Duke (1847–1909), 128, 129, 498n54

Volkonsky, Prince Sergei Mikhailovich (1860–1937) (director of Imperial Theaters), 240, 250, 258, 259, 279–80, 286, 510n42, 511n7

Voltaire, François Marie Arouet de (1694–1778), 30, 208

Von Bool, Nikolai Konstantovich (1860–1938) (comptroller of Imperial Theaters), 437, 466

Vorontsov-Dashko, Count Illarion Ivanovich (1837–1916) (minister), 102, 130

Vrubel, Mikhail Alexandrovich (1865–1910) (painter), 203, 205–6, 219, 283, 311, 365, 511n4

Vsevolozhsky, Ivan Alexandrovich (1835–1909) (dir. of the Imperial Theaters), 62–63, 77, 104, 116, 128, 129, 142, 143, 176, 177, 220, 498nn54,56

Vyazemskaya, Princess (mother of S. Dmitriyevich), 490n18

Vyshnegradsky, Alexander Ivanovich (amateur comp.): *Vision of St. Anthony,* 385

Wagner, Cosima (1837–1930) (wife of Richard Wagner), ix, 300

Wagner, Richard (1813–1883), x, xi, 9, 14, 27, 33, 34, 35, 36, 37, 39, 41, 43, 54, 69, 78, 83, 86–91, 93, 150, 156, 162, 173, 187, 209, 235, 254, 263–64, 268, 271–72, 300, 306, 338, 382–84, 419, 424, 432–33, 441, 482n9, 485n6, 509n26, 518n46, 530n29; *Eine Faust Ouverture,* 375; finale to overture to Gluck's *Iphigénie et Tauride,* 271; *Götterdämmerung,* 39, 187, 316, 384, 451; *Huldingungsmarsch,* 37; *Isoldens Liebestod,* 448; *Lohengrin,* 5, 27, 34, 39, 49–50, 95–96, 131, 294, 494n72, 509n39, 517n42; *Meistersinger, Die,* 14, 37, 201, 223, 224, 225, 231, 254, 281, 381, 391; *Parsifal,* 15, 39, 43, 183, 224, 239, 300, 333; *Rheingold, Das,* 21, 27, 40, 176, 384, 391, 448; *Rienzi,* 224; *Ring des Nibelungen, Der (Ring of the Nibelungen),* 5, 27, 34, 43, 50, 83–84, 131, 164, 182, 200, 224, 230–31, 450, 482n1, 501n22; *Siegfried,* 24, 32, 192, 198, 305, 306, 391, 449, 450, 504n15; *Tannhäuser,* 50, 51, 223–24, 305, 312, 510n39; *Tristan und Isolde,* 5, 27, 37, 51, 82, 151, 200, 220, 223, 225, 238, 251, 306, 384, 387, 448, 482n1, 501n22, 502n46, 510nn39,40, 518n3; *Waldweben,* 34, 83; *Walküre, Die,* 34, 62, 82, 151, 164, 192, 238, 250, 271, 384, 306, 391, 406, 447, 448, 511n8

Weber, Carl Maria von (1786–1826), 14, 39; *Freischütz, Der,* 117, 130, 217, 370, 509n26

Weber, Miroslav (1854–1906) (Czech violinist, comp.), 19, 482n13

Weingartner, Felix (1863–1942) (cond.), 217, 220, 226, 300, 533n32; *Getilde der Seligen, Die,* 217

Wihtol, Joseph Ivanovich (1862–1948) (comp.), 327, 403, 447, 497n37, 516n23, 518n5, 519n17; *Bard of Beverin,* 256; *Berceuse,* 395; *Dramatic Overture,* 215; *Feast of Ligo,* 385; Overture to *Spriditis,* 446

Wilde, Oscar (1854–1900), 454, 465

Wilder, Victor (1835–1892) (writer on music), 82

Winkler, Alexander Adolfovich (1865–1935)

(comp.), 497n37, 518n5; *Caprice,* 534n45; *Prelude,* 534n45

Wolf-Ferrari, Ermanno (1876–1948) (comp.): *Vita nuova, La,* 342

Wolf, Hugo, 350

Yakovlev (painter), 536n28

Yakolev (impressario), 527n33

Yakolev, I., (music critic), 537n43

Yakovlev, Leonid Georgyevich (1858–1919) (baritone), 214, 292–93, 304, 317, 471

Yakoleva, Arina Rodionovna (1758–1828) (Pushkin's nurse), 455, 536n34

Yanova, Maria Vladimirovna (chamber singer), 257, 360, 376

Yanovsky, Boris Karlovich (1875–1933) (comp., music critic), 341, 365

Yanovsky, Moisei Osipovich (1898–?) (writer on music), 528n28

Yaromir (tenor), 19

Yastrebtsev, Vasily Vasilyevich: articles, xi, 122, 225–26, 322, 352, 392, 434–35, 463, 469, 496n30, 507–8n12, 520n22, 534n47; articles on R-K, 272, 290; biographical information, ix–x; children of, 119, 165, 209, 450; desire to do biography of R-K, 434–35; monograph on harmony, 68; Orlov Whitsung song, 466; at Petersburg Conservatory, 5–10; wedding, 50

Yastrebtseva, Alina Andreyevna (second wife), 79, 92, 106, 193, 201, 206, 209, 223, 225, 235, 282, 288, 289, 306, 308, 516n30

Yastrebtseva, Nadezhda (née Shenshin) (first wife), 51, 63, 104, 138, 153, 165, 201, 276, 293, 320

Yermolenko, Natasha Stepanovna (1881–?) (dramatic soprano), 341

Yershov, Ivan Vasilyevich (1867–1943) (tenor), 132, 139, 317, 320, 374, 376, 403, 406, 419, 424

Yuferov, Sergei Vladimirovich (1865–?) (amateur comp.), 519n8

Yunosova, Julia Alexandrovna (mezzo-soprano), 214

Zabela (married name Vrubel), Nadezhda Ivanovna (1858–1910) (coloratura soprano), 195–

Zabela Nadezhda Ivanovna (*continued*)
96, 201–3, 206, 210, 213, 215–18, 225–26, 229, 266, 283, 339, 340–1, 342, 353, 365, 384, 386–87, 393, 394, 396–97, 399, 400, 402–3, 416, 418, 420, 433, 436, 446–48, 507*n*59, 508*n*18
Zapolsky (friend of Yastrebtsev), 2
Zaremba, Nikolai Ivanovich (1821–1879) (music theorist, comp.), 376
Zbruyeva, Yevgenia Ivanovna (1869–1936) (contralto), 374, 375, 403, 406, 418, 531*n*5
Zelyony (Zelenoi), V. A. (cond.), 438, 468
Zemanek, Wilhelm (cond.), 342
Zhdanov (bass), 163
Zhemchuzhnikov, Alexei Mikhailovich (1821–1908), *see* Kuzma (Kozma) Prutkov
Zhemchuzhnikov, Vladimir Mikhailovich (1830–1884), *see* Kuzma (Kozma) Prutkov

Zherebtsova Yevreinova, Anna Grigoreyvna (1868–1944) (mezzo-soprano), 66, 141, 191, 401
Zhukovsky, Vasily Andreyevich (1783–1852) (poet), 496*n*20; *Nal and Damayanti,* 25, 484*n*41, 496*n*20; *Rustem and Zorab,* 25
Zimbalist, Efrem (1889–1985) (violinist), 397, 401, 407
Zimin, Sergei Ivanovich (1875–1942) (1904–1917 head of Zimin's Private Russian Opera in Moscow), 434
Zimmerman, Mikhail Sergeyevich (singer), 438
Zolotarev, Vasily Andreyevich (1873–1964) (comp.), 255, 320, 434, 496*n*18; *Elegy,* 270; *Fête villageoise,* 340; quartet, 434
Zumpe, Hermann (1850–1903) (cond.), 514*n*45
Zverzhansky, Alexander Georgiyevich (engineer), 255

DATE DUE

DEMCO 38-297